An old fisherman once had said,
"This deep sea gives to me my daily bread;
where winds will blow, and seas will spray,
Its in my blood — It is my way."

Wooden Boats and Iron Men

History of Commercial Fishing
In Northern Lake Michigan
&
Door County 1850 – 2005

By

Trygvie Jensen

Paisa (Alt) Publishing Co.
De Pere, Wisconsin

Copies of Wooden Boats and Iron Men are available from:

Dennis Trygvie Jensen
1414 Crooks St.
Green Bay, WI 54301
(920) 433- 9136
(920) 609- 3396

Website: http://trygviejphoto.homestead.com
Email: trygvie38@yahoo.com

Published by Paisa (Alt) Publishing Co.
502 George Street
De Pere, WI 54115.
920.983.5326

Printed in the United States of America
Library of Congress Control Number 2007925312
ISBN 9780976478270
Second edition November, 2007
Book formatted by Douglas Hjorth
Cover by Trygvie Jensen and Douglas Hjorth
Front cover art by Door County Artist Malin Ekman
Back cover photo by Trygvie Jensen
All line art illustrations by Trygvie Jensen unless otherwise noted.

3 9082 10915 9577

Dedication

To my wife Tina and my children: Carrie, Autumn,
and Logan. A special dedication goes out to my Great
Grandparents Oliver Bjarnarson and Harry Hagen, two
prominent fishermen in their own right.

WOODEN BOATS AND IRON MEN

Foreword

How would you describe a commercial fishery? Many men in the fishery call it the last industry. It was the first industry in the Door County area to provide not only jobs and food, but the money needed to sustain a good living. Earliest records indicate that the waters around Washington Island and Door County were teeming with fish. The Coffey family told Ray McDonald that the early settlers came here because the whitefish were so abundant. As early as 1840 -50 the first fishermen were shipping barreled and salted fish by sail schooners to the Milwaukee and Chicago area, and the business expanded rapidly.

This book is the most complete history of the Door County commercial fishery ever published. The author is a class photographer who has done extensive research and has created a wonderful complete history of commercial fishing in the Door County area. Trygvie Jensen was born and raised on Washington Island and realized the need of recording the history of fishing in the area. Two of Tryg's great grandparents were prominent fishermen. Tryg's Icelandic, Norwegian, and Danish ancestry served him well in compiling this record of fishing history. "Mange Tussen Takk" Tryg! (Many thousand thanks). A way must be found to sustain this fishery that has provided quality lake fish for one hundred fifty years and must continue to provide these fine lake fish for the centuries ahead. You will enjoy this book.

Jake Ellefson

Author's note:

This book was helped made possible by a generous grant from the Door County Historical Society, Door County Community Foundation, and the Clifford and Clara Herlache Heritage Foundation. Every effort has been made in trying to maintain the accuracy to the names, dates, and overall history in this text. The text in this book is derived from personal interviews, books, periodicals, unpublished and published manuscripts, family trees, and research through local history and archive departments. Many sources had conflicting name spellings, and time lines, and further research had to be done. If there is any misspelling of names or inaccuracies in dates and stories, the author apologizes.

Trygvie Jensen

Trygvie Jensen was born on Washington Island, ensconced in a rich Scandinavian heritage, working class community, and strong family values, gave him the tools necessary to create his art and build his dreams. Photography, poetry, and history writing, is his way of depicting a sense of people and place in a once bucolic way of life in Door County. The inspiration for this book derived from the memory and spirit of Trygvie's Great Grandfathers Oliver Bjarnarson and Harry Hagen. Both were commercial fishermen at Washington Island, which during its zenith was the dominant industry and mainstay of Door County. Trygvie has a degree earned in Natural Resources and is currently working on several other books, including: "Through the Door: A Poetic Pictorial of Door County" and "Through Waves and Gales Come Fishermen's Tales."

Back Cover Photo: Hickey Brothers fish tug coming into Baileys Harbor.

Table of Contents

WOODEN BOATS AND IRON MEN

Preface

Let us close our eyes and try to imagine how it was one hundred forty years ago on a small island in northern Lake Michigan. Now we open our eyes and see two young fishermen loading a dozen wooden boxes, four of which are dry nets just off the reel, packed neatly in the two-by-four-foot boxes, and into their 26-foot Mackinaw boat, a common sight on Lake Michigan back before there were any motor driven boats, ten years before the steam powered fish tugs plied the waters. Back then iron wills and stamina was the character make-up of a fisherman, who relied on the wind and the strength in their arms to propel their wooden vessels.

No wind this particular day – the two young Norwegian fishermen know the deal, and begin to row the seven miles to where they set a four box gang of nets. A few days earlier they had a fresh wind to fill their sails on their boat named the *Fiske Yeager* (Fish Hunter). Maybe they could have waited another day, but without any weather reports, they couldn't take any chances on leaving their nets out any longer. I wonder what they talked about while they took turns rowing to their fishing grounds, some four hours away? "Oh Lord could you muster up a south wind to fill our sails?", maybe one of the fisherman called up to the heavens.

After reaching their nets, we see them pulling up their buoy line and begin the daunting task of retrieving their gill nets that lie in nearly one hundred feet of water. One by one they pull up the maitre and twine with sea weathered hands. One of the young fisherman's hands begins to bleed, but he continues on with his task without complaint pulling in the twine, and picking out the silvery whitefish that glisten in the afternoon sun. Not much in the first two nets, but as they pull in the third net, they forget about their aches and pains and bleeding hands, as the harvest is now looking good. After the last net is brought into the boat, and the last of the whitefish are cleared from the net, and stored into the one remaining fish box, they breathe a little sigh, but they know there isn't any time to take a break to eat their lunch and talk about the great harvest. What they were hoping for hadn't come – the lake was like glass – not a stitch of wind to give them a speedy return home. They were more concerned to make it back by nightfall, and knew that the last few miles they would be overcome in the darkness of a mid-October night.

While one rowed, the other fisherman began setting back the freshly packed linen nets into the water. The boat was now 600 pounds heavier with a cargo of wet nets and lively whitefish flopping in the boxes, but still not a word or complaint was uttered between the two men. They took turns spelling each other at the oars, and finally when the last net was lowered into Lake Michigan's cool depths, they quickly got the boat turned around and headed back home. The sun was dipping lower towards the horizon, and the sky was ablaze in color from the waning day, reflecting on the water in a myriad of colors. There were nearly a hundred hungry seagulls hovering over them, like a white cloud providing the men some company with their raucous banter.

Darkness fell upon them, the lantern was lit so they could check their bearing with a small compass they carried with them. After rowing a few hours in the chilly autumn night, they finally saw the lantern lights on the shore. Their wives had lit the lights to guide them back home safely. The hallowed light danced on the water, like a golden shimmering path to guide them safely home. Once the boat was pulled onto the shore, the fishermen carried the boxes of whitefish and wet nets into the shanty. After the boat was emptied of gear, they took a half hour break to eat their supper. Hastily eating their meal, the men came back down and dressed and salted the fish. Once dressed, they were put into the oak barrels that they purchased from the cooper, who had a shed further down the beach.

The wet nets were taken out of the boxes, and strung on to the net reels to dry for the next day of fishing. When the last net was spread open and reeled, the two fishermen said goodnight to one another, and proceeded to their little cabins. If they had any energy left, they would have a cup of coffee and spend some time with their family, before retiring to bed. The next day would begin before sun-up and maybe then there would be a little wind to accommodate them. Such was a possible day in the life of a fisherman in the 1860s. Let us imagine those same two Norwegian fishermen coming home battling a gale-force squall that suddenly whipped up, far away from home—just another day out on the lake, or now in modern times we like to say "just another day at the office."

Things have changed since then in the commercial fishery, but the one thing that hasn't changed is the fact that in order to be a successful commercial fisherman, it takes hard work, working long hours, sometimes seven days a week, and an iron will. Commercial fishing is one of the oldest professions known to man, in which the fishing industry has survived for nearly two-hundred years on the Great Lakes. A commercial fisherman epitomizes the American Dream, independent, ambitious, and hardworking. Not only were they fishermen, they had to be carpenters, navigators, electricians, mechanics, welders, among other things. As one commercial fisherman so eloquently put it, "We don't know how to do anything well, but we can do everything." For many of the commercial fishermen they were born into the business, which was carried down from generation to generation. At a young age they helped out at shore duties, and eventually accompanied their fathers on the boats, learning the craft first hand – assimilating into a way of life that proved to challenge one's physical and mental strength. "It's not the easiest life, but it's the only life as far as I'm concerned," says one old fisherman.

Commercial fishing on the Great Lakes has been a time honored tradition with it's beginnings around the early nineteenth century, and by the end of the century it became one of the most dominant industries on the lakes. By 1880, Lake Michigan had the most fisheries, and proved to be the dominant fish producing lake of all the Great Lakes. Commercial fishing, in general, evolved slowly from 1800 to 1850. After the Erie Canal and Welland Canal were built, steam boats began plying the waters from Buffalo to Chicago, bringing in a large influx of American and Europeans further inland. The early fishermen found the waters off northern Door County, near Washington, Rock, and St. Martin Islands teeming with whitefish and trout. By 1860 and 1870, Rock and St. Martin islands had large settlements of predominantly fishermen, many of whom were of Irish descent. By 1865, many left those islands for the much bigger island of Washington. Washington Island provided a sheltered harbor on its north end, and better access to ship fish on the schooners that frequented there twice a week. By 1850, Amos Saunders had a good size dock in Washington Harbor, and eventually had the first ice house on the island.

Over the next one hundred fifty years, the commercial fisheries evolved in many ways, and fishermen were put to many new challenges. This book will take you on a journey and history of the commercial fishing industry from 1850 up to present day. This book was written to take you back in time to see how the fisheries were an integral part of the Door County and Washington Island communities, and gives the reader an inside look at how a fishery operates; moreover it will give the reader a personal view of a day in the life of a fisherman. It covers the history of every facet of the industry from the evolution of the boats, common types of gear used in the last one hundred fifty years, the species of fish that made up the great harvests, and the invader species that almost wiped out the industry in the mid to latter part of the twentieth century. The harrowing stories of the fishermen caught in violent storms, ice shoves, and many other stories that will give you insight to what a commercial fisherman went through to eek out a living on the Great Lakes. It will give the reader a better understanding of what sort of challenges that befell commercial fishermen in the last century and a half and what the future may hold for the fisheries in the next century through many interviews and reflections by the few remaining commercial fishermen. You will see the rise and fall of a once powerful industry where Door County alone boasted over four hundred commercial fishermen around the turn of the century. In the last thirty five years the industry dwindled considerably and there are only a handful of fishermen left on Lake Michigan. The state of Michigan lost most of their commercial fishery in the late 1960s when Michigan's DNR emphasized the sport fishery and put the proverbial noose around the commercial fisherman's necks through tighter restrictions and regulations; banning the gill net; and zoning the lake making it impossible for them to make a living.

Acknowledgements

It was ten years ago when this book wasn't even a concept. I was sitting having coffee with my Grandfather Dale Bjarnarson. We got on the subject of some of the "old timers" on Washington Island and some of the good 'ole stories he remembered from when he was growing up, listening to the stories told by the older men of his day. He was telling me some of the toughest men were the commercial fishermen. As we sat there that morning I said "wouldn't it be a great idea to go around and interview some of the remaining older folks on the island, maybe even videotape them telling their stories and preserve some of the rich history that began here a century and a half ago." He said, "Someone should have done this years ago. Most of the stories have gone to the grave." He told me if you are going to do this you had better do it pretty soon, before more of the stories and history are gone. Unfortunately it was a year after my grandfather and I had that conversation, he passed away. I never had the pleasure to hear any of his stories about his years growing up on the island and fishing with his father, Oliver Bjarnarson who was a prominent commercial fisherman in his own right. From what I can remember of him, he was a colorful person who always had a story or a poem for us great grandchildren.

Several years later this concept of preserving some of the stories stayed with me, manifesting in me, but I just didn't know how I was going to present it, or what medium to best give the right color and hue. One day in the summer of 1999 I was taking pictures at Jackson Harbor and saw Jake Ellefson coming into the harbor with his fish tug, the *Miss Judy*. After he moored her up to the dock I walked over and talked to him for over an hour. It was then I had what some call an epiphany or what I call an awakening. Jake gave me almost one hundred years of history of commercial fishing and life on the island in that hour. I knew then somehow, some way I was going to create a book about the history of commercial fishing and the people and the communities that were an integral part of the fisheries. I was tremendously excited and a bit apprehensive of this daunting task that lay before me, but I remembered a passage I had read from Henry David Thoreau that gave me the confidence to do this labor of love and I knew then it wasn't going to be an endeavor but a wonderful journey.

If one advances confidently in the direction of his dreams,
And endeavors to live the life he imagined, he will meet
With a success unexpected in common hours ... In proportion
As he simplifies his life, the laws of the universe will appear
Less complex, the solitude will not be solitude, nor poverty poverty,

Nor weakness weakness; if you have built castles in the air,
Your work need not be lost; that is where they should be.
Now put foundations under them.

The first person I interviewed and must give, I feel, a considerable amount of the credit to, is Jacob Ellefson. He was the person who inspired me that warm summer day as I sat in his boat and listened like a pupil to a teacher with his poetic voice and vast knowledge of the fisheries and island life; no wonder, after all, he has lived the life and seen it all. Little did I know he was going to retire and sell his boat later that fall; maybe that was why he was so reflective, but at that moment Jake was the muse I was looking for and needed. I remember the first interview with Jake, it was the fall of 2001 and I went over to Jake and my Aunt Shirley's afflicted with a bad cold rendering me almost speechless. Thank goodness Jake did all the talking. We sat there for three hours eating smoked whitefish and drinking coffee, and already I knew this was going to be something wonderful.

I am most indebted to all the commercial fishermen, their widows and family members I have had the pleasure interviewing. These commercial fishermen with their reflections and vast knowledge of the lake make up the bulk of this book. Many stories they shared with me; battling heavy seas, snow storms, caught in ice shoves; the ebb and flow of fish cycles, the changing ecology, regulations among many other variables that they had to deal with and challenged their wills. From many of the interviews I noticed that these trials and tribulations only seemed to make the men tougher. I give many thanks to these sea-weathered men who gave me insight into their lives. The most enjoyable for me was sitting down with them, hearing their stories, looking at their pictures and allowing me to make copies of their photographs for my book. Some of the older fishermen I interviewed have since passed on and I am saddened that they wouldn't be able to read their story, but I guess they have lived it and now it can be shared to the readers of this book.

I especially like to thank some of the older fishermen and people who taxed their memory and provided me with information about the fisheries at the turn of the century, remembering stories they had heard from the fishermen in their generation. Thanks to Phil Albertson, Orval and Pat Orsted, Jacob Ellefson, Jim Cornell, Alvin "Gabby" Anderson, Donald Voight, "Gibby" Goodlet, and a special thanks to Elaine Johnson and Gretna Johns who entertained me with many a wonderful story and history of the fisheries. Ruby Weborg, Bennett Hagen, Harold and Arbutus Greenfeldt, Joy Gunnlaugsson, Dorothy Peterson, Walt Jorgenson, Carolyn Koyen, Richard and Marilyn Bjarnarson, Joe LeClair, Gert Young, Carol Jornt, Arni Richter, Dick Purinton, and Sylvia and George Nelson. A special thanks to Ross and Cathy Meader for providing me with some wonderful old pictures of Gasoline Town and video. Thanks to Charlie Miller for his photo contributions and Jewel Lee Grandy for photos and stories of Sunset Resort. To Kirby Foss for providing me with some history of Gas Town and a recording of an interview with Howard Foss by Paula McDonald when she interviewed Howard many years ago.

I would also like to thank the younger generation commercial fishermen. To Dennis and Jeff Hickey for their patience and time for interviews and me tagging along to witness first hand how a commercial fishery operates and I now understand what a multi-faceted industry this is. Many thanks to Jeff Weborg for his time and his colorful interviews and insight to help me further understand more of the business. To Charlie Henriksen with his honesty and candor, helping me to better understand the challenges with the markets and all the rules and regulations imposed on the fisheries. Also thanks to Ken Koyen, Rick Johnson, Neil Teskie, Leon and Lyle Voight, Tim Weborg, Jeff McDonald, all were very helpful and insightful.

I am most thankful and appreciate all the time from the staff members at the Washington Island Archives, Barb Ellefson, Marilyn Bjarnarson, and Jeanette Hutchins for their time and patience locating files, photos, of early island history and history of the island fisheries. A special thanks to Eric Kahlenberg of the Kahlenberg Brothers Company for the pictures and documents; The Manitowoc Maritime Museum, Sturgeon Bay Maritime Museum and a special thanks to Bill Olson and Harold Greenfeldt at the Jackson Harbor Maritime Museum for the use of their photos and records. Thanks to the genealogy and local history departments at the Joseph Mann Public Library, Brown County Public Library, and Sturgeon Bay Public Library and the Milwaukee Public Library. To Catherine McCardle; Mary Ann Johnson, thanks for the history of Baileys Harbor.

To Dave Hongisto and Jim Alt, I deeply appreciate their support in believing in this book, and helping my dream become a reality. To Doug Hjorth, my appreciation for designing and giving the book a good sail for the winds to get it on its way.

I would like to give a special thanks to my loving wife and family for their support, patience and understanding during all those long hours working up in the office and in the field collecting information. Trying to juggle family time, running a home building business, and writing this book at times was a bit daunting, but worth it to preserve a rich history in the Door County communities of an industry that was once the backbone of many communities around Lake Michigan and the Great Lakes. An industry that is now only a mere shadow of what it once was, and possibly becoming only a memory in the years ahead. Thank you to Dorothy Anderson for the original copy edit.

I

A General History of Commercial Fishing in Lake Michigan

Chapter 1

The Rise of Commercial Fishing

The Great Lakes make up the largest body of freshwater in the world. Together they comprise one-fifth of the world's fresh water. An impressive expanse of water that has provided a means of survival, travel, and livelihood since people came to its shores. In modern times, the five lakes have linked people, industries, and economies in North America. They cover eight states, border two nations, and provide an international lake-way for the resources of the North American continent.

The Great Lakes cover 94,250 square miles and hold 5,439 cubic miles of water. The shorelines of the five lakes stretch for 10,210 miles. Together the lakes drain a total of 94,460 square miles in Canada and the United States.[1] The primary outlet of the lake system is the Saint Lawrence River. Elevation varies with each lake and decreases to the south and east. Lake Superior, the deepest of the five lakes at 1,330 feet is the highest above sea level, at 600 feet. Lakes Michigan and Huron lie at the same elevation, 577 feet. Lake Erie, the warmest and shallowest of the Great Lakes, has an average depth of 62 feet and lies at 325 feet above sea level. Lake Ontario, the smallest of the lakes is 243 feet above sea level. (See figure 1.1)

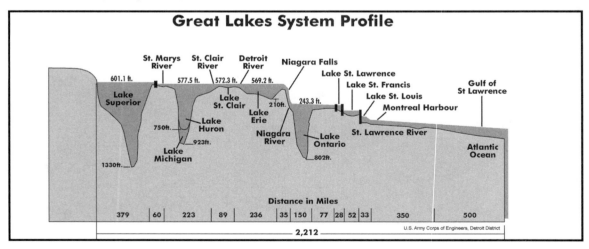

Fig.1.1 U.S. Army Corps of Engineers

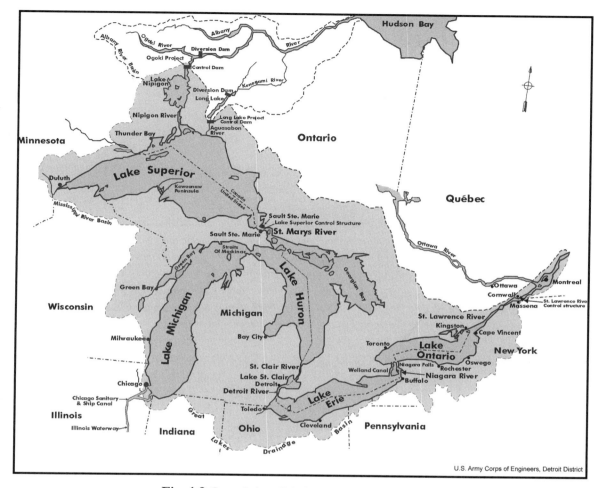

Fig. 1.2 Great Lakes, U.S. Army Corps of Engineers

The lakes are very different in physical appearance and geology and fall into two categories. The northern region and the southern region differ in terms of climate, soil type, topography, vegetation, and animal species. The northern region (Lake Superior, northern Lake Michigan, and Lake Huron) has a colder climate, granite bedrock, and acidic soil; the predominant vegetation type is coniferous forests. The southern region (Lake Erie, Lake Ontario, and the southern portions of Lake Huron and Lake Michigan) is limestone bedrock, fertile soil, a warmer climate, and deciduous forests interspersed with grasslands. The southern region is more habitable than the northern region.[2]

Lake Superior is the largest (2,900 cubic miles), coldest, and deepest of the Great Lakes averaging 483 feet; the deepest part of the lake is 1,330 feet deep. Its surface area is 31,700 square miles, about two-thirds of the lake is in the United States. It could contain all of the other four Great Lakes plus three more lakes the size of Lake Erie. The length of Lake Superior is 350 miles and it has a breadth of 160 miles.[3] Lake Superior has an irregular coastline with a number of large bays. Bold, rocky cliffs fringe the northern lakeshore, some rising a thousand feet above the water. The land around the western and southern shores is rich in minerals, especially iron ore (taconite and hematite), copper, nickel and silver. Lake Superior drains into Lake Huron from the southeast via the Saint Mary's River, which is navigable through the Sault Sainte Marie Canals. This lake seldom freezes over, but ice near its shores closes its ports from December to mid April.

Lake Michigan is the third largest of the Great Lakes (1,180 cubic miles) and the only one that is completely in the United States. It is bordered by Michigan on the north and east, Indiana on the south, and Illinois and Wisconsin on the west. The lake is 307 miles long and 118 miles wide, with an area of 22,300 square miles. The maximum depth is 925 feet and the surface is 577 feet above sea level.[4] Lake Michigan has a gentle coastline with rich marshland and fertile soil. For thousands of years, prevailing westerly winds have blown large quantities of shale and sandstone soils into great sand dunes that stretch from the Indiana border to the Straits of Mackinac. It is the largest accumulation of sand dunes on a freshwater lake anywhere in the world.[5]

The northern outlet of Lake Michigan is the Straits of Mackinac, which connect it to Lake Huron. Lake Michigan has a complex system of lighthouses, buoys, weather reports, and storm signal stations maintained by the federal government. Northern Lake Michigan has several islands where early travelers and explorers frequented. Colonies and small communities were established, and most of the early settlers were fishermen who found an abundance of trout, whitefish, herring, and other species for the taking.

The first fishermen on the Great Lakes and in Lake Michigan were the Native Americans. For thousands of years, well before the coming of the European explorers, the Indians depended on fish for food. Archeologists have found evidence that by 3,000 to 2,000 BC they used a wide range of fishing gear developed and adapted over long periods of time, including spears, gaffs, hooks, lines, and weirs. The Native Americans began using nets in Lake Michigan sometime around 300 to 200 BC. For the Lake Michigan tribes comprised of the First Nations: the Anishinabeg, (Ottawa, Potawatomi, Ojibwa or Chippewa) the Iroquois, Huron, Menominee, and Winnebago's, lake fish became a staple. For this reason, bands or tribes were concentrated around the inland shores. The fish were a predictable source of food, especially during the spring and fall spawning seasons. That spawning cycle, Anthropologist Charles E. Cleland believes, is "the key to understanding the evolution of subsistence and settlements of the upper Great Lakes Indians."[6]

In the seventeenth century, French explorers were making their way deeper into the Great Lakes system. They noted that the Native Americans were using a type of gill net when they fished through the ice and in open water with their birchbark canoes. Early explorers like Jean Nicolet, Radisson and Grosselliers observed and spent time with the indigenous peoples of the Door Peninsula. Nearly all of the Native American tribes around northern Lake Michigan used the birchbark canoe, a craft that was masterfully designed and awed many European explorers. The canoes had a white cedar structure; white birch bark skin or covering; coarse bindings made from spruce and tamarack roots; jack pine root for sewing the bark; and pine pitch with charcoal for sealing the seams.

Sometimes the Native Americans would set out in their canoes at night, as observed by these explorers, and spear fish using torchlight to spot them. They stood in the bow of the canoe and used

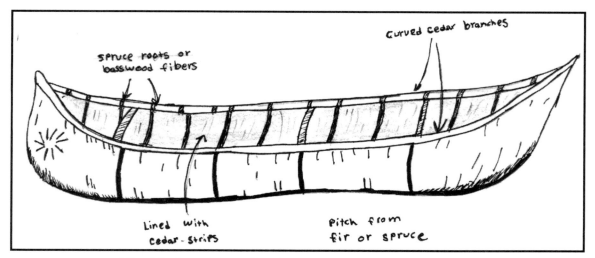

Fig. 1.3. One of the earliest fishing boats was the birch bark canoe

a spear. This was a common method of fishing, as observed in 1840 on the waters of Green Bay and on the Fox River.[7] The different tribes around Lake Michigan fished cooperatively. The women gathered nettles and hemp which they made into fine cord for netting by spinning and twisting it; the men made the gill nets from this cord. Antoine Denis Readout, a French official at Quebec, wrote in his memoirs in 1709 of the "savages of the northern regions:" "They are as skillful at fishing as at hunting; they say…. one of their divinities invented the way of making nets after attentively considering the spider when she worked to make her web to trap flies. They make these nets of nettles or wild hemp … it is with these nets that they take all sorts of fish."[8] The men did all the fishing while the women preserved and stored the catch. This was especially true of the Potawatomi. The Native Americans mainly fished for food. However, sometimes they used fish for barter between tribes.

Native Americans of the Great Lakes needed fish for nourishment, so it was in their best interest to take only what they needed. Their belief was, take only what you can use. Moreover, they believed animal and plants were embodiments of spirits and were part of the "Spirit that moves in all things." Early French explorers observed and documented many of the indigenous peoples of Lake Michigan and Lake Superior and reported that they held these beliefs. Father Allouez reported in the Jesuit Relations of 1666-67 pertaining to the Native Americans of the region: "They believe that the souls of the departed govern the fishes in the lake … and thus, from the earliest times, they have held the immortality of the souls of dead fishes, believing that they pass into other fishes' bodies. Therefore, they never throw their bones into the fire; for fear that they may offend their souls, so that they will cease to come into their nets."[9]

Things began to change, however, in the early nineteenth century in the northern Lake Michigan region. The Northwest Territory was created and five states were eventually from it. With statehood, more and more people moved to these areas. Ohio was admitted in 1803, Indiana in 1816, Illinois in 1818, Michigan in 1837, and Wisconsin in 1848. Congress drew up enabling acts for the admission of the states, and each law included state boundaries in Great Lake waters. These acts divided Lake

Michigan between Wisconsin and Michigan and gave a small portion to Indiana and Illinois.[10]

When Congress enacted the Northwest Ordinance in 1787 restructuring the government, the authority to regulate fisheries was not designated as an enumerated power of Congress. The states interpreted this as giving this power to them under the Tenth Amendment, and so it remains today. Each of the eight Great Lakes states – New York, Pennsylvania, Ohio, Indiana, Illinois, Michigan, Wisconsin and Minnesota – still make up fishery rules for their Great Lakes waters. This created problems in the unified regulation of fisheries. A total of nine governments – eight states and Canada made fishery rules and regulations, none of which are the same, despite efforts to achieve uniformity. These diverse regulations are a major impediment for present day management and regulation.

Commercial fishing in Lake Michigan and the Great Lakes in general evolved slowly until 1850. Then as more people began settling in and around Lake Michigan waters, wider markets and new harvest techniques provided fishermen with larger yields. The growth of commercial fishing in Lake Michigan varied considerably by regions, market demands, locations, and access had an impact on the growth of fisheries. Early in the nineteenth century patterns of growth were small, save for the larger cities around the lakeshores such as Chicago, Milwaukee, and Green Bay. Commercial fishing started to grow as communities began to increase in size and fish were sold locally to merchants who in turn traded or bartered with distant suppliers for needed goods. As populations grew in these communities people began fishing full time and selling their catch locally to consumers.

Sometime after 1830, fisheries became more abundant in the waters of Lake Michigan, since demand grew with a larger market base. On all the lakes, entrepreneurs found the waters had a great potential for wealth, but with communities few and far between, transporting fish to distant markets was costly and difficult. Most of the fish were bartered or sold within a single community.

When prosperity hit the nation in the 1830s and 40s, transportation started to improve and more public land became available, which allowed more people to settle around Lake Michigan. People were moving into lower Michigan and the southern shores of Lake Michigan to Indiana, Illinois, and Wisconsin, especially Chicago and Milwaukee. Markets for fish were becoming more available. The advent of steamboats in the early 1820s and the ever-expanding railroad system connecting the major cities had a great impact on the fisheries. Now steamboats could navigate from Buffalo, New York, to Chicago through the various canals on the Great Lakes. In 1825 the Erie Canal was completed; it connected Lake Erie and New York City by way of the Hudson River. The Welland Canal built in 1833, connected Lake Erie and Lake Ontario, bypassing the Niagara Falls. More canals greatly increased the potential markets for fish.[11]

In the late 1830s more entrepreneurs were opening up fish markets along Lake Michigan. Such names as John Clark and Alfred Booth were becoming well known to the early fishermen of Lake Michigan. John P. Clark, a Detroit merchant, fish dealer, and ship builder, established a fishing business in 1838 near Manitowoc, Wisconsin. Manitowoc was a recently established community, and many of its residents fished the whitefish rich waters.[12] Captain J.V. Edwards began fishing off the Point Beach area of Two Rivers in 1837 and found the waters abounding with whitefish. He became the first fisherman to adopt a viable fishery in Manitowoc County. Captain Edwards told John Clark of his success – he had just hauled in 2,000 pounds of whitefish with one net. After hearing this, Clark began using seine nets to test the waters. By 1838, Clark had his operation in full swing and formed a partnership with Edwards. The business became very profitable. It was reported that in one lift there were enough whitefish to fill 175 barrels holding 200 pounds each, and for a number of years the company's annual catch was approximately 2,000 barrels.[13]

Whitefish at this time were selling for $12 a barrel in Detroit. Clark acquired a schooner called the *Gazelle,* along with many fishing rigs. It was said that a Native American led John Clark to the Door County area at Whitefish Bay, where he soon established an operation in that area. Native Americans – mainly the Potawatomi – were employed by fishermen in many areas to show them some of the best fishing grounds and also to aid in harvesting the fish with seines. On Rock Island in the early 1830s, some of the early fisherman lived and fished harmoniously with a band of Chippewa Indians.[14] But by1850, most of the fishermen on northern Lake Michigan were of European descent.

Green Bay and Detroit fish dealers established a partnership that was reported to harvest 400,000 pounds of fish from Lake Michigan in a single season. The J.P. Clark Company thrived for fifteen years, not only with the fishery, but also buying fish from others and selling them to Detroit markets. This was a time when a system of merchant dealers would buy fish from remote locations and redistribute and sell the fish with a high markup to other markets. Some of these dealers worked with various types of fishermen, some were independent, and others would work on a share system, which continued well into the twentieth century.

By 1840 the fisheries entered a period of further growth because of more sizable harvests, growing regional markets, and better means of transportation to an ever growing national market. A growing economy and more people coming every day to the region marked the beginning of a more complex large scale fishing operation on Lake Michigan. Moreover, newly built rail connections vastly improved shipping fish to distant markets. In Milwaukee, Chicago, Detroit, Sandusky, Cleveland, Toronto, Buffalo, and many other Great Lakes ports, fish dealers were finding great success in their operations.

Table 1.1 Fishermen Employed on the Great Lakes (circa 1880)

Lake	Number
Lake Michigan	1,578
Lake Superior	414
Lake Huron	976
Lake Ontario	612
Lake Erie	1,470

(Compiled from Frederick W. True, Geographical Review of the Fisheries, Section II, in George Brown Goode, The Fisheries and Fishery Industries of the United States. United States Commission of Fish and Fisheries, 1887)

Lake Michigan produced the most fish and had more fisheries than any of the other of Great Lakes. From the rise of commercial fishing in 1830 to its expansive heyday in 1899, the waters of Lake Michigan were combed top to bottom for fish. The northern waters of Lake Michigan and all its islands were teeming with fisheries. Washington Island, Rock Island, St. Martin Island, and Beaver Island all had large fishing communities that started around the mid 1800s. Some of the first settlers in this area established themselves on Rock Island and St. Martin Island. The addition of the Pottawatomie Lighthouse on Rock Island in 1836 greatly improved navigation on the lake, which in turn brought more steamboats and people to this area.

In 1849 U. S. biologists took part in a study of Lake Michigan and Lake Superior fisheries, which was later given to Congress. The men set out in canoes and toured many of the fisheries in northern Lake Michigan and southern Lake Superior. They found ten boats and thirty men fishing at Rock Island, fourteen boats and fifty men at Washington Island, and six boats and twenty men at Pilot Island. On the western shores of northern Door County there were also some fisheries. They reported that most of the fish taken there were whitefish and trout. "The quantity of fish caught is variable. Fishermen say that the same ground is much better one year than another, so that they are obliged to shift their quarters."[15]

By 1845 Rock Island and St. Martin Island had approximately one hundred people, mostly fishermen.[16] These islands proved to be close to good fishing grounds for whitefish and trout. Nearly all the fishermen at this time were using sail powered "Mackinaw" boats. These boats were small enough that they could be pulled on to shore without a need for docks. By 1870 most of these island communities disbanded and sought out other places that offered sheltered harbors and better means of shipping their fish to markets. Some moved to northern Michigan and others to nearby Washington Harbor, located on the north end of Washington Island, where there was a good dock and steamboats and schooners stopped more frequently to pick up fish and cordwood.

By 1860, Washington Island was the major hub for fisheries in the northern Door County region and had three established docks and fishing communities. On the west side of Washington Harbor, Amos Saunders built a good size dock in 1846 where he could provide fishermen with mooring, salt, and barrels for packing their fish. Later the dock and property was owned by other men who expanded the commercial fishing operation and greatly improved the island's economy. Lake steamers stopped there to refuel with cordwood, and fish were shipped out on a regular basis. A letter that Albert Kalmbach wrote in 1939 gives a brief depiction of the early fisheries at Washington Harbor: "When I was a small boy, my parents moved to Washington Island at the tip of Door County, Wisconsin. This was a fishing community, the headquarters of many boats, and quantities of trout and whitefish were taken. The only means of shipping was the steamers which ran to Detroit and Buffalo during the summer months so the fish were all salted when caught and marketed in half barrels of 100 lbs. each."[17]

Dennis McDonald had a substantial dock at his property on the northwest side of Washington Island. This dock could handle the large steamboats and occasionally the big side-wheel Buffalo boats that would lay over to "wood-up" their boilers, drop off freight and pick up fish, and continue on their way to Green Bay or Chicago. Around that time, Andrew Irr had a large dock at his property on the north end of Washington Island. Irr's dock was frequented on a regular basis by the steamboats that carried whitefish and trout to the Chicago markets.

By the 1870s fish were harvested in the Great Lakes at a record pace. Commercial fishing exploded on the scene in both Canadian waters and American waters. Now both countries were starting to keep records that emphasized the size of the industry and total harvests in pounds. In 1872 the annual harvest in both Canadian and American waters totaled approximately 39,330,000 pounds, with a value of $1,819,849.[18] It was also around this time that the U.S. government created the Commission of Fish and Fisheries to oversee fishing operations and collect data.

The first appointed director to the U.S. Commission of Fish and Fisheries was Spencer Baird. He appointed James W. Milner, a biologist from Waukegan, Illinois, to prepare a special report on the American Great Lakes fishing industry that year. Milner's main area of expertise was Lake Michigan waters, where he had been doing studies for years. Milner compiled data by doing extensive fieldwork, interviews, observations, investigations, and studies of local records. The report was finally completed after twenty years of study of the growth in the commercial fisheries on the Great Lakes. Milner spent most of his time on Lake Michigan.

Milner found that the fishing industry comprised three major areas of operations: harvesting, processing, and marketing. Fishermen were the major factors in harvesting and did most of the work. They were the men in the boats, tending the nets in all kinds of weather from April through December and in some regions, working through the winter months if ice conditions weren't bad. The independent fishermen had their own gear and a crew of usually four or five men. Normally these independent fishermen were organized in partnerships and most often had investments of $300 to $20,000 in nets, boats, and shore properties.[19] Fishermen that did not have the capital to start a fishery worked for wages or on shares, and some worked for the fish dealers. By 1880 there were 1,578 fisheries on Lake Michigan, the most in any of the Great Lakes. Most of the fish were shipped fresh.

Table 1.2 Lake Michigan Fish Quantities and Values, 1880

Products	Quantity (lbs.)	Value
Fresh fish	10,728,250	$343,070
Salted fish	7,730,740	$203,425
Frozen fish	100,000	$6,000
Smoked fish	788,590	$52,930
Caviar	31,330	$6,620
Fish oil	200	$100

(Compiled from Frederick W. True, Section II, Geographical Review of the Fisheries; George Brown Goode, The Fisheries and Fishery Industry of the United States, United States Commission of Fish and Fisheries)

Fish dealers performed two operations in the commercial fishing industry – processing and marketing. Dealers had a large impact on the livelihood of all fishermen, who depended on them to buy their catch, process it, and send it to the markets. Dealers had great control of the prices and would pay fishermen based on the fishermen's expenses and on market price, and then affix their commission on top of that. However, competition among dealers acted as a control valve. Most of the dealers paid according to the quality and size of the fish. They also established territories where they could control the market, often sending steamboats to pick up the fish from various ports.

By 1870 Chicago was a major rail hub for the nation – Chicago and Buffalo were the dominant markets. In 1872 markets handled 7.5 million and 6.4 million pounds of fish, respectively. The major reasons for such dominance were good steamboat and railroad connections that enabled dealers to collect the harvests from producers and distribute the fish to faraway markets. Lake Michigan fish, as well as most of the other Great Lakes fish, went to New York City from Chicago or Buffalo. With newly developed means of freezing and cold storage units, it was possible to ship fresh whitefish and trout by rail to Cincinnati, St. Louis, Omaha, Washington D.C., and other cities. An 1879 summary of Frederick R. True's Geographical Review of the Fisheries Industries gives a breakdown of the fish that entered Chicago (table 1.3). The total amount of fish shipped in 1879 was 5,910,570 pounds; 2 million pounds were consumed in the city and surrounding areas.

Table 1.3 Fish Production in Chicago, 1879

Description	Quantity (pounds)
Fresh Fish:	
Whitefish	3,658,567
Trout	1,705,761
Sturgeon	42,560
Miscellaneous	274,162
River fish	230,520
Smoked fish:	
Whitefish	232,000
Sturgeon	300,000
Total	5,910,570

(Compiled from Frederick W. True, Geographical Review of the Fisheries; Section II, George Brown Goode, The Fisheries and Fishery Industries of the United States)

After 1882 there were several dealers in the northern Door County region. One on Washington Island saw many owners. At Washington Harbor, the first dealer was Captain Amos Saunders, who bought fish from the local fishermen, followed by James M. Craw, Willet P. Ranney, and John Furlong. Two firms in Sturgeon Bay bought fish from the regional fisheries, paying close to five cents a pound for trout. One firm shipped to Chicago and Milwaukee, and the other shipped to St. Louis and St. Joseph, Missouri, Kansas City, and Leavenworth, Kansas, and Denver, Colorado. There was also a dealer at Fish Creek that bought and shipped fish from 1859 to 1880[20] In 1873, Mr. Blakefield, of the firm Blakefield and Minor of Fish Creek, sold more than $4,000 worth of fresh fish from two small pound nets set in the vicinity of Chambers Island.[21]

By 1871 federal researchers began to see changes ahead. The future of Lake Michigan fisheries did not look good. "There is an alarming diminution of the food fisheries of the lakes," said one official in his report. The decrease of whitefish was becoming more evident. Lake trout stocks were decreasing as well. Compared to the previous twenty, the researchers noted, there would be a 50 percent decrease in fish stocks in the next twenty years. In their opinion this was due to harvesting large numbers of immature fish with pound nets, which were starting to become more prevalent.[22]

The first pound net was used in the Door County region around 1856, and by 1858 pound nets were being used at Menominee and Little Suamico. By the following year, pound nets were used on the Lake Michigan side of Door County at Whitefish Bay. It wasn't long before this type of apparatus was used all over the region. Pound net fishing became more established along the shores of northern Lake Michigan and was ideal for the fisheries, especially in November when whitefish schooled in preparation for the spawning season. The fish would come into the shallow waters near shore, making them easy to catch in the nets. Fishermen would also set their nets in the spring of the year, but spring harvest was never as good as the fall harvest.

An article in a November 10, 1859 *Green Bay Advocate* reported that hundreds of barrels of fish a day were being taken from the waters: "What effect this wholesale slaughter of fish will have on the supply, another season may tell." By April 1862, Wisconsin's legislature adopted regulations regarding pound nets, which prohibited the use of any pound net or trap net in more than 20 feet of water off, under, or on the south point of any bay or inlet on the west shore of Lake Michigan in Door County.

In the 1860s and 70s the waters of Green Bay along the western Door County coastline, there were an estimated two hundred pound nets set in the shallow waters. Whitefish and herring were a fairly consistent catch, and the harvests were always good up until the 1930s. The bay was an ideal location for setting pound nets, because the fishermen could easily drive their pound net stakes into the soft silt lake bottom. Pound nets were also used on the eastern coast of Door County; many rigs were set in and around Rowleys Bay, Sand Bay, North Bay, Baileys Harbor, Jacksonport and other areas.

Commercial fisheries in the northern sector of Door County and Washington Island saw some lean years from 1877 to the mid 1880s. Whitefish and trout harvests were down considerably. At Washington Island the fishing industry saw a decline in numbers of fishermen after 1877. From 1864 to 1877 there were about twenty-five crews of gill net fishermen, ten in 1884, and eight in 1885.[23] Save for a good year in 1881, the fishing was poor in the northern Door County waters. A May 15, 1879 *Door County Advocate* article states the sobering fact: "At Washington Island the fishing business is perfectly flattened out" and "It doesn't pay." An August 24, 1884 article stated: "Fishing is so completely played out that fishermen and coopers have got to leave or go to work at something else."

For many years the fishing grounds between Washington and St. Martin islands were considered to be the most productive in the bay and one of the best fishing grounds in northern Lake Michigan. During the summer months in the late 1860s and early 1870s there were as many as six hundred gill nets set in that region, and during the fall months there were close to twelve hundred. By 1874 there were four thousand to five thousand nets set in that area in the vicinity of Washington, Rock, and St. Martin Islands, generating almost $100,000 dollars in revenue. Then came the big decline and the fishing dropped off considerably due to a several causes, according to Frederick True's report of 1880: "Their abandonment was due to several causes, and not least to the terrible storm losses of nets which occurred there in the fall of several seasons. As many as three thousand nets have been lost in one autumn, carrying down with them 500,000 or 600,000 whitefish."[24] It was believed that the decaying fish in the nets at the bottom of the lake on the spawning beds drove away other spawning whitefish. Many nets were retrieved with grappling hooks the following spring, but were tossed overboard due to the stench of the rotting fish.

By 1887 there were signs of a slight improvement in the fisheries at Washington Island and northern Door County. March 3, 10, and 17, 1887 issue of the *Door County Advocate* stated that there were at least 35 tons of trout taken during the winter months, bringing about $6,000 to nearly a hundred fishermen. Another report in the November 19, 1887 *Door County Advocate* said that the season's whitefish harvest was very good after a lapse of many years. Further down the county, along both the bayside and the eastern shoreline, fishermen were fairing better than the Washington Island fishermen (table 1.4). "Along the entire eastern shore, in 1879, about 2,200 gill nets and 40 pound nets were employed, the total value of which was about $26,000, according to the estimates of the owners. For the management of these nets and for the preparation and storage of the fish taken, boats and other apparatus and accessories, worth about $15,000, were employed." [25]

Table 1.4   Yield of Fisheries (November 1, 1879)

Description	Pounds
Fresh Fish (whitefish and trout)	555,000
Salted Fish (whitefish and herring).	355,000
Smoked Fish	10,000
Total value:	**$33,000**

(Compiled by Frederick W. True, A Geographical Review of the Fisheries. Section II. George Brown Goode, The Fisheries and Fishery Industries of the United States, United States Commission of Fish and Fisheries, 1887)

Between 1885 and 1893 fish production was on the increase. It reached a high point in 1889 with a 146,284,000 pound harvest in the Great Lakes, a record that held until 1899 (table 1.6). The years from 1875 to 1893 saw improvements in refrigeration technology, more steamboats sailing the lakes, and larger capital investments. Moreover, there was a larger workforce employed in production and distribution. Dealers and entrepreneurs were becoming more prevalent and had more power and control over the industry – labor, capital, technology, and marketing of fish to consumers nation wide.

By the turn of the century, Door County was leading the state in the number of fisheries and fish being harvested from Lake Michigan. It became the most important industry, surpassing logging and farming. Gasoline engines were being installed in the boats, replacing the sail powered boats and steam tugs; thousands of dollars were being spent on nets and gear. By 1904 there were only a dozen small sailing craft, predominantly Mackinaw boats, in use on the peninsula by fishermen. A few years earlier there were many more Mackinaw boats, classed as being the fastest and best sea boats in the fishing business on the lake. The year of 1904, fishermen harvested 6,284,359 pounds of fish, which amounted to $ 151, 232. Following is statistics showing value of nets, number of fishermen, fish caught and their value for the year of 1904:

Number of men employed	342
Value of boats	$34,200
Value of nets	$65,364

Fish and their value.

Kinds of fish	Pounds	Value
Whitefish	18,214	$1,427
Lake trout	794,387	41,298
Blue Fins	89,404	3,466
Chubs	344,159	7,209
Herring	4,658,949	91,566
Menominees	71,700	2,169
Perch	232,528	3,303
Pike	1,000	60
Pickerel	6,933	276
Sturgeon	1,890	144
Suckers	15,200	319
Total	**6,234,359**	**$151,232**

There were more fish taken in pound nets than in other type of fishing gear; over 4,000,000 pounds of herring being taken in this manner. There were over 150 pound nets set along the shores of Door County— the greatest number of them being on the Green Bay shore line.[26]

The Rise of the A. Booth Fish Company

One of the most powerful and controversial entrepreneurs in the wholesale fish business was Alfred Booth. The A. Booth Fish Company, based in Chicago, had a great influence on the Lake Michigan fisheries as well as those of Lake Superior, Lake Huron, and Lake Erie. Booth became a multimillion dollar corporation before World War I and monopolized the fishing industry until the early

1920s. Many of the dealers were going out of business as a result of the depression of 1890, so the Booth Company initiated a merger designed to consolidate the major fisheries. At the close of the nineteenth century the Booth Company began a campaign to consolidate and dominate the entire fishing industry of the Great Lakes by controlling the majority of the fish dealers.

Alfred Booth, born in Glastonbury, England came to America when he was twenty-four years old. He first lived in Kenosha, Wisconsin, and in 1850 made the move to Chicago where he opened a small store and traded fish and vegetables. In 1857 he relocated his business to a larger building on Dearborn and Madison streets where he bought fish from Lake Michigan fishermen and sold them locally on the streets in a cart. After the Civil War, Chicago was a boomtown and showed steady population and economic growth. The fishing industry was also rising at a steady pace. Alfred Booth, an ambitious, hard driving man had grand visions for his company as being a leader in the wholesale food arena. His capital rating by 1862 was $8,000 to $10,000, and by 1871 he had $100,000 to $250,000 a year in annual sales.[27]

Booth started out buying and selling fish locally in the Chicago area. As the city's railroad hub expanded, he expanded his own horizons. As Chicago became one of the dominant markets in the Great Lakes region, Booth's business grew, becoming the largest wholesale fish business in the City. He also had a fleet of steam tugs and fishing crews that fished the southern region of the lake. He could bring in all the whitefish he could handle without going any farther north than Milwaukee.

By 1870 Booth began sending fleets of tugs to northern Lake Michigan. By 1870 he had operations on Washington Island, Green Bay, a freezer plant in Escanaba, and operations in Manistique, Michigan. He bought fish from fishermen in the entire northern Lake Michigan shoreline. He had two or three company steamboats bringing fish back to Chicago nearly twice a week. He also had pound net fisheries near Naubinway and gill net fisheries in the northern waters of the lake. Shipments of fresh and frozen fish from the Escanaba plant in 1884 reached over a million pounds. The company had a 90 foot steam tug that was used to pick up fish at Manistique, Michigan, St. Martin Island, and Washington Island then return to Chicago. This tug would make two trips a week and could travel at a speed of 19 miles per hour.

By 1907, Booth had operations in most regions of the Great Lakes. Its activities on Lake Erie gave the company an avenue to the markets on the East Coast by means of the railroad. Most of the fish in Lake Erie went to New York. On Lake Erie, the Booth Company ran fishing operations from Erie, Pennsylvania to Ohio and its marketing monopoly gave them the power to set prices directly from the nets. This was the modus operandi of most dealers and the reason why fishermen did not hold them in high regard.

In 1909 the company changed its name to Booth Fisheries and adopted policies and strategies to build up profits when markets were favorable. The omnipresent Booth Fisheries, with their diverse operations in many regions of Lake Michigan and Lake Superior, began to have an impact on fish populations. Fishermen in Port Arthur in Lake Superior resented this because of the amount of fish the company's fisheries were taking from the waters. The local fishermen felt that Booth was invading their domain. Fishermen in both Lake Superior and Lake Michigan had the same complaints about contracts the company offered for their catch. Prices were the major issue – fishermen felt that they were paid too little, as Booth was reselling the fish at a substantially higher price. The Booth Fisheries developed a reputation for intimidating overseers, breaking regulations, and fleecing the fishermen.

By 1912 the Booth Fisheries was facing many challenges from rival dealers. It was disliked by fishermen and had a bad reputation with the Department of Marine and Fisheries. Booth filed for bankruptcy in 1908 and reincorporated as the Booth Fisheries Company in 1909. They held on as a major company in the Great Lakes until the Great Depression, beginning in 1929, caused them to greatly reduce their operations. They filed once again for bankruptcy and recognized but never regained their once powerful status. By the 1960s they were a mere shadow of what they had been.

The years from 1896 to 1933 proved to be a dynamic time in the fisheries. Since that time commercial fishing has been threatened on three fronts: over fishing, pollution, and by the 1920s, invasive species. There was a decline in fish populations from over fishing, and many believed lake pollution from industries and the failure of any conservation programs had a large impact on Lake Michigan fisheries. The influx of non-native species such as smelt, alewife, German carp, and the sea lamprey helped to hasten the end of an era of great harvests of fish. In the latter part of the twentieth century certain species still thrived, although some species have been taken off the commercial market by the Department of Natural Resources. The native lake trout were nearly wiped out by the sea lamprey in 1948 and the herring were gone by the late 1950s from Lake Michigan waters. The non-native smelt were a major factor in the decline of herring, as these small predator fish consumed eggs and fry of the herring.

Pricing

Market forces that fueled the commercial fishing industry from 1896 to 1929 can be blamed for the downward slide of the valuable fish species of the Great Lakes. With the declining harvest of whitefish, herring, and trout, expanding markets, and improved marketing systems the demand for fish sent prices on an upward climb from the glutted market of the late nineteenth century.

Table 1.5 Lake Michigan Commercial Fish Production, 1879-1899 (thousands of pounds)

Species	Years						
	1879	1885	1889	1890	1893	1897	1899
Whitefish	12,030	8,653	5,524	4,564	2,446	3,345	1,770
Herring (Cisco)	3,050	3,312	9,569	7,480	20,085	23,814	24,745
Lake Trout	2,659	6,431	5,580	8,364	8,526	7,823	5,286

Data gathered from Norman S. Baldwin, Robert W. Saalfeld, Margaret A. Ross, and Howard J. Buettner, Commercial Fish Production in the Great Lakes, 1867-1977, Technical Report No. 3 (Ann Arbor Michigan; Great Lakes Fishery Commission, 1979)

After the turn of the century, fishermen found themselves in better times. World War I created a heavy demand for Great Lakes fish and demand sent prices on a steady increase that encouraged more fishermen to strive for larger harvests. Data gathered for the Great Lakes fishery showed a rise in fish dealers from 121 in 1899, to 183 in 1917, and then falling off to 159 in 1922.[28] A study by the U.S. Commission of Fish and Fisheries showed that between 1890 and 1892, the average price levels of the various species of fish began to rise. The price per pound increased again from the 1899 levels, with a greater increase from 1908 to 1917. Whitefish prices rose from seven cents a pound in 1899 to thirteen cents a pound in1917 to eighteen cents a pound in 1922. Most species sold for much more in 1923.

The harvest of commercial fish from the Great Lakes between 1896 and 1929 totaled well over 100 million pounds a year, except for 1926, and 1928, and 1929(Table 1.6). Herring, which were a major catch for decades, declined drastically in the mid 1930s in Lake Michigan, presumably due to the influx of smelt.

Table 1.6 Great Lakes Commercial Fish Production 1879-1929 (thousands of pounds)

Year	Whitefish	Lake trout	Herring
1879	24,336	7,997	18,040
1885	22,178	17,673	33,679
1890	19,098	18,473	59,820
1893	12,977	21,727	55,623
1899	9,002	17,898	72,723
1903	7,653	22,656	40,523
1908	10,931	19,123	56,089
1913	4,329	16,989	47,653
1918	9,802	17,218	76,712
1923	9,358	15,073	43,179
1924	8,472	17,962	25,874
1925	8,721	17,973	22,322
1926	9,544	17,546	30,264
1927	9,940	15,823	20,922
1928	10,547	15,823	25,571
1929	11,857	16,561	28,904

Data compiled from Commercial Fish Production of the Great Lakes (Technical report no. 3) by Norman S. Baldwin, Robert W. Saalfeld, Margaret Ross Dochoda, Howard J Buettner, and Randy L. Eshenroder; Great Lakes Fishery Commission.

Fishermen kept the total harvest at a constant level during the twentieth century by marketing different species of fish. Lake Michigan fishermen in the early 1900s began to fish for smelt as the market began to open up for this species and some were used to make fish oil. In the latter part of the twentieth century smelt became more marketable as other species started to decline. When herring and whitefish populations dropped in the 1960s many fishermen relied on chubs to sustain their fisheries, especially the fishermen of Washington Island and Door County.

Some rough fish became more marketable in the middle of the twentieth century, fish such as yellow perch, walleyed pike, sauger, carp, and suckers. Fisheries in the waters of Green Bay relied heavily on these species for their livelihood. Fifty years earlier these fish were not considered marketable and found uses as fishmeal, oil, and fertilizer. Yellow perch and walleye, in the latter part of the twentieth century, found a market in restaurants and supper clubs. Friday night fish fries are still popular today with many people in Wisconsin and Michigan.

In the twentieth century new technology allowed fishermen to harvest fish from greater depths and travel longer distances to new fishing grounds. Fishermen could comb the waters from top to bottom – the fish had nowhere to go but into the nets. The two innovations that greatly enhanced the fishing industry were the mechanical net lifter and gasoline and crude oil or semi diesel engines to power fishing boats.

Steam powered boats and net lifters had in use since 1870 on the Great Lakes but these were rarely used because of their high cost. Many fishermen could not afford them. Most of the steamboats operated around Washington Island, which at that time was a mecca for fishermen. One of the first steam tugs on Lake Michigan was the *Kitty Gaylord*, owned by John O'Neil of Washington Island. Shortly after O'Neil's tug was in service, five other fisheries started to use them. Two Washington Island fishermen operated steam tugs by 1871 and a few more were in use near Beaver Island.

Along with the steam engines, fishermen also used steam powered net lifters. They were introduced in 1869, and by 1899 nearly all the gill net fishermen were using these patented devices, which enabled fisherman to set more nets at greater depths. Now fishermen could set twice the gang of nets, as opposed to lifting by hand, and only able to handle a small gang of nets.

At the turn of the century another innovation, the gasoline marine engine, greatly improved commercial fishing. The gasoline engine was more affordable than the steam engines. Around the time gasoline engines were introduced, mechanical net lifters were perfected and replaced the steam net lifters. The mechanical net lifter typically ran off a separate engine, or the eccentrics of the boat's engine. With these two innovations, commercial fishing changed forever. On April 12, 1900, John LaFond, a fisherman from Two Rivers area received the first marine engine built by the Kahlenberg Brothers, an 8 horsepower marine internal combustion engine. Later that year, in the Door County region, two fishermen, Heald and Hayes, received an 8 horsepower engine.[29] In 1902, Matt Foss of Washington Island and his fishing partner Tom Johnson sailed their 28-foot mackinaw boat, *Laura*, to Two Rivers, where the Kahlenberg Brothers installed an 8 horsepower gas engine for $200. By 1917 nearly all the fishermen on Lake Michigan were using gas or oil engines.

Pollution and Changing Ecology

Commercial fishing in the northern region of Lake Michigan remained fairly steady through- out most of the twentieth century, primarily due to the federally funded restocking programs. From the early 1800s when commercial fishing began to the early 1920s, the ecology of the lake hadn't changed much, and fish populations remained fairly constant. It wasn't until invader species such as smelt, alewife, and sea lamprey began to infiltrate Lake Michigan and the other four Great Lakes that there was a noticeable impact on the ecology of the lakes, indirectly affecting the native species. Early records prove that the waters of Green Bay and northern Lake Michigan show the importance of whitefish production and contributed to half of the total lake production. Between 1894 and 1927 commercial harvests were relatively stable, approximately 1 million to 3 million pounds of fish were harvested. There was a strong increase in the late 1920s with production near 5.4 million; however, in the 1930s there was a steady decline and the 1939 – 1940 harvests were the second and third lowest since records had been kept.

Table 1.7 Total Commercial Fish Production in Lake Michigan, 1930-1980 (thousands of pounds)

Year	Species			
	Chubs	Whitefish	Lake Trout	Herring (Cisco)
1930	5,037	5,383	5441	
1932	3,123	3,836	5,470	2,948
1934	6,236	2,183	4,956	6,415
1936	5,675	1,026	4,763	4,796
1938	5,404	1,259	4,905	4,478
1940	1,648	955	6,266	2,674
1942	1,755	1,341	6,485	1,427
1944	2,608	1,753	6,497	
1946	4,524	2,558	3,975	5,550
1948	5,929	5,247	1,197	8,029
1950	9,291	2,361	54	7,492
1952	11,097	1,770	3	9,692
1954	10,568	789	0	7,728
1956	10,913	57	0	5,731
1958	9,583	49	0	2,026
1960	12,659	124	0	233
1962	11,115	266	0	116
1964	5,172	777	0	34
1966	7,227	1,422	0	53
1968	10,183	893	0	53
1970		1,729		12
1972	5,266	3,504		4
1974	3,267	3,405		6
1976	422	4,070		0
1978	397	4,092		0
1980	1,475	4,190	0	0

Data collected from Commercial Fish Production in the Great Lakes 1867-2000 (Technical Report No. 3) by Norman S. Baldwin, Robert W. Saalfeld, Margaret Ross Dochoda, Howard J. Buettner, and Randy L. Eshenroder; Great Lakes Fishery Commission.

From the late 1800s pollution was a major factor impacting the waters of Lake Michigan, and it progressively worsened in the next seventy years. Pollution from mining in northern Michigan and Wisconsin fouled the waters, and industrial pollution from industry and paper mills affected the southern region of the lake. By 1870, intense clear cutting of timber and development along the Fox River along with raw sewage pumped into the water led to a major pollution problem. Development of the Green Bay of Door County shore was intense, with clear cutting of the forests, then farmland being opened up as farmers and rail crews burned the cover from cleared land.

A drought hit the region during the summer and early fall of 1871, creating a very dangerous scenario. Many people were clearing land and burning the brush and ground cover. Then the unthinkable happened, on October 8 strong southwest winds fueled these small fires into one large inferno. It burned the eastern and western shores of Green Bay in a 40 to 50 mile front of hellish fire and smoke that raced as far north as Peshtigo and beyond. Over a thousand people and countless animals perished in the "Great Peshtigo Fire", one of the most destructive fires ever recorded in North America. The after-effect of the fire had serious environmental implications that lasted nearly a decade. A 110 mile stretch of land, starting north of Green Bay to just south of Escanaba had burned. Streams and rivers were polluted with ash and runoff, causing heavy silting in the rivers and shore areas, affecting spawning grounds for certain fish.

Another source of pollution that had an impact on the ecology of Lake Michigan was lumber operations, which reached large productions from 1880 to 1910. James Milner reported on the effects of this type of pollution: "The refuse from sawmills is thrown into the streams in immense quantities to float out and sink in the lake. It is having a very injurious effect on the fisheries. The waterlogged slabs … tear and carry away the nets. The sawdust covers the feeding and spawning grounds of the fish …"[30] In Wisconsin the logging boom hit around the 1870s and peaked around the mid 1880s. Logging and settlement activities caused one of the most profound environmental changes to Lake Michigan. Loss of fish habitats due to changes in the drainage systems with the numerous sawmills built near the rivers and tributaries. Many Lake Michigan tributaries were dammed hindering certain species of fish from their spawning grounds. Many of these fish were found concentrated in an area downstream and were more susceptible to over-fishing. Heavy logging increased soil erosion into streams making the water turbid, thus covering spawning areas and warming the waters, which further hindered spawning activity.

By the mid 1960s commercial fishing catches in Lake Michigan around northern Door County were at an all time low. The herring were literally wiped out by 1962; the lake trout were gone by 1948; and whitefish were in low supply. Many fishermen went out of business and had to find work elsewhere. The only commercial fisheries that made it through those troubled times were the ones who had out-of-state fishing licenses. Most fishermen began fishing for chubs during that time. By 1972 the whitefish started coming back in larger numbers, which saved many fisheries from going under. Whitefish chubs, and perch are the only native commercial species that still thrive in Lake Michigan, although the population has fluctuated over the years.

Chapter 1 Notes

[1] Great Lakes Information Network 1993-2004. http://www.great-lakes.net/lakes/ref/michfact.html.

[2] Margaret Beattie Bogue, *Fishing the Great Lakes: An environmental History, 1783 – 1933* (Madison, WI: University of Wisconsin Press, 2000), 4.

[3] Great Lakes Information Network; Lake Superior Brochure, 1990, Michigan Sea Grant.

[4] Great Lakes Atlas; Great Lakes Information Network 1993-2004. http://www.greatlakes.net/lakes/ref/michfact.html.

[5] Richard Olsenius, *Distant Shores*; (Bluestem Productions 1990), 18.

[6] Ibid, 5–6.

[7] Margaret Beattie Bogue, *Fishing The Great Lakes: An Environmental History 1783-1933*; (Madison, WI: University of Wisconsin Press, 2000), 7.

[8] Antoine Denis Raudot, "Memoir," etc., in W. Vernon Kineitz, The Indians of the Western Great Lakes 1616 – 1760 (Ann Arbor, 1965), pg. 369.

[9] Conan Bryant Eaton, "Door County Fisheries: The First Fifty Years," *Door County Almanac No. 3* (Sister Bay, WI: Dragonsbreath Press, 1986), 25.

[10] Margaret Beattie Bogue, Fishing The Great Lakes: An Environmental History 1783 – 1933 (Madison, WI: University of Wisconsin Press, 2000), 12.

[11] Margaret Beattie Bogue, *Fishing The Great Lakes: An Environmental History 1783 – 1933,* (Madison, WI: University of Wisconsin Press, 2000), 29.

[12] *Fishing in Manitowoc County* By Eugene Krejcarek ; Courtesy of Lester Public Library, Two Rivers, Wisconsin (1969 series Manitowoc County Historical Society).

[13] Ibid.

[14] Conan Bryant Eaton, *Rock Island Series*, revised addition 1979(Eaton, revised addition; Sturgeon Bay, WI: Bayprint Inc. 1988), 12. Jessie Minor, *Early Days on Washington Island* (Washington Island 1937).

[15] Conan Bryant Eaton, "Door County Fisheries: The First Fifty Years," *Door County Almanac No. 3* (Sister Bay, WI: Dragonsbreath Press 1986), 26.

[16] St Martin Island Census 1870.

[17] Mabel Kalmbach Spencer, "Fishing in Door County at the Turn of the Century; *The Peninsula, March 1958* (Door County Historical Society 1958), 3.

[18] Margaret Beattie Bogue, *Fishing The Great Lakes: An Environmental History 1783 – 1933* (Madison, WI: University of Wisconsin Press, 2000), 35.

[19] James W Milner, "Report on the Fisheries of the Great Lakes;" Margaret Bogue, *Fish of the Great Lakes*, (University of Wisconsin Press, 2000), 36.

[20] Conan Bryant Eaton, "Door County Fisheries," *Door County Almanac, No. 3* (Sister Bay, WI:

Dragonsbreath Press, 1986), 31.

[21] Frederick R. True, " Section II, A Geographical Review of the Fisheries Industries and Fishing Communities for the year 1880"; George Brown Goode, *The Fisheries and Fish Industries of the United States;* 645.

[22] Conan Bryant Eaton, "Door County Fisheries: The First Fifty Years," *Door County Almanac No. 3* (Sister Bay, WI: Dragonsbreath Press, 1986), 29.

[23] *Ibid.* 31.

[24] Frederick R True, Section II, "A Geographical Review of the Fisheries Industries and Fishing Communities for the Year 1880," George Brown Goode, *The Fisheries and Fish Industries of the United States,* (Washington Govt. Printing Office 1887), 645.

[25] Frederick R True, Section II, "A Geographical Review of the Fisheries Industries and Fishing Communities for the Year 1880." 646.

[26] *Door County Advocate,* 1904.

[27] Margaret Beattie Bogue, *Fishing the Great Lakes an Environmental History 1873 – 1933;* (Madison, WI: University of Wisconsin Press, 2000), 60.

[28] Ibid, 254.

[29] Scottie Dayton, "Kahlenberg Brothers Built Engines for Some of the Toughest Boats in the World"; *New Month, March/April* 1997 (New Month Magazine).

[30] Tom Kuchenberg, *Reflections In A Tarnished Mirror: The Use and Abuse of the Great Lakes;* (Sturgeon Bay, WI: Golden Glow Publishing, 1978), 36.

Chapter 2

Fishing Rigs

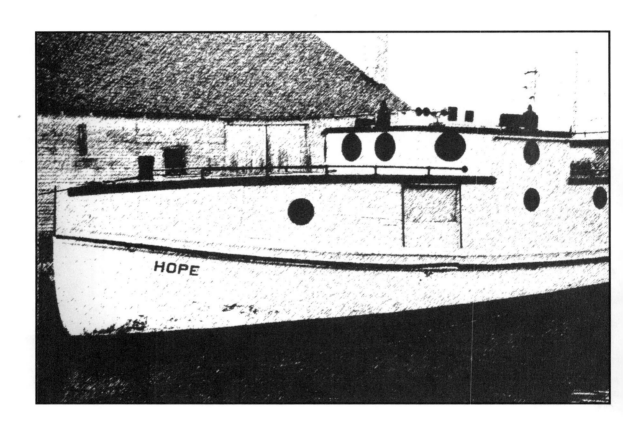

Commercial fishing has always required an effective way to harvest fish. Native Americans had already been using hoop-nets, hooks and lines, weirs, seines, gill nets, and spears, and they also had birchbark canoes as means of water transportation to fishing grounds. Such fishing methods were also known in Europe and were employed by the early fishermen of European descent who settled in the Great Lakes region, though they also adopted some ideas and techniques from the Native Americans, who were very skilled and knowledgeable about fishing these waters.

During the first forty years, between 1830 and 1870, the equipment and gear didn't change much. Fishermen had nets, a boat, and a means to preserve the fish for market. In the early years, the means of harvesting fish were limited and production was low compared to the expansive heyday that began in the late 1860s. Early fishermen relied on the wind and oars to power their boats, and on days without sufficient wind, rowing out to the fishing grounds was no easy task. The boats they used in the early days usually were small craft that could easily be brought onto the beach without a dock. Thus, a fisherman could fish close to home, and his net gear was usually a small gang of as many gill nets as he could handle. Such fishing was demanding work that required strength and stamina, and the days could be long.

Fishing Boats

Boats have always been critical to commercial fishermen, since they provide transportation to and from fishing grounds. Over the years, fishing boats have changed in many ways, but they have always had to be able to hold up in heavy seas and to bring their crews safely home. By the early 1850s, several styles of boats were in use for gill-net and pound-net fishing on Lake Michigan. The most common boats were the Mackinaw, the Huron or "square stern;" the Hayward, the Carvel, the Wheeler, and a boat called the Clinker after its construction style. Norwegian sloops were used by fishermen in some areas.

Mackinaw Boats

In 1850, most fishermen in northern Lake Michigan were using Mackinaw boats. The exceptions were mainly fishermen tending pound nets with skiffs and hand-made boats. Different regions of the Great Lakes had different styles, variations, and construction methods of the Mackinaw boat, but all evolved from a common prototype. Some experts believe they may have derived from a type of small

Fig. 2.1 Diagram of a Two Rivers style Mackinaw Boat

boat used in New England as early as 1800 which were referred to as "New England" boats, or "No-Man's-Land" boats. Other historians believe the Mackinaw boat originated in Canada along the shores of Georgian Bay.[1]

In the Lake Michigan region, Mackinaw boats were usually 22 to 26 feet long with hulls constructed with overlapping sideboards ("clinker" built). They could be double-ended or have square transoms. Most were built from local white cedar and white pine and typically were carvel-built double-ended schooners or cat ketches, rigged with lugsails. Another style used in northern Lake Michigan that was fairly close to the original design was a small carvel-built hull with a simple, cedar pole, cat ketch gaff rig. On Georgian Bay and Lake Superior, the common variety was a clinker-built double-ended craft of about 30 feet with a gaff schooner rig.

The French Canadians were the first to build flat-bottomed centerboard Mackinaw boats. They typically were double-enders with a simple hull design and double masts. According to William Radigan:

The early Mackinaw's were little more than barges with flat bottoms and rather blunt ends. Designed to take advantage of any puff of wind, they had a rudder that could be used at will and masts stout enough to take the shock of gusts on unstayed sails. Masts could be keyed into position quickly and easily by a Mackinaw skipper, and they also could be hoisted from the slot in a trice and laid aside while the sailor took to his oars.[2]

By 1880 the design of the Mackinaw had been modified and improved. Some were as little as 16 feet or as much as 34 feet in length, but typically they were 26 feet long. The usual rig was a gaff-headed ketch, but a few carried sloop rigs. There were two masts, generally about eighteen feet high with a gaff-rigged main and mizzen. Mackinaw boats in Lake Michigan often had a raked stern, and this probably shows Scandinavian influence. Mackinaw boats were well suited for fishermen and proved to be sound, seaworthy craft. They were in use longer and were safer than any other boat of that time. These boats normally had a three to four man crew and three to four boxes of nets. Biologist and Great Lakes expert, John Milner noted that:

The famous Mackinaw of the lakes has bow and stern sharp, a great deal of shear, the greatest beam forward of amidships, and tapers with little curve to the stern. It carries either schooner rig, or with a lug sail forward. It is fairly fast, the greatest surf-boat known, and with an experienced boatman will ride out any storm, or if necessary, beach with greater safety than any other boat. It is comparatively dry, and her sharp stern prevents the shipment of water aft when running with the sea. They have been longer and more extensively used on the upper lakes than any other boats, and with less loss of life or accident.[3]

Here is a list of observations concerning Mackinaw boats by two pioneer fishermen from the Two Rivers region, who relied on these boats for their livelihood:

Most of the boats were built by local carpenters or workmen. The Burger Boat Company built a few of these with a price tag of $120; (b) The De Pere boat yard turned out "clinker" or overlapping sideboards boats. Most of the Two Rivers boats were not clinker style but were simply made with butted sideboards; (c) The clinker style was given to leaking more easily than the butted style; (d) Most boats were 24 feet to 26 feet long, 4 feet deep, and 8 feet wide; (e) Decks were eventually added until some vessels had "storm shelters" under their decks; (f) The amount of canvas sail varied and this determined to a large extent the speed of the vessel; (g) The canvas sails were either red or white in color; (h) The color scheme of the boats followed a pattern. The entire boat was painted white except for a trim strip along the gunwales. John V. Allies' boat was white with a brown trim line. Other boats used white with green trim or white with maroon trim; (i) The boats were not usually unnamed nor [sic] did they bear a registration number. Some of the fishermen named their boats after their children; (j) Eighteen-foot oars were set in two staggered oar-locks so as to avoid a collision between the two rowers; (k) The main mast of a typical boat was 24 feet long from the keel to the top of the mast. A second mast was about 22 feet long placed astern; (l) Nets were lifted by using a hand roller; (m) The netting was purchased from salesmen of the American Net and Twine Company and the Linen Thread Company. It was manufactured in the eastern part of the country; (n) The entire family mended nets; (o) Each boat set 4 to 6 boxes of nets and for every box of nets in the lake there was another ashore. More money was invested in nets, etc. than in the boats themselves; (p) The gill net used lead sinkers tied along the bottom edge and wooden floats tied individually along the top edge of the net. The net was about 1,300 feet long and the netting most used was a 4 inch mesh. The nets were anchored and had a buoy on the water surface as a marker; (q) Each net had 140 leads, which were place 9 feet apart; (r) The boat usually fished in 15 to 30 fathoms of water and usually 3 to 4 miles from port; (s) The tendency was to fish in deeper water as more fish were obtained that way; (t) The netting was boiled in large outdoor boilers in order to remove slime, which, left on the nets, would rot them beyond repair; (u) Fishing was best off of a reef or rocky shelf where spawning took place. These reefs were spotted occasionally along the coastal waters of Lake Michigan. The bottom of the lake is generally sandy; (v) Buoys are about the same as the 1930s – made of cedar with a steel shaft and eyelet at the lower end and a taper running from the thinner lower end to the thicker upper end to the buoy. Attached to the upper end were a cedar pole and a small flag, sometimes with an identifying number on it.[4]

Huron, Hayward & Scandinavian Boats

The Huron boat was another style of craft used extensively by gill-net fishermen on Lake Michigan, less often on Lake Huron and only rarely on the east end of Lake Ontario. It was more or less a schooner-rigged sailboat, with less shear than the Mackinaw, but had ample room for net boxes, fish, and barrels. The better-built models were a little faster than the Mackinaw. They were generally 30 to 40 feet in length and fishermen would venture further out in the lake with the Huron boats. One inquiry into mishaps among Lake Michigan fishermen concluded that Huron boats had suffered the most accidents and fatalities, probably due to the fact that they made fishing runs out further from shore.[5]

The Hayward boat was found primarily on the eastern shore of Lake Michigan, though a number were in use at Thunder Bay, Lake Huron. This boat got its name from its maker and was typically 32 feet in length with an 8 or 9 foot beam. Hayward boats had two masts and were schooner rigged, with a gaff top sail, and some with jibs. The average cost of this type of boat was $200 to $300.

The Norwegian boat was used mainly by Scandinavian fishermen, who built this style of craft. They were cumbersome-looking boats but fared well out in the lake. They were predominantly used at Grand Haven, Michigan, though a few were reported at Racine.

The Norwegian is a huge unwieldy thing, with flaring bows, great shear and high sides, and is sloop-rigged. She is absolutely dry in all weather, and thought perfectly safe, and with ample room, is only used by the Scandinavian fishermen, most other fishermen objecting to her slowness and the great labor of rowing in time of calm.[6]

By the late 1890s the masts of many Mackinaws were hauled down and gasoline engines were installed on the boats. According to George LeClair, a fisherman from the Two Rivers area, the last Mackinaws received gasoline engines by about 1904. Other boats of this type were left in a state of disrepair and were soon disposed of as power tugs came into use. The last power Mackinaw ceased operation around 1911.[7]

Steam-powered boats had been present on the Great Lakes since 1818, but they were larger vessels used for hauling freight and passengers. The steam power revolution did not reach the northern islands of Lake Michigan until a decade after the Civil War, when fishermen on Washington Island were among the first to convert from sail-powered boats to steam power. Fishermen from that region had to venture further out in the lake and were forced to set their nets deeper to find fish. That was almost impossible in the old Mackinaw boats, and both Mackinaw and Huron boats paled in comparison to the new steam tugs that began to be used in northern Lake Michigan. The new tugs carried large rigs compared to the older sailing craft; as Milner noted:

Steam tugs usually carry from 250 to 400 nets, disposed in gangs of about 40 nets each. They are set from the stern of the boat while it steams slowly along, and are taken in over the bows, where rollers are arranged to lessen the hardship.[8]

In the fall of 1870, John O'Neil had a 41-foot steam-powered fish tug called the *Kitty Gaylord* built at Fort Howard, Wisconsin, for use on Green Bay. The official dimensions of this first-of-a-kind steam-powered fish tug (Official No. 14279) were length of 41.0 feet by 10.6 on the beam; 13 gross and 8 net tons,[9] and she was powered by a high-pressure steam engine. Many fishermen viewed this new type of craft with a certain reluctance because of its high price tag, but it proved a great success for fishermen around the islands. The cost was anywhere from $2,000 to $10,000 each and carried a weight of five to thirty tons. The forward section of the boat had bins for storing fish and boxes of ice, while the after third of the boat was housed over and used as a place to store net boxes. Rollers were arranged at the bow where the nets were pulled in and over the rollers. Using them, fishermen could double their capacity of nets and set them in far deeper water than before; they were also able to venture further out onto Lake Michigan.

Not long after the O'Neil's put their tug into service, other fishermen from Washington Harbor were putting in orders for such boats. In 1871, Ranney and Shipman had Captain H.L. Turner, a ship builder from Green Bay, Wisconsin, built them a propeller-type steam vessel measuring 51.6 feet by 11.6 on the beam and displacing 17 gross, 8 net tons. They named her the *Sarah R. Shipman* and used her for seventeen years, until she caught fire and burned in 1888.

Captain Turner also built another steam fish tug for Ranney and Bradner that same year. This boat was named the *Pottawatomie*, and was launched May 23, 1871 from Green Bay. She had a length of 48 feet by 11.6 and weighed 18 gross, 11 net tons. The machinery for this tug and most of the others was built by Sutton Brothers of Buffalo, New York, and was installed by Spencer and Emeigh, machinists from Green Bay, who had also fitted the *Shipman* with her engine. Their engines had a cylinder of 8 inches by 8 inches with a capacity of 12 horsepower. These steamboats performed very well and could reach speeds up to 10 miles per hour.[10]

The success of the new steam tugs prompted other fishermen from near-by islands to purchase their own. At St. Martin Island, the Driscoe Brothers Fishery had a similar vessel built, and the Noe Brothers of Beaver Island had one built by the Sorenson Co. in De Pere. Andrew Irr later bought the boat and had it in service for many years for his fishery on the north side of Washington Island.

These boats were all relatively small with flush decks and were devoid of any upper works which would be in the way in heavy weather. They didn't require much to operate; the engines used wood for fuel, and wood was available in great abundance on the islands. With the advent of the steam tugs, fisheries began harvesting many more fish from the lake, and by 1890, introduction of steam-powered net lifters to the fisheries almost doubled the harvests.

Lake Michigan, Georgian Bay, and Lake Erie were the three areas of the Great Lakes that had the highest production of fish. Lake Michigan became the most productive of the lakes because of its geographic and physical characteristics, market demand, and growing industry. Lake Michigan fisheries had the most extensive fleet of gill-net steamers; their numbers grew from five in 1873 to thirty in 1880 and eighty-two in 1885, but then declined to forty-eight boats by 1890.[11]

After the turn of the century another invention changed fishing boats forever and greatly enhanced commercial fishing – the introduction of gasoline and "semi-gasoline" (diesel) engines into fish tugs. Among the various companies and types of engines, the Kahlenberg engine was the most popular in northern Lake Michigan, but other common makes included Fairbanks and Morse, Straubel, Gray Marines, Cummins, and a few others.

After 1900, advances in the design of fishing boats made them more versatile. The boats were built bigger with houses attached that afforded more protection from the elements. In the early 1900s, the average size of a fishing tug was approximately 30 to 35 feet in length, with all-wood construction (usually white oak), a "barrel" type hull, and a round stern. They were not very good in heavy seas and had a tendency to roll quite a bit in high waves, according to one old Washington Island fisherman. It wasn't until the 1940s that steel hulls with a square or flat stern was introduced, giving the boat more stability in heavy seas. Both Burger and Marinette Marine built boats that had round sterns and consequently tended to roll quite a bit in heavy seas. Some local fishermen called them "Menominee Rollers."

A few boat builders around the upper Lake Michigan region specialized in building commercial fish tugs, including two located at Sturgeon Bay: Sturgeon Bay Boat Works, and the Peterson Boat Works Company.

Martin Peterson formed the Peterson Boat Works Company in 1907. His son Fred Peterson built his first boat, a commercial gill-net tug called the *Sally Lou*. During the First World War, the Peterson company closed its doors, and their employees went to work in other yards for the war effort. In 1918, the Peterson boat yard buildings caught fire and the company was destroyed.

After the Peterson company closed, Fred Peterson found work at the Smith Shipyard and then at Sturgeon Bay Boat Works, learning the craft of boat building. In 1933, he took out a loan for $1,500 and used the money to rebuild the buildings and resurrect Peterson Boat Works. They built commercial fishing boats, yachts and sailboats. Over the next few years the company grew, and during World War II they contracted with the Navy to build personnel carriers. The number of employees swelled to approximately 272. They built seventeen 110-foot submarine chasers and twelve 40-foot motor launches for the Navy and eight 85-foot rescue boats for the Army.[12]

Sturgeon Bay Boat Works was founded in 1903 by William Hayes and became one of Sturgeon Bay's most important industries. The company's early success can be credited to two master boatbuilders and craftsmen, Hans Johnson and Herman Gmack, who had learned the craft of building boats in Europe and brought their skill to this country. In its early years, the yard turned out rowing skiffs and commercial fishing boats. For nearly thirty years they were responsible for building many of the commercial fishing boats for the region and elsewhere around Lake Michigan.

Hans' son Palmer took over the company after his father passed away in 1931. In the 1930s, Sturgeon Bay Boat Works began building yachts and pleasure craft, turning out such illustrious yachts as *Last Buccaneer, Copperhead, Tahuna, Northern Light*, and *Samara*. During World War II, the company was awarded a government contract to build six 65-foot supply boats, fifteen 42-foot and twenty-two 45-foot aircraft rescue boats and won an Army Navy "E" for excellence.[13]

After the war, Sturgeon Bay Boat Works again began building yachts. They turned more exclusively to building Gilbert Dunham's "Stout Fella" design sloop and no longer built commercial fishing tugs. Palmer Johnson retired in 1956 and the company was sold to local businessmen. They changed the name of the company to Palmer Johnson because his name had become synonymous with the company and its reputation for craftsmanship. The company still thrives today, building yachts for clients scattered all over the globe. Mike Kelsey now runs the company. He took over from his father, Mike Kelsey Sr., long-time president, and Bill Parsons who kept the company prosperous for many years.

Another major builder of commercial fishing tugs was the Burger Boat Company based in Manitowoc. They built commercial fishing boats well into the 1950s. Marinette Marine Company in Marinette, Wisconsin, also built commercial fish tugs for several years, and the T. D. Vinette Company in Escanaba, Michigan, and builders at Muskegon, Michigan, by the name of Henry E. Danhof and Vern Kleiner also turned out a number of boats.

Lake Michigan and Lake Superior fishing tugs were built differently than those on the other Great Lakes. The upper Great Lakes (Michigan & Superior) tugs were built with open decks, in contrast to a closed deck with the engine placed beneath it typical of Lake Erie tugs. Any water that came on board the upper Great Lakes tugs was pumped out of the bilge rather than flowing out the scuppers as on a Lake Erie tug. Lake Michigan and Superior tugs were somewhat smaller in design, shorter in length and narrower in the beam than Lake Erie tugs, but were built to a heavier design. The frames and ribs were closer together and the hulls were clad with plating that was quarter-inch or heavier. They proved to be more seaworthy and were very good breaking through ice.[14] The engine was installed amidship and was located above the deck. Another difference was that the wheelhouse, or pilot house, was elevated and located either amidship or aft on the upper Great Lakes tugs. Engine sizes in the early days ranged from 10 to 70 horsepower, depending on the size of the boat. By the 1930s, diesel engines were being fitted into the fish tugs and the boats were being built either with steel hulls or with wooden hulls covered with quarter-inch inch steel sheets. This last is what fisherman called "tinning over."

Early fish tugs, built circa 1900, were built with the pilothouse towards the bow of the boat and the engine located amidship. There was normally a door or hatch in the side of the forward house for hauling in nets and where the mechanical net lifter was eventually housed, and there was another door in the aft section from which the fishermen would set their nets. In the 1920s, the design of a fish boat changed somewhat, placing a pilothouse and steering station amidship in some of the newer boats, while others had a rear pilothouse. Placing the house and steering station in the aft section eliminated one crew member, since it allowed the skipper to help set the nets, and it also provided a more comfortable ride in heavy seas than having it in the forward section of the boat.

Another type of fishing boat used in northern Lake Michigan was the pound-net boat or herring boat, which had a completely different design than that of a fish tug. Pound-net boats were somewhat like large open skiffs with small decks both forward and aft – the decks were usually about eight feet long at the stern and six feet at the bow – while the midsection of the boat remained open for the cargo of fish. Normally the boats were 28 feet in length so they could easily be maneuvered inside the "pot" area of the net; some pound-net boats were 30 or 32 feet long, but most were built at 28 feet. The depth of the boat from the gunwale to the bottom of the boat at mid-ship was approximately 4 feet, and it was about 3 feet at the bow and stern. Running along the inside on each side of the boat was a platform of planking located about a foot below the gunwale; it provided a place to stand when hauling in nets.

The pound-net boats on Green Bay circa 1870 were relatively large, flat-bottomed, and had broad beams. Their average length was about 28 feet with a 9-foot beam and a depth of about forty-two inches. They could carry anywhere from 60 to 80 boxes of fish. An average manageable load was 70 boxes, or approximately 10,500 pounds. Elsewhere on the lake there were many variations in the design of pound-net boats. Along the eastern shore of Green Bay they typically didn't have masts or sails, but were propelled by oars. On the western shore of Lake Michigan in the Two Rivers region, some had one mast and a gaff sail, while others had two masts. They tended to be somewhat better built than those used in the waters of the bay. The average cost of a pound net boat with masts and sails was about $200.[15]

In the early days of pound-net fishing in the Two Rivers area, the boats typically had flat bottoms and open decks, resembling oversized rowboats. On occasion, a round-bottom boat with a covered deck, known as a "whaleback," was used with another boat or scow or even a raft towed behind to hold the stakes and the pile driver, a derrick with a weighted hammer which was raised and lowered by three or four men to drive the stakes into the lake bed.[16]

Driving stakes is considered the hardest work connected with the pound-net fishery. Under the most favorable conditions, the weather being calm and the lake bottom clay, four men can drive about twenty stakes in a single day. On the west shore of Lake Michigan, in the vicinity of Two Rivers, the pile drivers are built more substantially than in some other localities. On account of frequent storms and heavy seas, they are not mounted on rafts, but on two pound-net boats lashed together.[17]

Around 1900, there were gradual improvements to the equipment used for pound-net fishing. Around 1895, steam hammers were installed on the scows, which allowed stakes to be more easily driven into the lake bottom. By 1904, gasoline engines were being installed in pound-net boats, which allowed nets to be set in deeper water; some were reported being set in as much as eighty feet of water. Setting the stakes in deeper water posed an additional problem in that it put more stress on the tamarack stakes (most often used in the early days) which as a result would break off. As a result, fishermen began to splice heavy hardwood stakes (oak, white ash, or elm) to the lighter softwood stakes. A splice was usually around seven feet in length and held together by nine bolts.

To remove fish from the "pot" of a pound net, a boat is maneuvered to the outside of the net, and the line holding the tunnel open is released. At each corner, the net is held in place by a rope and pulley system that are attached to the king stakes; these must be released and the corners raised. Then the side of the net is temporarily lowered so the boat can be maneuvered into the pot. After raising the inside corners the harvesting commences. Normally three or four men are required for this task; as they move the boat, fish gather toward the outside of the net and scoops are used to bring the fish aboard the boat.

Modern pound-net and trap-net boats are typically 30 to 40 feet in length and are constructed entirely of steel. They usually have a small pilothouse in the bow section of the boat while the rest of the boat is all deck, with the engine located in a hold at midship. Some boats have compartments under the deck for storing fish boxes and fish. Trap-net and pound-net boats are of relatively simple design and are very practical, built specifically for their task.

Prior to 1900 and the advent of the gasoline engines, pound-net boats relied on sails or oars for power. Under these conditions, pound nets were an ideal style of fishing because they were set near the shoreline and didn't require a fisherman to venture far out on the lake. A pound-net boat could hold approximately three tons of fish in the hold, and a fisherman had to be conscious of this fact and not overload the boat, since it could become unstable and might overturn if caught in bad weather. In Iceland the biggest loss of life of fishermen was due to overloading the boats with fish.

From the Mackinaw boat to the modern fish tug and trap net-boats, a fisherman's boat was designed for practicality and safety rather than for looks or comfort, and an inside look at a modern fish tug reveals that is technologically complex. Skippers no longer have to rely on clock and compass, as they did during the first half of the twentieth century. An automatic Loran-C receiver serves as a computerized navigation aid that not only establishes locations but also can determine course for the automatic pilot feature. A modern fish tug is also equipped with radar for navigation and sonar for sounding water depths, and many boats have a wood stove or (in later years) a furnace to provide heat during the colder months. "Everybody I know is convinced we freeze to death fishing in the winter," says commercial fisherman Charlie Henriksen. "We tell them we have heat in the boat. Sometimes it's so damn hot in there, you can hardly stand it."

Navigational Aids

Modern navigational aids have greatly improved fishermen's ability to navigate the lake with greater safety and ease. Lighthouses and range lights have fallen into disuse and are now mostly for nostalgic and aesthetic purposes. Sonar, radar, long-range navigational aids (Loran), and Global Positioning Systems have become standard equipment for mariners. They are a very precise and accurate and are relatively easy to use.

The Loran (Long Range Navigation) system relies on shore-based radio transmitters provided by the United States Coast Guard. A Loran chain consists of three to six transmitting stations separated by several hundred miles. A radio transmission signals to two distant secondary stations, and these stations then retransmit the signals. The loran receiver picks up both the original signal and the secondary transmission and measures the time between them. The elapsed time appears in microseconds on a display screen, and the differences in arrival times allows (automatic) calculation of the distances from the two points which in turn allows (automatic) plotting of the ship's position.[18]

Loran A, the first Loran system, was developed in the 1940s. In the early 1950s there began to be a demand for a longer-range electronic navigation system than the standard Loran-A system, and, as a result, the Loran C system was developed and became operational in 1957. Loran C uses a system employing synchronized pulses for both time difference and phase comparison. Today a mariner can use Loran C to navigate over long distances.

The Global Positioning System (GPS) is a satellite based radio-navigational system operated and controlled by the Department of Defense through the United States Air Force. GPS was formerly known as the Navstar Global Positioning System and was initiated in 1973 to reduce the proliferation of navigational aids. GPS consists of a constellation of twenty-four satellites orbiting earth in six planes of four satellites each, at an altitude of 109,000 miles. Mariners can expect to have seven to nine satellites available for use if they have an unrestricted view of the sky.[19] Because it has overcome the limitations of many existing navigational systems, GPS has attracted a broad spectrum of users. Because its capabilities are accessible with small, easily portable, inexpensive equipment, GPS is being used in many applications in addition to classical navigation.

GPS determines location by computing the difference between the time that a signal is sent and the time it is received. GPS satellites carry atomic clocks that provide extremely accurate time. The time information is placed in the codes broadcast by the satellite so that a receiver can continuously determine the time the signal was broadcast. The signal contains data that a receiver uses to compute the locations of the satellites and to make other adjustments needed for accurate positioning. The receiver uses the time difference between the time of signal reception and the broadcast time to compute the distance, or range, from the receiver to the satellite. The receiver must account for propagation delays, or decreases in the signal's speed caused by the ionosphere and the troposphere. With information about the ranges to three different satellites and the location of the satellites when their signals were sent, the receiver can compute its own three-dimensional position.

Radio Detection and Ranging (radar) is a navigational aid which uses radio waves of very short wavelength sent out as a narrow beam by a highly directional aerial. The aerial rotates, sending the beam out through a full 360 degrees, and any solid object of reasonable size will reflect the part of the beam back to the aerial. Precise measurement of elapsed time between the time the signal was sent and the time the reflected signal was received allows (automatic) calculation of the distance to the object along the line of the beam, which allows display of the object on the radar screen as a bright spot at that distance out along the rotating beam.

Engine Types

With the advent of the gasoline engine at the turn of the century more fishermen were installing them into their boats. Most of the early fishing boats had Kahlenberg gasoline and (later) diesel engines. The Kahlenberg engines were designed and built by the Kahlenberg brothers of Two Rivers, Wisconsin, and since its organization in 1895, the Kahlenberg Brothers Company has devoted its entire time and attention to the manufacture of heavy-duty internal combustion engines. These engines came in different sizes and horsepower ranging from 10 to 200 horsepower and from two to six cylinders. The engines are very heavy and actually provide ballast for a fish tug.

Two brothers, W. R. and Otto Kahlenberg, opened a small machine shop in Two Rivers, Wisconsin, in 1895 where they rebuilt marine steam engines and also built small vertical steam engines for marine craft. At this time fishermen were either using two-man 18-foot Mackinaw boats or steam-powered fish tugs. The brothers were very familiar with the steam engines being used and thought there had to be a more efficient and better way to power these marine boats.

It took reading an article about Karl Benz designing the first gasoline-powered boat that gave W. R. his own ideas. In December of 1899, W. R began working on what was to be the first gasoline-powered marine engine. The result of his four-month design was a single cylinder, twin stroke, and direct reversible engine with a gasoline vaporizer. W. R worked throughout the winter on tweaking this engine until every little detail was just right.

On April 12 the very first Kahlenberg engine was born and fitted into a local fisherman's boat. It was a single cylinder eight horsepower internal combustion engine that performed remarkably and reversed without stopping from full speed ahead to full astern, which was almost unheard for a gasoline engine to perform. The cost of the engine was $353.07 and at that time the cost of gas was 13 cents per gallon.[20]

Heald and Hayes, two fishermen from Door County, bought an eight horsepower gasoline engine from the Kahlenberg's on December 19, 1900 and commented, "We can run twice as many gill nets as heretofore, and make six lifts a week instead of three or four as is the case with sail. We make a trip from six to eight hours every day and our engine gives perfect satisfaction."[21]

It wasn't long before word spread all around Lake Michigan how dependable, easy to operate, and low-maintenance Kahlenberg engines were. By 1901, seventeen had been ordered and were paid for in two installments. At the turn of the century, Kahlenberg Brothers was one of the five firms manufacturing internal combustion engines for use in fishing boats. Over the years, many fishermen concluded that Kahlenberg engines were very durable and dependable and that they offered everything needed to run their boats in all kinds of conditions.

Kahlenberg

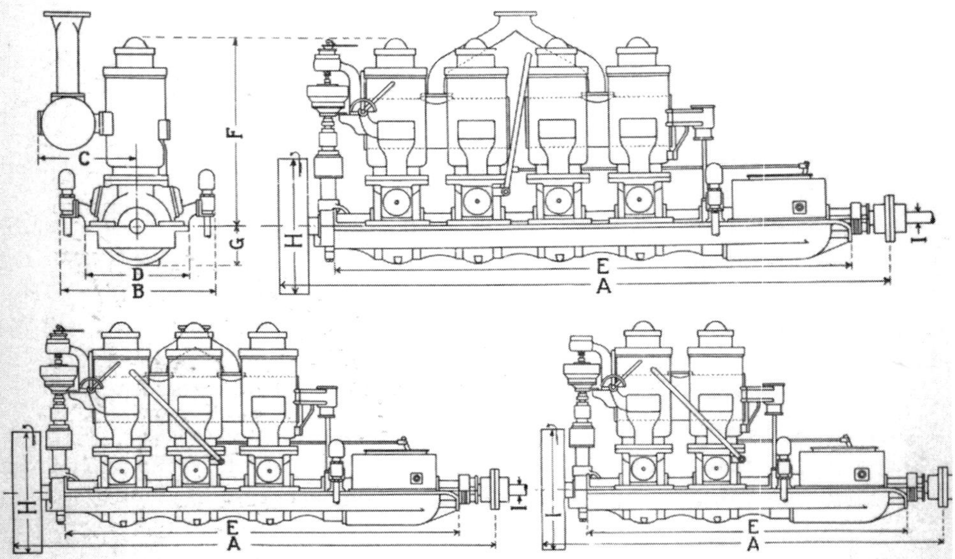

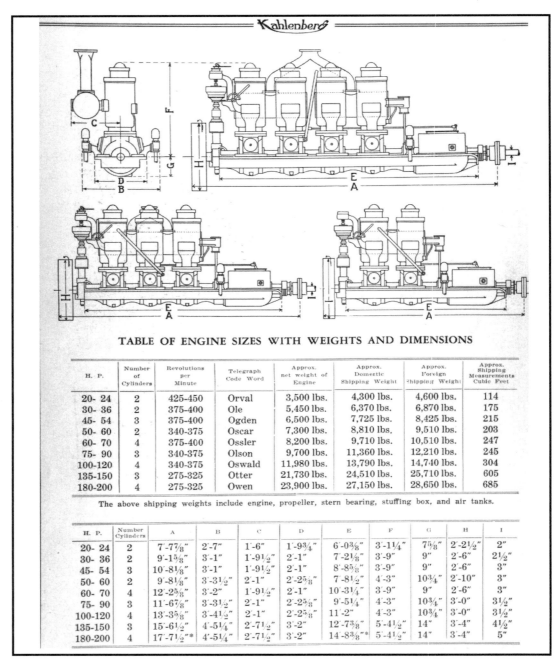

TABLE OF ENGINE SIZES WITH WEIGHTS AND DIMENSIONS

H. P.	Number of Cylinders	Revolutions per Minute	Telegraph Code Word	Approx. net weight of Engine	Approx. Domestic Shipping Weight	Approx. Foreign Shipping Weight	Approx. Shipping Measurements Cubic Feet
20- 24	2	425-450	Orval	3,500 lbs.	4,300 lbs.	4,600 lbs.	114
30- 36	2	375-400	Ole	5,450 lbs.	6,370 lbs.	6,870 lbs.	175
45- 54	3	375-400	Ogden	6,500 lbs.	7,725 lbs.	8,425 lbs.	215
50- 60	2	340-375	Oscar	7,300 lbs.	8,810 lbs.	9,510 lbs.	203
60- 70	4	375-400	Ossler	8,200 lbs.	9,710 lbs.	10,510 lbs.	247
75- 90	3	340-375	Olson	9,700 lbs.	11,360 lbs.	12,210 lbs.	245
100-120	4	340-375	Oswald	11,980 lbs.	13,790 lbs.	14,740 lbs.	304
135-150	3	275-325	Otter	21,730 lbs.	24,510 lbs.	25,710 lbs.	605
180-200	4	275-325	Owen	23,900 lbs.	27,150 lbs.	28,650 lbs.	685

The above shipping weights include engine, propeller, stern bearing, stuffing box, and air tanks.

H. P.	Number Cylinders	A	B	C	D	E	F	G	H	I
20- 24	2	7′-7⅞″	2′-7″	1′-6″	1′-9¾″	6′-0⅜″	3′-1¼″	7⅝″	2′-2½″	2″
30- 36	2	9′-1⅝″	3′-1″	1′-9½″	2′-1″	7′-2⅛″	3′-9″	9″	2′-6″	2½″
45- 54	3	10′-8⅛″	3′-1″	1′-9½″	2′-1″	8′-8⅝″	3′-9″	9″	2′-6″	3″
50- 60	2	9′-8⅛″	3′-3½″	2′-1″	2′-2⅝″	7′-8½″	4′-3″	10¾″	2′-10″	3″
60- 70	4	12′-2⅝″	3′-2″	1′-9½″	2′-1″	10′-3¼″	3′-9″	9″	2′-6″	3″
75- 90	3	11′-6⅞″	3′-3½″	2′-1″	2′-2⅝″	9′-5¼″	4′-3″	10¾″	3′-0″	3½″
100-120	4	13′-3⅝″	3′-4½″	2′-1″	2′-2⅝″	11′-2″	4′-3″	10¾″	3′-0″	3½″
135-150	3	15′-6½″	4′-5¼″	2′-7½″	3′-2″	12′-7⅜″	5′-4½″	14″	3′-4″	4½″
180-200	4	17′-7½″*	4′-5¼″	2′-7½″	3′-2″	14′-8⅜″*	5′-4½″	14″	3′-4″	5″

Fig 2.2 Courtesy of Kahlenberg Brothers Two Rivers, Wisconsin.

In 1912, W.R. introduced a semi-diesel engine that started on gasoline and then converted to injected #2 fuel oil after the engine warmed up. This new design had special cylinder heads and dual injection equipment. In 1914 the Kahlenbergs built a marine engine that ran on fuel-oil injection; it was designed, patented, and built by William R Kahlenberg. The engine was an experimental single-cylinder model that was tested in the plant for a year. By 1916 this heavy duty crude-oil design had been modified and was introduced as a two-cylinder engine and sold to Two Rivers commercial fishermen Art Luebke and Hugo Heller for their new boat the *Karlsruhe*. This engine design became very popular, and the Kahlenberg Brothers Company produced large numbers of them. The engines ranged from two to four cylinders for use in commercial fishing vessels, and there eventually were more Kahlenberg engines in commercial fishing vessels on the Great Lakes than all other makes combined. Moreover, the Kahlenbergs exported more engines than they sold domestically.

World War II brought the Kahlenberg plant large contracts, and they produced engines at a record pace to keep up with demand. One government order was for 300 Kahlenberg engines ranging from 120 to 250 horsepower. The company largely supplied the United States Transportation Corps, and as demand increased, the number of employees swelled to over one hundred and worked a seventy-hour week to keep their production schedule. By this time Kahlenberg Brothers Company was solely dedicated to the war effort, and they ceased production for other agencies and for private firms. After the war, a glutted market in marine engines caused a slump in domestic sales for the company, but they still produced steam whistles and propellers, and eventually marine engine sales picked up again, especially in Europe, Latin America, and the Philippines.

During the 1950s the Kahlenberg Brothers Company developed their turbo-charged model E engine designed by chief engineer, Roger Kahlenberg. The six-cylinder engine developed 600 to 900 horsepower in the 300 to 400 rpm range and was used mainly in larger tugboats, army transports, and tankers. Kahlenberg Brothers Company continued production until 1964, but then ceased making marine engines due to heavy competition. The company today still is successful producing quality air horns and propellers for marine craft.[22]

Kahlenberg engines had an unusual sound and their chugging rhythmic cadence was easily recognizable. The engine would run at a slow rpm, somewhere between 375 to 400 rpm and could propel the boat to speeds of six to ten miles per hour. "It was the most efficient, dependable engine, I think, that they ever had on the lake", says commercial fisherman Laurence Daubner. "When you opened it wide open, you knew you were going home."

According to Jake Ellefson it was quite a procedure to start these engines:

> To begin with, most of the fish tugs had their fuel tanks in the bow section of the boat, which provided gravity feed for the fuel to reach the engine because the tank was at a higher elevation. There was a separate fuel tank designed to fuel the blowtorches that were used to heat up the glow plugs on the engine; this tank was often called a torch tank and held a few gallons of fuel oil. On the top of each cylinder of the engine, behind a metal flap, there was a glow plug that was used for ignition purposes. The torches were used to heat the glow plugs until they were glowing with heat. Before heating the glow plugs each cylinder of the engine had to be primed

with fuel, which was done by a means of a small crank that pumped the fuel into the cylinder. After these two procedures were complete, then the next step was to introduce a blast of compressed air into the engine to turn the pistons, compressing the fuel air mixture, as the heated glow plug would ignite the mixture. There were typically two tanks four to five feet long that held 120 to 150 PSI of compressed air for starting purposes. The compressor, located at the back of the engine ran off the engine's eccentrics, which also operated the bilge pump and a water pump for cooling purposes. A small valve on top of the compressor was used to fill the tanks. At the end of the day a valve would be opened to refill the tank for the following day's starting procedure.[23]

There were many other makes and models of engines around besides the Kahlenberg. The Norge was a semi-diesel engine that was similar to the Kahlenberg and was popular with some fisheries. The Fairbanks and Morse engine was also very similar to the Kahlenberg and ran on gas or diesel; it was very dependable and was preferred by some fishermen. The Hagen brothers, Jule and Charlie Hagen, two fishermen from St. Ignace swore by these engines. They would often say, in a slight joking manner, "There's no other engine that can beat these engines. Those Kahlenberg's, the only good place for them is the bottom of the lake."

These older, heavier engines remained in use on fishing tugs until newer and more modern diesel engines became available. Both Caterpillar and Cummins diesel engines were far easier to start than the old semi-diesel and gasoline engines. On some boats there was a second engine that ran the mechanical net lifter, and this was usually no more than a 5 horsepower engine.

There were other popular marine diesel engines used in fishing tugs. One of the early ones was the Gray marine engine made during the first decade of the twentieth century by the Gray Motor Company of Detroit, Michigan. By 1908, the company had become an established manufacturer of marine engines and produced one, two, three, and four-cylinder engines. In that year, a 2.5 horsepower one-cylinder engine cost $67.50.[24] These early marine engines were used in small vessels and fishing boats.

Another popular engine used in the early fishing boats was the Straubel engine, built by the Straubel Machine Company in Green Bay, Wisconsin. They built one, two, and three-cylinder engines. The Kahlenbergs and the Straubel Machine Company were the two major northeastern Wisconsin manufacturers of internal combustion marine engines. However, in the 1940s and 1950s, Cummins, Buda, Chrysler, International, Volvo Penta, and Caterpillar diesel engines became popular for use in fish tugs; they offered more horsepower and were considerably lighter and smaller than their old iron predecessors. Kahlenberg Brothers ceased making engines in March of 1964, though they still produced parts for their engines. Times were definitely changing as the newer, lighter, and more powerful engines were installed in the fish tugs.

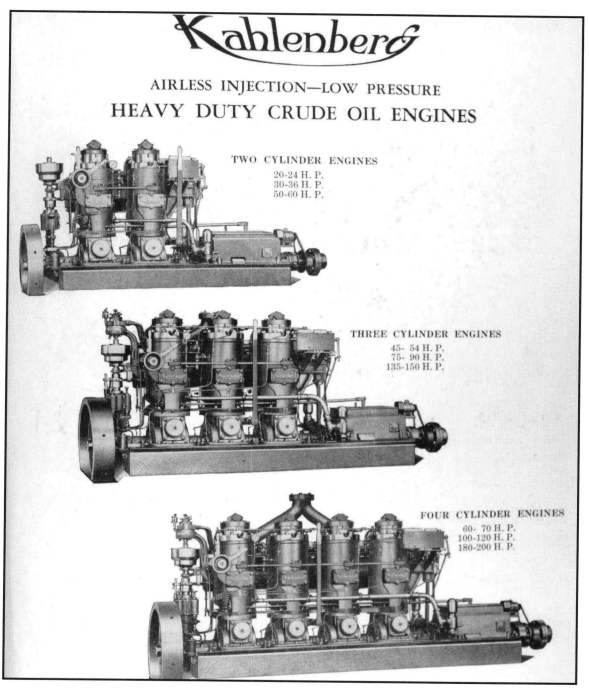

Fig. 2.3. Kahlenberg engines. Courtesy of Kahlenberg BrothersCo.

Mechanical Net Lifters

Fig 2.4 Mechanical net lifter and gill net in operation. Illustration by Gustaf T. Sandstrom; Bureau of Commercial Fisheries (Courtesy of Milwaukee Public Library)

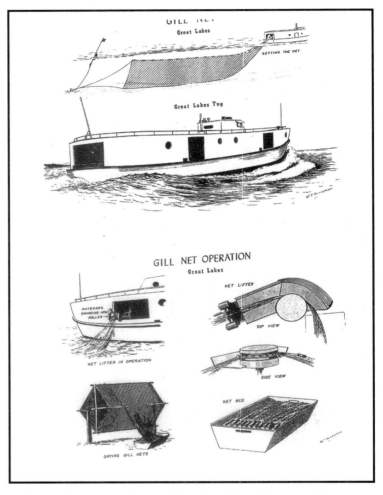

Mechanical net lifters transformed the commercial fishery into a viable industry by enabling a fisherman to double his net capacity and to use the nets at greater depths. They were introduced around 1900 and replaced steam net lifters that had been in service since about 1891. From 1870 to the turn of the century, fishermen working on steam tugs set the nets from the stern of the boat as it moved slowly ahead and retrieved the nets from the bow with the assistance of rollers and this new device.

Prior to using net lifters, fishermen had to pull the nets in by hand. Joe LeClair, a retired fisherman from Jacksonport, Wisconsin reflects:

I remember my dad used to lift by hand over a roller they had rigged up. They would open up the doors and throw out these large wooden rollers. The rollers were four to five feet long and six inches in diameter, which were braced to the boat. They would pull the nets over the rollers, sometimes in forty or fifty fathom – that was hard work. My mother made special heavy leather gloves for them to wear to protect their hands from getting split and bloody. They would only fish four or five boxes of nets back then – that was all they could handle.

Many fishermen who could afford the new mechanical lifters quickly installed them in their boats.

By 1910 nearly all the fisheries in Lake Michigan had them.

The two most popular lifters were the Crossley and the Pentwater, and both proved to be very reliable. A lifter was installed in the prow section of the boat just inside the bow hatch and was typically powered by a small engine. Once they reached the net, the fisherman would swing the roller out from the front steering station door, which typically is located about fifteen feet aft of the bow. The buoy line was pulled in with the net bridle, run through the roller, and then attached to the lifter, a twenty-four inch hydraulic winch that sat horizontally near the door. Between the roller and the drum there would be a pan along which the nets move along. The head of the winch rotates and grabs the net and pulls it from the water. The lifter has a cam in it that opens and closes dropping the net at the right position, usually half of the circumference of the lifter. Basically the net is dragged half way around the drum then the cam opens releasing the net on the table, where the fish are removed and put into one box and the net in another.

Fishing Nets and Gear

When the fisheries began in the early 1800s the common means of harvesting fish was by the use of nets. Two net types, the gill net and the pound net, were the most common and then eventually trap nets were used. In the 1830s seine nets set from a rowboat dominated the commercial fishing industry, but by 1850 fishermen began using gill nets and pound nets more frequently. Seining was effective when the fish came into shallow water near the shore or into rivers in large numbers to spawn. The seine was a simple technique and the least expensive of the nets. The net itself was a fine mesh comprised of cotton or linen. It ranged in length up to 900 to 1,000 feet. The seine net had wood floats called corks along the top of the net and lead weights attached along the bottom of the net. A fisherman would anchor one end of the net to the shore and with his rowboat he would take the other end of the net out past the shore, make a wide sweep, and return back to shore, trapping whatever fish in that area.[25] In some cases fishermen would pull the net ashore or rig up a device that used a capstan and a team of horses. As the years went by new types of nets that could harvest more fish became popular, and by 1850 seine nets were declining in popularity.

Pound Net

The pound net, short for impoundment gear was introduced to the fisheries of the Great Lakes sometime in the late 1830s. The pound net was developed in Scotland and became popular in North America as immigrants began arriving more frequently. Fishermen in the Connecticut River and in the Lake Ontario region, particularly the Black River region, were using this type of net as early as 1830.[26] By 1850 fishermen in Lake Huron and Lake Michigan adopted this new style net, harvesting whitefish, herring and lake trout. Compared to the seine net, the pound net was costly and very complex, and would entrap fish rather than entangle them. The average price for pound net gear in the 1870s was $500, and a pound net boat cost approximately $200. Today the average price for a pound net is

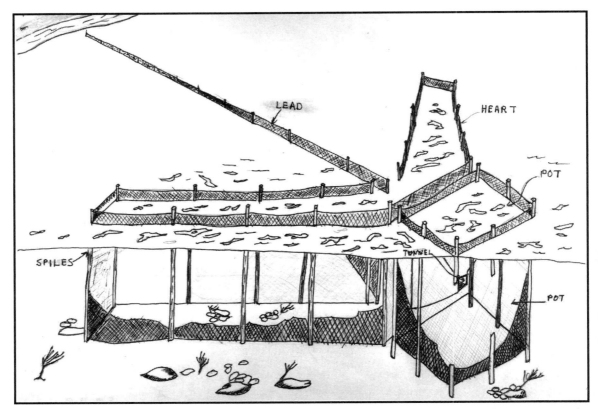

Fig.2.5 Pound net set up circa 1890 "spiles," or stakes were driven into the lake bed. The lead ran from shallow to deep water toward the heart and pot.

$8,000 and a boat, $150,000.

The pound net works on the principle that a fish encounters the lead, which is more or less an obstacle to them and instinctively heads for deeper water. This lead is typically 1,200 feet long and made of larger mesh netting (14 inch mesh). It is tapered to the slope of the bank. Floats keep the top of the net at the surface, while lead weights hold the bottom down. It is secured by anchored lines in deeper water and in the old days stakes were used in shallow water. The lead extends from shallow water, near the shoreline, to deeper water where the heart and pot portion of the net is located.

The pound net consists of three parts, the lead, the "heart" and tunnel, and the pot. For example, let's say a whitefish encounters the lead net, usually a 7 to 14-inch mesh; it will swim to the deeper end of the lead and into the other part of the net referred to as the "heart," which usually has a 6 to 11-inch mesh. The fish then swims into the top of the smaller mesh net area (4-inch mesh) and out of the bottom, which serves as a funnel to the pot or bowl section. The pot is the main part of the net where the fish are collected. The pot has a mesh size of 2 up to 4 inches and is suspended by stakes. They are formed by splicing a heavy maple post to a lighter stake of white ash. In the early days the stakes or, "spiles and sticks" as some fishermen called them, were made of tamarack. However, around the turn of the twentieth century as improvements to equipment were made, pound nets were set deeper. As a result, the lighter tamarack sticks tended to snap. Fishermen began splicing heavier hardwood with the tamarack or splicing two hardwood stakes together, thus allowing for sturdier, more stable stakes.[27]

Fig 2.6 diagram of a Two Rivers style pound net, showing location and distance of the stakes or spiles.

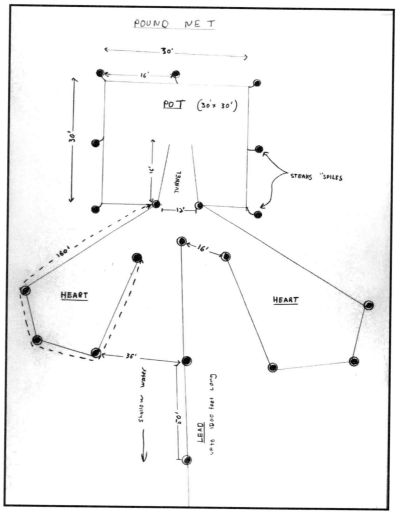

The "pot" or "bowl" is the main portion of the net and is 30 to 40 feet square and 25 to 30 feet deep. It has a mesh net bottom and is attached to the main stakes by a series of hoops. It can be lowered then raised for the harvesting of fish. The pots could be set as deep as 80 or 90 feet, normally they are set in about 40 to 60 feet, but most often they are set in about 30 feet of water.

When the time comes to harvest fish from the net, a boat designed for this type of fishing is positioned at the outside of the net. The line holding the tunnel or heart open is released. Each corner of the net is held in place by a rope and pulley system. The ropes are released and the corners are raised. One side of the net is lowered allowing the boat to be maneuvered over the pot. The corners of the net are then raised and the gathering begins. Typically, two fishermen are needed for scooping, sometimes three if there are a lot of fish. As the boat is moved, the fish are bunched toward the outside of the net where scoop nets are used to collect the fish.

Pound nets require many factors to properly function. First it's helpful to have calm seas when setting them, and to locate the net in an area of the lake that has a soft bottom in which to drive the stakes.   Years ago the nets were set and hung on stakes that were driven into the lake bed with a pile driver that was operated either by hand or by steam power. Driving the stakes was considered the most laborious task associated with pound net fishing. The Hickey Brothers, fishermen from Baileys Harbor, use a winch and the weight of their boat to drive the stakes into the lake bed.

The pile driver was a 25-foot wooden upright tower or derrick with a hammer attached to a rope that ran through an eyehook at the top of the rig. Four or five men would pull on the rope to raise the hammer. Then it was released, dropping down with all its weight to drive the stakes into the lake bed. The stakes would normally be driven into the bottom of the lake 6 or 7 feet.

Pound nets were set in the spring of the year, usually by the first of May, and left in until mid June. They were reset in the fall of the year, coinciding with the spawning season of whitefish and herring, in late October. It took a few days to set up a pound net; typically a day to set the stakes, and another day to set the twine. Spring harvests were never as abundant as those of the fall season. In late October pound nets were set and required two boats to carry all the twine. The nets were left in the water for about a month and a half or just before the close of the whitefish season. In the early days, the pound nets were left in until ice began to form on the lake.

The normal daily routine was to maneuver one of two or three 28 to 30-foot long open deck boats, directly over the pot portion of the pound net and then raised by hand to scoop out the fish. Jake Ellefson, a Washington Island fisherman related one incident:

> **O**ne time we put about 6 ton of herring on our 28-foot boat. We had a two-foot high gunwale off the deck on that boat and we had her loaded to the hilt. That day we had four men with us, Steve, Walt, Dale, and me. We had a little cabin over the engine, in the center of the boat, with two guys on each side of the cabin. The herring were up to our knees, and every now and then a herring would flip over the side of the boat because we were level full and then there were all the packing boxes besides. You talk about loaded...boy, we were loaded.[28]

The marketable whitefish or herring were removed from the net and others were released back into the lake. During the peak run of fish, fishermen would tend their nets twice a day, usually going out at daybreak to empty the pot and again in the early evening. This was demanding work that required heavy lifting, scooping, and pulling the pot to retrieve the fish. Pound net fishing required more equipment and labor than other methods of fishing. But this style of fishing was less risky and was more routine than gill net fishing. Pound net fishermen rarely had to travel far to their fishing grounds, but they had a large capital investment in their equipment.

After the pound nets were dismantled late in the fall or after the spring season, the old cotton and nylon nets required a certain degree of maintenance which proved to be a big task due to their size. It often took up to a month to do this. The size and weight of pound nets was very immense. The stakes could be as long as 90 feet, but were typically around 50 feet. In 1879, a pound net set off the north shore of St. Martin Island, at the entrance of the bay, was reported to be the deepest pound net on the Great Lakes. The pot stood in 97 feet of water and was enclosed by stakes 120 feet long with three splices.[29] The leads ranged from a 1,000 to 1,200 feet and the hearts are normally 175 feet long.

In the early days pound nets were made of cotton and had to be treated so they wouldn't rot from being submerged in the water for long periods of time. The nets were dipped into vats of tar and then spread out to dry. Once dried, the fishermen would repair any damaged nets. After all that was completed, they were put away for the following season.

Gill Net

Fig. 2.7 Gill nets stand like a fence along the bottom, but can also be suspended; contains floats along the top and weights along the bottom. Generally set perpendicular to shore and strung end to end in gangs. (Illustration by Trygvie Jensen)

Fishermen relied extensively on gill nets for fishing deeper waters. Native Americans developed and used this type of net for centuries. It was adapted for commercial use in the 1830s and became common by the 1840s. Gill net fishing demanded hard work and experience. Fishermen had to battle the elements that put their seamanship skills to the test when confronted with sudden storms, fog, and snowstorms. "As a class, the gill net fishermen are, perhaps, the most venturesome men, and at the same time the most skillful seamen, of the lakes. In certain regions they set their nets near the shore, but in other localities they invariably fish at a distance of 20 or 30 miles from land, and frequently encounter storms, which, were it not for their skill in managing their boats, would inevitably overwhelm them."[30] Gill nets have been the most common type of net gear used in Lake Michigan since its inception in the early 1800s due to its versatility. They are still used extensively by today's commercial fishermen. As recently as the 1970s, the gill net was the most common type of gear used.

Table 2.1 Percentage of Total Catch Landed by Various Types of Gear (circa 1970s)

Type of Gear	Percentage
Gill nets	38%
Trap and Pound net	33%
Trawl net	23%
Seines	2%
Fyke, hoops and other gear	4%

From Frank Prothero, *Men 'N' Boats*: The Fisheries of the Great Lakes.

In the early days of commercial fishing, gill nets were set from Mackinaw boats. This was a physically demanding job and proved to be dangerous as well. Fishermen were constantly exposed to the elements and could easily find themselves overwhelmed by a sudden storm or squall. In 1885 a report by the U.S. Commission of Fish and Fisheries noted that the average Lake Michigan sailboat carried 60 to 100 nets, while steam tugs after 1870 fished several times as many nets. In 1885, fishermen on the Great Lakes used 97,000 gill nets, covering 5,300 miles in length.[31] These gill net fishermen spent a great deal of their time maintaining and caring for their nets and boats. Most of the repair and maintenance to their rigs was done in the off-season or when fishing was slow.

Table 2.2 Capital Investment and Apparatus Summary on Lake Michigan, 1880.

Gear	Number	Value
Vessels and boats	642	$125,895
Pound nets	476	$185, 425
Gill nets	24,599	$124, 740
Seines	19	$2,040
Other apparatus		$8,935
Shore property		$104,100

Data compiled from Frederick W. True; Lake Michigan and Its Fisheries Statistical Summation; Section II A Geographical Review of the Fisheries Industries and Fishing Communities for the year 1880.

The gill net works on the principle that it entangles a fish when it comes in contact with the net. It is the most versatile of all gear types and can be set at any depth. Moreover, the lake bottom isn't an issue as it is with the pound nets. The gill net is similar in concept to a tennis net, and is usually 1,000 to 1,200 feet long and 10 feet wide, with a float line on top and a lead line on the bottom. These two lines that the net or twine are attached to is known as maitre lines. The lead line or bottom line is weighted down by lead weights and keeps the netting submerged near the lake bottom. The float line is the top line and keeps the netting extended to its full height or depth. With lake currents acting on the net there's always a little "bag" in the net. If the current is strong it can pull the net down. If there is less current, the net remains fairly straight. At each end of the net the bottom and top maitre are connected with a bridle, which is attached to a buoy or anchor line. A buoy marks each end of the net and is anchored to the bottom of the lake with an anchor line. Early buoys were made from wood and in later years, aluminum. The fisherman's license number is painted on the buoy. The buoy also has a 6-foot staff that holds a flag or flags.

Gill nets, years ago and some yet today, are packed and stored in a wood box measuring 2 feet by 4 feet and approximately 1-foot deep, with flared sides. Nets strung together form a "gang" that sometimes would extend nearly five miles. Set from the rear of the boat, these nets form incredibly long submerged fences that are marked on each end with flagged buoys. The end of the net closest to the shore is usually marked with a double flag, and a single flag on the buoy marks the end farthest from the shore. Fishermen would sometimes set as many as 6 to 8 boxes of nets in a gang that would stretch for nearly 5 miles and were typically set at a depth of over 100 feet; but 80 to 120 feet was the desired depth. Depending on the species of fish and where they were feeding dictated the depth to set the net. For whitefish and trout the nets were set near the lake bottom; chubs were fished as deep as 60 to 70 fathoms.

The first gill nets were called "float and stone nets," and were used on Lake Michigan sometime in the mid to late 1840s. In some of the early fisheries gill nets were almost entirely used for harvesting whitefish, so the nets were set where they would catch the least amount of lake trout, which caused considerable damage to the net with their sharp teeth. In the early days, gill nets were made by hand, as there were no knitting machines or manufactured nets available. Usually fishermen's wives and family members worked long hours making and mending nets. A fisherman was prudent and took very good care of his nets. By the late 1870s many of the nets were machine made and purchased from dealers. At Two Rivers, however, many of the town's women and children spent most of the winter months making nets for local fishermen and sold to other fishermen around Lake Michigan. The price of a cotton twine net in the 1870s was about $5.50, and linen nets were valued at $2.00 a piece.[32]

The first gill nets were made of natural fiber, mainly cotton, linen, hemp and manila were used for the maitre (float and lead lines). The first floats were made of cedar, which were 24 inches long, 1 1/2 inches wide, and 1/2 inch thick. One end of the float was tapered, and the other end was notched so it could easily be attached to the top line. They were set 10 feet apart. The weights were small beach stones held by a 6 inch strap and were fastened to the bottom maitre of the net every 8 or 10 feet. The floats and stones were removed from the nets every time they were pulled from the water and reattached before setting the nets again.[33] Many floats were lost and constantly had to be replaced. This proved to be a very time consuming operation.

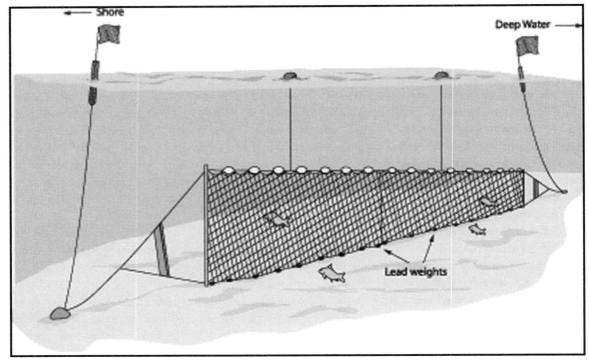

Fig. 2.8 Gill net showing net markings; (courtesy of Michigan Sea Grant University of Michigan.

Fig. 2.9 Net knots and needles U.S Fish and Wildlife
        Service; Illustration by Gustaf T Sundstrom.
        (Courtesy of Milwaukee Public Library)

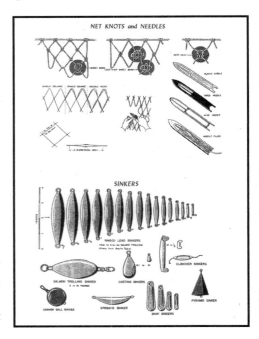

By 1880 wood floats were produced on lathes, and
were still made from cedar. These floats were 2 inches in
diameter, 4 to 5 inches long with a hole drilled through
the center of the float. The ends of the float were rounded over. A hole was drilled through the length of the float,
and a cord or float line was run through the hole, so the
floats could easily be removed when they got waterlogged. The wooden floats were dipped in linseed oil and
allowed to dry. The oil acted as a waterproofing and preservative to keep the floats from soaking up water. The
floats were usually replaced every few months, and new
ones were restrung on the nets. Weights at this time were
molded from lead, and measured 3/4 inches in diameter,
3 inches long with a slot to place through the lower net

cord and crimped closed.

By 1900 wood floats were being replaced with aluminum floats that were the same size and shape as the wood floats. These floats were attached to the float line with small chord and the weights were pipe leads. In the late 1800s, fishermen were using bottom lines with lead woven into them, but chaffing or dragging on the rock bottom was an issue that kept the pipe lead the most popular type of weight. By 1950, plastic floats came into use, and netting was made of nylon, which made the net less of a maintenance issue. Plastic floats are still in use today and in 1965 the monofilament gill net made its debut and has proven to be very successful with fisheries. These nets hold up better than cotton and are not susceptible to rotting like the cotton and nylon nets of years past.

Gill nets vary in mesh sizes, ranging from 2 1/2 inch mesh up to 6 inch mesh. Fishing regulations and fish species played a roll for which size of mesh could be used. For example chubs and herring required a 2 1/2 inch mesh, which the net mesh is actually 1 1/4 inches square, measured diagonally from the long point to long point. Whitefish could not be taken less than 17 inches in length and required a bigger mesh typically 4 1/2 inches, which had a 2 1/4 inch square opening in the mesh. Gill nets are generally set at depths of 120 feet for whitefish and lake trout. Chubs are found in deeper water and the nets are usually set at depths of 180 feet.

The common practice was to set the gill net close to the bottom where certain species of fish, such as whitefish, herring, and chubs feed. However, in the fall of the year when herring and whitefish began to make their way towards their spawning grounds they would feed higher in the water. Gill nets were suspended at different elevations of the lake using floatation devices, known as bobbers that were attached to the cork line. The bobbers were placed at intervals of 20 or 30 feet. They were made from plastic jugs, 14 inch long aluminum floats, and some fishermen even used air-filled cans — basically anything to keep the cork line suspended. This technique is called the "floating gill net," and fishermen began using this style in the early 1900s to enhance their production. It is still being used today by many fishermen. This technique was only used for a short duration, usually not more than a month in the fall of the year, and it proved to be an effective way to harvest whitefish.

In recent years the floating gill net hasn't changed much. Today the floats are plastic, typically 6 inches long by 3 inches in diameter. They are spaced every 50 feet on the top maitre. In the fall of the year when the whitefish are in shallow or surface water, the nets are suspended about 8 to 10 feet below the surface.

In 1905 a variation of the floating gill net emerged into what is known as the "bull net," designed to harvest fish in a wide range of lake depths. The height of the net was expanded to four times the normal height of a gill net and covered a larger vertical area in the water. The bull net was like a very tall submerged fence, capable of catching more fish. This net caught many young whitefish and trout and caused considerable controversy in the fisheries for years. Some people blame the use of the bull net for the decline of herring in the late 1920s, but there was never any proof to these allegations.

Gill nets in the early days were labor intensive and required a shore crew, usually two men to prepare them for setting. The early nets woven of cotton or linen required constant mending and cleaning. Tanning and boiling of the nets were performed every three or four weeks. Tanning was done to darken the nets, so they were less conspicuous to the fish. They were dipped in a mixture of boiling water and salt (to kill bacteria), creosote, (a preservative), and dyes. The dye was usually made from hemlock bark, and was added to the mixture that made the water a dark brown. This process known as "scalding" killed bacteria and removed the slime from the nets and to insure longevity.

Fires were started under large pans, something like a sap pan for making maple syrup. The nets were then placed into the boiling water, first being sprinkled with washing powder to dissolve the scum and dirt. After the scalding process, they were hung on the net reels to dry and then packed back into wooden boxes. The net reels were made of cedar or pine and were used for reeling the wet nets and then tipped upright to dry. The reels were approximately 8 feet wide and were placed on a cross buck that supported the central pole of the reel and could be turned to reel up the net. The next day the nets would be taken off the reel and packed neatly into the net boxes. When packing the nets, the corks were placed on one side of the box and the leads on the other. They were packed in such a way as to avoid any tangles when setting them out in the lake.

It was imperative that if the wet nets weren't set right back in the water they would have to be brought back to shore and dried. A box of wet nets, if left sitting in a box, would rot in three days, bacteria would literally rot the cotton, or linen fibers and destroy the net. It was a common practice for fishermen to reset half a gang of wet nets along with dry nets, then return to shore and reel up the wet nets for the next day. The wood floats, or corks, as they were called, were also dipped in this solution. The corks would usually last two to three months and would then have to be replaced, as they tended to become waterlogged. A special lathe was used to produce these floats in the early days and many fishermen made their own, all floats were made out of cedar because of its lightweight and a natural rot resistant quality. Now aluminum and plastic floats have replaced wood floats.

Monofilament nets were introduced to the fisheries in the 1960s and have revolutionized the fishing industry. With this new synthetic fiber, nets no longer have to be scalded and preserved. These nets are very durable and light and are less conspicuous to the fish in the water. It was a big advantage for the fishermen, which reduced the time and manpower for net maintenance.

Trap Net

The live entrapment gear, or trap net, is very similar to the pound net and works in the same manner but it has a few advantages over the pound net. Trap nets were used as early as 1885. The trap net is more versatile than the pound net. It can be set almost anywhere in the lake, unlike the pound net which requires a soft lake bed to drive the stakes and lake depths of not more than 90 feet. The trap net uses anchors instead of stakes and has a covered pot and heart. This is why the trap net was very popular as it could be set at greater depths without regarding what type of lake bed was down there. Trap nets generally have wing nets leading into a V-shaped heart, or house, and a box-shaped pot. The lead consists of a 14-inch mesh, similar to the pound net lead, and is usually 900 to 1,100 feet long. The fish follow the lead into the heart as in the pound net. Once in the house they eventually swim into the pot via a tunnel connecting the house and the pot of the net.

Trap nets today are made of a synthetic material known as marlex, which is durable and rot resistant. Trap nets can be set as deep as 150 feet of water, but must be set only in areas of the lake desig-

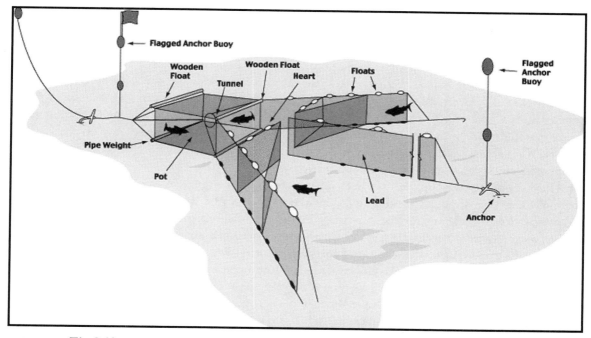

Fig.2.10 Trap net diagram, (Courtesy of Michigan Sea Grant; University of Michigan)

nated by the DNR for live entrapment. Whitefish are in deeper water most of the year, which makes the trap net a better gear to fish. "You still have to be careful how you handle the fish," commented commercial fisherman Dennis Hickey. "You don't want to bring them up from too deep of water, or they bloat and it can be very stressful on the live fish... It's hard on them and you don't want to rough handle them. We can only go as deep as 150 feet; they (DNR) don't want us to go any deeper than that because they might bloat or kill some legal fish and we don't want to do that either."

In the fall of the year some fishermen will set a trap net in shallow water when the whitefish move in to spawn. A 30-foot trap net can normally be set in 30 feet of water, the lead is right up to the surface and tapered toward the shore. Commercial fisherman Charlie Henriksen sets many of his trap nets in shallow water during the fall months. "We even modify some of our 45-footers, actually Neil Teskie had come up with this deal where you take the center of the cover and tee-pee it up, raising it up about 10 feet or more. So you can take a 50-foot trap net and set it in 60 feet of water. You fish the lead right to the surface, so what you're trying to do is fish it like a pound net."[34]

To lift the net a boat similar to a pound net boat is used, one having a broad, flat deck with an open hold for the fish. The main line (king line) is lifted over the side of the boat an attached to a winch. The pot is then moved across the back of the boat, concentrating all the fish into one area. A string that secures the pot cover is undone, the cover is removed and the fish are scooped out. To reset the net, the pot cover is closed, the pot is lowered back into the water, sliding the king line off the stern. Another advantage the trap net has over the pound net is it doesn't take nearly as long to assemble and dismantle. According to Dennis Hickey, "Setting a trap net, if you do it right and the conditions are just right, typically takes a few hours, sometimes more if there is a lot of current or there is a heavy sea. To take one out is usually an hour or so."

Trap nets are the least detrimental of all the types of gear to the fish and are recognized by the DNR as a safe and harmless method of harvesting trout and salmon for research and tagging. Once the trap net is set, it is marked with buoys, similar to those used for gill nets. Today the buoys are painted orange, a universal color. There is a double flag on the inside end of the lead and a single orange flag is on the pot. The king line may be any color. "We didn't know what would happen when we went with the bright orange marking system," said one fisherman. "But everyone seemed to catch on to it. We had the Sea Grant Program make up a brochure or publication to make sport fishermen and boaters understand the marking system of our nets."[35]

The history of the trap net has been marked with controversy, especially in the early 1930s between the gill net fishermen and pound net fishermen. Many of these fishermen were against the use of the deep-water trap net, or submarine nets (some fishermen called them "deep subs"). It sparked a controversy that lingered for decades. These fishermen argued that the deep trap net was very destructive and considered it to be a shortsighted form of technology.

The deepwater trap net was developed by Lake Huron commercial fisherman John Howard. He experimented to modify and improve the trap net to harvest more fish. In 1924 he began setting the new style nets he developed around Cape Vincent, New York.[36] This new net rig, with its larger capacity, giving it as much as 12 to 30 feet more of depth, did catch more fish than other types of nets, and found its way into the hands of the local fishermen.

Gill net fishermen were the first to protest that the trap net was being deliberately placed across their nets, disrupting the whitefish in their summer grounds. Some pound net fishermen also complained that the trap nets were being placed in such a manner that they blocked access to their gear.[37] At the time it divided a lot of fisheries and prompted an investigation by federal and state authorities. The Wisconsin and the Michigan bureau of fisheries reported that deep trap nets took too many adult whitefish, depleting the breeding stock, and destroyed too many small fish.

By 1930 the use of trap nets and deep water trap nets in northern Lake Michigan were becoming the new rage, and many fishermen who were using pound nets soon saw the potential of harvesting whitefish and herring by using this type of gear. They could broaden their fishing grounds and venture farther out into deeper waters. Whitefish production rose substantially in Lake Huron, nearly doubling the total harvest from 1.5 million pounds in 1929 to 2.9 million pounds in 1930. In 1928 it was reported that fishermen near Alpena, Michigan, were having catches resulting in incomes as high as $2,000 per week, which was a substantial sum at that time. Trap nets were only used for whitefish in their summer range. By 1930 this type of gear was beginning to be used along the U.S. shoreline of Lake Huron and in the bountiful whitefish grounds of Lake Michigan and Lake Superior.[38]

In 1932 the Michigan Conservation Department sent a questionnaire to all licensed fishermen. Only about 40 percent replied, roughly 492 fishermen. Of the 174 comments on the deep trap nets, 142 disapproved and only 32 were in favor of them. In wasn't long before a ban was put on the use of the deep trap nets, or "submarine nets." In the last fifty years the trap net has become very popular with many fishermen and all those inflamed tempers have nearly been forgotten.

For a period of twenty years the trap net was banned in Michigan and Wisconsin waters, but it was reinstated for use in the commercial fisheries in the early 1970s. The trap net quickly became popular with northern Door County fishermen and were used extensively along with gill nets. Today the trap net and gill net are the two most popular gear for harvesting whitefish. "I like them both," comments one fisherman. "Gill net and trap nets are to me a great way to harvest fish. I would not trade either one of them."[39]

Hook and Line Rig (Trot line)

The hook and line rig consisted of 1,400 to 2,000 hooks spaced 15 or 25 apart on "snoots," small lines attached to a main lead line, or maitre, that would form a gang and normally covered 4 to 6 miles. The hooks were baited with small herring, smelt, or bloaters that were caught in small mesh nets called bait nets, or chum nets. Chubs and herring 5 to 8 inches long were preferred for baiting these hooks. This type of gear was inexpensive, and many fishermen had great success with it, especially for lake trout.

During the late 1920s and 1930s when whitefish were scarce many fishermen used the hook and line rigs for lake trout. According to Marvin Weborg: "My dad and Frank Teskie began using hooks, setting bait nets or getting herring out of the pound nets, and then putting them on the hooks, and setting them for trout. There were a lot more trout than whitefish. Whitefish were very scarce at the time. After they went through the hooks, they went to floating hooks in the summertime, where they fished what we call floating hooks down about 18 feet so boats could go over the top of them. Back in my day, in the 1940s we fished out of Baileys Harbor, fishing floaters. We would average between 600 and 1,000 pounds per day. The floats were made out of wood. Every hundred hooks, you would run an anchor, a stone to the bottom with a line on to hold the line in place. You'd put a float about every tenth hook, and an anchor every hundredth hook to the bottom to hold that, because that was floating on the top, and the pressure would swing that back and forth, but they would only let it go so far."[40]

Over the years, the hook and line rig was a simple yet effective piece of gear for catching certain species of fish. There were a few modifications and variations to the gear between fishermen, but for the most part it was quite simple. Howard Weborg talks about the hook and line rig, which comes from an interview from the book "Fish For All" by Michael Chiarappa and Kristin Szylvian:

I started fishing hooks. Four hundred hooks on each line – all cotton too. When they wanted to lay them away, they put them on slats along the walls of the shed. We used hooks for lake trout. There is a hook every 20 feet on the heavy twine or maitre cord. Every 20 feet there is a 4-foot line with a hook tied to it. They call the four-foot line a snoot, which might be a Scandinavian name. We had 10,000 baits and so we set 10,000 hooks. We started outside the bluff out there and went all the way across to Michigan – we had a Michigan license. Then they went up to Door County with the lines and came in by Chambers Island and Fish Creek and then back down. You only can lift 3,000 hooks a day so that took a little over three days to lift all the lines. The lines would sit out for one or two nights. Then you would go out and pull them and take the trout off. They had pound nets that would catch little herring for bait. Then they would take the hook through the back and then come out through the cheek. We stopped using hooks in the 1920s. There are about 400 hooks on each one of the lines. You tie them together. At the time we set 10,000 hooks, all in one line. We would have to run those hooks over, you know. The trout tangled the lines up, so then before they could set them again, we had to run them over and put them in boxes. Us kids, nine to ten years old, would take all the tangles out and run them. We would space them out after they lifted them.[41]

A variation of this type of gear is the floating hook and line, or "floaters". Wooden floats were placed on the main line, or maitre at intervals of 20 feet to suspend the gear in the water. This was usually done when lake trout were feeding on bug hatch in the late spring and summer months. Fishermen would suspend the line usually 10 or 20 feet below the surface of the water.

Setting hooks most often required two people to efficiently handle this operation. One person baited hooks on one side of the line and the other person baited hooks on the other side. The line was released from the stern of the boat while the boat was moving at a gait of 4 to 6 miles per hour or sometimes a little faster if they were good. Like the floating gill net, the floating hook gear was used only during certain times of the year, late spring and early summer for the lake trout. Some fishermen had better catches if they relocated the hooks every day. Depending on the water temperature, the hook and line rig was set and left out for three to four days, a little longer if the water temperature was colder.

Ice Fishing

As far back as 1857 hook and line fishing through the ice on Green Bay and northern Door County was popular with some fishermen. It attracted many people, as far away as Milwaukee to catch whitefish and trout through the ice. Ice fishing helped bring in extra income for a number of fishermen and farmers in the Door County region, who used hook and lines and even gill nets to harvest the fish. The three-month harvest brought in as much as $75 to $100 of extra income.[42]

In 1870 the bay during the wintertime looked like a scattered small village, because of all the shanties that housed many of the ice fishermen. Each fisherman owned about 25 to 100 nets, which were set in gangs across the bay in about 60 fathoms of water. Fishermen would build small shanties of wood and canvas, approximately 7 feet by 12 feet, on steel runners that could be pulled out on the ice with a horse. The gill nets were set under the ice at intervals of 100 feet where a hole was cut. A pole with a line attached and long enough to reach the other hole was used to string the net along from hole to hole. This was repeated until all the nets were set. Two men could manage about thirty nets. The shanties were placed over the holes when they lifted the nets to extract the fish.[43]

Marvin Weborg remembers his father fishing for trout with hook and line through the ice. "Years ago, back in the twenties, lots of people made their living – that's all they did, fish on the ice in the wintertime. They would go out onto the ice, pull a shanty out there, and stay there for about a week. When the weather was good enough, they would come home for the weekend. Otherwise, they would live right there and they would take their fish and bury them right in the snow bank, and when they'd come ashore, they would take those same fish, box them up, and sell them; they used horses and sleighs at that time."[44]

Marvin's two sons, Jeff and Mark began their fishing career by taking out a loan to purchase two snowmobiles and gear that included eight boxes of twenty-eight mesh gill nets and thirty-two ice nets. They strung the nets out in the fall and winter of 1971-1972 and made enough money to satisfy the loan.

"I used to fish on the ice for the first nine years," says Mark Weborg. "That was a good living, but I learned a lot of things about the ice. Water is powerful, but ice is ten times more powerful." It was in the winter of 1973, Mark and Jeff had some nets set out about 10 miles from land and decided to scout out an area to set more nets. Mark went off in one direction with his snowmobile and found a smooth stretch of ice about a half mile away. The one mistake he made was he never thought to check the ice, and the snowmobile broke through as he ran over that smooth stretch. He suddenly found himself and his machine in open water. He quickly decided to gun the engine to reach a patch of ice that was twenty feet away but unfortunately came up short and the snowmobile went under. Mark couldn't swim, but luckily his snowmobile suit kept him buoyant in the water for a moment for him to try to kick and splash with his arms to reach the patch of ice. He got there before his suit filled up with water. He remembered how to get out of the water by rolling on top of the ice.

Jeff, who was talking to some fishermen, saw Mark stranded on the ice patch, raced out there, and pulled him off from the other side and almost lost his machine in the process. Mark's snowmobile suit was frozen solid, and he was fighting the effects of hypothermia. Luckily, the other fishermen had a shanty where Mark could warm up. Then Jeff raced Mark the 10 miles back to shore.[45]

Over the years, a number of fishermen who fished through the ice found themselves in precarious situations. Even the experienced person would be helpless when he found himself caught in fog, or a snowstorm, or set adrift when winds shifted and broke up the ice. Many years ago, three Gills Rock fishermen found themselves adrift on a large cake of ice. The wind was from the south, and they floated out past Washington Island. They managed to make a torch by burning the linings of their pockets and their gloves. It was after midnight when the Plum Island Coast Guard rescued them.

Two Norwegians from Washington Island were well known for catching trout in the winter of 1903. Their story was told by Ray McDonald in his book Four Islands:

> Charlie Anderson lived near Jackson Harbor, and his brother-in-law Elmer Anderson, who had just arrived from Norway, was staying with Charlie. He was twenty years old, blonde hair with rosy cheeks, and of medium build. There wasn't much work for the two that winter, save for cutting wood, which brought in a meager income, so they decided to try fishing for trout through the ice using hook and line. That winter was a very cold one and the lake had frozen over between Washington Island and an area known as the Dry Shoals, which was about four miles northeast of Jackson Harbor. The Fisherman's Shoal was also near that area and a deep channel ran between the

shoals and Washington Island. Normally the area was open, but that winter was exceptionally cold and it had frozen over.

Elmer and Charlie knew this was a good spot for trout, so they, along with another young Norwegian by the name of Harwick Carlson, started out early one morning traveling east with their gear on a wind sleigh. They came to an area along the channel bank and knew the depth was good for trout. After arriving to the spot they proceeded to cut holes through the fifteen- inch ice, baited their hooks, then lowered them down through the hole into the icy water; finding what they thought to be the proper depth where the trout were likely to feed. After fishing for some time without getting any bites, Elmer decided to check his bait and started to bring up his line; he had his line almost near the surface when suddenly something hit it hard. He knew right away that it had to be a trout and frantically pulled, hand over hand, the line to the surface. He pulled the fish through the ice and couldn't believe his eyes as it weighed close to 12 pounds. So Charlie and Elmer raised their lines and found the trout were hitting only a few fathoms beneath the ice.

By mid afternoon Charlie had caught forty-two trout and Elmer had thirty-eight trout that averaged about 10 pounds apiece. Harwick didn't do any fishing that day he just went along to help the boys out. Some of the fish were around four pounds and the largest was around 16 pounds so when they loaded them on to the sleigh they had a total of 800 pounds of trout to haul back to shore. The trout by that time were frozen solid and were piled on the sleigh like cordwood. The journey back was arduous to say the least for there had been some water on the ice a few days before and it had frozen, but not very good, so when they ran that 800 pound fish packed sleigh over it the runners broke through. With three men pulling it took them the rest of the day to make it back to shore. The next day they went back to the same spot, but this time Charlie brought his team of horses along to pull the sleigh. Unfortunately they didn't have as good luck as the day before, Charlie only caught five; however Elmer caught thirty-two.

Ice fishing today is now exclusively for the sport fisherman, but there are still a few commercial fishermen who use gill nets that are set through the ice to harvest whitefish. A few fishermen on Washington Island, in the last few decades made this an annual event and sometimes were quite successful at it. To set gill nets under the ice, first two holes had to be cut into the ice. The cork line is then attached to a wood pole or sometimes 2 by 4 inch lumber nailed together to guide the chord from hole to hole.

In 1978 a new device called a "creeper," was introduced to some of the island fishermen. Calvin Gunnlaugsson saw this device being used in Lake Superior and brought it to the island. The creeper with the cork line attached would guide the net along to the other hole. It resembled, what some described as a fly on the ceiling. It ran along under the ice and had a clicker so the fishermen knew where it was.

That winter (1978) several fishermen, including the Youngs, Koyens, Walt and Bill Jorgenson, used this device and had great success with it, catching whitefish off the west end of Washington Island. The Youngs that year caught 100 to 500 pounds per lift. The Koyens would lift two or three times a week and were also getting around 500 pounds of whitefish.

Nautical Definitions[46]

Afore - Forward

Aft - Near the stern or back of the vessel

Ballast - Any substantial weight placed in a vessel to provide desired draft and stability

Beam - Greatest width of a vessel

Bow - Front of the boat

Bowsprit - A spar projecting fro the upper end of the bow of a sailing vessel for holding the tacks of various jibs or stays

Breeze - Wind speed of 4 to 31 mph

Brig - A two-masted vessel, square-rigged on both masts

Brigantine - A two-masted vessel, foremast is square rigged, aft mast is fore and aft-rigged

Carvel-built - A vessels hull planks laid against one another to form a smooth exterior; flush at the seams.

Cat Ketch - Single mast forward with a single sail attached to a boom and two masts and sail with a shorter after mast

Check down - To impede motion of a vessel or slow down the speed

Clinker-built - When the boat's planks overlap one another; lap-straked construction

Clock - A clock used with the boat's compass for navigational purpose

Combers - A long wave that curls and crests in a foamy spray; a breaker.

Cork line - The top maitre or line of a net rig that the floats are attached

Draft - Depth to which the boat settles in the water bearing a full load

Fathom - Equates to six feet

Fender board - Short length of planking cantilevered laterally to provide a wider surface along the hull

Fore and aft - Pertaining to the length of a boat from stern to bow.

Fore and aft rigged - A sailing rig consisting of non-square sails set along the line of the keel.

Forecastle - A cabin or quarters located in the forward section of a vessel

Founder - The sinking of a vessel from taking on water

Fresh breeze - Wind speed of 19 to 24 mph

Fresh gale - Wind speed of 39 to 46 mph

Gaff - A spar holding the upper side of a four sided sail; the spar upon which the head of a fore and aft sail is extended

Gaff rigged - A four sided sail with a spar holding the upper side; typical of schooners, barquentine type vessels and Mackinaw fishing boats

Gale - Strong wind; moderate (32-38 mph), fresh (39-46 mph), strong (47-54 mph) whole (55-63 mph)

Gunwale (gunnel) - The upper edge planking, or uppermost strake of a vessel, along the top of the hull

Heavy sea - The body of water that contains large waves from high winds

Jib - A right triangular sail set on a headstay; a single headsail

Jib boom - A spar that forms an extension of the bowsprit

Keel - The main member at the bottom of the hull running fore to aft

Keelson - A structural member running fore and aft placed above the keel running parallel with it for strength

Ketch - A sailing vessel rigged fore and aft; two-masted rig with a shorter after mast

Knot - A unit of speed equal to 1.15 statute miles per hour

Landlubber - A person with little knowledge of the sea

Lapstrake - Overlapping the planking in construction of the vessels hull "clinker built"

Lead - A weight usually made of lead attached to the bottom maitre of a fisherman's net. A weight used to measure the depth of the sea

Lee - The side that is sheltered from the wind

Long line (Trot line) - A single fishing line (maitre) with as many as one hundred hooks attached on smaller lines that are ten feet long called snoots

Lugger - A container used to store fish, typically 2 x 4 feet, holding 100 pounds of fish.

Lugsail - A quadrilateral sail (four-sided) bent upon a hanging yard that crosses the mast obliquely

Main - The principal mast and sail

Mainmast - A sailing vessels primary mast

Marine engine - An internal combustion engine with a few modifications for marine use

Mast - A vertical spar or structure on a vessel on which the sails, spars, rigging, booms are attached

Maitre - A natural, or synthetic line that mesh from a net is attached.

Mizzen - A fore and aft sail set on the mizzen mast

Mizzen mast - The third mast (aftermost mast) from the forward on vessels with threeor more masts

Moderate breeze - Wind speeds of 13 to 18 mph

Moderate gale - Wind speeds of 32 to 38 mph

Nautical mile - 6,076 feet

Oilers - A fisherman's term for waterproof garments to keep the person dry from the elements

Planks - wood used in construction of the hulls and decks of a vessel

Port - The left side of a vessel

Porthole - typically a circular window in a boat

Prow - The front of the vessel, also called the bow or fore section

Rake or raked - The slant of a ship's bow, stern, or mast

Raked bow or stem - The stem of a vessel is at an angle to the waterline

Schooner - Fore-and-aft rigged vessel, with or without other masts. Having fore and aft sails on all lower masts

Scow - A barge-like vessel with a flat bottom and square ends with sloping ends; various   sizes

Screw - A propeller; sometimes called a wheel

Scupper - A drain hole at the edge of a vessels deck which allows water to run overboard.

Sea - Waves in a specific area caused by blowing wind

Sea cocks - A valve which penetrates the hull where water is taken in or discharged for engine cooling, waste disposal

Sea legs - Being able to maintain standing or walking aboard a vessel while it is tossed about in a sea

Skiff - A small boat which may be propelled by oars, sail or marine engine; may be open or decked over

Sloop - A boat having a single mast, with a mainsail and jib

Sprit - A small boom or gaff used with sails in small boats

Square-rigged - The vessel's primary sails (four sided) and set across the vessel.

Stay - To tack a vessel so that the wind is brought to the other side; to put on the other tack

In Stays - When a vessel is going from one tack to another; coming about

Starboard - Right side of the boat

Stem - The vertical post of the bow; an upright structural member to which the side timbers join

Stern - The back end of a vessel

Storm - Winds of 64 to 72 mph

Strake - Planks running fore and aft on a vessel

Strong breeze - A wind of 25 to 31 mph

Strong gale - A wind of 47 to 54 mph

Swell - Long, large wave that does not crest

Tack - A sailing maneuver changing the direction of the boat

Three Sisters - Sailors term for three large consecutive waves that sometimes occur in a heavy sea.

Trawl - A large, strong cone-shaped net dragged along the sea bottom in order to catch fish

Trawler - A boat used in trawl fishing

Trough - Depression in the water between two waves

Vessel - Any craft that rides on a body of water

Wash strake - Topmost plank on the side of a boat

Whole gale - Wind of 55 to 63 mph

Chapter 2 Notes

[1] Patrick Labadie, Brina J Agranat and Scott Anfinson; Adapted from the National Register's Multiple Property Documentation(MPDF) Minnesota's Lake Superior Shipwrecks A.D. 1650 -1945 "History and Development of Great Lakes Watercraft;" (Minnesota Historical Society).

[2] Evan Gagnon,"When the Mackinaws Sailed the Upper Lakes, " Joseph Mann Library; Two Rivers Wisconsin.

[3] Milner, "The Fisheries of the Great Lakes," Report U.S. Commissioner Fish and Fisheries, Part II, 1874; Appendix A, pp. 13-14.

[4] Evan Gagnon, "Point Beach Fishing Community" Joseph mann Library, Two Rivers, WI.

[5] Milner, "Report U.S Commissioner of Fish and Fisheries." Pt. II 1874, Appendix A. p. 14.

[6] Ibid.

[7] Ibid.

[8] Ludwig Kumlein, "Fisheries of the Great Lakes," The Fisheries and Fishing Industry of the United States; (Washington Government Printing office 1887), 764.

[9] Walter M. and Mary K. Hirthe, " The Conversion From Manpower to Steam Power in the Fishing Industry"; *Door County Almanac No. 3* (Dragonsreath Press 1986), 35.

[10] Ibid, 36.

[11] Smith and Snell, "Review of the Fisheries of the Great Lakes;" Margaret Beattie Bogue, Fishing the Great Lakes: An Environmental History 1783-1933: (University of Wisconsin Press 2000), 49.

[12] "Ship Building History," *Door County Advocate*, June 10, 1976.

[13] Carl Raymond Christianson, Ship Building and Boat Building In Sturgeon Bay, Wisconsin: From the Beginning to 1985 (Private printing, 1989), 14-20.

[14] Frank Prothero, Men 'N Boats: The Fisheries of the Great Lakes: (Great Lakes Fishermen,

Port Stanley Ontario), 143.

[15] Kumlein, "Fisheries of the Great Lakes." 759.

[16] Evan Gagnon, "Point Beach Fishing Community"; Joseph Mann Library, Two Rivers Wisconsin.

[17] Kumlein, "Fisheries of the Great Lakes," 760.

[18] Sturgeon Bay Maritime Museum, Navigational aid exhibit.

[19] Ibid.

[20] Scottie Dayton, "Kahlenberg Brothers Built Engines for Some of the Toughest Boats in the World", *New Month Magazine, March / April 1997.*

[21] Ibid.

[22] Ibid.

[23] Interview with Jake Ellefson, October 2, 2001.

[24] Manitowoc Maritme Museum, marine engine exhibit.

[25] Margaret Beattie Bogue, *Fishing The Great Lakes: An Environmental History 1783-1933* (Madison, WI: University of Wisconsin Press 2000), 38.

[26] Ibid, 39.

[27] Two Rivers Public Library; diagram of a pound net, drawn by a local fisherman.

[28] Interview with Jake Ellefson, October 2, 2001.

[29] Ludwig Kumlein and Frederick W. True, "section III, Fishing Grounds of North America" *The Fisheries and Fish Industry of the United States* (Washington 1887), 120.

[30] Kumlein, "Fisheries of the Great Lakes," 762.

31 Smith and Snell, "Review of the Fisheries of the Great Lakes." Margaret Beattie Bogue, *Fishing the Great Lakes: An Environmental History 1783- 1933*; (Madison, WI: University of Wisconsin Press, 2000), 97.

32 Kumlein, "Fisheries of the Great Lakes," 764.

33 Raymond McDonald, *Four Islands: A History of Detroit, Rock, St. Martins, and Washington Islands* (Sturtevant, WI: Wolfsong Publications, 1984), 6.

34 Interview with Charlie Henriksen, December 13, 2002.

35 Interview with Dennis Hickey, September 29, 2002.

36 John Van Oosten, Ralph Hile, and Frank Jobes, "The Whitefish Fishery of Lakes Huron and Michigan and Special Reference to the Deep Trap Net Fishery," *Fishery Bulletin 40* (Fish and Wildlife Service 1946) 50, 299. Tom Kuchenberg, *Reflections In A Tarnished Mirror* (Sturgeon Bay, WI: Golden Glow Publishing 1978), 30.

37 Tom Kuchenberg, *Reflections In A Tarnished Mirror* (Sturgeon Bay, WI: Golden Glow Publishing 1978), 30.

38 "The Deepwater Trap Net," *The Fisherman,* October, 1934, 1. Tom Kuchenberg, *Reflections In A Tarnished Mirror*; (Golden Glow Publishing 1978), 30.

39 Interview with Neil Teskie, July 3, 2003.

40 Lon Kopitzke, "An Interview with Marvin Weborg Along With His Son Mark," *Door County Almanac No. 3* (Dragosnbreath Press, 1986), 156-158.

41 Michael J. Chiarappa and Kristin M. Szylvian, *Fish For All An Oral History of Multiple Claims and Divided Sentiment on Lake Michigan* (East Lansing, MI: Michigan State University Press, 2003), 216-217.

42 Margaret Beattie Bogue, *Fishing the Great Lakes: An Environmental History 1783-1933* (Madison, WI: University of Wisconsin Press, 2000), 87.

43 Kumlein, "Fisheries of the Great Lakes." 764.

44 Lon Kopitzke, "An Interview with Marvin Weborg Along With His Son Mark," *Door County Almanac No.3* (Dragonsbreath Press, 1986), 156-158.

45 Ibid.

46 Joseph P. O'Flynn, *Nautical Dictionary* (Boyne City Michigan: Harbor House Publishers, Inc. 1992) Dictionary.com http://dictionary, reference.

Pic. 2.1 A fleet of Mackinaw boats in Algoma, circa 1870s. (Photo courtesy of the Wendell Wilke Collection)

Pic. 2.2 Steam tugs began replacing the sailing vessels around 1870. Steam power was used sparingly, because of the substantial cost. Picture of the *Tillie E.* owned by Torger Engelson from Washington Island. (Photo courtesy of the Sunset Resort Collection)

Pic. 2.3 In the early 1920s, gill-net tugs were modified with houses built on them to lend fisheremen protection from the elements. Pictured is a circa 1920s style tug with forward pilot house, and lifter station. The *Esther C.* was built by Sturgeon Bay Boat Works. She was a 40-foot all-wood construction and powered with a 30-36 Kahlenberg marine engine. (Photo Courtesy of the Sturgeon Bay Maritime Museum and Lighthouse Preservation Society)

Pic. 2.4 Another style of gill-net tug indicative to the 1930s and 1940s, was the midship pilothouse and forward steering station. The gill-net tug *Gloria* was built by the Burger Boat Company in 1929 at Manitowoc, Wisconsin. It was equipped with a 45-54 horsepower Kahlenberg marine oil engine. (Photo courtesy of the Kahlenberg Brothers Company)

Pic. 2.5 One of the last modifications to the gill-net tug, was an aft pilothouse and steel constructed hull and house. This gave a greater advantage for setting nets and often eliminated one crew member. Photo of the *Faith II* breaking ice at Gills Rock. (Photo courtesy of Donald Voight)

Pic. 2.6 Kahlenberg brothers standing outside of their marine engine plant in Two Rivers, where the famed Kahlenberg engine began production in 1895. (Photo courtesy of the Kahlenberg Brothers Company)

Pic 2.7 A two-cylinder 30-36 horsepower Kahlenberg marine oil engine in the gill-net tug *Jane Elizabeth*. (Photo courtesy of Harold and Arbutus Greenfeldt)

Pic. 2.8 Mechanical net lifter and forward steering station in the bow of the gill-net tug *Hope*, which is on display at the Gills Rock Maritime Museum. (Trygvie Jensen Photography)

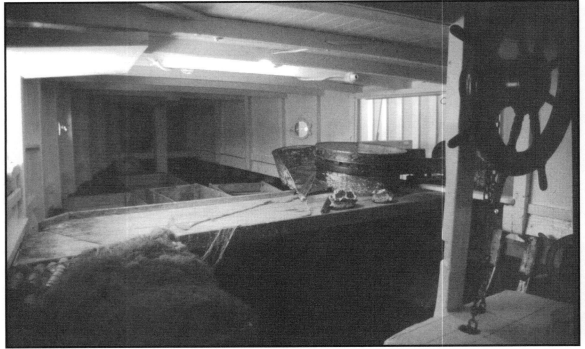

Pic. 2.9 Setting a gang of gill nets. Jake Ellefson (left) and Jeff Hagen in the venerable gill-net tug *Jane* owned by Jeff McDonald at Washington Island. (Trygvie Jensen Photography)

Pic. 2.10 Pound net set up in North Bay. (Trygvie Jensen Photography)

Pic. 2.11 Gill-net reel used for drying cotton and nylon nets. Pictured is Steve Ellefson reeling a box of gill nets at Jackson Harbor. (Photo courtesy of Jake Ellefson)

Pic. 2.12 Fisherman, Harry Hagen scalding gill nets to remove bacteria and scum in a large boiling pan. This was done once a month, or as necessary. (Photo courtesy of the Washington Island Archives)

Pic. 2.13 Fishermen lifting gill nets from the lifter station in the gill-net tug, *Dorothy*, circa 1927. (Photo courtesy of the Door County Maritime Museum and Lighthouse Preservation Society)

Pic. 2.14 Washington Island fishermen holding their prized catch of lake trout. (Photo courtesy of Jens Hansen)

Pic. 2.15 Jake Ellefson at the lifter trying to grasp a whitefish that sometimes escape the gill net, and a fisherman's hand. (Trygvie Jensen Photography)

Chapter 3
Commercial Fish Species (The Big Four)

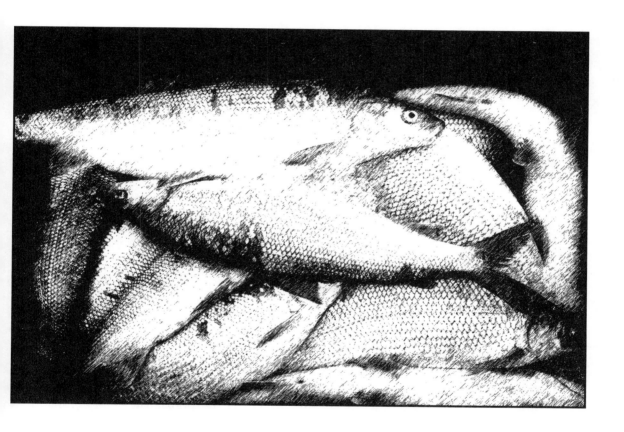

Since the dawn of commercial fishing in the Great Lakes, certain species were more abundant and more desirable for consumption than others. Whitefish, lake trout, herring, and later chubs, sturgeon, and yellow perch were mainstays in the commercial fishing industry. From 1830 to 1870 the populations of whitefish, trout, and herring did not fluctuate much. As the ecology of the lake started to change, so did the stocks of native fish. Changes were evident as far back as 1880 with declining lake trout and whitefish stocks. From the early 1900s the whitefish, lake trout, and herring populations were more cyclic, and by the 1960s most of the commercial fish stocks were in peril.

The lake whitefish is the most popular commercial fish species among consumers and fishermen.

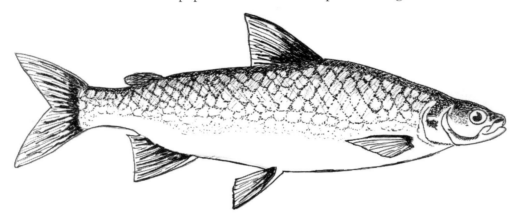

Fig. 3.1 Lake Whitefish (Coregonus clupeaformis)

Features: Silvery color with green-brownish back. Clear or lightly pigmented fins. Heavy amount of slime over the scales

Size: Average weight in the Great Lakes, 2 to 4 pounds; length approximately 18 to 22 inches

Adult Diet: Diporeia, small fish, and fish eggs

Spawns: November and December over rocky shoals

Common Names: whitefish, sault fish, gizzard fish, grande coregone, and attikumai (Chippewa)

The whitefish has long been known for the richness and delicacy of its flavor. Native Americans preferred this fish to others in the lakes and fished them for centuries. Chippewa Indians who lived near the St. Mary's River in the Sault St. Marie area lived on the whitefish from the river. It was said that two men in a canoe could catch as much as 5,000 pounds of whitefish in half a day by dipping scoop nets into the river. The Native Americans would then build fires and boil them. The wind carried the savory smell for miles attracting other Indians to join the feast.[1]

The excellence of whitefish as food made them the most highly regarded and sought-after fish in the fisheries. They bring the highest price of any fish on the market and are one of the most valued fish in North America next to the Pacific salmon. Whitefish are best known for their use in the traditional "fish boils." Whitefish eggs are highly regarded and marketed as caviar, and are shipped to Japan, Sweden, and other European countries.

Bella Hubbard, a well-known late nineteenth century geologist, voiced his opinion in 1878, about the future of whitefish. He observed that fifty years of commercial fishing had made whitefish available throughout the United States as well as markets in England, such as Liverpool. Moreover, prices were affordable for most consumers. He grew concerned that with such a big demand they would be overfished and possibly be exterminated from the waters. Figures compiled gave credence to Hubbard's observations. Commercial catches of whitefish showed a decline between 1879 and 1899 from 24 million to 9 million pounds.[2]

Whitefish were an easy species to catch with gill nets, second only to salmon. Whitefish by nature are gregarious and move in large schools. It isn't uncommon for fishermen to make their catch in only one or two boxes of nets out of a "gang" of gill nets consisting of eight or more boxes. Schools of whitefish tend to stay in one area; they do not wander over wide areas of the lake. They move slowly near the bottom feeding. Marine biologists consider the whitefish to be a shallow water species that inhabits depths ranging from 60 to 180 feet and occasionally deeper.

In 1872, James Milner working for the U.S Commission of Fish and Fisheries did extensive studies of whitefish behavior patterns. He observed that whitefish do not migrate along the coast, as many once believed, but move toward shore twice a year – in summer for a brief time to seek more oxygenated water, and in fall to spawn. They return to deeper water for the remainder of the year. According to Milner, spawning season was the best time for fishermen to harvest whitefish. They would follow the fish with their nets as they moved toward shore from deeper waters from October to December, depending on the region. In northern Lake Michigan spawning typically begins in late October and ceases in mid December. Once in shallow water the fish remain there to spawn. Spawning takes place at night when the fish became very active near the surface of the water, jumping and splashing. The fish rise to the surface, occasionally in pairs or sometimes in three comprised of one female and two males. The female releases the eggs and the smaller males discharge the milt after the eggs settle to the bottom of the lake. Milner also noted that they would spawn in late afternoon and at night in the shallow waters, 6 to 60 feet deep, often over gravel or honeycombed rocks.[3] Lake trout, burbot (lawyers), and northern pike were predators of young and adult whitefish. Occasionally perch and ciscoes fed on whitefish larvae, and whitefish sometimes were found to consume their own eggs. Milner observed that trout were partially responsible for the decline of whitefish in Lake Huron and Lake Michigan in the 1890s. He was convinced that the combined pressures of the destructive and wasteful methods of commercial fishing and the changing ecology of the lake due to pollution of the whitefish habitat had an impact on its population. In a report he noted:

As everywhere civilized man disturbs the balance of nature, and becomes the great enemy of all forms of life that do not conform to his artificial methods for their protection. Not only by the hundreds of artifices for the capture of whitefish, but in the foul drainage from the cities, smelting works, and manufactories, and the quantities of sawdust from the mills, they are driven from their favorite haunts and spawning grounds, and their food destroyed by waters tainted with fatal chemical combinations.[4]

Whitefish have always been highly sought after by commercial fishermen. From 1870 to the turn of the century, fishermen aggressively harvested whitefish, and there was a growing concern about overfishing. Annual harvests declined from 1879 to 1899. In 1899 the annual catch was down to 1.77 million pounds in Lake Michigan waters. In 1871, John Milner, in a study for the U. S. Commission of Fish and Fisheries, noted that whitefish had been aggressively harvested for two decades by an expanding commercial fishing industry. He also observed that already by 1870 the harvest of whitefish had peaked and was in decline.

Lake Whitefish were abundant in Lake Michigan until the late 1800s. In 1880 federal statistics showed a production in Lake Michigan of over 12 million pounds; the harvest in 1922 showed a decline to 1.5 million pounds.[5] After 1930 whitefish became cyclic in their population, and the reason is not clearly understood. There was a low point in the cycle in the 1930s and again in the 1960s. The largest catches since 1940 occurred in 1947, when 1,806,281 pounds were harvested. There was a decline to an all-time low of 9,219 pounds in 1958. Production gradually increased and by 1974 production climbed to 1,714,208 pounds of whitefish harvested.[6] The bulk of commercial harvests have always occurred in the Door County region, with gill nets and trap nets as the principal means of harvesting. Mid 1970s estimates of the North Bay and Moonlight Bay whitefish spawning stock (1.1 million) and of the Wisconsin areas of Lake Michigan whitefish population (1.2 to 1.5 million) indicate that this spawning stock was a major component of the Wisconsin Lake Michigan whitefish population.[7]

Coinciding with the great smelt die-off in the winter of 1942 - 1943, which left the whitefish free of predation from smelt, whitefish in Lake Michigan was found, that year to be abundant. By 1947 whitefish seemed to be doing well. But as the smelt recovered, the whitefish population began to decline. The lake trout population in the late 1940s collapsed due to sea lamprey predation, and whitefish may have also been victimized extensively by these aggressive parasites. Local fishermen found dead whitefish in their nets that showed extensive scarring by lamprey. It wasn't until the sea lamprey were controlled by lamprecides that whitefish numbers began to increase, but it took the whitefish almost a decade (1959-1970) to recover.

The lake trout was considered the most valuable commercial fish species in Lake Michigan from 1890 until the mid 1940s.[8] In the early years of the fishery, lake trout were once found to be less desirable than whitefish. It wasn't until the decline of whitefish that trout became more marketable. Early records show that in 1879, only 2.6 million pounds were harvested. Shortly after that, lake trout had a fifty-year run as a highly sought-after fish. In that period of time lake trout catches were the higher in Lake Michigan than in the other Great Lakes. From 1890 to 1911 the catch was consistently high,

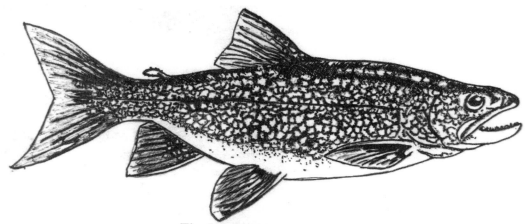

Fig. 3.2 Lake Trout *(Salvelinus namaycush)*

Features: Generally light green or gray in color with light spots on a darker background, irregular wavy markings on back and dorsal fin. Deeply forked caudal fin

Size: Average weight in Great Lakes 6 to12 pounds, but may exceed 60 pounds; approximately 23 to 29 inches long

Adult Diet: Chubs, lake herring, sticklebacks, alewives, smelt, sculpins, macroinvertebrates

Spawns: Fall, over open water rocky shoals

Common Names: Laker, togue, grey trout

averaging 8.2 million pounds. The average annual yield dropped to 7 million pounds from 1912 to 1926, and declined further to 5.3 million pounds in 1927 to 1939. The trend was reversed from 1940 to 1944 when the catch was above 6 million pounds in each year; the average was 6.6 million. The year 1945 marked the beginning of a precipitous decline: the catch was only 342,000 pounds in 1949 and a mere 34 pounds in 1954. Lake trout were extremely rare in 1955, and the species probably became extinct in the lake by 1956.[9]

Lake trout stocks were diminishing as far back as 1880 in northern Lake Michigan, and many experts believed it was the result of exploitation. The decrease in lake trout from 1893 to 1938 correlated with the increasing number of fishermen harvesting the lake. The phenomenal decline of the lake trout due to the pernicious lamprey began in 1943. This was the major factor in bringing the native lake trout to extinction.

Lake trout are voracious eaters consuming both small and large fish, one trout was found with the tail of another fish protruding from its mouth. Others were found to have jackknives, corncobs, and other indigestible articles contained in their belly. One fisherman said about a lake trout. "He always bites best when he's fullest."[10] Lake trout do not swim in schools like whitefish but hunt independently, sometimes in deep water. When insect larvae hatch in June they can be found at shallower depths. When Milner made his 1880 study on Lake Michigan he showed that herring not whitefish was the lake trout's main food source.

Lake trout are long lived and do not reach sexual maturity until six to eight years of age. In October they move into shallow water near the shoreline, selecting area of clay and rock, reefs, and honeycombed rock at depths from 40 to 100 feet to deposit their spawn. The Milwaukee and Sheboygan reefs were well-known spawning grounds for native lake trout. The eggs hatched in January or early February. The spawning ritual of the native lake trout, summarized by P. H. Eschmeyer:

> No nest or redd is built by lake trout. The males, which outnumber the females on
> the spawning ground, precede the females in congregating on the breeding area. They
> cruise over the bottom and clean it of debris, algal growth, and slime by fanning and
> rubbing the rocks… Most activity occurs between dusk and midnight and reaches its
> peak shortly after dark, although a few males may be present at all times of the day
> during the height of the breeding season. Lake trout are polygamous and there is no
> vigorous fighting or defense of territory. During courtship a marked, but transitory
> color change occurs among the males; the back becomes light and silvery while a
> dark, lustrous stripe appears along each side. Spawning may occur with only one or
> two males and one female taking part, or several males and several females may com-
> pose a compact spawning group. Typically, one or more males approach and nudge
> or nip at a female and then press against her side, with vents in close proximity. The
> bodies of the fish quiver, their mouths open, and the dorsal fin of the male is erect.
> Each act lasts for only a few seconds and must be repeated a number of times before
> spawning is completed. The fish breed at random over the cleaned area and no
> attempt is made to bury or otherwise care for the eggs, which sink into the crevices
> among the rocks. Individual male lake trout may remain on or near the spawning
> grounds for three weeks or more, but after the spawning is over the adults disperse
> widely from the breeding area. Although lake trout may move to distant points
> between breeding seasons, most return to the same spawning grounds each year.[11]

Since the mid 1950s, after the native lake trout were extirpated from Lake Michigan, and new stocks of trout were introduced there has been little or no natural reproduction occurring. In December, 2002, Phil Moy, Fisheries Specialist at the Wisconsin Sea Grant Institute commented: "Part of it seems to be that trout seem to have a certain area where they return to spawn every year; some-thing like salmon, but they don't die; and maybe these stocked lake trout can't find decent spawning areas."[12]

Changes in lake trout population were becoming evident in the 1940s as the sea lamprey infiltrat-ed Lake Michigan waters in 1938 (there was a report of one found near Milwaukee as early as 1936). After 1938 the lamprey population grew rapidly. Trout became easy prey for the sea lamprey due to the trout's slow moving nature. The best lake trout harvests occured in the late 1930s and peaked at 6.8 million in 1943. A decade later the native lake trout were, for the most part, gone from the lake. Table 3.1 shows the steady decline in numbers of trout caught from 1943 to 1952.

Table 3.1 Decline of Lake Trout in Lake Michigan

Year	Pounds
1943	6,860,000
1944	6,497,000
1945	5,437,000
1946	3,975,000
1947	2,425,000
1948	1,197,000
1949	342,000
1950	54,000
1951	11,000
1952	3,000

Data compiled from Commercial Fish Production in the Great Lakes 1867-2000 (Technical report N0. 3) by Norman S. Baldwin, Robert W. Saalfeld, Margaret Ross Dochoda, Howard J Buettner, and Randy L. Eshenroder; Great Lakes Fishery Commission.

In 1958, the United States and Canada both recognized the problem. The Lamprey Control Program was implemented, and scientists developed a chemical lamprecide called TFM. TFM was designed to kill lamprey larvae in streams, but would not harm other species. After fifteen years the sea lamprey were under control in Lake Michigan, lake trout were reintroduced in 1965 through restocking programs and in 1968 were taken off commercial fishing status. Lake trout were introduced in Lake Superior in the 1950s, Lake Michigan in the mid 1960s, Lake Huron and Lake Ontario in the 1970s, and Lake Erie in the 1980s. With the lamprey situation in check and the lakes restocked with hatchery reared lake trout, there were high hopes that the trout would begin to reproduce and eventually develop a healthy population.

Long-term monitoring of the status of lake trout relied heavily on catch records submitted by commercial fisheries prior to the species being decimated by the sea lamprey. Later monitoring of lake trout populations relied on the fisheries to asses the increase in abundance of stocked fish and naturally produced fish. Only Lake Superior showed evidence of widespread reproduction. In Lake Michigan and Lake Ontario, lake trout reproduced in only a few areas.[13] In Lake Michigan, only scattered evidence of lake trout reproduction, including egg deposits on the spawning grounds and newly hatched trout, has been found since the 1970s. The only place that showed production of lake trout more than one year old was the Grand Traverse Bay region during the early 1980s. However, because of overfishing by the local fisheries the wild lake trout population was soon wiped out, preventing any natural lake trout population to proliferate. Today, efforts to restore lake trout in Lake Michigan are focused on restocking the lake with a variety of lake trout strains in offshore refuges. This protects them from sport and local fishermen.

The lake herring, or cisco, is a small slender-bodied relative of the whitefish that schools in depths varying with seasonal temperatures. Herring are active fish, always searching for and consuming plankton (small water plants and animals), insect larvae, and fish eggs. They move from shallow to deeper

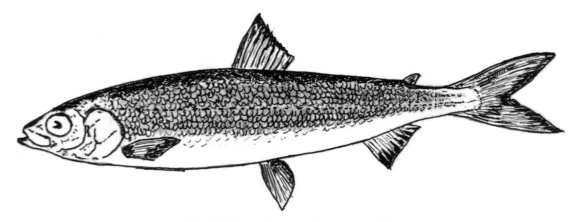

Fig 3.3 Lake Herring *(Coregonus artedii)*

Features: Silvery with pink to purple iridescence; similar to a bloater chub but with more gill rakers
Size: 11 to 15 inches long; weighs 6 ounces to 2 pounds
Adult Diet: Mainly zooplankton; Mysis relicta, Diporeia species
Spawns: Gathers in large schools to spawn in late November and early December
Common Names: Cisco, tullibee, freshwater herring

water during the warmest part of the summer. In Green Bay during the cool months of May and June, and September and October they congregate in shallow waters (30 to 40 feet). This is when they are the most vulnerable to fishermen's nets. The most active period for herring is in the late fall, when they move into their spawning grounds.

Water temperature plays a major role in spawning, which occurs from early November to mid December. Herring arrive on spawning grounds when the water temperature drops to 41 or 42 degrees Fahrenheit. Spawning reaches its peak when the temperature drops to 39 degrees Fahrenheit. In Green Bay most herring move into shallow waters ranging from 10 feet to 60 feet deep. Males arrive in the shallows a few days before females, and once the females arrive, spawning begins. Spawning takes place at night near the surface of the water. The eggs hatch in late April or early May. Herring typically reach maturity in two to three years. Young herring also fall victim to lake trout and larger herring.

Herring were once abundant in Lake Michigan especially in the shallow waters of Green Bay. In 1952, this region produced 38.7 percent of the lake herring catch from all U. S. waters of the Great Lakes. Lake herring became a popular commercial fish species in the latter part of the nineteenth century. Lightly pickled herring proved to be a delicacy. Improved methods of handling and curing made herring even more marketable in the early twentieth century, and they became more popular with fishermen, especially when whitefish populations were low. Most fishermen preferred using the pound net for catching herring. It wasn't long before there were a large number of herring fisheries along the shores of Green Bay, Washington Island, Rock Island, and St. Martin Island.

Fishermen believed herring populations were inexhaustible and that they could never be overfished, but the inevitable happened. After more than forty-five years of aggressive fishing and harvests, herring started to decline in numbers. In Lake Michigan, the production of herring from 1899 to 1908 averaged 20 million pounds and by 1952 it dropped to 6 million pounds. By the 1970s few were caught – 2,209 to 2,752 pounds in 1972 and 1973.[14] Pollution became a factor that had an impact on the herring as more runoff from farms and industrial pollution from paper mills and factories entered the lake.

Another factor in the decline of herring was the non-native smelt that made their way into Lake Michigan. These small fish were voracious predators that consumed a large number of herring fry and eggs. Jake Ellefson, a commercial fisherman from Washington Island recalled that in the 1930s, "The smelt were so thick in the nets it took nearly a day to remove all of them." By 1943 there was a major die-off of smelt, and the herring made a comeback. They were once again abundant until the smelt made a strong resurgence and once again were prevalent in Lake Michigan. The alewife, a species that infiltrated Lake Michigan waters by the early 1950s, posed a serious threat to the herring. They not only were a strong competitor for food but interfered with spawning and preyed on the young fry. Since the 1980s, with the alewife and smelt populations in decline, herring are thriving near the Apostle Islands in Lake Superior. There is also a growing number of herring in northern Lake Huron near the St. Mary's River.

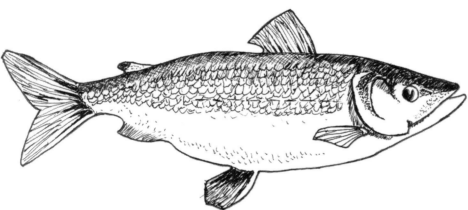

Fig. 3.4 Bloater "Chub" *(Coregonus hoi)*

Features: Long, deep-bodied fish with adipose fin; silvery with some pink and purple iridecence, with greenish tinge above the lateral line and silver white ventral surface
Size: 8 to 10 inches long; weighs 8 to12 ounces
Adult Diet: Mainly zooplankton; Mysis relicta, opossum shrimp, Diporeia species
Spawns: February through March
Common Names: bloater chub, bloat, chub, Hoy's cisco

Bloater chubs are small, soft-fleshed, oily fish that inhabit the underwater slopes of Lake Michigan and Lake Superior, far away from the shores of the mainland. In Lake Michigan the predominant chub grounds are found from Manitowoc to Kenosha in waters ranging in depth from 80 feet to 500 feet. Bloaters, until their third year, are found in midlevels of the lake; few bloaters less than 7 inches are found near the bottom. Most adult bloaters are found near the bottom of the lake at depths ranging from 300 to 400 feet. In Lake Michigan this species moves towards shore in May, and by July, large numbers are found in depths of 120 feet.

Spawning usually occurs in Lake Michigan at a depth of 167 feet, but some chubs may spawn in shallower or deeper water. In the southeastern portion of Lake Michigan, they typically spawn in 239 to 360 feet of water where a large number of alewives are found. Important breeding grounds exist off Milwaukee and Port Washington, Wisconsin, but there may be many other spawning grounds in Lake Michigan.

At one time there were as many as four species of ciscoes or "chubs," as commercial fishermen like to call them. The deepwater cisco – short nose cisco, blackfin cisco, longjaw cisco – once inhabited the deeper waters of Lake Michigan and were larger than the bloater or hoys cisco. For more than two decades the bloater constituted more than 90 percent of the chubs harvested by commercial fishermen.[15]

Because of their small size, bloaters survived while the other species of chubs disappeared, partly due to selective harvesting. The larger chubs fell victim to the sea lamprey in the 1940s and 1950s. Sea lampreys preyed heavily on the larger chub species after eliminating nearly all the larger lake trout and burbot, which were principal predators of the chub. Chubs were fished commercially as the lake trout disappeared and whitefish populations declined. With the two major predators of the ciscoes gone, the smaller bloater began to thrive. In more recent years the bloater has become the mainstay of the chub fishery. Fishery surveys of Lake Michigan show bloaters making up only 31 percent of the catch from 1930 to 1932, over 75 percent of the catch from 1950 to 1955, and 93 to 95 percent of the catch in experimental gill nets from 1960 to 1961.[16]

Two factors contributed to the decline of the bloater chub during the 1960s and 1970s and prompted the DNR to enact an emergency closure of the chub fishery, in 1976. Some experts believe the number one factor for the decline was the explosion of the alewife population in Lake Michigan during that time.[17] Alewives competed with bloaters for space and food and preyed upon immature bloaters. The alewife was believed to alter the zooplankton population by greatly reducing the availability of large zooplankton species that young bloaters fed on. The other factor that may have contributed to the plummeting chub stocks was an otter-trawl fishery that was created in 1959 to harvest small ciscoes for animal food and fishmeal. Gill net fishermen and this new trawl fishery, harvested nearly 12 million bloaters in 1960.

Lake Michigan Fish biologists concurred that the population of bloater chubs has been declining at the rate of 20 percent per year since 1969. There was a correlation of increased size of bloaters with their gradual decline in numbers. The increase in size was attributed, in the early 1960s, to faster growth, but it was also evident that there was a greater proportion of older fish. Concern was growing about the dwindling bloater population, which prompted state and federal agencies to protect and manage what was left of the stock in Lake Michigan. In 1974 the chub stocks were at an all time low, which led to the formation of the Lake Michigan Chub Technical Committee, endorsed by the Great Lakes Fishery Commission. As a result of reviewing available scientific data, the committee recommended that the fishery be closed until the chub population recovered sufficiently to provide a harvestable surplus. Efforts by the states to implement a lakewide ban on chub fishing were challenged by many in the fishing industry in the courts of Illinois, Michigan, and Wisconsin.[18]

On April 26, 1976, Anthony Earl, secretary of the state, closed by emergency order the commercial fishing season for chubs in Wisconsin waters of Lake Michigan. Michigan closed its chub fishery on August 7, and Illinois followed on January 20. The secretary of the Wisconsin DNR justified the closure by saying, "The department is obligated to protect by whatever legal means available those species of fish which it considers to be threatened."[19]

Following the technical committee's 1974 recommendation to ban chub fishing in Lake Michigan, Wisconsin, Illinois, and Michigan established and divided a quota to monitor the stocks during the impending closure. The Wisconsin DNR initiated a contract assessment program for chubs in Lake Michigan on April 1, 1977. Nine contracts were awarded for a total catch of 310,000 pounds, which was repeated in 1978. By late 1978, the chub population seemed to be recovering in some areas of the lake. In 1979, Wisconsin established a 1 million pound quota south of Kewaunee from April 1 to December 31, and it was increased to 2 million pounds by 1982, including a 250,000 pound quota for waters north of Kewaunee in 1981.[20]

Today in 2004, chub fishing is open year round. In the south end of Lake Michigan the season has been open since 1990 and the northern zone has been open since 1996. "The DNR keeps claiming there's a poor recruitment of chubs, but I don't think that's very accurate," claimed commercial fisherman Charlie Henriksen. "They have been aging them and claim that they're all old – even the little ones are old. What I noticed back, about six or seven years ago, there were so many chubs that were stunted - they weren't growing. For a while there were so many chubs – there was a bigger biomass of chubs than there was even alewives, in fact at one point they made up half the biomass of the lake. In a few years they kept growing and growing, and now they've dropped dramatically, although there's still a good population. Up here in the north end, there's so many small whitefish that I think it forces the chubs off of their summer grounds."[21]

Non-Native Species

The commercial "Big Four" – lake whitefish, lake trout, herring, and chubs – over the years were affected by aggressive fishing, pollution, and changes in their habitat. Another factor was further stressing whitefish, herring, and lake trout, and later the chub, and it was another result of man changing the lake ecology. By the early 1900s certain intruder species found their way into the Great Lakes. With the opening of the Erie Canal and the Welland Canal, these invaders eventually filtrated all of the Great Lakes. Fishery managers may have inadvertently introduced some non-native species to the lakes as well.

The alewife, smelt, carp, and sea lamprey, and more recently round gobies, zebra mussels, and white perch have found their way into Lake Michigan. It's been estimated that 130 non-indigenous species have been introduced into the Great Lakes since the opening of the Erie Canal and Welland Canal in the mid nineteenth century. Several species, especially the sea lamprey, alewife, smelt, carp, and milfoil have contributed to profound changes in Great Lakes fish and plant communities.[22] In the 1870s fish culturists were looking for ways to increase the commercial value of the fisheries and introduced two species that became abundant in the twentieth century – the German carp and the alewife.

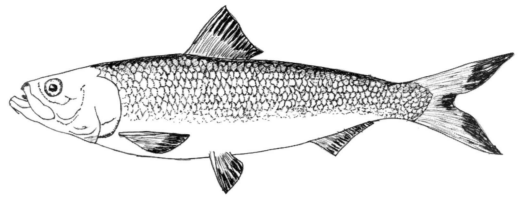

Fig. 3.5 Alewife *(Alosa psuedoharengus)*

Features: Silvery iridescence; single black spot behind head at eye level; blue green metallic luster on backs

Size: 6 to 8 inches long; weighs 4 to 6 ounces

Adult Diet: Plankton; may also eat small fish and fish eggs

Spawns: In shallows in late spring and early summer

Common Names: Mulhaden, grey herring, golden shad, Seth, skipjack

There are a few other theories as to how alewives found their way into the Great Lakes. Many believe a man named Seth Green introduced alewives into Lake Ontario in 1870 when he tried to introduce American shad into the waters, and the fry of the two species were intermixed inadvertently.[23] Some think they may have come on their own by way of the Hudson River and Erie Canal. By 1873, alewives were present in Lake Ontario, where they became numerous.

The alewife is native to the Atlantic Coast and may have entered the Great Lakes through the Welland Canal. Alewives were found in Lake Erie by the 1930s and in Lake Michigan in 1949. By the winter of 1956 and 1957 fishermen in the southern part of Lake Michigan were finding large numbers in their chub nets. There was a major infestation of alewives in the waters of Green Bay, evident by the commercial fish figures recorded in 1957 when 220 thousand pounds of alewives were harvested. In 1960, 2.4 million pounds of alewives were taken, in 1966, 29 million pounds were taken, and in 1973 there was an overwhelming harvest of 45 million pounds of alewives from the region. After the sea lampreys eliminated most of the large predator fish in Lake Michigan, the population of alewives exploded throughout the lake. Alewives are a prolific species. They compete with young whitefish, herring, chub, and perch for plankton and eat small fish as well.

During late spring, when the water temperatures reach 55 to 60 degrees Fahrenheit, these small fish spawn in harbors and near the shoreline. In summer and fall they migrate to deeper waters in the central part of the lake where they feed near the bottom. By mid March and April they come back to shallow waters near the shore, completing a yearly cycle. Alewives begin to spawn at two years of age. They do not die after they spawn and can live up to six or seven years. But when they move from deep water to shallow water near the shore, they are exposed to fluctuating temperatures. A drastic change in water temperature can cause the fish to die. Alewives swim in dense schools and have been a major food source for Lake Michigan's trout and salmon.

Lake Michigan and Lake Huron saw an explosion of these small silvery fish in the 1960s and 70s, but they never developed in Lake Superior. Some fish experts believe the lake is too cold for them. Another theory is that enough of the predator fish survived the lamprey invasion and kept them in check. Alewives are saltwater fish and are not well adapted to fresh water. In fresh water, the salt concentration in the alewive's body is higher than it is in the surrounding water. Water will normally diffuse into the cells of the fish (by osmosis), and freshwater fish must constantly pump water out of their bodies. Fish that are well adapted to fresh water have larger kidneys to remove excess water. However, alewives lack large kidneys and often die in great numbers in the early summer. In the spring of 1967 the alewives began to decline in numbers due to a great die-off similar to that of the smelt die-off of the 1940s. It was reported that approximately 70 percent of the population of alewife was decimated that year, however, by the mid 1970s the population rebounded.

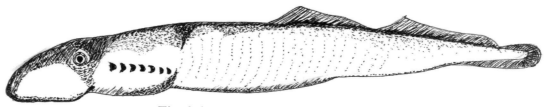

Fig. 3.6 Sea Lamprey *(Petromyzon marinus)*

Features: Grey-blue back, metallic violet on sides; lacks jaws; has circular, sucking mouth with
  rasping teeth
Size: 12 to 30 inches long; and weighs 8 to 13 ounces
Adult Diet: Fluids and tissues of large fish, particularly salmon, trout, and whitefish
Spawns: In rivers and streams in the spring; larval lamprey spend 3 to 6 years buried in sediments; migrate to open waters for adult parasitic life
Common Names: Great sea lamprey, lake lamprey, lamprey, lamprey eel

The sea lamprey, an ancient predatory fish that feeds on the blood of other fish, was well established in Lake Ontario in the early 1820s. It may have been native to the lake, or it may have entered from the Atlantic Ocean by way of the Erie Canal. By 1890 sea lamprey were abundant in Lake Ontario and were becoming a menace to whitefish. This was evident by the scars on whitefish and trout that were harvested by fishermen. In their natural habitat, sea lamprey, like salmon and alewives, are ocean fish that spawn in fresh water. Lake Ontario is open to the Atlantic Ocean by way of the St. Lawrence River.

In 1921, lampreys were found in Lake Erie for the first time. Evidently they came by way of the Welland Canal, connected Lake Erie and Lake Ontario. The spawning lamprey moved upstream in search of spawning grounds. The lamprey posed a threat to native fish, but didn't inflict that much damage. By 1930 the lamprey had moved up the St. Clair River, and by 1932 it was found in Lake Huron, where it devastated the whitefish and trout populations. By 1934 it was found in Lake Michigan where it exploded in numbers, and threatened the lake trout, whitefish, herring, and sturgeon. In a matter of ten years time the lamprey did its damage. By 1946 the lake trout were nearly wiped out in Lake Michigan, and the whitefish population was threatened as well.

The sea lamprey, an aggressive parasite, is native to the Atlantic Coast of the United States and Canada. The adult feeds on large fish as a parasite rather than as a predator. The lamprey has two life stages — larvae and adult. It spends a few years as a larva, living at the bottom of freshwater streams and feeding on insects, fish eggs, and fry. After it reaches a certain size and the water temperature changes, the larva undergoes a complete metamorphosis and becomes an adult. After one year as an adult in open water, it returns to a river to spawn.

The lamprey attaches itself to its prey by means of its disk-shaped mouth, which is full of sharp teeth. Its rasp-like tongue makes an opening in the skin of the fish and then releases an anticoagulant in its saliva, keeping the wound open as long as the lamprey stays attached to its prey. This can be weeks or until the fish dies. Usually only one in seven fish attacked by a lamprey survives. During its adult life as a parasite, a sea lamprey can kill forty or more pounds of fish. Those fish that die are killed either by fluid loss or by secondary infection from the wound.

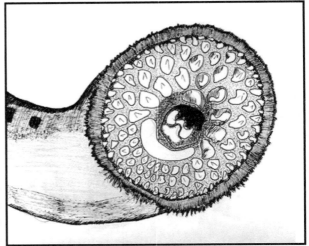

Fig. 3.7 Mouth of a sea lamprey revealing a myriad of teeth for rasping a hole in the host fish.

The sea lamprey had a tremendous effect on fish populations in the upper Great Lakes — Huron, Michigan, and Superior. In Lake Michigan the lamprey population exploded and seriously affected whitefish and lake trout populations. In 1946 the overall harvest of lake trout was 5.5 million pounds but in 1953 the annual harvest was only 402 pounds. Lake Michigan and Lake Huron trout fisheries were virtually wiped out in a decade. The sea lamprey, for some unknown reason, had no impact on fisheries in Lake Ontario.

In 1958, scientists developed a chemical called TFM (3-triflormethyl -4-nitro phenol) that selectively kills sea lamprey larvae in their spawning grounds. In ten years time the lamprey population was reduced to about 10 percent of their peak population in 1948.[24] Some scientists are concerned that these surviving lampreys might develop a resistance to the lamprecide or spawn in areas of deeper waters where the lamprecide is not effective. In addition to TFM other methods of controlling the sea lamprey were adopted. One was a barrier method to block spawning lampreys from ascending rivers. Traps and sterile-male release programs have been introduced since 1990 that have proved to be effective in the control of the lamprey.

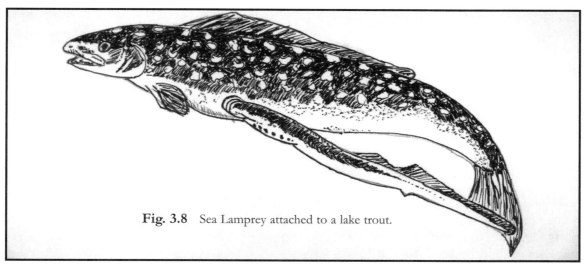

Fig. 3.8 Sea Lamprey attached to a lake trout.

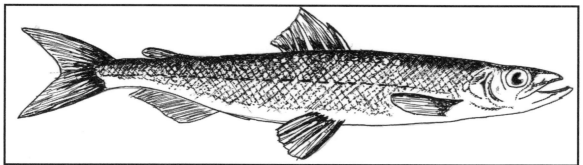

Fig. 3.9 Smelt (Osmerus mordax)

Features: Elongated body, silvery in color with purple, blue, and pink glittering reflections
Size: Average weight in the Great Lakes is 4to 8 ounces; to 7to 8 inches long
Adult diet: small fish, opossum shrimp, mysis relicta
Spawns: Spring, usually in streams, but also known to spawn offshore over gravel shoals.
Common names: freshwater smelt, lee fish

The rainbow smelt found in Lake Michigan descended from a stock of smelt that originally came from Green Lake, Maine. This species is a freshwater relative of a marine species found along the Atlantic Coast. In the early 1900s there were several attempts to introduce smelt into the upper Great Lakes. The present strain is thought to originate from the 1912 stocking of Crystal Lake in Michigan.[25] Rainbow smelt were first found off Lake Michigan's east shore near Frankfort, Michigan, in 1923. By 1924, they had spread to Big Bay de Noc, Michigan. They were found in Wisconsin waters in 1928 when a few were caught in fishermen's nets near Little Sturgeon Bay in Door County. A year later they were found at Gill's Rock and the Sturgeon Bay Canal; by 1930 they were reported in Manitowoc, Port Washington, Racine, and Kenosha.

During the Great Depression many people relied on these small fish as a food source, and to bring in some extra income. In 1947, John Van Oosten, fisheries biologist, noted: " The smelt, therefore, has not only added a new source of food for the people and fish of the Great Lakes area and a new source of revenue for the commercial fishermen and unemployed during the winter, and stimulated all types of business generally during a normally slack period of the year, but has provided additional recreation for the citizens during the fall and winter with hook and line, during the spring with dip nets and other paraphernalia, and even during the summer with fly fishing when the smelt school near the surface."[26]

The fisheries, regarded smelt as a nuisance and a threat to native whitefish and herring. However, some people welcomed them for recreational purposes. In the 1960s they were gaining more popularity as food, and people harvested them with dip nets and seine nets when the fish came to shallow waters to spawn. In the spring of the year, usually April or early May certain areas along the lakeshore would draw large crowds of people who harvested these little fish for smelt frys. The largest population of smelt in Lake Michigan is found in Green Bay. In the past twenty years the bay has provided in excess of 70 percent of the total Lake Michigan harvests. One of the major spawning runs occurs in the Menominee River, which forms the boundary between Wisconsin and Upper Michigan.

In Lake Michigan, young smelt, up to the end of their first year, inhabit the upperlevel waters until late summer or fall. After the first year they are commonly found at midlevels; after three years of age they live near the bottom. Smelt in northern Lake Michigan, where they are more abundant in than the southern portion of the lake, are often found at depths of 80 feet and sometimes at 150 to 210 feet, rarely are smelt found deeper than 300 feet.[27] Smelt begin to spawn in mid to late spring (March through late April to early May). Water temperature influences when the smelt spawn, typically 40 degrees Fahrenheit or higher. Spawning time varies as much as three weeks between the northern and southern regions of Lake Michigan. The spawning run in southern Green Bay is usually a week later than in northern Lake Michigan due to the bay freezing in the winter – it takes longer for the bay water to reach optimal spawning temperature.

Spawning smelt congregate in shallow waters near streams and migrate as far as a mile upstream. Smelt also spawn on gravel deltas in lakes, generally in about 2 feet of water. Spawning begins when there is a ratio of four males to one female; later in the season there is an equal number of males and females. Spawning takes place primarily at night. Females never release more than fifty eggs at one time.[28] Some female smelt are known to return to the lake still bearing eggs, and presumably they return for a second spawning run. Once spawning is completed, males and females return to the lake and seek deeper water.

When smelt made their way into Lake Michigan, their numbers rose rapidly and kept increasing until the early 1940s. Many fishermen in northern Lake Michigan caught smelt in small mesh gill nets and used them as bait for set hooks for lake trout. Fishermen actually preferred them to the native chubs. In 1942, smelt were almost nonexistent in the lake, and by 1943 and 1944 production was down to zero. This came to be known as the "smelt disaster," and its cause remains somewhat of a mystery. During that period, many fishermen from Washington Island and northern Door County pulled in thousands of pounds of dead smelt that had been caught in their gill nets.

Scientists concluded that the die-off was probably caused by a communicable disease.[29] The smelt population recovered to a record high by 1957-58, then dropped again in the 1960s. One factor thought to have an impact on the population increase was the lack of predation by lake trout, which were decimated by the sea lamprey. By the mid 1960s the smelt population declined once again, coinciding with the stocking of Pacific salmon. Throughout the 1980s and 1990s the smelt population fluctuated.

Since the 1990s, the smelt population has declined almost 95 percent in Lake Michigan. Lake wide trawl surveys conducted by the U.S. Geological Survey's Great Lakes Science Center indicated that a biomass of smelt declined almost 95 percent in a decade, from 46 million pounds in 1992 to less than 3 million pounds in 2001. Commercial harvests also showed a decline from 1.89 million pounds in 1991-92 to 316,000 pounds in 2001-02. This prompted the Wisconsin DNR, in 1993, to reduce the season by six weeks and lower the harvest limit in Green Bay from 351,993 pounds to 100,000 pounds.

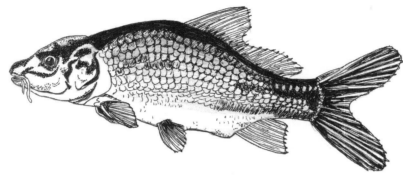

Fig. 3.10 Carp *(Cyprinus carpio)*

Features: Olive green on back, yellowish belly, large scales
Size: 15 to30 inches long; weighs 2 to 20 pounds
Adult Diet: Omnivorous – will eat almost anything; frogs, insects, fish eggs, and vegetation that grows in shallow water
Spawns: Late May and early June; congregates in the shallows
Common Names: German carp, European carp, mirror carp

In the latter part of the 1800s the U.S. Commission of Fish and Fisheries introduced the carp into North America, raising them in ponds for a food fish. Soon carp were found in growing numbers in the shallow waters of Lake Erie. In 1893, a reported 631, 000 pounds were shipped to markets, and by 1908 over 9 million pounds were shipped. Carp soon were found in Lake Michigan, Lake St. Clair, and Lake Huron.[30]

In the 1890s, fish culturists and the public were quick to condemn the introduction of carp, for they were not as pleasant to eat as trout and whitefish and they were also becoming a problem in streams and rivers. They began to inhabit the shallow, weedy shorelines, particularly along the south eastern end of Lake Michigan and in lower Green Bay, where they became abundant. These fish are notorious for destroying wetland areas, streams, and rivers because, they uproot vegetation, muddy the waters, and destroy vegetative foods and cover needed by other fish. Being omnivorous, carp will eat frogs, insects, spawn of other fish, and vegetation that grows on the bottom of shallow waters. Fishermen disdain these fish because they eat the spawn and young fry of commercial fish species. Carp in Lake Michigan were once harvested and sold commercially for food and fertilizer. Now many carp, especially those from southern Green Bay and the Fox River, contain relatively high levels of contaminants, and cannot be sold commercially.

Chapter 3 Notes

1 George C Becker, *Fishes of Wisconsin*; (Madison, WI: University of Wisconsin Press, 1983), 339.

2 Margaret Beattie Bogue, *Fishing the Great Lakes: An Environmental History 1783-1933* (Madison, WI: University of Wisconsin Press, 2000), 151.

3 James Milner, "Report on the Fisheries of the Great Lakes," 48-52; George C. Becker, *Fishes of Wisconsin*; (Madison, WI: University of Wisconsin Press, 1983), 336.

4 James Milner, "Report on the Fisheries of the Great Lakes" 64; Margaret Bogue, *Fishing the Great Lakes An Environmental History1783-1933*; (Madison, WI: University of Wisconsin Press 2000), 153.

5 W. Koelz, " Coregonid Fishes of Northeastern America 1929"; George C Becker, *Fishes of Wisconsin*; (University of Wisconsin Press, 1983), 339.

6 "Wisconsin Department of Natural Resources" 1976; George C. Becker, *Fishes of Wisconsin*; (Madison, WI: University of Wisconsin Press, 1983), 339.

7 Ibid., 340.

8 L. Wells, and A.L. McLain; 1973, "Lake Michigan ? Mans effect on Native Fish Stocks and other Biota." Tech. Report No.20; 55. George C. Becker, *Fishes of Wisconsin*; (University of Wisconsin Press, 1983), 328.

9 Ibid.

10 Margaret Beattie Bogue, *Fishing the Great Lakes An Environmental History 1873-1933*; (Madison, WI:

University of Wisconsin Press, 2000), 154.

[11] P.H Eschmeyer, "The lake trout; U.S Fish and Wildlife Service" George C. Becker, *Fishes of Wisconsin*; (Madison, WI: University of Wisconsin Press, 1983), 324.

[12] Interview with Phil Moy, Fisheries Specialist Wisconsin Sea Grant Institute; University of Wisconsin Manitowoc. January 9, 2003.

[13] Michael J. Hansen, National Biological Services and James W. Peck, Michigan Department of Natural Resources; "lake trout in the Great Lakes."

[14] L. Wells and A.L McLain, 1973, "Lake Michigan" Mans effect on native fish stocks and other biota." George C. Becker, *Fish of Wisconsin*; (University of Wisconsin Press, 1983), 346.

[15] Edward Brown Jr., Fish and Wildlife Service; Ronald W. Rybicki, Michigan Department of Natural Resources; and Ronald J. Poff Wisconsin Department of Natural Resources; "Population Dynamics and Interagency management of the Bloater in Lake Michigan 1967- 1982." Technical Report No. 44, Great Lakes Fishery Commission; Ann Arbor, Michigan.

[16] S.H. Smith 1964, "Status of the deep water cisco populations of Lake Michigan;" Trans. AM. Fish Soc. 93(2) 155-163.

[17] Edward Brown Jr., Ronald W. Rybiki, and Ronald Poff; "Population Dynamics and Interagency of the Bloater in Lake Michigan, 1967- 1982;" Technical Report No. 44.

[18] Ibid, 3.

[19] Letter from Anthony Earl to Elaine Johnson.

[20] Ibid, Technical Report no. 44, 30.

[21] Charlie Henriksen interview, December 12, 2002.

[22] "Nonindigineous Species Problem" Sea Grant Great Lakes Network.

[23] Margaret Beattie Bogue, *Fishing the Great Lakes: An Environmental History 1783- 1933* (Madison, WI: University of Wisconsin Press, 2000), 162.

24 "Sea Lamprey Control," Great Lakes Fishery Commission.

25 George C. Becker, *Fishes of Wisconsin* (Madison, WI: University of Wisconsin Press, 1983), 379.

26 Ibid, 383.

27 L. Wells 1968, "Seasonal depth distribution of fish in Lake Michigan," U.s. Fish and Wildlife Service; George C. Becker, *Fishes of Wisconsin* (University of Wisconsin Press, 1983), 382.

28 Ibid. 380.

29 John Van Oosten1947, "Mortality of smelt in Lakes Huron and Michigan during the fall and winter of 142-1943; Ibid, 383.

30 Margaret Beattie Bogue, *Fishing the Great Lakes: An Environmental History 1783 – 1933* (University of Wisconsin Press, 2000), 165.

Chapter 4

Ice Production

Cutting and storing ice was an integral part of the fishing business, since large amounts of it were needed throughout the summer and fall months for shipping fish. Compared to salting, ice was a far better way of preserving fish, and it was easily available during the winter. Thus, when the waning days of autumn had given way to winter cold and the boats (and some fishermen) retired for the season, attention turned to the production of ice.

Ice harvesting usually began in late January or early February when sufficient thickness of ice had developed in the harbors – fourteen to sixteen inches was optimal. Everyone lent a hand, for this was a task where teamwork was imperative. Speaking of it with some of the oldtimers, one can almost hear the saw blade singing through the ice and the men laughing and telling stories. Bennett Hagen remembers how, as a youngster, he couldn't wait to get home from school to run out to watch the men and maybe lend a hand. He recalls the ice harvest as a great time that provided some excitement to break the monotony of the long winter months.

The first step in harvesting ice was to find an area where ice conditions were suitable for making the blocks or "cakes." This meant finding ice that was fourteen inches thick in an area that was flat and relatively free of ice chunks and snow. Some years they could make ice right off the docks, which was ideal since it cut down on transport. In other years, they had to haul it from further away. Howard Foss remembers harvesting ice well down Washington Harbor, near where the wreck of the *Louisiana* was located, and one year they had to haul ice clear across the harbor from near Mt. Misery with five or six teams of horses hooked to a sleigh.[1]

Once a suitable area was found, the men would remove any snow and expose an area large enough to produce several hundred blocks of ice. Then they scored the ice with an "ice-plow," creating a grid pattern. The ice plow had curved twelve-inch blades that cut into the ice to mark the grid pattern for blocks. Different operations cut blocks of different sizes. For example, at Washington Harbor, Howard Foss ordinarily cut blocks twenty-two inches wide, forty-four inches long, and fourteen to sixteen inches thick, or however thick the ice was, but others preferred other sizes.

It was common for fishermen to help one another out making ice. Walt Jorgenson described making ice for Art Hanson:

> In the winter months, usually around the end of January or whenever the ice was twelve to fourteen inches thick we would clear the snow off an area. Art Nelson had a saw rig that Art Hanson would use to saw the cakes. It had a three-foot circular saw blade and would score the ice to a depth of twelve inches, but not all the way through. Otherwise it would throw water all over. This rig had a guide on one side

that would follow the saw cut and kept the cakes uniform in size. The ice cakes were normally cut eighteen inches wide by thirty-six inches in length, but sometimes a larger cake was cut that measured twenty inches by forty inches. Once the ice field was cut into a grid pattern the outer cakes were removed first with ice bars and picks, and then floated towards a ramp or slide where they were pulled out of the water. The ice cakes were stacked four high and hooked to a cable that was attached to the ice jack and pulled to the icehouse by the power take off unit of a truck or tractor engine. Ice harvesting operations would normally take one or two days to fill the ice house.[2]

If the distance was not too great, they might cut a channel slightly wider than the blocks leading to a ramp near the icehouse, and men with ice picks then moved the floating blocks along it. In later years, ice was often transported as described above, using an "ice jack," a tool with two iron finger-like hooks attached to a cable or rope by means of an eyehook, but in early years a team of horses might be used to run the ice to the icehouse.

Most often a door way or opening was left in the wall facing the waterfront to allow loading and unloading the ice cakes. Once the blocks arrived at the icehouse, they were either carried in through that opening or (later on) run in on a gas-powered winch or conveyer. Men working inside the icehouse stacked them in tiers, spreading a thin layer of sawdust between tiers and a thick layer all around the perimeter of the icehouse. They used planks across the opening to hold each tier from falling out, with sawdust between the planks and the outermost blocks. Eventually, the entire opening would be blocked with planks, since the icehouses were normally filled to the tops of the walls. After all the ice was in, the top was covered with a thick layer of sawdust to insulate and keep it from melting in the summer months. The outside walls and the floor of the icehouse would be lined with sawdust about fourteen to sixteen inches thick, but the top layer was thicker.

In the summer months, old sawdust (that had become soaked) was removed and fresh sawdust was applied to the ice on a weekly basis to keep the ice from melting. For use in packing fish, the sawdust was rinsed away before the blocks were run through a one-cylinder gas-powered ice chipper. In the days before such chippers were available, an ice shaver was used to process ice for packing fish.

However, not all the ice was used for packing fish. Some was sold to residents of Washington Island for their iceboxes, as there was no electricity to run refrigerators there until 1946 or 1947, and ice also was supplied to merchants on the island. For example, both Ted Gudmundsen, who had the harbor grocery, and the Koyen Brothers bought ice from Matt Foss for their coolers. In the early days, teams of horses pulled wagons or sleighs to supply the merchants and residents with ice, but trucks eventually replaced the horse-drawn vehicles. Charlie Jensen was one person who distributed ice on the island, and George Hanson in his Chevy truck was another.[3]

In Washington Harbor, Howard Foss made all the ice for his business, and there was another icehouse at the Furlong dock, where John Young did the ice harvesting. Sometimes these two men and their crews would help each other out; teamwork and camaraderie meant a lot in those days. Each harbor or region of the island had its own ice production.

Matt Foss had a large icehouse at his dock in Washington Harbor. It measured forty feet by sixty feet, with walls eighteen feet high. Matt, his son Howard, and their crew usually spent one or two days harvesting ice from the harbor to fill their icehouse with enough to last through the following seasons, but Howard recalls one year when they filled the icehouse in nine hours time – a record for them. Their operation normally required a crew of ten or twelve – six men in the icehouse taking ice off the ramp and stacking it, one "jack man," two men moving ice cakes through the channel, and two or three men cutting the blocks.

There were several icehouses at Jackson Harbor. Most fishing operations had their own icehouses, though a few fishermen purchased ice from Art Hanson. The Ellefsons had their own, as did the McDonalds, the Nelsons, Goodmander and Johnson, and John Christianson. Most of them were constructed with the studs and framing members on the exterior with the sheeting applied to the interior side of the studs. The sheeting was then coated with creosote to preserve the wood from the melting ice. This arrangement allowed air movement that helped to keep the interior cooler in the summer months. Only John Christianson's icehouse – made of concrete blocks – was constructed differently.

Art Hanson owned a dock at Jackson Harbor that many fishermen used, and he also harvested ice and stored it in a large icehouse. He retired from fishing after his brother Hans passed away and ran the dock and sold ice from the late 1940s until 1970, packing fish for some of the fishermen. The fish were normally packed in wooden crates that would hold a hundred pounds of fish, including the weight of the ice. During the years when herring were plentiful, they were first salted and then packed in crates or barrels, but otherwise nearly all the fish were packed with shaved or crushed ice. There also were a number of icehouses at Detroit Harbor. Fred Richter had his own icehouse on Detroit Island for his fishing operations, and John Cornell had an icehouse at his dock on Lobdell's Point. Also, Ole Christiansen, who lived in Detroit Harbor, had a small icehouse on his property

In fact, throughout Door County, towns and villages that were near the water annually cut and hauled ice. In Fish Creek, nearly everyone running a business had an icehouse. Farmers would come in and haul ice to make a little extra money. Ephraim was an ideal location for good ice because of the shallow waters. The locals in Ephraim rigged up saw blades on each side of the wheel hubs on the rear axle of a truck. The truck was pulled by two horses as the saw blades cut through the blue (clear) ice, and men behind cutting the cakes, picking them out, and loading them onto sleighs. Sometimes, if they were near enough to shore, they cut a channel and floated the cakes right to where they could be hauled up into the icehouses. Those blocks were cut to the width of the wheel hubs and then cut into forty-inch lengths.

Near Lily Bay, Ted Wester also modified an old automobile engine for cutting ice. He had started out cutting ice with a one-man saw, but after a few years he devised a saw rig from one of his old cars. He mounted a large saw blade on one of the rear wheels and locked the other wheel so it couldn't turn. He then sawed half-way through the ice in a grid pattern, and all the way through to the water along the first row. Ice blocks from the other rows were broken loose with needle bars.[4]

In Gills Rock, Lyle and Leon Voight talk about their grandfather cutting ice. His ice house was on the hill up from the dock. He owned the old farm up there and had a big building that was used as an icehouse. The ice was cut right out in the harbor.

Chapter 4 Notes

[1] Paula (Hansen) McDonald, "Interview with Howard Foss 1979."

[2]. Interview with Walter Jorgenson, May 5, 2005.

[3] Hannes Anderson, "Washington Island Through the Years," *Washinton Island Observer;* Gail Toerpe, "Harvesting Ice For the Icebox," *Washington Island Observer*, May 4, 2000, 1.

[4] John Enigl, "Fishbox Business Was a Spinoff for Ted Wester," *Door County Almanac No. 3* (Dragonsbreath Press, 1986), 142-146.

Chapter 5

A Day in the Life of a Fisherman

Commercial fishermen epitomize the American dream and working class hero – independent, hardworking, and tough – and they practice one of the oldest professions known to man. "It's not the easiest life, but it's the only life as far as I'm concerned – it's all I've ever done," says one old commercial fisherman. A fisherman must be and do many things to be successful. Besides fishing, he must be a weatherman, carpenter, welder, electrician, good pilot of his craft, navigator, and gambler. He needs an iron will, a strong body and a good pair of sea legs. As one fisherman puts it: "We may not know how to do anything well, but we can do everything."[1]

Fishermen on the Great Lakes have always been a tough bunch, especially in the early 1900s. Marvin Weborg and Cliff Wenniger, two Door County fishermen, liked to say that "years ago, they made iron men and wooden boats. Now they make iron boats and wooden men." Fishing was rough, hard work. A fisherman's day began very early and ended late, usually well into the evening, depending on the season, weather, and type of fishing. The life involved physical labor under all kinds of conditions, from sunny calm days to late fall storms and heavy seas, and was a true test of endurance in which both skill and luck played an integral part.

Experience was an important factor and played a major role in how a fisherman fared. Those who spent most of their lives on the lake acquired a great deal of practical knowledge about such things as where fish feed and spawn, lake currents, the most effective methods of harvesting fish, and basic lake ecology, which gave them a great advantage in a competitive industry.[2] The success of a fishery also depended on a having good crew, a sound boat and a good work ethic.

Alvin "Gabby" Anderson, a commercial fisherman from Milwaukee who grew up in Ellison Bay, spoke with me in January 2003 about the range of knowledge and experience which is needed to be a commercial fisherman:

> **A** true commercial fisherman has more knowledge, I don't care how much education you have; if you have two years, four years, or eight years. It takes common sense and knowledge of all that's around you. You've got to understand in this business, you can't be taught this in books – it's all experience, and you have to know what's happening all the time in order to understand it. In the old days all we had was a clock and a compass; I had an old alarm clock. There were no fathometers, radios, navigational aids, or sonar. You'd run into snowstorms, fog, what have you, and you had to know where you were by what you knew and what knowledge you gained through experience. I don't care if you've been out there five years or thirty-

five years you see something different every time you go out — you keep learning, always learning. There's always something different, but you learn and don't forget, you store that in your mind which gives you experience so when a situation arises you can say, ' I've seen this; I've been through this; and I know what to do.' A good captain observes everything and you learn from your experiences. You are never too old to learn. I've been out there for fifty-two years and I don't think there was hardly ever a day I haven't seen something or learned something new. It's unbelievable what you can learn.[3]

Many fishermen learn their trade at a young age, usually from their fathers or working with other fishermen. It was a career that was not learned from books but rather from firsthand experience as Laurence Daubner, a long-time commercial fisherman from Door County, explained:

You know, when I decided to go into fishing it was like on-the-job training; you couldn't find out anything about fishing by books, but rather you had to have it by experience. And that was handed down from the older generation to the younger generation. When you were out there, in the beginning, you got some pretty good seas. They had old Straubel engines that sneezed once in a while and you'd smell gas and you had to shut the door up and then you felt something in your stomach rolling around; and then it got worse and worse. First you were afraid you were gonna die, then you were afraid you weren't.[4]

There were lean times when fish populations declined, and bad weather kept fishermen idle. They learned in this profession that they had to take the bad with the good. As Marvin Weborg says, "you never know what you're going to catch – it's a gamble from day to day. You either get a good lift or you get nothing, and that's what you have to live with."[5] Jake Ellefson, a semi-retired commercial fisherman from Washington Island, remarks:

A commercial fisherman is a strange creature. You have to battle the elements, you know. It's something like being a farmer except that we're more exposed because we have to fight the wind and sea with our boats. We can be out on the water and of course can get involved with the worst weather – fog, snowstorms, heavy seas, high winds – and you have to find your way home under all those conditions.[6]

And a superintendent from the Wisconsin fish hatcheries spoke of the rigors of fishing in the 1800s:

The lives of lake fishermen are not easy. In all kinds of weather the nets must be looked after, and usually the catch is largest when the great gales sweep the lakes. In November the best run occurs as the herring, whitefish, lake trout, and blue fins leave deep water and seek the shallow spawning grounds. Oilskins sheeted with ice, numb fingers cut and bleeding from drawing in freezing nets, and faces frost bitten by icy spray are common experiences.[7]

"I guess we're a different breed of people," remarks Pete Le Clair, a commercial fisherman from Two Rivers, Wisconsin. "There are only so many in this business that have survived. If you're going to be a fisherman, you got to be tough."[8] So many variables affect a fisherman's livelihood and prosperity: life cycles of fish, seasonal temperatures, and long-term cycles of weather patterns, lake levels, and human activities that alter the lake's ecology. October and November, the spawning season for whitefish, herring, and trout were important months for fishermen. Spawning season is the one time of year when fishermen can count on a good run of fish. Years ago, when the native lake trout came to spawn on the Sheboygan and Milwaukee reefs in October, and the whitefish in the shallow waters in November, fishermen had a chance to make up for poor harvests earlier in the season.

The most common types of fishing gear on the Great Lakes are still in use today. They are gill nets, pound nets, and trap nets, each with their own challenges and procedures. Gill-net fisherman had to be willing to travel long distances in search of good fishing grounds. To be successful, gill-net fishing demanded hard work, skill, and experience. Gill-net fishermen could sometimes set them close to shore, while at other times they might have to travel as far as thirty or forty miles and then battle sudden storms and squalls that tested their skills and seamanship.

Pound-net and trap-net fishermen had a larger capital investment in their rigs compared to gill-net fisherman. They also lived a less risky, more routine way of life. They rarely had to travel far to their fishing ground. But theirs was still a physically demanding job. Some fishermen used both gill nets and pound nets. In the 1870s, the average price for a pound net-rig was about $500 compared to $225 for a gill-net rig. Today, the cost of a pound net or trap net is approximately $8,000.

A fisherman also has a sizable investment in his fishery. Besides his rig and gear, there's the cost of coolers, ice machines, vehicles, fuel, maintenance, buildings, docks, real estate, tools and other miscellaneous expenditures that add up to a substantial overhead. Today, it's not unusual to have a total investment of $500,000 to $750,000 in a fishery. Some fisheries have four or five boats, a number of gill nets and trap nets, and a sizable investment in processing the fish. The high costs make it difficult for someone to break into the business. In addition to the overhead, license fees, the problem of obtaining a quota, tighter regulations and other factors make it extremely difficult to make a profit. "It's not a profession to get wealthy. It's something that you have to love to do and work very hard to do it," as one fisherman explains.[9] Dennis Hickey, a commercial fisherman from Baileys Harbor, Wisconsin, put it like this:

I don't like to quote the price of fish or the size of our investment. Some people can't put things into perspective. We have a sizable investment in our operation. If I were to say I had ten trap nets at a certain dollar amount, some people might say, he must be making a lot of money – Yeah, if you work seven days a week, fourteen to sixteen hours a day, for a lifetime you can have that. You have to be careful what you say – I've seen in the past, how that all works. It's the same with farmers; people see a farmer with three or four Harvestor silos, a nice big red barn, a bunch of cattle, they don't realize the poor bugger is out there until 9:00 or 10:00 in the evening and out there again at 4:00 in the morning.[10]

According to Jeff Weborg,

One of the biggest misconceptions of a commercial fisherman is that he's rich simply because when you get a good lift everyone seems to know about it, and therefore
assumes you're making a lot of money. But what they don't realize or hear about is
all those times you're out there and never get any fish; or you go out there and your
nets are lost or ruined; or you blow an engine in your boat. Nobody hears about that.
But let me catch a few fish and they say, 'Oh look at the fish they got.' So there's some
real misconception there.[11]

Neil Teskie, a commercial fisherman from Gills Rock, remarks:

One of the biggest misconceptions about commercial fishermen I notice is that we
don't care about the fish. People think that we're just out there raping the lakes, so
to speak. Not caring about the stocks. People don't understand that we understand
that without those fish we don't have anything. We're more conservative or conser-
vationists than what people think, and I think the biggest misconception is that we've
destroyed the stocks and are destroyers. We're the first to say if the stocks are in jeopardy. I'll be the first to say, 'cut my quota' if I think the stocks are in jeopardy.
Sometimes the jeopardy is more people management than fish management.[12]

Retired Lake Michigan commercial fisherman Lorman Greenfeldt expressed similar sentiments:

People think we're trying to catch the last fish in the lake, which we're not. We are
as concerned about conservation as anyone else, so there [are] fish the next year and
the next year. Sports fishermen used to think that we're fishing out the lake, you
know. We had some wild meetings with the sport fishermen. "You're trying to rape
the waves," they said. The DNR would hold meetings in cities along Lake Michigan,
and the sport fishermen would be there protecting their interests, and that's all right
too. But they didn't have to think that the commercial fishermen were killing off
their sport. It was especially a problem when the trout were being attacked by the
lamprey eels, and finally it was determined that it wasn't the fishermen. We used to
spear those buggers off the back of the boat. The eels would latch on to the back
of the boat when we were setting our nets, and they'd love to catch hold of the boat
on the back end, and we'd take the spear and stab them.[13]

A Day in the Life of a Gill-Net Fisherman

The day begins early for a fisherman and his crew. Each fishery normally has a crew of three or four men and sometimes five or six, depending on the size of the harvest. Generally today there are three men on a boat. Years ago, there were usually two others who remained on shore to perform such tasks as scalding (boiling) nets to clean them, reeling nets, packing fish, and sometimes slugging (repairing or adding a new section to) nets. A few fisheries had only a crew of two or three men, but they didn't set as many nets as those with larger crews.

The crew of three or sometimes four is headed by the skipper, who pilots the boat. In the 1940s and 1950s, the skipper didn't do much but operate the boat, but that has changed somewhat. Nowadays, whoever runs the boat is expected to do much more. In the past, when the nets were lifted, the skipper would keep the boat up to the net steering from a forward station near the lifter, and would have a gaff hook or net in hand in case any fish fell out. The rest of the crew would separate fish from the nets at the sorting table and then set the nets back into the water. Some older boats required an extra man known as the engineer to run the engine if there wasn't any engine control from the pilothouse. The engineer would control the speed and motion of the boat following orders from the skipper, who transmitted them either with a bell or by voice. The bell system was more effective over the loud din of the engine, especially an old Kahlenberg engine. One bell signified neutral or clutch off; two bells meant reverse; three bells meant check down speed; and four or five bells called for more speed.

Prior to the 1960s and the use of modern navigational aids, a fisherman relied primarily on his wits and experience at sea. He had a compass for finding his bearing; a clock for determining time and distance traveled, and a logbook for keeping track of such things as bearing or reference points, range lights, lighthouses, water currents, and other bits of information to aid him in navigation. It was all he had and he became very adept at navigating. Many fishermen used landmarks such as a tall tree or other conspicuous objects for bearing points. In the 1940s and 1950s on Washington Island, many fishermen used Roger Gunnerson's silo as a reference point, and fishermen in Rowleys Bay used a pine tree that was taller than the other trees as a landmark to guide them into the harbor and stay clear of the reefs.

Today, a typical day on the lake for a gill-net fisherman begins at daybreak. He loads the boat with boxes of nets, empty boxes to hold the wet nets, boxes for the fish, and ice to keep the fish fresh. Before the 1960s, if the boat had a Kahlenberg engine, it would take some time to get the engine running. Each cylinder had to be primed with fuel, glow plugs were heated to ignite the fuel, and finally a shot of compressed air was introduced into the cylinders to start the pistons moving. Beginning in the 1950s, engines came to be equipped with batteries and a standard ignition, making them much easier to start.

According to Jeff Weborg:

> **A** normal day for me is, I wake up between 4:00 and 4:30 in the morning and I get up and start thinking about what I'm going to do. I'm looking at the weather, planning the day according to the weather, and then I head down to the shed fifteen or

twenty minutes ahead of the other guys in order to get things ready to go, so when they get there we can head right out on the lake. Once in the boat we head out to where our nets are and begin lifting. When the net is lifted, the desirable fish are picked out of the net and undesirable species or species that cannot be legally caught like the lake trout and salmon are thrown back in the lake. After the nets are lifted and reset, we dress the fish on our way back and pack them in boxes with a layer of ice. It's extremely important to keep them iced and handle them properly, or you won't have a decent product.

Unlike other workplaces, there's very little talk among the crew on a fishing boat. The members of an experienced crew know their responsibilities in any given situation; there's no need for orders or questions. Once back into port – typically around 3:00 or 4:00 in the afternoon – we unload the fish from the boat to our processing shed either at Gills Rock, our home port, or at our other one in Rowleys Bay. The fish are then processed, and after that it's a matter of doing any repairs to equipment. After my crew takes off and goes home, I usually make sure the fish are shipped out and make sure the boat is ready to go the next day. A day can go, we normally say, from 6:00 in the morning to 3:00 in the afternoon, but it doesn't always go that way.[14]

Lorman Greenfeldt and his older brother Harold began fishing with their father Anker at Washington Island when they were fourteen years old, and fished their entire lives on Lake Michigan. I sent a questionnaire to Lorman, who told his story to his son Eric. Lorman has owned a total of fourteen boats in his fifty plus years.

Eric: What is a typical days routine?
Lorman: Get up in the morning at 4:30, have breakfast, go down to the harbor, get on the boat, warm up the engine a little, head for the fishing grounds. Sometimes we shouldn't be out there, but… (laughs)
Eric: How did you heat the boat?
Lorman: Soon as it started getting cold in the fall we'd put the stove in.
Eric: Were the nets loaded on the boat the night before?
Lorman: Not always, we would have to load them in the morning.
Eric: Was it different if they were cotton or nylon nets?
Lorman: Could be either – no set routine. We would run our time and course on the compass, and when our time was up, our buoy was supposed to be there. Hunted around sometimes, pulled up the nets and picked fish, hopefully!
Eric: Anyone pull up anyone else's nets?
Lorman: Oh, it was known to happen.
Eric: Would someone set nets on top of yours?
Lorman: Oh yes, some more prone to do that than others.
Eric: If someone set their nets on yours what did you do?

Lorman: You would pull them up and pass them on top of yours. It made it harder to get yours out – it would wind them up.

Eric: Would most fishermen respect everyone else's buoy?

Lorman: Yes, one time we had four different strings of nets come up at one time – ours and three others. We had to figure out how to disentangle them. We may have cut our own nets and pass them under, I don't know. It was on a whitefish ground, over in Michigan. Fishing was especially good there then. So after we lifted, we set the same nets most of the time. We would gut the fish after we had reset. Used to reset half of what we lifted. If we lifted ten nets, we would reset five and take home five – mostly cotton ones. With nylon nets, you could throw them in a corner of the boat and leave them for a month or two. Now they have monofilament – stronger. We would take half of them (cotton) home. We would set mostly ten nets. Some guys would fish twelve or fourteen.

Eric: What time of day would you finish resetting the nets?

Lorman: We would be back home (back at the dock) at three o'clock.

Eric: All dressed by then?

Lorman: Depends on how many you would get. Most of the time we had them all cleaned by that time. Seagulls would clean up the guts. Back at the dock, we would take care of the fish; put them in boxes with ice and get them ready to ship out, and take care of what nets we brought home, put them on the reels to dry, and if we didn't have a shore crew, we'd have to pull off those that had dried a day or two before and put them in boxes. You weren't done 'till it was all over. I remember one time in Racine we had 5,000 pounds of perch. We took them all home and had to pick them. We had a little pick that we stuck in the eye and pulled them through the net. Had to get ice, pack them in boxes, and put them in the storage building, and took them to Chicago the next day. We had to do all that. I think it was midnight that night. We started at 4:30 in the morning, and the next day we started all over again. Those little perch! Pick, pick, pick! We didn't have to gut them. Schwartz Company in Sheboygan had women who gutted them. They had bony cheeks and a spiny back on them. I got blood poisoning being stabbed by them. If you weren't careful, you were stabbed to pieces. Usually you put a glove on; it was like needles sticking up, and their jaws were sharp – they could cut you.

Eric: What is the strangest thing you encountered?

Lorman: One of the strangest things was when I was fishing with Dad on the *Jane Elizabeth* we pulled up an old weather balloon, and we got it tangled in our nets. All the way from Minneapolis, Minnesota – General Mills was putting them up. The ball that had the instruments in it got caught in the net and we pulled up this huge - type thing that was carrying the gondola - type thing (instrument package). This big thing comes up, and it was full of water. I don't know how we ever done it. We got it up and pulled it into the boat. Of course the water came up as we were pulling it. For some reason, I called Ruby Cornell (island operator), and she contacted General Mills and I think we got a $25 reward. This was off the west side of the island in the late 1930s.

Another thing we picked up was the raft that is now in Washington Harbor. It was a big life raft off a freighter. That was a bugger to tow, and we donated it to the town. It sat out at Jackson Harbor for awhile. We found a canoe once. One summer a young man wanted to learn the fishing trade, and he was heaving over the side and he lost his glasses. Later that September, I found the same glasses and I brought them back to him! I saw him in town, and I said, "Here are your glasses." They had been broken and repaired with duct tape, so we knew they were his. He couldn't believe I had recovered his glasses. Nets pick up a lot of things. You name it, they come up. Bed springs. The current would pick up everything along the bottom. There was a lot of dirt in the nets then, dead fish, sticks, stones, stumps, clinkers (residue from the steamboats) ashes would form into a big thing we called a clinker – lots of sharp edges. The nets would fill right up with that. All kinds of moss and algae. Once my son, Eric, was reeling up the nets, and there was a rubber in the net. Absolutely astounding, the junk in the nets, even a bicycle.

Eric: What was the most dangerous situation you were in?

Lorman: One time we were caught in an ice shove east of Rock Island. It pushed the boat up a foot out of the water. It was grinding through the propeller and rudder. It sounded like being in a big steel drum. On the one side the ice was stable – was up against the shore, and on the other side, a big ice field was going from the shore out to the lake, and we just got caught in it. One ice field was stable and the other was moving; the current was moving it. We were in the *Betty*, and she got caught between the moving ice.

Eric: How did you get free?

Lorman: The current shifted and moved it off just enough so the boat dropped the water, and we went. It was about an hour of damn scary business. It was pile ice – it was really rough.

Modern navigational equipment like the new GPS and Automatic Loran-C receivers make locating the nets and finding the way home much easier, but before they were available a fisherman relied on a clock and a compass to navigate, and, in inclement weather, he had to use all his skills to do so. Jake Ellefson remembers heading out in many foggy days:

In foggy weather, you try not to worry about it. You just go out and try to find your nets and get a lift on them and you got to be on the ball. Dense fog, you still find your nets if you're a good skipper, that's the unskilled part of it (with a slight chuckle) and of course today it's much more simple as you have the long range navigational aids such as Loran-C. All you have to do is take the setting from the buoy and if you come back to that setting then the buoy should be there unless the current has moved it. When you set the boat for that point you know you are where the buoy should be and of course years ago we didn't know that for sure because we didn't have any real positive way to be sure.

These Loran-C units, you can set that thing when you're leaving where you set the nets, lets say Rock Island Bluff. You can punch the numbers at your buoy and it will tell you just what course to steer and how long it's going to take you. But I never did that because I wanted to test my skills, and so I would attempt to do it with a clock and compass to see how close I would come. When I got there, or fairly close, then I'd adjust my course and time a little bit if it looked like I wasn't going to be dead on the buoy. The Loran-C and the new GPS units are just pieces of equipment, and if they fail, then they are not going to find the buoy for you. I didn't rely on them much. They should be aids not the principal means of finding your way.[15]

Once the fisherman reaches his nets and the net buoy is located, the buoy is pulled inside the boat and the anchor line brought up to the surface. The net is then attached to the mechanical net lifter, sometimes operated by a separate engine. The skipper keeps the boat in the desired spot from a forward steering station and the crew takes to their stations behind the lifter at the sorting table. From the forward steering station, the skipper tries to keep the boat directly over the net being pulled up by the lifter. In a heavy sea, that is always a challenge. As the net is pulled in and onto the sorting table, the fish are removed from the net and the undesirable ones are tossed back into the water. Jake Ellefson spoke about getting a net full of undesirable fish:

Sometimes you can get a net full of suckers. It's bad news, because the shape of a sucker makes it very hard to get it out of the netting. Their fins are larger than those of the whitefish, which have more of a taper to them. Whitefish usually slide easily out of the net. A load of suckers is not what you want to see in your nets.[16]

The fish are put into boxes that can hold approximately 100 pounds, and the nets are loaded back into the net box to await resetting. When a box is filled with fish a little ice is sprinkled over them before they are set aside, and the process continues until all the gangs of nets are in. The new monofilament nets can be set right back into the water. The old cotton and nylon nets were brought back in to dry, although it was common practice to reset half of the wet ones and bring in the other half to dry. The nets are set back into the water from the aft section of the boat while the boat moves forward at her normal gate (speed). This procedure still normally requires three men – the skipper to drive the boat and two men to set the nets, however some fishermen did this all alone or with only one other crewmember. As the boat moves along, the nets are passed out the stern of the boat via a rear door and are strung over a bar or roller to keep the float and lead lines separate from one another. One crew member feeds the net from the box. Sometimes another man stands by to make sure there are no tangles, to tie the nets together when one box was almost empty, and to prepare the other box of nets to be set. The nets move rapidly, and Jeff Hickey talks about the dangers of this procedure:

> When you're resetting nets you can see why you don't wear wrist watches or rings; you could get pulled right out of the boat by the net. It happened to a lot of guys. It never happened to me, although one time we bought some chub nets from a guy up in Manistique, Michigan. For some reason they decided if they didn't tie on the brail that goes across the end of the net they wouldn't pick up so much junk in the nets. I found out that this could get caught or wrapped around your arm, so we had to take them off, especially with chub nets. Those things are really flying out of there.[17]

In a 2001 interview, Jake Ellefson spoke about the daily routine on the lake:

> They set the nets a little different in the old days compared to now. In those days they used a lot of packed nets, because cotton netting wasn't synthetic and needed to be taken ashore and scalded with hot water [between sets]. Some of these boats would set fourteen boxes of nets every day – dry ones, fourteen dry ones. They would take the wet ones in, or sometimes reset half the wet ones and take the other half in, and reel them up to dry. That's why they needed a shore crew, to reel all those nets. The next day there were usually two men to pack them into boxes, floats on one side and leads on the other, and they were careful to pack them so they could be easily set. Once out on the lake, they would go and get a lift on the nets that were set from the previous day or days. The nets were set out of the back of the boat and the guys who were really good at it could set the nets as fast as the boat could run. When one box of nets was nearly set they had to be tied to another box and were the work of the guy who was setting the floats. The guy who set the leads had all he could do just to keep those leads uniform. Some fishermen would let the cork line run freely, and whenever the guy setting the leads had a chance he'd tie the nets together, one box to the next. After he got that done he would continue setting, but for a while the cork line would be allowed to run freely with no help. Tying the nets together was a tricky procedure, especially when you got to the end of one box. Then you had to shift. The guy handling the leads would move the [new] box up on his end and the other guy on the cork end flipped the [old] box away, hanging on to the net and then moving his side [of the new box] up, all the while the boat is moving on her gate and sometimes bucking heavy seas. So it could be a very tricky procedure.[18]

Until the 1950s or so, fishermen would sometimes leave their nets out for as long as a week in the early spring because the water temperature was just above freezing and there was no danger that the fish would spoil. In the warmer months, however, the nets could only be left out for a few days. Jake Ellefson comments:

> **T**oday the DNR wants you to lift your nets every day. It's not the way to fish really. It's fine if there's a lot of fish, but whitefish are never really on the bottom one hundred percent of the time. You know they'll be down there good one night, then the next night they'll lift right off and there won't be any. Biologists say their feed is three feet off the bottom. Well ideally it is, but half the time it's not there because you know that they follow their feed, and if they're not at the bottom, their feed is off the bottom. It's as simple as that.[19]

Throughout the twentieth century, Lake Michigan gill-net fishermen prospered when whitefish were abundant. Whitefish brought in the most money at the market place, and they could be caught nearly year round except for a period in late fall that coincides with their spawning run. Fishermen would comb the waters for whitefish, setting nets through the ice during the winter months. If the ice wasn't too thick, many fishermen would run their boats for open water to set their nets, and some still do. However, the whitefish season is now closed to commercial fishermen from October 25 to December 1.

One Washington Island fisherman went out in the very cold December of 1870 to get a lift on his gill nets despite the danger of getting caught in the quickly forming ice. This story was told to Jake Ellefson by Angus Swenson, another Washington Island fisherman, about his grandfather, Andrew Irr:

> **A**ndrew Irr was 6 feet 5 inches tall, 300 pounds, and all bone and muscle – a real bear of a man. That family withstood cold very well. Angus would never wear gloves in the winter. In December of 1870, Andrew had pulled out his pound net and was fishing gill nets with a small Mackinaw boat a few miles north of Washington Island where the fishing had been excellent for some time. The weather got very cold a few days before Christmas. All fishermen worry that the ice will come and they will lose their nets. The nets were so important when you have to make one mesh at a time. Christmas day dawned bright and clear but very cold, one of the coldest days on record. The pancake ice was forming all along the shore, and Andrew realized he had to go and try to get his nets.
>
> He found the nets and got a lift on them. Andrew said it was so cold that the backs of the whitefish turned black when they came out of the water. He rowed in toward his dock but there was a lot of ice all along the shore, which made it impossible for him to land. He turned the boat around and headed for Rock Island and landed just south of the present site of the ranger's house. He had to leave about 800 pounds of fish for the fox but he had saved his nets. He spent the night with one of the Rock Island families and walked home across the ice the next day. There

were many fishermen that day that lost their nets, but Andrew wasn't one of them.[20]

There were great catches of whitefish every year until 1880, but after that time there was a cycle in the population. Whitefish would be abundant for a few years, then there would be hardly any for a few years, then they would be abundant again. In the 1930s, Cliff Wenniger began fishing whitefish with deep pound nets at Baileys Harbor. The waters off Baileys Harbor and Moonlight Bay are one of the most important spawning areas for whitefish in all of Lake Michigan. He was soon setting pound nets in Deaths Door and also up at Minneapolis Shoals where he was catching many whitefish. The Weborg's of Gills Rock were doing the same. Marvin Weborg saw many "comings and goings" of whitefish in his time. When Marvin's father Arthur and his two brothers Alfred and Willie began fishing in 1910, whitefish were scarce in the bay and lake, so they fished lake trout with hook and line. It wasn't until 1927 that fishermen began to harvest whitefish once again. In the early 1930s Marvin remembers getting lifts of whitefish exceeding 3,000 pounds, but by 1934 smelt had became so thick in the bay, clogging their nets, that it wasn't worthwhile to fish whitefish any more. The whitefish were there, but it was almost impossible to clear the nets of smelt.

The most successful fishing today is done with trap nets and pound nets. Jake Ellefson remembered a day late in the fall of 1947 when Dan Lindal and Steve Ellefson went out on the *Billy Jean*:

They went first to their pound net set northwest of Poverty Island and lifted about 2,500 pounds of whitefish. They then proceeded to their other net, which was set off the north shore of St. Martin Island, west of the lighthouse dock, and lifted almost 6,000 pounds there. So, between the two lifts they had over 8,000 pounds in their twenty-eight foot boat. That was considered a very big load.

The wind was calm on the north side of St. Martin Island, but it started to pick up from the southwest. They were loaded heavy in the bow and had not taken the time to transfer more fish aft as they headed back to Jackson Harbor. All the fish were above the deck. The hull was tight, but there were two hatches in the deck with covers on. They rounded the north end of St. Martin Island and found themselves in a small swell. The sea kept building and becoming more intense, and soon they had taken a pretty good sea over the bow. Because of the position of the load, the boat rose very slowly, and the swell filled the boat with water. One full box of fish had floated off. The bow finally raised, and they swung around and headed for the beach, moving slowly along the shoreline in very shallow water, so they could walk ashore if the boat started to sink.

The hatch covers were letting a lot of water into the bilge, and the self-bailer was clogged. Steve managed to clear the self-bailer, and they gradually got rid of the water. The lightkeeper at Rock Island had spotted them. He came out to help and brought in a ton of fish on the lighthouse boat. Then they reloaded the *Billy Jean* with most of the fish placed aft before they made their run back to Jackson harbor. Vic Goodlet, their shore crewman had his work cut out for him dressing all those fish. They weighed in at 8,600 pounds that day.[21]

There were some very big catches of whitefish with gill nets through the years. In December 1947 the McDonald Brothers from Washington Island caught about 5,500 pounds of whitefish with linen and cotton gill nets west of St. Martin Island. That was one of the truly great lifts, because linen and cotton weren't nearly as effective as the monofilament nets used twenty years later.

In 1974 and 1975 the Ellefson Brothers in the *Miss Judy* made two lifts of 5,500 pounds and several others of 3,000 to 4,000 pounds of whitefish; those were considered very good days of fishing. The record catch by gill nets on the island belongs to the Koyen Brothers, Kenny, Tom, and Harvey, all of Washington Island. They were fishing in the *Sea Diver* and came in with 7,800 pounds of whitefish one day in the spring of 1996. In March of 1978, the Ellefsons had a 5,000-pound day. These fish were all caught west of St Martin Island. Jake remembers:

> We managed to get up in a small area of open water and set our nets. A couple days later we could see from the lighthouse on Rock Island that we might be able to get a lift. There was a lot of ice between Rock Island and St. Martin Island, so we had to go out between the shoals and then up around the north side of St. Martin Island. We got to our nets about 9:00 AM. By 5:00 PM, Steve and I had picked out 5,000 pounds and had our nets set back in. We came by St. Martin light by 6:00 P.M., then had to come home through the ice. We finally made it back to the cut by 10:00 PM. A nice little bit of Navigation by Steve. A great day of fishing, although a very tough day.[22]

One of the largest whitefish Jake Ellefson remembers catching was over 15 pounds, caught in a deep trap net near shore close to Cedar River, on the western coast of the bay of Green Bay. Ray McDonald remembers catching one or two that were close to 19 pounds, and Tom Goodman had one in his net that weighed 17 pounds. Dennis Hickey, a fisherman from Baileys Harbor caught several whitefish over 20 pounds in pound nets. Apparently the bigger fish swim high in the water, because pound nets come all the way to the surface and seem always to catch more big fish than trap nets, which usually are well under the surface.

Fishing for chubs became an important part of the fishery after 1910. In the 1960s, chubs were about the only commercial species left to catch, as whitefish were scarce. After a botulism scare involving chubs in 1964, the commercial fishery for chubs almost closed down. Chubs are commercially valuable only when smoked. They didn't bring much, but it was enough to keep some fishermen going. In the 1960s, chubs were sometimes as low as eight or ten cents a pound. Alvin Anderson, a native-born Door County fisherman recalls those days:

> I think back through out the history of fishing on Lake Michigan and I have to say that the chub fishery was always the backbone of the industry. You know way back when, the whitefish and trout were more or less seasonal. It was so uncertain most of the time. If you wanted to try hard enough, you could always fish chubs. In the early 1960s, I think it was 1962–63, the lake froze over solid. I remember it was so doggone cold and snowy that winter. We had chub nets out that year of 1963 for almost seventy nights. We set January 9, 1963 and we didn't get out to get a lift on

them until the middle of March. We saved what we could of the chubs. Back then there wasn't much income – we had some tough times.[23]

Jake Ellefson remembers fishing chubs throughout the 1960s:

Soon as we got the *Miss Judy*, we then had a good long range boat so we were able to go out and fish for chubs, which were about the only fish out there to catch. The chub fishing grounds were found to be in the middle of Lake Michigan or beyond, in Michigan waters, which were over 30 miles away, or about three hours from the Rock Island bluff. So that's what we did then every summer, from the 1st of April to about the middle of September, we'd make that run two or three days a week.

At that time we had to have our fish on the 5:00 P.M. boat every night, because we didn't have refrigeration at the time. So that meant we were up at 2: 00 in the morning, leave the dock by 3:00 A.M., get back by 3:00 P.M., get the fish packed by 4:00, and have them to the ferry before 5:00 P.M. We did that for eight years, and then the whitefish started coming back. So then we fished primarily whitefish for the next twenty-five years. But when we were fishing chubs we never stopped. There was a closed season a few years in November, but after that we fished them hard straight through the winter. Most of the whitefish grounds were iced over in the winter, so the practical thing to do was fish for chubs, so that's what we did. We fished for chubs all winter, and that was a tough time. If you had a couple of weeks where it was real cold, you might not get a lift during that time, and when you did finally get out to lift them, the fish were usually no good. It's a very tough game, no question about it.[24]

Chub fishing was usually the best during the winter months, one of the worst of times to be out on the lake. The tough fishermen were the ones who went out and fished chubs. Freezing cold temperatures, heavy seas, ice forming on the boat sometimes 4 to 6 inches thick, and snowstorms made winter fishing a true challenge for the fishermen. For most of the fishermen in the northern Door County region, the chub grounds were two to three hours away. They had to navigate in the early morning darkness and often returned home in that same cold winter gloom.

Fishermen use a 2 1/2-inch mesh net for harvesting chubs and normally set the nets at depths over 100 feet. Before there were any regulations, fishermen used 2 3/8-inch mesh nets. When the Wisconsin Conservation Commission imposed the new 2 1/2-inch mesh size, many chub fishermen argued that it wasn't appropriate, because the normal adult size for a chub is a fish that's caught in a 2 3/8-inch mesh and couldn't be caught in the larger mesh size. Some fishermen continued to use the smaller mesh and had their nets confiscated by the authorities.

On Washington Island, many fishermen had a secret place to make illegal nets, which they continued to use despite the new regulations. One island resident recalled that:

In the late 1930s the fishermen were not getting many fish, so they kept making illegal nets. A man by the name of Frank Grasse would come to check the nets, but he never found an illegal small mesh. The fishermen had a field back in the woods called "Mabel's Room" where they took care of illegal nets. So, if you wanted a certain fisherman you couldn't find, it was always "he's up in Mabel's Room."[25]

Chapter 5 notes

[1] Interview with Jeff Weborg, December 13, 2002.

[2] Margaret Beattie Bogue, *Fishing the Great Lakes: An Environmental History 1783-1933* (University of Wisconsin Press, 2000), 94.

[3] Interview with Alvin "Gabby" Anderson, January 23, 2004.

[4] Laurence Daubner, An evening of story telling at the Wagon Trail Resort, Rowleys Bay; Video by Charlie Miller;(Courtesy of Elaine Johnson).

[5] Marvin Weborg, interview in the video *The Last Fisherman.*

[6] Jake Ellefson, quoted from the video *A Calming of Deaths Door* (HVS Productions).

[7] Wisconsin, Commissioners of Fisheries and State Fish and Game Warden, Fifteenth Biennial Report, 1893-1894 (Madison, Wisconsin; State Printer, 1895), 21. Ibid, Margaret Bogue, 93.

[8] Pete LeClair, quote from Harvesting the Inland Seas (video) Wisconsin Maritime Museum.

[9] Interview with Jeff Weborg, September 14, 2002.

[10] Interview with Dennis Hickey, September 29, 2002.

[11] Interview with Jeff Weborg, September 14, 2002.

[12] Interview with Neil Teskie, July 3, 2003.

[13] Interview with Lorman Greenfeldt conducted and transcribed by his son Eric.

[14] Interview with Jeff Weborg, December 13, 2002.

[15] Interview with Jake Ellefson, October 2, 2001.

[16] Ibid.

[17] Interview with Jeff Hickey, June 8, 2003.

[18] Interview with Jake Ellefson, October 2, 2001.

[19] Ibid.

[20] Interview with Jake Ellefson, May 4, 2003.

[21] Interview with Jake Ellefson, May 4, 2002.

[22] Interview with Jake Ellefson, October 2, 2001.

[23] Interview with Alvin Anderson, March 29, 2003.

[24] Interview with Jake Ellefson, March 1 &2, 2002.

[25] Letter to author from Joy Gunnlaugsson, April 2003.

Chapter 6

Through Waves and Gales Come Fishermen's Tales

In late autumn and early winter, fishermen on northern Lake Michigan found themselves in some tough situations when the autumn gales came to blow and fishermen were caught in them. Jake Ellefson remembers such experiences all too well:

Out on Lake Michigan in October can be a very windy month, and it can blow every day, northwest, north, southwest, what have you, for three to four days in a row and it will surely test your skills. When you have one of these windy falls, you'd see a lot of days when there would be 15 foot seas and every fall you'd see one or two days where there would be 20 foot seas. I used to judge the size of the sea. I'd look at it and say, well is it as high as the shed? And there were some days when the waves were that high. The peak of our shed is about eighteen feet.[1]

On a really bad day, a breaking sea forms on top of the big swell and continues to build until it is much larger than the average and then breaks like a breaker would on shore. There often are three big waves in a row ("Three Sisters") followed by one that is slightly smaller, then three larger ones, and so on. The best practice for a skipper caught in a heavy sea is to reduce speed and turn the boat into the wind to face the big waves coming in. Whether lifting nets or setting them, it made tough work for the crew, but keeping the bow into the wind lessens the impact of those big waves, or combers. As Jake Ellefson noted:

Those were the tough fishermen – the ones who had to fish chubs, because you had so far to go and you were exposed to the open sea. And boy, you couldn't be ashore very many days or your fish were going to rot in the nets. You have to fight the weather, that's all there is to it, and you suffer. One of the biggest satisfactions of being a commercial fisherman, for me anyway, is that challenge when you're fishing chubs. In the fall of the year, especially October, it can blow day after day and you're typically lifting in 10-foot seas; some days it can be a 20-foot sea. If you fish your entire life you'll see 30-foot seas once or twice. That's always a challenge. You have to handle the high waves while the boat pitches and rolls, and you get what is known as your sea legs, which is an old sailor expression for keeping your legs spread far apart to keep your balance as the boat rises and falls, pitches and rolls.

On the other hand, when you're fishing whitefish you're more in a confined area where the sea might not get as big. In the bay, the sea never gets as big as it does out in the middle of the lake. But it can be very nasty, because the swells are shorter and choppier, so of course you roll more. When you get out in the middle of the lake, the swells are longer and you don't roll quite as much, but they can be big.[2]

Another account of battling heavy seas was related by the late Hannes Hannesson, a commercial fisherman from Washington Island, who at the time was fishing with Leon Cornell on his new 48-foot boat the *Velox*. Leon fished chubs across Lake Michigan from Washington Island in the winter months during the early 1930s. Hannes remembers a particular day when they were lifting near the Manitou Islands in a huge south sea. One wave broke over the entire boat, and they took so much water down the exhaust pipe that the engine nearly stopped. At the same time the cabin shifted an inch. But then the next wave hit and the cabin shifted back into place.[3]

Working in rough weather is just part of the job for a commercial fisherman. Some are more cautious than others, but most fishermen are proud, confident individuals who have the utmost faith in themselves and their boats. One Door County fisherman summed up this attitude as follows:

Т he weather could just be awful, and it would look like nobody was going to be out on the lake that day. But, all it took was one boat to start up and head out, and then everyone else had to go. You couldn't be the one who lay on the beach. That was always a big deal, if you could get a lift on someone else; then you were king of the hill.[4]

Some storms were so fierce that fishermen did not venture out, and they were wise to heed the weather warnings. But, there were plenty of times when fishermen were caught unexpectedly by a big storm and had to just ride it out. This story is told by Alvin "Gabby" Anderson, a fisherman originally from Ellison Bay, about a time when he and his brother barely escaped death when they were caught in a three-day blow on Lake Superior:

Caught in a Northeaster

I was talking to my brother Clarence some time ago, and we got talking about the time we were both put to the test of endurance and seamanship. It was fifty-two years ago, in 1951. My brother Clarence and I got caught in a heavy northeaster while we were fishing out of Port Wing up in Lake Superior. We had the boat the *RVH* at the time. We had a Caterpillar [diesel] engine in her. It was around the time of the vernal equinox. I think it was the days of March 19, 20, and 21. At that time we were gone for a week fishing 40 miles out from Port Wing. We left Two Harbors that day and anchored for the night between Rocky and South Twin Islands. Earlier that afternoon, we ran into Norman and Harris Johnson in the *Roamer* as they were heading back to Port Wing the day before the storm. The *Margaret* was fishing way east of us. He come by us late that afternoon, so he stopped to see if everything was all right with us before heading back. He wanted to know when we were heading back in. I told him we got at least one more day of lifting before heading back. We pulled behind the islands that night and dropped anchor. That night she started to whistle out of the northeast – oh God, did she blow! We were between Rocky and South Twin Islands that night.

The next morning it was blowing a little harder than the night before, so we stayed put there until we saw what the weather was going to do. That afternoon the wind kept increasing, and our anchor wasn't holding by Rocky Island. So we thought we might try to get in the lea of South Twin Island. We headed over there, but that proved to be impossible over there. You couldn't imagine how the seas were building. It was late afternoon probably around 3:00 or 4:00, that we decided we had to get the hell out of there. So we scooted down between Rocky and, I want to say Bear Island, where we ran the boat and went as close as we could and dropped anchor for the night. That night it began to snow. Boy did it ever snow. When we threw the anchor we had it wrapped around the bow stem, which didn't work very well. We had no fathometer so we had to hold. We never stopped the engine. We had to hold a sounding line out the window to see if we were getting into deeper water. Every time we were getting into deeper water, we knew the anchor line wasn't holding, so we had to pull up. We couldn't see anything. My brother climbed up on the bow and left the clutch on and headed her back in towards the island. I kept hollering the depth and as soon as we got into shallower water, he'd drop the anchor again. That night it snowed even harder and the wind was still blowing gale force.

You know, I wake up yet at night thinking of that time, and every time I see my brother, we talk about that night. Anyway, it snowed so hard and blew so hard you couldn't see two feet in front of you. Little did we know, with the cold water and snow, we had ice and snow piling up on the boat. By morning the snow let up a little. Overnight, little did we know, the snow and ice were building up around the hull and sucking us down. We opened the door when it got to be daylight. Our rail was right down in the water. That's how far down we had sunk. If daylight hadn't come for another five hours, we would have sunk without even knowing what happened. We cleared the snow and ice off the best we could and kept the boat going. We never stopped the engine once. We kept her going for seventy-two hours. We had enough fuel. We always kept an extra barrel on board the boat.

We had an old coal stove on the boat for heat, but we were running low on coal. We had plenty of fish to eat and plenty of water to boil the fish in, but it was pretty hard to eat at a time like that. We never slept at all. I don't think we spoke a word to each other for thirty-six hours. We just knew what we had to do. The following day we tried to get out of there, but the seas were so tremendous that we had to head over by Bear Island. We laid on the southern end of Bear Island in a small cove and anchored there for another night. The next day we finally caught a break in the weather and headed back for Port Wing. You should have seen the faces on the people back at Port Wing when they saw us coming into the pier. They thought they saw a ghost ship. Norman Johnson had said the night before to some other fishermen that we were goners and that they'd never see those guys again – that there was no way anyone could have survived through that storm.[5]

For many years, Laurence Daubner worked for various fishermen like Lawrence Voight and Stanley Voight, from Gills Rock, and Cliff Wenniger of Baileys Harbor. In his many years of fishing on Lake Michigan, he had many brushes with death. The following took place on a bitterly cold December morning in 1941:

Adrift in a Skiff

We were fishing out of Sand Bay. It was a cold morning. Lake Michigan was steaming, and only three boats went out to lift nets. Most of the boats figured they couldn't find their nets that day because of the steam and the icy conditions. The three boats that went out were the *King,* owned by Richard and Victor Johnson, the *Golden Girl,* owned by Alfred and Willie Weborg, and Jim Peterson's boat [he couldn't remember the name]. About 3:30 in the afternoon, Jim Peterson came in with his boat and reported that the other two boats were aground, the *Golden Girl,* on the west side of Sand Bay on Larson's Reef, and the *King* on Newport Point Reef.

Roland and Vernon Johnson offered to take their boat, the *Ramona,* to try to pull them off. There was a small skiff lying on the beach that had about an inch of ice on the bottom. I think that's about all that held it together. We threw the skiff on board the *Ramona* with a couple of boards to use for paddles, as there were no oars around. We went first to rescue the *Golden Girl.* Lester Wickman and I boarded the skiff with a small line to pull a larger rope to attach to the *Golden Girl* for pulling it off the reef. It was a southwest wind and we were protected from the shore, so that the project went fairly well. We soon had it free off the reef and floating again.

Then we headed across the water to Newport Point, where the *King* was on the reef. The further we went, the worse the sea became. By the time we arrived close to the *King,* the waves were pretty high. We again threw the skiff in the water, and I asked George Lindal to accompany me to pull the small line to the *King.* By that time the waves were very threatening, and we didn't know what could happen in the rescue, so we threw a five gallon bucket in the boat in case we had to do some bailing. We took the small line and tied it to the bow of the boat, and off we went in the direction of the *King.* The only time we could see the *King* was when we were on the top deck of the *Ramona,* it was steaming so badly. Keep in mind that it was five degrees below zero that day.

Our companions on board the *Ramona* assured us, "if anything should happen to you so you feel you can't make it, or the boat fills with water, just jerk on the line and we'll pull you back to the boat." We started off on our rescue mission, but when we got about half way, all at once the boat snapped around and almost threw both of us overboard. We managed to stay in the skiff, but by flipping the boat around, it had filled about one-half with water. I told George not to worry; we'll just pull ourselves back to the *Ramona* with the line. I started to pull on the limp line, only to have the other end of the line appear at the edge of the skiff. We were adrift. We found out later that the *Ramona* had started to hit bottom as it was backing up to get ready to pull, and the man at the helm had abruptly put the drive in forward before the man on the line could release it from the tie-post. The sudden jerk broke the line, so we were completely disconnected from the base boat.

Now we were on our own, and it was bad. However, the wind was blowing us toward shore. We were concerned that if we were far enough out to miss the point and floated out into open water between the point and Spider Island, we would surely be goners. We kept drifting in the dark. We kept speculating how, if we came to the reef, we could walk on it to shore. But we were aware there was deeper water in places between the reef and the shore. All at once, we knew we were on the reef because the combers, large swells with whitecaps whipping on top of them, tossed our boat fiercely. After we crossed the reef, the water became calmer, and we kept drifting with the wind. When the boat had filled with water, our paddles had floated away. And we wouldn't have known which direction to push ourselves anyway.

George kept bailing and I laid up in the bow on my knees to let the water deflect off of my chest to keep it from entering the boat again. To this day, I still can't figure out how the boat stayed in the position it did. It was really a miracle. I'm sure there was a divine guidance that held it in the right position. We finally decided we needed something to test the depth of the water we were in. There was a narrow strip of lumber on the top edge of the side of the boat, which we tore off and used as our depth gauge. All we could do was sit silently and wait. Both George and I began to hear a sound like a "shh, shh, shh" at intermittent times. We concluded we were getting closer to shore but hoped it would be the mainland and not Spider Island. The sound became louder and louder, and then we washed up on the beach. We pulled the skiff up on shore and examined the rocks to detect where we possibly could be. Even in the dark we decided we were on Newport Point. We couldn't go through the woods because we couldn't see any trail. So we decided to walk the icy shore over to Schoenbrunn cottage, then up Juice Mill Road and over to Roy Wetterstom's farm. He wasn't home, so we walked to where Norman Strandel lived to get help. Norman took me home to Ellison Bay, and he took George to his home in Baileys Harbor.

I came into the house and my wife Emily observed that I was all icy and wet. "Oh, I fell into the lake," I said. "I'll put on some dry clothes and go and help the fellows with the large catch of fish we got." I then drove my car down to Sand Bay and saw the boat was all lit up. The fellows were still sitting there talking. They were conversing about the events of the afternoon and about George and my where-abouts. I opened the door of the boat and the fellows just looked. I'm sure they thought they were looking at a ghost. They didn't say a word, I betcha, for five minutes. They never dreamed they would ever see me again.[6]

Laurence Daubner told of another time when they went out to get a lift on some nets out past Pilot Island:

The Day the Waves Broke In

Willy [Johnson] and Stanley [Voight] had just got a brand new boat at the time, the *Roamer*. They also had the *Hope*. We were going out, and it was a southeast wind. Stanley and I and Harry Carlson Sr. were on the *Roamer*. Willy, Bernie Wentworth, and someone else were on the *Hope*. We headed out in the morning on the lake past Pilot Island. The southeast wind was picking up. We met the island boats coming back. "Too rough" for the *Johnny Bull*, the *J.W.*, and the *Richter*, the old-timers from the island. Johnny Cornell had the *J.W.*, which was the biggest boat around and even he was coming back. We kept a going. Willy wouldn't turn, and Stanley wouldn't turn. Neither of them would bow to being "chicken." We had to go about 1 1/2 miles out in the lake past Washington Island to lift chub nets. We tried five times to grab the buoy. We would go up and the buoy would go down. I finally grabbed hold of the buoy and we managed to lift the nets.

Then we started to head for home. There were some big combers out there. There were always three big ones that would come, and then there would be a calm for a ways, and you can watch them. Willy would put the bow up into them and ride them slow. Stanley would put the stern to them and ride down with them. We were so tossed about that we couldn't possibly dress any fish, as we always did on our return trips.

I arranged the fish boxes so I could have a comfortable, safe place to sleep. I was half-asleep when I heard a loud Ka-Bang! It knocked me out from about those boxes, and I flew down below the deck to the stove, there by the engine. I was in cold water, and I couldn't get my breath. I looked out, and I could see the water running out of the boat into the lake. It was just level with the lake. I looked, and Stanley and Harry were laying on the floor in the front. They were knocked out of the pilothouse. I saw that the nets were near the eccentrics of the engine and I didn't want them to tangle up and have the engine stop. It was a three-cylinder Kahlenberg engine, and it's a good thing we had that. So I got the nets out of there first. Stanley came to, and he climbed back up to the pilothouse. We were then lying like this. [He illustrated what looked like a thirty-degree tilt.]
Stanley put the boat up into the wind slowly, but then the motor started to miss. The

breathers were taking in water and we couldn't have that. I started up the blowtorches, which we used for starting, to heat the breathers. That method worked OK. Stanley, with great difficulty, did his best to keep the boat going straight, because we were leaning so much. Harry came back, and then we started to bail. He stood below, and I stood on the deck. We had two pumps pumping. He handed the five-gallon pails up to me on the deck, and I would dump them. We did this for forty-five minutes before we could make any time. All the ballast down below, the rocks and the chain, broke loose, causing the boat to list the way it did.

We finally got under way, but the others at the dock became concerned, so Willy started coming out to see if they could find us, because we were so late. We were in the area of Pilot Island when they met us coming slowly, and they followed us into the dock at Gills Rock. The next day we took out the floorboards in the bottom of the boat, put all the ballast back in place and replaced most of the bracing. It was a job to get it all back in order again.

You see, Stanley kept in the trough of the sea, and when the wave would come, he would turn the stern to it and ride it down. Well, this time he didn't turn fast enough, and a comber hit us. It knocked the two doors in on one side on his brand new boat, and even knocked out the doors on the other side. Splinters from the doors whirled around with such a force they stuck in the oak wood on the other side of the boat. We were lucky we didn't get killed.[7]

Jeff Weborg tells a story of going out to get a lift on some chub nets on a day when no one should have been out:

I was fishing for my cousin Leif [Lee], and we were fishing about one hour and ten minutes south of Kewaunee on the inside grounds for chubs. We were getting some big chubs on the inside. We got up in the morning, and it was blowing hard from the north, so we decided we were going out there to get the nets pulled out because they could get ruined in a north wind. We got down to the dock and got the boat started, and of course we had a Kahlenberg. As we were torching her up, the car ferry was waiting by the dock and the captain called us on the radio. "Where are you guys going?" [he asked.] I said "We're going out to lift." The captain said, "Are you guys nuts? We're registering 50 knots here at the dock, and she's blowing harder out on the lake." We ran down, made our lift. It took us an hour and twenty minutes to get to the nets, as we were riding with the sea, and it took almost four hours to get back home.

We got done lifting and were heading back. I said to Leif, should we run check [slowly]? He said, "Let her go!" I said, "I don't think we should." He said again, "Let her go, we should be fine. Let her go." I said OK and put her on her gate. She didn't run three minutes before she took a sea in the bow. I was standing in the front of the engine, and the sea came in the front port light and a solid stream of water came back and hit me – soaked me. The water came through so hard and fast it soaked Leif up in the pilothouse. After that, we wedged a board up there in the broken port light and ran check the rest of the way back. It took us almost four hours to get back home. That was a nasty storm.[8]

Retired fisherman Joe LeClair remembers one of the last rides he had in his father's boat, the *Bub*, in the late 1940s. She was a 40-foot wood hull boat formerly owned by Leslie Cornell of Washington Island built in 1926. By the time he's speaking of, she was getting a little rotten, as Joe so mildly put it:

One of the last rides I had on the *Bub*, we were getting a good run of fish in the fall of the year off of Cedar River [along the western shore of the bay of Green Bay]. We were lying in Fish Creek at the time. Stuart Woerfel was going over there to set nets, so we threw a gang of nets on his boat to save us a trip. We set a gang of nets off of Cedar River. We left early the next morning from Fish Creek to go lift them, when she started to blow from the southeast. At that time the old *Bub* was pretty rotten. We got off the northwest corner of Chambers Island, and it was so rough we were taking in water through the smoke stack, and one of the windows blew in. My dad was on the pump and Louie was bailing. We finally made it to the northwest end of Chambers Island. There was a little dock over there, so we pulled in there and found Emil Nelson and his guys lying in there with their pound-net boat. If Chambers Island wasn't there, I don't think we would have made it back. When that bay starts to build, it can get really nasty. You get a shorter, choppier sea than out on the lake.[9]

A fisherman usually will go out to lift his nets and reset them in tolerable conditions. He keeps a close eye on local and marine weather reports, and if the conditions are unfavorable or pose a threat to his crew and craft, he doesn't go out. On rare occasions, a fisherman will go out on a favorable day, then suddenly and unexpectedly get caught in a freak squall that seems to just whip up out of nowhere. Such was the case with Alvin Anderson and his brother Clarence one day in the 1950s.

From Dead Calm to Mountains

I remember one time when we were out fishing, up in Lake Superior. That was in December, probably around the middle of December. We were fishing out of Port Wing with our boat the *RVH*. Actually, for a December day, it was nice. It wasn't cold. It was more or less foggy, or hazy. The lake was dead calm. We were going way up west towards Superior. We had two gangs of nets set up there, fishing whitefish. We were running an hour and forty-five minutes to two hours west of there. Oh hell, it was such a beautiful morning, the boat didn't even wiggle, you know. We went by the one [net] buoy. We had two gangs – that wasn't the one we wanted to lift – and continued on to the other gang. They were a couple of miles apart.

All hell broke loose as soon as we went by that one buoy. The seas come out of nowhere – a northeast blow – unbelievable. They turned into mountains within minutes. From dead calm to mountainous seas. It was unbelievable. And it snowed. It was snowing so hard you couldn't see anything. Going back, well Port Wing didn't have a fog signal. There was a light, but that didn't mean nothing. It was snowing so hard you couldn't see the water. We had a clock and compass, but you couldn't tell how much time you were losing in that sea. My brother and I got talking and we figured out, we were never going to find Port Wing. So then we were thinking maybe we had a better chance if we set a course for Two Harbors [Minnesota], which is right straight across the lake about 22 miles. We thought we'd maybe go there, because they had a fog signal. Holy Christ Almighty, then we was going, more or less on the [Canadian] border, heading that way. We weren't sure where we were going to end up over there either. So we turned around again and didn't even think about looking for our other buoy.

We got turned right around and headed back, but Christ it took us forever. And then we didn't know where we were. We didn't have a fathometer – all we had was a lead weight on some twine that we dropped over every once in a while to get our depth. We had a clock and compass, [but] we didn't have any idea how much time we were loosing. We didn't have the slightest idea. My brother and I just kept going. We had one chance. If we would have missed it, it would have been all over right then. We just kept on agoing, just kept going hard enough. We figured we would haul her in for the beach and run her aground. We were going to make it or we were not going to make it. We had to do something, because it was so bad, it was just unbelievable. You couldn't imagine. We knew if we didn't see or hit the pier, we were going to beach her. We had no other choice; we didn't know where the hell we were!

My brother had his head out of the top hatch, and all of a sudden he hollered, "I see it! I see it! I see it!" And I didn't know what the hell he was talking about. "See what?" I said. I couldn't even see the damn water. I was looking out the porthole, looking down. It was snowing so hard and blowing, I couldn't see the water. "I see the pier!" he said. Well, my knees got like rubber bands. It was a one-shot deal, because if we would have been 100 feet either way we would have missed it. Man I tell you, we got in there, and Bobbie Voight come over – he seen us and came down by the dock – and said, "You guys are lucky to be here." [10]

Jeff Weborg remembered when his brother Mark and one of their crew were out in the late fall of 1981 and got caught in a heavy sea where a wave smashed in part of the boat's house:

Guardian Ship

My brother Mark and one of our guys were out lifting just west of Washington Island, about an hour north of Rowleys Bay. A stiff breeze started to blow, and some big swells started to form. At that time we had two boats, the *Seabird*, which they were in and the *JA Weborg*, which that day I had in Rowleys Bay. They were out lifting big mesh and I noticed it was getting nasty, so I called them and told them to get out of there. They told me they just had another box to lift; after they were done lifting they would be right in. I told them to call me when they got done. So then they called me awhile later and said, "We're done and we're on the run home now. We can't run gate speed, we're checking down." As he was talking to me, all of a sudden I heard him exclaim, "Oh No!" Then the radio fell silent. About a minute later he comes back on and said, "We just took in about six feet of our side, and we got the boat full of water. We're bailing by hand." I said to Mark, "Run with the sea. Don't try to fight it." I saw a freighter, the *Buffalo*, [out in the lake] and so I called them and asked, "Where are you guys heading?" It looked like they were going to Escanaba. The captain said, "We're heading for Sturgeon Bay. Why, what do you need?" I told him "I have a boat in trouble out west of Washington Island, about an hour north of you. I thought if you were heading to Escanaba, you could keep an eye out for them." The captain said, 'We'll go out there and look for them." I said "I'm heading out now in my other boat, if you could keep an eye on them until I get there."

They ran up there and found them right away. They turned and made a windbreak for them. The *Seabird* was idling coming down. Six feet was gone from the bow, about three feet back, all the way back to the lifting doors. The sea had smashed the stanchions, the plywood, the whole works. They took in 80 barrels of water. I was talking to the *Buffalo* on the radio. They said they would run with them until I got there. I caught up to them when they were halfway down and I called the skipper. He said, "Is that you coming toward us off our port bow in that little boat?" I said, "I'm forty five feet." He said, "Ah, I don't think you'll be much help to these guys. I think we'll stay with them until we get them into the beach." They ran with the *Seabird* all the way into the harbor. The next spring I saw him passing through on one of his trips, so I called him and said, "Do you remember me?" He said, 'Oh sure.' So I said "You mind checking down a bit? I have some whitefish to give you." We were grateful for his services. When that wave crashed in on the *Seabird* that day, the guy who was working for us was sitting on the edge of the engine box. When that sea hit it knocked him off the engine box and up against the shipside. He was OK. It washed him right off, and he had glasses on.

We never did find his glasses. I mean, we looked everywhere. We never did find them."[11]

Curt Johnson and Angus Swenson were fishing with Roy and Earl Richter on the *Fred* in the winter of 1928. They had lifted and were setting dry chub nets in a big south sea. The *Fred* took a bad roll, and Curt slid down on Angus and Angus slid over the side of the boat and into the water. It took them twenty minutes to get Angus back on board and almost a day to warm him up.[12]

Winter always poses a challenge for commercial fishermen, especially around the northern Door County and Washington Island region when the ice begins to form along the shores. Some years, Green Bay would freeze over solid from Door County to its western shore. On the lake side of the peninsula, depending on wind and temperatures, the ice was unpredictable and tended to move around with the wind. When there was a week or two of subzero temperatures and not much wind, ice would form fairly quickly in and around Washington Island, the Death's Door Passage, Northport and south of there to Rowleys Bay.

The Death's Door Passage, where Lake Michigan waters meet Green Bay waters is a very dangerous area. The current can be very strong through it, sometimes moving as fast as 8 miles per hour. In the winter months, the ice is always moving with the wind. One week there might be ice lying really heavy, and then the wind will change, and the next day the ice is gone. Westerly or northwesterly winds often cause huge ice shoves. Generally speaking, the ice is very unpredictable and dangerous in this region, and many fishermen have found themselves caught in the frozen grasp of winter.

The Weborgs experienced the dangers of shifting ice out in their fish tug the *Islander* one February in the late 1970s. They took the boat out of Rowleys Bay after the ice had cleared from the harbor to retrieve some nets they had set a few days before. After they retrieved the nets and were coming back in, the wind shifted, and the ice, which was over two feet thick, was pushed together in a slow-motion collision. They found themselves thrust on top of the ice, high and dry. Jeff recalled that day:

High and Dry on an Ice Floe

One of the most dangerous situations we ever were in was when we had our gill nets set under the ice and the ice went out. We took the *Islander* to go out and picked them up, [but then] the wind shifted. We tried to get back out and we got caught right off of table bluff. We were almost crushed. The ice made three shoves and shoved the boat up high and dry. It shoved ice down twelve feet and shoved the boat on top of the ice. I was in the boat while the ice was shoving and it pushed the sides of the hull in about 10 inches or more. And when the ice broke it went underneath the hull; if it would have broke and come over the top, it would have sheered the pilothouse right off – I probably wouldn't have got out in time.[13]

Marvin Weborg, Jeff's father, also left an account of that day:

The boat in Green Bay got caught in the ice shove. The boat weighed 30 tons, and it shoved it out just like you picked up a ton of wood and set it on top of the ice. My two boys took the boat out on the bay, that was in February. The ice had moved out and they had nets under the ice that they had set, and they wanted to go get the nets. So they got the nets all right, but about the time they were coming back by Wisconsin Bay, the ice was coming together and that ice was 25-30 inches thick. They didn't have much of a chance; it just shoved the boat high and dry. The ferry came over there three days later, and Teskie's boat, and the *Mesquite* from Sturgeon Bay, and they were all breaking ice around the boat. There was about 35-40 feet of water where the boat was. They couldn't even break her down from where she was shoved out. They were piled right down to the bottom, the ice. From where it was shoved, they could walk ashore. They ran a line to the shore, figuring the wind would shift, so the boat wouldn't get away, but they didn't have to worry about that. That boat wasn't going anywhere when the ice was piled to the bottom. When the *Mesquite* was there, they wondered how we were going to pull the boat off of there. He's got about 1200 horse-power in there. He didn't want to pull her out, because he didn't want the responsibility of anything happening. I told the captain on the boat that we had walkie-talkies, so we could talk back and forth. They put a pump on the boat, and they put two of their men on there, to see what condition she was in. The ice pushed the boat together on the sides. You couldn't even move the catch lever on the engine when she was being moved out. If she wouldn't have come up, it would have cut her right in two. I told him if he'd give me the line, I would put the line around the boat. I would take all the responsibility. "You won't have any problem," I said. "She isn't leaking that bad. The rudder might be damaged from the shove, but as far as the hull is concerned, she isn't that bad." So they brought in a line, three-inch nylon, and I put the line around the whole boat, right around the bow. He said, "You'll sink her when she comes off of there." But I said "Don't worry, she won't be sinking. She'll slide off of there." We tied the line up, so it couldn't drop down, and he pulled on her. We were talking back and forth on the walkie-talkies, and he said "She doesn't seem to be moving." And I said, "Well, you've got to let her go." "I got full throttle on 1200 horsepower," he said. And I said, "Well, just let the line slack up a bit because it could be frozen." It was cold. It was probably down to 10 or 12 degrees above zero that night. He just slacked it up a bit there, and when he pulled ahead, she slid off of there just like a cork. The stern never went down enough so it never went near the water. They started up the engine then, and ran it back to Rowleys Bay, and the next day we took her to the shipyards because the rudder and wheel were bent so we got that taken care of.[14]

Years ago, the bay side of the Door peninsula almost always froze up, which left most fishermen on that side of the county limited to setting nets through the ice. The fishermen out of Gills Rock would move over to Sand Bay or Rowleys Bay on the eastern side of the peninsula and fish from there through the winter months. On the shores facing Lake Michigan the water usually remained open except for the harbors freezing unless there was a long spell of subzero weather. Then ice could form several miles out on the lake. During the winter of 1935-36 the entire lake froze over for a time, but usually the lake remained open. In North Bay, Sand Bay, Moonlight Bay and Baileys Harbor, where most of the local commercial fishermen moored their boats, fishermen sometimes found it a challenge to break through the ice to reach open water. Some days they couldn't get out at all. Speaking of his experiences in Baileys Harbor, Dennis Hickey exclaimed:

> It's a bear in here breaking ice! When you get prevailing northwest winds coming across that harbor, it can make two feet of ice overnight in there. I mean its ice. In our boat the *Southwester*, we modified her for exactly those conditions. We took out the Kahlenberg and installed a 343 Caterpillar diesel engine that would gives us 600 horsepower. The *Southwester* has a nice round hull in the stern, which makes it great for backing up in the ice. Other boats have a square stern, and they are useless. You can't back up. There're times when the ice gets really thick in the harbor. We try to go out every day. That's why we repowered the boat. But some days we are the only ones out there fishing. We've got a 4 1/2 to 1 reduction gear – a big bull gear – it's like a river tug. You don't make any money breaking ice though. You have to take it easy and not give'er hell. Jeff usually runs her about one third throttle; he doesn't really give'er.[15]

Depending on ice conditions, most fishermen would continue to fish through the winter months. Most modern tugs with steel hulls and modern engines are able to break through ice 6 to 10 inches thick. The boat rides up a ways on the ice, and the weight of the boat breaks the ice. But it's still an arduous task, and there have been a few times when boats would get hung up or stranded. The older boats with wood hulls and Kahlenberg engines were always challenged by ice. "The Kahlenberg's weren't too good in the ice," said Laurence Daubner, a local commercial fisherman. "They got that big flywheel, and that was the power. When that got going, that was your power. You hit an ice cake and that flywheel slowed down, and it took a long while to wind up again."[16] Another danger for the men and their boats during the comparatively slow process of breaking ice was a buildup of ice forming on the boat from the sea spray. The ice could build up so heavy that it would literally make the boat unstable.

Dennis Hickey remembered a time in the 1980s when he and his brother Jeff were caught in heavy seas late in the season and couldn't get back to their home port of Baileys Harbor. They were in their 45-foot fish tug the *Southwester:*

> If I had to be in a storm, there is no other boat I'd rather be in than that boat [the *Southwester*]. It's a Burger-built boat, she rolls a bit, but hell, they all roll in a heavy

sea. One time we were out in her, I think it was the first of January, and we couldn't get back in here due to the ice conditions. So we ran down and tried to make it into Sturgeon Bay, but that was all iced in. It was night and she was blowing a gale from the southwest. The *Buffalo* was anchored off the canal, and she was iced up pretty bad. We decided to keep going to Algoma. It was blowing so hard from the southwest that we had to go past Algoma then turn to come in at an angle. Going through that break wall at night, man those seas were rolling right over everything there. By this time we were loaded heavy with ice. We didn't have much longer to go [before foundering]. We lucked out. When we got into Algoma and docked, we had 6 to 7 inches of ice covering the hull and roof.[17]

Jeff Weborg also recalled a precarious situation due to icing:

The worst situation I was ever in was the time we were out on the other [i.e. the eastern] side of the lake [Michigan] in the *JA Weborg*, fishing chubs. As we were coming back, we ran into a big sea. We were making ice pretty fast, so I checked her down and we were damn near idling. The engine was running at about 1,000 rpm. She was dropping off the seas pretty hard. There were times I lifted the floor boards underneath the pilot house, because I was sure we had split the hull wide open. It was like you dropped the boat on concrete. I thought there isn't any way the boat could handle that. By the time we got back to the shore over here with that northwest wind, I figured we had only a half hour left before the boat would have rolled over, she had so much ice on her. She would roll, then hesitate, then she'd come back and roll the other way, and hesitate for a moment, before coming back again.[18]

Joe LeClair told of a time when he and his father almost got crushed by the ice:

One day I was out with my dad. We had that damn old 30-foot wooden boat, the *R&D*. We were coming in. It was in the spring of the year, and there was a big ice floe coming down. The wind started up out of the north, and we started going through the ice, [but] that cake ice kept coming in and we got caught. The ice was squeezing us pretty tight. I don't know how that old *R&D* held together the way she did. I thought for sure that ice was going to bust the hull in. The Grovogels were coming in behind us in the *Sally Lou,* but hadn't followed us into the ice field. They threw us a line and managed to pull us out. We ended up running down to Sturgeon Bay and made it in there by eight o'clock at night. If it weren't for the Grovogel's pulling us out, we wouldn't have made it out of that situation.[19]

Sometimes fishermen have been stranded out on the lake for a day or two because of ice conditions. If the ice isn't that bad, a fisherman might maneuver into open water but then, upon returning later in the day, find that the wind shifted the ice around, making it impossible for the boat to break through. Back in the days when fishermen didn't have radios or ship-to-shore phones, this sort of thing could cause terrible concern when they didn't return that evening. Marvin Weborg tells of a time when he spent a night on his boat the *Islander*:

A Night in the *Islander*

One time I stayed out on the lake overnight, in Rowleys Bay, and that was in February 1962. We had lots of ice in windrows in Sand Bay, and it wasn't that much pressure on it, so we could get out. It was snowing in the morning. We went out and we lifted off Cana Island in Baileys Harbor with big mesh. We had about 350 pounds of whitefish. That afternoon when we were coming back, we got as far as Rowleys Bay. The wind had shifted to the southeast and was blowing 25 to 30 miles per hour. We got into the ice, and the boat wouldn't move anymore. That's as far as we could go. We had food along, and plenty of coal for the stove. We had a fellow by the name of Denny Strandel along with us, and he said that was the most peaceful night he had put in for in a long time. The next morning, the wind had shifted, and by daylight the ice had moved off. Of course, in the meantime, we didn't have ship-to-shore at the time, and everyone on shore was worried. They had sent out an airplane from Traverse City, to come and look for us along with the Coast Guard. The next morning, when we started up the engine, we could run right through the ice that was left there. We didn't have any problem getting in. We were about a quarter of the way in, when the airplane came right over the top of the boat. Scared us to death. He came down within a hundred feet of the boat, right over the top, to be sure it was the right boat. They called when they saw us and told everybody we were all right. We had a foot of snow that night. We didn't suffer at all. We boiled potatoes and whitefish on the boat for supper and had canned goods. We were perfectly all right.[20]

Howard Weborg was caught in moving ice in the *Golden Girl*:

Icebound in the *Golden Girl*

Our Dad was with us at the time. We left Sand Bay and went up into Green Bay area. We had open water. We went past Door Bluff out towards Whaleback Shoals. Then we struck more open water, and that's where we set our nets. On the way back in, we started in towards Death's Door, and when we got in so far, it showed an opening between two ice fields of about 100 feet. We thought we could break the ice and get to open water on the other side. We started, [but] we weren't no more than 100 feet from the edge when the one ice floe that was lodged against West Harbor and the other floe started moving. Well, it wasn't long before the *Golden Girl* was with the wheel [i.e. the propeller] out of the water. She was shaking and shuttering, so we crawled out of the boat on the deck. We didn't know if we were going to make it or not. But then it stopped, after it shot us out of the water. Well then, how are we going to get help? We didn't have any ship-to-shore radios then. I started walking on the ice to Ellstrom's, and went up there and called the Coast Guard. Phillip Carlson was on the *Bull* at the time [a Coast Guard boat at Plum Island]. Wasn't long before the *Bull* came and picked me up by Ellstrom's and we started out for the boat. In the meantime, the *King* was headed out for us. They thought they could get through, but then they got stuck. So the old *Bull* started breaking ice and had to break quite a bit of ice before she loosened it up all around the *Golden Girl*, so she could get out into the water again. And then we followed the *Bull* into Death's Door Passage and made it safely into Sand Bay.[21]

Jim Cornell, a retired fisherman from Washington Island, was caught in a snowstorm while fishing near St. Martin Island.

The Snowstorm

My brother Alvin and Fred Young were fishing with me back in the early 1960s. We left the cut in the morning on the 14th of February, and we were heading out to get a lift on some whitefish nets we had set off the west end of St. Martin Island. It has to be a northeast or east wind to lift there, because the ice would slide off. On this particular morning we knew we could get a lift. It took almost an hour to get out past the cut and get out of all that slush ice, so I knew we couldn't come back that way because it was going to keep packing with that northeast wind. We made it out to the nets and began lifting. I was moving at a pretty good clip when Alvin says "You better cut her down. She's full of ducks and sticks." I said "Not today. You might not know this, but there's a storm brewing, and it's going to hit us by three o clock."

By the time we lifted our nets, I knew we were going to have to get out of there. I looked to the northeast, and the sky was all gold. I said "Hell, let's set the nets back in," and so we did. As soon as we set the last net, it started to snow. And sure enough, the winds picked up, and it started to blow something fierce, and before we knew it we were in a big sea. I knew the only place to go was the west channel and to try to tie up at Andersons dock in Detroit Harbor. That was some 14 miles to our south.

At this time it was snowing so hard I couldn't see over the bow stem. When I got close to Rock Island point, I looked at the clock and said, "Set the clock [a windup clock set for sixty minutes with a ringer] but cut it off by five minutes," because the wind is northeast, and I pulled her out a half a degree on the compass. There were times I'd see the waves go by the bow and think "Are we that close to Hog Island?" It was just the sea. After the ringer went off on the clock, I checked her down and put her on a course to come in and then reset the clock. I knew I hadn't drifted, but we come up on what appeared to be a large white mass. Alvin thought it was ice. I said "I'll be damned if that's ice, that's a reef. But whose reef is it? So I hauled her to the east five or six minutes on the clock, and then I said to Alvin, "I'm going back to check that reef. I think that's Detroit Island Reef." And sure enough, it was. The sea was breaking all around it. I took my logbook out and looked at it to make sure. And then I headed straight in there between the reef and Pilot Island and down toward Plum Island. There's a reef in there too, but I knew where that was.

I set my minutes, adjusted my course and went right past the tripod [channel tower marking the channel with a light and a fog signal]. Never seen or heard the damn thing because it was snowing and blowing so hard. The snow was drifting on the channel ice something terrible, but I kept the boat on her gate and time and brought her in right into Anderson's dock, just as it was getting dark. Oliver Bjarnarson came down in his truck and said, "By God man, get in the truck." I said "Forget that! I'm so glad to see land, I'll just to sit on the back. We were either lucky that day or somebody was with us, or maybe both.[22]

It was fishing that first drew people to Door County, and for almost a generation other pursuits were largely neglected. Originally, they were able to catch all the fish they wanted in or near their home ports, but gradually, fishermen from the peninsula extended their range to include much of northern Lake Michigan and most, if not all, of the bay of Green Bay, always seeking and following the fish. However, in the late 1930s and early 1940s, many Gills Rock fishermen began fishing seasonally from a small town in northern Wisconsin called Port Wing, on Lake Superior. Phil Albertson and Clayton Johnson fished up there with Clyde Olson on the *Mallard*, a thirty-seven foot wood-hull boat built for the government sometime in the 1890s and converted into a fish tug in the 1930s. She was acquired by Harvey Olson in 1932 and was taken up to Port Wing in 1938 by Harvey's brother Clyde and by Phil Albertson. *Mallard* was considered an old vessel in 1940. Willie Johnson and Stanley Voight also moved their operation up to Port Wing, with their boats *Hope* and *Roamer*. So did Alick Johnson, who had the *Lindy*, and Lawrence Voight, fishing with the *Aloha*.

Phil Albertson recalled a day when some Gills Rock men experienced a "big blow" on Lake Superior:

Armistice Day Blow

We had the *Mallard* there. [It was] 1940, the November 11 blow. Us and the *Hope* were out that day. That's when we were fishing out of Port Wing. It was blowing hard, 105 mph when we were out on the lake. When we come in, well, we were so damn lucky. We only had about fifty-five minutes [going] out there, but it took us three hours to come in. The wind was out of the northeast. There was hardly a breath of wind when we went out. We got done lifting and she was blowing pretty well by then, but there was a steam boat coming by and we couldn't start setting until he went past us. I said to Clyde, "Damn it, we ain't gonna go no place unless we get some nets out of this old boat!" So we just set those damn things. If they got tangled, so what? We just set the whole damn gang. We had Clayton Johnson along. Hell, he passed out, and I had to tie him fast to the wall.

Damn, those seas were building fast! You see, you get four big seas — what sailors call the three sisters, or four sisters — which is four big waves following one another during a big blow. Every time you could see them coming, we had to check down and run straight into them. It's like the [Green] bay, or Lake Michigan, you get the same thing, but the lake here [i.e. Lake Michigan] you usually only get three. Sometimes in the bay by the Door you can get four of those bastards, but up there [Lake Superior] it was four. Oh hell, there were over thirty-foot waves — that old *Mallard* was a good sea boat. The *Hope*; they were east. They kind of came with it, but we were in before them. It was just us and the *Hope* out there that day. Lawrence was out, but he got sick, and they had to take him home in the *Aloha*. Alick Johnson wouldn't go out. Well, we didn't look at the barometer that morning. Alick saw it was down and falling, and he told the boys [Norman and Harris] "You can go out on the lake all you want to, but the boat stays at the dock." And it did. Norman was so happy though he said, "Once in awhile you got to believe the old man."

We got back in after 3:00, and when we were coming back it was raining. You know, that rain was driving sideways, it blew right through the cabin. What the hell you gonna do? Well Clyde, he wouldn't eat for three days afterwards. I'd been in many blows before, but I don't think he had ever been in any. We got in and tied up at the dock and started dressing the fish. We could hear some people hollering, so we figured the *Hope* was coming in. We opened up the door and looked out. You couldn't see nothing, it was snowing so hard. Then we heard the *Hope* coming in around the corner. You couldn't see her coming around the corner in the harbor, but they went up the river then, where their dock was.[23]

This story comes from H.R Holland's *History of Door County* - 1917, about three fishermen trying to make it back to their homes in Door County and get caught in some inclement weather. This event took place late one December back in 1860, when fishermen were using sailing craft, predominantly Mackinaw boats.

A Terrible Experience

For sixty or seventy years the Green Bay basin has been the most productive fresh water fishing grounds in the United States. The large rivers of clear cold water that poured into it from the great Wisconsin woods serve to make it the favorite feeding ground for the cunning trout, the wandering whitefish and the humble herring. Each year millions of fish have been taken out of its waters without showing any signs of depletion. It is common to talk of the "good old days" when the nets were always full and the sturgeon were stacked up like huge stone piles on the beach — unsalable because of their abundance. Yet even nowadays the fisherman frequently lifts a net that yields fifty or sixty half barrels in one lift.

It was the fishing that first drew people to Door County. For almost a generation this was considered her only possibility and the land was looked upon merely as a necessary point of attachment for their nets. From the ranks of the early fishermen many of Door County's best men were drawn to the more sedate but sure occupations of farming and business. Most of the fishermen, however, never got beyond that station in life. They were alert and indefatigable as beavers when on the water, enduring hardships innumerable without a whimper, but lazy and indifferent as porcupines when on land. They were an easy-coming, easy-going class. Their quick earnings were spent as quickly. Dauntless in danger when on the deep they often experienced thrilling adventures.

The best fishing has usually been found near the long, low shore north of Menominee. Frequently fishermen from Door County would cross over to this "West shore" and try their luck in the fall fishing, returning with their boats, nets and part of their profits to Door County shortly before Christmas to lay up for the winter.

One fall about 1860 there were among others three such fishermen on the west shore. They were Ingham Kinsey and Bill Stahl from Washington Island, and Allen Bradley with his boy, form Hedgehog Harbor (Gills Rock). They used gill nets, ten feet long, set in from six to ten feet of water. The whitefish were so numerous that fall that frequently the nets had to be cleared several times during the night. Two hundred whitefish, weighing from three to six pounds each, were frequently taken from a net at each lift.

Pleased with their success they kept on with their fishing until rather late in December. Finally the day came when they decided to pull up for home. They loaded their nets and winter's supplies into their boats and pushed off.

The day was a cold and cloudy one with a rather steady wind from the southwest which promised to land them on Washington Island in speedy time. It was their plan to keep the boats close together for Kinsey and Stahl alone in their respective boats, which rendered their navigation somewhat difficult. For a long time they got along very well. Finally it began to get dark and with that the wind swung around to the northeast, blowing briskly dead ahead. It soon veered to the north, blowing furiously while the weather became intensely cold, the mercury falling almost to zero. By this time the boats had become separated and lost sight of each other and each man struggled as best he could.

But it was a desperate and useless struggle. The flying spray had saturated their clothing and now every outer garment was frozen stiff. Their sails were also frozen and unmanageable and each rope, halyard and sheet was soon like a rod of steel. Meanwhile the wind was shrieking, the waves roaring, the mighty storm tossing their clumsy craft where it would. They felt the numbness of intense cold and despair creeping over them. Through the darkness of the night they were driving irresistibly onward to their doom.

Allen Bradley's boat had outdistanced the others, having two men to navigate it Bradley was moreover a tremendously strong man with the endurance of a wild animal. In the coldest weather he was never known to wear a coat, overcoat or mittens. As he sat in his ice encased garments, gradually feeling his limbs turn to the numbness of death, his ear suddenly detected a sound different from the roar of the storm. It was the booming of the sea on the rock-bound shore of Door County! With sudden life he jumped to the foremast and with a tremendous wrench tore it out of its frozen socket. Another jerk or two and the spar and foresail were also thrown overboard. He then seized the oars and seconded by the feeble but earnest efforts of his son he got the heavy ice laden, ice encrusted boat under control. Tugging incessantly at the oars with the flying spray turning into an ever increasing load of ice on the boat, he managed to keep it clear of the shore. After two hours of this work he was finally rewarded in turning the point of a little cove and found himself safe in Fish Creek.

There was a great surprise in the little village the next morning when it was learned that Allen Bradley had arrived during the night. The cold had been so intense and the gale so terrific that it seemed incredible that anyone could have survived it in an open boat covered with ice. It was generally agreed that the other two fishermen must have perished but some abortive attempts were made along the shore to discover their bodies. A heavy fall of snow, however, had covered everything with a cloak of white.

Toward evening a searching party saw a slowly moving body about a mile away. At first they thought it was a bear because it was moving on four legs. They approached nearer and to their surprise they saw it was a man moving painfully through the snow on his hands and knees. It was Ingham Kinsey! During the preceding night he had been hurled almost insensible with cold on the beach four miles south of Fish Creek. His boat had been smashed on the rocks. During the night and the next day he had staggered along the beach, first south, then north, vainly looking for a human habitation in the unsettled wilderness. Finally his limbs refused to support him and with the last figment of endurance he was crawling along, his hands and feet frozen, when he was discovered and saved.

Meanwhile, where was Bill Stahl? William Stahl was a famous water dog who had survived so many adventures on the water that he believed himself immune from death in that element. He built both his own boat and the one that Kinsey had and had unbounded faith in them. Yet he recalled now that his boats had a bad reputation. So many accidents had occurred with his boats that it was a common saying on Washington Island that a Bill Stahl boat and a bottle of whiskey were a combination which could kill anyone. He had the combination right there under him. Was it after all going to prove true with him?

As he felt his boat settling deeper with its load of ice becoming quite unmanageable, he gave up all attempts at navigating her and devoted all his energies to keeping his hands and feet from freezing. He was soaked with water and ice, more ice was forming around him. As he listened to the shrieking of the wind, the swish of the white caps and heavy thud of a wave striking his bow in the trough of the sea it seemed that the resistless cavalry of hell was hitched to his boat dragging it furiously onward to the brink where he would tumble over into the next world.

As he sat there with uncanny fancies flitting though his disordered mind, his boat suddenly struck hard on a rock! Before he realized what happened another wave followed, throwing the boat up on a rocky beach while he was thrown out into the water. The water seemed almost warm in comparison with the intensely cold wind he had been exposed to.

He scrambled out and looked around him but nothing could be seen in the darkness. However, now that he was on firm land he felt new hope within him. He would strike out at once following the shore till he came to a boat house or human habitation. He stumbled over driftwood that littered the shore, slipped on the stones but struggled on. He felt his limbs were not yet frozen and with good luck he would yet reach a shelter. Suddenly he stopped amazed! There in front of him was another overturned boat lying in exactly the same position as his! He reached in to the bow of the boat and pulled out an oblong box. It was his boat. Here was his toolbox!

He stared vacantly at the boat. How could it be his boat? He must have turned in his tracks and retraced his steps. Was he losing his mind? He started off along the shore once more, keeping the water on his left, and the land on his right. He walked carefully to avoid confusion. At the end of a half hour he was again in front of the boat! Suddenly he realized the situation. He was on an island and the reason he had come twice upon the boat was that he had walked twice around the island.

By this time it was beginning to get light in the east. Looking in that direction he could now distinguish the high cliffs of Door County. Straining his eyes northward he could also dimly discern a long low shore which must be Chambers Island. He now recognized where he was. He was cast ashore on Hat Island, a barren little rock growing a few stunted trees about five miles southwest of Fish Creek.

The dejection that followed upon this discovery struck him like a blow. He felt excessively weary. He had toiled and struggled and suffered all through the storm of the night before, his clothing was frozen stiff, he felt numb with cold to the marrow. He wanted to sink down and forget it all in a moment of slumber. Suddenly he started up. In his pocket was a match box filled with matches. There were birch trees on the island. He needed but a little bark and in a few moments he would have a fire.

Feverishly he stripped some bark off the birches, broke some dry twigs off the trees and struck a match. It refused to ignite. He struck another and another till the box was half empty. Still no success. Then he examined the matches carefully and found they were all water soaked. Still clinging to hope he struck the matches with greater care than before till the last one was tried in vain.

Almost stunned by this result he went through his pockets one after another. Some were so frozen he had to tear them apart with main force. What chance had he unless he could make a fire. In his exhausted condition he could not endure it another hour. In his hip pocket was his can of tobacco. It had a tight-fitting cover. But down there among the tobacco crumbs lay a match. He could see no sign of moisture inside of the can. He poured out a little tobacco in his hand and examined it critically. It seemed dry as ever. If the tobacco was dry it was likely that the match was dry also. He carefully refrained from touching it, however, lest his clumsy fingers might drop it in the snow. One humble forgotten match! Yet it might mean another lifetime for him.

With this thought in mind he once more made his preparations for fire. This time, however, he proceeded with much greater care than before. First he carefully picked out the spot on the island which seemed most sheltered from the wind. Then he made a windbreak out of his frozen sail which he propped up with a number of supports. Then he gathered a good sized pile of dry twigs and birch bark. Finally he carefully gathered up a lot of dry leaves which he found under a log. These he tested for dryness, one by one before he put them in their place. Finally he selected a flat dry stone, not too rough, under the same log. This was to strike his match on.

He took out the match but hesitated to strike. What if it were defective? What if it broke and fell into the snow? What if the tinder refused to ignite? No more boats would sail the bay until next spring. No travelers would pass on the ice for a month or two. He knew that within an hour or two his stiff limbs would be frozen. On the outcome of that match hung life or death.

Lifting the match in silent supplication to heaven, he scratched the stone gently. It failed to spark. He felt the sweat break out underneath his sodden garments and he tried again with greater force. The flame burst out and he thrust it down among the dry leaves. There followed an interminable interval. Finally the thin veil of white smoke was followed by a leaping flame. Carefully he fed the fire with birch bark, twigs and sticks until he soon had a large fire blazing. He was saved!

Toward evening it occurred to him that he ought to have his fire out on the beach where it might attract attention from the mainland. He made a roaring bonfire fed with stumps and logs, snatching a nap intermittently. This fire was soon seen from Fish Creek. When the good people of Fish Creek found Kinsey that evening they appointed a lookout to patrol the beach and keep a watch for Stahl. About midnight the village was electrified into life by hearing the lookout shout in the street. "Bill Stahl on Hat Island! Bonfire Blazing!"

Quickly a willing crowd gathered at the pier to lend a hand in the rescue. But how were they to launch a boat? The heavy gale had packed a sheet of anchor ice into the harbor a mile deep. This had frozen together in a solid mass in many places two feet thick. Meanwhile the storm was still roaring and it needed a good vessel to weather the seas. Axes were found and the whole village went to work to cut a channel. By nine o'clock the next morning a channel was cut a mile long and the best vessel in port was towed out. Sails were bent and by noon Bill Stahl saw sweeping down on him a white winged carrier of life.[24]

Anyone who has been out in a boat when the waves start rolling and bouncing the boat around may have discovered the unfortunate affliction known as sea-sickness. And, if the lake waves don't get you, the waves of nausea surely will. I found this out first-hand after many proud years of never having gotten sick out on the water, and it's a whole different ball game when you're out in a fish tug rolling around in twelve foot seas with a miasma of unpleasant aromas than to be larking along in a cabin cruiser. I was told by one Door County fisherman that if I was going to write a book about fishing; I had better get some experience to give myself some credibility, and I was invited to go along chub fishing on a day of blinding snow and a heavy northeast blow. In a very short time I was pretty sick of being sick, but I made it through, and I'm told that hardly anyone escapes getting seasick while chub fishing. Elaine Johnson likes to tell a story about a reporter for the Door County Advocate, a ride in a fish tug, and sea-sickness:

In 1976, I contacted the *Today Show*. The roving reporter at the time was a man by the name of Cunningham. I told him about the conflict that was going on in Michigan and Wisconsin and that commercial fishing was the first industry up here, along with lumbering, and farming. He asked if I could orchestrate something for them and they would come up and do an interview with some of the fisheries up here. They made a date to come up, so I got all the fishermen together and then I called Steve Ellefson and asked him if there was some way to take the *Miss Judy* and set nets off the island and set them so that no matter what the weather was that day, you would be in the lea of the wind. "Well sure," he said. "I can do that, Elaine."

They came up that one day and interviewed us. I was called "Sissy of the Fishery." Can you beat that? They interviewed a lot of the guys. Then I said "I got it set up for the island. They're going to lift some gill nets for you." He thought that was great. I said "One thing. We'll go along with anything you want, but we have a local reporter here by the name of Keta Steebs, who writes for the *Door County Advocate*, who would love to go along. She's been after me and is just crazy to go along with you guys." He said, "Oh God, we can't do that." I said "We sure would appreciate it. We have a local reporter who would love to write up the story – How often do we get the *Today Show* up here?" He agreed to let her go along.

I went down that morning, and the boat came, and here comes Keta. She was dressed to kill. She had this wig and long white gloves on. Keta thought she was really going to impress these New Yorkers. She went down to the gangplank and got on the *Miss Judy*, and away they went to the island. On Washington Island, they went all-out for the evening and were catered to by some of the islanders. They smoked fish. They fried fish. They broiled fish. Every imaginable way they could serve fish, they had it, along with beer and bitters. They filled Keta up pretty good on fish, beer and bitters. Then Steve said "At 6 o'clock in the morning, we're getting up and going fishing."

I had told Steve before, "When you get back to the island, call me right off the bat and let me know what happened and how it went. It was a tough time waiting for that call. He finally called and said everything went well lifting. He said he had lifted on the lea side of the island. "There was a swell, but we did OK, except we had one person who wasn't doing so well." I said, "What happened?" Steve said, "Well, the first thing, there came Keta down to the boat with white pumps on, a wavy chiffon dress with white gloves clear up to her elbows, and a great big hat on." He said "We got out north of the island. There was just a dead swell. He said "You couldn't get away from it. Keta was down there by the lifter." Steve said: "Keta, you have just got to go someplace else. You're right in the way. Go up in the bow." He had put a couple of clean boards across there. He said "Go up there and sit. You'll be out of the way when we're lifting." "All right," she said.

Keta went up and sat on a little plank that ran across the bow. They got out to the buoy and started to lift. They had probably lifted a half a box, when Steve kind of caught Keta out of the corner of his eye and could see her color was changing and her big hat was starting to tilt. So anyway, Steve was clearing nets and he turned around and looked up in the bow of the boat and there is Keta. She is ready to throw up. She is not going to make it. Steve said, "Keta Steebs, don't you dare throw up in my boat." He said that old wig had come around and was twisted so you could see about one eye and a half. Steve said "Keta looked at me with that one eye and she immediately took off one glove, and here it came." He said "She vomited, filled the glove right up. There was a porthole nearby, so she got that open and threw the glove out the porthole. There it went," said Steve. "It went by the lifter door and I could see that white glove going by." Steve said, "We continued to lift and, when we got on the last box, I looked back at her and she was really green, and a little white around the eyes." He said that wig had almost covered her entire face, so just part of one eye was now showing. It took three guys to get her off of that boat.[25]

Alvin "Gabby" Anderson and his crew were caught in a freak south wind generating a big sea on January 9, 1971, while fishing chubs out of Milwaukee. Gabby had the fish tug *Aloha* at that time.

The Rogue Wave

It wasn't that bad of a day to begin with, if I remember right. In my younger days, I went out no matter what. It didn't make any difference. If I thought it was dead calm, [or if] it would be blowing fifty – it never bothered me. But that day something happened – some freak sea hit us on the way home. It came up fast out of the south, and one big sea hit us and cleaned the doors right off her. Busted them right off the hinges – busted everything. She took so much water that she was right down to the rail in the water after it hit. That old Kahlenberg bilge pump clogged up and wasn't pumping. I couldn't believe it – the stern doors were gone – busted in! The port stern door come in immediately when we got hit by that south sea, and when she hit, the *Aloha* leaned so far over that the other door on the starboard side busted in. They were both gone!

The pilot house on that boat was in the stern. We had just stepped off the deck to go down and start to dress the fish. We just got down there. Roy Nelson was with Lee [Weborg] and me that day. We all just got down below the stern deck, when all of a sudden she hit and I didn't see nothing but blue sky and green water. I headed towards the front because everything was in such disarray. It was unbelievable. We had 2,700 pounds of chubs on board that day and they were all over the place. I got up into the pilot house by the wheel and everything was out, the radar, radio – everything was all wet and washed out. The bilge pump was out. We had the sump pump working, but we didn't have any side gas-powered pump to pump the water out. So, somehow Lee – I don't know how he did it–I'll never know. He got hold of a pipe wrench and crawled down in the bilge, back by the gear of the Kahlenberg with the shaft turning. He was all submerged in that cold water. He got that wrench on the plug and took the drain plug out of the seacock, pulled the seacock off, and got a little piece of screen. He stayed down in that ice cold water for hours and held that screen over the hole so we could start pumping the bilge water out with the engine.

Part of the rules of the road, when you get in a situation like that – caught in a big sea – you always have your bow into the seas. But, every time we hit a big sea with those doors gone, the *Aloha* was so low in the water that every time she went up on a sea, the water would come in through the opening. We were losing more every second. I hollered to Roy and Lee, "We're going to loose her this way. We got one chance and that's to get her turned around and go with it." It was completely against the rules of navigation. We were heading due north. Actually we were just north of Port Washington. I waited for the three big ones – the three bigger seas – and then gunned her, hoping it was going to work. I just kept heading with the sea. The *Aloha* had a fan-tail stern on her, you see, and when the seas came by they just blew away from the stern and washed by us. No water come in the side doors either, and I had to watch real close by the wheel, you know, that it didn't swing towards me. Lee must have been down in the bilge for 2 1/2 or 3 hours. I don't know how in the hell he did it. I have no idea.

After we got it pumped out, we got the boat turned around and headed back for Milwaukee. Funny thing, we had a little bottle of brandy that we got from the fish dealer in Chicago, wrapped in a Christmas box. We had it lying on one of the shelves right across from the wheel in the pilot house. After we got everything situated – I don't know when this happened, haven't got a clue – but when we got into the harbor, Roy and Lee were up getting things cleaned up. It was such a mess in there, you wouldn't believe it. Anyway I looked up to see what was going on, up forward. Here they had that bottle of brandy on top of the rooster tail – on top of the lifter – wasn't even a third left in that bottle and it was a big bottle. I don't know when they came and got it. I didn't ask any questions either.[26]

A fisherman out on the lake was not only at risk from the dangers of the elements, but was also at risk of being struck by another boat. This can easily happen when the boat is left unattended on automatic pilot while the crew are cleaning fish. In 1998, this sort of incident claimed the lives of three experienced fishermen on the fish tug *Linda E.* on Lake Michigan near Port Washington, Wisconsin. On December 11, 1998, Leif Weborg and his crewmembers, Warren Olsen and Scott Matta, went out to lift nets on a calm clear morning but didn't return that evening. Leif was an experienced fisherman who had fished with his father Emery and his uncle, Howard Weborg, from an early age in both Green Bay and Lake Michigan waters. He was a very good fisherman and an experienced skipper so that when the *Linda E.* didn't return home that evening, everyone knew something was amiss. The Coast Guard was notified and immediately began an intensive search that covered almost 3,000 square miles of the area where they were presumed to have been. The last contact with the *Linda E.* had been at 9:00 A.M. by cell phone between Leif and a representative of the Smith Brothers Fish Company in Port Washington, which was their home port. After two days of searching without finding any kind of debris or any sign, the Coast Guard suspended its search. That same day the Coast Guard opened a marine casualty investigation on the disappearance of the *Linda E.*[27]

Their investigation was intensive, but turned up no witnesses and no physical evidence of the fate of the *Linda E.*, though the Coast Guard questioned all commercial vessels traveling in that vicinity on December 11 and interviewed many commercial fishermen regarding normal fishing practices and routines. They also conducted experiments and stress tests on many fish tugs that were similar in size and design to the *Linda E.* Charlie Henriksen, a commercial fisherman from Baileys Harbor, spent a number of days with the Coast Guard during these investigations. He describes them as follows:

The Coast Guard came out here, measured my boat up, which was the sister ship to the *Linda E.*, and ran stability tests on her. They put weights on her to see how far she could lean, measured the doors, and performed flood rates. During the trial a few years later, the Coast Guard came up here again and put a guy on the roof of this house they were building here in Sand Bay, which is forty-two feet up in the air, and had us run out with our boat a distance supposedly where the watch had changed between the crewmen on the tug boat. What they found out was at four miles, this boat was more visible at ground level than it was forty-two feet up in the air. This boat disappeared into the background; and you couldn't pick it out. We got good radar on our boats and have an alarm on it to warn us of a collision, however, there still are many fishermen who never use it.[28]

The coast guard also gathered information on the repair and maintenance history of the *Linda E.* After all their investigation and studies, the Coast Guard determined that the most probable cause of the tragedy was either a collision with another boat or object, or structural failure. Two years later, Congressman Mark Green initiated a search and discovery effort using two US Navy minesweepers, and they combed the area where the *Linda E.* had disappeared eighteen months earlier. On June 18, 2000, the *Linda E.* was located and the Coast Guard reopened the investigation.

The Coast Guard sent a remote submarine down, and they shot both video and still photographs and obtained paint samples from the sunken fish tug. From this evidence, investigators came to the conclusion that the *Linda E.* sustained damage and was sunk by a collision with another vessel, and further investigation led to a tug and barge, the *Michigan/Great Lakes*, the only vessel that was in that specific area on that particular day. Paint samples taken from her that were consistent with paint found on the wreckage of the *Linda E.* After the hearings, the third ranking officer of the *Michigan/Great Lakes* agreed to a two-year suspension of his license and had to perform additional training. The Coast Guard concluded that the *Michigan/Great Lakes* should have detected the *Linda E.* on radar at least thirty minutes before the collision.

A similar tragedy nearly happened a few years later to Dennis and Jeff Hickey off Baileys Harbor while they were lifting nets on a calm winter day. Dennis tells the story:

> **I** think the most dangerous thing we are concerned about is the Great Lakes towing with the tugs and barges. They'll run you right down. We almost got ran down in 2001 by the sister ship [of the one] that ran down Leif Weborg and the crew of the *Linda E.* We were watching them. It was a calm, clear day in February, and I glanced over the lifter and saw them coming. I ran up to the pilothouse. All the radios were on and the radar was on, and I came back down and said to Jeff, "You know, he's on a collision course. He's coming right at us." We got to the end of setting our last box and I said to Jeff, "Let's wait here a bit." So we waited and got our buoy line up and buoy up. They never turned at all. Nothing on the radio, or anything, so we kept watching. Finally Jeff said, "He's going to run right through us." We threw the buoy on and ran up put the boat in reverse. He came so close that while we were backing up, the buoy banged all the way down the side of him. When we looked up, there wasn't a single soul in the pilothouse, or in the forward watch on the barge. There

wasn't a damn soul anywhere. They went straight out of sight, never turned around or anything, never acknowledged. They never saw us. We told the Coast Guard about it. I'm sure I could have hailed them, but I wanted to see if that would have still gone on, after what happened to Leif and his crew. And it almost happened to us, so we have to watch out. We never run without somebody in the pilothouse, if we're dressing fish or whatever. I know most chubber's – they run on autopilot, without anybody watching. We never do that. For now, we're not real concerned about getting run over, but what we're more concern about, up here, with the marinas and everything and the yacht club, is that we'll run somebody else down. Then we've got ourselves a mess.[29]

Fishermen were sometimes highly competitive about who had the best or fastest boat, as related by Laurence Daubner at an evening of storytelling hosted by Jeff Weborg at the Wagon Trail Resort:

Now, when they [Stanley Voight and Willie Johnson] got the *Hope* – and a lot of them got bigger boats right along – well then that got to be a thing. Then it was the racing – who had the fastest boat, you know – and that went on and on. The *Hope*, she was the fastest then. Then Art and Orville Weborg came in with a boat named the *Dierssen*; she was long and narrow. They had a Straubel engine, and she was fast, faster than the *Hope* on full gate, but they didn't want to challenge one another. So, one day we were coming through the Door [Death's Door passage] coming in, and Art was behind us in the *Dierssen* and he was gaining on us. Well the Kahlenberg had two oilers that you cranked to give them more oil, and then if you give her water in the breathers, she would turn that much more steam. Stanley Voight said, "You crank those oilers and I'll give 'er more water." You couldn't give her too much, because then it wouldn't slow down. So the *Dierssen* came up alongside of us, and down went that governor, wide open – Stanley on that, and I cranking and away we went. We were watching one another, but, by the time we got to the dock, we were half a boat length ahead.[30]

Elaine Johnson and Gretna Johns are fond of another story about a 1975 incident involving two fishermen and two game wardens. The following version is from an article by Keta Steebs:

The Keystone Wardens and the Forbidden Trout

Somewhere up north in a handleless locker lie six of the most sought-after fish in Door County. They are, the most impartial observer one would agree, beautiful specimens of lake trout. Caught last Wednesday, these fish have been tagged, photographed, identified, hugged, kissed, hidden, and searched for by two widely disparate parties – the commercial fishermen on one hand and the Department of

Natural Resources on the other.

Their whereabouts is a closely guarded secret, but when the time comes, the fishermen say, these trout will be on public display in court. They intend to prove that the DNR, guardians of public interest, violated one of their own most sacrosanct laws. Two wardens sold these trout to a restaurant for public consumption before bothering to measure them. Each fish is over 24 inches long, and, according to present health standards, contains too much PCB to be edible. PCB is, of course, polychlorinated biphenyls, a family of chemicals which can be found in fish. The Federal Food and Drug Administration have ruled that lake trout more than 24 inches in length contain an excess of PCB which is detrimental to health. For that reason commercial fishermen are not permitted to sell them and sport fishermen are urged to limit their consumption to one meal per week. Pregnant women are advised not to eat them at all.

These fish, the smallest measuring 24 1/2 inches, were sold to Woerfel's Restaurant in Sister Bay shortly after being confiscated by Wardens Charles Olson and Joel McOlash. Woerfel's paid the men (with a check made out to the DNR) 50 cents per pound. The fishermen say they weren't paid anything.

The story begins on Wednesday, August 6, [1975] when Alvin Anderson, Clayton Johnson and Alvin's 13-year-old son Steven caught a mess of whitefish and trout while fishing in the vicinity of Whaleback Shoals. The men say a strong wind the day before had kicked up quite a current in the bay, and their lift contained an unusually large amount of dead trout. Forbidden by law to throw any dead fish back in the bay, the fishermen had no alternative but to tag and ice the trout before bringing them in. They are permitted to keep 10 percent of their incidental catch (which would be 10 percent of the weight of the whitefish caught) and are entitled to be paid 15 cents per pound for the rest. This price, they say, is to compensate them for tagging and icing the fish properly before turning them over to the department.

On this particular day, Johnson and the two Andersons didn't have a chance to tie their lines before their fish boat *D&S* was boarded by McOlash, who began rifling through two boxes of fish. Alvin (better known as Gabby) maintains that McOlash had no right to search his boat without probable cause (or a warrant) and hadn't even bothered to ask permission before boarding.

The men said they told McOlash they had trout to turn over to the department, but would have to weigh them first. McOlash watched as they loaded their catch on Anderson's fish truck and proceeded to leave the dock. They had traveled perhaps 100 feet when Olsen, carrying what appeared to be either a sawed-off shotgun or a riot gun, approached on foot, joined McOlash and watched the fishermen leave.

Meantime, Elaine Johnson met the fishermen and said she needed whitefish for her restaurant clientele. Gabby said he'd deliver the fish to her shanty but had to go to the bank first. Elaine went home, the men went to the bank, but the wardens, not knowing of the unscheduled stop, apparently drove to Ellison Bay, the usual unloading point. It took them perhaps another 10 or 15 minutes to track down the fishermen who had by now backed up to Elaine's scale and informed her, "We have to wait for the wardens before unloading."

At this time the fishermen and Elaine were joined by Rueben Bergwin (called Dead-Eye because of his hunting ability) and Elaine's partner Gretna John. Bergwin helps the two women in their fish filleting operations and was on hand to help do the weighing-up. When Olson and McOlash appeared, all the fish were still on the truck, and Clayton said he asked Olson to bear in mind the fact that he and Gabby were allowed to keep 10 per cent incidental catch. Clayton says Olson told him he couldn't keep ANY of the trout and Clayton said after taking another look at Olson's artillery he wasn't in the mood to argue. The wardens asked Elaine for boxes and she says she found four old crates "a little on the dirty side" which were promptly filled with trout (unweighed) and placed on the wardens' truck. Un-iced and "far from sanitary containers," the fish were all set to be hauled away when Gretna asked Olson, "What happens to these fish?"

Olson reportedly said he sold them to persons and places, and, when pressed as to just what persons and places, replied "To people like my father-in-law or restaurants like Andre's." Gretna still curious, asked what price the DNR received and was told between 10 and 60 cents per pound. Not wishing to ask who paid the 60 cents (Olson's father-in-law or Andre's restaurant), Gretna said she shut up but was still anxious to find out what happened to this particular load of fish.

She was assured, she said, by Olson, that all fish measuring over 24 inches in length were destroyed "because of contamination." The next day Gabby learned from Craig Woerfel that at least 198 pounds of trout had found a home in Woerfel's market. Craig's wife Sue had been approached by the wardens and asked if she'd like to buy fresh trout for 50 cents a pound. Sue's scale only goes up to 25 pounds but she watched the wardens weigh the fish (without measuring) and wrote a check to the DNR for $99. She was not given, she says, a certificate of sale as required by law nor was she given a receipt. The fish, still tagged with the commercial fishermen's lot numbers, were placed in her freezer.

Once they found out where this "seized lot" was taken, Gabby and Elaine enlisted the help of a state official to measure and weigh them. The first trout measured 26 1/2 inches long and, according to Elaine, Gabby grabbed it, kissed it, and exclaimed, "Oh, you beautiful doll. Are we glad to see you!" After finding five more oversized trout, the fishermen quit looking, asked Woerfel's to turn the trout over to the association and called their lawyer Paul Jonjak. Jonjak notified John Brasch, director of DNR's Bureau of Fish and Wildlife Management in Madison of their wardens' inauspicious sale, and Madison apparently lost no time calling Green Bay. Warden Norman Hicks, supervisor of a five-county area, and Olson immediately drove to Sister Bay, and asked Susie to turn over an undersized trout she had inadvertently purchased from the wardens.[31]

In the earliest records, there are many stories about big trout. Some of them have been handed down through the generations and may have become somewhat embellished, but others are well documented. In 1862, William Cornell, who was fourteen years old at the time, caught seven trout, the smallest weighed 40 pounds and the largest weighed 48 pounds. In the winter of 1868, Godfrey Nelson caught one hundred trout one day and one hundred twenty the next, which amounted to $150.00 worth of trout in a three-week span. All these were caught through the ice on hook and line and a lot of muscle. In 1882, Edward and James, two brothers from Washington Island, were fishing near Fisherman's Shoal and caught two big trout – one weighed 58 pounds and the other 65 pounds. In the winter of 1870, a twelve-year-old boy by the name of George Irr caught a 38-pound trout. His father said, "Put your hook down quick." Young George said excitedly, "Not by a jugful. I'm going to show my Ma!" [32]

Jessie Miner fondly remembers his younger days catching large trout through the ice: [On April 11, 1871,] I went fishing near Rock Island with my father. I was going to cut a new hole, if he did not take aholt. Then the fish grabbed it and ran up the bait. I yelled, "I got the little scamp." The ice was smooth. The first thing I knew I was on my back. Father said, "Looks like the fish has got you." I lay on my back and hauled him in hand over hand. I got 29 that day. The largest weighed 26 pounds. Hauled the 29th just at sundown and he weighed 6 1/2 pounds – the smallest trout I had out of the 29. The largest number I ever caught in one day was 56, 1 1/2 miles northwest of Boyer's Bluff. They averaged about 5 pounds. This was the winter of 1868–1869. When I got home with my trout, Tom McBride met me on the ice and said, "Your water and night wood is carried in." I thought, Thank God for neighbors and let him pick out a trout. He picked the smallest one. I took it back and gave him one that dressed out at 15 pounds, which was just right for a family of eight."

In the winter of 1876, Charlie Goap caught 140 trout in one day – the largest number reported being caught by one person in a single day. That same winter, Nels Jepson had 106 in one day. They were caught off the north end of a little lake on the west side of Washington Island. In 1860, Joseph Cornell and Orson Nichols didn't know how big their trout was because the scale only went to 60 pounds. They thought it weighed close to 70 pounds. All these fish were caught through the ice using hook and line, save for Joseph Cornell's, which may have been caught in a net. J.W. Cornell caught a 43-pound trout that had two trout in its stomach, one weighed 2 pounds and the other about a pound and a half. So he caught one fish and shipped three. [33]

J.W. Cornell had the last heavy trout harvests from around Washington Island. Fishermen always tried to get their nets in early in the spring. One spring in the early 1930s, Claude Cornell owned a small airplane and took off to check the ice conditions in the bay and found open water somewhere in the vicinity of whaleback Shoal. John Cornell with his boat the *J.W Cornell* and the *Clara C.* made it out there and set their nets. Nearly every day for about three weeks they came in with lifts of 2,000 to 4,000 pounds of lake trout. The very largest lifts rarely exceeded 10,000 pounds, although one boat at Beaver Island once caught 14,000 pounds in a single day. [34]

[1] Interview with Jake Ellefson, October 2, 2001.

[2] Ibid.

[3] Letters from Jake Ellefson, March 2003.

[4] Interview with Jeff Weborg, September 14, 2002.

[5] Interview with Alvin "Gabby" Anderson, March 29, 2003.

[6] Leonard Peterson, *Rowleys Bay: Reliving the Heritage of Door County*, (Private printing, 1991), 158.

[7] Ibid, 164.

[8] Interview with Jeff Weborg, September 14, 2002.

[9] Interview with Joe LeClair, January 10, 2003.

[10] Interview with Alvin Anderson, March 29, 2003.

[11] Interview with Jeff Weborg, September 14, 2002.

[12] Letters from Jake Ellefson, March, 2003.

[13] Interview with Jeff Weborg, September 14, 2002.

[14] Lon Kopitzke, "An Interview With Marvin Weborg Along With His Son Mark," 1985 *Door County Almanac No. 3* (Dragonsbreath Press 1986), 156.

[15] Interview with Dennis Hickey, September 27, 2002.

[16] Laurence Daubner, An evening of story telling at the Wagon Trail Resort, Rowleys Bay; video by Charlie Miller (Courtesy of Elaine Johnson).

[17] Interview with Dennis Hickey, September 27, 2002.

[18] Interview with Jeff Weborg, December 13, 2002.

[19] Interview with Joe LeClair, January 10, 2003.

[20] Lon Kopitzke, An Interview With Marvin Weborg Along With His Son Mark, 1985; *Door County Almanac No. 3*, (Dragonsbreath Press, 1986), 156.

[21] Howard Weborg, An evening of story telling at the Wagon Trail Resort, Rowleys Bay; videotaped

by Charlie Miller (Courtesy of Elaine Johnson).

[22] Interview with Jim Cornell, May 4, 2002.

[23] Interview with Phil Albertson, March 7, 2003.

[24] H.R. Holland, "A Terrible Experience," History of Door County, Wisconsin, vol. 1 (Chicago, IL: S.J. Clarke Publishing Co, 1917), 362-366.

[25] Interview with Elaine Johnson, March 3, 2003.

[26] Interview with Alvin Anderson, February 28, 2003.

[27] Meg Jones, "Commercial Fishermen Look Out For Their Own," *Milwaukee Journal Sentinel*, December 16, 1998.

[28] Interview with Charlie Henriksen, December 13, 2003.

[29] Interview with Dennis Hickey, January 30, 2003.

[30] Laurence Daubner, An evening of story telling at the Wagon Trail Resort, video by Charlie Miller; (Courtesy of Elaine Johnson).

[31] Steebs, "The Keystone Wardens and the Forbidden Trout," *Door County Advocate*, August 12, 1975.

[32] Jessie Miner, Early Days on Washington *Island, Island Tales: An Anthology*, Prep. Cay Kurtis (Washington Island, 1937), 15-16.

[33] Jessie Miner, "Early Days on Washington Island," *Island Tales*, (Washington Island 1937), 15-16

[34] Letters by Jake Ellefson, March 2003.

Chapter 7

Attitudes, Reflections, and Observations

The nature of his work shaped the way a fisherman thought about fish. Some fishermen regarded the fish they caught as farmers viewed their harvest. Both ended up in the marketplace and provided income which provided for their families. Fishermen prepared their harvest of fish for the market without giving them much thought. They believed that they were using a resource as it was intended to be used. They worked hard to make their living in all kinds of weather, risking their lives and using all of their skills to do what they knew best.

Some fishermen developed an attitude toward certain species of fish. For example, lake trout with their voracious appetites. Fishermen often regarded lake trout as nothing but predators that ate just about anything. While dressing a lake trout, one fisherman pulled a whitefish from its mouth almost equal to its size, and another fisherman commented, "It's one of the dirtiest fish in the lake. It eats almost anything." Before 1900, gill-net fishermen complained that lake trout wrecked their nets, especially fishermen who sought only whitefish.[1]

In the early nineteenth century, another species of fish, the sturgeon, were regarded as a junk fish by some and were considered worthless pests that destroyed fishermen's nets. They were literally pulled from the nets and thrown on the shore to rot in the sun. Joe LeClair, a retired commercial fisherman from Door County remembers his grandfather netting sturgeon:

> They used to get a lot of sturgeon caught in their nets and at that time there
> wasn't any market for them. They would leave them piled up on the beach or dig
> holes in the sand and bury them. Some of the sturgeon got to be over 200
> pounds.[2]

Over the years, as the ecology of the lake changed, so did the attitude of the fishermen toward species that invaded the Great Lakes, such as smelt, sea lamprey, and alewives. Every fisherman had his own opinions about fish. Some planned to hand their business on to their sons and had concerns about conservation. They understood the "toleration level" for certain species – how many could safely be harvested, maturity levels of the fish, and certain times of the year when they should be fished. One experienced fisherman remarked, "I believe a man that is fishing and making a home here with the intention to live here will be likely to save his ground all he can, and if a man is merely here for a year or two, he will get all he can out of it. I live here and I will do all I can to save the fish."[3]

Commercial fishing, typically has been a family-oriented business handed down from generation to generation. Everyone in the family helps out, whether on their boat or as part of the shore crew. It's a team effort. Hard work, long hours, and teamwork are imperative to make a fishery thrive. Wives and children help out to support the family business any way that they can. Sons and daughters, when old enough, help out on the boat or packing and mending nets, packaging fish, or working on equipment. It's a family affair. "Once the business is gone," says one commercial fisherman, "you're never going to get it back. Its family oriented, and you grow into it. You develop certain things, and once you quit, there's no way back."[4]

A certain level of disdain and conflict has always existed between local fishermen and nonresident fishermen. When some of the larger fisheries expanded their operations to different regions of the lake, it caused a lot of controversy with the local fishermen. In the early 1900s, some of the larger fisheries on Lake Michigan were the A. Booth Fish Company out of Chicago and Albert Kalmbach based out of Sturgeon Bay. Both had operations in northern Lake Michigan. The resident fishermen regarded their fishing grounds somewhat like a farmer regards his land, and anyone intruding on it would be considered a trespasser. Like a farmer, a fisherman intended to use the resource and pass it along to the next generation of his family. In the late 1970s, limited entry and the quota system put an end to nonresident and transient fishermen.

Where I Live and What I Live For
(Reflections by Jake Ellefson)

My brothers and I were all in World War II. After the war we all came back to [Washington Island] and discovered we all wanted to live here. We decided to work together as the Ellefson Brothers and build upon our father's fishery. I don't think any of us regretted that decision. It was a hard life and we worked hard, and we had a wonderful life living and working together.

When I was young there were chubs, lake trout, herring, perch, and whitefish for us to catch. Green Bay and Lake Michigan were full of fish. Now Green Bay provides only a small percent of the Wisconsin commercial catch. Today, only chubs and whitefish remain for the commercial catch.

Beginning in the 1920s, there was a dramatic change in the ecology of Lake Michigan. First, the ocean fish smelt had a population explosion in the lake and were largely responsible for the decline of the herring and chub fishery in Green Bay, as well as depleting other species. Then the lamprey eel destroyed the lake trout. Later the alewives became very detrimental to all native species, consuming large amounts of spawn and plankton. Now the zebra mussels, gobies, white bass, white perch, and others continue to threaten the remaining chubs and whitefish. In addition to a good abundance of chubs and whitefish, the commercial fisherman needs to have more flexibility in his operation.

The fisheries resources of the state of Wisconsin have been governed by the Conservation Commission and for several decades now by the Department of Natural Resources. Many of the regulations are good. I'm referring to the size limits for whitefish, the mesh size of the whitefish gill nets, and also size of mesh and general design of both trap nets and pound nets. A number of years ago the Department issued rules creating a limited entry fishery. The limited entry was supposed to benefit the full-time fishermen. Some of the rules are too restrictive. We need to be able to fish gill nets, trap nets, and pound nets; moreover the catch requirements for license renewal should be removed. The chub net mesh size should be reduced until the plankton regains their former abundance. We need to have the 'one night lift' for whitefish removed and increased footage for whitefish gill nets permitted. The remaining fishermen need this flexibility to have a chance to survive.

The citizens of the state of Wisconsin have had a steady supply of Lake Michigan and Green Bay fish available throughout the history of the state. If indeed the fisheries resource is to be shared equally, then the consumer needs a steady supply of state fish available to purchase. The only way that can happen is for a healthy commercial fishery to survive.

The commercial fishery should also be assigned a quota of lake trout for each license. This would go a long way in assuring the future health of the fishery. It is entirely feasible and should have happened years ago. Perhaps the most glaring and potentially most detrimental mistake was the lack of regulation concerning removal of ballast water by ships using the St. Lawrence Seaway when the seaway was opened. The Great Lakes will be plagued with unwanted non-native species forever, because of this mistake. We can only hope that Lake Michigan will sustain successful fishing operations far into the future. Enlightened management by the DNR would go a long way towards making this happen.[5]

If you ask fishermen why they chose their profession, you get a variety of responses – "It's all I ever knew," or "my father was a fisherman as was his father before," or "a feeling of satisfaction from using all your skills and hard work to bring in a good lift," – but one common thread is an inner flame that burns in each and every one of them, consciously or subconsciously. It's a passion about fishing, working outdoors, and finding solace in nature. Says one Door County commercial fisherman: "I enjoy being able to do a lot of things. I'm not a professional at anything, but if I have to do something, I can do it. The fact that I'm not a college educated person, but being able to run a fairly good business is all the satisfaction I need."[6]

Fishermen are different from other people – ask any fisherman, and he'll agree. You could compare him to a farmer – both are independent, use natural resources for their livelihood, put in long days, and are not afraid to work hard. But a fisherman finds himself more exposed to the elements than a farmer, and is at the mercy of nature's elements. He's in it not to get rich, but for the love of the game. Says Marvin Weborg of Gills Rock, who spent nearly his entire life as a commercial fisherman as did his father:

It's not the easiest life, but it's the only life as far as I'm concerned – it's all I've ever done. I fished probably fifty-five or sixty-five years at least. With the kind of boats we've had, I've fished gill nets, pound nets, trap nets, hooks, and herring nets, floating herring nets, pound nets for herring, and all the rest of it. I've had a good life as far as fishing is concerned. We've caught an awful lot of fish. I've enjoyed it – the fresh air. I've never been afraid to be on the water and the winds – you might as well stay there once you're out there, because the winds are just as bad [going in]. The time you get the worst ride is going out or coming in, when you're traveling any speed. As far as lifting is concerned, we've had waves take and throw a roller when we were lifting nets and throw it right back into the boat, and the water land right through the lifter door on the other side of the boat. "Put it back out there, and keep right on lifting," I'd say. Sometimes the nets have snapped right off, [and} we had to go to the other end or grapple them up. Of course, on an occasion like that you don't stay there anymore, you head for home.[7]

The History of Regulation of the Fisheries

As early as 1801, New York legislators passed laws disallowing the use of seines, nets, weirs and other apparatus to divert salmon from moving up the rivers that fed into Lake Ontario and Lake Erie to spawn. However, during the first half of the nineteenth century, fishermen on the Great Lakes had pretty much a free run. Such regulations as existed were loosely enforced, and licenses were not required. By the mid nineteenth century, commercial fish species were noticeably diminishing, and fish experts concluded that it was only going to get worse. This prompted policymakers to pass more restrictive state policies. Over the second half of the nineteenth century, New York passed twenty-three more laws regarding the salmon in Lake Ontario. But, these laws were still often hard to enforce and were applied piecemeal at best.[8] By the 1870s, things began to change, and heated battles between fishermen and regulators began and were to continue right up to the present.

Three states – Wisconsin, Michigan, and Ohio – were largely responsible for the evolution of state regulation of the Great Lakes fisheries during the nineteenth century. These three states controlled the largest portion of the Great Lake waters which also produced the largest annual income for commercial fishermen. However, the three states had different policies and regulations regarding types of fisheries, their geographic locations, and enforcement of laws. By 1865, all three states began regulating fish harvests in specific locations and specified the type of nets to be used, but they left enforcement of the regulations to local authorities.

After 1865, legislation noticeably changed the face of the commercial fishing industry. In Michigan, legislators passed a law protecting whitefish, which had been heavily fished. It specified a certain mesh size on pound nets for harvesting whitefish, but placed no restrictions on gill nets. Also, for the first time, it imposed a fee of fifty dollars for a non-resident fishing license. These regulations covered all of Michigan waters and the responsibility for enforcement was left to individual County Boards of Supervisors.[9]

Both Wisconsin and Michigan required nets to be registered with the local county Registrar of Deeds, and pound-net fishermen were required to have their fishing locations plainly marked and to have a registration number on their markers. The fishermen from Washington Island, in the northern waters of Lake Michigan, typically inscribed their names on pieces of wood or timber which they erected near the beach for the purpose of claiming the waters in Green Bay for fishing with a pound net. Their names were registered at the courthouse in Sturgeon Bay in much the way a deed on piece of land was.[10] Wisconsin's legislators passed a law that prohibited setting a pound or trap net in more than 20 feet of water off, under, or on the south point of any bay or inlet on the west shore of Lake Michigan in Door County. Each offense could bring a $10 or $15 fine. In 1867, a law was passed in Wisconsin that provided for state fish inspectors – one more thing to widen an already growing rift between fishermen and regulators. Under this new law, packed fish could not be removed from the county until inspected and branded by the inspector or his deputy. Moreover, all barrels were to be well hooped with ten good hoops, quarter or half barrels had to have eight hoops.[11]

By 1870, there was growing concern about dwindling commercial fish populations and the need for conservation to preserve the fisheries for long-term use. In 1871, the federal government established the United States Commission of Fish and Fisheries, headed by Spencer F. Baird. This commission worked with the governments of states bordering the Great Lakes on conservation issues, especially on artificial propagation and restocking programs, but also on the introduction of nonnative species. Baird appointed a biologist from Waukegan, Illinois, named James W. Milner to conduct studies of the Great Lakes fisheries. Milner's findings from a two-year study were furnished to the states' legislatures, and he was instrumental in getting individual states to establish state fishery commissions to work with the US Commission of Fish and Fisheries. The states launched their own fishery commissions based on Milner's suggestions and studies. Milner was specifically concerned about declining whitefish populations.

The most successful innovations that came out of the state fishery commissions were the hatchery and stocking programs. They were, for the most part, funded by the states with minimal federal contribution except technical support and breeding programs. But, it wasn't long before a storm began to brew among the commercial fisheries and fish dealers. Fishermen argued that the regulations could not be enforced equally and thoroughly over such a large area as the Great Lakes. Moreover, they believed that those who did follow the regulations were at an economic disadvantage because others disregarded regulations and reaped larger harvests. Theirs was highly competitive, and those fishermen who achieved the largest production were the most profitable. Fishermen had to obtain high yields to survive. They came to be squeezed between low prices for fish and increasing costs for boats and rigs, especially as the technology began to change.

In 1871, the commissioner of the US Commission of Fish and Fisheries toured the entire shoreline of Lake Michigan, including the islands, interviewing local fishermen and observing fishing practices around the lake. He wanted to establish the condition of the fisheries at that time relative to prior years, and he discovered that risks made their income variable, but their investments compared favorably with farming, nor is there any truth in the aspersion on the class of men, who are industrious, hardworking citizens, and considering the hardships and exposures incident to their calling, singularly free from the habit of hard drinking. He also noted that,

> Fishermen suffered frequent loss or injury to their stocks, and their season's success
> depended much on the weather. [Moreover,] alternation of abundance and scarcity

does not develop the provident faculty that accumulates property. Though as a class not given to dissipation, they spend their money freely for comfort and good living when the fishing is prosperous. In spite of all these unfavorable conditions many attain comfortable circumstances.[12]

Attitudes Toward Regulation of the Fisheries

The twentieth century proved to have the same problems regarding restrictions, regulations, and conservation programs, and there were still heated battles between fishermen and policymakers. At the turn of the century, more regulations were imposed on the fishery. In the 1920s and 1930s, gear restrictions eliminated the use of deep trap nets and bull nets in some areas. Some of these restrictions were based on poor research. Fishermen felt that their traditional grounds were being invaded and that too many young fish were being caught with the bull nets and deep trap nets. The loudest complaints were from old time gill-net and pound-net fishermen who didn't want to see change.

Lake Michigan fishermen were becoming more adversarial toward and distrusting of the Wisconsin State Fishery Commission, or the Conservation Commission, as it came to be known by the early twentieth century. Each state imposed its own regulations and restrictions. Fishermen who carried both Wisconsin and Michigan licenses, for example, had to abide by the regulations of both states. Boundary settlements had given eight states a share of the US coastline of the Great Lakes. Clearly, a coordinated effort between the states for a single jurisdiction and uniform regulations was needed.

As far back as 1883, some efforts were made toward establishing uniform regulations on the Great Lakes. That year, representatives from Minnesota, Wisconsin, Ohio, and Michigan met along with the US Fish and Game Commission in Detroit – thirteen recommendations were brought to the table, but not one was adopted by the states. Between 1883 and 1941, more meetings were held, including twenty-seven international and interstate conferences, and resolutions came and went, but nothing came of them.[13]

It eventually became obvious that a "single jurisdiction" approach was not going to work. At a conference in 1904, there was a recommendation to pass state resolutions to give control of the commercial fisheries to the federal government, in an attempt to promote uniform regulations. Wisconsin and Minnesota were the only states that actually passed the measure. In February of 1938, representatives of all the Great Lakes states plus the Province of Ontario and the US State Department assembled an international board of inquiry to find some common ground on this issue. The board considered various ideas, interstate agreements, and compacts that were drawn up by the US Congress, and also took into consideration the opinions of commercial fishermen. Fishermen were asked what factors they believed were causing the decline of native species. They said that pollution was the most important factor, followed by small-mesh nets, over-fishing, the effects of the deep-trap net, and, finally, fishing during the spawning season. The fishermen were also given a chance to make a list of recommendations for measures to control the fisheries. Of the approximately 6,500 suggestions or recommendations from Great Lakes fishermen, the top five were: (1) strictly controlling closed seasons during the spawning of fish; (2) eliminating habitual violators; (3) preventing pollution; (4) planting more fry; and (5) planting of more large fish.[14]

After all the meetings were held and information gathered, a treaty between the US and Canada was drawn up, signed, and submitted to the U.S Senate. It eventually was withdrawn by President Eisenhower. Fishermen helped to defeat this treaty by uniting and voicing their opposition. They thought they would be better off leaving the power of regulation at the state level, and feared that politics would overshadow issues that were important to them.[15]

In 1921, Michigan reorganized their fish commission into a new unit called the Michigan Department of Conservation. Legislators gave the department more power to enforce laws to save the dwindling stocks of whitefish and lake trout. The commission began licensing commercial fishermen, imposing size limits, establishing closed seasons, and regulating gear. Wisconsin soon followed Michigan's lead and created the Wisconsin Department of Conservation in 1927, and the department soon began research on commercial fishing on the Great Lakes.[16]

In the 1920s, one of the best-known fish biologists was Dr. John Van Oosten, who had earned a PHD from the University of Michigan in 1926. He worked for the Bureau of Commercial Fisheries of the US Fish and Wildlife Service, devoting his entire career to the study of fish and fisheries. His area of expertise was the study of fisheries and the effect of pollution on species. His studies over the course of forty years proved invaluable to the Great Lakes fishery. His area of expertise was fisheries and the effect of pollution on species. He paved the way for federal government involvement in the Great Lakes fisheries, and he brought fishery issues to both national and international attention. He was instrumental in drafting the American Fisheries Society's North American Fish Policy in 1938.[17]

By the late 1950s, the commercial fisheries of the Great Lakes were in a tough situation. Most of the native species that were valued for commercial use either were gone or occurred in such low numbers that many commercial fishermen were forced out of business. The sea lamprey had decimated nearly all of the native lake trout and were preying on whitefish and deepwater chubs. Up to this point, the US Department of Conservation had focused their research on pollution, and had largely overlooked the problems of the changing ecology of the Great Lakes and the dwindling commercial fish populations. But the population crisis now spurred both national and international conservation organizations to begin addressing this problem managing the great lakes in a unified effort, and in 1955, the US and Canada organized the Great Lakes Fishery Commission. Following is an interview with Howard Tanner, formerly with the Michigan DNR and Michigan State University:

The Great Lakes Fishery Commission was formed in 1955 in response to what was perceived as a crisis, the collapse of the various fisheries in the lakes. Sea lamprey and over fishing were some of the factors blamed. Smelt was an important factor, in my opinion. The establishment of this joint commission between Canada and the United States would mean uniform management of the Great Lakes. Each state would have to voluntarily give the Great Lakes Fishery Commission its management authority over their portion of the Great Lakes. Seven states and the province of Ontario agreed. One state said no. That state was Ohio. Ohio had a significant sport fishery for walleye and perch in Lake Erie and a commercial fishery, and the state refused to turn its management authority over to anybody. The Great Lakes Fishery Commission decided it would manage Ohio's share of Lake Erie and so they went ahead with the formation of the commission without its management authority.

The principal mission of the Great Lakes Fishery Commission was to control sea lamprey. Secondarily their mission was to rehabilitate lake trout populations. Those are the only two missions they ever really had. Now in order to fulfill their mission, they have conducted research. Back in the early days, there was a technology portion to their laboratory where they helped develop markets for fish products as part of an effort to help sustain a very floundering commercial fishery. The fishermen could not make a living. There was nothing left to fish for. By the early 1960s, alewife made up the vast bulk of weight of fisheries in Lake Michigan.

The Great Lakes Fishery Commission was located in Ann Arbor. The U.S Bureau of Commercial Fisheries was still there at the Institute for Fisheries Research. The Great Lakes Fishery Commission was pretty much totally oriented toward commercial fishing. The problem was the sea lamprey and the need to rehabilitate the principal predacious fish, the lake trout. That is very understandable; it was the way things had been and the way they were going to continue. That is why Claude Ver Duin was Michigan's representative on the Great Lakes Fishery Commission.[18]

Each of the states bordering the Great Lakes was to give the commission its management authority over their section(s) of the Great Lakes. Seven states and the Province of Ontario agreed, but the State of Ohio did not. Ohio was concerned about both its commercial fishery and its sport fishery for perch and walleye in Lake Erie, so the commission ultimately had to go ahead without Ohio's management authority. Their main goal was to control the sea lamprey, with a secondary concern for helping the lake trout populations to recover, and those were the only two missions they ever really had.[19]

During the 1960s, Wisconsin, Minnesota, and Michigan reorganized and renamed their conservation departments, each as a state Department of Natural Resources (DNR). Particularly with the formation of the Michigan DNR in 1966, the fisheries of the Great Lakes came under close scrutiny. According to DNR biologists, almost all of the fish stocks had been depleted. Policies and perspectives began to change.

First, the department saw great potential for economic benefits from recreational fishing. They perceived commercial fishing as only one aspect of the management problem, and not the main interest. The Michigan Department of Conservation had begun introducing pacific salmon into the lakes, the use of gill nets was being controlled, and sea lamprey programs had reduced the lamprey population enough to allow steelhead trout to thrive once again. The Michigan legislature amended their basic commercial fishing statutes to provide direct controls on the fisheries. Coho salmon were introduced into Lake Michigan streams in the spring of 1966, and Chinook salmon by 1967. In a few years time they proved very prolific and created a burst of interest among sport fishermen and generated a substantial economic boost to local lakeshore economies from the influx of tourists and sport fishermen.

Michigan's bias in favor of the sport fishery and the success that their new policies appeared to be having prompted the Wisconsin Department of Conservation, which became the Wisconsin Department of Natural Resources (DNR) in 1968, to follow suit. The Wisconsin DNR soon also began programs that benefited the sport fisheries. For example, Coho salmon were planted in Lake Michigan tributaries. However, by 1970, Wisconsin began also to help the commercial fisheries. Jeff Weborg, a commercial fisherman from Gills Rock, Wisconsin, proclaims, There's no area in the entire Great Lakes system that is fished more heavily, commercially, than northern Door County. Yet this is one of the most thriving sport fisheries as well. That shows they can coexist in harmony. But if you went to a meeting before the senate or the assembly with the DNR and leaders of the sport fishing industry present, they'd try to promote this argument that a great conflict exists. There isn't a conflict. There's room for both on the lake, and we've proven that right here.[20]

In the early 1980s there were approximately 180 commercial fishing licenses issued in Wisconsin, representing over $10 million of Wisconsin's economy. There were about 500 licenses issued to charter boat operators that cater to sport fishermen, and some 200,000 Great Lakes Trout and Salmon Stamps were issued to sport fishermen, which generated a lot of revenue to sustain the stocking operations and other programs that benefit the sport fishery.[21]

Attitudes Towards Regulations

Rules and regulations have long been part of a fisherman's life, and even though there was a lot of grumbling and inflamed tempers, they still had to abide by them. Fishermen always tended to be very independent and were proud of this fact. Unfortunately, this independence contributed to their downfall when all the restrictions and regulations came in. Their independent natures made it difficult to organize a collective voice in opposition to the regulatory agencies. Says Jake Ellefson:

We know why we have fallen victim to all these regulations. We have no degrees behind our names, and we have no clout. If we had a lot of clout like a hundred thousand farmers, it might have been a little different. With no clout you haven't got a chance.[22]

Commercial fishermen did not organize collectively for various reasons, including regional differences between fisherman that used different gear types and the fact that they were scattered over a very large area including eight state jurisdictions. Also, they are sometimes jealous of one another, and may be afraid that another fisherman might find out how much they're catching. Whatever the reasons for it, their failure to organize collectively left them at a major disadvantage when dealing with state agencies and with sport fishing organizations.

In the 1970s, fishermen finally did organize associations to voice their opinions to the DNR, partly because they found themselves in rough waters again in 1972 over state policy favoring the sport fishermen. It seemed evident to the commercial fishermen that the DNR was trying to squeeze them out. The number of commercial fishermen in Michigan already had dwindled from 1100 to 30. In northern Wisconsin on Lake Superior, there had been a decline from 560 to 19 commercial fishermen, and Illinois and Indiana had only a few left. However, Door County still had roughly 300 active fishermen, and they were adamant about maintaining that number.

In 1974, nearly three hundred commercial fishermen united and formed the Northeast Wisconsin Commercial Fisheries Association (NWCFA). Prior to that time, there were loosely scattered associations organized by region that had never really achieved any substantial collective bargaining power. The NWCFA was born at a meeting in Sturgeon Bay, where, a formal election was held and officers were installed. Elaine Johnson, who became secretary at the time recalled:

We formed the [NWCFA] in 1974. Prior to this we – the Door County fisheries – had our little group. We were the whitefish people. To the south, around Two Rivers to Racine, that was mainly chub fishermen, and southern Green Bay was perch fishermen. We all had our own little associations before we unified and went to a state association. I used to write the newsletters, so I think we had close to 300 fishermen in our association. The department [DNR] claims we only had 211.[23]

Today, the NWCFA isn't as active as it once was. They meet only a few times a year, or as necessary, and have a fish boil to raise some money for the association. Rick Johnson was president of the local association in 2004. He comments:

We don't have a very active association anymore; we're pretty much under the Wisconsin Commercial Fishing Association, which is our state organization. Our local association was real active for a long time, but the numbers are dwindling. Basically everything is done through our state association.[24]

Of the four regional associations – Southern Lake Michigan, Door County, Green Bay, and Lake Superior – all have limited membership, and only the Door County and Southern Lake Michigan associations are really functioning. There are only a few independent fishermen participating in the Green Bay association.

The Wisconsin Commercial Fishing Association represents all the commercial fishermen in the state of Wisconsin. Commercial fisherman Charlie Henriksen was president of the state association in the 1990s and held meetings when necessary. They hired a lobbyist several years ago to help the commercial fishermen with certain issues. The associations have made a difference, and the DNR now listens to the commercial fishermen.

The Lake Michigan Commercial Fishing Board was appointed by the governor when limited entry and quotas were established. It is made up of seven members, predominantly commercial fishermen from the Wisconsin Commercial Fishing Association, and functions mainly to allocate quotas among the fishermen, though it recently has been serving as an advisory group to the DNR on commercial fishing issues.

In 2004, the Lake Michigan Fisheries Forum was designated by the DNR to address issues related to Lake Michigan fisheries. It has seventeen members, seven of whom are selected by the DNR and represent various organizations, plus ten others selected to work collectively and constructively with the department. The forum has no rule-making authority and serves only in an advisory capacity to the Wisconsin DNR and the DNR Lake Michigan Fisheries Team. Its stated purpose to: (1) facilitate information exchange between the department and interested groups or individuals; (2) provide a forum for discussion of issues of concern; (3) develop consensus among diverse interests on matters of common concern; and (4) develop public advocacy for policies of general interest.[25]

Among the seventeen members of the forum are three commercial fishermen who have actively participated and helped in creating some rule changes for the good of commercial fisheries. One of them, Charlie Henriksen, commented that:

> We [have] actually done some good things with the regulations in the last few years. We were able to change a rule so we could fish our trap nets in deeper water. We're working on a regulation change for chub fishing. It used to be, when the chub fishery was open year round, there were some fishermen didn't want it open and they argued that (fishermen sometimes being their worst enemy) if you let guys fish year round they would catch too many trout. One of the guys, rather than saying something sensible, like "we'll fish outside of forty fathom and not kill any trout," he said "we'll fish outside of sixty fathom." Well for ten years, during a six-week period we had to fish outside of sixty fathom, which really kills a big part of the fishery. We tried and tried to get that rule changed, and after some time, things began to move in our direction with that. As of January 15, 2002 we no longer have to fish outside of sixty fathoms, and now we can fish in as far as forty-five fathom. In a sense we made a trade-off based on incidental kill. We took forty-five fathom for twelve weeks instead of sixty fathom for six weeks.[26]

Fishermen's associations and lobbyists working for the fisheries have given fishermen more clout and bargaining power, but it's still a challenge to get the DNR to change a rule or just to be heard according to Charlie Henriksen:

> We have to almost beat the issue to death with them to get some of these regulations changed – everything's a political issue. That's why we have a lobbyist to stay on top of things. For many years, it seemed like we kept stepping back and stepping back, but in the last five years [1998-2003] we've done some positives for the commercial fishery. It used to be that the DNR would show up with a package and say, "it's like this or like that." Now we have better input into the process.[27]

Another aspect of the difficulties commercial fishermen experienced with the regulating agencies was the reports they were required to file. With the reorganization of the DNR in the late 1960s, fishermen not only had to deal with the low commercial harvests, they were faced with increased paperwork required by the DNR. Every fisherman had to submit a monthly quota report for chubs and perch to the Bureau of Fish Management, and weekly reports on chubs which were sent to the Milwaukee district office. Today (2003), fisherman submit one report every two weeks. One fisherman remembered:

When I was young, my Dad had to file a monthly fishing report. Now we file one every two weeks, and of course the fishermen in those days were always scared to death of the DNR – it was the Conservation Commission in those days. The fishermen didn't record half the fish they caught, and their records weren't worth a damn because of that.[28]

Regulation During the Decisive 1970s and Later

By the early 1970s, the Michigan commercial fisheries were in a very precarious position. Their livelihoods were threatened by the sport fishery. The Michigan DNR favored the sport fishery because, economically, that policy was in the best interest of the state. Over the next decade, commercial fishermen in Michigan waters were slowly and methodically driven out by regulations and restrictions. Sport fishermen supported these restrictions with great enthusiasm, while commercial fishermen looked at them with horror. Wisconsin and other states soon followed similar restriction programs, which fall into several categories: (1) limited entry; (2) geographic restrictions; (3) restrictions on species and imposition of quotas; (4) restriction of net types; (5) restriction of net mesh size; (6) restriction of maximum fish length.[29] We will discuss these categories in turn.

Limited Entry

One of the first restrictions on commercial fishing in Michigan and then in Wisconsin was the Limited Entry Program. Limited entry was already being enforced in Lake Superior and had reduced the number of fishermen eligible for licenses from 50 to 30. On Lake Superior, limited entry required that, in order to retain a license for two years, a fisherman had to prove that he fished 50 days per year and had at least $5,000 invested in commercial fishing gear. To be eligible for a third year he needed an investment of $7,500, and for the fourth year, $10,000.[30] This had the effect of weeding out part-time fishermen. The program was opposed by some commercial fishermen who could not meet these requirements, but it did weed out part-time fishermen.

In 1975, at the recommendations of a task force and state agencies, a bill eventually materialized, Senate Bill 409. This bill clearly defined regulations by the DNR. Bill 409 would establish limited entry, allow the DNR to close certain areas of Lake Michigan to commercial fishing, and impose stiffer penalties for sport and commercial fisheries. Taken from a 1999 interview from Michael Chiarappa and Kristin Szylvian's book, "Fish for All," with Ron Poff, Wisconsin DNR Fishery official, commented on the genesis of limited entry and quotas with the birth of Bill 409:

When the Wisconsin DNR instituted limited entry on Lake Michigan, we worked through Larry Van Sistine, a legislator from Green Bay. He was the one who finally agreed to consider some legislation. The agency cannot draft the legislation; it has got to be drafted by somebody other than us if it is going to get anywhere. The first lim-ited-entry legislation proposed for Lake Michigan was called Senate Bill 409 or SB 409. I actually appeared in opposition at a public hearing on it in Racine. I said it had a lot of good points, but it went too far in some respects. Then the bill came back as an assembly bill in a revised version. Both houses supported it with some fairly mod-est amendments and it was all a matter of just working across the street with a few legislators. My boss at the time was Jim Addis and that was his forte. He realized his strong point was in the political arena, so he spent his time working over there. I spent my time working with the fishermen. It worked out real well. Clyde Porter, the legislator up in the Door County – Green Bay area, introduced twenty-six proposed amendments to this piece of legislation, and they all failed. And once the word got out that he was doing this, every one failed a bit worse than the one before it, till by the end, there were not any votes in favor except probably his own. His comment was agents Poff and Addis are in the back room rubbing their thumbs. We got out of the legislature about five p.m. that night after a long day.

After this came a long series of meetings with the commercial fishermen on the administrative rules. The statute established limited entry and created a fee struc-ture for license and relicensing fees. It said that the state should establish relicensing criteria, so we had to develop administrative rules. NR25 is the part of the adminis-trative code that contains commercial fishing regulations and rules determining our operating procedures, how the fishery is going to be licensed, how we are going to regulate it, and the kinds of gear that can be used. The statute allows us to regulate such things as the kinds and amounts of gear. It also gave the right to limited entry and the quantity of fish that could be harvested and those sorts of things.

In order for an agency to develop a set of administrative rules, I held seven meetings, night meetings, with commercial fishermen. I think we had well over 150 commercial fishermen attending the meetings in fish houses. They were tough. We started at 7:00 p.m. and a lot of times, we didn't get done until midnight. Then we broke out the smoked chubs or the smoked bullheads. My job was to go through that rough draft and get their reaction to any changes from previous commercial fishing regulations. I would come back from every one of those meetings with a big pile of paper that was just my own notes.

We made a lot of points with the industry in doing things that way. We had a lot of supporters. They recognized the value of limited-entry and playing an active role in developing the rules to go with it. But it is hard. You can read things into what they are saying, so you have to be careful what you say. The key is not to create a whole lot of enemies in the fishery. It makes you work that much harder. You can have enemies, but they can be friendly enemies. They can be the ones who are not afraid to debate you in public.[31]

A majority of commercial fishermen still thought this bill was not going to benefit the commercial fishery. Furthermore, it would have a great impact on a fisherman's livelihood. Jeff Weborg voiced his disappointment in the state's bureaucratic inadequacies and indifference:

When Senate Bill 409 passed, I happen to know how it passed. I was very active in our association. I was going to Madison all the time testifying. When Senate Bill 409 passed; it was brought up in the senate chambers. Most of the guys weren't even in chambers; there was absolutely no discussion on it and when they called on the vote, the people ran in from the corridors and rang the bell yes and ran back out again.

It was shortly after that was passed that there was a joint meeting of the senate and the house on the natural resources and I was to testify on another issue. I would say in the two committees there were probably ten, twelve people, maybe more than that. I stood up and said, "You know, the state of politics in the state of Wisconsin makes me sick." You could see their hair rising. "What just happened recently makes me sick to my stomach on what's going on here with the bill that was passed, Senate Bill 409." I said. "Now, I'm not going to embarrass you and ask you what that bill says, none of you could tell me what that bill says, and yet you all sitting here voted for it. That bill affects my livelihood more than you'll ever know, and yet you guys didn't even have the courtesy to sit in chambers and listen to the bill being read. You were outside the chambers and when the bell was rung, you ran in and voted for it. You know you people make me sick." There was hardly a face looking at me. They couldn't argue with me, it was true. What are they going to say? So that was the start of me being involved in a lot of different things.[32]

"Bill 409 was very controversial," says Charlie Henriksen. "When 409 passed in 1979, and limited entry, quotas, closed seasons were implemented that was a sore spot for many of us. It brought more rules and regulations, but at that point it was either make a deal… they had enough sport fishing clubs… it would have been all or nothing, they would have tried to ban commercial fishing."[33]

Bill 409 provided the DNR greater legal authority to impose tighter controls on sport, charter, and commercial fisheries. The limited entry program was designed to eliminate the part-time fishermen. It was believed to actually benefit full-time commercial fisherman, as would increased license fees. The department assured commercial fishermen that limited entry would be flexible and allow fishermen that fished through the ice to continue fishing with a crew card issued to the license holder, which allowed a four-person crew to fish. James Moore, a local Wisconsin DNR fish manager explained that when limited entry became law, it would give the DNR authority to establish criteria which might or might not be the same on Lake Superior and Lake Michigan. To determine the most effective criteria for Lake Michigan, input would be gathered by a commercial fishery advisory board.

In the 1970s, Wisconsin fishermen were regulated on the number of lifts during a season. In order to keep your license, you had to have fifty lifts. But, once that number was reached, a fisherman could no longer use that license, which imposed a real limit on his income. Some fishermen complained that the use of catch records submitted by fishermen to determine eligibility was very arbitrary, as some fishermen would combine up to a week's time in a single report.[34] But the real crux of the matter was expressed by commercial fisherman Charlie Henriksen: "It was the whole idea of accepting limits on what you could do. You know fishermen – when the fish are there, you want to catch them, and you have no control over that. It was very hard to accept that, and it's still hovering over us."[35]

But some fishermen denied that limited entry was even a viable option. Said commercial fisherman Jake Ellefson, "Limited entry wasn't really necessary, because people need the fishery all the time. It's not as though there was a large number of people trying to get into the business."[36]

However, Dennis Hickey, a commercial fisherman from Baileys Harbor sees some benefit to smaller fishing operations:

> One of the biggest things that happened in the state of Wisconsin was when the fisheries went to a limited entry system. In a sense it was somewhat like farming, you know, the person either decided to get bigger or get out. With the quota system, some fishermen were actually in favor of that because what that allowed was that the smaller guys were not just run out of business, they would be able to be bought out. The DNR had no money, so they let other fishermen buy them out. The guys were able to sell. Otherwise they wouldn't have gotten anything. They would have been run right out of business.[37]

Jeff Weborg elaborated the point:

> When they went to a quota and limited entry fishery, the only way to get a license was to buy one from another fisherman or from somebody selling a license. However, to be qualified to buy that license, you needed to have two years crew card experience. The only way to really break into the business [was], say, I give you a crew card, you work for me for two years or someone else for two years. [Then] you could come back and buy a license. Back when all this came about, we had (and still carry) five licenses. The reason we carried them at that point was simply because of the stuff that was going on. They could jerk your license, if they felt like it, and so we had that many licenses simply for insurance policies. So if they jerk one, we could fish on another. I'm not concerned with that anymore. We keep five licenses now simply because if there is or comes a point and time where we decide to sell off a license, or split off a few nets, a quota, or a boat we still would have enough licenses to keep going.[38]

The DNR maintained that part-time fisheries were a detriment to the economic well-being of the industry. James Moore understood that most commercial fishermen regarded limited entry as a way to eliminate commercial fishing, and he tried to assure them this was not the case.

> This bill is designed to make commercial fishing more professional and accountable. Bill 409 won't hurt bona fide fishermen, but it will eliminate their "rowboat competitors." This is the department's name for people who hear the fishing is good, pay

$16 for a commercial license, go out in a rowboat with inadequate equipment, take what they can and quit. These are the people who also aren't careful about lifting their nets regularly."[39]

Some Door County fishermen were in favor of limited entry and quotas. Commercial fisherman Dennis Hickey explained how limited entry and quotas benefited commercial fisheries: "Limited entry was set up in a way so that somebody who wanted to fish could fish, and the other guys who didn't know what they wanted to do or just wanted to fish part of the time… they were gone. The way this benefited some of these small fishermen who had a hard time making their quota was that they had something to sell. Otherwise they would be just out of business. They could sell their quota to some other guy."[40]

By 1977 there were varied responses from commercial fishermen and sport fishermen as well as other interest groups to this proposed bill. Commercial fishermen united and voiced emphatically some of their views, which created two amendments to Bill 409. The first amendment provided that a seven member board of the commercial fishing regulatory commission include five commercial fishermen and two others. The second amendment provided for prior legislative consideration and approval of any administrative rule set up by the DNR to implement Bill 409. In 1978 both houses of the state legislature adopted the bill by wide margins.

Ron Poff worked for the DNR for forty-one years and dealt with both commercial fishermen and sport fishermen. Ron described how limited-entry and the quota system came to be:

In the late 1950s and early 1960s I worked mostly inland. I knew the Great Lakes Fishery had been somewhat depleted for years and years. The Great Lakes Fisheries were going to hell. They were over fished. There were hundreds and hundreds of miles of gill nets being set in the Great Lakes. In 1874, the federal government established fish commissioners, and the states created a department and a state fish commission, and we started getting fish from the federal government to plant. During the first year of its operation the Wisconsin Fish Commission spent under four hundred dollars to plant fish. The Federal Government provided millions and millions of fry, and even eye eggs at the time. It was an effort strictly aimed at replenishing what was considered a food supply, partly, perhaps, because there were a lot of immigrants coming into the country and they needed food. The Government perceived this need for food, and the stocks were already over-fished at the time. Over-fishing went on and on, throughout a series of ups and downs and regulations until finally, in 1967, Lake Superior became limited entry. Lake Michigan became limited entry in the mid-1970s.

The philosophy that came out of limited entry was that if you are going to have limited entry, you have to have quota control, and you probably will eventually need some system so that quotas have value. They can be transferred to maintain a viable fishery. When I started, there were sixty-eight licenses on Lake Superior and about two hundred sixty on Lake Michigan. I had been hired for the Great Lakes position to implement limited entry. The legislature passed a resolution around 1967 that said the state should limit entry to the fishery. The first thing we did was freeze the number of licenses. Then we had to work on a process in order to be constitutional that would allow a way for new fishermen to get into the fishery. Some sort of criteria or test that had never been run before had to be established for them to meet. It had to give them a chance to compete for a position in this fishery. The rules were that the fishermen had to show an investment of a certain size or amount of gear in order to get a license, or they had worked as a member of a crew for a number of years as though they were apprenticing into the fishery. It worked out pretty well. We lost the fishermen who were pretty much part-time fishermen. We lost some through attrition; these were the people getting older and could not fish anymore. And we created a fishing board to review the license process, and if somebody had a definite hardship, the board could address that and allow them to keep their license.[41]

Commercial fishermen Neil Teskie from, from Gills Rock, held one of the biggest quotas when the quota system was implemented in 1980. He has a bittersweet attitude towards limited entry and the quota system:

In 1979 we went to limited entry and a quota system shortly there after. It did cut us all back; we were catching more fish before we went to quotas. I don't catch my quota every year. There are a lot of guys who don't. It's not because the fish aren't there; it's just the markets take a certain size. I don't know how many thousands of pounds of fish I dumped back this spring; because they were too small for markets. You know when I first started – when our quotas were smaller – my quota was 150,000 pounds. They took a five-year average and then they gave you a percentage. With the onset of the quota system, I had the largest one. I had my dad's license, I had one, and then I bought John Young's quota and rig.

There were some people in the industry that wanted this to eliminate some of the undesirable fishermen, the part-timers. It was not very popular at some of the meetings about the quotas. I went to the task force and submitted a proposal. Basically what it said was with every pound … if you caught one pound you should get a certain percentage of that. If a guy gets 250 pounds of quota at least he can sell that 250 pounds for his investment and it should be based upon how much he caught. The guys that produce the most probably have the most investment, because they have most of the equipment and are the ones that will continue fishing. That's what I proposed. When Paul Goodman sold out, he had 7000 pounds of quota. It gave the guys who were forced out a chance to recoup some of their investment. Really, the quota system cleaned up the fisheries. It got rid of some of the bad fishermen. You just can't be a permanent violator and stay in business.[42]

Geographic Restrictions

The second phase of control was the establishment of a zone management program. Michigan-controlled waters (as well as some areas in Wisconsin waters) were divided into different zones of management — sport, recreational, commercial and rehabilitation zones. Sport zones were for sport fishermen, except for selective harvesting of food and rough fish. Commercial zones were for the commercial fisheries, and all conventional gear was allowed to be used. Rehabilitation zones were the vast majority of Michigan's waters, and in these zones, only impoundment gear, not gill nets, was allowed. Once again, commercial fishermen felt slighted, feeling that they were being forced into narrowly confined areas. The majority of the state's waters were put into rehabilitation zones or sport fishery development zones. In those areas, commercial fishermen were only allowed to use impoundment gear for whitefish, which was viewed by the Michigan DNR as a selective harvest, though commercial fishermen were allowed to take lake trout and salmon on an incidental catch basis.[43]

Commercial fishermen still operating in northern Lake Michigan have come to terms with the regulations and limits, but in 1985, there was still a good deal of active resentment of the new systems. At that time, Marvin Weborg said:

I wouldn't recommend commercial fishing for my grandchildren. There could possibly be a future in it, but according to the rules and regulations, and all the restrictions we have now, they're closing the lake off in lots of areas because of the trout they have planted. We have quotas on chubs, and they're talking quotas on whitefish. They have quotas on perch, and it seems everything is on a quota system. They want to do away with commercial fishing, where they can restrict how many fishermen there can be — limited entry they call it. The license fees we've been paying, $200 a boat is supposed to be $300 this year, and go as high as $1,000 within the next three years. That's another drawback — what about the small fisherman that fishes with a rowboat, fishes under the ice, or whatever situation, he can't afford to have a license under those circumstances.[44]

Restriction of Species Caught & Establishment of Quotas

The third phase was to control the catch of individual species and to establish quotas on certain species. This eliminated some species from commercial status in some regions. With Michigan commercial fishing already dwindling, the Michigan DNR put another nail in the coffin by taking yellow perch and walleye off the commercial list and giving them exclusively sport status. Also, by the mid-1970s, the chub fishery was closed by the Wisconsin DNR, and the Lake Michigan Chub Technical Committee was established in 1974 to address the problem of declining numbers of bloaters and other deepwater ciscoes, or "chubs," as commercial fishermen called them. The committee recommended a lake-wide ban on chub fishing that was then fully enacted by Illinois, Michigan, and Wisconsin in 1976. By 1978, the chub population was showing signs of recovery, and in 1979 chub fishing was once again allowed under a quota system. Wisconsin established a liberal TAC (total allowable catch) of one million pounds (dressed weight) for its chub fishery south of Kewaunee, requiring that no more than one-third be harvested within each successive three-month interval from April 1 to December 31. The TAC, which was increased each year, reached two million pounds in 1982, including 250,000 pounds for waters north of Kewaunee beginning in 1981.[45] Moreover, some of the commercial fishermen remained suspicious and resentful of the chub quota system:

> They closed the chub season for no particular reason. They said it was an endangered species, [but] the boats were running 2,000, 2,500, 3,000 pounds to the lift. The chubs were running so big; they were averaging about two to the pound, which has never been seen since we've been fishing chubs. They closed the season for a year, and then put them on a quota system. It started out that three months you could fish, and now it's up to nine months. When your quota is filled, you have to quit. At first, you could fish chubs only in the fall, but now you can fish from April to December. We always had a full season for chubs during November, which is the spawning season, but now they've changed everything all around. Then they went back to the quota system, and there were plenty of chubs. The reason they shortened the season was because they thought the alewives were depleting, and they wanted to save the chubs for the trout. They were afraid the trout were going to run out of food, and that's the reason they actually closed the season.[46]

Another fisherman wrote letters to the DNR, voicing his opinions:

> I tried to tell them for years when the whitefish were really thick. I told them in letters, probably half a dozen years in a row, what's going to happen here. These fish are going to eat themselves out of food and starve. Let us catch the darn things before that happens – it could be much healthier for them. "No Way!" was more or less their reaction. After the abundance was far enough down, so we couldn't catch them, then they give us all kinds of quotas.
>
> We know why this is happening, [but] we have no clout, and of course there are only a few fishermen and there are 400,000 sport fishermen, and so of course they're [the DNR] trying to take care of the resource. But that's not quite the way to look at it. You've got five million people in this state that should be able to buy a fish when they want to eat one, and they can't buy a Wisconsin fish most of the time. It's a shame, especially when the resource is there.[47]

The biggest controversy began when trout were given sport status, and commercial fishermen could no longer harvest them. After the sea lamprey was controlled in the mid-1960s, lake trout were reintroduced into Lake Michigan through federally funded stocking programs to try to restore the lake trout fishery for both commercial and sport fishermen. However, because lake trout showed no sign of reproducing naturally, they were never given commercial status, and this drew heavy criticism from the commercial fishermen. The DNR view was that they shouldn't be commercially harvested until natural reproduction was documented. However, the commercial fishermen had their own ideas about lake trout, and they saw the issues quite differently. For example:

> **Y**ou know the government has spent millions of dollars on this reproduction program for the lake trout and nobody seems to get any benefits. The sport fisheries can utilize them and the charter boat businesses. How is the John Doe public supposed to get some of their tax dollars back, if you can't produce lake trout and put them on the market? We don't want everything. All we're asking for is maybe a small quota. We're willing to pay so much per fish for replanting. They [the DNR] have to do something. They're wasting so much of a natural resource, it's terrible. I could cry when I think about it. It makes no sense. When a farmer's grain gets ripe, he has to harvest it. When the crop is ripe, you got to harvest it or you lose it.[48]

And again:

> **W**hen the lake trout were eliminated by the lamprey, they had to restock the lake. There's been no natural reproduction since, and they couldn't figure out why. But there just isn't any, not here. In Lake Superior, but not here. We tried to convince them that they should let us pay for some of the cost of raising the fish to fingerling size and then give us a quota on them. I think it's a big mistake that they didn't.
>
> The Michigan DNR started planting salmon thirty years ago [in the 1970s], and of course they did do a real number on the alewives and provided a great sport fishery. Had they [the Wisconsin DNR] spent all that time and effort on lake trout, [they could] have been partially harvested by commercial fishermen. It's a traditional commercial fish. What we tried to do, we tried to tell them you're not getting any natural reproduction, why don't you let us pay for stocking and then give us a quota. That's what could have been done. How many people go out and catch their own fish? Maybe two percent of the population? Here we could have provided good protein food for the consumer. We got a lot of good arguments but no clout, and it could have been very feasible if it worked. They would have been able to propagate the trout no problem. They think they got to do it all with natural reproduction. Well it's not happening. Might as well get used to it. Even if it did, there's a real question if they would ever give us any.[49]

And again:

> **T**hey restocked the lake for trout, and we've never been able to take one trout. The sport fishermen can fish them, which we have no regrets over. There were plenty of trout for the sports fishermen, but we should have been entitled to a percentage, a quota. The money that was used to kill the lampreys by the federal government, the restocking of the lake by the federal government [was] for commercial and sport fish-

ermen. So, the commercial fishermen should have had the advantage to that point. We told them [that] when they planted the fish, which they got from Lake Superior, reared them in a hatchery, and brought them down and planted them. We had them on the pound nets, the trap nets, the gill-net boats – they tagged and tagged, and they tagged. All that has been going on for twenty-two years. As far as we know, they have never found reproduction, as far as the trout are concerned. We told them that when they started – there was something wrong with hatchery plantings. They wouldn't reproduce. They've got not only the lake trout, but the salmon, the brook trout, the German brown trout. And the only way they could keep them going is restocking.[50]

Since 1968 the Michigan DNR has had a general policy of reserving lake trout for sport fishermen and excluding their commercial harvest. This has been a bone of contention between commercial fishermen and the DNR ever since, and it lingers to a small extent today.

On December 15, 1975, a civil action was filed regarding the management of the Lake Michigan trout fishery. The plaintiffs were a diverse group of special interest groups and individuals, including Door County fisherman Jeff Weborg, Elaine Johnson, who represented commercial fish processors and wholesale fish dealers operating in Wisconsin, Martha Cook, who represented herself a purchaser and consumer of fish, Al Johnson, who represented commercial restaurant operators who serve fish in the state of Wisconsin; Laddie Fiala, who represented commercial fish market operators in the state of Wisconsin; and Pritz Behlert, who represented grocery store owners and operators who wanted to offer fish for retail sale.

The plaintiffs were up against seventeen defendants, including both individuals and state and federal government agencies, including the Wisconsin DNR, the Wisconsin Secretary of Commerce, the US Secretary of the Interior, the US Secretary of State, the US Fish and Wildlife Service, sport fishing associations, and several other agencies and interest groups. The suit eventually was dismissed by the judge on the grounds that the states had the authority to regulate the fishery.

Restrictions on Gill Nets

The fourth and most controversial control on commercial fishing was the proposal to eliminate the use of gill nets. In 1971, small-mesh gill nets were banned from Lake Huron except in Saginaw Bay by the Michigan DNR. In 1972, they banned all gill nets in all fisheries under Michigan jurisdiction, though there was a four-year grace period to convert to impoundment gear.

There was heated disagreement between sport fishermen and commercial fishermen regarding gill nets. Sport fishermen argued that gill nets were unselective and caught too many fish that were excluded from commercial status. They said that gill nets kill too many fish, since the fish are caught by the gills and die before the net is lifted from the water. They also argued that the nets interfere with sport fishing and recreational boating by limiting access to bays and harbors, and that the use of the new monofilament material for nets was so much more effective that it raised the likelihood of overfishing.[51] The sport fishermen wanted to completely outlaw gill nets and force commercial fishermen to convert to entrapment gear, such as pound nets and trap nets.[52]

Commercial fishermen believed these arguments were based on ignorance of how gill nets work. The gill net was and is the most commonly used type of gear in the commercial fishery. It is as old as the industry itself. Commercial fishermen argued that in certain areas and seasons gill nets are very selective, and they are the only nets that can be effectively used in the lake waters. University of Wisconsin/Madison biologist Ross Horrall sides with the commercial fisherman on this issue, saying, "Ninety-five percent of Lake Michigan cannot be fished with pound nets. Both practically and legally, they can't be used in water deeper than eighty feet, and this restricts their use to just six or eight weeks of the year." He also believes that gill nets can be very selective depending upon the size of mesh and where the net is placed. "A few tenths of an inch difference in mesh size can eliminate a whole species or size of fish [from being caught]," he adds.[53]

Wisconsin was under considerable pressure to follow Michigan's lead, but the Wisconsin DNR investigated the issue thoroughly and decided against banning gill nets, with the express purpose of maintaining a viable commercial fishery. Fisheries Biologist Mike Toneys comments on the state's decision to retain the use of gill nets:

It has been our position to work towards a viable commercial fishery on Lake Michigan's Wisconsin waters. One of the things we have tried to do was to make regulations as flexible as possible for the commercial fishermen so they had a variety of gear to use out there. One type of gear does not fit all situations for harvesting. And yet we have tried to control the amount of gill net used and where it was used, to minimize incidental kill. Fishermen from other states around Wisconsin have put pressure on sport fishermen here to put pressure on the DNR to get rid of the killer gill net. It has caused a lot of headaches over the years, and we have spent a lot of time trying to defend our position on the use of gill nets in the commercial fishery.

It is probably fifty-fifty right now, although the last ten years or so, it has gone more towards trap nets. There are some years when some of the fishermen feel compelled to go back to gill nets, because trap nets are not getting the fish they need. They are not getting deep enough with them. We have probably gone more to an entrapment-gear fishery than a gill-net fishery, but the fishermen like to have the option of using both. We have allowed them to continue using both, although it has created a lot of management headaches and user conflicts. We have tried to walk a fine line and leave those options out there, and yet try to placate sport fishermen and keep the lake trout program going. It is much more difficult to administer than Michigan policy; they just outlawed the gear, period.[54]

The gill-net ban spread through Michigan's waters like a giant wave that was poised to wipe out many of the gill-netters. The Michigan legislature adopted a compensation bill that allocated $1.5 million for the commercial fisheries, but the amount was cut in order to balance the 1974-75 budget. The Michigan DNR was instructed not to implement the gill-net ban until funds became available. The

Michigan DNR figured that approximately 86 licensed gill-net fishermen would receive compensation which would be paid out to fishermen who fell into three categories: large-mesh, small-mesh, and those who used both. The compensation fund was based on the total value of fish caught in gill nets during the three-year period 1971-1973. It amounted to about 83 percent of a fisherman's average annual catch over the three years, and it helped some fishermen to buy new gear and some older fishermen who were ready to retire to supplement their retirement funds. But, for fishermen who hadn't been fishing too hard, it was really no help at all.[55]

Restriction of Net Mesh Size

During the late 1930s, new regulations were issued concerning the mesh size of gill nets for certain commercial species. Specifically, in 1939 in the southern part of Green Bay, gill nets for herring, bluefin, chubs, perch, menominees, and smelt had to have a mesh of not less than 2 3/8 inches and not more than 2 3/4 inches, and effective July 1, 1940, such nets had to have a mesh not less than 2 1/2 inches, though smelt had a special rule when fished between January 1 and April 14. In Lake Michigan and in the northern part of Green Bay, effective November 21, 1939, gill nets for lake trout, whitefish, suckers, and carp had to have a mesh not less than 4 1/2 inches, flexible rule measure, and gill nets for herring, bluefins, chubs, perch, menominees, and smelt were required to have a mesh not less than 2 1/2 inches and not more than 2 3/4 inches, flexible rule measure, though here too smelt had special rules January 1 to April 14. Gill nets used under the ice for herring were allowed from 1 December until the ice went out, were required to have a mesh of not less than 2 1/4 inches, and had to be suspended from the ice so as to remain at least five feet off the bottom of the lake or bay – furthermore, effective July 1, 1940, the mesh of such gill nets had to be not less than 2 1/2 inches nor more than 2 3/4 inches, flexible rule measure.[56] Mesh size limits did not sit well with many of the gill-net fishermen:

> There's no question that we thought that some of the regulations were way off base. The Conservation Commission reached an arbitrary size of mesh for chubs [in 1939], which was 2 1/2 inches, and a lot of the old fishermen said that's not appropriate, because the normal adult size for a chub is a fish that is caught in a 2 3/8 inch mesh. We went to a smaller mesh and the DNR confiscated a lot of our nets. Now the same thing is happening right now [2003]. For years and years there were plenty of chubs and you could catch them in a 2 1/2 inch mesh. Now we are going with a tighter mesh. They confiscated a lot of nets, and we thought that they were way off base. The market took care of a lot of the problem. There was very little sale for small fish, because there were so many, and so you needed to catch bigger fish. You really didn't need the regulations, but the DNR went out of their way to seize equipment and confiscate gear and what not. This day they don't fool around at all. They'll confiscate your boat.[57]

In 1969, the Wisconsin DNR closed nearly the entire lake to large-mesh gill-net fishing. The only area to remain open to large-mesh fishing was an area north of Baileys Harbor in northern Door County, and the waters of Green Bay. As a result of this action, large-mesh fishing activity, which previously ranged from Rock Island in Door County to the Illinois state boundary was now limited to the northeast corner of the state's waters. Several years later, this led to a confrontation between the NWCFA and the DNR. Because some gill nets had been found in the restricted zone, the DNR set up a "red can" buoy at Baileys Harbor and restricted commercial fishing south of it. The "Red Can" case went to court, and, in April 1977, a circuit court judge voided part of the DNR regulations, but the DNR was able to continue to enforce the policy, and anyone fishing south of Baileys Harbor could be subject to arrest, confiscation of fishing gear, and impoundment of all fish.[58]

During the 1970s and 1980s, many commercial fishermen feared and loathed the DNR, and many felt they had to keep an eye out – that there was a warden behind every tree. To many commercial fishermen, some wardens seemed to carry out their duties in a militia style, searching fish boats at random, carrying out "sting" operations, and seizing equipment and rigs. New regulations were being passed providing for increased license fees and stiffer penalties for commercial fishing violations. By the 1980s, a commercial fisherman automatically lost his license for a second conviction in a period of three years for taking an illegal fish or using illegal gear. But, there were times when fishermen inadvertently harvested undersized fish, or when gear may have become illegal for reasons over which the fisherman had no control, such as gill-net mesh shrinking under regulation size, or currents causing a net to possibly drift into a closed zone. It is true that some fishermen were knowingly violating the rules and deserved their penalties, as any honest fisherman would concur, and not all the wardens were out to get the fishermen. But there were some that seemed to abuse their power and authority. One incident occurred when a DNR informant tried to get a commercial fisherman to sell lake trout illegally:

> They had a woman with a tape recorder on her. One of our crewmembers was on the boat then. I went to the shed to work on nets, and he stayed on the boat to sell fish. They [had] approached us before and wanted a – she wouldn't say trout – she wanted a big fish to give to her boyfriend. So we gave her a trout. Well, she and her party came back, and they wanted to buy a couple of hundred pounds for a fish boil up in Minnesota. They said they were from Minnesota, you see, which was a lie. And so then we gave them the fish, well then they came back and wanted a thousand pounds of trout – we couldn't get a thousand pounds for them. We had another fisherman saving some for us, and he almost got in trouble too. They boarded him and were looking for trout, but they didn't find any. Anyway, that particular day when they were going to put the sting on us, our crewmember took them to where the fish were. They got the fish. There were fourteen game wardens at the dock, the district attorney, and the sheriff. There were twenty guys there to take the boat away from us. I remember one of the wardens along with my partner came to the shed where I was working and said if we [didn't] admit that we were selling these trout, they would take our boat. And so I had to admit to it. We got to court with them, and

before the trial came up, the judge threw it out. He said you don't know where these trout were caught – if they were caught in Michigan waters or Wisconsin waters. And so then they tried again to take us to court and again it was thrown out, because it was entrapment. So they lost the case.[59]

In summary, it is fair to say that there was a good deal of animosity and hard feelings between wardens and commercial fishermen, and there even were incidents where physical altercations took place between them, but their relationship was not all conflict and discord.[60] Jeff recalled one particular incident back in the 1970s when an altercation developed:

> One fall we were out in nasty weather and we were coming into Rowleys Bay with the boat. At that time the DNR wardens were arresting you for anything and everything that they could figure out. What it boiled down to, for example, if you were out driving on the road and the speed limit was 55 and you were going 57, you got pinched. Those years, a couple of pinches, you could lose your license. There were things going on that I didn't think was right. One of the things I didn't agree with was wardens searching the boats and that particular day we came in and docked in Rowleys Bay, and here they show up. There were two of them, and they were going to search our boat. I asked them if they had a warrant. They told me they didn't need a warrant. "Well, yes you do," I said. "Maybe on another boat, you don't, but on this boat you do. If you don't have a warrant I'm going to go about my business. If you got a warrant you can do what you want until such time you can get out of here." Well, it ended up I turned my back to them and started back to my boat when one of them jumped on my back. The other one was going to hit me with his club. We got into a bit of a scuffle. We ended up taking our boat back out and coming over here to Gills Rock with the fish on the boat, and then we were taken to Sturgeon Bay. We ended up going to court and beat them with a jury trial. At that point, that was the turning point in the whole war with the DNR. [61]

In the mid 1970s, Wisconsin, with its substantial commercial fisheries, had the most lenient policies and regulations of any state in the Great Lakes jurisdiction. For a time in the late 1960s, Wisconsin followed Michigan's lead on certain policies, but Wisconsin never implemented a total gillnet ban, though there was mounting pressure from regional and local sport groups, commercial fishermen, researchers, and lakeside communities for common Lake Michigan policies and regulations.

In the early 1970s, Wisconsin's Lieutenant Governor, Martin Schreiber, proposed some ideas that were a breath of fresh air for the commercial fishing industry and were far different from neighboring states' policies. For one thing, he disapproved of the ban on chubs in regional areas, and was a strong advocate for sustaining the commercial fishery in the state. He thought that a commercial quota on lake trout should be considered to help keep the commercial fishing industry going. He was in favor of the "put and take" concept for lake trout, which meant, more or less, planting and harvesting trout on a strictly controlled basis, with the commercial fisheries bearing the cost of planting the species.[62] He also stressed that commercial fishermen should have due process in all aspects of their dealings with the DNR However, though Schreiber had some good ideas when he was Lieutenant Governor, they seemed to fishermen to fall somewhat to the wayside after he became Governor.

The Present and Future Fisheries Forecast

As long as there are commercial fishermen and healthy fish stocks there will be a commercial fishery. This seems easy to predict, but it's hard to give a true forecast. The ecology of the lakes is forever changing, commercial fish stocks are cyclic, markets ebb and flow; and many other variables will affect the future of the fisheries.

In 2004, the whitefish population in Lake Michigan is abundant, but it has varied dramatically over the past century, and still varies in the short term with weather conditions. During the late 1800s, the annual commercial whitefish harvest averaged around 600,000 pounds. By 1958, it had declined to around 9,000 pounds, but there was a major recovery in the early 1970s, when it rose to 300,000 pounds.   In 1999, the statistics show a staggering 1.9 million pounds of whitefish were harvested. Today, in 2006, there are fewer fishermen fishing the waters of Lake Michigan than at any time in the past one hundred years. In Wisconsin in 2002, there were only 80 whitefish licenses in three zones.[63]

Commercial fisherman Jeff Weborg commented:

> The whitefish stocks seem to be good for now. We seem to be getting good recruitment, but growth rates are much slower, because we feel there isn't enough feed. There are so many things that are affecting the lake. To say how it is? Nobody knows, and tomorrow they could be gone. Why? Well if it was twenty years ago, I could tell you why this happened, or what's going to happen, because you had a track record. What's going on in the lake now, there is no track record. It seems now there are too many things that are affecting the ecology to define what's going on. The whitefish today are switching their diet to zebra mussels. When they started doing that a few years ago, the fish were incredibly skinny, now they have more fat on them. They're a little bit healthier fish now. The other issue is marketing. Marketing has become very difficult.[64]

Phil Moy, a fisheries specialist from the University of Manitowoc Sea Grant Program, noticed a change in the feeding habits of the whitefish that probably accounts for part of the reason the fish appeared rather thin a few years back:

> We've noticed the *Pontoporeia* shrimp, which is a major food source of the whitefish, disappearing. It was found in [populations of] tens of thousands per square meter on the bottom of the lake, now it's down to zero in a lot of areas. There seem to be more along the west coast of Lake Michigan than other parts of the lake, so we're lucky here. The whitefish now have been feeding on quagga mussels, which are relat-

ed to the zebra mussels, but smaller and found in deeper water.[65]

However, Dennis Hickey disagrees about the shortage of certain food species for the whitefish:

Somebody did a study and they weren't finding any *Pontoporeia* one year. I just got done picking that stuff off the chub eggs. The chubs are just full of them, when you go to dress them. They just explode, they're feeding so heavy. They [the experts] do this. It gets you so damn mad. They get everyone all worried. How do they know this? They never checked this before; they say it's declining — we've got a problem here. How do they know it's not supposed to be that way? The chubs are full of it. We told them last year. Just because where they went to look for them they weren't there, doesn't mean that it's declining.[66]

Speaking of the future of commercial fishing and the changing ecology of the lake with the new exotic species such as the zebra mussels, white perch, and round gobies, Rick Johnson, a commercial fisherman from Gills Rock said:

Now they claim there's more whitefish than ever before in the lake, but if you go by our catches in the last couple of years, [2001-03] you wouldn't think so. As far as the future of commercial fishing, I think it has a lot to do with the ecology of the lake. It's a little scary. You don't see the whitefish in the areas where you used to see them, like North Bay. The pound netters and trap netters used to really catch them in there during the spring of the year. The last few springs, that area has been just terrible. I keep hoping it will turn around and get back to the way it was about six years ago, when you could go out in the bay with just three or four boxes of nets. It seems like the Dead Sea now. For several years in a row, you knew where the fish were, and you could almost follow them. You knew where they were going to be. That's the scary part of fishing now, is the changes in the lake.[67]

When asked what it was going to take to be a commercial fishermen in the twenty-first century, most concur that fishermen are going to have to change their ways to some degree. Jeff Weborg commented:

In order to be a fisherman in the twenty-first century you're going to have to be a businessman and not a fisherman. I mean that in a respectful way. The old fishermen – and we still have a few of them around, not older guys but [guys] still operating under the old thought pattern – think if I catch one hundred pounds of fish and I get a dollar a pound, I made a hundred dollars – I'm rich. But, [what if] the price of fish goes down to fifty cents a pound and I have to double the amount of gear I have in the water and hire another guy to help me and spend more time in getting double the fish and I still get my one hundred dollars? He never takes into account what it costs to produce those two hundred pounds of fish, so he never took that into consideration. That was the old tradition – if the price goes down, I have to catch more fish. You just can't do that any more. Now days you have to figure out how to catch less and get more. It's not how many fish I can catch, but how to get more for what I catch, and that's a real challenge. Marketing has become a real issue, and that's what I see as the biggest challenge for today and tomorrow.[68]

Rick Johnson basically agreed:

You definitely have to be a better businessman and cater to the public buying your product. The only thing that kept me going for the last three or four years has been selling locally. You have to do more work in processing the fish for fish boils. You know in the long run it's worth it. You have to deal with people that way and cater to their needs. In my case, it entails driving to Ephraim once a day to deliver fish.[69]

Neil Teskie of Gills Rock commented:

I came into the business through my dad. I had a starting point, just like the Weborg's. They got into the business through their dad, just like many other fishermen. There was a starting point. If you had to go out and buy everything, it's a tremendous overhead. The markets haven't been that good the last few years. There are not [as many] buyers as there once were. Fulton market in New York used to have whitefish all up and down the state. Now it's all ocean fish, and a lot of salmon is readily available because it's farm raised. I sell locally here for the fishboils. I have a couple of sizable accounts, and it's a pretty big draw here. I sell fresh whitefish, chubs, and smoked whitefish and chubs.

　　　　If I could change anything to improve the fishery, I would have to say market conditions. I've been doing this for thirty-eight years, and I would say the market prices haven't changed that much during that time. It could be better for us. Our markets haven't kept up with inflation, and we're selling fish at prices that shouldn't be. Prices should be a little higher. I actually found, like other guys have, some other ways to market differently, like selling larger fish only and not harvesting the small ones. I don't think the future is bad. I think the industry all the way around right now in Door County is going through a little rough time, which is not unusual. It's not with the fish so much, but the markets.[70]

Charlie Henriksen said emphatically that the biggest problem is:

Market conditions! The last two years have been [2001-03] horrible. There are two things happening. One was when the tribes took over all the fisheries up in Michigan. We thought they'd produce less, but they opened up all kinds of new fishing grounds and they actually produced a considerable amount of fish, which eventually began to flood the markets. But really the weakness of the dollar is killing us. We're not talking nickel and dime stuff here. We expect to get an average price of a dollar, and when you're only getting 70 cents that makes a big difference. We produce 200,000 pounds of whitefish a year. That's big money. We're selling a lot of whitefish and chub roe to Sweden, but the dollar is worth only half of what it was ten years ago [against the kroner]. The salmon really put a dent in our market as well. The production of salmon has skyrocketed in the last ten or twelve years, there is so much salmon worldwide. You can get salmon at every restaurant in this country.[71]

Dennis Hickey, a commercial fisherman from Baileys Harbor, remarked:

Today [2002] the market is so unstable we just don't know how it's going to be tomorrow. I haven't set as many trap nets this year, because we're not sure how the markets are going to be. The Indian fishery, the way it is in northern Michigan, they generally flood the markets. There's no sense trying to fish. We're competing with that, so you can hardly sell the fish. Last year we wound up scooping a lot of fish overboard. I couldn't sell them, thousands of pounds we let go. We're only fishing half of our trap nets. Between the boats and our trap-net rigs we have the potential to harvest a lot of fish. But what's the sense? You wind up flooding the market, and some days the market won't even take any. I don't understand why some of the fishermen in the county are doing that. They're going nuts and pounding the nets in there. I said what the hell, I'd as soon fish less nets. Some of those guys have big crews. I have all part-time help, and young guys working the nets. Otherwise you end up bleeding the hell out of yourself all year.[72]

Jake Ellefson added:

I would have loved to have my boys on the island making their living here – give them our outfit. But it doesn't do much good if there isn't enough fish to make a living. It's not easy. That's the way it is now [2002]. In Michigan, it's all tribal fishing. We knew that it was going to happen. That's why I couldn't encourage my boys. We had a great outfit, but what good is that if you can't make a living. I figured I would have had to invest $200,000 to get a good entrapment rig. To have a good boat you can spend $100,000, and you have to have a good boat here on the island [because you] have to travel to areas like Big Bay. You need to have at least thirty entrapment nets and a darn good man to run them to stay competitive in this day and age. I figured the boys could have done that, but what happens when you run out of fish? I was just lucky, you know, really lucky that I was able to make my living. That there was enough fish to sustain my career.[73]

With fewer commercial fisheries in the state of Wisconsin and only six full-time fishermen left in Door County, there's a general need for commercial fishermen not to supply consumers, but also to aid the DNR in monitoring the status of the lake.
Said Dennis Hickey:

I think with the reduction in the number of commercial licenses, they [the DNR] are going to have to work more with us. Things are going to change in the next few years. They're going to have to recognize us as a viable research tool for them. They're starting to go to state licensing, or trying to anyway. They've been working on it for three or four years now, but then they're going to have to start protecting the fishermen in order to monitor what's going on out in the lake. If they totally lost the fishery, there is no way the DNR, with their boats and only going out one or two days a month, that they're ever going to know what's going on. We're the best source of information they could get as far as monitoring what the status is out on the lake.[74]

Some new proposals are being introduced that could affect the commercial fisheries in a positive way. However, many fishermen believe that to survive tomorrow in this business the DNR has to give them more slack to run their businesses. Asked what could be done to improve the fishery, one Door County fisherman said:

The biggest thing would be to get the DNR to relax some of their trivial regulations. For example, we had a couple of fishermen up here get cited for not having their license number displayed properly on their net buoys. Something like that you shouldn't be able to lose your license over. Stuff like that would make life a little easier and also the reporting. If you sell somebody ten pounds of fish, or fifteen, they want you to write their name and address down and submit it to them.[75]

There are changes in the works that will benefit commercial fishermen, including changing to an electronic reporting system. Also, the DNR and the commercial fishermen reached a compromise that alters the chub fishing "60 fathoms for six weeks" rule by changing it to 45 fathoms for a twelve week period.
Said Dennis Hickey:

We have five licenses for our five boats. We have to pay a license fee anyway, so now what we're working on with the DNR is trying to get electronic recording and also trying to get the fleet license put into effect so that you actually record all five boats as one license. It would cut down on the amount of paperwork and be a lot easier for the department to keep track of. Now we're filling out daily, weekly, monthly, biweekly, and wholesale reports too. You have to have the daily report all filled in before you hit the dock with the estimated pounds. Then, when you weigh them, you have to have the actual weight on there. The same thing with electronic recording. We'll have to call in before we get ashore, and then we'll have to call in the total catch for the day. With the system we have now, with multiple licenses, you're totaling all your fish. It gets so complex. That's why we have to simplify it to make it easier on us, and I'm sure it would be a heck of a lot easier for them. They've got mountains of paper work generated by all these reports. They can't even look at it all and don't even know what half of it is.[76]

Commented Rick Johnson, on the subject of electronic reporting:

> **I** think in the long run it will be beneficial to us. It will give us some credibility. I was on the task force that recommended that. However, now a couple of the head guys from the DNR that were on that committee leading the way have retired, and now there's a couple of new guys in there adding their own spin to it. So it sounds like we'll have electronic reporting and still have a bunch of paperwork besides.[77]

Neil Teskie remarked:

> **T**here are certain regulations that should be improved. There are some unnecessary regulations. I don't see any harm in harvesting lake trout. We don't catch many now, but it would be nice to offer the consumer lake trout. There not really a sport fish. I don't know if it would be an improvement or not, but it's better than throwing them away dead, if you're catching them. I still think some of the regulations need to be looked at. I'm in favor of this electronic reporting. We want this. Now, the way it's set up, if I want to transfer fish from the *Frances* to the *Betty*, or if I want to use another boat, or if I want to fish more gear off the *Betty* than I got the license for, I have to transfer a license. Electronic reporting is going to make multiple licenses under one heading. All my gear will be interchangeable. As a matter of fact they were going to issue me a citation because I fished 2000 more feet of gill net one day last year than I should have. But I have three licenses, I can fish 12,000 feet per license, so I should be able to set 36,000 feet of gill nets, which I'm not going to do. If I had the fleet reporting system I wouldn't have this citation. There has been a number of people getting citations or have been inconvenienced by not being able to transfer fish.[78]

Commercial fisherman Ken Koyen from Washington Island had a ready response when asked one thing that he would change to improve the commercial fishery:

> **S**almon. Allowing salmon to be caught instead of dying and rotting away. I'm not talking about incidental catch or anything. I'm talking about come fall now when salmon are spawning, they should be fished with an 8 1/2 inch mesh gill net so you would only catch fish twenty pounds or bigger. [Keep track of them] with tags. I don't care if they were ten dollars a tag. Sell the fish. The DNR gets their share of the money for replanting. It's ridiculous. If you want salmon, you have to buy it from Alaska.[79]

One thing is very evident now compared to the past. There are fewer fishermen harvesting the waters of Lake Michigan. Some say the future looks pretty bleak, and the way things are going with all the restrictions and regulations, and without any of the younger guys breaking into this profession, there may not be a commercial fishery left by 2050. According to retired commercial fisherman Alvin Anderson:

You have to have rules, but some of these regulations and rules we're under now, there's no call for them whatsoever. It's all politics and it's a waste of a resource. I don't know if it will ever change. Probably after it's too late. You know, you count all the fishermen left today. How old are they, and how old are the youngest ones? Maybe forty? All the rest of them are older. The average age is probably fifty-five or sixty. Twenty years from now, 99 percent of all the fishermen will be beyond sixty-five. Then what's going to happen? The industry is dead. It's over! I've been thinking about this quite seriously. I've been trying to figure out what the average age is. By 2025, all you'll see is a bunch of boats lying by the dock that 99 percent of the people won't even know what they were or what they were used for. That's what will happen.[80]

The Last Fish Tug

Morning breaks with her devout silence
Over the harbor like amber glass;
Yesterdays storm and white-capped waves relents,
Leaving the harbors hull a placid mass.

A weathered dock moors no boats
And slips down more to waters side,
A seasoned reflection still floats
Where once fish tugs used to reside.

No nets spun out to dry on racks
That stands like crosses for a grave,
And sounds of sparrows sift through cracks
Of an empty shed's weathered staves.

Smell of wood smoke in the distance –
Redolent of something I knew yesterday,
Takes me back there for an instant
Where chubs were smoked and hung in gold display.

To see once more the tugs returning,
Splitting water from wooden hulls;
Hear once again the hungry calling,

Overhead, the white cloud of gulls.

Morning goes down like a sinking stone –
One old fish tug, all that remains,
Idle in her slip moored alone,
Paint-peeled and forgotten by name.

A fish box, empty, gone to gray;
A sad reminder so it seems,
How everything fades away,
Like some old fishermen's dreams.

Chapter 7 Notes

1. Margaret Beattie Bogue, *Fishing the Great Lakes* (University of Wisconsin Press, 2000), 98.

2. Interview with Joe LeClair, January 10, 2002.

3. Margaret Bogue, Op. cit., 99.

4. Pete LeClair, "Harvesting the Inland Seas: Great Lakes Commercial Fishing" video Wisconsin Maritime Museum.

5. Jacob Ellefson, handwritten letter, March, 2003.

6. Interview with Jeff Weborg, December 13, 2002.

7. Lon Kopitzke, "Interview with Marvin Weborg," *Door County Almanac No. 3* (Dragonsbreath Press, 1986), 304.

8. Margeret Beattie Bogue, *Fishing the Great Lakes* (Madison, WI: University of Wisconsin Press,2000), 175-176.

9. Margaret Bogue, *Fishing the Great Lakes*, 181.

10. Conan Bryant Eaton, *Washington Island 1836-1876*, 3rd edition (Jackson Harbor Press, 1997), 70.

11. The next several paragraphs are drawn largely from Conan Bryant Eaton, "Door County Fisheries: The First Fifty Years," *Door County Almanac, No.3* (Dragonsbreath Press, 1986), 25-33.

12. Ibid., 28.

13. Tom Kuchenberg, *Reflections In A Tarnished Mirror*, (Golden Glow Press, 1978), 43.

14. Ibid.

15. Ibid.

16. Michael J Chiarappa and Kristin M. Szlvian, *Fish For All: An Oral History of Multiple Claims and Divided Sentiment on Lake Michigan*, (East Lansing, MI: University of Michigan Press, 2003), 492.

17. Ibid., 495.

18. Ibid, 531-532.

19. Ibid., 531-532.

20. Tom Davis, "To Preserve a Way of Life," *Door County Almanac No. 3*; (Sister Bay, WI: Dragonsbreath Press, 1986), 105.

21. Ibid.

22. Interview with Jake Ellefson, July 5, 2003.

23. Interview with Elaine Johnson, January 16, 2003.

24. Interview with Rick Johnson, January 1, 2003.

25. Lake Michigan Fisheries Forum.

26. Interview with Charlie Henriksen, December 13, 2002.

27. Interview with Charlie Henriksen, December 13, 2002.

28. Interview with Jake Ellefson, May 4, 2003.

29. Tom Kuchenberg, *Reflections In A Tarnished Mirror*, 88.

30. Keta Steebs, "Local Fish Manager Tells Why DNR Supports Senate Bill 409," *Door County Advocate*,

31. Chiarrappa and Szylvian, *Fish For All* (Michigan State University Press, 2003), 625.

32. Interview with Jeff Weborg, December 13, 2002.

[33] Interview with Charlie Henriksen, December 13, 2002.

[34]. Chiarappa and Szylvian, *Fish For All*, 628.

[35] Interview with Charlie Henriksen, December 13, 2002.

[36]. Interview with Jake Ellefson, May 4, 2002.

[37]. Interview with Dennis Hickey, September 27, 2002.

[38]. Interview with Jeff Weborg, September 14, 2002.

[39]. Keta Steebs, "Senate Bill 409," *Door County Advocate*,

[40] Interview with Dennis Hickey September 27, 2002.

[41] Chiarappa and Szylvian, *Fish For All*, (Michigan State University Press, 2003), 629.

[42] Interview with Neil Teskie, July 2, 2003.

[43]. Chiarappa & Szylvian, *Fish For All*, (Michigan State University Press 2003), 120.

[44]. Lon Kopitzke, "An Interview With Marvin Weborg Along With His Son Mark," *Door County Almanac No.3* (Dragonsbreath Press, 1986), 156-158.

[45]. Edward H. Brown, Ronald W. Rybicki, and Ronald Poff, "Population Dynamics and Interagency Management of the Bloater In Lake Michigan, 1967-1982," *Technical Report No. 44*, (Great Lakes Fishery Commission 1985), 30.

[46]. Lon Kopitzke, "An Interview With Marvin Weborg Along With His Son Mark," *Door County Almanac No.3*, 156-158.

[47]. Interview with Jake Ellefson, October 2, 2001.

[48]. Interview with Alvin Anderson, March 29, 2003.

49. Interview with Jake Ellefson, May 4, 2003.

50. Lon Kopitzke, Op. cit.

51. Tom Kuchenberg, *Reflections In A Tarnished Mirror*, 90.

52. Linda Weimer, "Pound Nets Impractical Says DNR Fish Manger", *Door County Advocate*, January 22, 1976.

53. Ibid.

54. Michael Chiarappa and Kristen Szylvian, *Fish For All*, 618.

55. Tom Kuchenberg, *Reflections In A Tarnished Mirror*, 92.

56. *Commercial Fishing Regulations sheet*, Nov, 1939, Obtained from the Washington Island Archives.

57. Interview with Jake Ellefson, October 2, 2003.

58. "Local Fish Manager Tells Why DNR Supports Senate Bill 409," *Door County Advocate*.

59. Interview with Harold Greenfeldt, July 5, 2003.

60. Interview with Jeff Weborg, September, 2002.

61 Interview with Jeff Weborg, December 13, 2002.

62. Kuchenberg, *Reflections In a Tarnished Mirror*, 104.

63. *Green Bay Press Gazzette*, Oct 20, 2002.

64. Interview with Jeff Weborg, December 13, 2002.

65. Interview with Phil Moy, January 9, 2003.

66. Interview with Dennis Hickey, February 10, 2003.

67. Interview with Rick Johnson, March 14, 2003.

68. Interview with Jeff Weborg, December 13, 2002.

69. Interview with Rick Johnson, March 14, 2003.

70. Interview with Neil Teskie, July 2003.

71. Interview with Charlie Henriksen, December 13, 2002.

72. Interview with Dennis Hickey, September 27, 2002.

73. Interview with Jake Ellefson, July 4, 2002.

74. Interview with Dennis Hickey, September 27, 2002.

75. Interview with Neil Teskie, July 3, 2003.

76. Interview with Dennis Hickey, October 12, 2002.

77. Interview with Rick Johnson, March 14, 2003.

78. Interview with Neil Teskie, July 3, 2003.

79. Interview with Ken Koyen, May 4, 2002.

80. Interview with Alvin "Gabby" Anderson, April 26, 2005.

Part II — Washington Island

Chapter 8

Washington Harbor

Washington Harbor, with its deep waters and white wave-worn shores, lies on the northern end of Washington Island. It is one of the most beautiful geographic creations the glaciers formed out of Lake Michigan. A shoreline of white limestone cobbles, rounded and worn smooth by the waves, is one of the attractions of this splendidly sheltered harbor. A fringe of cedar trees keeps vigil along the azure water, and then, back from the water, gives way to an association of mixed hardwoods that host a rich variety of bird and animal life.

At the northwest end of the harbor looms Bowyers Bluff, a 200-foot escarpment rising out of the waters of Green Bay and sheltering the harbor from the westerly fall gales. South of Bowyers Bluff is a clearing called Mount Misery, named by the Potawatomi Indians who inhabited Washington Island for many years. Jesse Miner, one of the island's first residents, recalls in his diary that he went up there to borrow a headdress to be used in a school project.[1]

The bluff at the northeastern end of the harbor was known as Rowe's Point. A limestone quarry operated there until 1870. The southern shore of the harbor is lower and gradually rises into rolling hills. Today, the harbor presents few reminders of the thriving community that once was there. Personal watercraft, speedboats, water skiers, and sport fisherman have claimed these waters, and the harbor is now merely recreational, where once it was a means of survival and prosperity. For both the indigenous inhabitants, the Potawatomi Indians, and the German, Irish, and Scandinavian immigrants who came later, this was an ideal place for a settlement and community.

One of the first settlers and landowners in Washington Harbor was Amos Saunders, a steamboat captain from Green Bay who sailed for ten years on the Great Lakes before settling on Washington Island in 1844. He had been looking to get out of sailing and thought he might dabble in real estate, so he purchased land on Rock Island, but then sold his Rock Island holdings to John Boon and purchased three government lots around Washington Harbor in 1846. Saunders built a dock there and constructed a slip to protect it from storms and moving ice. He also had an icehouse, and he shipped cordwood and fish from the dock. Fishermen were continuously arriving in the area, perhaps due to Lapham's book *Wisconsin*, which attracted many immigrants to the region,[2] By 1849, a government geological survey under Foster and Whitney reported that there were fourteen boats with fifty fishermen at Washington Island, and ten boats with thirty fishermen at Rock Island. [3]

In 1848, Wisconsin entered the union and thus became an even more promising area for settlement. Europe at this time was in a bad political and economic state, and large numbers of immigrants were settling in this region. Steam vessels plying Lake Michigan were glad to fuel their boilers with cordwood that was abundant on the island, and this became a profitable business for some of the islanders, beginning in the 1850s. Whitefish and lake trout were present in great abundance and were easy to catch, and for the first time, fisherman actually received cash for their fish, and the prices were good. Gone were the days of shipping fish to Chicago markets to barter for flour and other goods.

Throughout the early history of Washington Harbor, men who had money monopolized the land and held it in large tracts. However, some early settlers had built cabins, docks, and other structures without purchasing the land, and many were still occupying it, their scattered shacks, sheds, and docks arranged in village-like clusters. The following is extracted from an article that appeared in the *Green Bay Advocate* in 1851:

Lake Michigan Fisheries

Very few, we believe, are aware of the extent to which fishing is carried along the shores of Green Bay, and the numerous islands near it. The principal fishing points on and near the route from Green Bay to Mackinac are at Grand Traverse, Fish Creek, Washington Harbor, Rock Island, and the Fox and Beaver Islands. Here far away from civilized life, the hardy fisherman seeks a favorable location, cuts away the pines sufficiently to give room for his little house and for the drying of his nets, and commences his laborious and hazardous work. His life is a life of chance. Chance sends him large or small "hauls." Chance regulates the visits of vessels or steamers to his little dock for the purchase of his stock, and it's a good chance which furnishes him with flour and the comforts of life as he needs them. But chance, it seems, deals well with him generally. He is hale and hearty; his fish command a ready sale in the market; and we have never seen better pictures of cozy and contented life than those fishing establishments, with their white lake beach, their snug houses surrounded with long lines of nets in course of drying, their little piers, the handsome boats drawn up on shore. . . .

The perfect cleanliness about these establishments is worthy of note. The beach is white and clean, and the water which drives in upon it is uncontaminated by even a particle of offal. . . . The high price of fish this spring has naturally increased the force employed in the business, and stimulated all to the most active exertion. The statistics of the trade for the present year will probably show figures already exceeding those of the whole of any previous year.

While upon this subject, we cannot forbear to mention the fishery belonging to our townsman, Captain Saunders, at Washington Harbor. He has got the finest harbor on the route, and the place, with its storehouse, boarding, cooper, and fish houses, has the appearance of an active little village. There is also a fine wharf, well laden with dry wood, and an icehouse, containing some forty cords of such ice as is only found in these northern waters.[4]

In June of 1850, a small group of islanders met on Rock Island at Henry Miner's cabin and decided that a township should be formed to establish some law and order on the island, to keep records of property rights, and perform a census. Thus, in 1850, the Town of Washington was born, and Amos Saunders became the first chairperson. In his diary, Jessie Miners gives an account of how, when and why Washington Island became a township:

The town of Washington was organized on June 20, 1850, on Rock Island, on lot 2, section 23, at the home of Henry D. Miner. I blessed the meeting. I was two weeks old. The men disagreed about something and they made quite a racket and I began to bawl, and my mother told them they must make less noise or go outside in a hurry, so they concluded to keep quieter. Amos Saunders was appointed Town Chairman; H. D. Miner, Town Clerk; John A. Boon, Justice of the Peace. I cannot find the name of the constables, assessor, etc.

It has been told that the town was organized to prevent the Indians from getting whiskey. When the white men were on the lake and the Indians, about seventy-five of them, got filled up on Forty Rod or Squirrel Whiskey, the white ladies got nervous. All you ladies know how it is yourself. John Oliver and his brother Andrew was [sic] selling stuff to the Indians, but Andrew would not let an Indian have a drop of Skuta Waba (fire water), or whiskey.[5]

In 1851, James M. Craw, a Cleveland, Ohio native ninety years of age, purchased 350 acres in Washington Harbor from Amos Saunders and later added another 172 acres to his holdings. James Craw, although being well up in years was a vibrant and enthusiastic man with many business interests. He became the postmaster to this region and was one of the first land barons, who owned most of the northwest region of Washington Island and all the land around Jackson Harbor. James built up the dock, adding a warehouse, fish sheds, and a sawmill, which was located just up from the dock. He had a boarding house built for workers who he employed. He hired a man by the name of Godfrey Kalmbach, who was in the hotel business from Cleveland, [to] come to the island and run it for him. He also had several fishing crews fishing pound nets and gill nets.

From his best lumber, he built a very large home that he used for a hotel for people stopping over on the passenger boats. This came to be known as the White House and was one of the most prominent landmarks in Door County and remained on that site until 1950. James Craw had invested $3,000 in building a very large barn. The barn caught fire around the middle of February of 1856 and was a total loss. The fire was always said to be very suspicious, and a man by the name of Joel Westbrook was arrested and suspected of arson, and spent eight months in a Green Bay jail, but was cleared of any wrongdoing. Westbrook was going over to get some hay to replace what he had lost when some of Craw's men had taken some hay from his property earlier that fall. It was also at that time two young men went over to the Craws store from St. Martin Island to retrieve some Wig Wag whiskey manufactured by J. M. Craw and Son. The boys were found frozen with the whiskey on the sleigh by Westbrook, who went back to Washington Harbor to report the incident and was taken into custody.[6]

James M. Craw never really recouped emotionally and financially and lost his desire to stay on Washington Island. In 1858, he and William Craw began selling their 1,800 island acres. Their first sale, according to an abstract of sales and deeds, was the dock, White House, and the mill tract on the harbor's west side to New Yorker Frank S. Wilson. In 1860 he was operating the former Craw enterprises, but never found the success that James Craw had. Until late in 1863, ownership of the Craw's former holdings is clouded by apparent duplicate sales and unkept agreements.[7]

In 1863, Willet P. Ranney paid the Door County sheriff $260 for title to the former Craw dock and business property, located on the west side of Jackson Harbor. By 1865, the Ranney brothers had gained title to five government lots of 240 acres and at that time owned land all around Washington Harbor.[8] By the early 1870s the island's population had swelled to more than three hundred people, many dependent on fishing for their livelihood.

W. P. Ranney and his brother Dalbert Ranney had a store in Washington Harbor and bought fish extensively from the fishermen. They shipped as much as two thousand packages annually. Their dock was the island's major metropolis. Dalbert Ranney was well liked and respected by the island citizens, and he was known to be very generous. He set up the first "deferred payment plan"[9] to help out landowners and fishermen when money was tight. When the fishermen needed anything, they went to Ranney and got it on a line of credit. There was trust between W.P. Ranney and the fishermen, and he also worked with some of the local farmers on the same basis. The Ranneys had quite a business operation at Washington Harbor, including a store, a large warehouse, an icehouse, and fifteen to twenty small cottages and dry-houses up on the hill. The Ranney residence was the large White House built by James Craw ten years previously. There were a half-dozen fish boats moored on the dock, and it was there that the Goodrich passenger steamships landed.[10]

A little village of log cabins and a few frame houses were scattered around the dock, some just up the hill, others just north and south of it. Most of the families living around the Ranney dock were Irish, and the settlement was known as the "Irish village." Irish families living there at that time were Tom and Tim Coffey, the Guinan's, Hugh McFadden, the O'Neil's, the McDonald's, and a few other families. They enlivened the area with their vibrant personalities and every now and then they would have a jig competition down on the dock, cheap entertainment and the delight of the coopers, fishermen, sailors, and others who came to see this spectacle.[11]

Some of these fishermen had moved over from St. Martin Island, finding that Washington Harbor had more to offer for their fishing operations. This became the largest fishing community in Door County and northern Lake Michigan. By the turn of the twentieth century, a great number of the Irish, Yankees (easterners, mainly from the New York area), and some Germans had moved away from Washington Island. However, a few of the Irish families remained there and continued to fish and farm. Tim Coffey, Tom Guinen, the McDonalds, and the Kincaids were some of the Irish families that stayed on[12].

In the last days of June, 1870, Michigan's state geologist Alexander Winchell sailed to Washington Island and neighboring islands to make observations, especially about Washington Island:

June 25, 1870 — Washington Harbor I am told by Souci, a Frenchman who fishes from this harbor in Lake Michigan and owns land at this place that there are about three hundred fishermen on the island and one hundred boats. They are "Yankees," Irishmen, Germans, and Danes. He is the only Frenchman on the island. A settlement of several families of Danes and Norwegians is on the west side of the island . . . .

Washington Harbor (camp) — Monday, June 27, 1870 A threatening thunder cloud and gale of wind approaching drove us into an early camp in this beautiful little harbor. Propellers from Buffalo and Green Bay make regular stops at this harbor, taking away great Quantities of fish. Ranney & Co. is the buyers and shippers.

Here I find numerous fishing boats, whose owners are just now considerably agitated about the annual boat race to come off at Beaver Island July 4th. It is expected several fishing boats from this place will compete for prizes . . . .

Washington Harbor village is much scattered about the bay, and contains but two or three good houses, one church, schoolhouse, post office, store, fishermen's houses, cooper shops and warehouses for inspecting and repacking fish.[13]

Prior to the latter part of the nineteenth century, fishermen often used sailing vessels called Mackinaw boats. They were usually 22 to 26 feet in length, and equipped with a tiller and rudder at the stern. Each boat carried two sails. These boats were very seaworthy and had been in use for a very long time on the Great Lakes. Other types of sailboats were in use, such as the square-sterned Huron boat and the Norwegian boat, with large gill-net rigs, but they were not as good as the Mackinaw boat.

The fishermen on Washington Island were the first in Lake Michigan to convert from sail-powered Mackinaw boats to steam power. It occurred during a period of decline of whitefish, and fishermen were seeking better fishing grounds that often meant traveling long distances. Some traveled as far as 15 or 20 miles to set their nets, which made it very difficult to operate in sail-powered craft. With an open sailing vessel, much depended on the wind and weather. Gill nets often were set 10 or even 20 miles from shore, and, in calm weather, fishermen might spend the whole day, sometimes until late at night, rowing out to their nets, overhauling them, and rowing home again. Fishermen often worked all night because the fish had to be dressed and packed before they could call it a night. With a steam engine, a crew could easily handle their tasks and increase both their capacity of nets and the amount of fish harvested. The new steam-powered fishing boats marked a new era of fishing. The first one on Washington Island was the *Kitty Gaylord*, owned by John O' Neil and sons. John O'Neil was a cooper from Ireland and made the trip to the United Stated in 1860 to become a resident of the town of Washington. He lived in the Washington Harbor region with his wife and ten children.

On September 15, 1870 his boys launched a steam tug in the Fox River that had been built to their order in Green Bay. Named the *Kitty Gaylord*, she made her maiden voyage to her home port of Washington Harbor. Her official vessel number was 14279; she was 41 feet by 10.6 feet on the beam, and displaced 13 gross, 8 net tons. She had a high-pressure steam engine with return flues.[14] The local newspaper took note of the new boat:

> Gill net fishing at Washington Island is poorer than it has been for fourteen years.
>
> The nets have to be placed out a distance of 14 or 15 miles and, in some instances, seventy fathoms of water. This makes it a work of difficulty to reach them, one fishing boat having been rowed for ten hours in one trip out to the gangs. The sons of Mr. John O'Neil are fitting up a small propeller to be used in going out to the nets, which promise to be a great success.[15]

The *Kitty Gaylord* was the first fishing steamer on Lake Michigan and was named after the young daughter of Captain G. A. Gaylord, commander of the *Rocket*. The *Rocket* was a steam propeller that brought freight and passengers to Washington Harbor region; she was converted to a barge in 1877. The O'Neil boys began fishing from the *Kitty Gaylord* right away and found they could double their capacity of nets and expand their fishing grounds tremendously. Jesse Miner wrote in his *History of the Town of Washington and Adjacent Islands*, "In the fall of 1870, O'Neil's tug *Kitty Gaylord*, with what would be five two-hundred lead boxes, got 42 barrels of whitefish . . . about the 18th of December.[16]

By the early 1870s pound-net fisheries were becoming more prevalent in the region, as indicated by the number of fishermen acquiring fishing claims from the justices of the peace and then registering them at the courthouse, somewhat like land deeds. To mark such claims, fishermen would inscribe their names on a monument such as a stake or a piece of timber on the beach near their fishing grounds. Some of the men filing fishing claims in 1874 were John Boyce, S. Gunderson and B. Lind, Andrew Irr and Ferdinand LaBack; Patrick O'Neill, Loyal Baker, and Hugh O'Neill, who used the schoolhouse on the beach as a bearing in describing his location.[17]

In the early summer of 1873, a correspondent of Milwaukee's *Journal of Commerce* provided an account of Washington Island and Washington Harbor life, paying close attention to the Ranney dock and operations. At that time the Ranney dock was the major hub of fishing and commerce at Washington Island, though there also was a smaller wood dock on the southeast side of the harbor owned by John Nolan where cord wood was picked up. Eaton discusses the account:

> He was disappointed in not finding the colony of Icelanders he had expected, and was told that only one such remained – a fisherman on Detroit Island. The others were said to have moved on, leaving behind a good reputation; they were so polite, the school master told him, that the other people used to laugh at them.
>
> At the dock in Washington Harbor, the island's "metropolis," the reporter saw the store and warehouse of D.W. Ranney, seemingly the only merchant and principal proprietor of the place. On the steep hillside were clustered fifteen or twenty weather-beaten, gray cottages and dry-houses with stone chimneys. The Ranney residence, [a] large white house with a piazza, looked out prominently among them. Piles of cord wood filled the foreground, and on the dock stood rows of fish barrels just delivered from the steamer. A half dozen fishing boats were tied to a smaller

dock built up with picturesque fish houses of logs and bark, and easterly across the harbor were more boats and scattered gray houses.

The population, including Detroit and Rock Islands and even St. Martin, was estimated at between 250 and 300, with [the] greater number engaged in gill-net or pound-net fishing. Mr. Ranney estimated for him [that] during the past year, Islanders had got out 2,700 cords of wood, 3,500 telegraph poles, 25,000 cedar posts, and 13,000 packages of fish. From 5,000 to 7,000 barrels of salt and 8,000 half barrels were sold per annum, the merchant told him.[18]

In 1873, the Ranney Company sold their extensive fishing establishment and store to John Furlong, a Milwaukee native, for $10,000. The island's economy was faring pretty well, despite low fish prices, but John Furlong saw great potential for the island. In 1874, his work crews were already fixing up the old Ranney dock and buildings. Furlong also bought up most of St. Martin Island and four or five more sections on Washington Island, and in the spring he had purchased the steam tug *Emma Dyer* for his fishery. Thus, in a short period of time he had acquired most of the land around Washington Harbor. He was not well received by some of the island people, since he introduced laws and stipulations that the fishermen and farmers did not like, causing hard feelings.

For example, in 1876 Furlong had seven local island residents charged for trespassing violations. These men had built a dock and a road leading down to it on the harbor's southeast side for transporting cordwood and their goods to markets. Some of these men were well-respected citizens of the island, and one of them was John Larson, who served on the town board. Furlong didn't like them moving in on his business and brought charges of criminal trespass. The men were freed after a few months in jail and had to pay Furlong $15 in damages. A few years later the Furlongs moved back to Milwaukee, though the land remained in the hands of the estate until 1948 when a portion of it was sold to Haldor Gudmundsen.[19]

The largest influx of immigrants to Washington Island came in the 1870s. They were predominately Norwegian, Danish and Icelandic. Most of the newcomers arrived with only a few belongings and not much money, but they brought strong wills and convictions. At that time, many immigrants to this area came first to Milwaukee and from there scattered throughout the state finding jobs as lumberjacks, farmers, fisherman, and laborers.[20]

By April of 1875, the town of Washington election saw more Scandinavians being elected to office. Except for town clerk Robert Severs and Justice Henry Miner, every office was occupied by a Scandinavian. The three-man board of supervisors was Danish, with William Wickman as chairman. John Gislason, an Icelander, became the highway overseer and continued to lay out roads on the island. One new road started from the water on the west side and followed the township line eastward for three miles. Later that year, the town board split the island into two districts, separated by an east-west line from the bay to the lake situated a half mile north of the township line. The land to the south of that line was to be known as School District No. 2. School District No. 1, to the north of it, was served by the school located at Washington Harbor.[21]

That summer a July 4th picnic was held at the Bethel Church grove and was well received by the islanders. Many visitors came that day on the Goodrich Company boat *De Pere*. The picnic was to welcome the Scandinavian newcomers to the island. The summer of 1875 also saw a surge in fish production on the lake. Fishing started slowly in the spring, but then exploded in June. The O'Neils caught ninety-nine packages (kegs) of fish from one haul, leaving twenty kegs for the next day. Other island fishermen were also enjoying high catches of fish.[22]

By the 1870s, Washington Harbor was a self-sufficient community with a small store, a school-house, and a church. Two sawmills furnished lumber cut from the abundant local stands of white pine and hardwood for the docks and buildings. The Craw-Ranney mill was located up the hill from the docks and began operating around 1854. The other mill, located south of the Ranney mill, was owned by Chris (Olson) Saabye, and was later moved to Saabye's property in the middle of the island. Chris Olson had changed his name to Saabye in honor of his native town in Denmark.[23]

In 1900, Washington Harbor was a bustling community. Passenger liners, freighters (locally known as "hookers"), and fishing boats operated to and from this location, making it a major hub of commerce for the islanders, as it had been forty years earlier. Many people, both visitors and new residents, arrived on the regularly scheduled passenger liners, which were steam-propelled boats that plied the Great Lakes. It was quite an event on the island when one of them arrived, and often drew a good crowd. The captain usually would bring newspapers for islanders, since there were no local publications in such a remote area of Door County. The papers were often a few weeks old, but they were current enough for islanders.[24]

During the 1880s, several Hart Line steamboats frequented the port of Washington Harbor. They carried both freight and passengers. Beginning from Green Bay, they went first to Marinette and Menominee, then across the bay to Egg Harbor and up the shore to Fish Creek, Ephraim, Sister Bay, and Ellison Bay before proceeding on to Washington Island, and they sometimes went as far north as Manistique, Michigan, before returning south. The Hart Line was owned by three brothers in Sturgeon Bay. They had several ships in operation to haul passengers and freight to and from the ports they served, and they also carried fresh whitefish and lake trout to markets in Green Bay.[25] At one time, the Hart Line had eight boats in operation: *Eugene Hart, Fanny Heart, Charles MacVea, City of Marquette, Bon Ami, Sailor Boy, Thistle*, and *Petosky*. The Hart Line continued their runs for many years but ceased operations in 1919. They visited Washington Island weekly during the shipping season, including stops both at Washington Harbor and at Detroit Harbor.[26]

Another passenger line that served Washington Harbor was the Goodrich Company based in Chicago. Their ships hauled both freight and passengers and called twice a week at Washington Harbor, stopping both coming from Chicago to Mackinac Island and on the return trip. These were large, impressive boats that always drew a crowd when they arrived. Several different boats stopped at Washington Harbor, including *Carolina, De Pere*, and *Truesdell*. These large steam-powered passenger liners started out from Chicago, touched at various ports along the Wisconsin coast of Lake Michigan, then passed through the ship canal (opened in 1871) at Sturgeon Bay and proceeded to Fish Creek, Ephraim, Sister Bay and Washington Island on their way to Mackinac Island., where they turned around and retraced the route back to Chicago.[27] They carried fish to the Chicago markets on these return trips, and so were very beneficial to the local fishermen. Around 1900, some fishermen packed their fish in thousand-pound boxes that were loaded onto the Goodrich boats. Bill Cornell packed such boxes for his father, John Cornell, and saw them loaded with wheeled dollies, but a few years later, they packed only a hundred pounds of fish per box.[28]

Washington Harbor also provided a shipping point for timber cutters, who exported cordwood to different markets, and for farmers who, during the late 1800s and early 1900s, exported thousands of bushels of potatoes to markets in Milwaukee and Chicago. These early farmers were nearly all Norwegians or Icelanders, who found that farming involved familiar challenges on the island, due to the shallow topsoil and the labor of clearing trees. However, the potatoes grown on the island were some of the finest produced in the entire country. In the fall of the year, the farmers would haul them by wagon to the Furlong dock, where they were weighed and then loaded onto schooners. During harvest time, the farmers who got to the docks earliest had a chance to get an extra load in by the end of the day. The potatoes were shipped in November, and the schooners would lay over at the docks in Milwaukee and Chicago for the winter, while the potatoes were unloaded. The farmers on the island did not receive payment until the following spring and thus had to wait five months to receive the fruits of their labors. In the early 1900s, a bushel of potatoes usually sold for twelve to fifteen cents.[29]

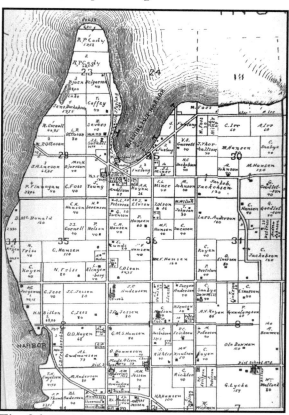

Fig. 8.1 Washington Island Real Estate map, 1899 (Courtesy of the Washington Island Archives)

The Furlong Dock

The Furlong dock, sometimes called the Ranney dock because it originally was owned by Dalbert and Willet Ranney, was located on the west side of Washington Harbor. It had a well-constructed slip to protect the docks and boats from northerly winds and ice shoves. There was a large warehouse, an icehouse, and some fish sheds on the property. During the 1870s or earlier, the A. Booth Fish Company from Chicago ran a 95-foot steam tug from there called the *A. Booth*. Twice a week, she would run to Manistique, then to St. Martin Island, and then to Washington Island, loading fish to take to market in Chicago.[30] It was also the dock where the Hart Line and Goodrich steamers loaded and unloaded.

Jim Cornell well remembers the Goodrich boat *Carolina* arriving at the Furlong dock. As a youngster, he had a hard time containing his excitement. He particularly recalls a day when he was fishing for rock bass in the slip when the African-American cook aboard the *Carolina* offered him twenty-five cents for each bass he could catch – a fortune for a young boy. He also remembers the captain of the boat, an Irishman named Daniel J. McCarty, who would always acknowledge him. Passenger and freight ships continued to use the dock until the mid 1930s. After that they couldn't compete. Business had slackened, tourists were traveling by rail and automobile, and most of the fish were sent to market via trucks or on smaller boats called hookers. Most of the fish and freight went to or through Green Bay.

Apparently named after similar craft used on the "Hook" of Holland in Europe, hookers were 50 to 60 feet in length and relatively shallow draft boats, originally sail-powered but usually quipped with gas or diesel engines by the 1920s. They had been modified for cargo holds and sleeping quarters, and the pilothouse, galley, and sleeping quarters were in the aft end of the boat. One of the first such boats converted over to haul freight in these waters was the *Wisconsin*, owned by Bill Jepson and Carl Christiansen. There was also the Anderson Brothers, Chris, Ray, and Roy who operated the hooker, *Wisconsin*. They acquired the boat from Bill Jepson in 1928. Bill sold it after building a new boat, the *Welcome* for a car ferry. The *Wisconsin* was a wooden boat built in Green Bay and powered by a 50-60 Kahlenberg oil engine. The Anderson brothers ran freight and oil for nearly twenty years. Many of the freight boats owned by Washington island men operated from Detroit Harbor.

Another island boat that ran freight was the *Marion*, owned by Carl Hanson. Captain Ole Christiansen had the schooner *Flotilla* and earlier the *Madonna*. Another freight boat, the *American Girl*, was owned by John Anderson, and later, by his two sons, Cecil and Jack. The boats took turns on these runs to ensure that fresh fish would arrive daily at Green Bay markets, and they brought back fuel and commodities for the islanders. Eventually, most of the fish were trucked to Green Bay from Gills Rock at the tip of the peninsula, eliminating their cargo of fish, but they continued to carry gasoline and fuel oil from Green Bay to the island.[31]

John or "Jack" Anderson was born on Washington Island in 1886. His parents, George and Elsie Anderson were among several of the Danish immigrants settling at Washington Island from the Schleswig – Holstein region. In his early years, Jack worked for Captain Ole Christiansen on the schooner *Madonna*. During those years he developed a love of being out on the lake, and decided it was a career he would choose to follow the rest of his life of 87 years. He joined up with Al Shellswick and formed a partnership, and they purchased the 65 foot wooden yacht *Diana*, which they converted to a hooker. After the *Diana* was wrecked near the west side of Detroit Island in 1922, Jack and Al amicably dissolved the partnership.[32]

Al kept the *Diana* and continued to run freight with her, while Jack purchased the 42 foot wooden boat the *Agnes H*, built by Rasmus Hanson in 1914 over at Jackson Harbor. Jack's sons helped out in the freight business. When they were old enough, they accompanied their father on runs to Green Bay and back. They typically made three trips a week and carried a wide array of cargo including fish, oil, furniture, dry goods and other sundries.

Tragedy struck the family when Jack's 14-year-old son Elliot was struck by lightning and drowned July 22, 1932. Approximately 3:00 p.m., a thunderstorm developed and lightning struck the boy while he was being towed in a small skiff behind his fathers boat *Diana*. They were midway between Plum Island and Detroit Harbor when the lightning struck, and blew him out of the boat, unconscious and he drowned instantly. His father recovered his son with a couple of trout hooks in 60 feet of water just before dark. Captain Anderson and his two sons, Cecil and Elliot had delivered barrels of oil to the Plum Island Coast Guard station earlier that afternoon. They were returning back to Detroit Harbor to their home port, halfway across the two mile passage, when the storm hit. The lightning bolt first struck the stern light post and part of the charge gleaned the row boat. It then followed up an aerial on the *Diana,* snapping off a wire narrowly missing one of the men.[33]

In the early 1930s, Jack bought the *Diana* from Al Shellswick after he decided to pursue the commercial fishing trade. Jack ran his operation from the Standard Oil dock at Detroit Harbor. For nearly ten years they continued making the Green Bay run stopping at various ports along the way with the *Diana.* In the late fall of 1943 the *Diana* met her fate when she was struck by a fish tug in Jackson Harbor. Jack and his son Cecil were returning back to Jackson Harbor after delivering some coal at Rock Island. They were following behind Dan Lindal's fish tug *R.E. Helen.* Dan left the pilothouse momentarily and the vessel swung around veering into the *Diana* at midship. They were brought back to Jackson Harbor on the slightly damaged *R.E Helen* without injury. The following day the *Diana* was retrieved by the aid of the Plum Island Coast Guard and several local fishermen and their tugs.[34]

In 1947, Jack purchased the 56-foot steel-hulled hooker *American Girl* from the William Walker Company from Chicago, Illinois. A few years later, he acquired the 64-foot tank barge, *Oil Queen.* They continued the runs to Green Bay and back, three times a week, especially during the busy times of the year. By this time his two sons, Cecil and Jack were a part of the family business. They installed bunks and a stove to give some comfort on the nine hour trips from the island to Green Bay. On the return trips it took as long as twelve or thirteen hours. In the fall of the year during potato harvests, they would run 90 mile round trips, daily to Sturgeon Bay and Menominee. During World War II, they were contracted to deliver all the oil to the upper Lake Michigan lighthouses. Cecil's son Jim Anderson remembered a story told to him by his father:

> **D**ad, Jack and Grandpa were headed for Menominee, Michigan in the *American*
> *Girl* in the late fall. They were hauling a load of potatoes for Ed Anderson. I think
> it was 1957. They normally carried 1100 sacks of potatoes, which put the rail down
> nearly to the water. They were headed into a big sea, and the temperature was below
> freezing, so the spray coming over the bow froze to the boat, weighing it down even
> more. Dad had to get out on the top of the foredeck several times and chop holes
> in the ice beneath the pipe rails, so the water could drain off. He said they didn't dare
> turn around for fear of rolling her over. When they finally got into Menominee safe-
> ly, the doors and hatches were so frozen shut that the men on the dock had to chip
> the ice off to let them out.[35]

In 1955, Jack sold the *American Girl* and *Oil Queen* to his son Cecil, who continued the operation until 1971. He then sold the boats to the Gillespie Oil and Transit Company of St. James on Beaver Island. On June 10, 1973, the *Oil Queen* was in tow of the *American Girl* when she capsized in a storm on a run to Beaver Island from Charlevoix, Michigan. It was righted on June 12, after 24,800 gallons of gasoline were pumped out, and then towed into St. James, Michigan at Beaver Island.[36]

Even after the decline of the large passenger and freight boats in the late 1920s and early 1930s, the Furlong dock was still a busy place because of the numerous fishing operations that took place there. Fishermen came from other parts of the state to fish during the summer months, and many of them leased dock space from the Furlong Company. One of the boats that operated from the Furlong dock was the *Sylvia* owned by Albert Kalmbach from Sturgeon Bay. He had a crew fishing there from 1912 to 1914. Also, the Booth Fish Company had a fish boat named the *Peter Coates* operated by James Denio running out of the Furlong dock from 1909 to 1912, and the *Elsie M*, a fish tug from Kewaunee, Wisconsin, owned by the Allen Brothers also fished from the Furlong dock for a few seasons.[37]

Tom Guinen was one of the early settlers on the island who based his operation at the Furlong dock from the early 1900s on. Guinen fished from that dock for many years and owned a number of steam tugs, the *Liberty,* the *Unknown,* and the *Brooks.* Like many others, he fished off the north end of Washington Island for whitefish and had a successful career as a fisherman. In his day, he was known to be quite a drinker who knew how to have a good time. One night in the fall of 1912, he and Jesse Helgarson were drinking in the warehouse and got into a fight. A lantern tipped over, and the place caught on fire. Soon, barrels of gasoline on the dock caught fire, and before long the whole place was ablaze. The warehouse and icehouse burned to the ground, and an agent buying fish for the A. Booth Company was asleep in an office in the rear of the building and perished in the fire.[38] Officially, the cause of the fire was not established, and Tom Guinen was not charged, but some believed he had caused it. The following spring, Mr. Furlong built a new 40 by 60 foot warehouse and a modern icehouse and made extensive repairs to the dock. Tom Guinen retired from fishing around 1915 and moved to Rock Island, where he became the caretaker for Chester Thordarson's estate.[39]

An article from the Door County Advocate from the October 10, 1912 issue describes some of the events of that evening:

Man Burns to Death

Aldine Outland loses his life when dock burns at Washington Harbor. Washington Island was visited with the most serious conflagration in its history Friday night, Oct. 4 when the warehouse docks, icehouse and net shed burned, the catastrophe happening along about eleven o'clock. But the most serious loss of all was the death of A. R Outland, the local manager of the Booth Fishing Co., whose home was in Green Bay. He was asleep in the building. The body was found near the door, the exit from the office.

Mr. Outland had been an employee of the Booth co. for fifteen years, the last three having been spent on Washington Island, during the fishing season. Among the heavy losers of freight contained in the building are W. M Jess, George O. Mann and Rev. J. McElroy.

The latter is the new pastor of the Baptist church, who had sent his furniture ahead, and all excepting the piano and stool were lost in the common ruin; also some books. There was of course no insurance on the property. The Booth Co., which had leased the dock property for a term of years, has its representative on the ground again looking after their interests. Undoubtedly the landing and buildings will be reconstructed.

John Cornell, who was born in 1865, grew up in the Washington Harbor region and began fishing at a young age. He was a quiet man and strongly devoted to his profession. He kept his boats and equipment in peak condition, and was very successful in this business. Like many others in the late 1800s, he fished from sailboats. It was not until 1895 that he bought the steam tug *Welcome*, which enabled him to expand his fishing grounds. John and another fisherman named Delos Smith from Port Washington leased the Furlong dock property from 1900 to 1905.[40]

In 1905, Cornell sold the *Welcome* to Tom Goodman, who fished from the Foss dock across the harbor, and then bought the steam tug *Henry Gust,* for which he paid $4,400 in $100 bills. After 1905, he moved his operations to Detroit Island and leased Fred Richter's dock, and then finally bought some property on Lobdells Point, where he built a dock, net buildings, and an icehouse. Cornell eventually sold the *Henry Gust* and had a new tug, *Clara C.*, built. A few years later, he also had built the *J. W. Cornell.* All these boats were equipped with Kahlenberg oil engines. John fished from Lobdells Point for many years. He retired in the late 1930s.[41]

Jacob Young was born in Germany and came to America at the age of sixteen. After a tumultuous 42-day voyage to New York, he came to Wisconsin and settled in New Berlin, where his father had settled a few years earlier. In 1864 Jacob enlisted in the Ninth Wisconsin Regiment and fought in a battle at Falls Church, Virginia[42]. After a six-month tour of duty in the army, he returned home and moved to Washington Island, where he found work in the fisheries and, in the winter months, worked with the timber crews. He was also employed by the lighthouse service for a few years.[43]

Jacob Young went into partnership with John Larson for a number of years in the 1870s and fished off the west end of Washington Island for lake trout. They had a small skiff with sail and oars to use in case there wasn't any wind. They used gill nets that were hand made during the winter months, with stones attached to the bottom lines as weights and sticks tied to the top line for floats. Like many fisherman of that time, the two men began their day before sunup and sailed or rowed out to where their nets were set. They pulled the nets in by hand, picking out the trout and discarding the other fish, a task that required strong men with strong wills. After hauling in and resetting their nets, they returned to shore, packaged the fish in kegs, and hauled them to the Furlong dock via horse and wagon. From there, the fish were sent to various markets.

In 1869, Jacob Young had married Mary Ann Wade, a widow who already had five girls ranging in age from two to seven. They had five more children of their own: Charles, Mary, John, Fredrick, and Robert. Jacob had to work at jobs other than fishing, especially during the winter months, to support his large family. He worked at the stone quarry and also cut wood. Robert and Charles both moved off the island in later years, but Fred and John stayed and followed their father into the fishery. Jacob was a strong Republican his entire life and voted for Abe Lincoln when he was only nineteen years of age.

Mary Ann Wade Young died in 1894, and Jacob Young remarried in 1897 to Annie Foss, thus expanding his family further. She was also a widow and had four children: Steena, Nettie, Mathew, and Ruby. Jacob Young eventually retired from fishing and lived out the rest of his life on the island.

John Young, a son of Jacob Young, also fished from the Furlong dock. John was raised in a house at Washington Harbor, only a short walk from the Furlong dock, and spent his youth absorbing knowledge about fishing and the fishing business. Eventually he rented and managed the Furlong dock, later called the J.B Young dock. He did all the fish packaging and dock maintenance, and, in the winter months he harvested ice from the harbor and stored it in the icehouse near the dock. He married Agnes Jess, and together they raised five sons and three daughters: Art, Lloyd, Mabel, Ruth, Percy, Howard (Fred), Laura, and Clifford. John Young and his family also lived near Washington Harbor, and his sons would eventually follow in their father's footsteps and become successful fisherman on their own.

The Young boys spent their spare time at the dock, helping their father and other fishermen. This became a classroom and playground for them. They made their own nets from old nets given to them by the fishermen. They set them in the boat slip and proudly took home their catch of suckers and perch. In the evening, they helped their mother to repair nets and to string new nets in the living and dining rooms of their home. They also spent evenings filling wooden needles (for repairing nets) with cord – this was called "winding maitres" as it consisted of making balls of maitre cord from skeins – and attaching lead weights onto the nets.[44]

Art and Lloyd, the two oldest sons, fished with their father on the *Rainbow* and were later joined by Cliff, the youngest son. Cliff later moved to Chicago for a year and fished with Fred Weimer, who owned a fish store in the city. Cliff then moved on to Kenosha and fished with the McDonald Brothers. The other two sons, Fred and Percy, bought their own boat named the *Sea Queen* and fished from the Furlong dock for a few years.

During the years of the Great Depression (1929-1935), John Young lost a considerable amount of money when the Goodrich Company went bankrupt and was unable to pay docking fees. Around that time, most of the fishermen from the Furlong dock moved to Jackson Harbor on the northeastern corner of the island, and the dock at Washington Harbor fell into a state of disrepair. John Young and his sons Art and Lloyd fished from the Furlong dock until the late 1930s and then moved their fishing operations to Jackson Harbor. By that time, most of the other fishermen also left the area for other fishing locations. Originally, the Youngs had the fish tug *Darlene,* but it was sold George Nelson and his sons Russ and Spencer at Jackson Harbor. In 1924, they had the *Rainbow* built by Rasmus Hanson, a boat builder at Jackson Harbor. The *Rainbow* was a 34-foot wood-hull boat with 10 feet on the beam, powered by a 28 horsepower Straubel gasoline engine. In the winter months John still cut ice in the harbor to stock the icehouse for the following year, but this was a task that required only a few days and a small crew.

Many fishermen operated from the Furlong dock over the years. Anker Greenfeldt and sons Harold and Lorman had the boats *Jane Elizabeth*, *Yankee*, and *Betty*, but they eventually moved their operations to Jackson Harbor. Many fishermen moved their boats to Detroit harbor before the winter ice formed in Washington Harbor. Ice shoves could be detrimental to the boats and buildings. On some occasions, when northerly winds prevailed, ice shoves would reach high as the gables of the warehouse.

Severt and Johnny Barnes fished from Furlong dock for quite a few years between 1900 and the

1930s. Their family had come from Iceland and settled in the Washington Harbor region, and they had shortened their name from Bjarnarson to Barnes when they arrived in America. Ellsworth Cornell was another fisherman to use that dock, along with his brothers Alfred and Newell. The Cornells owned the *Helen*, and *Lady Grace*, and late in 1908, Alfred and Newell built a small schooner called the *Lillian*, 50 feet in length, that later was sold to a man at Gills Rock.

By the 1940s, the Furlong dock was a shadow of its former self. Most of the fishermen were gone, and the big freighters and passenger liners no longer stopped. The dock was in disrepair. Though the slip was still in fairly good shape, the buildings were neglected and falling down. For nearly a hundred years the Furlong dock held its own against the forces of nature and saw many changes in fishing and commerce. Today, there is hardly any evidence that it was there at all.

The Wood Dock (East Side Dock or Nolan Dock)

On the east side of Washington Harbor was a smaller dock known as the eastside dock or wood dock. It was built in the early 1860s by the Nolan Brothers, who used it for their fishing and cordwood operations. The Nolans had a well-built dock and warehouse and a little store where they sold potatoes that were grown on their property.[45] During the early years, a large amount of cordwood and timber were hauled from there, hence the name "wood dock." Most of the fishermen that used the dock lived nearby. In the fall of 1913, it was nearly destroyed by a strong northerly storm, which later became known as one of the most intense storms of the century. It started on Saturday, November 5, and blew four days, with winds gusting up to 70 miles per hour that forced many lake steamers and sailing vessels to find safe harbor from the tempest. The steamer *Louisiana* came into Washington Harbor for shelter. An article in the *Green Bay Advocate* describes the event:

Steamer Louisiana Burns

The steamer *Louisiana* was totally destroyed by fire Sunday morning at Washington Harbor, Wisconsin. Her crew of seventeen men got ashore without much assistance. The boat got beached but a couple of rods from the shore, the water being very bold at that point.

The *Louisiana* had delivered a cargo of coal at Milwaukee and was bound from there to Escanaba for ore. The storm, which broke over this section about midnight Saturday night, struck the *Louisiana* in all its fury and she was not able to keep her course, so an effort was made to get into Washington Harbor for anchorage.

This was done but the tremendous wind and sea was too much for her and she dragged closer to the beach by morning. Then it was discovered that there was a fire in the hold and after an ineffectual attempt to extinguish the flames the craft was abandoned.[46]

Fortunately, no lives were lost, but the ship was a total loss, with an estimated value of about $15,000. The *Louisiana* was built in 1887 at Marine City, Michigan. She was 267 feet long, with a 31-foot beam, and had a draft of 20 feet. She was owned Frank M. Osborne of Cleveland. The wreckage remained in Washington Harbor for a long time until the waves and ice finally broke her apart. Today, most of the wreckage still lies in about 15 feet of water off the southeastern shoreline of Washington Harbor and has become a diver's delight.

During the same storm, the sailing vessel *Halstead* was towed into the harbor by a small steamer that dropped her off and continued on for a safer harbor. The *Halstead* ended up on the south shore of Washington Harbor, on what is now called Schoolhouse beach. Everyone aboard her survived the storm, and the boat was salvaged the following spring. *The Green Bay Advocate* reported:

Barge Halstead Beached

The barge *Halstead*, consort of the steamer *Prentice* was driven ashore at Washington Island during the storm Saturday night. The boats were light and bound north when overtaken by the gale, which swept over this region. The tow line parted and the *Halstead* went adrift. The anchors were dropped, but in the terrific storm were unable to hold the boat, which dragged and the vessel was cast on the beach of Washington Harbor. She is four feet out forward and two feet aft. The *Halstead* is the property of the Hines Lumber Company of Chicago.

The Plum Island life-savers under Captain William Robinson made valiant efforts to secure the imperiled seamen on the *Halstead*. A line was shot over the vessel during the height if the gale, but before the breeches buoy could be rigged up the boat was picked up on the top of a tremendous wave and carried bodily up on the beach. It was a thrilling time for the crew of the *Halstead*, who momentarily expected their craft to be thrown upon the rocks and smashed. The seas that run into the harbor were the largest within the memory of the oldest inhabitant.

Two more schooners were still then out at anchor, the *J. M Stevens* and the *Minerva*, which had come in before the storm, and so the lifesavers remained on the scene for 48 hours watching these boats and prepared to save the crews if the hooks would not hold. Eyewitnesses said it was the most thrilling sight they had ever seen, the two vessels at one moment being on the crest of an enormous billow and the next going out of sight in a smother of foam. How they weathered the storm is a mystery, it being little short of a miracle.[47]

The storm proved to be one of the deadliest in history. Nearly 300 people lost their lives, and many boats were lost or severely damaged. After the wood dock was destroyed by the storm, some of the fishermen that used it moved to the Foss dock just to the north, while others moved to other harbors.

John Ellefson fished from the East Side dock for a few years, along with his son Ernest. John Ellefson was born in Norway and sailed the oceans in large schooners as a young man. He came to America and settled on Washington Island in 1896. He eventually took up fishing. In the winters of 1903 and 1904, with the help of Stein Lunde, he built a wooden boat which they called the *Viking*. They built it in the Anderson barn, and, once it was completed, they transported it on a sleigh to Gasoline Town, the dock also called the Foss dock on Washington Harbor. They had a two-cylinder gasoline engine in it, and John Ellefson and Charlie Hagen formed a partnership and fished together with the *Viking* until 1910 from the Gas Town docks owned by Matt Foss. After the partnership dissolved, Charlie kept the boat and renamed it the *Darlene*, and John kept the nets.

John soon built another tug, which he named the *Ragna* after his daughter. He began fishing from the wood dock along with his sons. The *Ragna* was a 22-foot wood hull boat with a six horsepower gasoline engine and was operated with a three-man crew. When his sons Swerra, Julian, and George were out of school, they joined their father's fishing operation. All the nets were set and lifted by hand in those days. Mechanical net lifters were just coming in, but many fishermen couldn't afford them. In 1915 John Ellefson sold the *Ragna* to Morris Hanson and moved to Lobdells Point where he built the *Mayflower* along with Nels Jepson. John fished there until the mid-1920s, then sold the *Mayflower* to a fisherman from Milwaukee and moved to Kenosha, Wisconsin. He eventually moved to Chicago, where he lived out the rest of his life.[48]

The Pat Chambers family fished from the Wood dock from 1906 to 1913 and had the steam tug *L.P Hill*. They moved from Fish Creek to Washington Island where they bought a house and property up the hill from the wood dock. Pat Chambers fished for chubs, whitefish, trout, or whatever was most abundant at the time. He had a boat called the *Search* built in 1912, a large boat painted white, with a pilothouse on the upper deck. The boat measured 74 feet and was powered by a steam engine, later replaced with a Kahlenberg engine. Chambers eventually decided to move their fishing operations to Detroit Harbor since the wood dock was not in good condition.[49]

Junius Garret fished for some time from the wood dock. He had a small scow schooner named the *Martha G*, which was built for him in Fish Creek. Junius was born on Washington Island and lived up the hill, not far from the wood dock. He was out fishing one day, and suffered an acute appendicitis attack. By the time he made it back to the dock and was taken to Sturgeon Bay, his appendix had burst and he later died. His boat was sold to the Graham brothers of Fish Creek, who had built it. They used her for salvage operations.[50]

Hannes Johnson fished for some time from the wood dock, though he kept his boat at night at the Furlong dock, because it offered better protection. The wood dock never had a protective break or seawall, which led to its early demise. After a time, Johnson moved to the Foss dock in Gasoline town. One of his first boats was the *Seabird*, built in 1912 and powered by an 8 horsepower gasoline engine. She was a wood hull craft, as were all the boats at that time, and had a length of 28 feet. In 1925, Hannes had the *Service* built at Marinette, Wisconsin. This was a bigger boat, with a length of 42 feet and a three-cylinder 45-54 Kahlenberg engine that gave her 45 horsepower.[51]

Gasoline Town (Foss Dock)

On the northeast side of Washington Harbor, out near Rowe's Point, there was another busy fishing community that came to be known as Gasoline Town because of the many gas-powered boats that were docked there. Limestone bluffs line the northeast end of the harbor, and cedar trees and hardwoods loom behind the bluffs. At least half a dozen boats were moored at the Foss dock, which became the busiest fishing dock in Washington Harbor after 1900.

Around 1870, a man named Peter McBride began a quarry operation along the northeast section of the harbor. For about fifteen years, limestone was removed from this site, loaded onto large schooners, and shipped away. The quarry had a small wood dock that had to be rebuilt each year, due to constant ice damage and storms. The schooners could be loaded only in good weather, so a large dock eventually became necessary. When the quarry operations ceased, the large flat area that was left served as a foundation for some of the buildings at Gas Town. Another advantage of the site was a road that had been built down to the shore that connected to the island's main roads. There was still plenty of limestone in the back of the quarry, and there were trees above it. Matt Foss saw the potential of the area, and, in 1888, he purchased 72 acres from John Furlong and began work on the docks and buildings.

Matt Foss was born October 10, 1858, in the small town of Christianfeld in the county of Shleswig Holstein, Denmark. He attended the common schools of Denmark until he was fourteen, and then came to America. He resided in Bedford, Massachusetts, and labored in a tannery. While working there, he made enough money to send for his older brother Henry, and when he arrived, they both worked at the tannery and made enough money to send for their sister Mary and their parents. In 1880, Matt Foss moved to Washington Island and worked in a quarry for a time before he began fishing.

In 1891 Matt married Minnie Jacobson Allen, a widow whose first husband, Frank Allen, had drowned somewhere between St. Martin Island and Washington Island. Allen, his hired man Willie Hideman, and another man by the name of Peter Anderson left St. Martin Island in Allen's fish boat early in the morning on a very windy day, and never made it back. He left behind a wife and a child, Curtis Allen. There is some confusion by different sources as to who was on the boat that day. A reporter from the Door County Advocate has Frank's son named on that ill fated day. The November 30, 1889 issue of the Door County Advocate reported:

Unknown Fishing Vessel, Foundered November 16, 1889

A small fishing boat sank on its way to St. Martin Island with a load of hay. The vessel's owner, a Mr. Allen, his son and a hired hand had been aboard. Apparently they were taking on water. Witnesses following a mile behind said they saw the three throw out the hay, make sail, and run for the beach. The boat sank before it reached shore. The two men were found near a bale of hay and, it was thought they floated to shore with it but were too exhausted to drag themselves from the water. The boy presumably went down with the boat.[52]

Matt's son Howard Foss tells the story of that ill-fated day: "My mother was married to Frank Allen, a fisherman over at St. Martin Island. She had three children with him – Curtis, Ozzy, and Agnes who died while young. Ozzy fell off the dock when he was four years old and drowned. One day Frank and his hired man decided to go over to Washington Harbor to get a load of hay. A squall came up and must have capsized their boat. They were never found or heard from again. Then my mother decided to move over to Washington Island and – I don't know if she had that store built or if it was already there, but she ran a general store down at Schoolhouse beach. Well, then she married Matt Foss and sold the store to Arbec Koyen. Then the store was moved up the hill to its present-day location."[53]

Matt and his new wife had a home built up the hill from the dock. It was a great location, with a grand view of Washington Harbor. They raised seven children there, three boys – Curtis, Howard, and Raymond – and four girls – Mary (Mamie), Agnes, Irma, and Laura. The children loved to go down to the docks, climb the bluffs, swim, and bother the fishermen.

January, 1913, Matt Foss decided to retire from fishing, so he sold his fish rig and his boat, the *Irma Jeanette*, to Charlie, Jule, and Harry Hagen. Even though he didn't fish anymore, Matt hadn't got out of fishing altogether. He still managed the dock and warehouse. There was also the large ice-house to provide the fishermen with ice for packing their fish. Matt and his son Howard did all the packing for the fishermen and also managed the warehouse operation.

Howard loved working with his father at the dock. He would come home from school and race down to the dock to help his father pack fish. In his spare time, he helped the other fishermen. He remembers one time, when he was ten years old, helping Jule Hagen pack nets, when Tom Goodman came into the shed and said, "Say, I see you like to pack nets. How would you like to do this every day? I'll give you a nickel a box." Howard said, "Why sure." Howard recalls, "Boy, sixty cents a day I was making. Was I into the money!"[54]

In the summer of his thirteenth year, Howard became a regular at the dock. Matt Foss had just let his hired man go, so Howard took over his position. It was a demanding job, and sometimes he worked long hours. At one time there were seven fisheries operating from the Foss dock, and there would be 5 to 6 tons of fish leaving there nearly every day. Fishermen would come in from their daily lifts, and Matt and Howard would soon be at work shaving ice, weighing-in the fish, and packing them for the fishermen. Later they acquired a gas-powered ice chipper to speed up the packing. The average price for whitefish and trout in the early 1920s was ten to twelve cents a pound. Chubs were going for six cents a pound (however, those prices fluctuated year to year).

Matt never charged fishermen for docking or property rental, but he did charge them for packing fish, normally fifteen cents per 100 pounds of fish. He packed the fish and then put a tag on the boxes, marked for the fish company the fishermen wanted them sold to. The fish were all shipped on consignment to markets at Green Bay. At that time, there were four major markets that the fishermen were selling to: Johnson Fish Company, Frank Schilling Fish Company, Fisher Company, and the A. Booth Fish Company.[55]

For nearly thirty years, from 1900 to 1930 or so, all the fish were sent to market on steamboats and hookers. A number of steamboats came to the Foss dock three times a week to deliver freight and pick up fish. Both Hart Transportation and the Hill Company had boats that frequented Foss's dock. The hookers normally carried empty fish boxes, but sometimes hauled fish to Green Bay. John Anderson had two boats for this operation, the *American Girl* and the *Agnes H*.

Another marketable by-product of fish was oil produced from the viscera. Howard Foss remembers putting the guts, especially the chub guts (which held a lot of oil) into a steel barrel. Then a fire was lit underneath the barrel. Once the contents began to boil, the oil would accumulate at the top. The next day, the oil was collected, put into another barrel, and sold to be used for stain or paint. Some of the fish sheds at Gas Town were coated with fish oil. Roy Cornell applied this oil to Tom Goodman's sheds to preserve the wood. Jens Hansen also made fish and sold fish oil at Gas Town.

Howard Foss recalls a favorite snack that he and some of the fishermen often prepared for themselves in the sheds:

In the fall of the year the fishermen always had a fire going in their stoves in the reeling sheds. We'd take a whitefish and split it open and chuck it full of onions and put some salt in it, regular old rock salt was all we had down there. Then we'd wrap it in newspaper, wet it, and throw it on the stove. Once the paper started to burn, we'd sprinkle water on it. We'd let it cook for an hour then open it up. The skin would stick to the paper and you had yourself a nice little snack. Boy, that was good.[56]

This was considered a delicacy amongst fishermen all around the Great Lakes, and many fishermen called this little snack "domers."[57]

When Howard began working for his father, Matt told him that he would set up a partnership with him. Howard would receive 25 percent of what they made. After a few years, when some of the fishermen had left, Matt and Howard split the profit evenly. During the years of the Great Depression, money was tight and fishermen were moving to Jackson Harbor. Matt and Howard were in a tight situation. Matt decided to retire and told Howard, "You take 75 percent and I'll take 25 percent. I really don't need the money." Eventually Howard performed odd jobs just to survive. He drove trucks on the side and, in 1939, he moved to Chicago, where he began his sailing career.[58]

Matt Foss was well up in years when he finally thought about retiring. His wife Minnie had passed away, and, after living alone for a few years, Matt moved in with his daughter Irma. Matt died in October of 1948 at the age of ninety. He had a long and successful career and was known as a kind and decent man. He was well respected by the Washington Island community and had many friends. He was a stockholder and director of the island telephone company and served as a director of voting in District 1.[59]

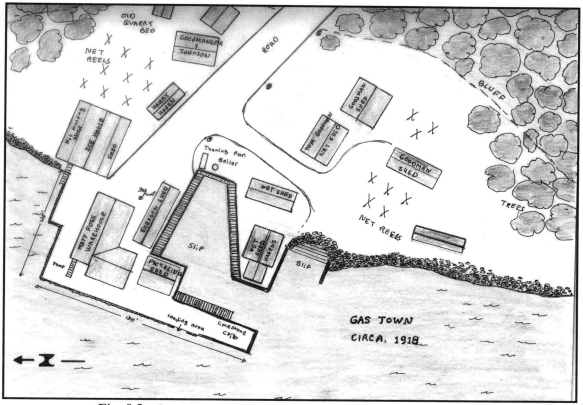

Fig. 8.2. Gasoline Town layout of docks and buildings. (Trygvie Jensen)

Buildings and Dock Activity

Matt Foss owned the dock and buildings that would become Gasoline Town. The dock had been well built to stand up to the powerful fall storms that raged from the north and west and also winter ice shoves. There was a need for a well-protected slip for boats. To the north of the property was a natural breakwater, or reef, that provided some shelter from the northerly winds and winter ice shoves. This breakwater remained there until 1920, when the Roan Company came in and dredged the area for the stone. There were no regulations to stop the company, and after a short time the reef was gone, allowing the forces of nature to more easily get at the docks and buildings.[60]

The dock was built during the winter months. Cribs were constructed of cedar and oak were presumably built on the ice and then filled with limestone slabs and boulders. When the ice gave way in the spring, they sank into place. The submerged part was built of oak and the upper part of cedar. The outside of the cribs were covered with an oak facing or "ice shield." made by sawing 12 to16 inch logs in half and installing them flat side out. This helped to protect the dock from pounding waves and from moving ice and ice shoves in the wintertime. The dock facing had to be replaced every five or six years, especially the parts facing north and west. The main breakwater crib, or L section of the dock, rose twelve feet out of the water. The dock jutted out from shore 125 feet to the west and then ran 150 feet to the south. Inside the main dock were low docks for mooring the fish tugs for easy loading and unloading. These lower docks and walkways stood 3 or 4 feet from the water. (See fig. 8.2)

Prior to 1900, nearly all fishing boats were powered by wind or steam. Matt Foss was fishing with his sailboat *Laura* when he decided to install an engine in her. He and Tom Johnson sailed the *Laura* down to Two Rivers, Wisconsin, and had an 8 horsepower Kahlenberg gas engine installed at a cost of $450. The Kahlenberg Brothers Company manufactured these innovative engines, and the *Laura* was the first fishing boat on Washington Island to have one.

After Matt got his boat fitted with a gasoline engine, other local fishermen took an interest in how they could improve their own fishing operations. A year later, Hannes Johnson and Sons also had a Kahlenberg engine installed in their boat, the *Seabird*, and within a few years all of the boats that fished from the Foss dock were equipped with marine engines. In fact, by 1907, most fishing boats were powered by gas engines, which greatly enhanced the fishery by making it easier to get to and from the fishing grounds. At the Foss dock, as many as six or seven boats would be docked in the slip behind the main dock, and that area of Washington Harbor soon became known as Gasoline Town. Some of the fishermen lived just up the hill, so it really was a small community onto itself.

The buildings of Gasoline Town served many purposes for the fisherman and the island community. On the main portion of the dock, Matt Foss had a 40 by 64 foot warehouse used for freight, dry goods, and produce storage that came in on the Hill boats and those of the Hart Transportation Line. In the fall of the year, the warehouse was filled to the rafters with produce, which would serve the islanders in the winter months. The icehouse sat north and east of the warehouse, where ice was stored for fish packing and distribution to the local stores. The icehouse was large, measuring approximately 40 by 60 feet. Two sheds were attached to the icehouse, one on the south side and one on the north. The south shed was for general storage, and the other one was used for stringing and mending nets, as well to store feed and flour. Matt's daughters, Mamie, Laura, and Aggie, would usually help out with the nets.

Two other sheds on the main dock were used for fish packing and box storage. In the long narrow one – approximately 18 feet wide by 50 feet long – fish were packed into 100-pound boxes. This was alongside the large warehouse (inside the slip) and ran along the dock for easy loading and unloading. The smaller one measured 16 by 22 feet and was just to the south of the warehouse.

In the area adjacent to the docks, the fishermen had their own sheds for repairing and storing nets and equipment. The smaller dock crib that made up the south portion of the slip held two buildings. The Hagen shed, a small 12 by 12 foot structure with two open walls, was used for net box storage and was located at the tip of the limestone crib. A walkway followed the inside of the slip at shore level, a few feet above the water. Behind the Hagen shed was a 12 by 14 foot shed used for fuel and oil for the boats. A pump stood outside the building, and there was a gas pump in front of the warehouse where Matt sold gasoline to the fisherman. On the shore near the slip was a boiler and tanning pan for treating nets. It was necessary to sterilize and clean the nets because algae and fungus would accumulate on them.

Tom Goodman owned the sheds just south of the road that led to the main dock. At one time there were four or five sheds on that side. Another prominent feature around the dock area was collection of net reels. They were made from wood and used to hold the nets for drying, and were scattered about the property. Each fisherman had a number of reels.

Harry Hagen had a shed on the north side of the road, up from the dock. It measured about 20 by 18 feet. Also on that side of the road, where the old quarry used to be, were sheds owned by Swara Hagen, Albert Goodmander, and Haldon Johnson. There were also several outhouses back there.

All these buildings were "stick" framed, using rough-cut two-by-fours milled on the island, and sided with pine or cedar clapboard. The cedar-shingled roofs were steeply pitched to shed the snow and rain. After most of the fisherman moved to other harbors or retired, the buildings were no longer maintained and were left to the mercy of the weather. Some were dismantled and relocated, as was the case with Swara Hagen's shed. In 1948, he moved it to his property on Jackson Harbor Road, where it was used as a woodshed. Tom Goodman also relocated a few of his sheds. Some of the sheds and the dock cribs were destroyed by the fall storms, and the rest slowly collapsed. A big blow in 1952 took down the warehouse, the packaging sheds, and most of the dock. By 1955, there were no buildings left on the main dock. In 2005, only one shed was left on the old dock property, which is now owned by Ross and Cathy Meader. Ross is a grandson of the late Harry Hagen. Looking now at the property, we see almost no evidence of the buildings and activity that once was there.

Gasoline Town Fishermen and Their Boats

The Hagen Brothers (Charles, Jule, Harry, and Swara)[61]

Carl Johann (Charlie) Hagen was born in Oslo, Norway on November 17, 1881, the first child of Ole and Fanny Hagen. While still quite young, he traveled with his mother, father and grandmother to the United States and eventually to Washington Island, where they settled in West Harbor. When Charlie was thirteen years old, he took a job on the schooner *J.V. Taylor*, loading and unloading pulpwood. He sailed for almost six years. His sailing career was cut short when he contracted typhoid fever while loading pulpwood out of Carp River, Michigan. After he recovered from this illness, he moved back to Washington Island, where he started fishing in 1902.

Charlie Hagen owned the fish tug *Darlene* (formerly named *Viking*) and fished from the Foss dock. He formed a partnership with his younger brother Jule, who fished with him on shares. Charlie and Jule fished together using gill nets in the waters north of Washington Island and Rock Island. It was hard work lifting and setting nets by hand on a daily schedule, but a love of fishing kept their spirits high. They made a good living at it and had many prosperous years together. In 1905, Jule moved to Chicago, and Charlie was left to fish alone until Jule returned in 1911 and continued their partnership. Charlie fished alone and then with John Ellefson for a while until Jule came back to the island. In 1913, Charlie and Jule sold the *Darlene* to John Young, who was fishing from the Furlong dock. With their younger brother Harry, they bought the *Irma Jeanette* from Matt Foss, including the nets and all the equipment. She was a fine boat with a solid wood hull, 32 feet long and powered by an 18-horse-power Kahlenberg gas engine. In 1916, they had the *F. Hunter* (Fish Hunter) built to their specifications at the Peterson Boat Works in Sturgeon Bay. She was a 45-foot gill-net boat with a 12-foot beam and a cabin. They had paid $1,100 dollars for her, which included a 25-horsepower Straubel gasoline engine and two coats of paint. The Hagens fished with the *F. Hunter* for thirty-eight seasons and replaced four engines during that time.

On June 30, 1904, Charlie Hagen married Thora Anita Hansen of Washington Island, and they moved into a large white house overlooking the east shore of Washington Harbor. They lived there and raised five children, until the family and fishing operations moved to St. Ignace, Michigan, in 1923. They rented a few different houses before buying one in St. Ignace, where they lived for the rest of their lives.

Charlie was a popular member of his family and community. He served in various posts of conservation organizations and was a member of a lobbying group responsible for pushing through legislation restricting the use of submarine (entrapment) nets during the 1930s. For more than a half century of commercial fishing, Charlie kept his engines running at peak form. He always had a special talent for mechanics and had the skill needed to replace an engine himself when the time came for a new one. It is a tribute to his mechanical skill that there was only one time in all those years that he had to be towed in.

The only serious accident Charlie had in all his years of fishing happened in 1905. He had some fingers cut off while driving pound-net stakes off Washington Island. He carried the fingers home in the hat he was wearing and his wife fetched the doctor. The only painkiller he had while the doctor reattached and sewed up his fingers was a few snorts of whiskey.

Jule Hagen was born July 4, 1883, on Washington Island, the second child of Ole and Fanny Hagen. While a child, he developed a strong love and appreciation for nature. Jule loved to hunt and fish, and he and Charlie provided a lot of fish and game for the family. It was during his early years that Jule developed habits that guided him in his later years, especially prudence and safety with knives, axes and guns. He developed a healthy respect for both the woods and water and understood where the dangers were. Jule was adamant about conservation and thought it a sin to shoot an animal or catch a fish that was not to be used on his or a friend's table. This was a common trait among Scandinavians.

When he turned seventeen, Jule sailed out of Milwaukee on a freighter named the *J.C. Case*, which was carrying a load of grain to Buffalo, New York. He came down with dysentery, and a doctor advised him to go home, so he sailed for home on the *Cheboygan*, a side-wheel steamboat of the Goodrich Line.

After returning to Washington Island, Jule worked for Ted Engelson cutting cordwood and helping in the fishing operation. Jule made $1 a day and thought it to be a good wage at the time. Later, he worked for the Smith Brothers, fishing from the Furlong docks in the summer months. The Smith Brothers based their fishing operations in Port Washington, Wisconsin.

In 1903, Jule started fishing with his older brother Charlie on a share basis. This is a system in the fishing business where the owner of the boats and nets generally takes one third of the money earned for his capital investment, while the remaining two thirds is split among the people actually performing the fishing operations. Later that same year, Jule became a full partner in the business, and Jule and Charlie fished together for a few years. Then Jule decided to move to Chicago and took a job as a steamfitter's helper.

Jule returned to the island each summer, where he played on the Washington Island baseball team along with his brothers Hank and Harry. After each game, their father Ole would get together with his sons and go over the game play by play. Another reason for Jule's lengthy summer visits was to continue his courtship with an island gal, Lillie Gudmundsen, whose father was a family friend of the Hagens. Lillie eventually moved to Chicago and soon after, she and Jule were married. They had two children there before moving back to Washington Island in 1911. Jule was considered a handsome man and, in 1922, won the prize for best-looking man on Washington Island. He stood at an even 6 feet and weighed 180 pounds.

After his return to the Island, Jule resumed his partnership with his brother Charlie. It was to become one of the most congenial and successful associations between two brothers in the Lake Michigan fishing community. They fished together for nearly fifty years before their retirement in 1954.

In 1913, the year Jule, Charlie, and Harry Hagen bought the *Irma Jeanette* from Matt Foss, Jule purchased a home on the hill overlooking the east shore of Washington Harbor. It was rather a strange transaction since he bought only the house, not the land. The land was owned by the Furlong family, and they would only give him a long-term lease. Jule later installed electricity at the house and thus became the first person on the island to have electricity. In 1916, Jule bought a Ford Model T, and thereby became the first person to own an automobile. At the time of the sale he was commissioned by the dealer to sell Fords on the island, for which he was to receive 5 percent of the selling price. He sold his first car to Tom Goodman, who drove it for years and then converted it to a truck.

In January of 1923, Jule, Charlie, and Harry took a trip to northern Michigan to scout out new fishing grounds. They thought that St. Ignace and Naubinway, Michigan, had potential for a fishing operation. St. Ignace proved to be the best location, since it was close to Lake Huron as well as Lake Michigan and to the famous whitefish banks. The following spring the brothers and their families moved to St. Ignace, though, after a few years, Harry sold out his share and moved back to the island.

Jule, Charlie and Harry found the St. Ignace area to have an abundance of whitefish. Pound nets were used along the whitefish banks by most of the fishermen in this region, and they could only be used seasonally. Most of the whitefish were being shipped during periods of glutted markets when prices were low. Using their gill nets, they could easily follow the movement of the fish, so the Hagens way of fishing was adaptable to different areas and to all seasons. In the winter months, Jule and Charlie used a team of dogs and a sled to haul gill nets and gear to different fishing grounds and set their nets through the ice. The Hagens fished six days a week and always kept their nets, boat, and other gear in top condition, which helped give them more fish production. Jule and Charlie also introduced other innovations to the local fishing industry. They were the first to market whitefish livers and the first to smoke fish for the retail trade, and they would fillet and bone the fish so they were ready for the pan. Another innovation was their diesel engine, which ran their boat at about one-sixth the fuel cost of the other boats.

One foggy fall morning, a reporter went along with the brothers fishing on a day when all the other boats were moored up:

> **W**ith only occasional glances at watch and compass they would calmly steer their
> wallowing boat fifteen or twenty miles out in either Lake Huron or Michigan and pick
> up a buoy which many a sailor with papers would have had difficulty locating on a
> clear day. Their knowledge of weather conditions, water depths, and movement of
> fish appeared to rest more on instinct than on any scientific data at their command.
> I used to watch in amazement as they debated the best place to set their nets.
>
>   We would be so far from land that the mainland would appear as only a
> black line on the horizon. The wind would be blowing up a sea that would periodi-
> cally send our wide beamed, 45-foot long boat up on the crest of the wave only to
> have it slide heavily into the trough at the next moment. Scudding clouds would
> obscure the sky, which might have offered some clue to our location. "We should
> have fifteen fathom here," Jule would say as Charlie threw out the one-pound sound-
> ing lead and then waited as it was pulled up and the fathoms counted off. "Fifteen
> fathom," Charlie would say. "With the moon going dark, the whitefish will be mov-
> ing down the bank. We'd better run nor' west a little. Should have about twenty fath-
> om." After a few minutes run he'd slow the motor down and once again the lead
> would go over the side.[62]

After 1935, Jule spent the winter months in Florida, giving up his winter fishing operation. He
spent a good share of his time mackerel fishing and oyster digging. He finally retired in 1954, after a
long career in fishing, as did his brother Charlie. The *Detroit Free Press* published an article about the
Hagen brothers at the time of their retirement:

Brothers In Fishing Business Never Argued In 60 Years

ST. IGNACE MICH. – Two brothers, who began fishing at Washington Island nearly 60 years ago, are retiring this fall after a half-century of commercial fishing – without one quarrel to mar their fishing partnership.

   They are Charles and Jule Hagen, 72 and 71 years of age, respectively, the
sons of Norwegian Immigrants who were among the early settlers of Washington
Island. The brothers and their families moved to St. Ignace in 1923 and operated the
Hagen Fish Company. "If we ever disagreed, we stopped talking, so we never quar-
reled," said Charles. They recently sold their 42-foot boat, the *Fish Hunter* that had
served them continuously for 38 seasons. Through the years they wore out four
engines – a Straubel 25-horsepower gasoline engine, a Straubel 40-horsepower gasoline engine, a Fairbanks and Morse 30-horsepower diesel engine, and a Fairbanks and
Morse 40-horsepower diesel engine. The last engine they purchased, and which was
in the *Hunter* when she was sold, was a Chrysler gasoline engine. However, only once
did engine failure require them to be towed into port – in 1953, Charlie and Jule had

to be towed in by Jule's son Dick, because of engine failure. They were able to set one box of nets, fortunately for them, for that one box was caught in a bad storm and practically ruined by black moss.

Exciting adventures? They had none "Because we were careful," Jule said.

The Hagen brothers have seen progress and distress in the fishing industry on the Great Lakes since they first set and lifted nets from a little sailboat at Washington Island. Nets are now made of nylon instead of cotton and floats are of plastic rather than wood; the sea lamprey has virtually destroyed the lake trout but the once worthless sturgeon now brings up to a dollar per pound.

The Hagens believe there is still a future in the commercial fishing business despite the sea lamprey menace. In fact, they expect to set nets from a rowboat next summer, just to keep their hand in the business on a part time basis.

Swara Oswald Hagen also fished from the Foss dock at Gasoline Town for most of his life, except for a few years when he moved his operation to Naubinway, Michigan. Swara was born on Washington Island on May 2, 1887 and was the third son of Ole and Fanny Hagen. He was a mild-mannered individual and was close to his older brother Jule. When he turned eighteen, he began fishing with his brother Charlie and fished with him until 1913. Then he became co-owner of a farming operation near Washington Harbor that belonged to his brother-in-law. However, after a few years of farming, he sold out his share and resumed fishing. Swara bought a gill-net boat named the *Mascot*. She was a 30-foot wood boat, powered by a 20 horsepower Straubel gasoline engine, and had been built at Green Bay.

Swara kept his fishing operation overhead to a minimum. He would have one hired man on the boat with him and run eight boxes of nets a day, though sometimes he reset half of his nets and brought four boxes back in with him. Swara generally fished whitefish and trout from the "inside bank," which was north of Washington Harbor. His son Bennett remembers going out with him early in the morning before school and lifting eight boxes of nets and then setting eight more boxes of dry nets. It was a lot easier to set dry nets than to reset nets that had just been lifted, since the dry nets were packed neatly in the boxes with floats on one side and the lead weights on the other.

Nets were set as the boat was moving, and usually the person or persons setting had to keep with the speed of the boat. Bennett was always amazed at how fast his father could set nets. Swara would do this alone, working both cork line and lead line, while the other crew member drove the boat and slid the boxes to Swara. When a box was almost empty the net would have to be tied to the next one, and tied in a hurry. This took skill, especially when done alone or when using a small crew.

On June 17, 1915, Swara married Agnes Foss, one of Matt Foss's daughters, at a small ceremony at Sturgeon Bay, Wisconsin. They had four children, all born and raised on the island. In 1924, Swara decided to try fishing elsewhere. His brothers who had moved a year earlier told him how great the fishing was in waters off northern Michigan. Swara moved his family to Naubinway, Michigan, and fished there for two seasons. However, Swara didn't find the area to be profitable for him, so he moved his family back to Washington Island.

Swara picked up where he had left off two years earlier in the fishing business in Gas Town. He sold the *Mascot* and began fixing up a boat that was beached on the east side of Washington Harbor that once belonged to Tine (Valentine) Irr. It sat for many years covered up on shore near the wood dock. Swara and Newell Cornell replaced boards and rebuilt the pilot house on what was left of the old wooden hull. He took the Straubel engine out of the *Mascot* and installed it in the rebuilt one. Swara called her the *Hagen* and used her for thirteen years. Then, in 1946, before moving to Chicago, he sold her to Dave Lucke, who fished with it at Jackson Harbor.

Swara's two sons, Donald and Bennett, lived in Chicago and were thinking of starting a fish store. Swara, being a generous man and a good father, loaned them $10,000 to start their business. He mortgaged his house and got the money from the town insurance company. Ray Krauss was the treasurer then and was pleasantly surprised at how fast they paid back the loan. In less than two years, and it was all paid off. Swara helped out in the fish store for a year, then moved back to the island and bought the *K.E.M Jacob* from Jake Ellefson. He fished for himself until 1949, then sold his boat and worked for various island fishermen and for the Ed Anderson Potato Company.

Harold Trygvie (Harry) Hagen was born on Washington Island on March 16, 1889. Harry loved to hunt, fish, and play baseball when he was growing up, activities that he learned from his father Ole. Harry played on the island baseball team, along with his brothers Jule and Henry. Harry was a rather good second baseman and played for several seasons.

On October 7, 1914, Harry married Mamie (Amelia) Foss, another daughter of Matt Foss and a sister to Agnes Foss, who would marry Harry's brother Swara a year later. They bought a house near Gas Town, next door to Matt Foss's house. They had four children, Harold, Clarice, Roger, and Shirley.

Harry Hagen began fishing from Gas Town and formed a partnership with his brothers Jule and Charlie. They fished together through the 1922 season, and the following spring they moved their fishing operations to St. Ignace, Michigan. After a few years fishing there, Harry decided to move back to the island. He sold out his share to his brothers. He was homesick for the island – a place he loved and would always call home.

Upon returning to the island in the spring of 1925, Harry resumed fishing from Gas Town. He had the 45-foot *Majestic* built at Sturgeon Bay Boat Works. It's said that he named the boat after a De Pere movie theatre. She had a 30-36 horsepower Kahlenberg crude oil engine, which was later replaced with a Fairbanks & Morse gasoline engine. The Hagens liked these engines, and all the brothers used them. With a new boat and a new start, Harry hired a crew of four to help him with his fishing operation. He had a two-man shore crew and two men on the boat. Oliver Bjarnarson and Alex Koyen worked for Harry for a while. One of his crewmembers, Ted Paulsen, was accidentally killed early one morning. While they were backing out from the dock during the dark hours of the early morning, Ted stuck his head out of a porthole and was crushed by the dock pilings. Ted was only twenty-three years old.

Harry was a successful whitefish fisherman and seemed always to know where the whitefish were. He was an early riser and liked to get out and set his nets before the wind picked up. Harry developed a technique for setting nets in a large "swing," or U pattern. It was only effective in places where the current wasn't strong. Harry seemed to know where it could work and where not. His brother Swara also used this technique. He would set four boxes of nets and then swing the boat and set four more opposite the others. Jake Ellefson remarked that "Harry was an excellent fisherman. He knew where he could make this effective and where he couldn't. He was probably the most successful whitefish fisherman in the area. That's partly because he didn't fish or like to fish chubs, so he was at it [fishing for whitefish] year after year."[63]

In the winter, before the ice set in, Harry and Swara and most of the other fishermen from Washington Harbor relocated their boats to Detroit Harbor for the winter months. Howard Foss remembers what a big day it was when the fishermen made they're way back to Gasoline Town in the springtime. Howard sometimes even set off charges of dynamite to break up the ice around the dock for them.

Harry was known for his fondness for beer. Harry's nephew, Bennett Hagen, remembers that Harry would come down some mornings with a bottle of beer in his hand. Every now and then they would load up the truck with beer bottles and cans and dump them in the woods behind the house. This came to be known as "Kingsbury Hill" since there were many such deposits made there over the years.

Another story about Harry was told by Irvin Goodlet, an island resident, farmer and fisherman:

At one time on [Washington] Island there had to be twenty-five gill-net boats fishing chubs, which meant there were about 250 fish boxes a day being shipped out, never to return, and as a result the M & M box factory in Marinette, Wisconsin supplied the island with fish boxes. The Coffey brothers, originally from the island, owned the factory. In appreciation for this business, they sent an annual keg of beer to the Island fishermen. The keg was stored in the icehouse at Matt Foss's, who was in charge of packing fish for Washington Harbor fishermen. A party was then held for all the fishermen. It would have been better for the fishermen if the party were to have been held as soon as the keg arrived. On the day of the party, with about fifty thirsty fishermen seated in a circle around the beer keg, those present were on their first glass. Swara Hagen was about five minutes late for the party. He found a glass and went over to fill it up and only got a hiss 'What the hell is this?' he asked. Closer examination showed the keg was bone dry. An investigation showed that the bunghole had several punctures in the cork, which meant whoever was in charge of the icehouse was strictly on a liquid diet. It was ironic when at a later date Swara found out it was his brother Harry who had helped Howard Foss consume the contents.[64]

Harry fished from the Foss dock most of his life, save for a few years at St. Ignace and a few years at Jackson Harbor. He moved to Jackson Harbor in 1946 and continued to fish for another ten years, then retired in 1956. He sold the *Majestic* to Lorman Greenfeldt, and in 1957 Lorman sold it to Frank Eichler, a fisherman from Kenosha. It was finally abandoned in 1976. Harry and Swara were two of the last fishermen to use the Foss dock.

Tom Goodman came to Gas Town from the Furlong dock in 1905 after buying the *Welcome* from John Cornell. Tom also had a gas tug called the *Gertrude* that he kept at the Furlong dock. Like many other fishermen of that region, Tom fished for whitefish, trout and chubs. He had a four-man crew, including Orville Wyllie, Burt Cornell; later on, Tom's two sons, Harold and Paul, worked with him. Tom was born on Washington Island, as was his brother Albert, and three sisters. Tom changed his last name from Gudmunder to Goodman; his brother Albert kept their father's name, Gudmunder, but changed the spelling.

Their father was an Icelandic immigrant who settled in Milwaukee upon arriving from Iceland in 1870. He fished for some time at Jones Island and later settled on Washington Island. He did a little fishing from the island, but then, getting on in years, he turned to making new nets for the fisherman. The following is a personal account of his immigration from Iceland to the United States as told to friends before he passed away:

An Icelandic gentleman and the Danish consul at Milwaukee had married sisters. And so it came that the Icelander went to visit his kinsmen in Milwaukee. He wrote back to Iceland and this is what he said: "All the gold in the mountains of California cannot equal the wealth that is to be found in the waters of Lake Michigan." He meant fish. I was a young man living on the south coast of Iceland, where my family had moved from my childhood home in the shadows of Mount Hekla. I was thirty years old, a fisherman and a net-maker, and I had my own fishing boat. I heard the letter from Milwaukee read aloud, and I decided to see for myself if the fishing were as good as the letter said. So I came across the sea, although my friends in Iceland feared I would be scalped by Indians in the little known, to us, region of Wisconsin. That was in 1869. For a year I fished at Jones Island, Milwaukee. The next summer I was one of a crew of four who took a fishing boat up to the Door of Death. We landed on Washington Island and found the fishing good. So I settled here. Gudmunder's letter to friends back in Iceland interested them and eventually they came over to the United States and settled on Washington Island. This influx of Icelanders to Washington Island would mark a spot in History and give the Island some notoriety as being the oldest Icelandic settlement in the region. Some of the people that settled on the Island were: Sigurd Sigurdson, Hannes Johnson, Arni Gudmundsen, John Gislason, Hans Johnson, John Johnson, John Gunnlaugsson, Peter Gunnlaugsson, "Yes-Yes" Einarson, Tom Einarson, John Einarson, and Magnus Johnson.[65]

After moving to the Foss dock, Tom Goodman used the small dock just south of the slip, since this area was close to his net sheds. After selling the *Gertrude,* Tom acquired a 34-foot wood fish tug at Green Bay and renamed it the *Big Peder* after his father-in-law Captain Peder Hanson. He moored the *Big Peder* on the outside of the slip at the main dock because the water was deeper there. In 1926, Tom had the *Hans* built at Sturgeon Bay Boat Works. This was a modern tug with a 45-54 Kahlenberg engine, the pride of his fleet, he called her. In the early 1940s, Tom and his sons moved their fishing operation to Jackson Harbor and fished from the Hanson dock for a number of years before retiring in the mid 1960s.

Tom's grandson, Paul Goodman, remembers fishing with his father and grandfather from Jackson

Harbor on the *Hans*. Paul was about thirteen years old, and at that time fishermen were catching only chubs. After a botulism scare in the early 1960s which nearly shut down the chub fishery, Paul's father moved off the island. He got out of fishing and worked in a plant north of Milwaukee.

Paul got into fishing in 1975 when he was twenty-three years old. He went into partnership with his cousin Charlie Voight. Together they bought a gill-net tug called the *Susie*. She was built in Saginaw, Michigan, in the 1940s, a 38-foot, all steel boat with a gasoline engine. They later replaced the engine with a Volvo diesel. Paul and Charlie fished together several years from Gills Rock, then Paul sold his share and bought another fish tug called the *Falcon* and fished with Lyle Teskie a few years. In 1990, Paul found out what it meant to be squeezed out of the business by the quota system. He sold what quota he had to Charlie Henriksen, and made the transition to the sport fishery. Paul enjoys commercial fishing, which has been in his family for more than a hundred years, but he also enjoys running his charter service and fish market in Gills Rock.

Albert Goodmander, Tom's brother, also pursued a fishing career nearly all his life. He began fishing with his father, Gudmunder Gudmundsen from a sailboat when he was ten years old. They fished mainly for trout, using hook and line rigs and occasionally a few gill nets. He and his brother Tom fished together for a while, until Albert went into partnership with Haldon Johnson and they began to fish from Gas Town in 1915. Albert and Haldon had the *R.E. Helen*, built by the Burger Boat Company at Manitowoc, Wisconsin, a 34-foot boat with a 30-36 two-cylinder Kahlenberg engine. In 1936, Albert and Haldon decided to have another boat built, at Peterson Boat Works, a 42 by 12 foot all-wood vessel with a three-cylinder 60-70 Kahlenberg oil engine that they called the *Islander*.

Albert and Haldon had a successful partnership and fished for many years from the Foss dock. In the mid 1940s they decided to move their operation to Milwaukee and fished there for a few years before the sea lamprey started to deplete the lake trout population. Many Door County fishermen moved their operations to Milwaukee during the winter months, and Alvin Anderson, a native Door County fisherman, remembers those days: "I remember when some of those guy's came down here [Milwaukee] to fish lake trout. We pretty much all did. Those guys had seven, eight, and ten gangs in the water – fourteen- to sixteen-box gangs they were running. The old *Islander*, Albert Goodmander and Johnson, I think they used to have eleven or twelve eighteen- to twenty-box gangs in around the time of Lent. They had a big crew. "[66]

Albert and Haldon moved back to Washington Island in 1947 and resumed fishing from Jackson Harbor. With the trout nearly gone, they fished for whitefish, herring and chubs. They had a four-man crew. Haldon's two sons, Rupert and Percy, worked in the business until 1960, when their father passed away from cancer and Albert retired. An older gentleman who lived on the east side of Washington Island would walk every day to Gasoline Town and help Haldon and Albert. It was a passion with him. He loved the camaraderie among the fishermen.

Joe Johnson and his brother Ben fished from Gasoline Town for some time. They had a 34-foot wood boat named the *Una* that had a 10-horsepower gasoline engine. Joe and Ben also had purchased the *Ragna* from John Ellefson and fished with her from the Foss dock. After a few years, they moved to Jackson Harbor, where Ben fished with Fred Bjarnarson.

Irr's Dock and Indian Point

On the northern side Washington island, between Washington Harbor and Jackson Harbor there is a stretch of land with cobblestone shores and heavily wooded forests. Over the years various fishermen succeeded in fishing from this remote area, even though there was no protection from the elements. Winter ice and northerly winds were hard on the fishermen's docks and buildings, but the region is close to one of the best fishing grounds in northern Lake Michigan. In the latter part of nineteenth century, when the Mackinaw boats were in use, it was a great advantage to be close to the fishing grounds, and some of the best whitefish and herring fishing was to found a short distance off the shore.

Andrew Irr and his bride moved to this region of the island from Quinnesec, Michigan in in 1858, and were among the first settlers to do so. Irr accquired a large tract of land on the north end of the island, and they found that this area suited them well. Andrew was soon felling trees from which he built a house and a good size dock. Irr was a very large and powerful man, and it wasn't long before he had a little farm from which to provide for his family. Irr also built a store, and began fishing for whitefish, using both pound and gill nets. In the winter, he cut cordwood and sold it to steam-powered freight boats that frequently stopped over. Passenger boats running from Green Bay to Buffalo, New York also frequented Irr's dock to replenish their wood fuel, and sometimes the steamers would lie over for the night and the passengers would stay in the Irr home. However, the house was rather small, and Irr eventually built a bigger house and a store to accommodate his guests.[67]

Andrew had a successful fishery complete with an icehouse, cooperage, and net sheds. He shipped out several tons of whitefish and kept a half dozen island men busy making barrels and packing fish. At first, he salted the fish, but later packed them in ice. At this time on Washington Island, Irr's dock and those at Ranney's and Foss's were the only ones to have ice houses, and most of the fish were shipped out from those locations. Andrew and his wife left Washington Island and moved back to Quinesec, Michigan in the late 1870s, and his wife became ill there and passed away. Andrew then moved back to the island and settled back into his house. He fished and farmed the rest of his life on Washington Island.

The Irrs had five children: Valentine, Nan, Caroline, Francis, and George. George died at the age of fourteen from small pox. There were also three children form Mrs. Irr's first marriage, a son named Loyal Baker and two girls. All the Irr boys grew up to become fishermen. The only one of their children to marry was Francis Irr, who married Andrew Swenson, and lived with her husband on Washington Island in the big house that her father had built. They raised five children: Sherman, Georgian, Janie, Angus, and Caroline. Andrew fished for herring in the fall of the year and also farmed and ran a small cherry and apple orchard. He was known for his cherry wine and story telling, and had entertained many friends and visitors.[68]

The Irr boys remained bachelors all their lives and their sister Caroline lived with them and kept the house. Nan and Tine Irr followed in their father's footsteps and took over the fishery after their father passed away. They continued to catch whitefish with gill nets and pound nets, and they also began fishing for herring in the fall of the year. In 1906 they bought the *Active*, a gasoline-powered tug, from James Denio and they later acquired the *F. Bittner*. Eventually, they moved their boats to Washington Harbor because it offered better protection from the elements. They were well up in years when they finally sold their boats and retired after many long years of fishing.

Chapter 8 Notes

1 Jessie Miner, "History and Anecdotes of Washington Island;" *Island Tales: an Anthology* prep. Kay Curtis (Washington Island, 1937), 10.

2 Conan Bryant Eaton, *Washington Island 1836-1876* (Conan Bryant Eaton 1972), 4. I.A. Lapham, "Wisconsin" (Milwaukee, 1846), 25.

3 Foster and Whitney, *Rock Island*, cited in Conan Bryant Eaton, *Washington Island 1836-1876*, (Conan Bryant Eaton, 1972), 5.

4 *Green Bay Advocate*, February 27, 1851. (Cited in Eaton, *Washington Island 1836-1876*, 7)

5 Jessie Miner, "Jessie Bosses Organization of Town, "History and Anecdotes of Washington Island," *Island Tales,* Washington Island, 1937), 7.

6 Ibid. & Hjalmer R. Holand, *History of Door County, vol. 1* (Chicago, Illinois: S.J. Publishing Company, 1917), 279.

7 Eaton, *Washington Island 1836 – 1876*, footnote # 46, p. 17.

8 Eaton, *Washington Island 1836-1876*, p.22.

9 Anne T. Whitney, *Lets Talk About Washington Island 1850- 1950* (Town Of Washington 1995), 25.

10. Arthur and Evelyn Knudson, "A gleam Across the Wave," *Island Tales: an Anthology*, Kay Curtis, eds.& comp., 58.

11. Ibid.

12. Ray McDonald, *Four Islands* (Wolfsong Publications, 1984), 22.

13 Conan Bryant Eaton, *Washington Island 1836- 1837: The Island Series* (Eaton, 1972 reprint, Bayprint Inc., Sturgeon Bay, Wisconsin, 1988), 31-32 footnote no. 74. Special Note by Conan Eaton, He adds: Demos Soucie(variously spelled) is possibly the only avowed "Frenchmen" to spend a considerable period of years in the town; (1870's census, shows him born in Maine). His 300 acres seem questionable; town records verify his owning eighty acres on today's Mountain Road in 1875. Soucie's figures on boats and fishermen also appear bloated; 1870 census lists 47 fishermen, not 300, implying possibly 16 boats not 100. Additional note: Arthur & Evelyn Knudsen, "A Gleam Across the Wave," *Island Tales: an Anthology*, 60. (Authors note: according to pg. 60, Demas Soucie at that time lived near the Nolan's property at the southeast end of Washington Harbor, circa 1860s. He fished by himself in a mackinaw boat.)

14 Walter M. and Mary K. Hirthe, "The Conversion from Manpower to Steam Power in the Fishing Industry"; *Door County Almanac No. 3* (Dragonsbreath Press, 1986), 34.

15. *Door County Advocate*, August 10, 1870.

16. Hirthe & Hirthe discuss the O'Neils and cite Jesse Miner. Op. cit. 16.

17 Eaton, *Washington Island 1836-1876*, 40, footnote # 95.

18. Ibid, 38.

19. Ibid, 44 & Interview with Bernadette Rainsford, October, 2003.

20. Interview with Jake Ellefson, June 12, 2004.

21. Eaton, *Washington Island 1836-1876: The Island Series*, 41.

22 Eaton, Ibid, 41-42.

23. Interview with Bennet Hagen, January 8, 2002.

24. Ray McDonald, *Four Islands*, 12-13.

25. Ibid.

26. See Schreiber, Edward & Lois, *Fish Creek Voices: An Oral History of a Door County Village* (Wm Caxton Ltd, Ellison Bay, 1990) for information on the Hart Line and for reminiscences of experiences with the Goodrich steamers and with boats operated by the Hill Steamboat Line.

27. See Elliott, James, *Red Stacks Over the Horizon* (Ellison Bay, WI: Wm Caxton Ltd, 2005) for a comprehensive history of the Goodrich Transit Company.

28. Interview with Jake Ellefson, June 12, 2004.

29 Ray McDonald, *Four Islands: A History of Detroit, Rock, St. Martins, and Washington Islands* (Wolfsong Publications, 1984), 24.

30. Ibid, 7.

31. Interview with Jim Cornell, May 4, 2002. Ray McDonald, *Four Islands*, 26.

32 Cheryl Ganz, "Anderson's Island Transit," *Door County Advocate* (Dragonsbreath Press), 234.

33 Anderson, Hannes; Washington Island, Through the Years. *Washington Island Observer* October 12, 2006.

34 Ibid, 235.

35 Richard Purinton, *Over and Back: Picture History of Transportation to Washington Island* (De Pere, WI: Independent Printing, 1990), 66.

36 Historical Collections of the Great Lakes; Great Lakes Vessels Online Index University Libraries Bowling Green State University; http:/digin.bgsu.edu/cgi-win/xvsl.exe

37. Ray McDonald, *Four Islands*, 20.

38. "Man Burns to Death," *Door County Advocate*, October 10, 1912. Additional source, a speculative story told to the author during an interview with Jim Cornell, May 4, 2002.

39. Ray McDonald, *Four Islands*, 14.

40 Ibid, 14-15.

41. Ibid, 14.

42. Ibid, 17.

[43] Lorel Gordon, "Fishing – A Young Family Tradition," *Door County Almanac No. 3*; (Dragonsbreath Press 1986), 64-69.

[44] Ibid, 66.

[45] Arthur and Evelyn Knudsen, "A Gleam Across the Wave: The biography of Martin Nicolai Knudsen," Chapter 5 Washington Harbor. *Island Tales*; 59-60.

[46]. *Green Bay Advocate*, November 10, 1913.

[47]. *Green Bay Advocate*, November 10, 1913.

[48]. Ray McDonald, *Four Islands*, 36-37. & Washington Island Observer.

[49] Interview with Carol Jornt, July 3, 2004. Also see Chapter 10 Detroit Harbor.

[50]. Ray McDonald, *Four Islands*, 37.

[51]. Ibid, 39 & Fishtug web page: Fishtug www.airstream.comm.net/fishtug/

[52] Paul J. Creviere, Jr., *Wild Gales and Tattered Sails* (Creviere, 1997), 122.

[53] Paula McDonald, *Interview with Howard Foss*, 1979.

[54]. Ibid; also an interview with Kirby Foss, March 2, 2002.

[55] Interview with Kirby Foss, March 2, 2002.

[56] Howard Foss interview conducted by Paula (Hansen) McDonald, 1979.

[57] The term "Domers" originated from an old commercial fisherman's snack, when he took one of the fish, and prepared it with onions and salt, then soaked the paper-wrapped fish in water, and place it on the steam dome of the steam engine. It's how the fishboil came to be.

[58] Interview with Kirby Foss, March 2, 2002.

[59] Ray McDonald, *Four Islands*, 43.

60. Interview with Kirby Foss, March 2, 2002.

61. Percy Hagen, "The Hagen/Gudmundsen Story," (1950) family compilation prepared by Percy Hagen. Cites the Hagen brothers biographies.

62. The Hagen Family 1883 to 2005, comp. by Cathy Meader (2005). Revised from Percy Hagen's, "The Hagen/Gudmundsen Story," 1950.

63. Interview with Jake Ellefson, October 2, 2001.

64. Vic Goodlet, *Kill The Umpire*; (Vic Goodlet 2001), 60.

65. Fred L. Holmes, *Old World Wisconsin: Around Europe in the Badger State* (Wisconsin House Ltd), 220-221.

66. Interview with Alvin Anderson, January 23, 2004.

67. Ray McDonald, *Four Islands*, 45-46.

68. Ibid.

Pic. 8.1 Goodrich boat *Carolina* entering Washington Harbor, circa 1920s. Warehouse and icehouse at the Furlong dock located on the west side of Washington harbor. (Photo courtesy of Washington Island Archives)

Pic 8.2 Fred and Percy Young's boat *Sea Queen* moored inside the slip at the furlong dock, looking south, circa 1938. Jim Cornell's small boat the *Don Deloris* moored up on the west side of the slip. (Photo courtesy Washington Island Archives)

Pic 8.3 Art and Lloyd Young's boat *Rainbow* coming into the slip at the Furlong dock. *Jane Elizabeth,* in the foreground, circa 1930s. (Photo courtesy of Washington Island Archives)

Pic 8.4 The "Big Blow" of 1913 lasted four days. Photo of the *Halstead* and the *J.H Stevens* left of her and in the background near the furlong dock the *Minerva* seeking shelter from the storm, looking northwest. (Photo courtesy of the Washington Island Archives)

Pic 8.5 The *Halstead* beached after the November blow of 1913. Background is the present day Schoolhouse beach at Washington Harbor. (Photo courtesy of the Washington Island Archives)

Pic 8.6 Early Gasoline Town fishing fleet in the slip circa 1912. Hagen Brothers standing on the *Viking*. Hannes Johnson aboard the *Sea Bird* in the background. (Photo Courtesy of Ross and Cathy Meader)

Pic. 8.7 Fish tugs moored up in the slip at Gasoline Town circa 1907. L to R *Ragna*, unknown, *Irma Jeanette*, and the steam tug *Welcome* in the background owned by Tom Goodman. (Photo courtesy of Ross and Cathy Meader)

Pic 8.8 Gasoline Town circa 1917 looking west from the bluff above the old quarry bed where Gasoline Town was built. Net reels in the foreground; men standing at the slip in the foreground. Icehouse on the right. (Photo Courtesy of the Washington Island Archives)

Pic 8.9   Gasoline Town looking west the day after the November 1913 blow. Notice the ice cladding on the north side of the building roofs and two boats overturned and lay at the bottom in the slip. Packaging shed is on the left in the background, the warehouse to the right and John Ellefson's shed ahead of the warehouse. (Photo courtesy of Ross and Cathy Meader)

Pic. 8.10   Westerly view of Gasoline Town. Icehouse to the right and the warehouse is in the background. Notice a team of horses and wagon backed up to the warehouse. (Photo courtesy of the Washington Island Archives**)**

Pic.8.11 Hannes and his brother "Yonsi" Johnson aboard their gill-net tug *Hazel Jeanette*. (Photo courtesy of Ross and Cathy Meader)

Pic 8.12 Aerial view of Gasoline Town Circa 1950s after all the fishermen ceased their operations and moved to Jackson Harbor. Most of the buildings including the large warehouse and packaging shed are gone and the icehouse stands with no roof. (Photo Courtesy of Jens Hansen)

Pic. 8.13 Hagen Brothers enjoying a cold one after a hard days work. L to R. Charlie Hagen, Jule Hagen, Ole Swenson, and Harry Hagen. (Photo courtesy of Ross and Cathy Meader)

Pic. 8.14 Swara Hagen standing and Harry relaxing on the bow of his boat *Majestic* in the slip, circa 1930s. Swara's boat the *Hagen* is to the left. A net shed is on the left and the packaging shed is in the back ground. (Photo courtesy of Ross and Cathy Meader)

Pic. 8.15 Showing off the days catch of native lake trout. From left, Haldon Johnson standing on the *R.E. Helen*, Hannes Johnson Sr., Albert Goodmander holding trout, Junius Garret, and Wesley Peterson in the background. (Photo courtesy of Ross and Cathy Meader)

Pic. 8.16 Gasoline Town fishermen standing atop Tom Goodman's gill-net tug, *Big Peder*, named after his father-in-law, Peder Hanson. Notice one of the fishermen holding a case of Rahrs beer, circa 1920s. (Photo courtesy of Ross and Cathy Meader)

Chapter 9

Jackson Harbor

Jackson Harbor is on the northeast side of Washington Island. Its shallow waters and sandy shore-line are edged with a mixed coniferous and hardwood forest. The entrance in to Jackson Harbor is shallower than the water inside the harbor, which posed problems for the larger draft boats that began to frequent this region. However, outside the harbor, the depth drops considerably to the north and west. Rock Island, with its 900 wooded acres, lies about one mile north east of Jackson Harbor. To the south and east of Rock Island, the lake is relatively shallower, and the north and west is consider-ably deeper with depths of 100 feet and more.

Jackson Harbor offers better protection from high winds and moving ice than does Washington Harbor. However, for nearly a century from 1850 to 1950, most of the fishermen used Washington Harbor because of its deeper water allowed large freight boats to have better dockage. The settlers and fishermen on Rock Island and St. Martin Island began to relocate in the late 1860s. Most were fisher-men seeking protective harbors and docks where freight could come in and out. Jackson Harbor was close by, but there was no settlement or docks there in the late 1860s. According to Jessie Miner's jour-nals, a Civil War veteran named Edwin Richmond fished from Jackson Harbor in the early 1870s and the 1870 census includes the Vermont- born fisherman, his wife and a child.[1] But, Washington Harbor had a major dock and other facilities for a fishery to operate successfully; therefore most fishermen went there rather than to Jackson Harbor. Jackson Harbor was settled much later than Washington Harbor; sometime in the late 1880s, where some settlers found it to be ideal for pound net fishing, and others made their living cutting cordwood.

There were no improved roads connecting Jackson Harbor to the rest of the island, and every-thing therefore had to be shipped in and out by boat. According to the island real estate map of 1903 there were two roads that connected Jackson Harbor at that time to a main road that ran from the west end of the island, from the shore of the John Larson property, due east, and terminating south and east of Jackson Harbor at the Ole Christiansen property. (See Fig. 9.1)

After 1900, fishing and logging gradually became more prevalent at Jackson Harbor. In 1900, there was only one gill-net fishing boat, owned by John Christianson and Curt Johnson. A few other fishermen used pound-net rigs, but after about 1905 fishing activities started to increase. More people saw opportunity at Jackson Harbor, especially fishermen. There was also plenty timber to be cut for cordwood and lumber.

Each spring, the woodcutters would have 500 cords or more of wood piled in front of the Rasmus Hanson homestead, awaiting shipment to southern ports of Lake Michigan. Out on the McDonald property, there were also a large number of log piles. In the spring and summer, small steamboats would come in to pick up the cordwood, and the logs would be floated out to the boats

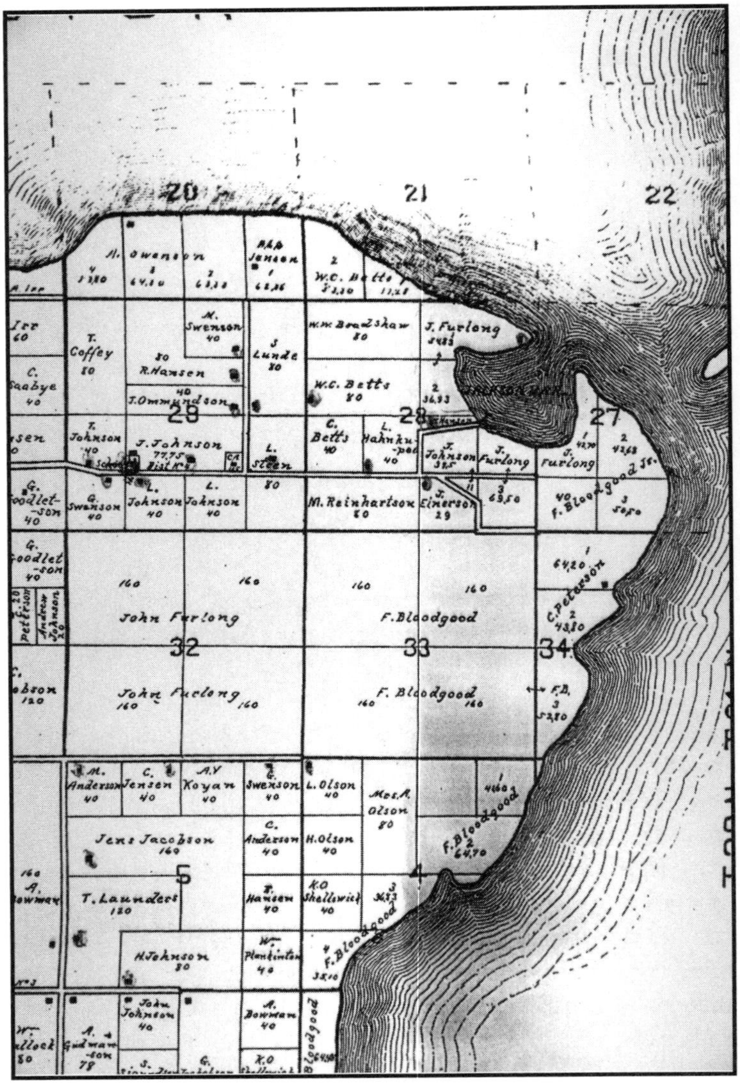

Fig. 9.1 Island real estate map 1899 (Courtesy Washington Island Archives)

and then loaded into the holds. Two of the steamboats that frequented Jackson Harbor in the early days were the *J.S Course*, owned by Charles Anderson from Frankfort, Michigan, and the *Addie Wade* owned by Joseph LaMere of Jacksonport, Wisconsin.[2]

A Norwegian immigrant named Eric Lunde lived at Jackson Harbor and operated a small schooner called the *Harvey Ransome*, frequently hauling wood during the summer months. The *Harvey Ransome* was built in 1887 at South Haven, Michigan. She was a 60-foot two-masted schooner with 16 feet on the beam. In 1913, it sank during a storm in Green Bay. Another sailing vessel that hauled mainly four-foot cordwood from Jackson Harbor was the *Lucy Graham*. Her owner and operator was a hardy sailor by the name of Captain Goodlet Goodletson. Captain Goodletson was born in Norway and had moved to the United States with his mother, father, and uncle. After serving in the infantry during the Civil War, he moved to Washington Island, acquired the schooner *Lucy Graham*, and sailed her for many years.[3]

During the first decade of the twentieth century, there were only a few landowners in Jackson Harbor. Charlie McDonald owned 55 acres on the northwest side of the harbor. Rasmus Hanson owned 76 acres on the south end of the harbor, which he acquired from Jim Denio. Bo Anderson and Ole Christiansen owned all the property on the southeast end of the harbor, each having owned approximately 40 acres.[4]

Early Fishermen and Landowners

Before 1870, there were few inhabitants besides seagulls and waterfowl at Jackson Harbor. A shallow placid harbor with clear blue waters and tree-lined shores was its identity. To this day people are still struck with its natural beauty, and in time, a few fishermen and sailors from neighboring islands began to take notice of the secluded place, and some eventually settled there. These first settlers and landowners built the docks and buildings that made Jackson Harbor into a thriving place for fishing from the turn of the century into the late 1970s. Over the years, many people have come and gone from Jackson Harbor, but some stayed, and their families still live there today.

Chris Klingenberg

According to early records, one of the first landowners at Jackson Harbor was a schooner skipper named Chris Klingenberg, who came to the island from Schlesvig Holstein. He sailed for many years on his schooner, the *Pride*. In 1884, Klingenberg bought approximately 60 acres of land from John Furlong, who by 1879 owned all the land in the southern portion of Jackson Harbor.[5] A few years after he purchased the land, he built a dock – thought to have been the first dock at Jackson Harbor — that was completed in March of 1887. His dock was built where the town dock is today. At that time there were only a few squatters living there, doing a little fishing and cutting wood.

At the time, the lake levels were at a record high. In 1886 it was the highest in recorded history; and the next time the lake would reach that level again would be in 1952, and then again in 1986. The lake remained high for nearly ten years. The natural bar or reef at the entrance of Jackson Harbor was only six feet below the surface at normal lake levels, but high lake levels provided more clearance and enabled a big schooner to enter the harbor. The reef ran from a point of land on the northwest end of the harbor to a point of land on the southeast end. Klingenberg must have known there was logging going on in that region and decided he could utilize the area for his own logging operation. He realized the area had great potential, and he eventually made a good sum of money there. It was said that, "everything went into the Klingenberg jackpot."[6] He knew how to bargain and made deals and trades with other boat owners who came to Jackson Harbor. He used the *Pride* to haul wood for barrel staves to Green Bay.

For many years, Chris used Jackson Harbor for his operations. In 1902, he sold all his property in Jackson Harbor. It was around that time his schooner was wrecked in Washington Harbor. His schooner, *Pride*, was wrecked in Washington Harbor November 22, 1901. She was fully loaded with a cargo of 900 bushels of potatoes and a few cords of wood. On that morning there was a fresh northwest breeze, which made tacking out of the harbor difficult. Evidently there was a failure of the rudder and steering mechanism, and she went aground just north of the Foss dock. The schooner and cargo were a total loss and lacking insurance, the farmers were out their cash crop for the year. Klingenberg sold his property in Jackson Harbor, mostly to John Johnson, to cover his debts. He and his wife Mary then moved to Racine, Wisconsin, where he found work in a factory. Many islanders were sad to see him leave. His wife was a good nurse and had helped many people, and they were both well liked by the island community. Over time he eventually cleared his dept by paying each farmer who had lost their harvest.[7]

Klingenberg sold his land to John Johnson except a few small parcels that went to a few pound-net fishermen. John Johnson later sold the Klingenberg property to James Denio, who later sold it to Rasmus Hanson in 1904. Real estate often changed hands frequently in those days. Some people found Jackson Harbor a desirable location, and others couldn't make a go of it and moved on. One of the small parcels was sold to Morten Jorgenson, who operated a pound-net. Morten held the property for only a year and then decided to move on. He sold his property to Gunner Jensen, who built a dock and operated a pound-net outside of the harbor. Gunner later sold it to Jacob Ellefson in 1907, who has had the property ever since.

Another small parcel was sold to Tim Coffey who owned it for two years before selling it John Christianson. Coffey was an Irish immigrant who left his native land of County Clare, Ireland, with his brother Tom and Tom's wife Catherine. They had heard that the fishing grounds off of Washington Island were good, prompting them to settle at the "Irish village" at the west end of Washington Harbor. Tim Coffey raised a family with his wife Mary Sanford Coffey and had nine children. He fished many years from Washington Harbor, and then moved over to Jackson Harbor, where he bought the property from Klingenberg in 1894 and built a small dock where he fished a few years. Tim and his family moved off the island in 1898, and later sold his property to John Christianson in 1904. He and his wife settled at Marinette, Wisconsin, where he lived out the rest of his life; passing away November 18, 1909.

John Christianson

John Christianson, or "Johnny Chris" as many islanders called him, was born in Norway on October 31, 1880, and arrived on Washington Island with his family as a young boy. As a young man he spent some years sailing both on the Great Lakes and also on the ocean. He had many adventures and told many a story about them years later. One story he told from his sailing days was of a time when he and a few others had gone ashore, found a local tavern and commenced to drink. Before long they were in a big brawl, and the next morning he woke up in the morgue with "dead people all around me." [8] It wasn't long after that incident that he moved back the island and began his fishing career.

Christianson returned to Jackson Harbor region in 1902 and fished from the former Tim Coffey property. He first leased the land from him, and then bought the property in 1904, paying $25 for 2 1/2 acres of land with water frontage. There was a dock built but no buildings on the property, so he built a house, an icehouse, and some net sheds. Adolph Moe, a mason who lived on the island, built the house and icehouse from concrete blocks that he made himself, a building technique unique on the island at that time. The buildings still stand today, just southeast of the town dock. John Christianson had a small shed at the end of the dock, and also had laid 300 feet of steel tracks from his house to his packaging shed. He used an 8-foot cart that ran on the tracks to haul fish and net boxes to and from the boat, a real convenience when he came in from a day of fishing. He had his icehouse right at the dock and also used the cart to transport ice to his packaging shed.[9]

John formed a partnership with another fisherman named Curtis Johnson, and they fished together until 1917. Both were bachelors for most of their lives. The first boat John had built was a 22-foot Mackinaw sailboat. He and Curt used it for many years, but when they had heard that Matt Foss had his sailboat, the *Laura,* equipped with a gasoline engine, it wasn't long before John had a gasoline engine in his boat.[10]

John and Chris made frequent trips to Washington Harbor in the early days, a five mile journey by water. Washington Harbor was the closest place from which they shipped their fish and obtained empty fish boxes. On one trip to pick up fish boxes, they set out early one morning when a south wind lent them a smooth sail over. However, as they picked up their supply of empty boxes and headed back, the wind increased and became very gusty. As they neared Indian Point they were overcome by a large gust and the boat tipped on her side with the sails lying in the water. They were unable to right the boat, and their boxes were floating away when John Cornell in his fish tug *Welcome* spotted them as he came in from fishing off Rock Island. Cornell picked them up and towed their boat to Jackson Harbor. They were both very lucky only to lose a few boxes and not their lives.[11]

Around 1912 John Christianson acquired a 32-foot fish tug called the *Pirate*. It was built by his father on Christianson's property just east of the "mountain", a high point of land in the middle of the island. John and Curt fished from that boat until 1917 when Curt sold his share out to John. John then decided he needed a larger boat so he had Rasmus Hanson build him a 40-foot boat, also named the *Pirate*, which he used until he retired from fishing around 1954.

In 1924, John Christianson married Mary Anderson, who had lost her husband a year earlier during a flu epidemic on the island. Her husband Pete had been the mail carrier, and they had five small children together. After Pete died, John began courting Mary and they soon were married, ending John's forty years of bachelorhood. John was a good provider for the children, being a successful fisherman, and as the children got older they helped him fish periodically until they eventually moved off the island.

During the last years of John's fishing career, he called on his long-time buddy, Andrew Nelson, known to everyone as "Little Boy." Little Boy was just that, a short man — nearly a foot shorter than John — and had also sailed in his youth on various schooners, and helped John out until they both retired. Islanders tell of an incident when John had "Little Boy" at the helm of the boat, which was by far a whole different ballgame for him, accustomed as he was to sailing ships and unfamiliar with operating a fishing boat. John was running the engine and "Little Boy" was at the wheel; as they came into the dock. Little Boy began shouting to the people on the dock, "I can handle er ha?" But in his moment of glory, he mistakenly gave the signal for full power instead of idle and the boat hit the dock with a tremendous blow. He hit the outside crib causing the dock to have a ten-inch slant and that became known as "Little Boy's Landing."[12]

Rasmus Hanson

Rasmus Hanson was, for a lack of a better word, a jack-of-all-trades. He was a merchant, sailor, boat builder, carpenter, real estate dabbler, and a family man. Born in Fyn, Denmark, in 1855, he came to America in 1880, landing in Milwaukee, Wisconsin when he was twenty-five years of age. There, he found a job as a boat builder. Three years later, he moved to Washington Island, where he changed the spelling of his last name from Hansen to Hanson with an O (to avoid confusion by the post office since there were already several Hansen's on the island at that time). Rasmus had three brothers – Chris, Knut and Hans – who eventually followed him to the island but kept the spelling of their last name as Hansen. Chris was a sailor, and Knut and Hans B. became farmers; Hans had one of the finest farms on the island, which he later sold to Ed Anderson, the "Potato King."

Rasmus Hanson bought 30 acres of land on the northeast side of Washington Island and started to clear the land of timber and built a house. He used some of the timber to build his first boat, which he named the *Flotilla*. He and his brother Hans started work on it in 1890, and it took them nearly a year to complete. They used two-man crosscut saws to make the planking and framework from large oak and pine logs, a laborious task that required great stamina and strength. In this setup, a log was placed on a frame well above the ground, while one man stood on the ground below the log and the other stood on a platform above it and each worked on one end of the saw. It was a relatively primitive way of sawing logs into lumber, but it really was the only way available to them, since there were no sawmills near by at that time.

The *Flotilla* was a sturdy, well built schooner measuring 55 feet in length and 12 feet across the beam. She had a mainsail, foresail, and jib. Hanson first used his boat for hauling freight, but also used her for several years as a floating store, and would sail her to various ports selling groceries and other items. Around 1904, he had the *Flotilla* equipped with a Kahlenberg gasoline engine, which enabled him to travel more efficiently.

In 1898, Rasmus had gone back to his hometown of Denmark and met woman named Rasmine Rasmussen. She returned with him to Washington Island, and they were married a year later. In 1904, Rasmus bought the Jim Denio property in Jackson Harbor, which had a dock for his schooner and a good-sized house. He converted a large room off the west side of the house into a store and sold groceries. It was a great convenience for local residents at that time, since there were no motor vehicles and the nearest store was the Koyen's store five miles away at Washington Harbor. Going there meant either a long walk or hitching up the horse and buggy. Hanson sold a wide array of sundries, from groceries to hardware, and he also had the store on the *Flotilla*.

In 1906, Rasmus Hanson bought 600 acres on Rock Island, which at that time was a substantial amount of property. It became quite evident that Rasmus was becoming somewhat of an entrepreneur. George Larson of Ephraim owned a small sawmill on Rock Island. Rasmus bought it and moved it to his property at Jackson Harbor. He later sold it to Mads Swenson and John Einarson, who relocated it to Ole Christiansen's property near the lumber camp. Swenson and Einarson sawed timber there and both used it and also sold some locally. After several years John Einarson sold his share to Benny Jensen, and Swenson and Jensen moved the sawmill back to its original location on the Hanson property.

In 1910 Rasmus Hanson sold all his property on Rock Island to Chester Thordarson, an Icelandic inventor and entrepreneur. Thordarson was born in Iceland, came to America when he was five years old, and grew up in Chicago. He became an electrical scientist who held more than one hundred patents and was a good friend of Thomas Edison. After buying Rock Island, he let the place revert to a natural area, though he built several buildings, including a stately stone boathouse which was a scaled-down replica of a great Scandinavian hall in Iceland. He was a nature advocate and believed strongly in the preservation. He once said, "Man can live for two reasons, to create beauty or destroy it. I live to create beauty."[13]

In the spring of the year, there were enormous piles of hardwood cut into four-foot lengths piled on Hanson's dock. It was not unusual for him to have more than five hundred cord or more piled there awaiting shipment. The wood was cut in the winter months hauled to the dock using teams of horses hitched to sleighs. Ole Christiansen also stockpiled huge numbers of logs at his dock and would transport them to southern ports during the summer months.

Rasmine Hanson died in 1910 from complications of pneumonia. She was homesick and had taken a trip back to her native Denmark. One of the reasons Rasmus sold his holdings on Rock Island was to help pay for his wife's trip. Those who knew her said she never really found happiness over in the new country and she always seemed to be very melancholy. She came back to the United States in December and had a very bad cold. By the time she arrived at Sturgeon Bay, her condition had grown worse. A few days later, she died in a hotel at Sister Bay, without having made it back to Washington Island. She was only thirty-two years old and left behind a daughter, Agnes, and three small boys Hans, Art, and Willie.

Greif-stricken, Rasmus made a trip to Denmark in 1912 to find a housekeeper. He hired Anne Christensen, and they set sail back to the United States. But they were stopped in Canada and were told that in order for Miss Christensen to enter the country they had to be married. So they were married by the ship's captain and then made their way back to Washington Island. Three months later, Rasmus lost his young son Willie, who died when he accidentally fell into a large pot of boiling water used for boiling a pig.

Rasmus built another boat in 1914, calling it the *Agnes H*, after his daughter. He installed a 40-horsepower Straubel engine in the boat and used it for hauling freight. Rasmus later sold the *Agnes H* to John Anderson at Detroit Harbor. Rasmus also built boats for other fishermen on the island, such as the *Pirate 11* for John Christianson, the *Rainbow* for the Youngs, who fished from Washington Harbor.

Rasmus Hanson's two sons, Hans and Art worked with Rasmus from the time they were young boys, but in 1919, the two boys decided to start their own business. They moved to Southwest Bay at St. Martin Island, fixed up an old cabin, and started a pound-net operation. After working a few years with little success, they moved back to Jackson Harbor and began working with their father again.

In 1926, Rasmus, with the help of Hans and Art, built a 38-foot fish tug called the *Welcome* and powered her with a 40-horsepower Straubel engine. With this boat, they fished gill nets out of Jackson Harbor and spent a few winters in Kenosha, fishing for whitefish and lake trout. Rasmus continued to improve his dock, adding a few more buildings. He had a large warehouse, icehouse, and net sheds. It was a substantial dock for the time, and in later years many other fishermen used it for their operations. Rasmus passed away in 1937 at the age of eighty-two.

Ole Christiansen

Another early landowner at Jackson Harbor was a schooner captain named Ole Christiansen. Ole emigrated from Norway in 1882 and eventually settled on Washington Island. The first schooner Captain Christiansen acquired was the *Laurel,* built in 1852 at Plaster Bend, Ohio. She was a scow-schooner type with a length of 80 feet and 20 feet on the beam. Ole sailed to various ports hauling cordwood and other cargo. In 1900, he and Bo Anderson purchased over 80 acres from Charles Forester, who had acquired it from John Furlong a few years before. It is believed that Ole once owned over 800 acres on Washington Island.

The land at Jackson Harbor was a heavily timbered area at the northeast end of the harbor, and Ole saw potential there for a logging operation. He built a large dock just inside the harbor near a point of land at the harbor's entrance now known as Carlin's point. The dock extended 200 feet into the harbor, then north a few hundred feet cutting, back into the shore. From there, Ole hauled large quantities of cordwood with his schooner the *Madonna.* He acquired the *Madonna* a short time after the *Laurel* was stranded in bad weather in December of 1891. The *Madonna* was built at Milwaukee in 1871 and was a two-masted schooner with a length of 80 feet and 24 feet on the beam. Ole had a logging camp on his property and employed a number of men to cut wood in the winter months. These men lived in small buildings and would cut cordwood into four foot lengths using cross cut saws and then would split the logs transporting it to the docks where it would be stacked for shipment in the spring and summer months.

Ole was a sailor — you might say sailing was in his blood. It was his passion in life. He was known to say, "I'll always be ready to sail when the wind is ready." With his schooner *Madonna,* he transported cordwood to various cities on Lake Michigan. Some of the wood was sold to brickyards in cities along the west shore of Lake Michigan as far south as Chicago. It was a successful business, and when his boys were old enough, they sailed with him. Ole had five sons and one daughter. His sons became part of the crew of the *Madonna* at an early age. Story has it, Ole took full advantage of shore leave, but never allowed his sons to partake and share the adventures in the various ports of call. So his sons would sneak ashore to go on their own adventures.

One time Ole found out and confronted them. The next time Ole returned from his shore leave, his boys threatened to tie him up and throw him in the drink if he didn't ease up a little. Ole relented and allowed his sons shore privileges. Unfortunately Chris and Iener were only twenty-two and Norman and Arnold only twenty-three years of age, when they died of tuberculosis. Carl was the only son who survived the disease, and lived to be fifty. It was a great hardship for Ole, since he also lost his wife and daughter to the disease later on.[14]

In the spring of 1914, the *Madonna* was showing her age, and Ole decided to retire his faithful vessel and he sank her in Detroit Harbor near his home. He purchased the *Oscar Newhouse,* a 78-foot, two-masted schooner. She was built in 1876 by Martin Olson at Sheboygan Wisconsin. In May of 1910, the *Oscar Newhouse* was equipped with a gasoline engine. Ole used that boat only for a few years before selling it to a party in Manitowoc, Wisconsin. He then bought Rasmus Hanson's *Flotilla* and used her to haul fish from Washington Island to Green Bay until his retirement in 1918. Ole lived another twenty years and died in 1938.

Ole sold all his property in Jackson Harbor in 1914 to Gladys Dixon and Ruth Seifkin from St. Lois, Missouri, and they turned the property into a girl's camp. They fixed up some of the cabins that were used in the logging operations and made quite a success of it. About 1922, it was purchased by Mr. Carlin and became, a boy's camp, and it is now a part of a nature preserve. If you would walk through the property today, you may still find the remains of one of those old cabins.[15]

Charlie McDonald

Charlie McDonald was born in 1864 on the west side of Washington Island. His father, Dennis McDonald, was a fisherman who moved to the area in 1853 from Ireland. He left Ireland as a boy and made the voyage in seven weeks to New York City, then moved on to Kenosha where his brother Patrick worked on a farm, before finally settling on Washington Island. Dennis McDonald married Mary Mason from Waukegan, Illinois, in 1855, and in 1860 they bought property on the west side of Washington Island, facing the waters of Green Bay. He built a pier, then constructed a slip to the south of it. He started fishing using Mackinaw boats fishing for trout and whitefish not far from his property, since this was close to good fishing grounds. They had their own coopers shop for making barrels to pack fish and they also cut cordwood in the winter months. This was a very busy dock seeing that many of the steamboats, the "Buffalo Boats" would make stops there and refuel with cordwood. This was a precarious place for a dock, due to the constant barrage of winds, waves, and ice shoves. Over the years it had taken its toll on the dock and buildings. Dennis moved to Marinette in 1890 with his two youngest daughters after his wife Mary passed away at the age of forty-one. Dennis moved back to Washington Island in 1908 and lived with his son Charlie in Jackson Harbor until he died in 1916.[16]

Charlie McDonald began fishing with his father at a young age. He attended the Washington Harbor School for a few years, but soon left his studies to help out on the farm. At the age of nine, he was working in the family fishing business. In his younger days, Charlie was known to be an excellent swimmer, and he also attended many social events on the island where he could show off his dancing prowess. However, he was always bashful around the women. In 1896, when Charlie was thirty-two years old, he overcame his bashfulness enough to marry an island girl named Mary Francis Young.[17] The couple moved to a house in West Harbor, and Charlie bought a small steam tug called the *Fish Hawk* and fished out of there for a few years. Charles and Mary had three boys, Dennis, Raymond, and George, who all became fishermen.

Charlie McDonald moved his family to Jackson Harbor in 1903 from the west side of the island. He bought 55 acres of land at the northwest end of the harbor for $300 and could have purchased the rest of the harbor for an additional $300. There was a small dock on the property and a small house where the Bergerson Brothers ran a small pound net operation. Charlie built a larger house, which still stands there today, and he also extended the dock some 300 feet further out on the point. He became the second fisherman to fish with gill nets in Jackson Harbor.

A year later, in 1904, Charlie acquired the fish tug *Stewart Edward*. It had a length of 50 feet and drew over 7 feet of water, which made it a rather large boat for that time. It also had one of the first power net lifters. This new invention really made the fishing industry take off. There were many area fishermen having them installed in their boats. When the *Stewart Edward* was fully loaded with nets, crew, and gear she had a hard time maneuvering in the shallow waters of the harbor and would often scrape hard on the rocky bottom. Charlie knew he had to dredge the area to facilitate proper mooring.

Ole Christiansen's large sailing vessel, the *Madonna*, which he used to haul cordwood to southern ports during the summer months, also had a hard time getting in and out of the harbor because of the shallow water. In the spring of 1904, Charlie, Ole, and Rasmus Hanson, decided to dredge a channel deep enough to accommodate some of the large boats. They called in the Reiboldt and Welter Dredge Company from Sturgeon Bay to do the work, and a large dredge and dump scows were brought to Jackson Harbor by the tug *Lorena*. They dredged the channel to a depth of 10 feet and approximately 50 feet wide, to allow deep draft steamers and sailing vessels to enter the harbor. The work required only three days to complete, at a cost of $300. Charlie, Ole, and Rasmus, each had contributed $100 for the operation. In 1908, Rasmus had a company from Oshkosh, Wisconsin dredge the channel to his dock a little deeper and also had it widened.

Charlie and his sons fished for many years out of Jackson Harbor. Charlie was a very charismatic man and a great conversationalist, with a robust, booming voice that would carry over the harbor's still waters in the early morning hours. Jake Ellefson often said, "Old Charlie had a voice like a fog horn; you could hear him half way across the Harbor." An article in the 1927 Paul's Netting Gazette that described him best:

Charlie McDonald – Colorful Personage!

Mr. Charley [sic] McDonald, one of the best-known "Charlie's" around the lakes, is a veteran fisherman of 63, though his youthful looks belie the truth. He was a school days chum of John Cornell. A great conversationalist, clever and progressive in many of his ideas, Mr. McDonald makes a decidedly favorable impression without trying to unnaturally do so. Kindness of heart, courage, skill, and ability has won him life's reward of wealth.

He possesses a 55- ft. tug with a fourteen-foot beam. Previously he operated 40- footer, the *Maritana*. McDonald owns three boats and a large 40-foot scow. His operations are principally gill net, pound net, and hook. Starting at the age of nine, later fishing via sailboat, Charley has gone through the vicissitudes of life and business with a veteran nonchalance good to look upon.[18]

Independently wealthy, he still fishes... and how!

Once on a Chicago visit, Mayor William Hale Thompson introduced him to 2,000 people on a loop stage at a big political rally, which is excitement enough in one day for anybody.

In the early 1920s, the *Stewart Edward* was beginning to show her age, so Charlie and his sons bought a boat called the *Maritana* to replace her. The *Stewart Edward* was later burned intentionally to the water line out in the harbor. The steam boiler remained on the beach between the house and reel shed for many years before being taken away for scrap in the 1980s. Before the McDonald's bought the *Maritana* from a man called "Windjim," she was used to shuttle people across the Sturgeon Bay canal before the bridge was built.[19] The *Maritana* was a 40-foot wood boat with a Kahlenberg gasoline engine. They replaced the engine in 1926 with a 30-36 Kahlenberg crude oil engine and sold the old Kahlenberg engine to Tom Goodman who installed it in the *Big Peder*. In 1934, the McDonald's made a trade with the Richters at Detroit Harbor. They traded the *Maritana* for Earl and Roy Richter's larger boat the *Fred*, which was 47 feet long and had a 45-54 Kahlenberg oil engine. They fished the *Fred* until 1945 then sold her to Wilbert Wade, a fisherman from Kenosha.

By 1910 Charlie's boys, Raymond, Dennis, and George were all helping out in the family fishing business. Dennis, the oldest son, was seven years old when they moved to Jackson Harbor. He completed six years of grammar school, but then joined his father in the fishing business. It was not uncommon for male children to complete only eight years of schooling, as the young men were expected to help out in their family's farm or fishery.

Dennis was about ten years old when he began his career as a commercial fisherman. His father gave him the job as fireman on the steamboat *Stewart Edward,* and he became a very good fisherman and an exceptional navigator. Dennis was known for his dedication and devotion to his family, faith, and the love for fishing. He was concerned for the welfare of his fellow fishermen and did not hesitate to venture out on the lake in inclement weather to assist another fisherman in trouble. It was also a standard practice for Dennis to call other fishermen in the evening to find out what they caught, how many, and where they caught the fish.

Ray McDonald, the second son to Charlie and Mary McDonald, was the only one of their children to graduate from the eighth grade. After that, he went right into the family business with his brother Dennis and his father aboard the *Stewart Edward*. Ray left the Island in 1920 to pursue a career in sailing on the ore boats. However, that didn't last too long, and he settled in Kenosha where he went back into commercial fishing. He owned the fish tugs *Arbutus* and the *JW McDonald*. During the 1940s he moved his operations to Racine and fished from that port until the lampreys decimated the lake trout. Ray's son Jim followed the fishing tradition and eventually bought the gill net tug *Richard E.* from Frank Eichler. Now Ray's grandson Jeff McDonald, a forth generation fisherman carries on the legacy at Washington Island with his boat the *Jane*.

George McDonald, the youngest of Charlie's and Mary's three boys, began fishing when he was midway through the eighth grade. He became the engineer on the boat and was adept at working on Kahlenberg engines. Spencer Nelson, a commercial fisherman from Jackson Harbor said George was the strongest man in the harbor and was nicknamed "The Bull."[20] After their father died in 1931, Dennis and George took over the family fishery. They fished from their dock in Jackson Harbor many years and also spent some years fishing from Kenosha and Racine. During the winter months in the 1940s they would fish from Kenosha for lake trout and chubs, then return to the island come spring. They left Washington Island in 1957 due to poor fishing and fished from Kenosha for a few years. They were ready to go back to the island in the spring of 1961 to resume fishing along with Dennis's son "Buzz" McDonald, but Dennis passed away from a heart attack.

In 1945, Dennis and George sold the *Fred* and had a new boat, The *McDonald Brothers*, built by the Burger Boat Company of Manitowoc, Wisconsin. It was a 48-foot all-steel boat with a three cylinder 75-90 Kahlenberg engine and a mid-ship pilothouse. They later sold the boat to the Voight Brothers in 1960 and it was still in service in 2005, renamed the *Apache*, and owned by Larry Anshutz of Baileys Harbor. In the 1970s it was repowered with a four-cylinder turbocharged Murphy diesel engine.

The McDonald name will always be synonymous with Jackson Harbor, for the family fished almost sixty years from that region. They had a number of boats through their careers, with such names *Stewart Edward, Arbutus, Maritana, Fred,* and *McDonald Brothers*. Besides fishing, in the early days they hauled fish with the *Stewart Edward*, to the Matt Foss dock where they packaged fish for the Jackson Harbor fishermen, assisted many distressed boats, and made some daring rescues. Ray McDonald told a story about the McDonald's assisting the lake steamer *Cepheus* when it ran aground on a reef in the St. Martin passage:

In 1913, the steamer *Cepheus* was coming out of Escanaba with a load of iron ore. She came out of the St. Martin passage. After passing the lighthouse on St. Martin Island, they changed course to enter Lake Michigan. Whatever happened is unknown, but they swung too far south and she ran hard on the reef, which was all rock and extremely hard and flat. She slid up a long way before she stopped. She was out six feet forward and three feet aft. There had been some fog that morning, but not bad.

The *Stewart Edward* was coming in out of the lake east of Rock Island when we spied this ship and knew she was stranded from the direction she was headed. We were about five miles south of the ship when we headed down for her. It was blowing quite hard from the south. We rounded up near the stern as close as possible. They motioned someone wanted to get aboard. This was a very dangerous thing to attempt; however, the mate timed it so when the tug came up high on a sea, he made his jump and landed on the forecastle. We took the mate in to Jackson Harbor to a telephone. He called the coast guard on Plum Island and the owners. Shortly after this we took the mate back to St. Martin Island. It was blowing a gale at this time. There was a dock by the lighthouse and it was in the lee, so we could lie there without hitting bottom. The mate got off here because it would be impossible to put him back on his ship later that night or the next morning.

The steamer *Hyacinth*, a government buoy tender, was out to the *Cepheus* and had a line on her and was pulling on her. We started back for Jackson Harbor since there was nothing we could do. It was getting dark now, and as we rounded the west end of the island we ran into a squall from the south; one of the worst any of our crew had ever seen. I think we took tons of water over the bow. After running a half hour, we began to get the worst of it. It was during this squall with the *Hyacinth* pulling and mountainous seas from the south, and water a foot or two higher, that the *Cepheus* slid off. She finished her trip, not too badly damaged, and then she put into dry-dock for repairs.[21]

Ray also wrote of another incident that occurred in 1905 while the McDonalds were pulling nets with the *Stewart Edward* out near the Whaleback shoals. They spotted smoke coming from the are of the reef and quickly finished pulling their nets to head to the scene, which was about five miles away. When they arrived they found a badly burned ship, though the crew had managed to abandon their burning boat. The crew were most pleased to see the McDonalds, who took them to Menominee, Michigan.

John Omundson

Another early settler at Jackson Harbor was John Omundson. John had come from Norway and settled on the island in 1890 with his wife, two daughters, Emma and Tillie, and a son, Oman. He bought property just west of the Klingenberg land at Jackson Harbor. This was a great place to raise his family, since it had everything they needed. John was a carpenter by trade, and had soon built a house. He then built a dock and a few small sheds for his pound-net gear. He fished herring for a few years from Jackson Harbor, but then sold his rig to start building boats and houses.

John was a true craftsman and a diligent worker. He had built a number of homes in Jackson Harbor that still stand today. He also had built fish tugs for various fishermen, and even a small pleasure boat. In 1897, he built a 28-foot sailboat for Matt Foss called the *Laura*, that became the first boat on Washington Island to have one of the new gasoline engines installed. In 1909, he built a second boat for Matt Foss called the *Irma Jeanette*. John was also responsible for bringing to Washington Island a number of other Norwegian families. He sold his property to George Nelson in 1913 and moved to Seattle, Washington, where his brother was living. He and his brother built houses together and had a successful business for many years.

William Betts

William Betts came to Jackson Harbor in 1887 after serving as a lighthouse keeper at the Pottawatomie lighthouse for seventeen years. His wife Emily was an assistant lighthouse keeper over there and helped in all the daily chores of running a lighthouse. One such task was to keep the wicks burning in the lantern room. In those days, lighthouses used rather large lamps that burned lard for fuel, and in cold weather the lard would harden and would not burn. It was up to William and Emily to warm the lard and wrap towels around the bowl and rush it up the steps to light the lamp. They did this (and all the other duties of keeping a lighthouse) for nearly ten years, until kerosene replaced lard for fuel for the lamps. Besides the lighthouse duties, she took care of her two children that were born there.[22]

William Betts had met Emily on one of his visits to Pilot Island, where his friend Victor Rohn was keeper. They fell in love and were married in September of 1871, and they had two children while they lived on Rock Island. Emily cared for the children, and since there was no school on Rock Island, she taught them to read and write. Life on Rock Island wasn't easy back then, especially because it was such a remote area. The lighthouse was located on a bluff overlooking Lake Michigan and Green Bay waters and was the first lighthouse on Lake Michigan when it was put into service in 1836. It had to be rebuilt in 1858, presumably due to poor construction. The keepers had to carry water from the lake, and they usually had to climb the two hundred steps up the stairway from the beach, several times a day. Betts would travel 6 miles by boat to Washington Harbor for supplies once or twice a week, and they had to haul everything up the stairs. They eventually brought a cow over to Rock Island, which cut down on some of the runs for supplies.[23]

Like many other lighthouse keepers, William Betts served in the Union Army during the Civil War. He enlisted in 1861 and served through the entire war without serious injury. He fought many battles such as Baton Rouge, Fort Bizlin, Port Hudson, Mobile, Vicksburg and many others. He even shook hands with President Lincoln while he was in Washington, DC, escorting a prisoner of war. His ancestors fought in the Revolutionary war and the War of 1812 – his grandfather fought with General Washington at the battle of Yorktown and witnessed the surrender of the British general Cornwallis. So, Betts came from a long line of soldiers and was very proud of his heritage.

As a veteran he was able to acquire a considerable amount of government land at a very low cost. Most of the lots he bought were on the northeast side of Washington Island, and for that reason they eventually settled in Jackson Harbor. Betts fished using pound nets for three or four years, and his wife Emily kept busy teaching the children – they had seven more children in the years they lived on Washington Island after 1887 – and serving as a nurse to the people in the Jackson Harbor region.

They moved from Jackson Harbor around 1910 and relocated to the Detroit Harbor area where William fished for some time. William and Emily Betts eventually moved to Sturgeon Bay where they lived up until his death in 1930 at the age of ninety-eight. Emily died in 1950 at ninety-five years of age.

Jacob Ellefson and Sons

Ellefson is another name synonymous with Jackson Harbor, since the Ellefson family fished from there for nearly a century. Jake Ellefson Jr. is still fishing to this day (2006), though he retired in 1999 and sold his boat the *Miss Judy* after a long career in the fishing business. He continues to fish with Jeff McDonald and Jeff Hagen aboard McDonald's venerable boat the *Jane*. You could say Jake is the last of the true old-school fishermen. He has seen years when fish were very abundant and other years when the only thing that kept the business afloat was his father's license to fish chubs in Michigan waters. Not only fighting the challenge of fish cycles, there were other challenges such as fluctuating market prices, new regulations, stormy seas, fog, ice, equipment maintenance, and many other factors that have made this fisherman tougher than an old dock spike.

Jacob Ellefson Sr. came to Washington Island from Norway in 1902 after hearing about the island from friends who already lived there. Jacob left his family farm, located south of Oslo Norway, in1820 after several years of drought. The years of drought had severely damaged their hay production and they could not feed their livestock. The family had been forced to borrow money to buy hay for their stock and had mortgaged the land to a big timber company and had to lease it until 1907. Jacob had heard about the prosperity one could achieve in the United States, and he left Norway for what he thought would be the promised land, where he could make enough money to buy back the farm. He came to Washington Island and fished with Matt Foss for a year, then worked at various jobs, including sailing with Ole Christiansen on the *Madonna* one summer. Jacob saw that there was money in the fishing business and decided to try his hand at it.

In the spring of 1907, Jake and a friend named Harwick Carlson formed a partnership. They found some property just outside of Jackson Harbor, a little north and west of Charlie McDonald's property and started to build a dock. On a calm, quiet morning Jacob was working on the dock crib and noticed the *Stewart Edward* heading out of the harbor. He couldn't help but hear Charlie McDonald, in a booming voice that carried like a foghorn, say to his engineer Jim Boyce, "Those boys are making a terrible mistake. They ought to go in the harbor and buy that lot of Gunner's. The ice will take that dock out every winter." Jacob ceased his work, bought the property from Gunner Jensen, and has owned it ever since.

The property they bought included the pound-net rig, dock, and a few small buildings. Jacob started out in a partnership with Andrew and Mads Swenson, and Harwick Carlson, but he eventually bought them all out and became sole owner of the fishing business in 1923. In 1909 Jacob went back to Norway and spent the summer at the family farm. In the fall of that year he came back to the island with his brother Paul. They made it back in time to set their pound nets for the fall run. That winter Jacob and Paul worked up in the swamps at Escanaba, Michigan, cutting cedar for a lumber company.

In the spring of 1910, they were headed home on a train bound from Escanaba to Green Bay, but when they arrived at the Green Bay depot, a government land agent boarded the train and exclaimed, "Head er west boys, the government just opened up a million acres for homesteading in the Dakotas and Montana!" This was all too appealing for the Ellefson brothers, and they went west instead of north to go back home. The train took several days to get to Montana, and Jacob finally couldn't stand the ride any more and got off the train. His brother Paul wanted to keep going and continued on the journey. Paul ended up in Spokane, Washington where he got a job with the Great Northern Railroad and worked for them for 40 years. Jacob found a job on a sheep ranch in Montana and worked there for two years. As a ranch hand, his duties were to destroy beaver dams that were hindering the flow of water in the streams that provided water for the 2,200 head of sheep. All the time he was there, Jacob continued looking for some land to homestead.

Jacob finally found 160 acres he liked. Under the Homestead Act, certain criteria had to be met in order to acquire the land. The first one was there had to be a working well, then a building had to be constructed, and then crops had to be planted that first year. Jake couldn't meet all the conditions and eventually had to pay a dollar an acre for the property. In 1912, he returned to the island, thus ending his short stint as a rancher. He came back in the fall of the year, just in time to set his pound nets. So there he was, out setting his nets while sporting a Stetson hat and cowboy boots.

In 1914, Jacob married Grace Hahnkuper, and they moved into the house that John Omundson had built on the property, believed to be built around 1910. In that house Jacob and Grace raised their five children. Everett (Steve), Klemmet (Kay), Martha, Jacob (Jake), and Grace Ann. The boys all grew up around fishing and helped their father with various tasks, which eventually led them out on to the lake with their father, and soon were fishermen themselves.

Jacob fished many years exclusively with pound nets. Then in 1929, he began to work into the gill net fishery and purchased a 32-foot gasoline powered boat that he named (after his first four children) *KEM Jacob*. Jacob developed back problems that plagued him for many years, but luckily he had help from his boys, and by the mid 1930s they were all on their way to running the business. During World War II, the boys volunteered for service and spent several years away from home.

When the war ended, Jacob's sons decided they wanted to move back to the island and take over their father's fishery. When they returned in 1945, they were blessed with a bounty of whitefish and herring that lasted about eight years. In 1947, Steve went into business with Dan Lindal and fished herring with their pound nets. They had a pound-net boat built for them at Marinette Marine in early of 1947 named the *Billy Jean*. They fished pound nets with her until 1955 when Dan moved to Bayfield, Wisconsin and Steve went back to fishing with his brothers. They used the *Billy Jean* for pound nets for many years, and then in 1978 they had her lengthened to 44 feet and fished trap nets. Jake sold the trap net rig in 1991 to the Peterson Brothers Fishery.

During the early 1900s at Jackson Harbor many fishermen, including the Ellefsons noticed great changes in the fishery. The first large change clearly evident in the 1930s was an influx of smelt into Lake Michigan. Smelt were making their way through the upper Great Lakes, and by the late 1930s were disrupting the once bountiful herring and whitefish populations. However, in the early 1940s the smelt started dying off in large numbers, and by 1946, whitefish had made a remarkable recovery that gave fishermen eight years of great fishing. The herring stock also recovered and became very abundant by 1948. However, the smelt were not gone completely, and began to propagate in large numbers, again impacting the whitefish and herring. The decline in whitefish and herring was partly due to the smelt and partly due to the sea lampreys, which were destroying most of the lake trout.

When the Ellefson brothers started fishing after the war, they used their father's boat the *KEM Jacob*, and the first two years of fishing proved very good. They turned a profit, which enabled them to expand the fishery. In 1946 the cedar crib dock needed repair, so they tore down the building on the dock and built a new dock and a few more buildings. They bought more nets and a larger boat, which helped them to become well established. In 1948 they bought the fish tug *Esther C*, a 40-foot wooden hull boat with a 30 -36 horsepower Kahlenberg engine. They purchased the boat from George Kohlbeck, a fisherman from Algoma, and brought it back to the island where they completely rebuilt her.

When Steve joined his brothers in 1955, they had their best catches of herring and whitefish. That fall they set seven pound nets for herring in November. One was set west of Indian Point and another just east of there. Two were set in the Rock Island passage, and a few out by the cut. During that fall run they caught over 200 tons of herring. Jake remembers a day they had 61,500 pounds of herring from four nets, which filled 500 boxes or kegs. The next day they caught over 30,000 pounds of herring. They hired Dale Bjarnarson and Walt Jorgenson to help with all the herring, and they made about $2,000 during a run that lasted nearly a month. The herring weren't worth that much at the time, only about three cents a pound. One month of setting nets and one month worth of fishing and another month of taking down and putting away, that was what it was worth. The next year, the herring fishing wasn't good, and the following year they went back to gill net fishing.

In 1965, the Ellefsons had a quandary. The *Esther C* needed repairs, and they had to decide whether to stick more money into her or buy a more dependable boat. At that time the fishing was poor, and it was a tough decision for the brothers. They decided to take a chance, so they borrowed money and bought the fish tug *Miss Judy*, a 46-foot boat with a new style steel hull that had a square stern. Compared to the older boats with the barrel bottom hulls, the newer style hulls were more stable in heavy seas. The *Miss Judy* was only five years old at that time and had a caterpillar diesel engine that gave them sufficient power.

The following spring, the Ellefsons began fishing chubs in Michigan waters. They had a boat with sufficient power and speed to get them to the chub grounds, 40 or 50 miles away, they were fortunate enough to have the Michigan non-resident fishing license that their father obtained in 1930. They made the long runs at least two or three times a week, from April until mid-September. Typically, they left the dock at 3 a.m. and tried to get back by 5 p.m. in order to get their fish on the last ferry boat.

By 1972, whitefish had made a remarkable recovery, and the Ellefsons could fish closer to port. They also started a mink ranch in 1960, but the business was marginal at best. Klemmet managed the business and for many years raising mink for the pelts. Steve Ellefson died in 1978, and Randall Sorenson began fishing with Jake. They fished together for fourteen years. In 1980, the state of Michigan closed their gill-net fishery, which forced Jake to invest in trap nets in order to fish in Michigan waters. Jake still had his pound-net boat, the *Billy Jean*, which he used for several years for trap-net fishing. He sold his trap net fishery in 1991 to the Peterson brothers.

After Randy Sorenson began fishing on his own, Jake Ellefson hired Walter Jorgenson to fish with him. Walt was a good fisherman and very experienced, having fished with many other fishermen. Jake continued fishing throughout the 1990s, but in 1999 decided to retire, ending his long illustrious career in the fishing business. He sold the *Miss Judy* to Ted Eggebraaten of Baileys Harbor. Jake still continues to fish today (2006) with Jeff McDonald and still has his sheds and dock. Fishing is still in is blood; a man who lives part on land and part at sea; the lake has made him who he is. That's his story.

Pound net locations

1. McDonalds had a 60-foot pound net near the Rock Island Bluff. Last fished by Charlie and Lee in the mid 1950s.
2. Benny and Nels Jensen and Mads Swenson fished a 40-foot net until the mid 1930s, and then fished by the Ellefsons.
3. James Denio and Gunner Jensen fished a 40-foot net there from 1890 to 1906. Jacob Ellefson used that location from 1907 to the mid 1930s. The Ellefson Brothers ran two 60-foot nets in a row in the mid 1950s.
4. William Betts had a 30-foot pound net set, and then Pete Peterson had 40-foot net set there until 1935.
5. Ellefson Brothers had a forty-foot pound net set from 1952 to 1958.
6. James Denio had a pound net set at that location, which was located northeast of the harbor. George Nelson fished a 50-foot net from there until 1934. The McDonald's also had fished from there, in the mid 1950s.
7. Ellefson Brothers had a 30-foot net set out from Steve Ellefson's home in about 40 feet of water.

8. In the early 1900s, John Omundson and Mads Swenson had a 50-foot net set just west of Indians Point. Ellefson Brothers had a 50-foot net set there in the 1950s.

9. Nels and Benny Jensen Fished pound nets in that location to about 1935, and then the Ellefson Brothers fished with a 50-foot pound net there in the mid 1950s and also fished with a 75-foot gill net for whitefish.

10. Andrew Irr had 75-foot and a 90-foot pound net set for whitefish in that location, which was near his property. His sons, Nan and Tine, fished two herring nets and also his son-in-law, Andrew Swenson had one out from the dock.

Pound-net Fishing in Jackson Harbor

From 1890 to 1918, most of the Jackson Harbor fishermen were fishing for herring using pound nets, which were ideal for both herring and whitefish. In November, the fish would school during the annual

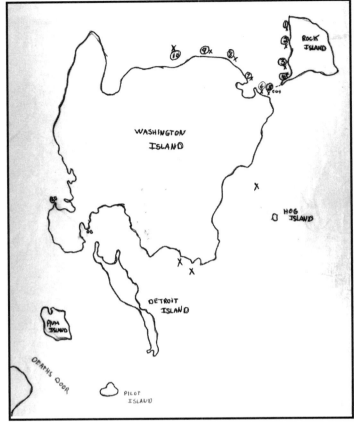

Fig. 9.2 Docks and fishery sites at Jackson Harbor

spawning season and come into the shallows, almost up to the beach. One area that was popular for harvesting herring and whitefish was just outside Jackson Harbor, along the Rock Island shore and the northern shore of Washington Island. As many as seven pound-net rigs could be found there. Fishermen set their pound nets in the spring of the year, after the ice was out, and left them until summer, when they were taken out of the water for cleaning and repairs. However, the spring and summer fishing was not nearly as productive as in the fall, when they would reset their pound nets. Their most abundant catches were usually in the late fall during herring spawning run. This usually started around Thanksgiving in northern Lake Michigan, and for at least a month, Jackson Harbor was a beehive of activity until the spawning run was over, sometime in December. Various boats arrived and departed, bringing in salt and barrels and carrying away freshly packed barrels of herring ready for market.

Herring were dressed and salted, then packed in wooden barrels that held 100 pounds of fish. Approximately 480 herring would fill one package or "keg." Herring were dressed flat, on a custom-made table and dressing station. Next step was to put the herring so its back was to the dresser and flip the head off with the knife and then cut along the backbone, cutting right through the backbone into the cavity without cutting the stomach and run the blade of the knife down until the herring flopped open like a butterfly fillet. There was a hole in the dressing table and a barrel beneath where the guts were disposed. Next the tail and guts were removed. The herring were cleaned in a water trough, then sent to the salting station. The "salter" would salt the open fillets, then placed them in a barrel until it was full. The salting station was a table made up of boards on a small incline. The person doing the salting had a small paddle on the end of a stick and used this to pull the herring over to them. There was a ridge all around the inside of the salting table in order to hold the salt so it didn't wash down to the middle part of the table where the fish were at. The "salter" would line the outer rim of the bottom of the barrel with three heaps of herring and one in the middle and would do this until the barrel was full. After leaving the herring packed for a few weeks, the barrel would be repacked with a few more herring to compensate for settling. Once fully packed, the barrels were sealed and ready for shipment.

From 1900 to 1910, herring prices fluctuated enough that fishermen might make a profit one year, then barely make ends meet the following year. During good years, herring sold for $1.50 to $1.60 a package, but when the prices fell to $1.25, fishermen were very lucky to have any profit at all after deducting the cost of package, salt, and labor. A day's wage for a good dresser was $1.00 to $1.50, and a "salter" could demand eighty to ninety-five cents per day.[24]

Herring had proved to be a predictable species, especially when and where they would spawn, and their population had remained fairly consistent from 1870 to 1930. However, by the mid 1920s smelt had made their way into Lake Michigan and soon began decimating the herring population. Smelt consumed large quantities of herring fry and spawn, depleting the herring so much that in a few years they were nearly gone. Ray McDonald recalls in the 1930s, the smelt were so numerous in Green Bay that it was just about impossible to continue fishing for herring and whitefish. The smelt were so thick they clogged the nets, and it took several days to clear them. Smelt affected not only the herring, but also whitefish and chubs. The smelt began to die off for some unknown reason and by the mid 1940s. Fishermen using small mesh gill nets were pulling them off the lake bottom by the thousands.

Jake Ellefson remembers pulling up chub nets that were laden with dead and rotting smelt when fishing off the Rock Island bluff with his father in the *K.E.M. Jacob*. Whitefish made a strong recovery by 1946, and the herring population came back strong by 1948. Herring remained abundant for almost ten years, but then the smelt started to make a come back and once again wiped out the herring in a very short time. By 1960, no one was fishing for herring.

During the peak herring run, each fishery would require eight to ten men to handle all the fish. They would work well into the night or early morning, go home for a few hours, rest and return in the morning to start again. Fisherman George Nelson was known to work well into the morning hours and during herring season he and his crew sometimes worked until 2 a.m. and then would tell his crew, "Have a good night boys, be down early", which meant in a few hours.

1948 was a good year for the fishermen, especially Dan Lindal and Steve Ellefson who began fishing with seven pound nets, and a new pound-net boat. That fall, they had all their nets set and had some great lifts. It was not unusual for them to haul in 4,000 to 5,000 pounds a day, and one day they had nearly 15,000 pounds to their credit.

Some of the island folk, including farmers, would lend a hand during this busy time. Ray McDonald recalled two men who were, in his opinion, the fastest herring dressers on the island. One was Lawrence Anderson, who lived in Jackson Harbor, was considered the fastest dresser. Another farmer, Lyman Johnson, was considered to be the fastest "salter." There was always a little friendly competition between the fisheries.

Once the fish were packaged, they would be shipped to their destinations including Marinette, Wisconsin and Menominee, Michigan. The Dennison brothers of Green Bay hauled some of the herring to market. They had two steamboats in the early 1900s. One was the *Nettie Dennison*, and the other was the *John Dennison*. The Johnson brothers, who owned the *Two Myrtles,* made trips from the city of Green Bay to Jackson Harbor and then to Menominee, hauling freight and fish. In the 1940s and 1950s, most of the herring were shipped to Marinette, Wisconsin, and Escanaba, Michigan. The Washington Island ferry *Griffon* and the hooker *American Girl*, owned and operated by Cecil Anderson, also came into Jackson Harbor to load fresh herring and deliver them to Escanaba.

Pound-net fishing was demanding work that required heavy lifting, scooping, and pulling to retrieve the fish. Quite a few fishermen on Washington Island adopted this style of fishing, and many were from Jackson Harbor. Pound-net fishing went on in Jackson Harbor for nearly fifty years, but waned in the 1950s when the herring disappeared. The early pound net fishermen included the McDonalds, Bergerson brothers, William Betts, Jim Denio, Gunner Jensen, Mads Swenson, and others that came and went over the years. Jackson Harbor was an ideal location for both pound-net fishing and gill-net fishing, because it was close to the fishing grounds. McDonald's had a slightly different style of setting up a pound net, indicative to outside of Jackson Harbor near Rock Island:

The pot or pound required nine wooden stakes driven in the bottom of the bay.

These stakes were set in a 30- foot square area and the pot was hung inside the stakes, approximately 28 feet square, allowing it ample clearance from the stakes which kept the net from rubbing on the stakes in rough water. The inside of the pot faced the shore in water that was around 46 feet deep. The stakes would be driven into the bottom of the lakebed using the pile driver. They would be driven in 6 or 7 feet, providing the lakebed allowed it. The outside of the pot was in deeper water, usually around 60 or 70 feet. Sometimes out in the deeper water the driving was poor where there was sometimes soft mud, or a rocky bottom. In these conditions, anchors and lines were attached, called Norwegian anchors. The outside stakes needed these otherwise they would pull over in a bad storm. We made our own Norwegian anchors, crude but good.

On this net two anchors were put on each corner stake with about 250 feet of good line attached to each one. The stake between the two corner stakes was known as the King Stake. On this stake, only one anchor was attached, an extra heavy one and a longer line, making five anchors in all. They really did a good job in a bad blow. These three outside stakes were in excess of 80 feet long and the stakes were all in two parts. A piece 40 feet or better was spliced on the bottom of a tamarack stake about the same length. These butts were made of beech, maple, or ironwood. They were heavy and would sink, helping to lift up the top, making for easier handling when driving them. If the water were less than 40 feet, the stakes would be one piece. It was difficult to find tamarack stakes long enough to drive in depths of 50 or more feet of water. After the stakes were all in, the nets were then set, which hung and were fastened to the stakes. All this required about two weeks worth of work before the herring run. As soon as the herring run was over, depending on what time of the month it was, the nets and stakes were all pulled out. Fisherman would normally have their pound nets out before ice would start forming, which was typically a few weeks before Christmas.[25]

Severt and Martin Bergerson fished from the McDonald property in the years 1898 to 1903, and then sold their pound-net rig to Charlie McDonald and Gunner Jensen. Charlie was a silent partner in the pound-net fishing business; he mainly fished with gill nets in a small steam tug called the *Fish Hawk*, but he sometimes lent a hand with the pound nets. After three years, Charlie decided to sell his share to his partner and to concentrate on gill-net fishing. However, in 1917, Charlie started fishing again with pound nets to expand his fishing operations and profits.

Gunner Jensen and his brother Benny were both Norwegian immigrants and both fished herring using pound nets through the first decade of the twentieth century, though Benny fished off of Indian Point, and Gunner had his operations in Jackson Harbor. Benny and Mads Swenson fished together for many years off Indian Point, which is northwest of Jackson Harbor. Their brother Gunner sold his fishing rig to them in 1907 and moved back to Norway with his wife and daughter. He sold his property to Jacob Ellefson, who started his own pound-net fishery.

During his sojourn at Jackson Harbor (1896 to 1904), Jim Denio operated a few pound nets and also used gill nets with his fish tug *Active*. Jim Denio sold his property to Rasmus Hanson along with his pound-net rigs. Rasmus sold half of the pound-net interest to George Nelson, who would operate his pound-net fishery from the Hanson dock for many years. Other pound-net fishermen in the early days of Jackson Harbor included William Betts Sr., Amy Duclon, and William Betts Jr. John Omundson had a pound-net rig he used for a few years from his own dock. He sold it to Eric Lunde and Nels Jensen in 1908.

The Docks and Buildings

The first known dock in Jackson Harbor was built by Chris Klingenberg in the spring of 1887. Chris hauled cordwood from this dock in his schooner *Pride*. He owned most of the land at the south end of the harbor. In 1902, he sold the dock to John Johnson. Around this time, other docks were built by Tim Coffey, Severt Bergerson, William Betts, William Bradshaw, and John Omundson had a small dock for his pound-net fishery. Between 1890 and 1902 there were four docks and a few buildings in Jackson Harbor. By 1904, Charlie McDonald and Ole Christiansen had two large docks in place.

The early docks were rock-filled cedar cribs, often placed several feet apart with stringers in between. They were either planked over, or cedar poles were set side by side to form a walkway.

Typically, white cedar was used for the cribs above the waterline and for the decking. Below the waterline, oak or other hardwood was used as it would not rot away so long as it was not exposed to the air. The docks required periodic maintenance, especially after high water or ice pressure, though ice wasn't nearly as destructive in Jackson Harbor as it was in Washington Harbor. Jackson Harbor was more sheltered and shallower, and ice shoves were not ordinarily a problem.

On July 19, 1952, Jackson Harbor was hit by a seiche, a rare phenomenon somewhat like a small tidal wave. The seiche was caused by a sudden afternoon squall and hit the harbor in the mid afternoon, pushing boats out of the water and damaging docks and buildings. Fortunately most of the fishing boats were out on the lake and weren't damaged. Only a few had to be put back into the water. But most of the docks, especially the Ellefsons', were hit hard and had to be rebuilt. This happened during a period of high water, which only made matters worse.

Charlie McDonald and Ole Christiansen each had large docks located almost opposite one another at the entrance of the harbor near the reef. Charlie's was a long wooden structure with a net and packaging shed out near the end of it. There was already a small dock on the property when he purchased it that had been built by Severt and Martin Bergerson where the two had a small pound-net fishery. Charlie extended that dock and built a nice house and some sheds. Later he built another dock further inside the harbor and used it in the high-water years. The dock still exists today, (2005) along with the net sheds.

Ole Christiansen's large dock was just inside the eastern entrance of the harbor. From there, he hauled cordwood with his schooner *Madonna*. This dock ran west 200 feet, then north 200 feet, then back toward the shore. Ole purchased the property in 1900 and built the dock soon after. By 1920 there was nothing left of the dock. Ole left the area in 1914, and the dock soon fell apart. Today there is little evidence of its existence except a few logs left from the cribs.

John Christianson owned the property south and east of the Hanson dock and had a 60-foot dock on it. He also had a small icehouse, which still stands today, on a small jetty of land. John had a rail track with a cart that he used to transport fish boxes and nets back to the sheds near his home. When he retired in the 1950s, he sold the property to Art Hanson, and it now belongs to the town of Washington Island and is part of the Ridges Sanctuary.

Rasmus Hanson and his sons, Art and Hans had, had the most substantial dock and buildings at Jackson Harbor. For years, numerous fishing boats moored at their dock, sometimes as many as six or seven boats at one time. The Hansons built a large icehouse in the early 1940s, approximately 40 feet wide and 60 feet long, just a short way in from their dock. The icehouse was built with the studs exposed on the exterior, and the interior walls were lined with wood sheeting. Creosote or linseed oil was applied to the walls to preserve them. Two net sheds located just behind and east of the icehouse were leased to other fishermen. Hannes Hannesson and Oliver Bjarnarson leased one of them, which is now the Jackson Harbor Maritime Museum. A 30-foot by 40-foot shed on the dock was used for packaging fish. The dock was well built and had a slip about 100 feet long that separated the Hanson dock from the Ellefson dock. In the early years this dock was made up of rock cribs with a plank and pole walkway. Originally built of rock cribs with a plank pole walk-way, the dock was improved in the 1940s and again in 1991, when steel sheet piling was installed around it.

West of the Hanson dock, the Ellefsons had a small dock with a few net sheds in the 1920s and

1930s. They rebuilt that dock three times in the course of eighty years. During years when the water levels were low, they had the area near the dock dredged. In 1908, Rasmus Hanson had the Reibolt Company dredge the harbor out from his dock, and every twenty years he would have it dredged again. Jacob Ellefson Sr. had two large buildings on the dock, but after years of high water the foundations gave way and they had to be torn down. During that time, the Ellefsons rebuilt the dock, and in 1946 they built a new net shed, icehouse, and storage shed. In 1994, Jake Ellefson had steel sheet piling installed along the edge of the dock.

West of the Ellefson's shed, Dan Lindal had a dock and a few net sheds built in the 1940s. This was the last dock to be built in Jackson Harbor. Eventually, Dan moved away and the state bought the property and dock. This is the dock from which the passenger ferry *Karfi*, originally owned by Jim Cornell and then his son Jack, transports passengers to and from Rock Island State Park. Three other docks in the northwestern part of the harbor changed owners several times over the years. That area of Jackson Harbor is shallow, and most of those docks couldn't be used in the years of low water. Pete Peterson had the dock just northwest of Lindal's. Pete had a pound-net boat and fished pound nets for many years. He bought the property from William Betts, who was the original owner and builder of the dock.

The next dock over was on the John Omundson property. He later sold it to George Nelson, who fished many years with his sons, Russ and Spencer. Over the years they added new sheds to the property. They had a large packaging shed and a few storage sheds. During the years of low water, the Nelsons used the Hanson dock. The last dock was the Lindgren dock, originally on the William Bradshaw property.

Changing Times

By the mid 1930's, Jackson Harbor was beginning to change. The established fisheries at the time included George Nelson and Sons, Art and Hans Hanson had their fishery, the Ellefson Brothers, B & H Fishery, (Haness Hannesson and Oliver Bjarnarson), and John Christianson, and McDonalds. Fishermen were still fishing with pound nets at this time, but more and more of them were using gill nets and hook and line fishing (trot lines). John Christianson was one of the first to use gill nets in Jackson Harbor, and in 1917, he began to use the floating gill nets for herring in the Rock Island passage. Other fishermen saw the success he was having with this type of fishing and began using the floating gill nets. This was a faster way of catching herring, compared to the rigorous and time-consuming pound nets and was actually more economical. A pound-net rig was twice as expensive compared to a gill-net rig and it didn't take as many gill nets to produce a bounty of herring. John Christianson continued using floating gill nets until he retired.[26]

In the 1930s and 1940s, Jackson Harbor was the primary base location for most of the fisheries. Gone were the days of the schooners and hookers sailing in and leaving with cordwood, and the steam-powered vessels were replaced by boats with gasoline engines. Fishermen were using gasoline and crude oil-powered tugs, and they all had mechanical net lifters installed on their boats. The last steam tug was Charlie McDonald's, *Stewart Edward*, and that was decommissioned in the 1920s. The freighters had ceased their operations in Jackson Harbor, because automobiles could now deliver fish to the ferry dock to be shipped out via the ferryboats. The only exception was in the fall of the year during the herring runs. At that time, the Washington Island ferry *Griffon* would haul fish to Menominee or Escanaba, Michigan, and the *American Girl*, owned and operated by John Anderson, took herring over to Escanaba.

In the late 1930s and 1940s changes became evident when many of the fishermen left Washington Harbor for Jackson Harbor. Half a dozen came to Jackson Harbor at that time. There were several reasons for the exodus, but the primary one was that the big docks at Washington Harbor were falling into a state of disrepair. By the late 1930s, the Furlong dock was in bad condition. The slip was eroding from yearly storms and ice shoves. Also, the Great Depression gripped the country, and money was hard to come by. It was no longer feasible to maintain the docks and buildings. Fishermen needed a sheltered area from which to base their operations, and Jackson Harbor was close to some of their fishing grounds.

Among the first to leave were Lloyd and Arthur Young with the *Rainbow*, Percy and Fred Young fished one year then moved to Jackson Harbor with the *Sea Queen*. Anker Greenfeldt and his sons Lorman and Harold left the Furlong dock in 1941. They had the *Betty, Yankee,* and *Jane Elizabeth,* and decided Jackson Harbor would be closer to their fishing grounds. Gasoline Town had become a ghost town. By 1947, only one fisherman remained, Jack Young. The buildings were in shambles, and ice had ruined the once-fine docks and slip. Matt Foss had retired and Howard Foss no longer found it profitable to pack fish. In the early 1940s, Tom Goodman moved to Jackson Harbor. His brother Albert Goodmander and partner Haldon Johnson moved to Milwaukee with their tug *Islander* in 1945. In 1947, they came back to the island and started fishing in Jackson Harbor. Harry Hagen decided it was no longer worthwhile to operate from the Foss dock and left in 1945 for Jackson Harbor with his boat the *Majestic*. By 1945, nearly all the fishermen had left Washington Harbor. The Goodrich line was bankrupt, freight and fish were being shipped on trucks. The island had good roads and a ferry service to the mainland, which proved to be a cheaper means of shipping.

Jackson Harbor had become a major hub for island fishermen and their fisheries. Fishing was excellent from 1946 to 1957, because whitefish and herring were abundant, though lake trout were becoming scarce and were all but completely gone by 1954. Many fishermen were turning profits at this time; moreover, fishing was still a good way to make a living on the island. At least forty-two boats operated from Washington Island during the 1940s and 1950s, and the majority were operating from Jackson Harbor, though some for only a short time.[27] In 1950, there were at least fourteen fisheries operating from Jackson Harbor and this continued until the mid 1960s. .Most of the fishermen that came to Jackson Harbor from Washington Harbor used the Hanson dock, and Jackson Harbor fisheries employed as many as fifty Island men, adding more during the autumn herring run.

Some men worked for various fishermen over the years, and some went into business for themselves. There were some part-time fishermen, and some fished alone, such as Bert Hahnkuper, who fished with a small boat called the *Omar* for perch. Bert used the Ellefson dock and was considered a part-time fisherman. Laurence and Arnold Hahnkuper also had a small-scale fishery and fished for a few years out of Jackson Harbor, also mooring at the Ellefson dock.

Some fishermen started their own fishery after working for others. Harold Zoellner had worked for the McDonalds for many years, and went into business with Len Ellerbrock in the late 1940s. They bought the tug *Ranger* and fished for several years before moving away. In 1952 they sold the *Ranger* to Lloyd Young, who sold her to Jack Young in 1955, who fished her until 1962. Jack then sold the *Ranger* to Harold Greenfeldt and Cliff Young. Jim Cornell also worked for the McDonalds many years before he went into business for himself and bought the fish tugs *JN Cornell* and the *Welcome*.

A few fishermen used Jackson Harbor sporadically for their operations. Glen and Alvin Sorenson fished for a while from Gasoline Town in 1946, then came over to Jackson Harbor for a few years with the fish tug *Velox*. They had the new 35-foot, steel hull boat named the *Sorenson Brothers* built at Marinette, Wisconsin and fished with it for a year from Jackson Harbor, but then moved elsewhere. David Lucke and Milton Dulong, also fished for some years from Jackson Harbor with their boats, the *Hagen* and *Louise*.

Fishing tugs often changed hands over the years and were sold to other fishermen, and sometimes exchanged hands four or five times, as was the case with the *Sea Queen*. She was built in 1906, and her first owner was Peter Christianson. Lawrence Voight owned it and then sold it, in 1934 to George Nelson. Over the years she provided service for Fred Bjarnarson and Ben Johnson, for B & H Fishery, and for Fred and Percy Young. Most fishermen couldn't afford new rigs so they bought used boats and fixed them up. Fishermen normally kept the same name on the boats when they bought them. However, if a boat were new or was being built for that person then a name would be given to her. It was an old sailor superstition not to change the name of a boat once it changed ownership, because it could bring bad luck, or worse, a terrible fate to the vessel.

The *Jane* was another boat that provided service for many fishermen. The *Jane* is one of the last boats still in operation at Jackson Harbor (2005) and provided service for Jeff McDonald until the spring of 2005, when he sold it to a maritime museum in Duluth, Minnesota. Sturgeon Bay Boat Works (Palmer Johnson Company) built the *Jane* in 1929 for Nels Sorenson, who fished in Kewaunee at the time. In 1942 the *Jane* was sold to George Nelson and Sons Fishery and moved to Jackson Harbor.[28] She had a Kahlenberg engine that was replaced in 1986 with a Caterpillar diesel engine. The Nelsons used the *Jane* for many years, and in 1962 they had the hull covered with 1/4-inch steel, as was done with most of the old wood hull boats at the time. When Spencer and Russ retired, they sold her to Randy Sorenson, who fished with her from 1992 to 1998 and then sold her to Jeff McDonald. Jeff fished with her until her last time out in the fall of 2004. The following spring she made her last voyage on the Great Lakes after seventy-six years of service.

During the prosperous years from 1946 to 1957 when herring and whitefish were abundant, hundreds of tons of fish went out of Jackson Harbor annually. Then, in the late 1950s, fish populations dropped. The years from 1955 to 1965 were a very tough time in the commercial fishing industry. By the early 1960s, fishermen found it hard to keep their fisheries solvent. Everyone started to fish chubs, which sold for five or six cents a pound. As Jake Ellefson said, "there were quite a few chubs to catch, but you could hardly give them away."[29] By 1962, there were only half a dozen fisheries still in operation at Jackson Harbor.

Another factor that forced some fishermen to get out the fishing business was the cost of replacing or overhauling their boats. Some, like the Ellefsons, took a chance and invested in a new boat. If they hadn't fished for chubs they would have lost everything. But they stuck it out and got lucky, as the whitefish started coming back in the late 1960s and early 1970s. By 1968, only a few remained, such as the Ellefsons, Oliver Bjarnarson and Hannes Hannesson, Russ and Spencer Nelson, Harold Greenfeldt and Cliff Young. By 1972, fishing improved and a few fishermen returned to Jackson Harbor.

Jackson Harbor Fisheries (1930-1990)

B & H Fish Company

Oliver Bjarnarson and Hannes Hannesson formed a partnership in 1934 and fished together for nearly thirty-five years. Oliver and Hannes both honed their craft from years of fishing with other fishermen in their younger days. They were tough Icelanders, and sailing and fishing seemed to be in their blood. Hannes worked for Leon Cornell throughout the 1920s and also fished with George Nelson.

Hannes developed his toughness with Leon and Les Cornell, who were known to fish throughout the winter for chubs, in all kinds of weather, in northern and western Lake Michigan. Hannes remembered a time when they were fishing from Leon's new 43-foot boat, the *Velox*, near the Manitou Islands. It was the dead of winter, and the days were short and bitterly cold. They were lifting nets in a huge south sea when a large swell broke over the entire boat, and a large amount of water went down the exhaust pipe nearly stopping the engine. The cabin shifted bout an inch by the wave, but then they were hit by another one that shifted the cabin back in place. They were happy to get back in to shore that day.

In his youth, Oliver sailed on the Great Lakes ore boats for a few years, all the time corresponding with his girl friend, Esther Hansen. They married after his brief sailing career, and had a family of three children, Dale, Shirley, and Richard. When the boys were old enough they fished with their father. Oliver fished for many years with Harry Hagen on the *Majestic*. He started out as part of the shore crew, and then he became the skipper.

Hannes and Oliver were friends, and both were eager to run their own fishery, so they formed a partnership in 1935. Oliver borrowed money from Pete and Laura Peterson and bought a rig from George Nelson, the 38-foot fishing tug *Sea Queen*, with a 30-36 Kahlenberg engine. They began fishing for lake trout with a hook-and-line rig because of its low cost, and because they both knew this technique well. Jake Ellefson recalls that, "they were experts at this style and fishing in general." They could run their boat right on her normal gait (speed) of 8 or 10 miles per hour and set the hooks without missing a beat, all the while baiting each hook as the line was flying out the back of the boat.. Oliver would bait one hook on one side of the boat, while Hannes would bait the next hook on the other side. The hooks were attached to a line that was tied to a lead line and spaced about 15 feet apart, and were set from the aft of the boat.

A hook-and-line rig or trot line as some called it, consisted of 1,400 to 2,000 hooks spaced 15 feet apart on "snoots" or small lines, attached to a main lead line, or maitre, to form a "gang" that extended four to six miles. The hooks were baited with small herring, smelt, or bloaters that were caught in small-mesh bait nets, or chum nets. In early summer, lake trout would be feeding on the bug hatch higher in the water, so Oliver and Hannes used a "floater" technique, where the maitre line was equipped with wooden floats every 100 feet that suspended the line 10 to 50 feet below the surface. Weights or leads kept the gang from floating off. Hannes and Oliver used this style periodically throughout the years, but within a few years they invested in gill nets and began fishing for lake trout, chubs, and sometimes herring.

Oliver and Hannes sold the *Sea Queen* to Fred and Percy Young in 1939 and purchased the *Clara C.* from John Cornell of Detroit Harbor. The *Clara C.* had a 30-36 horsepower Kahlenberg engine 39 feet long. In 1953, they bought the *CW Lind* from Clarence Lind of Ellison Bay and renamed it the *Esterlou*, after their wives. The Sturgeon Bay Shipbuilding and Dry Dock Co built the boat in 1945. The *Esterlou* was 40 feet long with an all-steel hull and house, and was powered by a 45-54 horsepower Kahlenberg oil engine. According to Walt Jorgenson, who was part of Oliver and Haness's crew, "She was a roller in heavy seas, but a good sound boat with a good captain and engineer."[31]

Oliver and Hannes had a crew of five men. Oliver was the skipper and would navigate and steer, while Hannes was the engineer. Oliver rang a bell to signal to the engineer for engine speed, forward, and reverse. The bell could be heard over the din of the engine. One day, Wes Peterson, who was part of their shore crew, was on board, as he sometimes was when they were short a crewman. Oliver let Wesley steer the boat coming back in that day, and as they got closer to the dock, Wesley was getting nervous as the dock grew closer. Oliver hadn't come up to the pilothouse to take over, so Wesley rang the bell frantically to check down, meanwhile Oliver still hadn't come up yet. Hannes finally slowed the engine, but it was too late, Wes ran the boat right into the dock. That was the last time Wes got to pilot the boat.[32]

Their crew consisted of three or four men on the boat and two ashore. Wes Peterson and Vic Goodlet made up the shore crew, taking care of the nets and packing. Walter Jorgenson and Oliver's, sons Dale and Dick, became part of the boat crew. Oliver took fishing very serious and taught his boys how to fish only one way and that was the right way and could sometimes be hard on his sons. Although Dale and Dick spent their youth fishing with their father, they eventually pursued other careers. Oliver somehow knew the outlook for fishing was bleak and persuaded his boys to seek another trade. Dick remembers going out on a rough day with his dad when he was twelve years old.

I was with him one day and it was rougher than hell and dad and Hannes always had a box on the side where you'd put your lunch box. Well the boat took a hell of a roll, rolled the windows under, and then rolled back up and hit another wave that rolled her hard again, causing my lunch box to fly down into the eccentrics of the engine and smashed it all to pieces. I went up and told the old man. I said, "Everyone else has turned around, damn it! Why don't you turn around?" He grins and says," Ya know laddy, we'll get a lift on those boys today. Here, I'll share my lunch with you." He wouldn't turn around. As soon as we got out to the nets and started lifting, wouldn't you know it, it got calmer than can be.[32]

During the lean years when whitefish, herring, and trout were scarce, Oliver and Hannes had a Michigan fishing license, like many other fishermen at the time, and began fishing chubs. A fisherman had to travel many miles to the chub grounds, but chubs kept many fisheries going when the white-fish were in low numbers. One year, just before the season closed for the month of November, the wind blew hard for several days. Oliver and Hannes knew they had a gang of nets full of chubs that had to be pulled. The Goodmans already had their nets pulled out for the season, so Oliver asked Tom Goodman if he would help them out. Goodmans with their boat *Hans*, started on one end, and Oliver and Hannes started on the other end with the *Esterlou*. When they met in the middle of the gang, each boat had about 2,500 pounds aboard.[33]

The late fall and winter months were the most difficult times and challenging times to be out on the water. Dick Bjarnarson remembers a time when it was blowing a gale and they went out. Walt Jorgenson was out on the lake with Oliver, Hannes, and Dale. (Oliver always called Walt "Sonny Boy.")

It was rougher than hell and Walt was looking out the window and seen the McDonald Brothers turn around and head back home, the Goodmander's turned around and went back home. Walt went up and talked to my Dad. 'You know I saw, McDonalds turn around and go back in and I saw the Goodmander's turn around and go back in. Oliver says, you know Sonny Boy, I don't think they were going to lift our nets anyway." And they headed out and got a lift on the nets that day.[34]

Oliver and Hannes rented a shed from Art Hanson, who had retired from fishing and was now dock manager and packed fish for many of the fishermen that used his dock. Oliver and Hannes packed their own fish, but they did buy ice from Art who supplied most of the ice in Jackson Harbor, except for the Ellefsons, Nelsons, and McDonalds who had their own icehouses. Later on many of the fishermen invested in ice machines. Oliver and Hannes ran a good business and were successful for many years. They sold their fish to a number of suppliers on consignment, which was a common practice in those days. Oliver kept a daily log that showed the date, how many nets were set, how many nights out, size of the mesh, the price per pound, how many pounds, the buyer and remarks, a simple but an effective

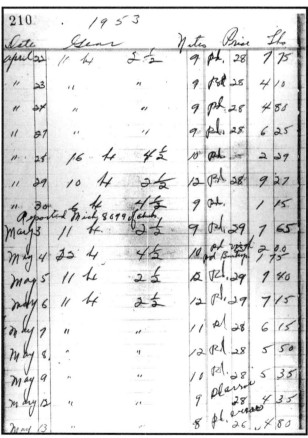

Fig 9.4 Oliver Bjarnarson log book

way of bookkeeping.

Even during the bad times in the 1960s when there was nothing to catch except chubs, Oliver and Hannes kept their full crew. Dale and Dick moved on and found different careers. By 1970, Hannes and Oliver decided to retire. They sold their boat to Melvin Keller, a fisherman from Algoma, who renamed the boat the *Kelly*. Oliver and Hannes, after a lifetime of fishing, sailed on into retirement.

Art and Hans Hanson

Hans and Art Hanson grew up in Jackson Harbor. They worked with their father, Rasmus, when they were young boys, and they began fishing on their own when they came of age. In 1918, they moved to Southwest Bay on St. Martin Island and took up residence in an abandoned cabin.[35] They spent a few summers there fishing with a pound-net, but didn't have much success and soon returned to Jackson Harbor.

In 1926, Hans and Arthur helped their father build a boat, the *Welcome*, for gill net fishing. She was a 36-foot wood boat with 10 feet on the beam. They installed a 40-horsepower gasoline engine in her. It was to be the last boat that Rasmus built. The *Welcome* was built in Jackson Harbor, in the woods where Rasmus had a sawmill, then moved it from the worksite out onto the ice. In the spring, when the ice melted, the boat was officially launched and put into service. The Hansons fished with gill nets on a full-time basis. Some winters they fished near Kenosha, where whitefish and trout were plentiful and they didn't have to contend with the ice.

In winter, most Jackson Harbor fishermen left their boats out near the "cut", a narrow channel through a reef that runs from Washington Island, northeast of the entrance of Jackson Harbor, to a point of land on the southeast end of Rock Island. The channel was dredged in 1938, by the Army Corps of Engineers. As many as fourteen boats would be tied up at the cut, and the fishermen would drive out to their boats in trucks when the ice had formed in the harbor. They tied their boats together, so that in case the ice broke up, they wouldn't drift out to open water or carried by moving ice. The men had easy access to the lake as the current through the cut kept it open.

Around 1930, Hans and Art had the *Gloria* built by Burger Boat Company at Manitowoc, Wisconsin. She was 45 feet long and had a 45-54 Kahlenberg engine. A little bigger than the *Welcome*, the *Gloria* proved to be a dependable boat. They sold the *Welcome* to Carl Richter, who used it for many years hauling freight and mail. The Hansons continued to fish for many years from their father's dock and off of Kenosha throughout the 1940s. They liked Kenosha, because there were good docks, a lighthouse, Coast Guard, with much less ice than on Washington Island.

The Hansons had one of the best docks in Jackson Harbor, with many buildings for packing and net storage. On the dock was a building where they packed the fish. Their home was a few hundred yards south of the dock. Many years earlier, Rasmus had a small general store in the house that provided many Jackson Harbor residents with provisions.

The two brothers continued fishing together up until 1947, when Hans died suddenly of a heart attack in Sturgeon Bay. Art gave up fishing and sold the *Gloria* to Dean Hansen. Art decided to start a business packing fish and selling ice to the fishermen who used his dock. By that time, most of the

Washington Harbor fishermen had relocated to Jackson Harbor and were using his dock for their fishing operations. Goodmander and Johnson used it, as did Tom Goodman, Hannes Hannesson, Oliver Bjarnarson, Fred and Percy Young, Alvin Cornell, Cliff and Lloyd Young, and the Greenfeldt's. Harry Hagen also fished a few years before he retired. This proved to be a very good business for Art Hanson.

Art leased the buildings to various fishermen. Oliver and Hannes rented one, and so did Tom Goodman, the Youngs, and other fisherman. This meant that there were large quantities of fish to be packed, and Art had a crew for icing and packing fish, and, in the fall of the year, they also salted and packed herring. Oliver and Hannes did their own packing, but they bought ice from Art. He also built several cottages on his property and rented them out in the summer. When John Christianson retired, Art bought his property and buildings, thus becoming the owner of most of the land in Jackson Harbor.

In 1972, Art decided to retire from the business after a long successful career as a fisherman, boat builder, and dock manager. Few fishermen were left by this time. The fishermen that used his docks years before had retired or moved away. He sold all his property to the town of Washington Island. The land to the south and east became a wildlife area called the Ridges, where people can hike, swim in the warm shallow water, and sun on the fine sandy beach.

George Nelson and Sons

George Nelson came to America from a small town near Bergen, Norway, when he was eighteen years old. He lived for some time near Hedgehog Harbor, now called Gills Rock, then moved to Milwaukee, where he met his wife Martha. They finally settled on Washington Island in 1901, where they stayed with the Jacob Richter family before acquiring some property from Gunner Swenson a mile southwest of Jackson Harbor. He worked the land and took up farming.

Not long after moving to the island, George Nelson bought some pound nets from Rasmus Hanson. He used them to fish out of Jackson Harbor for many seasons. He used the Hanson dock for several years, and then bought the John Omundson property located a little west of Rasmus Hanson's dock. There he improved the existing dock and sheds and built a few new sheds. In 1920, George began fishing with gill nets as well as pound nets, and he also used hook-and-line for trout a few years. In the fall of the year, he would fish for herring with pound nets near the cut, just outside the harbor. That area proved to be prolific for herring, and he fished from there many years. George built a small cabin near Jackson Harbor, and during the herring and whitefish run in the fall of the year, he and his two sons, Russ and Spencer would stay there.

Russ and Spencer began fishing with their father before the age of ten and soon became fine fishermen in their own right. George Nelson was an early riser and Russ and Spencer would be up at the crack of dawn to do their chores and accompany their father out on the lake when they were not in school. George liked to be out on the lake before the other fishermen headed out. If another boat were out before his, he would have fits – he had to be the first one out. After a day of fishing, George would be on the phone with Dennis McDonald, another fisherman from Jackson Harbor, for an hour, talking about the day's catch. Sylvia Nelson, Spencer Nelson's wife remembers this vividly:

> George would call every night to Den McDonald to find out how many fish they'd caught, where they'd caught them, and how the other fisherman fared that day. George would stand and talk and after awhile one leg would get tired and he'd shift and lean on the other foot, but he would never sit.[36]

The herring run in the fall was a busy time for the Nelsons and they would sometimes pack fish until 3 a.m., then sleep a few hours and go back to work. Sylvia taught at the Jackson Harbor school and would let some of her students out early to help out with the herring processing. Everyone lent a hand during that time. The women and children did a lot of the salting and net mending.

One year the Nelsons had so many herring in their pound nets that they sought help from Stuart Woerfel, a fisherman from Fish Creek. They would combine crews to harvest the herring until the season was over. Young George Nelson, Spencer's son, remembers helping out one day when they brought in almost 29 tons of herring. He says that you were literally up to your knees in herring when you scooped them out of the net and into the boat. Spencer Nelson told of one time fishing herring off of Burnt Bluff late in the fall of the year:

> We got so many herring. We just finished lifting before dusk. George Moe was in herring up to his hips. Just after we started home it began to snow. Russ steered a course for Ranney's then we used the lead line to find our way east to Jackson Harbor. You couldn't even see the bow of the boat. By the time we got in, it was dark and it had already snowed four inches. It was Thanksgiving, so we just tied the boat up and went home...left the fish until the next morning.[37]

Over the years, the Nelsons fished with many boats. Their first boat was the *Rambler*, which they used for pound-net fishing. Then in 1926, they bought the *Darlene* from John Young at Washington Harbor. They also had the *Sea Queen* and used her for a gill net boat for a year, then sold her to Oliver Bjarnarson and Hannes Hannesson in 1935. They also owned a tug named the *George Nelson* before ending up with the *Jane*. Sturgeon Bay Boat Works (Palmer Johnson Company) built the *Jane* in 1929 for Nels Sorenson, who had it for many years, then sold it to Clarence LaFond from Algoma who sold it to Russ and Spencer Nelson in 1942. The *Jane* was a 40-foot all wood boat powered with a 30-36 Kahlenberg engine.

George, Russ, and Spencer Nelson had many people work for them through the years, including Thorwald Johnson, Byron Cornell, Ervin Gunnlaugsson, Lester Johnson, Wes Peterson, Dave Cota, Neil Gauthier, and Harold "Lefty" Johnson, and a few others. Lefty Johnson was the most vibrant and impetuous of the men who worked for them. Spencer's son George commented:

> Lefty was one who would like to get an early start. If my Dad or Russ wasn't there, he'd be right on the phone and tell them to get your so and so down to the dock or he would walk right into the bedroom and wake either Russ or Dad up. In the winter time, out on the lake, Lefty always had cheese sandwiches for lunch and would

always slap them up on the side of the wood stove in the boat and hold it on there until it was black and then turn it over and burn the other side and eat them like that. He was definitely a character all right.[38]

Russ and Spencer took over the business in early 1941, and became one of the best partnerships in the commercial fishing business. They worked together very well, but were contrasting individuals. Russ was the better fisherman, and Spencer was more an engineer and mechanic. Spencer was adamant about keeping the boat and equipment well maintained, but he never much cared for fishing. Spencer was much more interested woodworking and painting. Russ was a fisherman at heart and was just as excited on his last day of fishing as he was on his first. He loved every second of it and together they were a good team.

They kept their boat *Jane* in peak condition. Spencer always made sure she got a fresh coat of paint every year or so, and the interior was spotless – not a fish scale could be found anywhere. There was a known affinity between Spencer and the *Jane*. The Kahlenberg engine was maintained regularly, he made sure of that. He kept that engine oiled and greased, which is why it lasted for nearly 40 years. Sylvia said she knew the distinctive sound of that engine and could differentiate the *Jane* from all the other boats in Jackson Harbor. She recalled: "I could open the door and hear the *Jane* coming in. There were probably a half dozen Kahlenberg engines in the various boats, and each one had their own unique sound." In 1962, they had the hull on the *Jane* covered with 1/4-inch steel, which protected the hull when going through ice.[39]

The *Jane* was known to be a roller in a heavy sea. Spencer and Russ were out one time in some bad weather, and both port and starboard windows were smashed in from rolling side-to-side, hitting the water. Another time they were out and lost a box of nets. The boat was rolling so bad, that bar used to secure the hatch flipped up and the hatch opened and a box of nets flew overboard. When the boat rolled back the other way the door closed back shut and the bar flipped back down securing it. They didn't know they lost a box of nets until they got back to shore.[40]

After many years of fishing, Spencer retired in the early 1980s to pursue his woodworking and many other projects. He continued to make sure the *Jane* was well maintained and lent a hand fishing now and then. Russ continued to fish for a few more years and hired Neil Gauthier and Dave Cota to help him. Russ retired in 1989, and Neil tried obtaining a Wisconsin License to continue fishing with the *Jane,* but was denied a commercial fishing license. The *Jane* was sold to Randy Sorenson of Washington Island. Randy fished with the Jane through the 1990s for whitefish. He later sold the boat to Jeff McDonald.

Jim Cornell

Jim Cornell came from a fishing family. His father, Newell Cornell, was a fisherman from Washington Island who fished out of Washington Harbor from the Furlong dock. Jim and his two brothers, Alvin and Vic, both followed in the fishing business. When they were older, they all fished out of Jackson Harbor. Alvin periodically fished with Jim and other fishermen, as well as by himself.

Jim began fishing with the McDonalds in the early 1930s. He bought a 20-foot wood boat called the *Don Delores* in 1941. In the evening, after fishing with the McDonalds, he often set a few nets for chubs or whitefish near Denny's bluff. He moored his small boat at the Furlong dock, but moved to Jackson Harbor soon afterward, as many others also did.

Jim bought his first gill-net boat in 1945 in Kenosha and renamed it the *J.N. Cornell*. He began fishing for chubs at that time and continued to do so for most of his life as a fisherman.

The *J.N. Cornell* was a dandy of a boat," Jim commented with a proud look on his face. "She was a better sea boat than the *Welcome*. She wasn't as long and big as the welcome, but she handled nice. The J.N originally… when I first got it had a Van Beak engine – great big iron outfit. The Van Beak was an unusual engine, it had two separate blocks. It was a four cylinder – two cylinders on each block, then it had a great big magneto on it. There was a starter but to save the starter I'd stick the crank in it and give it a kick with my foot, but that was dangerous at it would tend to kick back. One time I was on my way out to lift chub nets; my wife Doris fished with me for awhile. She was along that day too. All of a sudden she quit running, way outside the gas buoy. Well, I said I got to do something here. I put a lot of rags around the engine and took that magneto apart. You ought to have seen the springs and stuff in it, that's why I packed the cloth rags around it. By God, I got her going and we got a lift on our nets.[41]

Jim fished with the *J.N Cornell* for five years, mooring it at Art Hanson's dock. He re-powered the boat with a four-cylinder 456 Gray marine engine that was removed from Fred Bjarnarson's boat the *Sea Queen* and overhauled it at Green Bay. Jim paid $300 for the engine, which included the wheel and the propeller. In 1950, Jim bought the *Welcome* from Carl Richter who had used her for hauling freight and fish. The *Welcome* was the last boat that was built by Rasmus Hanson in 1926.

The *Welcome* was a bigger and more powerful than the *J.N. Cornell*. After a time, Jim decided to remove the forward pilot house and construct a rear pilot house. This gave an advantage as he could set nets with just one crew member, or by himself, if he had to. Jim had a 105-horsepower, 6 -cylinder Gray marine engine in the *Welcome*. He said:

She was good in the ice. She would go through 8 to 10 inches of ice; you had to back up and go ahead all the time. We had 3/16-inch steel on her hull. When I first bought her from Carl, he said there's good steel on her; he figured it would last her for ten years. It was 1960 I had her re-steeled, it cost me damn near what I paid for the boat. I kept her painted every year.[42]

Jim fished with a small crew, typically one hired crew member or sometimes two men. Over the years, many island men worked for him, and his wife Doris helped out for several years. Roy Richter worked for him for a time, as did Royal Johnson, Tom Johnson, Marvin Bjarnarson, David Goodmander, and later, Fred Young, and his brother Alvin Cornell Jim said:

All those guys were hard workers, as were many of the fishermen around here then. I always liked to fish with a two-man crew, we fished chubs pretty hard back then. I typically set three or four gang of chub nets. Some of the other guys had six gang in the water – the McDonalds, Goodmans. We fished about eight boxes in the gang. We set half dry ones and reset half wet ones after clearing the fish. We didn't have time to reel a whole gang. Sometimes we'd get in late and I didn't have a shore crew, so we'd have to reel the nets to dry for the next day [ourselves]. That's why we reset half of them. Once every three to four weeks we would scald the cotton nets in a pan to get the slime off of them.[43]

When the fishing slacked off during the 1960s, Jim fished some winters down by Milwaukee and Kenosha. In 1967 he had a passenger ferry built called the *Karfi*. He started the ferry service in 1968, transporting passengers from Jackson Harbor to Rock Island State Park – a business he ran for over twenty years. Then it was operated by his son Jack, and is now owned and operated by his grandson Jeff Cornell. Jim sold the *Welcome* in 1972 to Alex Koyen ending his long career as a commercial fisherman. Through out the 1980s and 1990s he carried the title and duties of Dock Master at Jackson Harbor.

Youngs and Greenfeldts

Art and Lloyd Young moved over to Jackson Harbor in 1941, fishing from their father's boat the *Rainbow*. Cliff young served three years in the army during World War II. When he returned, he was soon fishing with Art and Lloyd. In 1949, Art and his family moved to New Mexico, leaving Cliff to buy out his share of the fishery. In 1953, Cliff and Lloyd sold the *Rainbow* and purchased the *Ranger* from Harold Zoellner and Len Ellerbrock. They fished from the Hanson dock and were quite successful.

Tragedy struck in 1955 when Lloyd and two friends went out fishing for perch in Washington Harbor. It was a Sunday afternoon after the island ballgame. Lloyd, Tom Johnson and his brother Dick went where they had a small perch net set a few hundred feet off "Mount Misery," on the northwest side of Washington Harbor. They went out to lift the net in a small aluminum boat. A northeast wind was blowing, and when they lifted the net, the boat flipped over. Lloyd was a strong swimmer, but he got caught in the rope that was attached to the anchor stone and was immediately pulled under the water. Tom was able to swim ashore, but unfortunately his brother Dick, who couldn't swim, held on to the boat as long as he could, but evidently panicked and drowned.

After Lloyd's death, Cliff continued fishing with Art's son Jack Young, with the *Ranger*. Harold Greenfeldt began fishing with Cliff in the late 1950s, and in 1962 they formed a partnership that lasted for many years. The fishing at this time was very poor, forcing Cliff and Harold as well as other fishermen to work other jobs in order to make ends meet.

Some winters, Cliff fished in the Racine and Kenosha area. Cliff often said during that time, "I think you could have stretched a net from Washington Island to Escanaba and not caught one fish."[44] By the early 1970s the fishing improved and Harold and Cliff were soon fishing together again from Jackson Harbor. In 1972 they sold the *Ranger* and bought another boat they re-named the *Ranger*. This boat was a 45-foot steel hull design with a 400-horsepower turbo charged Allis Chalmers diesel engine. Harold and Cliff continued fishing throughout the 1970s and retired from commercial fishing in 1981. They sold the *Ranger* to Jeff Weborg, a commercial fisherman from Gills Rock.

Harold Greenfeldt was a second-generation fisherman who began his career when he was a young man. At an early age, he was often down at the Furlong dock in Washington Harbor helping his father, Anker Greenfeldt. Harold's brother Lorman also followed his father into fishing, and the boys were soon working full-time with their father. Anker bought the *Jane Elizabeth* in 1925 and ran his fishery from the Furlong dock. In 1941, they bought the *Yankee* at Gladstone, Michigan, and moved that same year to the Hanson dock in Jackson Harbor. Lorman and Harold continued fishing after their father retired, and they sold the *Yankee* to Glen and Alvin Sorenson in 1947. They bought another boat they named the *Betty,* built by the Burger Boat Company in 1945. The *Betty* was an all-steel hull design, originally powered by a Chrysler Royal gasoline engine with a 3:1 reduction gear. They later repowered her with a 45-54 Kahlenberg engine. Harold and Lorman fished together for a number of years until 1956, they moved their operation to Racine.

After a year, Harold moved back to the island and acquired the fish tug *Falcon* from Bill Jepson, who acquired it from Glen and Alvin Sorenson in 1953. Glen and Alvin Sorenson had her (*Sorenson Brothers*) built in 1947 by Marinette Marine Corporation in Marinette, Wisconsin. The *Sorenson Brothers* was a 32-foot, all-steel hull boat powered by a Chrysler Crown gasoline marine engine. Lorman remained in Racine and over the years, and fished in many locations with numerous boats and crews. Harold continued to fish at Jackson Harbor with Leland Johnson with their boat *Falcon* until 1961, when he sold her to Richard Hagen from St. Ignace. In 1962, Harold formed a partnership with Cliff Young that lasted many years.

Fred and Percy Young were third generation fishermen and fished with their father John Young when they were teenagers. In 1938, Fred worked briefly for Bill Cornell as one of his shore crew. This was during the Great Depression, and there wasn't much work on the island, so Fred decided to sail for a year on the Great Lakes ore boats. Also that year, he had married Gert Jorgenson and in order to raise a family and buy a house he needed some money. He came back to the island in January of 1939, and he and his brother, Percy bought the *Sea Queen* from Oliver Bjarnarson and Hannes Hannesson. Their partnership lasted many years.

Fred and Percy based their operation from the Furlong dock for a few years, then they moved to Jackson Harbor in 1943, like so many fishermen from that area. They moored at the Hanson dock and used one of the Nelsons net sheds. In 1946, Fred moved his family to Jackson Harbor and built a house close to the harbor. A few years later, he built a net shed on his own property. In 1953, Fred and Percy sold the *Sea Queen* and bought a boat called the *Franklin D. Roosevelt* from James Garrison, a fisherman in Waukegan, Illinois. This boat was built March 16, 1934 by Peterson Boat Works and was of all-wood construction. The *Franklin D. Roosevelt* was 42 feet long and 12 feet on the beam and was powered by a 85-horsepower Buda gasoline engine. But, that same year they bought the boat, Percy died of a brain hemorrhage. He was out fishing when it happened. Fred immediately brought the tug back to port, but Percy died a few days later.

After Percy's death, Alvin Cornell began fishing with Fred. Milton Dulong and Chuck Jorgenson also helped out. In the winter months Fred along with his sons, Howard (Butch) Bob, Larry, and Dennis fished with gill nets through the ice off the north and west end of Washington Island. They continued this tradition for nearly three decades. After selling his boat in the late 1950s, Fred continued fishing through the mid 1960s working for Jim Cornell, before finding employment with the Town of Washington Island. Fred's fishing shed still remained useful, and came to be known as Fred's Shed. It was the place where the island men gathered once a year in mid February for the annual men's day celebration and fish boil. This has been a tradition with the island men that has been going on for nearly a century. Fred's Shed is also used for a hunting shack during the opening weekend of deer hunting season.

Koyen Fishery

In 1971, fishermen were starting to see the whitefish returning in good numbers. Alex Koyen had been a farmer for thirty years, but saw the island's dairy industry fade like the setting sun. He decided there was no future in it. In the fall of that year, he asked his eighteen-year-old son Ken, who had just completed a year of vocational school, if he wanted to go fishing. Ken remembers that particular day:

> **I** was eighteen years old when I started fishing. I had gone to vocational school for basic electronics, and then I worked for the Ferry Line. One day my dad said to me – this was in October. He said, "Do you want to go fishing?" I said, "Yeah let's go." I headed over to the fishing poles. "No," he said, "commercial fishing." "Can I do it?" My dad said, "Hold out your hands, yep they're big enough." That's how I ended up fishing.[45]

Alex Koyen fished part-time nearly his entire life. He began fishing at a very young age, and through the years, he worked for various island fishermen. Alex fished nearly every part of Lake Michigan from Chicago all the way up to the upper peninsula of Michigan. It was what he knew and loved to do best. Ken recalls:

> **D**ad fished almost all his life, even during the years when he farmed he still fished part time, especially in the fall of the year during the herring runs. When he and my mother were married he found himself at a crossroads. He had to make a decision whether to keep fishing or farm for a living. He chose farming and did that for thirty years. Then when the dairy farming fell apart up here, he went back to fishing.[46]

Alex was nearly sixty years old when he got back into fishing full time. The timing was right. Whitefish were making a come back, and his sons were old enough to help him out in the business.

In 1971, he bought the fish tug *Welcome* and thirty-five boxes of nets from Jim Cornell for $3500. That fall, Alex and Ken began fishing with the venerable boat built nearly forty-five years earlier by Rasmus Hanson. A few years later Alex's son Tom helped out, and so did his brother Harvey, who was fishing part-time with Lorman Greenfeldt and Jack Young.

Ken recalls those early days:

> We had a 6-cylinder Gray marine engine in the *Welcome* at the time. We used 70 gallons of gas a day in that boat. During the winter months we tied out at the cut and would haul the gas out to her on our truck in milk cans. We fished chubs in the wintertime and whitefish the rest of the year.

The Koyens fished from the Hanson dock, now the Town Dock. When the town bought the dock and property, the fishermen were told that they could use the dock at no cost. However, that proved to be short-lived and the fishermen got a letter from the town saying they would have to pay a fee for using the dock. Carolyn Koyen said, "When we fished from Art Hanson's dock we paid $35.00 a month for the use of the dock. After it was sold to the town we were told there would be no charge, but it wasn't long after that we got a letter saying there would be a dock fee, which was the same as what we were paying Art Hanson."[47]

In 1986, the Koyens bought another fish tug to replace the *Welcome*, Which was beginning to show her age. They bought the *Sea Diver*, which was dry-docked in Kenosha, Wisconsin, for $800. The *Sea Diver* was built in Erie, Pennsylvania and was used for a while as a dive boat. When the Koyens bought it they made some modifications to it. "The first time I saw the boat it was used for a dive boat," said Ken Koyen. "It was all one deck and the steering was in the bow section. It was originally built for commercial fishing but then it was modified for a different use. We raised the aft house, put the deck in, and moved the steering back."[48]

Alex Koyen passed away from cancer a few years before they bought the *Sea Diver*. "Dad never saw this boat [*Sea Diver*]. He died in 1984 a year or so before we bought the boat. We would have never gotten Dad off the water if he were still alive to be on this one. The only way we got Dad off the *Welcome* was he finally got so bad one day. He was standing by the wheel and forgot where he was and what he was doing. We decided it was time to get him off the boat. It was tough we had to sneak out of the house, because he always wanted to go out on the lake."[49]

In 2005, Ken still continues to fish for whitefish, though he has found a new market for a different species of fish called burbot or "lawyer," which he sells in his restaurant, KK Fiske and bar called the Granary. The burbot is a freshwater member of the cod family, and too many people who have tried it, they have found it delicious. Ken fishes alone nearly every day, year round, and is one of the last commercial fishermen on Washington Island. He says "When they pry my cold dead hands from the wheel of my boat, only then will I retire."[50]

In 2003, Ken was in the process of getting the old fish tug *Welcome* back into service where she once plied the waters for more than half a century. He has done extensive work to the old boat, including a new paint job, rebuilding the engine, and revamping the wiring. By the spring of 2005 he hopes to have the *Welcome* back in service. Ken plans to fish with her as well as his other boat the *Sea Diver*.

As long as there are whitefish and lawyer left in the lake Ken will be out there setting his nets.

The Hagens

Roger ("Roddy") Hagen began fishing when he was a boy learning the business from his father Harry Hagen. He started fishing from Jackson Harbor in 1974. He moved to the island from Milwaukee, Wisconsin, where he and his family owned and operated the Hagen Fish Store for many years. In November of 1973, Roddy and Howard Foss made a trip up to Lake Superior and picked up the *Alex C* that he bought from a fisherman at Ontonagon, Michigan, a 35-foot Marinette Marine originally powered by a Chrysler Crown gasoline engine. In 1956 she was repowered with a 4-cylinder Caterpillar diesel engine following a gasoline explosion that bowed the roof of the boat up 3 inches. Roddy was excited about this trip and planned to have a cook out on the way back on his new boat. Unfortunately the weather wasn't cooperative, and Roddy and Howard were soon fighting the elements. The weather was turning worse and soon they were caught in a heavy sea. The previous owner had oiled the deck, and they were sliding all over the place. After a long day of battling the sea, they finally made it into the shelter of Jackson Harbor.

Roddy moored the boat at the Town Dock and fished for whitefish and chubs. Marvin Bjarnarson worked for him for several years, and after he retired, Walt Jorgenson fished with Roddy. Roddy continued to fish out of Jackson Harbor through the early 1980s then retired and sold his rig. Today his boat sits outside the Maritime Fishing Museum at Jackson Harbor. It was renamed the *Ginny* after he sold it.

Jeff McDonald

A third generation fisherman and home-design builder, Jeff McDonald continues a legacy that began on Washington Island with his great, great grandfather, Dennis McDonald, nearly 150 years ago. Commercial fishing has been in his family all through out his family's history. Jeff's grandfather, Ray McDonald, fished with his father and brothers as a boy and young man on the island before moving to Kenosha in 1920. After working on Great Lakes ore boats a few years, he began commercial fishing with the fish tug *Arbutus*. He acquired the *Arbutus* from a man named Frank Stroh, who lived in Kenosha. The boat was built at Peterson Boat Works in 1913 as a pleasure boat, and Ray converted it into a fish tug. In March of 1934 Ray had the fish tug *J.W McDonald* built, and sold the *Arbutus* to a fisherman from Milwaukee. Ray named the boat after his two sons, James and William. The *J.W. McDonald* was built at Peterson Boat Works, and was 40 feet long and measured 12 feet on the beam. With a 65-85 horsepower Buda diesel marine engine, she could maintain 12 MPH.[51] Ray fished from Kenosha for a few years then moved to Racine.

Ray's son, Jim McDonald, fished with his father on the *J.W. McDonald*. Jim graduated from Kenosha High School and then began fishing with his father out of Racine. Jim eventually had his own boat built, after the *J.W. McDonald* was showing its age, and named her the *Richard E.* She was built in 1944 by the Burger Boat Company and was the first boat built after WWII contracts were completed at the yard. She was a 50-foot by 14-foot, all-steel design powered by a 75-90 Kahlenberg oil engine. Jim bought it from Frank Eichler in 1958 and fished with it for a year, then sold her to Rueben Peterson at Harbor Beach, Michigan.

Jeff grew up in both Kenosha and Racine and remembers fishing with his father Jim:

> **I** went with my dad a few times on the *J.W. McDonald*. That was the boat my Grandpa
> Ray had built at Peterson's at Sturgeon Bay. It's interesting, I have a picture of it next
> to the *McDonald Brothers* boat and the *J.W. Cornell* was a completely different design –
> it had a flat bottom with a square or flat stern. It was a real good sea boat. It was built
> similar to the *Miss Judy* and the *Ranger*. The *J.W.* didn't last to long. It kind of rotted
> away. I guess it wasn't built with the best lumber – it didn't last long at all for a wood
> boat – maybe twenty years. I remember asking my Grandpa about that, and he told
> me that down there it was different. You had to keep them all locked up. It's not like
> here, where the boat gets pretty wet, but all the doors are open and things can dry
> out. But down there you got to lock up your boat when you're done and it stays
> damp.[52]

Jeff moved to Washington Island permanently after graduating with a degree in architecture from the University of Wisconsin at Milwaukee in 1989. Jeff started his own construction business and also worked at his father-in-law Ray Hansen's business part-time doing book work. In 1999, Jeff decided to try commercial fishing. He bought the old fish tug *Jane* from Randy Sorenson, who was getting out of the fishing business. The boat was showing its age and had been a constant effort to keep her running. At that time, the *Jane* was seventy years old, the oldest boat still in operation in northern Door County. Jeff rebuilt some of the decks and part of the house and bow section. Jeff commented:

> **W**e're pretty much a fair-weather fishery with a fair-weather boat and crew, except
> for Jake [Ellefson]. The *Jane* is fine in the summer when you're fishing off the beach.
> If something happens you can take a swim, but it's a whole different ball game when
> that water is cold you don't want to be fooling around, bad things happen quick.

Jeff McDonald and Ken Koyen are the last of the commercial fishermen left on Washington Island. Jeff is considered to be a part-time fisherman, though he goes out on a fairly regular basis when weather permits. He has a good crew who help him out and alternate fishing with him. Jeff Hagen and Jake Ellefson split time with him on the boat. Jeff Hagen's father, Roger "Roddy" Hagen was one of the last fishermen to fish from Jackson Harbor, and Jake Ellefson was the last of the original fishermen to fish from Jackson Harbor. Jake retired in 1999 and sold his rig to Ted Eggebraaten from Baileys Harbor. But, it wasn't long before Jake was back out on the lake where he was most at ease and in his element.

In November 2003, Jeff acquired another fish tug, the *C&R*, from the widow of Joseph Bray, a fisherman from Munising Michigan. The boat sat idle for seven years and, for the most part, was still in good shape. The *C & R* was built in 1958 for Carl Halberg by the T.D Vinette Company at

Escanaba, Michigan. She's a 40 by 14-foot steel-hull vessel powered by a 4-cylinder Caterpillar diesel engine. Jeff rebuilt the house and rebuilt the engine during 2004 and began fishing from her later that summer.

Chapter 9 notes

1 Eaton, *Washington Island 1836-1876*; footnote no. 74, p. 32 Jessie Miner's journal entry.

2 Raymond McDonald, Four Islands (Wolfsong Publications 1984), 57.

3 Ibid, 104.

4 Interview with Jake Ellefson, March 22, 2002.

5 1879 Platte Map, Washington Island (Washington Island Archives).

6 Anne T. Whitney, *Let's Talk About Washington Island 1850-1950* (Town of Washington 1995), 99.

7 Interview With Jake Ellefson, June 12, 2004; Richard Purinton, *Over and Back* (Independent Printing 1990), 11.

8 "Gibby" Goodlet, *Kill The Umpire: Memories of Door County Baseball and Life on Washington Island*; ("Gibby" Goodlet 2001), 60.

9 Ray McDonald, *Four Islands*, 31; Interview and letters by Jake Ellefson, March 1 &2, 2002.

10 Interview with Jake Ellefson, March 2, 2002.

11 Ray McDonald, *Four Islands*, 76.

[12] Goodlet, *Kill the Umpire*, 61.

[13] Ann T Whitney, *Let's Talk About Washington Island,* 102.

[14] Ray McDonald, *Four Islands*, 74.

[15] Ray McDonald, *Four Islands*, 75.

[16] Mary Jeanne (McDonald) Frenzel and Kathleen Rae Bennet, *From One Island to Another,* 30.

[17] Mary Jeanne(McDonald) Frenzel and Kathleen Rae Bennett, *From One Island to Another*, McDonald Family Biographies, 30.

[18] Paul's Netting Gazette, Vol.4 (Sept 1927), 1.

[19] McDonald Family Biographies, *From One Island to Another*, 136.

[20] Ibid, 136.

[21] Ray McDonald, *Four Islands* (Wolfsong Publications, 1984) 86-87.

[22] Ann T Whitney, 48. Steven Karges, *Keepers of the Lights: Lighthouse Keepers and Their Families, Door County, Wisconsin* (Wm Caxton Ltd 2000), 94-95.

[23] Ibid.

[24] *Door County Advocate* June 1900.

[25] Ray McDonald, *Four Islands*, 65-66.

[26] Ray McDonald, *Four Islands*, 71.

[27] Sylvia Nelson, *Fishermen and Their Boats* (Jackson Harbor Press, 1999), 5.

[28] Ibid.

[29] Interview with Jake Ellefson, March 1, 2002.

[30] Interview with Walt Jorgenson, May 5, 2002.

[31] Interview with Dick Bjarnarson, December 20, 2001.

[32] Ibid.

[33] Interview with Jim Cornell, May 4, 2002.

[34] Interview with Dick Bjarnarson, December 20, 2001.

[35] Ray McDonald, *Four Islands*, 8.

[36] Interview with Sylvia Nelson October 2, 2001.

[37] Dick Purinton, *Over and Back: A Picture History of Transportation to Washington Island*, (Independent Printing, De Pere, WI, 1990), 48.

[38] Interview with George Nelson Jr., May 5, 2002.

[39] Interview with Sylvia and George Nelson, May 5, 2002.

[40] Ibid.

[41] Interview with Jim Cornell, May 4, 2002.

[42] Ibid.

[43] Ibid.

[44] Lorel Gordon, "Fishing ? A Young Family Tradition,? *Door County Almanac*, No. 3(Sister Bay, WI: Dragonsbreath Press, 1986), 68.

[45] Interview with Ken Koyen May 4, 2002.

[46] Ibid.

[47] Interview with Carolyn Koyen, July 4, 2003.

[48] Interview with Ken Koyen, May 4, 2005.

[49] Interview with Ken Koyen, July 3, 2003.

[50] Interview with Ken Koyen, May 3, 2002.

[51] Hannes Anderson, "Through the Years," *Washington Island Observer*, December 21, 2006.

[52] Interview with Jeff McDonald, September 22, 2003.

Pic 9.1 Rasmus Hanson, master boat builder and merchant. (Photo courtesy of the Washington Island Archives.)

Pic. 9.2 Charlie McDonald's fifty foot Steam tug *Stewart Edward* undergoing repairs at his dock in Jackson Harbor circa 1910. (Photo courtesy of the McDonald family.)

Pic. 9.3 Charlie McDonald with a block of ice he retrieved from his icehouse. (Photo courtesy of the McDonald family.)

Pic. 9.4 Jackson Harbor, circa 1930, looking southeast toward the Ellefson dock and the Hanson dock. Bow section of a pound-net boat and skiff in the foreground and a derrick for pounding stakes located at the Ellefson dock. (Photo courtesy of Washington Island Archives)

Pic. 9.5 Jackson Harbor, circa 1930, looking northwest towards Lindal dock in the foreground followed by Peterson's dock, Nelson's dock and Lindgren's dock. Pound-net boat moored up at Lindal dock. Notice the wreck of the schooner *Iris* protruding from the water at the right. (Photo courtesy Washington Island Archives.)

Pic. 9.6 Ellefson dock circa 1912, looking north towards Rock Island; McDonalds' steam tug *Stewart Edward* in the background. Pound-net boats and stakes at the waters edge in the foreground. (Photo courtesy of Jake Ellefson)

Pic. 9.7 Jacob Ellefson SR's fish tug *K.E.M Jacob* moored at the Ellefson dock. The boat was named after Jacob's children Klemmet, Everett, Martha and Jacob (KEM Jacob). (Photo courtesy of Jake Ellefson).

Pic. 9.8 *Miss Judy* and the *Ranger* breaking ice. (Photo courtesy of Jake Ellefson)

Pic. 9.9 Jackson Harbor circa 1910.
(Photo courtesy of the
Washington Island Archives)

Pic. 9.10 Oliver Bjarnarson standing in
his shed, now the Jackson
Harbor Maritime Museum.
(Photo Courtesy of Dick and
Marilyn Bjarnarson)

Pic. 9.11 Art and Hans Hanson's dock and packaging shed circa 1957. *Ranger, Islander* and Lorman Greenfeldt's tug the *Kathy* behind the *Ranger*. (Photo courtesy of Kari Bjarnarson)

Pic. 9.12 During the winter months, fishermen often tied their boats together and fastened them to the ice at the Rock Island passage known as the cut. Circa 1950s. (Photo courtesy of Jake Ellefson)

Pic. 9.13 The crew of the *Ranger*, unhitching the lines and loading boxes of nets out by the cut. (Photo courtesy of Harold and Arbutus Greenfeldt)

Pic. 9.14 The *Jane* moored to the ice out by the cut; a fuel pump in the foreground was brought out to the boats for fueling purposes. (Photo courtesy of Jake Ellefson.)

Pic. 9.15 The *Jane* and her skipper Russ Nelson returning to Jackson Harbor after a day of fishing. (Photo courtesy of Dick and Marilyn Bjarnarson.)

Pic. 9.16 Alvin Cornell making his way back to port through the ice on a winter's day. (Photo courtesy of Jim Cornell.)

Pic. 9.17 The *Welcome* stuck in the ice after her drive shaft was bent, ca. 1960. (Photo courtesy of Jim Cornell.)

Pic. 9.18 Jim Cornell fueling up the *Welcome* at Detroit Harbor. (Photo courtesy of Jim Cornell.)

Pic. 9.19 Cliff Young standing on the bow of the *Ranger* coming into the entrance of Jackson Harbor; Rock Island in the distance. (Photo courtesy of Jackson Harbor Maritime Museum)

Pic. 9.20. Harold Greenfeldt (left) and Cliff Young, clearing whitefish from a gill net at the lifter table in the gill-net tug, *Betty*. (Photo courtesy of Harold and Arbutus Greenfeldt)

Pic. 9.21 Anker Greenfeldt at the wheel in the gill-net tug *Jane Elizabeth*. (Photo courtesy of Harold and Arbutus Greenfeldt)

Pic. 9.22 Alex Koyen packing fish at Jackson Harbor. (Photo courtesy of Jim Cornell)

Chapter 10

Detroit Harbor & Detroit Island

Detroit Harbor is on the south end of Washington Island and, like Washington Harbor, became a busy place for early settlers and fishermen. Detroit Harbor's shallow waters offer protection from wind and waves from almost any direction. The north end of Detroit Island is about half a mile south of Detroit Harbor and helps to protect it from southerly blows. On both sides of Detroit Island, which is long and narrow, there are channels. The east channel runs due south and is very shallow, with an average depth, depending on the lake level, of about 6 or 7 feet, a problem for deeper draft vessels entering the harbor via this route. On the opposite end of the harbor, the west channel is considerably deeper and became the major route for schooners and steamboats.

The Icelanders

In the 1870s, Detroit Harbor saw an influx of Icelandic immigrants, mostly due to a man named William Wickman, who left Eyrarbakki, Iceland, in the early 1860s and sailed for America to visit his sister, whose husband was the Danish Consul in Milwaukee. In Milwaukee, Wickman found employment in the grocery business, and during his sojourn there, he corresponded with friends back in Iceland and persuaded them to come to Milwaukee. Those friends were three brothers – Jon, Arni, and Gudmunder Gudmundsson (Gudmundson – dropped a "s" after arriving to the states) – and Jon Einarson. All were in their early twenties and eager for adventure, and they met at Reykjavik before embarking. Some of their families and friends told wild stories of how they would be subjected to cannibals and slavery, and would only find hard times, but they left anyway and set sail in May of 1870.[1]

When the young men arrived in Milwaukee they found the language barrier to be their greatest obstacle. Adjusting to this new culture proved difficult. They tried fishing at Jones Island, a major fishing community near Milwaukee, but the way they fished there was entirely different from what they were accustomed to. William Wickman tried to help them and discussed the situation with the captain of a lake schooner. The captain told him of an island in the northern waters of Lake Michigan where the fishing was good and land was available for the taking.

William Wickman took one of the Goodrich boats to see for himself this little island, known as Washington Island. Wickman was impressed with the surroundings and the natural beauty of the place. He met Victor Rohn, a lighthouse keeper on Pilot Island, before traveling to Washington Island. Rohn had a homestead on Washington Island, and Wickman stayed there a few nights. He was introduced to a Mr. Fuller, who owned several acres of land, complete with a house, dock, boats, and nets.

Wickman thought this would be ideal for him and his friends, and to Wickman's surprise, Fuller was willing to sell. Wickman went back to Milwaukee, sold his business, rounded up his friends and they all left for Washington Island. They were the first Icelanders who made Washington Island their home.[2]

The only one of the Icelanders who had success in fishing was Gudmunder Gudmundson, who had been an experienced fisherman in Iceland. In 1874, he married Gudrun Invarsdatter, who was also from Iceland, and bought property on the southeast end of Washington Harbor with a log house. They later added clapboard siding and painted it white. Gudmunder fished for a time, then began making nets for other fishermen. However, he was happiest writing verse and articles for publications. He and Gudrun loved entertaining their friends living around Washington Harbor. They had five children, and the two boys, Tom and Albert, became successful fishermen after learning the business from their father. Tom shortened his last name, Gudmundson, to Goodman, while his brother Albert changed the spelling to Goodmander. Arni, Gudmund's brother, also dropped an "s" to spell his name Gudmundson. This sort of thing was a common practice among Scandinavians when they relocated. For example, there were quite a few Scandinavians on Washington Island with the same last name of Olson, so the Chris Olson family changed their name from Olson to Saabye, after Chris Olson's native village in Denmark. Also, there were two families with members named Mads Hanson, so one became known as Norwegian Mads Hanson and the other as Danish Mads Hanson. And there were several families of Johnsons. John Johnson had a black beard and went by the name "Black John," to distinguish him from the Norwegian John Johnson who had curly blond hair and was called "Curly Chris."

William Wickman was instrumental in bringing a number of Icelanders to this region and helping them to settle. Some stayed only a short time, but others found Washington Island a hospitable place. Wickman had a local Irishmen from the north side of the island teach some of the newcomers the craft of felling trees and cutting cordwood. He recalls:

> The following spring, I took more Icelanders to the island, together with provisions, fishing nets, and other necessaries, and built a house for headquarters. They liked the country very much, and soon Icelanders began to come to me in big loads.[3]

Wickman remained on the island, and in 1875 he was elected Town Chairman of Washington Island, the first Icelander to hold that office.

John Gislason, another Icelander, was elected highway overseer in the same election. After arriving on the island, Gislason bought a store on the southeast end of Detroit Harbor from James Corrigan. It soon became very successful, with a well-stocked inventory of dry goods, hats, caps, clothing, shoes, jewelry, drugs, furniture, crockery, hardware, and just about anything else anyone might need. Gislason also rented summer cottages with dock privileges and built a good dock for the schooners that frequented the harbor. Years later the Hart Line passenger and freight boats would dock at Gislason's. In 1876, he attended the University of Wisconsin to improve his English skills. He was involved in various civic organizations on the island and had a family of nine children.[4]

Arni Gudmundson worked in the woods cutting cordwood after coming to the island. He and his wife Haldora lived for some time in a large house built for the immigrant Icelandic families. It was there that their daughter Ann was born. Not long after Ann's birth, they moved to Milwaukee. Arni became an American citizen in 1882, and by that time the Gudmundsons had returned to Washington Island. That year, he was elected justice of the peace, and he later became Town Treasurer, a position he held for almost thirty-five years.   Arni had persuaded his brother, Thordur, to immigrate to the island. Thordur was a doctor in Iceland and gave up his practice there to start over on the island.[5] He arrived in 1885 and was soon practicing medicine. His presence gave the islanders extra peace of mind that may have influenced more Icelanders to come to the remote island.[6] His first patients were a man with a broken arm and another man who had cut off two toes with an axe.

Icelandic Castle[7]

In 1872, Magnusson arrived on Washington Island with a vision – he wanted to build a large boarding house for the newly arriving Icelandic immigrants. The building came to be called the Icelandic Castle, allegedly in reference to a Shakespearean quote.[8] Lumber was shipped from Sheboygan and construction began in the summer of 1875. Peter Gunnlaugsson and Arnie Legrove built a spacious two-story house.

Oddur Magnusson was a bachelor who stayed in the house for some years. Another resident was Peter Gunnlaugsson, who eventually married Oddur's sister Magnena Magnusson. The first family to stay at the house was Nils Peterson and his wife. While there, they had two children, a boy and a girl. Many families came and went from the Castle, and the place became a haven in a strange and some-times harsh land for these Icelandic immigrants. There was a sign over the door with the inscription *Athabold,* meaning everyone welcome, and the house remained a place of welcome for a long time.[9]

Early Years at Detroit Harbor

From before the turn of the century until the 1930s, Detroit Harbor was a busy part of Washington Island. Many people passed through Detroit Harbor on the Hill boats and Goodrich boats, and some liked it well enough to return and built summer homes and cottages. The harbor proved ideal for swimming, fishing and sailing and has long been a fine place for sport fishing, with abundant small-mouth bass, rock bass, perch, walleye, and northern pike.

Several hotels were built to accommodate people who came to the area on the passenger liners, and they proved to be successful businesses. The first hotel on Washington Island, was on the southern shore of Detroit Harbor and was called the Ida Bo Inn after the proprietors, Bo L. Anderson and his wife Ida Francis Washburn Anderson. Bo Anderson had been born in Sweden and came to Washington Island in 1883. He was knowledgeable and well educated, and those traits were beneficial in his many ventures. When Bo Anderson first arrived, he sailed for a number of years on the brig *Gladiator* with his father. In 1889, he accepted the position as the first postmaster of Detroit Harbor. In 1894, he and his wife opened the doors of their new hotel, the Ida Bo Inn. Bo later built a large store on the property and became a merchant as well as a hotel proprietor. The store was stocked with a large inventory of general goods. In 1901, he extended an existing dock a few hundred feet so that the larger boats could moor there. He later had a channel dredged so that the Hill boats could land there as well.[10]

Bo Anderson invested in land in partnership with Ole Christiansen. Together they had substantial holdings on Lobdell's Point and around Jackson Harbor. Bo also was involved in civic organizations. He was Town Chairman for a number of years, and was instrumental in establishing a creamery on the island. He circulated a petition and got enough signatures to have telephone service brought to the island. The local telephone company was organized on August 17, 1909, and a government cable was laid across Death's Door to the island to serve stations from which accidents or warnings to the Coast Guard, stationed on Plum Island, could be reported. The stations were located at Koyen's store in Washington Harbor, Bo Anderson's hotel in Detroit Harbor, and Rasmus Hanson's establishment at Jackson Harbor.[11]

When Bo Anderson died in 1923, The Ida Bo Inn was inherited by the Shellswicks (Bo's sister, Aurora married Nor Shellswick). It sat vacant until Mrs. Henry Einarson bought it in 1928. Einarsons sold it in 1946 to Lester Betz, then in 1950, the Ida Bo Inn was sold to Al Stalter, and renamed Holiday Inn. They eventually sold it to the Findley family, who renamed it Findley's Holiday Inn. Despite a fire in 1988, which nearly destroyed it, it remains an historic landmark.[12]

The Spring Beach Hotel, also in Detroit Harbor, was owned and operated by Nor and Aurora Shellswick. The hotel was built in 1900. A natural spring was found on the shore, and it was aptly named Spring Beach Hotel. Nor's father Knud O. Shellswick was a sailor in Norway and came to America in 1862, and settled in Chicago. Knud remarried after his first wife Clara died, and he and his Norwegian bride Birgette had a son named Nor, who was born in 1869. In 1875, Knud and his family moved to Washington Island. He bought a parcel of land, which he named Fagerwick, meaning "beautiful place" in Norwegian.[13] Knud changed his last name from Olson to Shellswick, since there were already many Olsons – he opted for a name change to avoid confusion. He chose that particular name, after his family farm called Skjelsvig in southern Norway. Through several spellings, Knud Olson became Knud Shellswick. After Knud settled on Washington Island, he sailed Bo Anderson's schooner *Iris* for many years, as well as farmed and cut timber. In 1881, he built a post office under the name Fagerwick and was elected three times as Justice of the Peace.

Knud's son Nor carried on the operations at Fagerwick, and built the hotel at the turn of the twentieth century. He married Aurora Anderson, a sister to Bo Anderson, and had three children, Alfred, Leon, and John. For many years the hotel and property attracted many people with its beautiful shoreline and grand view of the harbor. A large garden on the grounds provided guests with fresh vegetables and fruit. Unfortunately, the hotel burned to the ground in the winter of 1932, after a chimney fire spread to the structure. Nor's son Leon eventually built a nice home on the site of the old hotel, where he and his wife lived for many years.[14] Nor Shellswick built another pier on property he owned on the south end of Washington Island and operated pound nets from there for many years. Nor owned many wooded acres around the South Point property, and for many winters he cut timber, which was shipped out in the spring of the year. During the winter months, the Shellswick family lived in a small log cabin located on the shore of South Point, while they cut timber. It remains to this day a secluded haven on the rocky shoreline.

Washington Hotel was opened to the public in 1904 and had all the conveniences of that time, a nice bathhouse, and pleasant décor. The owners, Ben and Evelyn Johnson, were island residents and good hosts. Ben was an accomplished storyteller and cook, especially of fish, and entertained his guests with many stories about the lake. Evelyn Johnson was a daughter of John Gislason, who ran a general store and owned a dock a short distance from the hotel. The hotel was always busy during the summer. During the off-season, Ben sailed on a lake carrier as a cook and returned to the island in the winter months while the ship laid up until spring. After Evelyn passed away in 1937, Ben sold the hotel to the Wrasses, who operated it for many years.[15]

Early Homesteads and Fisheries

Soon after Washington Island became a town in the 1850s, more people began settling on the island. Washington Harbor was the first area settlement to become established, but people soon also began settling on the south side of the island, and one of the first to do so was Godfrey Kalmbach and his family. Godfrey and his wife Christina came to this country from Wittenberg, Germany, settling first in Cleveland, Ohio, and moving to Washington Island in 1857. Godfrey first was employed by James Craw and then worked for Delbert Ranney. Godfrey purchased land on a little bay in Detroit Harbor, a secluded place, almost hidden in the rushes, but also a beautiful place where wild rice grew and cranes and herons were often to be seen.[16]

Godfrey built a house and a good-sized dock that became a refueling stop for some of the steamships frequenting the harbor. He sold cordwood to fuel their boilers and also shipped cordwood to various markets, but, after 1860, he turned his attention more to farming. The Kalmbach home was a gathering place for some of the harbor folk, and many afternoons and evenings were spent entertaining guests. Godfrey and Christina had five children – three girls, Mary, Minnie, and Susan, and two boys, Michael and Albert. The little islands just out from their bay were later called the Susie Islands after the Kalmbach's youngest daughter.

As the boys grew up, they became interested in the fishing business. Albert began fishing by himself when he was sixteen years old and marketed his own catch from the Ranney dock in Washington Harbor. A letter he wrote in 1939 tells of these early years:

> My job as a boy of seven or eight was to spread the stones and cedar floats on racks to dry the nets when the boats came in. These nets were 40 fathoms long, 12 meshes deep, 4 1/2-inch mesh, and, as it was long before the invention of knitting machinery, they were knit by hand at home. It was the regular stint of every school boy and girl to knit a net a week after school hours. When I was sixteen years old, I bought my first boat and fished alone, handling ten nets and salting the catch. A few years later, I went to work for my brother as captain of the schooner *Lettie May* picking up the packages of salted fish from the fishing grounds. This schooner I later purchased and went into the wholesale fish business on my own account in Sturgeon Bay,

Wisconsin.[17]

Albert was one of the first fishermen in the area to voice concern for the future of the fisheries. He tried for many years, but found it difficult to obtain laws to protect the fisheries. Years later his actions were finally recognized and he was appointed as a member of an advisory board to the Conservation Commission.

> **I** am eighty years old and have been working in some capacity in the fishing industry for more than seventy of those years. I have watched the transition from the day of sail boats and hand knitted nets through steam tugs to gasoline and diesel engines and have owned and fished each type as it came to popularity. The days of waste and plenty have been followed by scarcity and a belated effort to conserve the industry for future generations.[18]

Albert never forgot Washington Island, and visited frequently.

Mary Kalmbach married Jacob Richter in 1858. One story handed down claims that he proposed at Mary's woodpile. Jacob saw Mary splitting wood and said, "Why don't you get a man for yourself?" Mary replied, "Oh, no one would have me." Jacob replied, "I most certainly will." So began a long and flourishing relationship with eight children.[19] There were five boys, Fred, Carl, Albert, Frank and Vernon, and three girls Anna, Ada, and Mary. Fred, Carl, and Frank followed the fishing business, while Vernon ran the family farm, helping out in his brother Fred's fishery now and then. Albert moved away from the island and settled in Racine. The girls married island fishermen — Anna married James Denio, Ada married Amy Duclon, who fished pound nets for a while, and Mary (Mamie) married Albert Goodmander.[20]

Detroit Island

In the spring of 1834, two young fishermen landed on Detroit Island and built a small log cabin. They fished the waters off the west end of the island. In the summer of 1835, they came under attack by a small band of Potawatomi Indians. An arrow killed one of them, but the other found safety in the cabin. By morning, the Indians withdrew, and a government steamer that was passing picked up the sole survivor. The crew of the government boat investigated his story and found arrows imbedded in the logs of the cabin.[21]

In the late 1800s, a number of families lived on Detroit Island. It had a sheltered harbor on the north end, facing Washington Island's Detroit Harbor, and each family had a small house and outbuildings for their livestock, usually a few chickens and a cow for milk. Children went to Washington Island to attend the Detroit Harbor school. In the winter, they walked across the ice. Despite the lack of its own school, it was a pleasant place to live. Most of the men relied on fishing and cutting cordwood to provide for their families.

Some of the families that resided there were the Morten Jorgensens, the James Denios, and the

William Gierkes. Gierke owned a substantial amount of timber land. In the 1890s, Fred Richter bought land on Detroit Island, built a dock and many fish sheds, and started a successful fishery. The Hill Boat Line owned some property and had a dock built on the northwestern tip of Detroit Island, just inside the harbor, in 1891. The company also had another dock, built in 1883, on the other end of the harbor where they picked up fish.[22]

A name that became woven into the fabric of Detroit Island history was that of Captain C. O. Peterson. Captain Peterson came from Oslo, Norway, and settled on Detroit Island in 1887. He married Julia Anderson from Ephraim, and together they raised their children on the island. Captain Peterson sailed for many years on a schooner he built in Detroit Harbor called the *Agnes Berhmann*, which he used to haul cordwood and freight. He built the schooner in the spring of 1883. She measured 92 feet in length and was 25 feet on the beam. He lost this vessel during a storm on October 30, 1898 at Hedgehog Harbor (Gills Rock).[23] Captain Peterson then bought a three-masted scow-schooner called the *Ferrand Williams*, which he used to haul wood from the island to southern lake ports. The *Ferrand Williams* was built at Manitowoc, Wisconsin, in 1882. She had a length of 82 feet and measured 22 feet on the beam. Captain Peterson encountered a bad storm in 1900 and lost the *Ferrand Williams* near Horseshoe Bay. In 1901, he began a fish-oil business called Try Works. For a few years he was quite successful and found a market for the oil in Chicago. After he died, his wife Julia moved to Washington Island and settled in a home near the Holiday Inn in Detroit Harbor.[24]

Detroit Harbor Fisheries

In 1901, there was considerable fishing activity at Detroit Harbor:

> A conservative estimate places the average daily catch around Washington Island at something like three tons. There are five tugs operating out of Detroit Harbor, two from West Harbor. Each one of these tugs handles about 150 gill nets per day, and as they [the nets] average forty-five fathoms in length it will be seen that they cover a good deal of territory. Trout and chubs are about the only fish caught. Prices are six cents for trout and three cents per pound for chubs. Under the stimulus of these good prices fishing operations in that part of the lake and bay are the liveliest they have been in many a year.[25]

Detroit Harbor was an ideal location for a fishery with its sheltered harbor, and accessibility, even though it was farther from the best fishing grounds than Washington Harbor and Jackson Harbor. During the winter, most Washington Harbor fishermen brought their boats to Detroit Harbor because of its better protection from the elements. By the late 1800s, nearly a dozen docks in and around Detroit Harbor served fishermen, passenger boats, and freight liners as well as yachts and sailboats. Most of the fishing docks were on the west end of the harbor and on Detroit Island, near the west channel where the water was deeper. After the turn of the century, a few fishermen built docks on Lobdell's Point, which was owned by Ole Christiansen and Bo Anderson.[26]

Ole Christiansen had a small shipyard where the ferry dock is now. From there he operated a ship repair business. He also had a large dock in Jackson Harbor. In 1907 John W. Cornell purchased land just north of Christiansen's and built a dock and sheds for his fishery. Not long after John Cornell's fishery began operating, Pat Chambers acquired land north of Cornell's dock and began operating his own fishery, building a small dock and some buildings.[27]

Fred Richter

Fred Richter began fishing when he was in his early teens, and, by the time he was in his early twenties, he purchased the peninsula of land on the northwest end of Detroit Island, which is long and narrow with good waterfront overlooking the west channel and the inside harbor of Detroit Island. He began work immediately on a house, dock, net buildings and icehouse, and over the years kept adding more buildings to his land.

After he left Washington Harbor, John Cornell used Fred's dock for a few years, about the time that John acquired a large steam tug the *Henry Gust*, for his fishery. Albert Kalmbach, formerly from the island but then living in Sturgeon Bay, kept his ties with the Richter family and operated two pound nets from their dock. Jim Denio and Amy Duclon operated several pound-nets in the spring and fall for Albert's fishery, but only for a few years. Fisheries from other areas also used the Fred Richter dock. January Gagnon from Racine operated a 65-foot steam tug named the *J.S Gagnon* from there in the 1920s, and Charlie Wondrasek from Sturgeon Bay had the *Ralph Cooper*, a 60-foot steam tug.[28]

Fred Richter was well liked. He was generous with his dock property, allowing many fishermen from other lake ports to use his dock. However, some island fishermen did not want outsiders coming into the area to fish:

> The influx of fishermen from abroad is not at all satisfactory to the islanders, who say that these people come here to take what fish they can, and afterward pull up stakes without benefiting the community a particle. Those who are permanently stationed here expend all they make, besides helping to keep the town, county, and state governments. While there is no law against this sort of thing, there is growing sentiment that some ways and means should be devised for keeping out the interlopers – who are here one day, and somewhere else the next.[29]

Fred Richter married John Cornell's sister Ida. She and Fred had three children, a daughter named Pearl and two sons named Earl and Roy. Pearl married George O. Mann of Washington Island and owned and operated the George Mann Store. When they were old enough, Earl and Roy followed their father's path and became fishermen, taking over Fred's fishery when he retired. Fred's wife Ida also worked in the fishery with Fred and was very adept at it. Ida had her own boat, the *Dutchman*, which had an inboard engine, Ida also retained her femininity:

> One day when Ida was out fishing . . . she actually fished with regular nets by herself . . . her skirt got caught in the drive shaft and it was torn off her. In those days it was custom that women wore more than one petticoat . . . but that didn't matter to

Ida, for she was pretty modest and when she got into the dock, she called for someone to go up to the house and get her something to cover up with. She wasn't about
to come out of her boat otherwise.[30]

Fred employed a few men in his fishery and fished with gill nets, hooks, and (in the fall of the
year) with pound nets for herring and whitefish. He had a well-built dock with various nets and packaging sheds and a good-sized icehouse. It was no wonder why many fishermen were drawn to this
location.

In 1905 Fred was one of the first on the island to use a saw rig for harvesting ice. It consisted of
a gasoline engine mounted on a hand sleigh that powered a circular saw blade. With that machine, one
man could saw more ice than ten men could with hand saws. It also cut the ice in uniform-size blocks.

Fred owned several fish tugs over the years. The first one he had was the *Pearl,* built of wood in
1906, which had an 8-horsepower gasoline engine, and was 30 feet long and 8 feet on the beam. Three
years later, Fred acquired the *Two Brothers,* which was a larger boat – 30 feet long, wood construction,
with a 20-horsepower gasoline engine. In 1927, Fred Richter acquired another tug named the *Fred,*
which was 47 feet long and 12 feet on the beam, equipped with a 45-54 Kahlenberg engine. In 1930,
he sold the *Fred* to his son Roy. Roy sold it to Dennis McDonald in 1934, at the time he bought the
Maritana from the McDonalds.[31]

Roy took over the fishery after Fred retired, assisted by his brother Earl. The two brothers were
known for having a good time and enjoying their beer. One day Roy Richter and Tom Goodman had
a race in their fish tugs:

> Tom Goodman and Roy were going out fishing; Tom had the *Hans,* and Roy had
> the *Fred.* Well, Tom was ahead of Roy on the inside of him nearest of the shore and
> Roy was creeping up on him as if provoking him to race. Tom, seeing that Roy was
> going to pass him, started turning the boat toward shore causing Roy to turn as well
> and steered him into the shallows where Roy had to slow down and maneuver behind
> the *Hans.* The race was over before it barely began. The winner by skillful maneu-
> vering – Tom Goodman.[32]

Fred and Robert Young

Fred and Robert Young fished together and lived next to one another in Detroit Harbor. They
followed their father, Jacob Young, into fishing, as did their older brother John, who fished from the
Furlong dock in Washington Harbor. Fred and Robert used the Fred Richter dock in the early 1900s.
They had a fish tug called the *Messenger,* which they sold in 1906 at the time they bought the steam tug,
Clifford. They fished together until Robert entered the Lighthouse Service in 1923 on Pilot Island,
leaving Fred to fish on his own.[33]

Fred sold the *Clifford* to a company in Upper Michigan that used her for towing logs. He was out
of the fishing business for a few years, but then acquired a small gas fish tug in 1914 and named her

the *Nor*, after Nor Shellswick. The *Nor* was a wood boat, 28 feet long with a 7-horsepower gasoline engine. Tradition has it that Mr. Shellswick made a deal with Fred that if he would name the tug after him, Fred could use his dock at no charge. Fred agreed and fished from the Shellswick dock for about four years, then went back to the Fred Richter dock and fished from there until he retired from fishing in the 1940s.

Carl and Frank Richter

Carl Godfried Richter and his brother Frank grew up near Detroit Harbor. Their older brother Fred already had a fishery on Detroit Island when the two younger brothers started fishing. Frank left the island in 1901 while in his early twenties and moved to Manistique, Michigan, where he began fishing with his brother-in-law, Lawrence Figenscau. Frank became the engineer on Lawrence's boat the *Stewart Edward*, which was sold to Charlie McDonald in 1904.[34]

Frank Richter moved back to Detroit Island with his bride, Iva Mae Young, whom he had met while living in Manistique. Frank and his brother Carl bought a gasoline-powered fish tug from Two Rivers and named it the *Iona Estelle*, after their daughters. Carl and Frank fished together until 1917, when they decided to part ways and sell the business. Carl sailed on several different schooners for a few years, while Frank continued fishing with other fishermen and then moved his family to Chicago.

Frank's three sons lived in Chicago and were working on a fish tug called the *Indian*. In 1937, the Richters moved to South Haven, Michigan, and continued fishing from that location for many years. Frank's son Harold was fishing in the *Indian* when he was caught in the famous November 11, 1940, gale later known as the "Armistice Day Blow." The *Indian* and her entire crew were lost in that terrible storm, as were many other boats, including many fishing boats.[35]

Frank continued fishing with his other two sons, Glen and Warren, and lived in South Haven for the rest of his life. Frank also had had another son, Royal, who was lost at sea when he was only sixteen years of age. Royal was working on a freighter owned by Irvin Anderson, a brother of Jack and Cecil Anderson. The freighter was en route from Benton Harbor, Michigan, with a load of fruit bound for Milwaukee when they encountered gale force winds. The boat was heavily loaded and probably was overcome by the wind and waves and capsized. The entire crew was lost that day, as well as Irvin Anderson's wife of only one month.

Carl Godfried Richter was born in August 1881, the second son of Jacob and Marie Richter. Carl found his calling in life at a very young age, for when he turned sixteen years of age he already had a job sailing with Ole Christiansen on the Schooner *Laurel*. Ole offered Carl the job as Ole was loading cordwood at the Gislason dock, bound for Milwaukee. Ole needed a cook. Carl told a small lie, and said that he could cook and was hired on the spot. As he later explained:

I knew very little about cooking, but they were in a hurry to get started, so my mother tried to teach me while I was packing my turkey [sailors sack]. She told me how to make pancakes and such stuff. I was the cook all that season, and I remember the pay was twenty dollars a month.[36]

Even though he was the cook, Carl learned the ropes as a crewmember and became a good sea-man. As part of the crew of a sailing vessel, he had to learn and remember the location and function of each part of the rigging so thoroughly that they could find the right rope instantly, even on a moon-less night or in a howling gale. This knowledge was something Carl never lost, even when he was no longer sailing; it served him well when he was a commercial fisherman. Carl said, "To this day I could walk blindfold along the deck and name each line correctly."[37] When Carl was sailing in schooners, there were no weather bulletins or radio communications to warn of bad weather:

> All we did was – each boat had its own glass [barometer] on board and we watched that. They had made a mark on it to show how low it had gone before a bad storm, and if it started getting near that mark, we made for shelter. Of course, you could tell if a squall was coming by watching the clouds. These things were all we had to go by.[38]

Carl told of being caught in a storm as they were heading for Milwaukee:

> One fall a few years after I started sailing (I was a mate) we loaded up with cord-wood for our last trip to Milwaukee to bring in all the winter supplies for Gislason's general store. We got as far as Cana Island, but the sky looked bad so we came all the way back and anchored out by the gas buoy. The others went ashore, but the cook and I decided to stay on board. During the night, it blew a living gale from the west. The fluke broke off the anchor, and we went aground on Detroit Island. The load of cordwood was strewn all along the beach, and the cook and I were on board two days and nights before we could get ashore.[39]

And he told of another blow he was in:

> One storm I will never forget was on the 18th of May. It blew 72 miles an hour out of the north northwest. I was mate on the *Iris*. We came into Milwaukee the next day and outside of the old breakwater was the *Cummings* with just her spars above water and her crew of seven, including the woman cook, frozen to death in the rig-ging. They had climbed up and tied themselves there during the storm when the cabin went under water. During the night it had turned cold and snowed, and the Coast Guard hadn't been able to get out to them because of the seas.[40]

Carl gave up sailing in 1895 and began a new career in commercial fishing with his brother Frank, except for the years 1917 and 1918 when he sailed on ore carriers. In 1905, Carl married Margaret Gudmundson, the daughter of Arni Gudmundson. Carl and Maggie (as she was usually known) had five children – two sons, Paul and Arni Jacob, who later fished with Carl, and three daughters, Estelle, Margaret, and Evelyn.

After Carl and Frank sold their fishing business in 1918 and Frank moved away, Carl bought the fish tug *Shine-on* from Al and Leon Shellswick. After a brief period of fishing on Detroit Island, Carl and his family moved to St. Ignace, where he fished several years but then sold his rig and returned to the island. For the next decade, Carl fished with several different fishermen, including Fred Young. Carl and Fred Richter had a boat called the *Elsa M* that they used for several years and sold it in 1923.

In 1931, Carl decided he needed a change of pace and began carrying mail between Washington Island and Ellison Bay on the Door Peninsula under contract with the US government. He also carried freight and passengers on his boat the *Welcome*, which he bought from Rasmus Hanson. During the winter, he transported fish from Washington Island to Europe Bay, which could sometimes be a treacherous route with the constantly shifting ice. Carl's son Arni recalled one particularly memorable day in 1935:

> **B**efore we officially had the ferry service, Dad and I operated the *Welcome,* which Dad bought from Bill Jepson in 1931 and we would carry the mail, fish and some freight. We would take the fish across the Door and on over to Europe Bay. There was no dock over there at the time so we would drop anchor and put the fish or the goods on a skiff and row it ashore. One day we went over there and it was all packed in with heavy ice, about two feet thick that went north all the way up along the shore to North Port. We finally got the boat wiggled in and got the sleigh out. The Plum Island Coast Guard station was still open for the season, and we would take some of the crew, on their day off and take them to the mainland and then back again. Well, this day, as we were ready to leave there was a Coast Guard Service man with his wife and a five-day-old baby. There was a lot of ice cakes in the bay – they were jagged and in between them there was only an inch of ice, so you had to be careful where you stepped. I took her and her small suitcase and began walking out on the ice with her to the boat. The man and his baby followed behind. Just as we got to the boat and I helped her aboard, I heard the man holler. He had stepped off the ice cake onto a thin piece of ice and down he went into twenty feet of water with the baby in his arms. I ran back to the spot and got there when they came back up. It was just lucky that they came back up in that same spot. I grabbed the baby and ran back to shore. I took some of the outer clothes off; fortunately the cold water hadn't gotten inside to the baby, so he was doing alright. The father made it out fine as well.
>
> Many years later in 1990 it was our 50th year in operation, we got a call from a reporter in Green Bay and he wanted to do a story about the Ferry Line and he asked if there was something that happened in that fifty years that would make a good story. I chuckled and said, "Yeah, I think I have quite a few of them." So I told him we ran a smaller boat called the *Welcome* from 1931 to 1940 and about that episode. He ran with the story and it went out in publication. About two days later I got a call from a man in Milwaukee and he wanted to talk to me. I got to talking to him and he said, "You know, I think I'm the baby you saved fifty-five years ago.[41]

In 1940, Carl and his son Arni bought the ferry line, including all the docks and property, from Bill Jepson. Two boats were included in the deal that were used to haul autos, trucks, freight, passengers, the US Mail, and whatever else needed to be brought to and from Washington Island. These two boats were the *Welcome* and the *North Shore*. In 1946, Carl and Arni had a new steel boat built, called the *Griffon*. In 1950, the *C.G Richter* was built and is still in use today; mainly used as a winter boat.

Carl retired in 1953 at the age of eighty-three, and his son Arni became sole owner of the Washington Island Ferry Line. The ferryboats ran between their home dock in Detroit Harbor and Gills Rock, located on the northern tip of Door County. During the winter months, the ferry boat *C.G. Richter* would dock at Northport which was closer to the island than Gills Rock, although there were still the heavy seas and ice to contend with at that location overlooking the Death's Door Passage.

In 1960, the *Voyageur* was added to the fleet and christened on May 19, 1960 by Arni's twin daughters, Adelle and Estelle Richter. The new all-steel ferry boat had a "flattop" design, which offered a wider beam, and ramps both forward and aft for easier loading and unloading. In 1970, the *Eyrarbakki* was built and added to the fleet, named after the town in Iceland where the first Icelanders to settle on Washington Island came from. When the *Robert Noble* was built and put into service in 1980, it was the largest boat in the fleet, with a length of 90 feet and a 35-foot beam. But then the *Washington*, substantially larger than the *Robert Noble*, was added and put into service in 1990. In the early 1980s, the Washington Island Ferry Line discontinued running to Gills Rock and began sending all the ferries to and from North Port. In 1993, they constructed a breakwall at North Port to form a protected docking site.[42]

The ferry line is still running strong, with a fleet of five boats including a new winter boat called the *Arni J.* After Arni retired, his son-in-law, Richard Purinton became president of the company, and his son Hoyt as vice president. The ferries are the only means of transporting autos to and from the island, and the mail, lumber, fuel, and freight are still being brought from the mainland via the ferryboats.

J. W. Cornell

John William Cornell was born on Washington Island on December 12, 1865, the son of William and Hannah Johnson Cornell. They lived in the old Tim Coffey house in Washington Harbor. John's father died in 1888 at the age of forty, and John was left to take care of his mother, seven brothers and three sisters. In 1895, his mother remarried to Jessie Miner, the lighthouse keeper on Rock Island. At the age of fourteen, John began fishing, using sail-powered Mackinaw boats out of Washington Harbor, and he eventually bought the steam tug *Welcome* in 1898.[43] A year before he acquired the *Welcome*, John Cornell and a small crew went out one morning to lift some chub nets that were set 8 miles north of Rock Island.

They left Washington Harbor early in the morning and found a steady wind to fill the sails of the Mackinaw boat. Jessie Miner the lighthouse keeper and his friend and unofficial assistant Jens Jacobsen at the Pottowatomie lighthouse watched them sail by that morning. In the afternoon, when they had finished setting the nets, the wind suddenly died, so they began rowing back. When the lighthouse keepers did not see them return that evening, they knew what the situation was. The men rowed all night and by first light were in sight of Rock Island and the lighthouse keepers. Jessie told Jens to whip up a batch of pancakes and a lot of coffee and to go down the steps and holler for the boys to come up for flap jacks and hot coffee. John Cornell said that it was the best breakfast he had had in a long time. Not long after that episode he bought the *Welcome*. John sold the *Welcome* to Tom Goodman in 1905 and moved his operation to Detroit Harbor.

One of the reasons John left Washington Harbor was a heavy northeast blow that nearly destroyed the Furlong dock and many of the fishing boats that were moored there. As Bill Cornell told Jake Ellefson:

> Johnny Cornell had the *Welcome* then, a 35-foot steam tug. The Furlong dock construction was wood cribs with beach stone filled up to the top of the cribs. Well the water come up real high, as it often does with a northeaster – sometimes up two or three feet. At that time the boats were tied to the top log of the crib, and the dock would have [had] to be rebuilt continually as the top logs would tend to lift off the dock spikes, and that's what happened. They were tied up to the top logs, the water came up as did the logs with the extra lift from the boats rising as well and they washed up on shore and when the water receded the boats were left high and dry. It was shortly after that John decided to relocate his base of operations prompting him to head to Detroit Harbor.[44]

After leaving Washington Harbor, John bought another steam tug called the *Henry Gust* and operated it for two years from Fred Richter's dock. In 1907, John Cornell bought land on Lobdell's Point and soon after he was busy constructing a dock, a large icehouse, and a few buildings for net storage and fish packing. The docks and buildings were located just north of where the Standard Oil dock is today, just north of the ferry dock.

John was a good fisherman. He took it very seriously. He kept his boats and equipment in fine condition, and well maintained. John was a quiet man, well liked by many, and well known throughout the county by his peers as an experienced fisherman. In 1916, John sold the *Henry Gust*, and had a gasoline tug built, naming her the *Clara C* after his wife. The *Clara C* was a 39-foot wood hull and house constructed boat equipped with a 30-36 horsepower Kahlenberg oil engine. John later sold the boat to Oliver Bjarnarson in Jackson Harbor. A few years after the *Clara C.* was built, he had a few more boats added to his operation – the *J.W. Cornell*, and the *Bub*, named for his youngest son John William. In 1925, John had the fish tug *Sunrise* built, which his sons operated for many years. The *Sunrise* measured 33 feet in length and 10 feet on the beam, with a 30-36 horsepower Kahlenberg oil engine.

John Cornell married Clara Jess of Washington Island, and together they raised a family of five boys; William, George Henry, Claude, Harvey, and John William, and four girls; Ethel, Myrtle, Mary, and Audrey. The boys learned the trade from their father and fished with him until his retirement. They then took over the business, though Harvey left the fishing business to become a schoolteacher.

John's youngest son, John William, worked with him a short while until his untimely death in 1935. On March 10 of that year, John William and five other young men from Washington Island were returning home after playing a basketball game in Ellison Bay when their car plunged through the ice in Death's Door passage. They apparently got off the marked road that was made for safe passage across the ice and were lost. Another car made it across safely that night, and when they arrived to the island they noticed that the other car hadn't returned. It was a tragedy for the families of the six boys and for the island community. Lost that night were: John W. Cornell Jr., twenty-two, a fisherman; Norman Nelson, twenty; Raymond Anton Richter, twenty; son of Mr. and Mrs. Earl Richter of the island; Leroy Einarson, twenty-one, son of Henry Einarson, a fisherman; Roy Stover, twenty; and Ralph Wade, twenty-eight.[45]

Leon and Les Cornell

Leon and Lesley Cornell grew up in the fishing business. They were cousins of John Cornell, and their father, Elza Cornell, was a commercial fisherman who lived and fished from Washington Harbor. Leon and Les accompanied their father at a young age and learned the business like so many other children of fishermen.

Leon and Les began fishing together in 1920, using their cousin John's dock. The first boat they operated was one of John's boats, the *Bub*, and worked for shares. Three years later, they bought the boat and rig from John. They were both excellent fisherman and often fished far from the island. In 1926, Leon and Les decided that they would each have a boat. Les had a new fish tug built and named her the *Leila C*, after his only child. The *Leila C* was 40 feet long by 12 feet on the beam; built at the Sturgeon Bay Boat Works in 1926 with a wood hull and a 30-36-horsepower Kahlenberg oil engine. Leon had a 41-foot fish tug built at the Sturgeon Bay Boat Works, with a Kahlenberg oil engine and a wood hull design. Leon named her the *Velox*.

Only four days after Les had his boat in service, the unthinkable happened while he and his crew-man, Alfred Johnson, were out fishing. The two men were cleaning fish and had left the boat drifting when the steamship *Coolidge* slammed into them. Both men escaped from the sinking tug and were picked up a few hours later. Alfred couldn't swim, but he managed to cling to some boxes[46]. The *Leila C* was never recovered. The estimated loss was $8,000. It is worth mentioning that the captain of the *Coolidge* and Les where schoolmates, and both had gone to the Washington Harbor School many years earlier. Les had another boat built and soon was out fishing again. A few years later, Leslie Cornell had a new boat built by the Burger Boat Company which he named the *Dawn*, 44 feet in length, 11 feet on the beam and powered by a 45-54 horsepower Kahlenberg diesel engine. In 1940, Leslie and Leon moved to Bayfield, Wisconsin. Leon left after a year and moved to Sheboygan, Wisconsin, where he fished until his death. He died on February 2, 1943. Leslie fished from Bayfield for many years with the *Dawn* until his retirement 1966. When he retired, he sold the boat to Gaylord Schultz, who operated from Black River Harbor, Michigan.

Leon and Les were tough, skilled fishermen and good navigators. For the most part, they fished with hooks for lake trout, traveling far out onto the lake, sometimes as far as the South Manitou

Islands, nearly forty miles from Washington Island, though they later changed over to gill nets and began fishing chubs. Hannes Hannesson fished with them for many years before he and Oliver Bjarnarson began their own fishery.

The Chambers Family

To provide for their families or sustain their livelihood, fishermen had to be willing to relocate. Many Door County fishermen have had to move away and fish from different ports. Caroline Chambers Jornt referred to her grandfather Pat and his brother Don Chambers and their families as gypsies.

The Chambers family descended from Mormon settlers on Beaver Island in northern Lake Michigan. Minada Seaman, Pat Chamber's mother, was of Scottish descent and settled on Beaver Island in the early 1850s. Minada's mother, Lovina Smith, was said to be related to Joseph Smith, founder of the Mormon church. The Beaver Island settlement was a schismatic sect of Mormons led by James Jessie Strang, who took his followers to Beaver Island after Joseph Smith was killed at Carthage, Illinois, in 1844. Minada was sought after by "King" Strang for his second wife, though she was only sixteen years old. Daniel Murray Seaman, Minada's father, knew King Strang had enough power so that Minada would end up as his wife. In 1852, Daniel gathered his family and their belongings and left Beaver Island in his schooner, the *Seaman*, and moved to Drummond Island in northern Lake Huron, far from Strang's tyranny.

After living for some time on Drummond Island, the Chambers family and the Ludlow Hill family relocated to Fish Creek, on the western shore of the Door peninsula, where they found the waters of Green Bay ideal for setting pound nets. The Hills and the Chambers were cousins, as Minada Chambers and Ludlow Hill's wife Cecelia were sisters. Pat Chambers was born on Drummond Island and grew up in Fish Creek, where he began fishing with his father, Sam, at a young age. Pat and his father fished in a Mackinaw boat. They carried rocks for ballast, and the crew would move the rocks from one side of the boat to the other when they changed course under sail.[47]

When Pat started fishing on his own, he purchased a 65-foot steam boat from Ludlow Hill and converted it into a fishing boat called the *L. P. Hill*. According to Pat's granddaughter, Carol Chambers, his wife Anna began asking him to build a house, not long after they were married:

> **M**y grandmother wanted a new house, but they didn't have the money. She kept after him – she wanted that house. In one lift, on the Michigan side near the Manitou Islands [Pat had no Michigan license] he had an exceptional lift. He hit the market just right in Chicago and paid for the house with that one lift! It was a grand home which was built in close proximity to where the C. C. Club now stands. The house burnt down many years ago.[48]

Pat Chambers and his wife raised five children, Walter, Clifford, Lloyd, Howard, and their sister Edith. Walter, Clifford and Lloyd fished with their father for many years. It was truly a family business. When Pat decided to move his operation, his sons and their families moved as well.

In 1906 Pat Chambers moved to Washington Island for the deep harbor and proximity to the chub fishing grounds in northern Lake Michigan. The *L. P. Hill* was a large steam tug with a deep draft that led him to moor her at the Wood dock on the southeast side of Washington Harbor. He rented land near the dock that had a log cabin on it. Pat and his sons fished for several years from Washington Harbor, and they had the largest and most unusual fishing boat in the region. The November 1913 blow that raged for over three days damaged the Wood dock beyond repair. The large steam tug *Louisiana* went aground and burned a few hundred feet from the dock. After the storm, Pat Chambers moved his operation to the southern part of Washington Island, where he bought property on Lobdell's Point.

That year Pat decided to have a new fish tug built. Earlier in the year, he had traveled to Fayette, Michigan, on the Garden peninsula north of Washington Island, and had marked oak trees he wanted cut to make the keel and hull of his new boat. The Burger Boat Company at Manitowoc, Wisconsin, built the boat they named the *Search*, and the engines from the *L. P. Hill* were removed and installed in the new tug. The new 70-foot steam tug was an unusual design for a fishing boat in that it had a lower and an upper deck. Carolyn Chambers Jornt, Pat's granddaughter, recalls the boat:

> The *Search* was a grand boat. She was built to resemble somewhat the *L. P. Hill*. The hull was the same as the *L. P. Hill*, except they lengthened her 4 feet and then Grandpa designed a different house. He didn't want the whaleback design. The pilot house was rather big and had sleeping quarters with four bunks. There was a big galley down below where they cooked food, and I did a lot of cooking for the men. I used to cook a lot of pancakes down there, and there was also a bunk down there. I remember another time when I was younger, I worked the wheel on the *Search*. The *Search* was cross-chained, so when you wanted to go starboard, you had to turn to the left. One time I was out on the lake there was a little seagull flying ahead of me and Grandpa was down with the men setting nets. All at once he comes up and says "What ya doing up here?" He told me to stay on this line on the compass, but the boat would go off course some, and I'd overcompensate. The boat would go one way and I'd turn her the other way, so the nets were not in what you'd call a straight line. I just couldn't keep her straight.[49]

:

In the spring of 1914, Pat Chambers began fishing from Detroit Harbor. He used the Fred Richter dock while docks, sheds and another house were being built on his property. The Chambers family lived on Detroit Island near Captain C. O. Peterson's home until their own house was finished. Pat bought property just north of John Cornell's dock and fishery. The area in front of the dock had to be dredged to about 12 feet for the *Search* to navigate. The *Search* drew about 10 feet of water. That was one of the reasons that Pat later removed the steam engine and replaced it with a Kahlenberg oil engine. The Chambers eventually had four houses on their property. One was already there when they acquired the land, and they built the other three. Walter, Clifford, Lloyd, and Pat and their families all lived there.

In the fall of 1919, Pat was out fishing in the *Search* about 20 miles southwest of Washington Island. The wind was blowing strong, making for a big sea. Pat saw what he thought was a hot-air balloon heading down toward the water some distance away. He left his nets and headed toward the object. It was indeed a hot-air balloon, with two men aboard, and they were already low enough to touch the waves. Pat throttled up the *Search* and gave her full steam in time to save the crew as well as the balloon. The two men aboard the balloon told Captain Chambers that they were in a balloon race that had started in St Louis, Missouri. They found out later that they had traveled the farthest and won the race. Thanks to Pat Chambers, they won it and were still alive. Captain Chambers was awarded a commendation from Washington, DC, for saving their lives[50]. Carol recalls the day and what a thrill it was:

> **G**randpa and the boys were out fishing on the lake with the *Search* that day lifting
> nets, and there was a pretty good sea. She still had the steam engine in her and they
> were out in Lake Michigan – I don't recall where exactly – way out anyways, and all
> at once they saw this big thing coming down in the water. Grandpa went over to
> where they were coming down, and when they got close to it before it hit the water,
> the guys in the basket of this big balloon kept waving them off. There were two men
> aboard and they kept motioning them to go away. First Grandpa couldn't figure it
> out; "Crazy fools, they're not going to make it back up again, they'll drown." Finally
> it dawned on him what was the matter. The balloon was full of hydrogen gas and
> they had to get all the gas out of that big balloon. He could see the balloon coming
> down further as the gas escaped and finally after the gas was released they hailed
> them back. They were in this great big wicker basket – oh was that exciting for us
> kids. It was real rough that day. They had trouble getting it aboard. If it hadn't been
> for the *Search* out there that day they wouldn't have got her aboard. They got the big
> balloon and everything on the top deck and the basket they got in the stern doors.
> That was heaven for us kids. Those guys were living on Horlicks malted milk tablets
> – almost like the malt-o-milk balls today and they gave them to us. You know we
> never got anywhere near a candy store. When they come in, I can remember we had
> a big cook stove and a warming oven in the kitchen, and they had the cook stove and
> warming oven full of money, drying out. We couldn't believe it. They actually won
> the race. They made it the furthest. I believe they were from St. Louis, Missouri.
> Then they packed everything up and shipped it all back.[51]

In November 1921, the Chambers family moved their operation down to Kenosha where they were able to fish year around and didn't have to contend with the ice conditions that sometimes made it impossible to fish for several months at Washington Island. The Hills, the Chambers cousins from Fish Creek, told Pat the fishing was good off of Kenosha, prompting Pat to load the family and their belongings into the *Search*. Lloyd's family had the forward part of the boat, Walter's family had the aft, and Cliff's family was up in the pilothouse. The following spring they returned to Washington Island and their home in Detroit Harbor. They did this for three years before they moved permanently to

Kenosha. Carol recalls, "We were like Gypsies, traveling so much with all the families and belongings. I remember leaving in the late fall and would return to the island in May. I couldn't wait to come back. I didn't care for the city much. When we got back to the island in May, the island kids were out of school, so we had a little more summer vacation".[52]

In the late 1920s, the Chambers family moved their operation to Grand Marais and fished the waters of Lake Superior. One summer they fished from Shelldrake. Carol, Walter Chambers' daughter, remembers a trip to Chicago to deliver fish to market:

I hauled fish one year for my Dad when they fished up in Grand Marais, Michigan. I hauled fish from Grand Marais to Chicago. Twice a week I'd take the truck down. I was eighteen at the time. It was an old Diamond two-ton truck. That used to be fun – I was just a kid then, and I wasn't very big either. I'd get to Chicago and the guys down at the wholesale fish market would see me coming and one of the guys down at the Lakeside Fish Market dock would say, "See that truck? Take a look and see who's driving it." They'd see it was me driving – just a young kid driving. "Make you a bet," the one would say, "Make you a bet she can back that damn thing down in here. " Well I had gotten that thing down in there many times and had it down pat, so I'd just back in and down I went. And you know, the guy – Concannon was his name – he won more money making a bet on that. I never got a nickel out of it either.[53]

Pat Chambers died in 1926, and his boys continued the fishing business. In 1927, Cliff had a steel tug

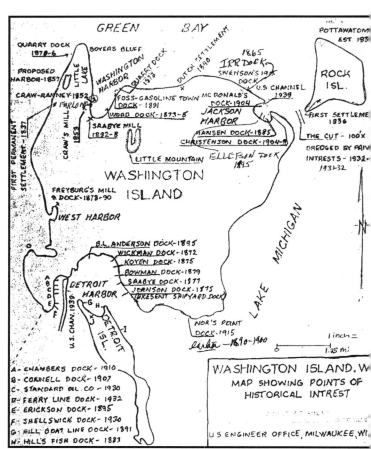

Fig. 10.1. Points of interest map. U.S. Engineers Office, Milwaukee, WI. (Courtesy of the Washington Island Archives)

built at Burger Boat Company called the *Chambers Brothers*. In the 1930s, they moved to Holland, Michigan. Walter and Lloyd eventually got out of the fishing business. The brothers all lived well into their eighties.

A Few Other Fisheries

Berendt Anderson was a sailor in his younger days, but in 1906 he began to fish commercially. He operated for a while from a small dock in Detroit Harbor near the Shellswick dock, and later moved to Detroit Island and fished from the Fred Richter dock for many years. He had the fish tug *Liberty* while he was operating from the Richter dock. Berendt and his wife Dorothy had several children. One of their sons, Milton, helped his father fish and took over the business when his father retired.

Milton "Cap" Anderson loved being around the water and ships. When he wasn't fishing during the winter months he found employment at shipyards in Milwaukee and Chicago. He built the fish tug *Namycush* one winter when he was in Milwaukee, an all-steel cruiser with a length of 50 feet. That spring he brought her to the island and began a charter service for lake trout. He sometimes took the *Namycush* with him when he went to work at a shipyard, so he could live on the boat. In 1949, Milton returned to Washington Island and bought property in Detroit Harbor, just south of the ferry dock. He built a marina and docks, and he had a skiff rental business as well. His place accommodated sport fishermen who were coming to the region more frequently. Cap was always to be seen working on boats or anything to do with sailing.[54]

Other fishermen of the Detroit Harbor region were Fred Hanson, who had the fish tug *Rosemary*, and Henry Einarson who fished with the tug *Petrollia*. Also, it was not unusual to see some of the Washington Harbor fishermen – Tom Goodman, Swara and Harry Hagen, among others – who would moor their boats either at Fred Richter's dock or Cornell's dock for the winter.

Al Shellswick had the *Palmer* built in 1926 after selling the hooker, *Diana*, which was used for hauling freight. Al dredged south point and created a small harbor to better facilitate mooring for fishing boats and other vessels. Besides his commercial fishing operation, Al built roads around his South Point property and also constructed Green Bay road on Lobdells Point. He fished out of Detroit Harbor for several years before moving to Kenosha, then on to Waukegan, Illinois. Al continued to fish from Waukegan, and owned several Chicago fish markets. In 1935, Al had the gill-net tug *Al Shellswick* built at Peterson Boat Works. The boat was 46 feet in length with a beam of 13 feet, and powered by a 125 hp Buda diesel marine engine. However, in 1936 he repowered the boat with a 60-70 hp Kahlenberg engine.

By the late 1950s and early 1960s, most of the fisherman had left Detroit Harbor. They either retired or fell victim to the scarcity of whitefish and herring. Earl and Roy Richter retired, and Leon and Les Cornell moved away. By the late 1960s most of the fishing was done by sport fishermen. The big docks that were built at the turn of the century were gone, except for Gislason's dock, which became a marina. On Detroit Island there are only a few old buildings left to mark where Fred Richter's big fishery was.

Chapter 10 Detroit Harbor

1 Conan Bryant Eaton, *Washington 1836 – 1876*, Appendix A.; 52-53.

2 Ann T. Whitney*, Let's Talk about Washington Island*, 36-37.

3 Conan Bryant Eaton, *Washinton Island 1836-1876: The Island Series* (Sturgeon Bay, WI: Bayprint Inc., 1972), Appendix A; Icelanders, 55.

4. Eaton, *Washington Island 1836-1876*, 55. Richard Purinton, *Over and Back: History of Transportation to Washington Island*, (De Pere, WI: Independent Printing, 1990), 31.

5 Ibid, 70.

6. *Door County Advocate*, September 3, 1885.

7. Ann T. Whitney, *Let's Talk About Washington Island: 1850-1950*, (Town of Washington, 1995), 40-41.

8 Ann T. Whitney, *Let's Talk About Washington Island: 1850-1950*, 42.

9. Ibid, 40. *Athabold* Icelandic for, Everyone Welcome.

10 Ann T. Whitney, *Let's Talk About Washington Island*, 53. Ray McDonald, *Four Islands*, 125-126.

11. Ibid, 53.

12 Washington Island Archives correspondence.

13 Dick Purinton, "Shellswick Family History," Washington Island Observer, January 11, 2007.

14 Ray McDonald, *Four Islands*, 126.

15. Ann T. Whiney, *Let's Talk About Washington Island 1850-1950*, 69-70.

16 Mabel Kalmbach Spencer, "Fishing in Door County at the Turn of the Century," *The Peninsula, March 1958* (Door County Historical Society 1958), 3. Ann T Whitney, *Let's Talk About Washington Island*, 27.

[17] Ibid, 3. Letter written by her father in 1939.

[18] Ibid.

[19] Ann T. Whitney, *Let's Talk About Washington Island 1850-1950*, 27.

[20] Ray McDonald, *Four Islands*, 128-129.

[21] Jessie Miner, "History and Anecdotes of Washington Island"; *Island Tales*, (Washington Island), The First settlement, 6.

[22] U.S Engineer Office, Milwaukee, Wisconsin; Map showing points of historical interest on Washington Island, 1939.

[23] Great Lakes Vessels Online Index; http://digin.bgsu.edu/cgi-win/us195x.exe.

[24] *Door County Advocate*, 24, August 1901.

[25] *Door County Advocate*, September 14, 1901.

[26] Interview with Jim Cornell, May 4, 2002.

[27] Interview with Carol Jornt, July 3, 2004. Richard Purinton, *Over and Back,* 26.

[28] Ray McDonald, *Four Islands,* 130.

[29] *Green Bay Advocate*, April 11, 1907.

[30] Richard Purinton, *Over and Back* (De Pere, WI: Independent Printing, 1990), 49.

[31] Fishing file, Washington Island Archives, fishermen's boats and specs.

[32] Interview with Bennet Hagen, December January 8, 2002.

[33] Ray McDonald, *Four Islands*, 133. Interview with Arni Richter, June 12, 2004.

[34] Interview with Arni Richter, June 12, 2004.

[35] Ray McDonald, *Four Islands*, 135-136.

[36] Sarah Magnusson, "Washington Island's Veteran Sailor Carl Richter Has Many Tales to Tell";

Door County Advocate. Washington Island Archives document file (Richter)

37. Ibid. Washington Island Archives document file (Richter).

38 Ibid.

39 Ibid.

40 Ibid.

41. Interview with Arni Richter, June 12, 2004.

42 Richard Purinton, *Over and Back,* 71

43 Interview with Jake Ellefson, July 4, 2004. Ray McDonald, *Four Islands.*

44. Interview with Jake Ellefson, July 4, 2004. Ann T. Whitney, *Lets Talk About Washington Island.* Island Archive correspondence with Barb Ellefson.

45 "All Bodies Found By Coast Guards"; *Door County Advocate,* March 10, 1935.

46 Ray McDonald, *Four Islands,* 139.

47. Interview, July3, 2004, and letters from Carol Jornt November 4, 2004.

48. Interview with Carol (Chambers) Jornt, July 3, 2004.

49. Ibid.

50 Ray McDonald, *Four Islands,* 140-141. Interview with Carol Jornt, July 3, 2004.

51. Interview with Carol (Chambers) Jornt, July 3, 2004.

52. Ibid.

53. Ibid.

54. Ray McDonald, *Four Islands,*

Pic.10.1 Fred Richter's fishery located on the northwest peninsula of Detroit Island; looking east across Detroit Harbor towards Jensenville and Gislason's store, now the Shipyard Island Marina. (Photo courtesy of the Washington Island Archives)

Pic. 10.2 Shore crew reeling nets at Detroit Island circa 1910; Fred Richter's Fishery. (Photo courtesy of Washington Island Archives)

Pic. 10.3 Fred Richter's fish tug *Two Brothers*, circa 1910; Bo Anderson dock Detroit Harbor. (Photo courtesy Washington Island Archives)

Pic. 10.4 Fred Young heading back to Detroit Harbor with his boat the *Nor* going through the west channel. (Photo courtesy of the Washington Island Archives.)

Pic. 10.5 Captain Carl boarding his boat the *Welcome* built by Rasmus Hanson at Jackson Harbor in 1926. (Photo courtesy of Washington Island Archives)

Pic. 10.6 John Cornell and his crew aboard his steam tug *Henry Gust* at his dock in Detroit Harbor ca. 1910. (Photo courtesy of the Washington Island Archives)

Pic. 10.7 Detroit Harbor fishing scene looking east. Cornell dock at the right Fred Richter's dock over at Detroit Island in the background circa 1915. (Photo courtesy of Washington Island Archives)

Pic. 10.8 The *Clara C* and *J W Cornell* moored at John Cornell's dock at Detroit Harbor. Jack Anderson's hooker *Diana* is in the background ca. August 1932. (Photo courtesy of the Door County Maritime Museum and Lighthouse Preservation Society)

Pic. 10. 9 Leon Cornell's 42-foot fish tug *Velox* encased in ice after a trip from Washington Island to Kewaunee in the winter of 1927. Built in 1926 for Leon Cornell, *Velox* was powered by a 50-60 Kahlenberg diesel engine. (Photo courtesy of Kahlenberg Brothers Company)

Pic. 10.10 Pat Chamber's seventy-foot steam fish tug *Search* at his dock in Detroit Harbor, ca. 1920. Notice the unusual construction with an upper deck and midship pilothouse. (Photo courtesy of Sunset Resort photo collection.)

Pic. 10.11 Fish tug being repaired in Jackson Harbor, circa 1940's. (Photo courtesy of the Sturgeon Bay Maritime Museum and Lighthouse Preservation Society)

Chapter 11

West Side of Washington Island

The west side of Washington Island faces the bay of Green Bay and is exposed to the prevailing westerly winds and winter ice shoves, which made it a real challenge for early fishermen. The only shelter on the west side is West Harbor and a little bay on the northwest side of Lobdell's point called Figenscau Bay. Both of these harbors are too shallow for larger boats. West Harbor is on the southwest end of Washington Island and is rather small. It provides protection from northwesterly and southwesterly winds, which attracted commercial fishermen in the late 1800s. West Harbor is ideal for resorts, and there have been several located there, overlooking the picturesque waters of Green Bay.

Among the first big landowners of the region were Charles B. Freyberg and his wife Caroline who had purchased a large tract of land from Andrew Frandsen in October of 1879. The Freyberg's arrived from Sheboygan, Wisconsin, where they had a furniture factory. They soon began constructing buildings, and then had a sawmill shipped to the property and assembled near the harbor. Freyberg hired a large crew to harvest the virgin timber on the island, and soon had a prosperous business. During an average ten-day period, they sawed 30,000 board feet of lumber; 60,000 shingles, and several thousand laths, all which were shipped to Sheboygan and sold in their lumber yard. Freyberg built a large boarding house inside the harbor to accommodate his workers.[1]

By 1880, the mill was operating, and Freyberg had constructed a pier out to the deeper water of the bay to accommodate large schooners to haul his lumber. Some passenger boats of the Hill and Goodrich lines would later call there. They carried on their lumber operation until the early 1890s, then shut down the mill and moved back to Sheboygan. In 1900, the land was sold to John Paulson.

John Paulson turned the Freyberg's boarding house into the West Harbor Hotel and tried to have the harbor dredged so that the Goodrich boats could land at the dock, near the hotel. However, the dredging operations ran into solid bedrock in the harbor and ceased. After John's wife died in 1919, he sold the property to Jim and Martha Sorenson, who ran the hotel for nearly twenty-five years before they sold it to Frank and Pearl Gibson in 1947. It is still being run by their son Herb and his wife Mary Ann Gibson.[2]

There were a few fisheries at West Harbor in the late 1800s, although not as many as at the other harbors of Washington Island. Charlie Paulson had a Mackinaw boat from which he set gill nets off the west end of Washington Island. Charlie McDonald fished from West Harbor in the late 1890s before moving his operation to Jackson Harbor. At that time Charlie had a small steam tug called the *Fish Hawk*.

Torger Engelson

Torger Engelson came to America with his Wife Anna when he was twenty years old. He left Bergen, Norway, where he had been a carpenter's apprentice and cabinetmaker, and moved to Chicago, where he found employment as a cabinetmaker. After working for some time to accumulate enough money, Torger built a house on Halstead Street, and raised a family with four children, Martin, Tillie, Anna, and William. Torger used his house as collateral to sign a note for a friend, but soon found that he had been taken advantage of when his friend defaulted on the note and he had to sell the house to cover the debt.[3]

A friend of Torger's told him about property that was available on Washington Island, complete with a house, outbuildings, and forty acres of land. Torger purchased the property without seeing it with the money that was left from selling the house. The description reminded him of Norway, and he and his family packed their furniture and belongings and headed to Washington Island on a passenger boat. They arrived on June 4, 1894, and found to their surprise that a family was living in the house. Torger gave them a month to vacate the premises, and in the meantime moved to St. Martin Island, which was nearly deserted at this time. Twenty years earlier, it had been a thriving fishing community, but it consisted then of empty cabins and small houses. Torger and his family occupied one of them until they could move into their own house.

They moved into their own house on July 18, and Torger began farming and working at Plum Island doing carpentry work. He heard that the fishing was good around the island and began fishing for a few local fishermen before building his own boat, a small sailboat that he named the *Express*. He used this boat several years for catching whitefish. Being a carpenter by trade, Torger improved the house and built a dock, net sheds, and a long shed to house his net drying reels down by the beachfront.

In the fall of 1899, Torger began building a hotel by adding on to the existing house. The money he made from farming and fishing wasn't enough for the expansion, so he borrowed from his friend Bo Anderson, and by 1902, the Pine Beach Retreat was open for business. It offered a spectacular view of the harbor and bay and became a very busy place in the summer months. It also became a gathering place for island social functions.

The Pine beach Retreat offered seven guest rooms, a large dining room, a music room, and a lounge. Guests were charged $1 per day for lodging, which included three meals. Anna and her daughters ran the hotel while Torger and his sons Bill and Martin ran the fishery. Besides his fishing business, Torger also maintained the buildings, ran the farm, and did many other tasks, and he especially liked the carpentry work. He and his family had a fine business and enjoyed their guests.

After using his sailboat *Express* for several years, Torger acquired a small steam tug the *Jessie Jackson*. With the new boat he was able to expand his fishery, using more nets and fishing further out in the lake. In 1904, he sold the *Jessie Jackson* and bought a larger steam tug, nearly 50 feet in length, and named her the *Tillie E.*, after his daughter. Torger and his sons Martin and Bill fished together for many years. Martin and Bill both married island girls – Bill married Dora Einarson, and Martin married Mildred Christiansen.

In 1921, the Engelsons decided to retire the *Tillie E.* and had a steam tug built by the Hemming

Larsen Boat Company of Marinette, Wisconsin, which they called the *Buick*. They took the steam engine out of the old boat and installed it in the new one. In 1923, Torger moved his family to Kenosha, Wisconsin, so that he could fish all year round. In Kenosha, Torger had a diesel engine installed in the *Buick*, making it a more dependable boat. He continued to fish and passed away in 1936 at the age of seventy-eight.

In 1938 Bill Engelson and his family returned to Washington Island and began fixing up the old Pine Beach Retreat that they had left some fifteen years earlier. He and his wife Dora ran the resort until they passed away, when it was taken over by their daughters Maxine and Lois. Maxine married John Engstrom, and Lois married Roger Hagen, a fisherman from the island and son of Harry Hagen. Bill, the youngest son, also helped out at the resort, which they renamed Sunset Resort. Maxine and Lois had a long and successful partnership, and the Sunset Resort is still operating.

The Bilton and Jorgenson Fisheries

North of West Harbor there lived a few families that relied on commercial fishing for their livelihood – the Bilton family and, to the north of them, the Jorgenson family. Henry Bilton came to Washington Island in 1870 from Toronto. There he met his wife, Laura Jacobsen, and they settled on the west end of the island overlooking the waters of Green Bay.

Henry cleared his land, built a house and a dock with a slip and sheds for his nets, and began his career as a commercial fisherman. The exposure to wind, waves, and ice shoves caused considerable damage, but despite his battles with the elements, he still ran a successful fishery. Henry and Laura raised five children: Jacob, Lars, Henry, Nettie, and May. The boys all became fishermen and fished near their home off the west side of the island. They mainly fished for whitefish with gill nets. Jake and Lars Bilton were quite a pair, like salt and pepper you might say, since they never seemed to agree on anything. If Jake said something was white, Lars would say it was black. Jake was devoutly religious and sometimes could be heard singing bible hymns at the top of his voice from his boat. Joy Gunnlaugsson remembered a story about them:

> Jake and Lars Bilton had a dock on the west side of the island that they fished from and also sometimes they would take people over to Escanaba to shop and buy Oleo, which was illegal in Wisconsin. Jake was a very religious man. One time the boat started to leak, so Lars is hollering bail, but Jake just sang Jesus Saves with all he had. One lady sat and wrote out her will, but they made it back to the dock.[4]

The Bilton's fished from that location for many years, but eventually moved away. The property was later sold to Harold and Edith Flath in 1950, after Lars Bilton died in January 1950. The property was turned into a resort that included cabin rentals.

A little north of the Bilton property was the home of Hans Christian Jorgenson, who arrived on the island in 1883 from his home in Jutland, Denmark. His wife and two sons, Carl and Walter and a daughter Freda, accompanied him to the island. He bought property on the west side of the island

and began farming and working at odd jobs to support his family. As his boys grew they showed interest in commercial fishing and they built a dock and some sheds on their property.[5]

Walter (Wallie) married Carrie Ottosen in 1924 and raised two children, Walter and Carolyn. Walter grew up fishing with his father and would go out with him in the summer months fishing with a gill net rig for whitefish. Wallie had a small wood gasoline-powered tug with a 20-horsepower Straubel engine in it that was named the *Leo B.* After Wallie died in 1946, Walter fished with Oliver Bjarnarson and Hannes Hannesson for several years before taking a job at the Ed Anderson potato farm. However, he never strayed far from commercial fishing, and, in the 1970s when the whitefish were coming back, he worked with Roger Hagen for several years and then with Jake Ellefson in the 1980s.

Carolyn married Alex Koyen, who fished with various fishermen throughout his life. He quit fishing altogether to pursue dairy farming, but after the island dairy industry collapsed on the island in the late 1960s, he got back into commercial fishing. He fished with his sons after buying Jim Cornell's gill net boat the *Welcome* in 1971.

Chapter 11 Notes

[1] Ann T. Whitney, *Lets Talk About Washington Island: 1850-1950*, 63.

[2] Cathy Meader, *The Hagen Family: 1883-2005*, Hagen Family Biographies.

[3] History of Sunset Resort; interview with Jewel Lee (Hagen) Grandy, July 5, 2003.

[4] Interview with Carolyn Koyen, July 3, 2003.

[5] Ray McDonald, *Four Islands*, 168.

Pic. 11.1 Torger Engelson's steam-tug *Tillie E.*, at his dock at the Pine Beach Retreat, which is now Sunset Resort, on Washington Island. (Photo courtesy of the Sunset Resort Collection)

Part III

Fisheries of Northern Door County

Chapter 12

Tip-of-the-Thumb Fisheries
(Gills Rock, Ellison Bay, & Sand Bay)

Door County during the twentieth century boasted more fisheries than any other county border-ing Lake Michigan. In 2006, there were approximately seventy-five licenses issued to commercial fish-ermen in the state of Wisconsin, and Door County fishermen hold about two-thirds of them. At one time there were more than four hundred Door County fishermen. Some were farmers who fished in spring and fall with pound nets for herring and whitefish or fished in the winter months on the frozen waters of Green Bay, which could bring in $100 to $200 of extra income. During the early days in Door County, a person's livelihood depended on commercial fishing, lumbering, or farming and some-times all three. In each Door County community there were as many as twenty full-time and part-time fishermen, and many other people were employed by the fisheries as part of a boat crew or as a shore hand. Other jobs associated with the fisheries included coopers, boat builders, fish box builders, and freight handlers. Washington Island once had more than forty fisheries which employed nearly half of the island men and some women.

At the northern end of Door County, the hamlet of Gills Rock is located on a rocky spit of land rising out of the waters of Green Bay. Gills Rock was originally called "Hedgehog Harbor," a name given it by Washington Island fisherman Amos Lovejoy. Amos fished the waters off Washington Island and around the northern tip of Door County, and he especially liked to fish from a small cove on the northeastern part of the peninsula. Late in the fall of 1855, Amos left his small sloop on the shore of this harbor for the winter, planning to return in the spring to resume fishing. That winter a family of porcupines, or "hedgehogs," moved into his upturned boat and found it to be not only a nice home but sustenance as well. When Amos returned the following spring, he launched the sloop without noticing the holes chewed in the hull until the boat began to take on water, forcing him to return to shore.[1] Thus the cove came to be known, as "Hedgehog Harbor" until it was renamed Gills Rock in 1870 in honor of Elias Gill, who settled there around 1860 and is thought to be one of the men who started a marble quarry at Door Bluff. He had owned close to a thousand acres of land in the vicinity.[2]

The Potawatomi called this area Wah-ya-qua-kah-me-kong meaning "lands end" or "head of the land."[3] Gills Rock is situated on the waters of Hedgehog Harbor, where it is somewhat sheltered by Death's Door bluff rising nearly two hundred feet above the water about a mile to the west. On the east side is Table Bluff, somewhat lower and clad with white cedar and birch giving way to a hardwood maple forest. By the 1850s, a few people had found the area, mainly fishermen and lumbermen. One of the earliest fishermen on record was Allen Bradley and another was Avle Simonson, who lived up on the hill east of Hedgehog Harbor and is said to have been one of the early settlers who both farmed and fished. He was also one of the men who formed the stone quarry colony at Table Bluff. Simonson died while making his way back from Detroit Harbor on Washington Island:

One morning in February, 1877, Avle Simonson and his son Alfred sailed from Ellison Bay in their fishing boat with a passenger for Detroit Harbor. The passenger was Miss Dora Higgins (later Mrs. Albert Kalmbach) who was going to Washington Island to teach school. They arrived at Detroit Harbor about noon, and as the wind was fair, they started immediately for home. They had not gone far, however, before a blinding snowstorm out of the northwest descended upon them. They were caught in ice flows which made their route almost impossible with the moving ice. Back at Ellison Bay their friends waited for them, but as nightfall came they still hadn't returned, and after two days had passed they were given up for lost.

About the middle of March the ice began to break up and was driven southward into Lake Michigan close to shore. One day William Sanderson, the lighthouse keeper of Cana Island, chanced to look out with his binoculars and saw a boat drifting by imbedded in the ice. In the boat sat two men, and their positions were so natural that the light keeper at first thought they were alive. As the boat drew closer, he saw that they were frozen stiff in an upright position and knew there was no chance of them being alive. Mr. Sanderson saw an old man in the stern of the boat with his arms folded, slightly bent forward, resting them on his knees. His face, with the expression of one straining to see or hear something, was turned toward the shore. On his cap was some snow, and icicles hung from his grey hair and beard. The young man, like his father had the same countenance, looking directly ahead of him with glassy eyes. There was no way to retrieve them and the bodies drifted by and they were never found, nor was the boat ever found.[4]

One of the first fishermen who settled in Hedgehog Harbor was a Norwegian immigrant, Andrew Weborg, whose family name is still prominent in Gills Rock. In the twentieth century, Gills Rock boasted many other fishing families, including the Johnsons, Teskies, Voights, and Larsons.

The Weborg Family[5]

Andrew Weborg and his wife Anna (Simondson), arrived in the peninsula in 1860 from Hammer, Norway. Along with his parents and two brothers, they bought land from Increase Claflin near Fish

Creek, which came to be known as Weborg Point and is now in Peninsula State Park. After a few years, Andrew and his wife moved north to Hedgehog Harbor (Gills Rock), where Andrew began with only a rowboat and a few nets that his wife had made. She made the nets by hand from cotton thread and then attached them to a top and bottom maitre cord. For floats, Andrew used cedar sticks, and for weights he attached stones to the bottom maitre. The nets were crude and small by today's standards, but they worked well enough to provide them with fish to eat and sell. The first winter at Hedgehog Harbor, Andrew chopped a hole in the ice and fished for trout and lawyers using hook and line, and he also occasionally set nets through the ice. The fish he caught were either salted or frozen until they could be shipped in the spring.[6]

When Andrew's three sons – Alfred, Arthur, and Willie – were old enough, they accompanied their father out on the lake and soon learned the fishing trade for themselves. By around 1900, the young Weborg brothers were fishing pound nets for herring, together with their father. They set the nets in bays in the northern end of Door County, and they had a dock and packing shed at Northport where they salted the herring. At that time, herring were all flat-dressed, salted, and stored in "packages" (small barrels holding 160 pounds of herring) to await shipment, usually in the spring of the year, though if the weather remained mild, they might ship them to Green Bay or Chicago from there most of them were sent by rail to the southern states.[7]

At Gills Rock, Alfred, Arthur, and Willie Weborg continued to improve their fishery by building up the dock and adding a few more buildings. In 1910, they had a small 35-foot steam tug called the *A.A. Weborg* built locally at Gills Rock at a small shipyard owned by the Ommondsons. It was built from aspen, birch and red oak, materials that didn't hold up well, and so they soon had another boat built. It was called the *G.W. Joyce* after William's and Alfred's children. They removed the steam engine from the *A.A. Weborg* and installed it in their new boat. They fished in the spring of the year from Detroit Harbor on Washington Island and also near Sturgeon Bay in the waters of Green Bay. For the winter months, the boat was moved either to Sturgeon Bay or to Detroit Harbor. In the spring and fall they continued to fish herring with pound nets, and they also fished for lake trout using hook and line rigs. During the summer months, they switched to using floating hooks, which proved successful when the trout were feeding on bug hatch near the surface of the water.[8]

During the early 1920s, Arthur fished with hook and line through the ice for lake trout, as did many other fishermen on the Green Bay side of the Door County peninsula. The fishermen would pull shanties out on the ice and stay out there all week if weather and ice conditions permitted and then return home on weekends. They stored the fish they caught in the snow until they returned home. Then the fish were boxed and shipped to Green Bay by horse and sleigh. During the spring, summer, and fall months, the fish were picked up almost daily by the Goodrich boats or other freighters that stopped frequently at Gills Rock, Ellison Bay, Sister Bay, Fish Creek, and Egg Harbor. The *Merrill Two* was one of the freighters that made a number of stops weekly at these ports to pick up fish and take them to Green Bay or Chicago.

The brothers fished together until 1921 when Art Weborg decided to fish on his own. He later fished with Frank Teskie for a few years in the mid-1920s. Art bought his first boat, the *Dahlia*, at this time. It was a small wood boat powered by a 28-horsepower Straubel engine. Art and Frank fished for lake trout using hook and line and also a few cotton gill nets that were only 15 to 18 meshes deep.

They had great success catching lake trout. The average trout was 20 to 25 pounds, especially late in the season when big trout came off the reefs after spawning. The trout were near the surface, so Art and Frank floated the hooks. During spring and summer, the trout they caught averaged 4 to 5 pounds, nowhere near as big as they were in the fall.[9]

In 1932, Art Weborg and his sons, Orville, Marvin, Laurence, and a partner named Andrew Woerfel began fishing in Jacksonport using the LeClair dock. Marvin was 15 years old when he began fishing on a full-time basis with his father and older brother. They built a small fish shed to store their nets and boxes and acquired a 42-foot gill-net tug called the *Dierssen* that was equipped with a Straubel engine. They fished out of Jacksonport from 1932 to 1939 using gill nets, hook and line rigs, and pound nets. In 1936 they went to Oconto and set chub nets for herring during the early season. The local fishermen thought they were crazy. The Weborgs' set eight boxes of chub nets and harvested a thousand pounds of herring, averaging about 1 1/2 pounds each. At that time they were getting 18 cents a pound for herring. The next day, the local fishermen were using chub nets too!

In 1937 and 1938 the Weborgs began fishing for perch commercially using a small flat-bottom pound-net boat, but in the fall of 1939 they lost all their nets in a storm off Jacksonport. During that time, Arthur developed ulcers that made it hard for him to work. He went to a doctor in Milwaukee, but there wasn't much that could be done for him. Orville, Lawrence and Marvin took the *Dierssen* to Sturgeon Bay that year and called it quits. One of Arthur's sons found a job at a meat market in Milwaukee, and Andrew Woerfel returned to Sheboygan and went back to painting. Arthur Weborg and his son Marvin started fishing for perch again at Sand Bay when the season reopened in June. They fished there for a month, then moved to Baileys Harbor and fished for perch there. They sold the perch locally and received about 20 cents a pound for dressed fish.[10] Marvin Weborg recalled his early years as a commercial fisherman:

On April 11, 1939 I married Eleanor Strandell. I was then working for Alfred Anclam, fishing float hooks in Baileys Harbor. I fished in the spring for Anclam with pound nets in North Bay. In the fall of 1940, Dad was feeling better and both he and I fished floating hooks with Anclam. That fall we moved to Baileys Harbor and Dad came to live with us. In the spring of the year Dad and I went fishing on our own. We started fishing perch with Red Saunder's pound boat at Rowleys Bay. In the fall of the year we bought the *C.L. Gladys*. This boat had a twin horse Straubel engine. We took it out and put in a Model A Ford engine. From perch fishing we went to big mesh and fished trout.

In the Armistice Day blow of 1941, many boats in Baileys Harbor went up on the beach. The *C. L Gladys* was one of them. The lampreys had destroyed the trout, especially the larger size caught on hooks. We rented the *Pelican* from Anclam and that winter we went to Racine and fished there until spring of 1943. Then we came back to Baileys Harbor. With no place to rent, Dad moved the log cabin, which we had been using to make wooden barrels and floats. We moved that building to Baileys Harbor, where we bought two lots from Gene Heald. We raised the log building two logs to make room for a bedroom upstairs. We lived together with Dad and

Mother that summer, until we finished our house in 1943. Dad then built an addition of 14 by 20 feet for living space. That building has now been torn down. Our house was built of logs and was 24 by 24 feet. It had two floors and was quite comfortable. This was during World War II and lumber was scarce.

That summer after we came back from Racine we fished the *C.L Gladys* for trout and whitefish. [Also] that summer we bought a boat, which had been a pound-net boat and we had Elmer Anderson build a house on it for gill-net fishing. In 1945 we fished this boat which we called the *Ark*. We had it powered by a Chrysler marine engine.

In the fall of 1945, we bought two pound nets from Joe Cote and Everett Olson. We planned to set for fall fishing, but the stakes were too short. We had now bought Jake Johnson's flat bottom pound boat. That winter we strung up two new pound nets, one a 75-foot and one 90 feet deep. In the spring we spliced the stakes and started pound-net fishing. We started with the four nets, took the house off the *Ark*, and used this boat and also the flat-bottom pound boat.

In 1947 we had a new steel boat built. We named it the *Joy* for the girl we planned to have shortly, but it turned out to be a boy we named Jeffrey. The girl didn't arrive until thirteen years later! The *Joy* had a straight-8 Chrysler marine engine and was about 35 feet long. It ran 18 miles per hour. We also had a Michigan license and set two nets near Cedar River. The first time we lifted them, Dad and Gordy had 4,500 pounds of whitefish. We had fourteen, deep pound nets at the peak of our operation. We also had the first ice machine in our area.

In the fall of 1952, we strung up three herring pots. We had one set off Appleport. On October 28, we went to pull it and it seemed to be stuck. That particular day we had Roger Johnson, Elmer Johnson, and Gordy lifting with us. We did get it up and found it was full of herring. We had the boat loaded to capacity and the crew feared we might sink. That was the day Roger and Elmer said they "walked on water." That fall we caught a total of 240,000 pounds of herring in two weeks. It was October 12, 1952, my dad, my partner, died.[11]

By the spring of 1952, whitefish were eluding the fishermen's nets and seemed almost to have disappeared. Marvin Weborg hadn't fished much in those early months of spring, but he decided to buy Richard Johnson's share of the gill-net rig, including the boat *King* jointly owned with Ed McOlash. The *King* at the time was powered by a 30-36 horsepower Kahlenberg, and they used it to fish chubs that winter. The next several years proved to be challenging for Marvin and many other fisherman in the county; chubs were about the only fish left to harvest.

From the mid 1950s, commercial fishermen in the region watched the fish slowly disappear from the waters. Lake trout were already gone, and the herring were the next to fade from the scene. By 1955, few fishermen were finding herring in their nets. Some believed that smelt had decimated the once plentiful herring, though others – like Marvin Weborg – thought that alewives played a major role in the decline of herring. Marvin believed that alewives ate the herring spawn and ruined their spawning grounds. Many fishermen began fishing chubs or moved to other areas of Lake Michigan. Marvin recalled that in his lifetime the whitefish seemed to run in cycles. "Three times I've seen them come and go. Seems they run in seven year cycles coinciding with high and low lake levels."[12]

Marvin sold the *King* in 1960 and then bought the gill-net tug *Islander* from Albert Goodmander, a commercial fisherman from Washington Island. The *Islander* was built in 1936 at Sturgeon Bay Boat Works. It had a 42- foot wood hull and was powered by a 60 -70 horsepower Kahlenberg engine. By this time Marvin's sons Jeff and Mark helped out on weekends and in the summer months. Jeff said, "We started with Dad and Eddie at a young age. There wasn't much else to do up here at that time. In order to do something, you worked for a fisherman. I started out when I was real young working in the smokehouse, helping pack chubs. That led into helping Dad in the summertime and on weekends. I did everything from packing nets, to rubbing roe, to dressing chubs. After school we would string nets, slug nets, and whatever there was to do. By the time we were in high school, we helped Dad and Eddie on the boat fishing chubs."[13]

In the early 1960s, chubs were about the only commercial species that seemed to be left in the lake, which was one of the reasons Marvin Weborg bought the *Islander*, a bigger boat for the long distances to the chub grounds. Jeff recalled:

> **I** know when I was still in high school. I was fishing chubs with Dad, and the big mesh were all stacked in the shed. I told my Dad's partner Eddie, coming off the lake one day, "those are the nets that are going to be the money makers." He said, 'They'll never see the water again – there isn't enough fish out there to fill them." It was only a matter of a couple of years when a few whitefish started showing up in the nets, then Dad set some pound nets in Ellison Bay around 1972 and caught 1300 pounds one day. That was the start of the whitefish coming back.[14]

The Weborgs also began harvesting alewives and shad with other local fishermen. They tried to get a processing plant going in Sturgeon Bay, but were not successful. Jeff recalls:

> **W**e set some pound nets for harvesting alewives, which were used for fertilizer. There was a man in the process of making a fertilizer out of them. [Pound-net fishing for alewives] was a backbreaking job. You're pulling the net by hand and scooping them out. There were a lot of them in the nets. We had to use small twine – it was somewhat like a blanket – you had to shake them out of there and bag them in the net and scoop them out. There was a boat on the outside of the pot and one on the inside, so you'd be scooping with both boats – it was all by hand.[15]

Jeff and Mark Weborg continued to fish with their father until they got out of high school. Then, after they graduated, they went their separate ways. Jeff worked the summer after he graduated from high school with his father and Ed McOlash, and remembered telling Eddie after coming home from chub fishing that fall: "You know I'm sick of this – I'm going to go out and get a real job, where I don't have to work twelve hours a day, six days a week. I'm going to get a job where I can put my forty hours in and have the weekends off – I'm done with fishing. I remember Eddie – we were standing there dressing – and he chuckled a little and said, "yeah, you may be done with fishing, but fishing isn't done with you."[16]

It proved to be a prophetic statement. After a six-year hiatus, Jeff and Mark were once again in the fishing business. During those six years, Jeff worked various jobs around the country and attended college in 1969 in British Columbia where he met his future wife. In 1970, Jeff moved back to Gills Rock while his wife Betty finished earning her degree. In the winter of 1971, Jeff and Mark began fishing gill nets through the ice. Jeff recalls, "Mark and I started fishing with eight boxes of 28-mesh gill nets, thirty-two ice nets, and two snowmobiles. We took a loan out for the snowmobiles and some equipment. We strung the nets out in the fall of 1971 then fished all that winter making enough to pay off the loan. That was the beginning of many loans to expand the fishery."[17]

The following spring, Jeff and Mark bought the *Islander* from their father and bought out Ed McOlash's share. The Weborgs diversified their business somewhat – Jeff started fishing gill nets with Eddie on the *Islander*, while Mark and Marvin concentrated on the pound nets. Marvin and Mark, along with two local fishermen, Clayton Johnson and Frank Teskie, began the Northern Door Pound Net Company, which lasted for several years until Marvin, Jeff, and Mark began implementing trap nets in their fishery. Some of the pound-net boats Marvin and his sons had at the time were the *Joy*, the *Liza* and the *Ark*. They set pound nets for whitefish, which had made a strong comeback by 1970, in many parts of the bay – near Chambers Island, Ellison Bay, and Door Bluff, and in the Death's Door area around Northport. Marvin and Mark continued setting pound nets in the early 1970s then went into the trap net business.

Jeff fished with the *Islander* until 1977 then sold it to buy the *M & R* from Gerald Casey, a fisherman from Manistique Michigan, renaming her the *J.A. Weborg*. The Burger Boat Company in Manitowoc, Wisconsin had built this 45-foot all-steel boat in 1945. Shortly after buying the *M & R*, Jeff also bought a gill-net tug called the *Seabird* from Lorman Greenfeldt; he fished with that boat for several years before selling it to the Caseys in Manistique, Michigan. Jeff also sold the *J.A. Weborg*, and in 1980, acquired the *Ranger* from Cliff Young and Harold Greenfeldt, fishermen from Washington Island. The *Ranger* was a fairly new boat, built in 1972 by T.D. Vinette Co. of Escanaba, Michigan. It had an Allis Chalmers engine that Jeff later replaced with a Caterpillar diesel engine. "The bigger the seas, the better she rides," commented Jeff. "I replaced the original engine with a more powerful Cat engine. She's a good winter boat for breaking through the ice."[18]

By the early 1980s, the J & M Fish Company was growing. They began acquiring more gear, boats, and processing equipment, including a scaling machine, a filleting machine, a band saw (for chunking whitefish for fish boils), and stainless steel dressing tables. Jeff Weborg noted, "We [reduce] our processing time considerably with this new equipment. If we're in there cleaning whitefish for a fish boil, by the time one hundred pounds go through the scaler, until it's chunked it has taken only five minutes. When we did it by hand it would take me almost twenty minutes to do one hundred pounds."[19]

At this time, Jeff and Mark were fishing more trap nets. They eventually gave up on pound nets and concentrated on trap nets, which, by the mid 1970s became legal in Wisconsin. They fished with trap nets on the lake side as far south as Whitefish Bay and on the bay side, down to Chambers Island. Jeff recalls:

For years we were fishing gill nets and pound nets, and then we decided to try trap nets. They were being used in Michigan, but there wasn't anybody around here using them. We were really the first ones to use the trap nets in this region. Dad, Neil, and Mark were still using the pound nets, and then Dad and Mark went on their own after converting over to the trap nets. We bought a boat, the *Liza*, one of Cliff Wenniger's old boats. It was a charter boat when we got it and we tore it apart and made a trap-net boat out of it.[20]

The Weborgs later renamed her *Heather J,* and have since extended it, adding 7 feet and a new engine. In 1987 Jeff had the *Robyn B* built in Louisiana.

As of 2006, Jeff and Mark are still fishing and carrying a tradition that has spanned nearly a century and a half. It may possibly end when their days of fishing come to an end. In the spring of 2006, Mark suffered an accident while he and his crew were fishing trap nets in North Bay. His arm was nearly torn off at his shoulder by a hydraulic winch used to haul in the trap net. He was immediately brought back in to shore and was rushed to a Milwaukee hospital where they performed surgery to try and save his arm. Marvin passed away in December, 1993, leaving a proud legacy to be carried on by his sons. Marvin was truly devoted to his craft. He loved to fish. Marvin once said, "Fishermen are the greatest sailors in the world, as far as storms are concerned. We've seen them all, and we've always made it back home safe. We've had, perhaps, the doors cave in, port lights smashed, and water come in by the barrels, but that's nothing that would bother you."[21]

Jeff described the attitude of his father and many of the fishermen of the area:

You could go down to the dock and the weather that day was just awful — nobody seemed to be going out. All it took was one boat to start up, and then everyone else would head out. That was always a big deal, when you could get a lift on someone else. Then you were the "King of the Hill." I remember Dad would always say when it was blowing real hard, "We'll go out and take a look at it." You knew when he said that, we were going to go out and get a lift on the nets.[22]

"What I learned from my father", said Jeff pensively, "was that you do an honest days work for an honest days pay." Marvin taught his boys what he was taught by his father – through hard work and perseverance you'd find a sense of freedom and independence that no one could take away from you, and he believed that once you were in it, it stayed with you as long as you lived. As Jeff can surely attest from those long-ago prophetic words by his father's partner, "You may be done with fishing, but fishing isn't done with you."[23]

Alfred and Willie Weborg fished together for several years, and then, in 1921, they bought the fish tug *Golden Girl.* Built at Sturgeon Bay Boat Works for another fisherman, *Golden Girl* was 43 feet long, with a hull of white oak. A Fairbanks Morse engine powered the boat for all its years in service. Alfred and Willie loved to fish and worked together for many years, and their love of fishing rubbed off on Alfred's sons, Glen, Wallace, Howard, and Emery, who were all out on the lake at an early age learning the trade. By the time they were teenagers, Howard and Emery were serious about making fishing their career. Alfred had a small farm in Gills Rock that his wife Minda tended while the men were out on the lake fishing. They fished from Gills Rock most of the year, except when winter froze the harbor and bay. The Weborgs then moved their operation to Sand Bay, as did many bayside fishermen.

There wasn't anything that would keep Alfred from going out on the lake, not even a heart condition. His doctor gave him stern orders not to fish anymore, but Alfred would not give up what he loved to do best. Alfred and his sons were out fishing on Howard's birthday, when his Alfred had an angina attack, and even though Howard and Emery gave him their whole supply of nitro tablets, it did not help. Their father passed away doing what he loved to do. Emery said that he died where he was the happiest. Alfred was only sixty-four years old.

Howard and Emery continued to fish in the *Golden Girl* with their Uncle Willie. Their mother, Minda, was still part owner of the rig. Ruby explained: "Howard and Emery were considered hired men and worked for Willie and their father. I know when we got married in 1936 they were making $65 a month, and we managed to save most of that." After five years, Willie decided to sell his share of the business to Howard and Emery. Ruby stated that Willie didn't see any point in sticking any more money into a boat that had seen her days, so to speak. So, Howard and Emery bought the *Golden Girl* in 1944. They fished for another year before realizing it was time for a new boat.

Howard and Emery sold the *Golden Girl* in 1945. The boat was getting fairly soft (a fisherman's term meaning that the wood had begun to rot), and they had a new boat built to their specifications at the Sturgeon Bay Shipbuilding and Dry-dock Company. The new boat had a 42-foot steel hull and was powered by a 30-36 horsepower Kahlenberg oil engine. It cost them $12,000, and they proudly named her the *Skipper* after their father, who had carried that nickname for many years. The *Skipper* was the first all-steel boat to fish out of Gills Rock. According to Ruby they would drive down to Sturgeon Bay every Sunday after church to see how work was progressing. They began fishing with her as soon as she was finished that fall.

A typical day for Howard and Emery started at Weborg's wharf at 5:30 am. They loaded the nets and fish boxes, torched the engine, and departed by 6:00 am. They did this for six days a week, six to seven months a year; rarely missing a day on the lake. They were known to go out in all kinds of weather, even when the Washington Island Ferry was laid up, they would still go out to lift their nets. Their partnership lasted for over fifty years. Ruby Weborg recalled:

> They worked together all those years with hardly an argument. Howard was the leader and Emery was the follower. He was two years younger than Howard. Howard would always be the first one down to the dock in the morning. He would leave the house at 5:30 in the morning and go down and torch the engine in the boat. Then as soon as Emery would show up they'd head out.[24] It became such a routine that one day when Emery was a little late getting down to the dock, Howard left without him and didn't even notice for a short time that Emery wasn't with him. During the off-season, Howard, Ruby, Emery, and his wife Grace went to Florida. Ruby and Grace were first cousins.

Out on the lake, Howard and Emery normally would lift eight boxes of nets, remove the fish, and set the nets back. They strung their own nets, either at Gills Rock or at their shed in Sand Bay. The two of them could string a new net of 1,200 feet in a day. Ruby and Grace would help out several days a week in the sheds. Ruby said:

Grace and I would mend nets, reel the nets, we did everything except dress the fish.

I remember when they fished in Sand Bay and would come back in with their nets full of clinkers [iron ore deposits dropped from the ore boats]. They were very hard to get out of the nets – they were so picky and your fingers would get raw from picking them out.[25]

Howard and Emery fished together for nearly fifty years, forty of them from just one boat, the *Skipper,* which will be on display at the Maritime Fishing Museum located at Gills Rock. Emery retired from fishing due to health reasons in the mid 1980s, but Howard continued to fish with Rick Johnson until he was well into his nineties. Howard began fishing in 1917 at a young age, and in 1999 decided it was time to hang up his oilers.

Wallace Weborg fished with his father, Alfred, and brothers until he was eighteen years old. His father had a 45-foot steam tug called the *GW Joyce.* Wallace completed eight years of schooling at Newport School. He and his brothers had to walk two miles every day. It was during the First World War, when most of his father's hired help left to join the war effort, that Wallace and his brother Glen quit school and began helping their father in the fishery, working for a dollar a day. When Wallace turned eighteen, he decided to join the U.S. Coast Guard and was stationed for a year at Plum Island. He relocated to Jackson Park in Chicago for two years. After his Coast Guard service, he and Glen started a fur business, acquiring two silver foxes from Canada for $1,000. The fox pelts were valuable, and the brothers were on their way to establishing the Silver Fox Company. Wallace married Gladys Strandell in 1928, and she helped out in the business, feeding the animals. After they were married, they continued to live on the farm, and, after building their own place, they raised their family, which included four boys: John, David, Tim, and Tom.

In 1930, Wallace decided to get back into fishing. He bought a 24-foot fishing boat called the *Emery L* from Andy Johnson and began fishing gill nets with the help of Ralph "Cap" Larson. A year later, Glen moved back from Oregon, and he and Harvey Hanson teamed up with Wallace. Wallace bought in with his father and Bill Weborg and fished with the *Golden Girl* for several years. In 1936, Wallace, Glen and Harvey Hanson had the 36-foot fish tug *Gem* built at Sturgeon Bay Boat Works, now the Palmer Johnson Company. *Gem* had a 100-horsepower Chrysler marine engine, and, according to Tim Weborg, Wallace's son, "she was built in 1936, and the reason dad picked 36 feet was that was the year she was built." The *Gem* was named for Gladys, Esther, and Margaret, the wives of the three men. In the 1940s, Wallace, Glen, and Harvey moved to Kenosha during the winter and fished chubs and lake trout off the Milwaukee and Kenosha reef. In the spring they came back to Gills Rock and fished whitefish, and, in the fall, herring.[26]

Wallace bought another boat, the *Cherokee,* after Glen and Harvey took the *Gem* to fish out of Kenosha. The *Cherokee* nearly claimed the life of Kermit Strandell when the boat exploded. Tim Weborg, Wallace's son, told the story:

It was in December of 1952, I believe, and they were going to take her down to the shipyard to have some tin put on her. My uncle Kermit was with my dad that day and my dad was up in the fish shed getting some rope and he told Kermit to go fuel up the boat and build a fire in the stove. Kermit was cold so he built the fire in the stove first then proceeded to fuel the boat up. There was a wood dish on the top of the tank; he put the nozzle on the top of the tank instead of in the hole, and so the gas went all over running down the floorboards toward the stove, and then she blew. It broke the windows of the house nearby. My dad came running out of the shed, pulled Kermit out, and rolled him in the snow to extinguish the flames. Then he wrapped some water-soaked rags around his face and hands so he wouldn't get burned and went back into the burning boat to retrieve the boat's valuable compass. Kermit was lucky to escape with only third degree burns and not lose his life. She burned out in the harbor all the way down to the water line. She's at the bottom of Wisconsin Bay now – that's where they sunk her.[27]

In 1953 Wallace Weborg and Harvey Hanson sold the *Gem* to Clarence Lind (who, in turn, sold the *C.W. Lind* to Oliver Bjarnarson and Hannes Hannesson at Washington Island). They then bought the *Freitag Brothers* for $8,500 from Otis and Warren Freitag of South Haven, Michigan. The boat was built by Henry, Kleiner, and Vern Danhof at Muskegon, Michigan and originally had been named the *Bonnie Lou* before being sold in 1951 to the Freitag brothers, who aptly renamed it *Freitag Brothers*. It had a 40-foot steel hull and a Kahlenberg engine. When Wallace, Glen, and Harvey bought it, they decided not to change the name. Some fishermen believe that if a boat's name isn't changed, it would bring good luck. Tim Weborg said the Freitag's were so proud of the fact that they kept the name that they told them it would always bring good luck if the boat didn't change names after new ownership.[28] After Wallace retired, Tim used the boat and years later replaced the Kahlenberg with a 220 Volvo Penta marine engine. Wallace, Harvey, and Glen fished together until the mid 1950s when Glen was stricken with arthritis. His wife Margaret helped out for a while, but after Glen was involved in a car accident he was unable to work any more.

Wallace, Glen, Howard, Emery, and Harvey also fished pound nets and formed the Door Fisheries Pound Net Company, which included two pound-net boats, the *Leo* and the *Rastus,* which once belonged to Cliff Wenniger. The *Leo* was a steel boat, and the *Rastus* was a wood boat. Tim said the *Rastus* leaked and they had to use a sump pump to keep the water out. "She leaked pretty badly," he said. "It seemed like we pumped the bay through her once a year and Lake Michigan through her once a year." The *Rastus* was a fast boat with twin 100-horsepower Chrysler engines that Cliff Wenniger had installed for fishing pound nets near the Manitou Islands many years earlier. The *Rastus* is still on the beach in Gills Rock near the Weborg wharf.

For many years, Wallace, Glen, and Harvey had many people working with them – Laurence, Bob, and Leo Daubner, among others. They had pound nets set as far away as the Whaleback shoals, Cedar River, and Minneapolis shoals, some fifteen miles west of Washington Island. Tim Weborg began fishing with his father full time when he was eighteen years old and remembered the pound-net days:

I fished pound nets with my dad and Harvey Hansen. We usually had a pretty good crew helping us. Howard and Emery helped us a few years, but they were more gill-net fishermen. We had two pound nets set in the Door near Northport – we had a 75-foot and a 55-foot net there. We had a 75-foot pound net set near Table Bluff, some near Door Bluff and a 45[-foot] off of Porcupine Bluff by Ellison Bay. We had one out by Whaleback Shoals and Cedar River Michigan. Years ago, Dad had seven or eight set out by Minneapolis Shoals and Cedar River, and even though Dad had a Michigan license, some of the locals didn't like him fishing there and wrecked his nets. That was a big loss – at that time the cost of a pound net was around $4,000.[29]

Wallace and his wife ran a smoked fish business in Gills Rock for more than thirty years. They had a smokehouse on Isle View road, and for years they provided both tourists and local people with fresh smoked chubs and whitefish. Wallace retired after sixty years of fishing on the lake and sold the business to his sons Tim and Jeff Weborg. Jeff had bought Harvey Hanson's share after Harvey passed away from cancer. Rick Johnson was hired by Jeff to fish with Tim on the *Freitag Brothers*, and in 1979 Jeff sold his share to Rick Johnson, who eventually bought out Tim. Tim Weborg retired from the business nine years later.

Teskie Fishery

Frank Teskie began fishing with his father, Frank Teskie, Sr., when he was just a boy of twelve, and then worked for Howard and Emery Weborg. Frank fished intermittently and worked as a laborer in shipyards before he spent four years in the navy during World War II. After the war, he came back to Gills Rock where he met Joyce and was soon married. Frank and Joyce had two sons, Neil and Lyle, who found out what commercial fishing was all about at an early age. Neil commented:

There wasn't much to do around here when we were growing up but hang out with the fishermen. I would go down to Weborg's wharf and sit with Howard and Emery when they were working in their shed or go over to Johnson's smokehouse and get some fresh smoked chubs or whitefish.[30]

In the same interview, Neil related some of his family's history:

My father, Frank, started fishing when he was twelve years old. He fished with his dad and also with Howard and Emery on the *Golden Girl*. As long as I've known him, he's fished and did some farming or cooking. He used to cook at Claytons Supper Club. He would go to Florida some winters and cook down there when times were lean up here.

My Dad started fishing basically on his own in the late 1950s, building his own rig. He built a shed and started fishing [with] the *Gem*, a fish tug he bought from Clarence Lind in 1959. My dad did a lot of work to fix it up, and then right away the fishing was poor around here. He held a Michigan license so he moved up to St. Ignace and fished chubs. Not long after that, the botulism episode closed the chub fishery up there, so he had to come home. He fished some whitefish here for a while. I helped him for a while, as did my brother Lyle. In my early years of high school we moved over to Frankfort, Michigan, for about four or five years. I went to college in 1967 and dad continued to fish in Frankfort until about 1970. After the DDT scare, which again was another scare that almost wiped out the fishery there, my dad moved back here.

When I was young I remember getting off the bus and going down to the shed and reel chub nets at night and boiling them. I especially remember reeling them in late October and November when it got cold and how warm they were when they came out of the scalding pan. My dad had all cotton maitre, and we had to boil them all the time. As a matter of fact, when I started fishing in 1971, we had a whole shed full of cotton chub nets that we had peppered and stored away, and we only had six boxes of nylon chub nets. We had a lot of cotton maitres. I remember in 1971, when I got out of college and started fishing, we didn't have much nylon or monofilament. We usually brought three or four dry nets along and would keep putting the dry ones out when setting and at the other end we'd always take the wet nets off, so there were always three or four dry ones to set back. Some fishermen with full crews would bring the whole gang of wet nets back and set dry ones every time.

My dad and Clayton Johnson fished together using pound nets. They picked up a pound-net rig in Two Rivers. I still have the boat and some of the nets left. The boat was called the *Tiger,* which they adapted to a pound net boat. It was called the *Tiger* because they took the little six cylinder Hercules engine out of it and put in a big 430 Buick engine. She really hummed – that was the fastest boat on the lake. It was a 29-foot boat with a flat bottom, so Howard and Emery called them the "flying tigers" because they were flying around everywhere.

In 1971, I got out of college and my dad offered me a job. "What are your plans?" he asked. "Do you want to come back and fish?" I said, "Sure. Why not?" He said, "It's starting to look good for whitefish again." I got out of college in the spring, and we started catching quite a few whitefish. When we first started, we fished gill nets. Then, in 1972, we started with the pound nets. We joined up with Marvin Weborg and his son Mark setting pound nets. We set in the bay and in the Door on the lake side. One spring we set eight or nine pound nets. We had one or two 60-foot pound nets and the rest were 75[-foot] and 80-foot nets. Marvin had his pound-net boat the *Joy*, and we had the *Tiger*.[31]

We started setting trap nets in 1974, about the time they were legalized. Compared to the pound net, trap nets can be set up a lot quicker. We can set up a trap net in about two hours. We have a small skiff that we use along with the *Frances* for setting the king line and anchor lines. I modified my nets over the years for certain areas where I fish. I made certain modifications where I was able to catch more fish with half the nets. I was doing this eight or ten years before anyone figured it out. It was only a minor change, but you could fish closer to the surface and, boy, what a big difference. I used all nylon nets for years. In the past year, I bought five marlex nets, and what a difference that made. I'd like to get a few more, but they're expensive. One nice thing is they're less maintenance. You don't have to dip them in net coating. However, they're a little harder to pull out. They tend to be a little more slippery when you handle them.[32]

In 1979, Frank and Neil bought the gill-net tug *Betty* from Clyde and Jim Olson. *Betty* originally was from Washington Island, built for Anker Greenfeldt in 1945 by the Burger Boat Company in Manitowoc, Wisconsin. Lorman Greenfeldt fished with it in Racine in 1957, and then sold it to Clyde Olson the following year. "They had an old 165 Cummins truck engine in her," said Neil, and we just replaced it a few years ago. It's a good boat. I like using the *Betty*. It's a useful tool. I can run gill nets in December and use her for chub fishing in the winter months."[33]

Frank and Neil continued fishing successfully through the 1990s and saw a lot of changes in the fishery, especially in the late 1970s — changing regulations, the enactment of quotas and limited entry, the closing of the chub fishery for a time. They managed, as did many fishermen, to thrive in challenging times. A fisherman learns to be optimistic and hopeful — it's all part of the package. Frank retired in 1997 after a long career as a fisherman.

Johnson Fishery

Over the years, many fishermen from the Gills Rock region have come and gone. Their names are woven into the fabric of the community and the stories and memories of the local folk. Victor Johnson and his brother Richard fished from Gills Rock in the 1920s, 1930s, and 1940s. They had a 36-foot wood fish tug called *King* built in 1920 at Sturgeon Bay Boat Works. They owned *King* for thirty-two years, then sold it to Marvin Weborg and Eddie McOlash in 1952. Richard Johnson's grandson Rick still fishes today with his gill-net boat *Freitag Brothers* and a trap-net boat called *Joyce*.

After Richard Johnson sold the *King* to Marvin Weborg, Richard's son Roger remained in the fishing business and worked for Marvin for several years in the pound-net fishery. Rick recalled tagging along on the wooden pound-net boat when he was seven years old, helping his father and Marvin:

They were fishing alewives in the early 1960s. I always enjoyed going out with my father and Marvin. I liked Marvin, we always got along well, although he was known to holler plenty, so you had to keep on your toes. I remember going along as a kid when they were catching alewives. They had an old wood boat that was fairly long. They would have that thing loaded to the rails with alewife and then they would bring them in and scoop them out onto a grain elevator and on a truck. They used them for mink feed, I believe.

> I remember my father telling me about when he worked for Marvin. They were out scooping herring from a pound net in the month of December outside of Sand Bay and nearly sank the boat. Marvin didn't figure that there would be that many fish in there and had the boat overloaded. There was herring right to the top of the gunwales. They were coming in and got caught in a swell and almost swamped the boat. They lost some fish but were fortunate enough to make it back in.[34]

Rick worked as a carpenter for a year after high school. Then, in 1975, he began fishing:

> **I** began working with Jeff Weborg and Ray Strege in Ray's boat the *Bonnie S*. It was around 1975. Ray came up here along with many other fishermen from the southern part of Lake Michigan. They all moved up here and fished whitefish for several years since the fishing was poor down there. There were a lot of fishermen here during that time. The bay was like a cedar forest with all the net buoys. After limited entry and the quota system were enacted, some of the fishermen got some of the quota up here, and the others sold theirs and went back to their home ports. Dan Anderson still has some quota up here.[35]

Rick bought the 40-foot steel fish tug *Freitag Brothers* from Jeff and Tim Weborg in 1979 and began his career as a commercial fisherman. The original Kahlenberg had been replaced with a Volvo Penta marine engine by Jeff and Tim.

Rick began fishing with trap nets which he bought from Jeff Weborg in 1999. As of 2005, he is fishing with eight. He has a trap-net boat called the *Joyce*, which was Marvin Weborg's old pound-net boat, and has a young man named Andy Stuten working with him. During the winter months, Rick fishes chubs with his gill-net tug *Freitag Brothers*. Then, in the spring, he resumes his trap-net fishery for whitefish. The Weborgs help Rick with his trap-net operation, and, in return, Rick will often lend them a hand. Jeff has the equipment, such as tractors and forklifts, to unload the fish.

Rick has made fishing his livelihood and remains cautiously optimistic about the future. He takes an active role in various associations that help preserve this dwindling industry and profession. In 2004, he was elected president of the Northeast Wisconsin Commercial Fishing Association and was chairman of the Lake Michigan Commercial Fishing Board, which was appointed by the governor to allocate quotas. The board also functions as an advisory group to the DNR on commercial fishing issues. Rick commented:

> **T**he last few years there hasn't been too many controversial issues. It's kind of died down. The board has been active ever since the quotas have been in place. It's basically five fishermen, one wholesaler, and one citizen. We allocated whitefish and chub quotas for all Wisconsin's Lake Michigan waters. The DNR sets the quotas and has final approval. Basically, it is left up to the fishing board to set how much quota each

fisherman receives. We held the meetings at the Manitowoc Courthouse. Some of those meetings got pretty ugly. We started at 7:00 at night and sometimes didn't get out of there until 3:00 in the morning. It was a tough job when you're meddling with somebody's livelihood. You felt sorry for some of those guys. In some cases, you were putting them out of their livelihood. The quota was set up and based upon a fisherman's previous five-year total production. For the guys who just started fishing their production was obviously lower than the fishermen who have been around a long time. It definitely didn't benefit certain fishermen, especially fishermen who didn't fish that hard when the price was down, me included, and a guy like Jake Ellefson was that way. If the price went down to 30 or 40 cents a pound for whitefish, you cut back. Why fish them for nothing? [But] there were guys up in this area, if the price was low they set twice as many nets. We figured we were conserving whitefish and the guy who kept pounding them in there, they were awarded a lot bigger quota than the rest of us.

I and Lee Peterson were on the board back when we started allocating whitefish quotas, and the meetings got pretty ugly. One time we had ethics charges brought against us, which came out of Two Rivers. The DNR told us – there was always a DNR lawyer there and DNR advisors at the meetings – and they advised us that as long as we were acting on behalf of the state that we couldn't be singled out, which was a lie. Lee and I were singled out. We were sweating there for awhile. It got to a point that we were going to have to hire a lawyer. It never amounted to anything, but it was one of the worst times of my life.[36]

Voight & Johnson Fishery

Two other prominent families involved in commercial fishing at Gills Rock were the Voights and Johnsons. Stanley Voight was born in 1893 to Gotleib and Mary Voight. Stanley's father, a postmaster, died when Stanley was eleven years old, which forced Stanley to quit school and begin his career as a commercial fisherman. Besides fishing he spent some time in the U. S. Coast Guard where he met his wife Edith Beckstrom. Stanley worked in the steel mills in Gary, Indiana, before moving back to Gills Rock and raising four children. Stanley began fishing with Willie Johnson and Alick Johnson in the early 1920s, and they soon formed a partnership. The first boat they owned was a small wood vessel called *Minnie S*. After several years, Alick began fishing on his own with his sons and had the *Lindy* built in 1927 at Sturgeon Bay Boat Works. In 1939 Alick moved his operation to Port Wing, Wisconsin, on Lake Superior. Stanley and Willie then formed Johnson and Voight Fisheries and purchased the *Sea Queen*. That boat later was sold to Stanley's brother Lawrence, who had a small boat called the *Nellie*. Stanley and Willie had a dock in Gills Rock, just north of the Weborg dock. Alick Johnson also had a shed and icehouse at that location. After selling the *Sea Queen* to Lawrence, Stanley and Willie acquired the *Howard L*, a small wood fish tug built in 1920, which they later sold to Willie's nephews, Roland, Verner, and Penny. Laurence Daubner, who was working for Stanley and Willie at that time recalled one of their last ventures out with the *Howard L*:

After fishing with Lawrence Voight who had the *Sea Queen* for several years, I began working with Stanley Voight and Willie Johnson. They had a boat named the *Howard L*, quite a small boat, you know. One time down at Sand Bay they got her stuck in the ice and couldn't get in. The next day they went down to Sturgeon Bay Boat Works to have a new boat built.[37]

That was 1930, and the boat they had built was named *Hope*, an all-wood vessel with a 50-60 two-cylinder Kahlenberg engine. *Hope* measured 43 feet in length and 12 feet on the beam, weighed 26 tons, and cost $3,500.00. During those lean Depression years, many people refused to give up hope, which seemed a fitting name for the new boat. *Hope* gave Stanley and, later, Stanley's son Donald many years of service until being taken out of service in 1992 and being moved to a final resting place at the Door County Fishing Museum in her home port of Gills Rock. Laurence Daubner recalled the day they first brought *Hope* home to Gills Rock:

> Stanley, Willie, and I brought the boat back when it was built. There was a big crowd there – I think all the people of Gills Rock were at the dock. It was a beautiful boat. It was quite a bit different from the one they had. I knew then we were in for some pretty rough rides – rides out on the lake – because I figured we weren't going to lay in much with that boat.[38]

Donald Voight recalled the glory years with their fish tug *Hope*:

> The *Hope* had a 50 Kahlenberg. It had two cylinders, each with 25 horsepower. Over the years, we bored out the cylinders and installed oversized pistons. When they got wore out we just bored out the cylinders. I was only four when the *Hope* was built, however I do remember when I was just a kid my father would sometimes get me out of bed early in the morning to go fishing with he and Willy when one of the guys didn't show up. They used to run across to the Manitous, you know, around 2:30 in the morning. If one of the crew didn't show up, they used to roll me out of the sack. We took some awful hard winds over there and got caught, you know. I guess you don't think too much about it, you just go out and do your job. Oh I used to get sea-sick, but you just try and forget it. The *Hope* was a fine boat. It never let us down.[39]

Besides having a dock at Gills Rock, Stanley and Willie had a dock at Sand Bay, which they used in the winter months to escape the heavy ice that locked in the bay. On a cold December day in 1934, Stanley and Willie took the *Hope* for a day of fishing and tried to break through heavy ice out of Sand Bay to reach open water to lift their nets. They developed engine trouble, and were soon adrift:

> **Gills Rock** — After battling a mile of heavy lake ice at Sand Bay, three fish boats finally went to the rescue of the fish tug *Hope* owned by Willie Johnson and Stanley Voight of this place Wednesday evening and saved the motor disabled craft from going on the dangerous Spider Island Reef.
>
> Failure on the part of the boat to get out into to open water would have meant

a possible disaster, because the only chance of rescue was by the Canal Coast Guard about twenty-five miles away. Plum Island guardsmen were helpless to give assistance, hemmed in by about three miles of solid ice caused by a severe cold snap this week. The *Hope* was the only boat at Sand Bay that attempted to get out Wednesday morning, breaking a channel from her own dock. The other boats, the *King,* owned by Victor and Richard Johnson, the *Howard L,* owned by Roland and Verner Johnson, and the *Sea Queen,* owned by L.E. Voight were at another dock and thought it was futile to try to break through. When they saw the flare go up from the Hope about 4:30 in the afternoon, however, they lost no time starting out. It took them 2 1/2 hours to reach open water.[40]

Donald Voight recalled his early days at Sand Bay, "There were four or five shanties in Sand Bay. Dad had a shanty there. They stayed there in the winter, and on the weekends they'd walk home. They used to walk across the Mink River Basin – come back up through to their home in Gills Rock. They would bring enough food for the week."[41]

In1936, Stanley and Willie had another boat built at Sturgeon Bay Boat Works named the *Roamer,* a 42-foot wood boat equipped with a 45-54 Kahlenberg engine. With two boats they decided to split the crews. Stanley operated *Roamer* with Laurence Daubner and Harry Carlson as crew members. Operating *Hope,* were Willie Johnson, Benny Wentworth, and Wilford Beckstrom. Laurence Daubner recalled the early days of chub fishing in the area:

> **A**t that time we were averaging about a thousand pounds of fish a day and they were – that was pile run. I don't know if you know the terms of the old fishermen, but it means that they were shipped as they come. Now your grading is number 1, number 2, and number 3. The pile run fish is from the smallest to the biggest, all in the same box. They were ten cents a pound then – the chubs, so that was $100 a day, but that $100 a day , back then, in the 30s was quite a bit of money.[42]

Stanley and Willie moved their operation to Port Wing in 1940, as did a few other area fishermen at the time, due to poor whitefish and chub harvests. Donald Voight recalled that another reason for moving away from Gills Rock was that "they changed the mesh size for chubs from 2 3/8to 2 1/2 [inches], which rendered all our gear illegal in these waters, so we moved to Port Wing, Wisconsin, and fished in Lake Superior waters where they were legal."[43]

The partnership between Stanley and Willie dissolved in 1948 after Stanley, Donald and Donald's brother Gerald bought out their Uncle Willie Johnson's share, and the fishery became known as S.R. Voight and Sons. The *Hope* was brought back to Gills Rock and the *Roamer* was traded for a tract of land on Table Bluff. Donald recalled:

> **M**y brother and I bought out my uncle back in 1948, and we moved back to Gills Rock with the *Hope.* We began fishing chubs again with our father. In 1958 my brother passed away, so it was just my father and I. We moved over to Frankfort, Michigan, in 1959 and fished chubs from there for eighteen years. Then we came

back to Gills Rock in 1976 and have been here ever since. Now my boys have taken over the business and fish these waters.[44]

Stanley continued to fish at Gills Rock with his son Donald, who bought the *Hope* from his father in 1959. Stanley retired in 1968 after spending nearly his entire life in commercial fishing. Donald left Gills Rock in 1959 and moved his family to Frankfort, Michigan, for better fishing grounds. After moving around and fishing in different areas, they came back to Gills Rock in 1976 when gill nets were banned in Michigan waters and they were more or less forced out of fishing there. Donald and his sons Leon and Lyle fished the waters of Green Bay and Lake Michigan with the *Hope*, alternating between the dock at Gills Rock and the one at Sand Bay. Shortly after they returned to Gills Rock, they bought the *Faith II* from the Mollhagens, who fished out of St. Joseph, Michigan. Donald retired from fishing in 1984, but Leon and Lyle continue in the business, as of 2006. The *Faith II* was purchased to replace the aging *Hope*, which made its last run on June 11, 1992, and is now on display at the Maritime Museum at Gills Rock. Donald recalled:

W e used both boats for awhile, but the *Faith II* is a good sea boat and doesn't roll as much. We replaced the Kahlenberg eleven years ago with a 250 Cummins diesel engine. We had to cut a hole in the roof and removed the original Kahlenberg with a crane, then modified the mounts for the new engine. I still have the original Kahlenberg in my backyard and start it occasionally to keep it alive. The museum, here would like to have it, but I couldn't part with it yet.[45]

Lawrence Voight, Stanley Voight's brother, was another fisherman in the Gills Rock fishing community. He began fishing with a small wooden fish tug called the *Nellie*. Later, he owned the *Sea Queen*. Laurence Daubner fished with him when he was just starting out and recalled a time when they had only six boxes of gill nets, which they slugged (repaired or added new mesh), dried, and stored in the upstairs of his home until he could build a shed. Lawrence had the *Faith* built at Sturgeon Bay Boat Works in 1934. It had a 35-foot wood hull and was equipped with a 30-36 Kahlenberg engine. He sold the *Faith* in 1938 to John Mollhagen from St. Joseph, Michigan. This was the same family from whom Lawrence's nephew Donald bought the *Faith II* many years later. In 1937, Lawrence had the *Aloha* built at Sturgeon Bay Boat Works, a 45-foot wood-hull vessel with a 50-60 horsepower Kahlenberg engine. Lawrence fished from Port Wing for several years, then fished from Sheboygan in the late 1950s and 1960s. Lawrence's sons, Bob, Leo, and Walter took over the business and became the Voight Brothers. They sold the *Aloha* to Dennis McDonald, who, in turn sold it to Alvin "Gabby" Anderson. Alvin remarked, "I don't even think the ink got dry, it changed hands so fast."[46] Gabby owned *Aloha* from 1961 to 1971, then sold it to Roy Nelson.

The Johnsons – Verner, Roland, and Pensfield (Penny) – began fishing together in the late 1920s. Their father, Leonard Johnson, was a farmer in Gills Rock who fished with pound nets in the spring and fall of the year. He was a brother to Willie and Alick Johnson. As young men, the brothers formed a partnership and bought the *Howard L.* from their uncle Willie and fished with that boat. Then they bought the fish tug *Ramona* from Maurice Martin of Washington Island. *Ramona* was a 42-

foot wood boat built at Sturgeon Bay Boat works in 1929. The brothers fished together all their lives at Gills Rock and Sand Bay, and they also ran a cherry orchard. They ran the Gills Rock Fish Company for many years, selling fresh and smoked fish to tourists waiting for the Washington Island car ferries that once frequented Gills Rock.

Alick Johnson & Sons

Alick Johnson came to the port of Gills Rock as a boy of twelve. Not long after he and his family arrived, he found work as a fisherman, as did many young men of that region. Alick fished with his brother Willie Johnson and Stanley Voight for some years before deciding it was time he fished on his own. In 1927, Alick had his first boat built by master boat builder Hans Johnson of Sturgeon Bay Boat Works. Alick named it the *Lindy* after Charles Lindberg who had just made his daring and historic transatlantic flight. *Lindy* was 40 feet long, with a forward pilothouse and a strong oak hull. *Lindy*'s actual documented length was 39 feet 10 inches, which was common practice at the time to elude a tax that was assessed on all vessels over 40 feet in length.[47] *Lindy* was powered by a two-cylinder 30-36 Kahlenberg engine. A few years later, Alick modified the *Lindy*, moving the pilothouse to the stern. This made it safer and offered some shelter when setting a gang of nets. In boats with forward houses, fishermen were exposed at the stern when setting nets. Another factor that may have encouraged fishermen and boat builders to alter their designs was that during the Depression fisheries often tried to reduce the size of crews on the boats; with the pilothouse at the stern, they could eliminate one or two crew members.[48]

With the *Lindy*, Alick had a good sea boat with a solid white oak hull and a dependable Kahlenberg engine. Alick's three sons, Norman, Everett, and Harris, began accompanying their father on the lake at a young age. They fished mostly for chubs and lake trout, as whitefish were scarce during the 1920s and 1930s. They typically fished six gangs of nets, which consisted of twelve boxes of 1,500-foot nets to the gang. They exchanged six boxes of dry nets for six wet ones every lift, which was a common practice among fishermen with cotton and linen nets.

Alick's sons Everett and Norman eventually bought a pound-net boat that Hilder Erickson had built in Ellison Bay. They built a house on it and hauled it to Cornucopia, Wisconsin, in the summer of 1938. The next year they returned to Gills Rock and, along with their father Alick, moved to Port Wing, Wisconsin. When the Wisconsin Conservation Commission changed the mesh size from 2 3/8inch to 2 1/2 inch for chub nets, it prompted several local fishermen to move to Port Wing to fish Lake Superior where they could still use their nets. Alick and his sons found the waters of Lake Superior bountiful with lake trout and chubs and enjoyed many prosperous years there. Everett bought the *Margaret* in 1944 from Kenosha fisherman Frank Eichler. The *Margaret*, built by the Peterson Boat Works Company at Sturgeon Bay in 1934, was 45 feet long and was powered by a 45-54 Kahlenberg engine. In 1948, they traded some land at Gills Rock to Stanley Voight and Willie Johnson for the *Roamer*. After Alick retired, Norman and Harris continued fishing with the *Roamer* and the *Lindy*.

After the trout fishing collapsed in the late 1940s, Norman and Harris decided to take a chance, and they moved their fishing operation down to the Gulf of Mexico and fished for red snapper. In 1951, Norman and Harris took the *Lindy* down the Mississippi River and began their operation from Pensacola, Florida. After a year of fishing, they noticed that worms and other sea invertebrates were damaging the *Lindy*'s white-oak hull. They sold the boat in 1952 to a local fisherman named Robert Loveall and returned to Port Wing. The *Lindy* remained in Pensacola and was taken out of documentation in 1963.[49]

After Norman and Harris returned to Port Wing, they operated the *Roamer* for nearly twenty-five years until July of 1975 when the boat was found burned at her moorings. Shortly after that, Norman acquired the fish tug *Allie Brothers* which still had its original 30-36 Kahlenberg oil engine. The *Allie Brothers* had a 40-foot wood hull that was later tinned. It was built in 1934 by Peterson Boat Works. After the Kahlenberg wore out, Norman installed a GM 3-71 diesel engine which he used until his death in the fall of 1987.

Rowleys Bay and Sand Bay

In close proximity to Gills Rock and Ellison Bay, Rowleys Bay and Sand Bay became integral to the fishing families of northern Door County. Rowleys Bay is located on the east side of the peninsula, approximately six miles southwest from the tip of the Door, and Sand Bay is a half mile south of Rowleys Bay. Sand Bay is a shallow harbor with numerous rocky reefs. In fog or snow, navigation is difficult and hazardous without modern sonar and radar. Fishing tugs often went aground there before they had these navigational aids. Alvin "Gabby" Anderson spoke about the precarious nature of that area:

> That could be tricky sometimes coming in there. All they had was sticks for markers in those days. There was no fathometers on the boats then, and all you had was clock and compass. You'd come back in snowstorms and heavy weather, fog, or blowing a gale – you know its funny the whole fleet didn't end up on the rock piles in there. If you were off by a couple hundred of feet, you'd had it. You had to keep track of your time and heading. I remember Howard Weborg and Harvey Olson and many others would go between those markers by the second. If you run too far or not far enough, you might end up on the rocks. Harvey Olson on his boat the *Lone Eagle* had his time and bearings scribbled down on the wall of his pilothouse – so many minutes to that buoy and that one and that one. If someone would have come in and erased all those, I don't know what he would have done.[50]

On the west side of the harbor is Larson's reef, and on the other side is the Newport Point reef. Many fishermen used a tall pine tree as a landmark to guide them through the reefs as well as the marker sticks. The winter months posed many challenges. When ice formed, a south or southeast wind could push pack ice that would extend down nearly to the bottom of the harbor. However, Rowleys Bay and Sand Bay provided fishermen protection from the prevailing northwest and westerly winds.

During the 1920s and 1930s, Sand Bay became a very busy place, not only in the summer months, but throughout the year. During the winter months, many fishermen who fished in the waters of Green Bay moved their operations to Sand Bay. The only way to Sand Bay by land was a widened trail through the woods starting from the cemetery at Rowleys Bay. In the summer months, trucks would pick up the fish, but in the winter there was no snow plow service and, if the roads became impassible for trucks, horse-drawn sleighs transported the fish from Sand Bay.

Ruby Weborg told of Gills Rock and Ellison Bay fishermen and their "bachelor shanties," as they came to be known:

> In the winter they stayed in Sand Bay. They all had their own cabins or shanties.
>
> When Howard and I were first going together, he would stay there all week and come home on weekends. All the fishermen had their own cabins – there was Richard and Victor Johnson; Alfred Weborg and his boys had their own; the Petersons; Harvey and Clyde Olson. My brothers Roland, Penny, and Verner Johnson had a shanty there. They stocked up on food and had wood stoves for heat. Usually, Friday afternoon or Saturday they would return home, sometimes by foot or on skis. The pastor would go down there and hold services for the fishermen.[51]

One can imagine the stories shared amongst the fishermen sitting around a woodstove on a cold winter night. There was a little card playing and talk about the catch of the day before they retired. Many fishermen shared Sand Bay as base of winter operations, including Jim Peterson and his sons Percy and Lee; Emil, Lexy, and Johnny Nelson; Willie Johnson and Stanley Voight; Alfred and Willie Weborg along with Alfred's sons, Howard, Wallace, Glen, and Emery; Verner, Roland, and Penny Johnson; Marvin Weborg; and Harvey and Clyde Olson. Jim and Percy Peterson began fishing from Sand Bay in the early 1930s. They docked at a slip that was built by Emil Nelson and Alex Albertson. Later on, the dock and property at Sand Bay was purchased and shared by Jim and Percy Petersen (who owned a share), Wally Weborg and Harvey Hanson (who owned a share), and Harvey and Clyde Olson (who owned a share). This partnership lasted nearly forty years before any of the shares were sold to other fishermen. Harvey Hanson sold his share to Tim Weborg and Rick Johnson in the mid 1970s, but the rest of the original partners held ownership until about 2002. At that time, Percy Petersen retired and Paul Saunders bought out his share and rig, including the gill-net boat *Kelly*. Charlie Henriksen bought Harvey Olson's share from his estate; prior to this he was renting dock space from Clyde Olson's son.

Many fishermen came and went from Sand Bay, and in 2006, a number of fishermen still use the dock for their operations. The dock has been improved, and more and more houses line the shore, but there is still a quaint feel about this quiet bay that still harbors the few remaining fish tugs – the *Mercury*, owned by Charlie Henriksen; the *Betty*, owned by Neil Teskie; the *Freitag Brothers,* owned by Rick Johnson; and the *Kelly*, owned by Paul Saunders, was sold in the fall of 2004 to Dan Anderson at Milwaukee, Wisconsin. She was renamed the *Alicia Rae* and it is used for fishing chubs. There is also the *Faith*, owned by Lyle and Leon Voight, who fish from the dock at the end of Waters End road (which is called New Sand Bay). Both their father and their grandfather were among the fishermen who called at these docks. There was also a dock just north of the dock at the end of Waters End road which was owned and shared by Howard and Emery Weborg and Roland, Verner, and Penny Johnson. That dock is no longer there.

Charlie Henriksen Fishery

Through hard work, strong convictions, and many years of experience, Charlie Henriksen has become one of the younger successful commercial fishermen of the area. He began his journey when he was twenty-one years old, working for Clayton Johnson and helped him set nets through the ice in the winter of 1973. The next year his father passed away, so he went back to Chicago for a time, then came back and fished with Jeff and Mark Weborg, setting gill nets out on the frozen waters of Green Bay. During the next several years, Charlie worked for several of the fishermen from the Gills Rock region. He worked with Charlie Voight and Paul Goodman for a time. He fished with Jack Schmirler for a time and then worked for Frank Teskie. During this time Charlie became very adept in the fishing business.

He began working for the Teskies fishing chubs off Kewaunee in the winter months during the 1980s. From 1985 to 1989, Charlie ran the Teskies' trap-net rig and fished his own nets using Neil's trap-net boat the *Frances*. In 1989 Charlie decided to fish on his own. He had gained a considerable knowledge of the business and knew and understood the challenges he faced. In some ways, being a commercial fisherman was like being a warrior. There were many fronts and battles to fight. A fisherman has to fight the weather; deal with ecological changes in the lake, battle the DNR, adjust to changing regulations, and battle the unpredictability of the markets.

In August of 1989, Charlie bought a 37-foot trap-net boat called the *Search LM* from Mike LeClair at Jacksonport. It came with four trap nets and 30,000 pounds of whitefish quota. That fall he fished his new boat (renamed the *Karen*) and also the *Frances* for whitefish. He also bought some whitefish quota from Paul Goodman who was getting out of the commercial fishing business. Charlie recalled that first year of fishing:

> **I** had been running Teskie's trap-net rig for five years. We were running on quotas then, and there just wasn't enough quota to do what we have been doing. I actually bought the trap-net boat for the quota. Then we fished it a little bit. Neil decided he was going to fish his own trap nets. One thing led to another, so I bought the *Mercury,* actually for the quota. It turned out we did an awful lot of chub fishing with it. When I bought the trap-net boat from Mike, it had a lay down Volvo engine in it. I changed it over to a Cummins. Those Volvos, we always referred to them as the "Swedish nightmare." That first year we didn't do much work to it. I remember we were fishing in North Bay and I went to turn 'er hard over and the rudder fell off; so I waded to shore to Cana Island. I had my guy run me in with the skiff as far as he could then I walked to shore and went and got the *Frances*. Dick Bergwin was working with me then, so we finished lifting with the *Frances* then towed her in and pulled her out. We rebuilt the keel, strut, and rudder that fall. The next spring we put a new

house on her.[52]

In late November, the Friday before gun deer season, Charlie purchased the gill-net tug *Mercury* from Ray Strege. The *Mercury* is a 42-foot steel-hull vessel and had a 250 Cummins engine which was replaced a few years ago with a rebuilt Cummins engine. It was built by Burger Boat Company in 1936. Said Charlie:

> **I** was told that was the first welded steel hull fish tug built by Burger. She was the sister ship to the *Linda E*. It was re-measured when Bob LeClair had it and was documented at 39.4 feet, but everything I have on it says it's 42 feet. The Coast Guard says it's 42 feet, same as the *Linda E*.[53]

After acquiring the *Mercury*, Charlie rented dock space at Sand Bay from Annette Olson, the widow of Jim Olson. Several years after Harvey Olson passed away, his dock and land shares went up for sale, prompting Charlie to buy it from his estate. Eventually Charlie, along with commercial fisherman Rick Johnson, bought up the acreage around the docks at Sand Bay. Rick bought one-third of the quarter and Charlie bought two-thirds.

Later that fall (1989), Charlie fished some big mesh in Green Bay before bringing the *Mercury* down to Algoma for the winter months. For nine years Charlie tied up at Emil Pagel's dock for the winter and fished chubs out on the lake. He and his long-time crewman, Chip Dickelman, fished chubs from the first of December through the middle of April, then returned to Sand Bay to resume trap netting for whitefish. They typically started setting them from the first of May until October 25, when whitefish can no longer be caught legally until the season reopens on December 1. Charlie recalled:

> **W**e went down there nine years straight and fished chubs. One year we fished out of Kewaunee. We'd come back to Sand Bay after Easter. That was a deal I worked out with a guy in Chicago who bought chubs from me. Then after that we'd bring the boat back. Then with the whitefish quota, we had 100,000 pounds so we started fishing whitefish around the first of May, so it worked out pretty good. We fished chubs pretty hard. We worked five to six days a week from December until April.[54]

Those years fishing chubs were some of the most challenging. Many times they were caught in bad weather. One time in particular that sticks out in Charlie's mind is what he calls his wildest ride:

> **W**e were fishing out of Algoma at the time, and we were fishing chubs right off Kewaunee when a southeast wind came up. The seas just got huge – I've never seen them build up that quick – southwest from time to time they can really get big but, boy; they really got big that day. Inside the reef here they build up fast from the southwest. It's a weird place to be. We headed back to Algoma in our boat the *Mercury* and started running normal gate. We were afraid to run her hard even with the sea, so we let her go. We were surfing all the way back. We got back and came

through the break wall and shot through the entrance. We couldn't see it, but I guess there was a wall of water behind us about fifteen to twenty feet. There was some tourists watching us come in and later they told us they thought we were goners. We lifted and set back that day. It really wasn't that bad in the morning. The sea just gradually built. There never was enough wind to explain why the sea was so big, but it was like ocean swells.[55]

In 2006, Charlie continues to fish whitefish in the spring, summer, and fall. When winter sets in and the trap nets are packed away for the year, he switches gears and fishes for chubs. Besides processing fish, roe is processed from both whitefish and chubs and sold to markets in Sweden. Charlie stays active in all facets of commercial fishing and is president of the Wisconsin Commercial Fishing Association, and participates in the local Northeast Wisconsin Commercial Fishing Association. He also serves as a member of the Lake Michigan Commercial Fishing Board and on the Fisheries Forum as a member at large. "Our local association – we're not as active. There are four regional groups – Lake Superior, Southern Lake Michigan, Green Bay, and Door County. Now it's just Door County and southern Lake Michigan. Rick Johnson is president of that association. Years ago in our state association we hired a lobbyist. Actually Charlie Voight and Lee Peterson hired a lobbyist instead of a lawyer. That was before I got involved, and it made a difference. If we had a crisis we at least had someone who could be our voice and the DNR definitely recognized us."[56]

Ellison Bay

The Native Americans called this area, Joe-Sahbe Bay. Sahbe was the son of Neatoshing otherwise known as Mishicott, a Native American Chief.[57] In 1865, federal surveyors recorded it as Ellison Bay, named after Johan Eliason, who came from Denmark and settled in Buffalo, New York. While there, he bought land in northern Door County from the U. S. Government, but the land officer mistakenly recorded his name as John Ellison on the abstract, and the small harbor was from then on called Ellison Bay. The first people who settled there were mainly fishermen and lumbermen. The town is situated near a 200-foot escarpment rising behind the southern edge of the harbor.[58]

The first commercial fishing from Ellison Bay began in about 1868. Fishermen using hooks and lines through the ice during the winter caught mainly lake trout. Some of the fish were salted in wooden kegs ("packages") that held about 125 pounds and were hauled across the ice to Menominee, Michigan, but most of the fish caught were kept frozen until shipped. Typically, a fisherman would bury his catch in the snow at the end of the day, and the fish were picked up every few weeks by a man with a team of horses and sleigh. The sleigh would go from Gills Rock all the way to Fish Creek, picking up fish from the various fishermen and then transporting them to Menominee, Sturgeon Bay, or Green Bay. The fish were stored in 125-pound boxes at that time.

By 1880, the fishermen in Ellison Bay began fishing year around with boats, typically Mackinaw boats. They used gill nets and pound nets extensively around this time. Hook and line fishing was still being done, but was more seasonal, and they were using boats to set gangs of hooks. The fishermen used herring that were caught in small-mesh gill nets for bait. Sometimes they caught so many herring that they began selling them in Menominee. By the end of the century, the herring fishery had become one of the largest industries in Ellison Bay. Fishermen began using pound nets to harvest herring, and, by the turn of the century, pound nets were quite a common sight in the bay. Some local fishermen even set pound nets through the ice in the harbor. This required cutting a hole in the ice the size of the pot and heart and a channel for the lead. It was a lot of work that required a large crew. Herring were important through the mid 1950s.

Some of the fishermen who fished from Ellison Bay around the turn of the century were recalled by one-time resident and fisherman Phil Albertson:

> There was Ed Evanson, who fished pound nets and had the dock that Harvey and Clyde Olson later owned. Emil Nelson, Johnny Nelson, Lexy Nelson, and Oscar Knutson also fished both gill nets and pound nets. Oscar had a gill net tug called *Laughing Water*. At the big dock there were Leslie Wickman, Harvey Seivert, and Alfred Wickman. My father Alex fished with Jim Peterson for a while.[59]

By the 1920s, there were a number of fishermen established in Ellison Bay fishing both pound nets and gill-net rigs. Prominent were the Olson brothers, Clyde and Harvey. They had a well-built dock, a packing shed, net sheds, and an icehouse to supply the local fishermen with ice for packing. Harvey and Clyde over the years also had their own rigs. One of the first boats Harvey had was an old government tug called the *Mallard*, built in the 1890s, which he bought in 1932. It was a 37-foot wood vessel and was used as a fish tug in Algoma in 1930. Harvey used the *Mallard* until 1936, when his brother Clyde and Phillip Albertson took it up to Port Wing, Wisconsin, to fish in Lake Superior for several years. Harvey had the *Lone Eagle* built at Sturgeon Bay Boat Works in 1936. This was a 38-foot all wood boat with a Kahlenberg engine. Harvey fished with that boat until 1971.

Harvey's brother Clyde bought the fish tug *Rex* from Edward Bohman of Algoma in 1943. Built in 1938 at Sturgeon Bay Boat Works, *Rex* was 35 feet long, an all-wood vessel with a Kahlenberg engine. Clyde fished the *Rex* until 1947 and then sold her to a fisherman from Two Rivers, Wisconsin. The next boat he had was the *Faith*, which he bought from Peter Adelson in 1950. The *Faith* was built in 1934 at Sturgeon Bay Boat Works and was 36 feet long with a 30-36 horsepower Kahlenberg engine. Clyde fished with the *Faith* for many years, then sold it in 1958 and bought the *Betty* from Lorman Greenfeldt and fished with that boat for many more.

Clyde and Harvey also fished at Sand Bay for part of the year. They also fished out of Milwaukee for lake trout and chubs during the winter months between 1943 and 1948. They would return to Ellison Bay in the spring and resume fishing from their docks in Ellison Bay and Sand Bay. They also dabbled in real estate. Harvey bought land at Sand Bay in 1932 from Jay Rogers and then formed a partnership with three other parties. Harvey fished only part time during the 1960s, as did his brother Clyde. By that time they had accumulated many properties in Door County. Their father was the sheriff of Door County for many years.

Other fishermen who called at Ellison Bay were Emil, Lexy, and Johnny Nelson, who fished from Ellison Bay and Sand Bay. Emil later moved his operation to Sturgeon Bay. Emil Nelson had the *Neptune* built in 1932 by the Burger Boat Company, in Manitowoc, Wisconsin. *Neptune* was a 42-foot wood vessel with a 45-54 Kahlenberg engine. In 1942, Emil's son Roy acquired ownership of the boat and used it in his operation based from Sturgeon Bay. In 1946, *Neptune* was sold to some Canadian fishermen. The Nelson brothers fished together for some years, both at Ellison Bay and at Sand Bay where Emil, Alex Albertson, and Alex's father Jim had built a small slip and dock. Lexy and Johnny Nelson eventually went on to fish with other fishermen in the county.

Clarence Lind fished for many years from Ellison Bay. Clarence was a "regional fisherman" in that he never ventured far from his home port. In his early years (1940s and 1950s), he fished through the ice out on the bay. Then he acquired a gill-net rig that he used seasonally. He had the gill-net boat *C.W. Lind* built in 1945 at Sturgeon Bay Ship Building and Dry Dock Company. The *C. W. Lind* was the sister ship to Howard and Emery's boat the *Skipper*. According to Phil Alberstson, the two boats were built at the same time, but the *C.W Lind* was a little faster. He remembered a time when they were both out on the bay:

> Clarence had his boat the *C.W Lind* built at the same time as Howard and Emery's boat the *Skipper*. You know, when they were out in the bay after they were built that year, Clarence blew by the *Skipper*, and he then checked her down because he thought the engine was turning too fast. I don't know the reason why she was faster, they both had 30-36 Kahlenberg's, although Clarence had a rebuilt engine in his boat.[60]

The *C.W Lind* was a 40-foot steel-hull boat with a 30-36 Kahlenberg engine. Clarence later sold the boat to Oliver Bjarnarson and Hannes Hannesson, two fishermen from Washington Island, who renamed it *Esterlou*. In 1970 it was sold to Melvin Keller from Algoma, and renamed the *Kelly*. Years later the boat was purchased by Percy Petersen of Ellison Bay who sold it to Paul Saunders in the late 1990s. Paul replaced the original Kahlenberg engine with a diesel engine and only used the *Kelly* for a few years. He sold it to Dan Anderson, fisherman from Milwaukee, who renamed it the *Alicia Rae*.

Jim Peterson lived and fished in Ellison Bay nearly his entire life. He fished pound nets for herring and gill nets for whitefish and chubs, and he fished lake trout through the ice, like so many fishermen did at the time. His son Percy began working with him in 1929 during the summers while in high school. After graduating in 1932, Percy began a lifelong career as a commercial fishermen. He was joined years later by his brother Lee, who was almost twenty years younger. Jim Peterson had an old wood fish tug named the *Ole*, which he and his son, Percy fished with for many years. It was a 35-foot wood boat powered with a Wolverine three-cylinder gasoline engine. Their home port was Ellison Bay where they used Harvey Olson's dock, which is still there, up the shore from the Ellison Bay town dock. Phil Albertson and his father Alex also used that dock, and they fished with Jim and Percy for a short time. Later, Phil fished with Clyde and Harvey Olson, and, in 1943, he worked for Cliff Wenniger.

In 1932, the Petersons began operations at Sand Bay as well as at Ellison Bay. At first, they used a small slip that had been built by Emil Nelson, but, before long, they bought a share of the property at old Sand Bay with Wallace Weborg, Harvey Hanson, and the Olson brothers. They bought the *Allie Brothers* from Walter and Elmer Allie at Sturgeon Bay. Built in 1934 by Peterson Boat Works, *Allie Brothers* had a length of 40 feet and a 30-36 Kahlenberg engine. The last boat Percy and Lee operated was the *Kelly*, which they bought from Melvin Keller of Algoma in 1975.

During the 1930s, many of the local men who fished out of Sand Bay during the winter stayed in small cabins (shanties). Jim and Percy stayed in the shanties only a few times during the winter months. They usually went back to their homes in Ellison Bay each night, though, if the weather was very bad, they might stay over in their shanty. Percy remembered the winter of 1935–36 as being unusually cold, and nights in the shanty were not pleasant. The wood-burning stove barely kept them warm. That was the year Lake Michigan froze completely from shore to shore.[61]

Percy and Lee Peterson encountered a few dangerous situations. They were very experienced and conscientious fishermen and knew the local waters well, but Percy's wife Dorothy recalled one evening in February of 1939 when they did not return home. At that time, they didn't have radios on the boats to communicate with folks on shore. Percy and his father got caught in heavy fog while fishing chubs about 10 miles out. They moved into about thirty fathoms of water and laid out there overnight. The next morning, when the fog cleared, they found that they were near Cana Island.[62]

Percy and Lee worked well together despite their age difference. Lee liked to sing while he worked. Tim Weborg described a day he spent fishing with Lee:

> **I** fished with Lee one time on a Sunday when Bob LeClair failed to show up. So I
> went out with him that day to fish chubs. I had heard Lee liked to sing, and, sure
> enough, he broke into song. He began to sing *In the Misty Moonlight*. "There she was,
> standing in the misty moonlight," he would sing at the top of his lungs while picking
> chubs. He'd be so happy singing and clearing chubs from the net that he never
> noticed the sea building and the boat rocking and rolling. I said, "Lee I think it's a
> little more than misty." That's when a big sea hit us and knocked the wood door in,
> flooding the forward section. We were standing in a foot of water. "You're singing
> 'standing in the misty moonlight,'" I said. "It's standing in the flooded moonlight."
> We're sinking like the *Bismarck*.[63]

Percy and Lee fished together for more than fifty years, until Lee passed away in the mid 1990s. Then Percy decided to retire from fishing and sold his boat, the *Kelly*, to Paul Saunders, a young commercial fisherman from the area. Percy's wife Dorothy said that in all the years her husband fished on the lake, she was on a fishing boat only a few times. Her father, Charley Anderson owned and operated a trucking company in Ellison Bay and transported fish to Chicago markets for the fishermen in Door County. He began the company in 1929, and, by the mid 1930s, he had several trucks that ran daily trips to Chicago and back. Sometimes they hauled freight on the return trips. In the winter months, in order to get the fish from Sand Bay, Charley Anderson hired Albert Hanson, and they would travel down the snow-covered trail with a team of horses and a sleigh to pick up the fish and bring them back to the trucks at Ellison Bay for shipment to the markets.

Alvin "Gabby" Anderson described what it was like growing up in Ellison Bay:

> **I** was born and raised halfway between Ellison Bay and Gills Rock. My father fished
> some pound nets and fished through the ice for lake trout. He also worked for other
> fishermen with the pound nets for herring. In my day and before, most of the fish-

ermen used gill nets and pound nets. I remember Wallace Weborg fished pound nets through the ice out here in the bay. It was quite a chore, but in those years you had to work hard, but you never gave it much thought, you were just happy to have a job. I was eight years old when I began fishing; working for Clarence Lind in Ellison Bay. I was so happy when Clarence Lind came down to the house that summer to ask me if I wanted to help him. Oh man, this was right before cherry-picking time, and the cherry trees and I didn't get along. I didn't want anything to do with cherry picking, so I went fishing.

When I was eleven years old, I worked for Howard and Emery Weborg. They had the *Golden Girl* at the time. The *Skipper* was being built that summer. By this time the *Golden Girl* wasn't in the best shape, she was getting pretty soft. For the weather that Howard and Emery pushed her through, I tell you, she was like a floating coffin. I think they had a Fairbanks and Morse engine in her at the time and she rumbled and she shook. I liked working for Howard and Emery, they got along real well, but you know, Howard was the boss. Emery was a hard worker – they both were. Thinking back – for an eleven year old in the mid 1940s, I had it pretty good working for some great fishermen. Those days you never asked what you were going to be paid. If someone asked you to work, you were just doggone happy to be working. Whatever they gave, you had to be satisfied. I'll never forget the check Howard gave to me after the first week. I wish I had a copy of that check. I couldn't believe it, $9 a day, $54 dollars a week. I thought I was the first millionaire to hit Door County.

My brothers and I started fishing on our own when I was fourteen. The first boat we had was the *Pelican*, Alfred Anclam's old boat. It was a 40-footer with a gasoline engine. We fished gill nets for whitefish, chubs, and some perch in the early 1940s. We used the clubhouse dock. Then we fished the winter months out of Milwaukee for many years. By 1949, the whitefish were pretty scarce around here, so my older brother and I bought a boat out of Grand Marais, Michigan, called the *R.V.H* and fished that boat up in Port Wing, Wisconsin. My other two brothers stayed and fished out of Baileys Harbor for some time and then moved to Algoma. In 1955 we bought the *H.W. Hocks* and fished her out of Milwaukee and Algoma.[64]

Chapter 12 notes

[1] Conan Bryant Eaton, *Rock Island: The Island Series*; (Conan Bryant Eaton 1969, Bay Print Inc), 12-13.

[2] Hjalmar R. Holand, *Old Peninsula Days,* eighth revised edition; (Twayne Publishers 1959), 188.

[3] Robert E. Gard & L.G. Sorden, *The Romance of Wisconsin Place Names* (New York: October House Publishers, 1968), 47.

[4]. Hjalmar R. Holand, *History of Door County Vol. 1;* (Chicago IL: S.J Clarke Publishing Co. 1917), 371-372.

[5]. The majority of the information on the Weborgs came from several sources including: Interviews with Ruby Weborg, Jeff Weborg, Tim Weborg, Charlie Miller, and the Weborg family tree book (privately printed).

[6].Weborg family tree manuscript, Courtesy of Ruby Weborg, (Unpublished).

[7] Lon Kopitzke, "An Interview With Marvin Weborg Along With His Son, Mark," *Door County Almanac No.3* (Sister Bay, WI: Dragonsbreath Press, 1986), 157.

[8] Interview with Tim Weborg, December 3, 2003.

[9]. Lon Kopitzke, "An Interview with Marvin Weborg," *Door County Almanac No. 3*, 156-159.

[10] Ibid, 298.

[11]. Weborg Family Tree Manuscript, Courtesy of the Weborg family (Unpublished).

[12]. Lon Kopitzke, "An Interview With Marvin Weborg Along With His Son Mark," *Door County Almanac, No.3*, 304.

[13]. Interview with Jeff Weborg, September 14, 2002.

[14]. Ibid.

15. Ibid.

16. Ibid.

17. Ibid.

18. Ibid.

19. Ibid.

20. Ibid.

21. From *The Last Fisherman*, (video)

22. Interview with Jeff Weborg, September 14, 2002.

23. Ibid.

24. Interview with Ruby Weborg, January 16, 2003.

25. Ibid.

26. Interview with Tim Weborg, December 3, 2003.

27. Interview with Tim Weborg, December 3, 2003.

28. Ibid.

29. Ibid.

30. Interview with Neil Teskie, 3 July 2003.

31. Ibid.

32. Ibid.

33. Ibid.

[34]. Interview with Rick Johnson, January 20, 2004.

[35]. Ibid.

[36]. Ibid.

[37]. Laurence Daubner, An evening of story telling at the Wagon Trail Resort, Rowleys Bay; video taped by Charlie Miller (Courtesy of Elaine Johnson).

[38]. Ibid.

[39] Interview with Donald Voight, June 20, 2003.

[40]. "Battle Heavy Ice To Save Fish Boat: Gills Rock Fishermen Almost Drifted on Spider Reef,",*Door County Advocate*, March, 1934.

[41]. Interview with Donald Voight, June 20, 2003.

[42]. Laurence Daubner, An evening of story telling, videotaped by Charlie Miller, (1997 at the Wagon Trail Resort, Rowleys Bay).

[43]. Interview with Donald Voight, December 20, 2003.

[44]. Ibid.

[45]. Ibid.

[46]. Interview with Alvin "Gabby" Anderson, March 29, 2003.

[47] Robert C. Grunst, Feature Article 1927, *Anchor News*, November/ December 1984, 134.

[48] Ibid, 134.

[49] Ibid, 136.

[50]. Interview with Alvin Anderson, March 29, 2003.

51. Interview with Ruby Weborg, January, 30 2003.

52. Interview with Charlie Henriksen, December 20, 2003.

53. Ibid.

54. Ibid.

55. Ibid.

56. Ibid.

57 Robert E. Gard & L.G. Sorden, *The Romance of Wisconsin Place Names*, (October House Publishers, NewYork, 1968), 37.

58. *A Century in Gods Country 1866-1966: Ellison Bay*, (Ellison Bay Historical Committee, 1966).

59. Interview with Phil Albertson, March 7, 2003.

60. Ibid.

61. Leonard Peterson, *Rowleys Bay* (privately published, Ellison Bay, WI, 1991), 167.

62. Ibid.

63. Interview with Tim Weborg, December 2, 2004.

64. Interview with Alvin "Gabby" Anderson, 23 January 2003.

Pic.12.1 Fishing fleet at Gills Rock, ca. 1905. In the background, (men standing on the boat) is Chris Anderson's boat the *Eagle*. In the foreground, Max Peil's boat *Marion*, Alick Johnson's first boat *Elijah*, and Jack and Andy Johnson in the *Jonnie Bell*. In the background on the right is Alfred and Willie Weborg's steam tug *A.A Weborg*, and Willie Johnson's boat the *Rock Bass*. (Photo courtesy of Ruby Weborg.)

Pic. 12.2 Arthur Weborg's first fish tug *Dahlia* on skids on the ice at Gills Rock, ca. 1920s. Fish tug *King* and Alick Johnson's fish tug *Lindy* in the background. (Photo courtesy Donald Voight)

Pic. 12.3 Marvin Weborg at his fish shed.
(Photo courtesy of Eleanor Weborg)

Pic. 12.4 Gills Rock fishermen, from left, Howard
Weborg, Emery Weborg, Tim Weborg, and
Rick Johnson.(Photo courtesy of Ruby
Weborg)

Pic. 12.5 Sisterships, *Skipper* (Howard and Emery Weborg) and the *C.W. Lind* (Clarence Lind) built in 1945 at Sturgeon Bay Ship Building and Dry Dock Company. Both were 42-foot all-steel constructed and powered by 30-36 horsepower Kahlenberg oil engines. (Photo courtesy of Kahlenberg Brothers Company)

Pic. 12.6 Richard and Victor Johnson's 36-foot gill net tug the *King*, built by Sturgeon Bay Boat Works in 1920 and powered by a 30-36 Kahlenberg oil engine. She was sold to Marvin Weborg and Ed McOlash in 1953. (Photo courtesy of Kahlenberg Brothers Company)

Pic. 12.7   The *Hope* and *Faith* sided by side at Sand Bay. The *Hope* on the left was built for Stanley Voight and Willie Johnson in 1930 by Sturgeon Bay Boat Works and powered by a 50-60 Kahlenberg engine. The *Faith* was built for Lawrence Voight in 1934, also by Sturgeon Bay Boat Works. (Photo courtesy of Donald Voight)

Pic. 12.8   Fishing scene at Gills Rock, ca. 1920s – pound-net boats and gill-net tugs iced in the slip. Stanley Voight is to the left, with his brother Lawrence Voight on the right. (Photo courtesy of Donald Voight)

Pic. 12.9 Jeff Weborg breaking ice in Death's Door Passage in his gill-net tug *Ranger*. (Photo courtesy of Charlie Miller)

Pic. 12.10. Wallace Weborg working a pound net. (Photo courtesy of Ruby Weborg)

Pic. 12.11 Gills Rock fisherman, holding up two lake trout. (Photo courtesy of Gills Rock Maritime Museum)

Pic. 12.12 Fishermen at Sand Bay, ca 1950s. Left to right, Howard Weborg, Roland, Verner, Penny Johnson; standing on the *Ramona* is Emery Weborg. (Photo courtesy of Ruby Weborg)

Pic. 12.13 Roland, Penny, and Verner Johnson's fish tug *Ramona*, built at Sturgeon Bay Boat Works in 1929. She was originally built for Maurice Martin of Washington Island, then sold to Verner Johnson in 1937. She was powered by a 30-36 Kahlenberg diesel engine. (Photo courtesy of Kahlenberg Brothers Company.)

Pic. 12.14 Charlie Henriksen coming into Sand Bay with his fish tug *Mercury*.

Chapter 13

Sister Bay, Ephraim, & Fish Creek

The communities of Sister Bay, Ephraim, and Fish Creek have all had commercial fishing boats and fisheries over the years. In the 1870s, pound netters were predominant, and fishermen fished through the ice during the winter months. Most of the fisheries were in Fish Creek, but some of them also used docks in Sister Bay. As in Ellison Bay, it was not uncommon to see several dozen pound nets set in and around Sister Bay, Eagle Harbor, Nicolet Bay, and Fish Creek. The soft, shallow bottoms of those bays and harbors provided ideal sites for pound nets. The area between Fish Creek and Ephraim which is now Peninsula State Park was one of the first large settlements in Door County. Most of the people were farmers and fishermen, and, especially near Nicolet Bay, many of the farmers had a pound net boat and a few pound nets they would set. Sometimes families would go together to fish for herring in the spring and fall runs, which provided both food and extra income for their families.[1] During the Great Depression, the people in this region did not suffer as much as those in urban areas. There was always enough food and a little extra money to be had for those who could harvest lake trout, whitefish, and herring in the lake and bay waters.

Northern Light Fish Company

Robbie Kodanko & the Fisher Women of Sister Bay

Since the early days of commercial fishing, harvesting fish typically was considered to be a man's job. Women would lend a hand mending, reeling, and packing nets for the men to reset. But try telling Elaine Johnson and her cousin, Gretna Johns, that setting and lifting fish nets was a job for men only. The two women became known as the "fisher ladies" of Sister Bay. They began in the early 1950s, fishing perch from a small skiff that belonged to Melvin Knutson with a 5-horsepower Johnson outboard motor that belonged to Reuben Bergwin, their uncle. With their friend Robbie Kodanko, they made a trip to Washington Island, where they bought a few gill nets, a reel, and some net boxes from a fisherman at Jackson Harbor. The nets were 1,200 feet long and too heavy for the women to lift by hand, so they cut them in half, made new bridles, and got smaller net boxes. It wasn't long before they made their way out on the bay and into the annals of commercial fishing history.[2] To better understand the desire of these two cousins to fish commercially, we have to know their beginnings. Their great-great-grandparents were Norwegian immigrants, Torkel and Olia Knudson, who came from the town of Larvik, in southern Norway. They arrived at Eagle Island (Horseshoe Island) in August of 1854 and lived in a small cabin in what became known as "Shanty Town." That year an epidemic of cholera occurred and many people died. After it was over, Torkel and Olia moved to Ephraim where Torkel fished, farmed, and did some carpentry.

Ingebrett Johnson was a fisherman and farmer on Washington Island. According to Elaine, he was a half-breed – half Swede and half Norwegian. He moved to the mainland and married Inga Marie, Torkel and Olia's daughter. Ingebrett and Inga homesteaded in Liberty Grove, near the cross-roads of Old Stage road and County Z. Elaine's and Gretna's grandfather, Charlie Bergwin, married Ingebrett's and Inga's daughter Martilda and was given some property across the road from the Johnson's, where they farmed the land and he worked in the woods. They had two daughters, Julia (Elaine's mother) and Helen (Gretna's mother). Julia moved to Nebraska and married Ed Johnson. Elaine was born and grew up in Nebraska. Gretna's mother, Helen Bergwin, stayed in Door County and married a local man, Johns. Elaine recalled:

> We came to visit my grandmother [Martilda Bergwin] when I was four, and one
> more time when I was seven. Gretna came out [to Nebraska] after high school and
> lived with us. When I got out of high school, we both worked various jobs out there.
> We worked in a missile factory and other jobs, but we somehow always made our way
> back to Door County in the summer months. When we moved back permanently, I
> was twenty-two and Gretna was twenty-four. That's when we met Robbie [Kodanko]
> and we became a threesome. We all hung out together.[3]

Robbie Kodanko fished for perch and whitefish in the bay at that time. He had the fish tug *Hagen*, which once belonged to Swara Hagen, a fisherman from Washington Island. Elaine and Gretna accompanied Robbie out on the lake, and Robbie showed Elaine and Gretna the ropes of commercial fishing. They helped to clear the nets of perch and whitefish, to slug nets, and to dress the fish. Robbie became a good friend and teacher. Elaine recalled fishing with Robbie after he sold the *Hagen* to the Erickson Brothers and bought the *Osprey* from Fred Bjarnarson at Washington Island:

> I remember that boat. It had a gasoline engine to start it. Then he'd get that old belt
> on her and try and get that old Kahlenberg to turn over. He'd tell me to get ready
> and squirt ether in the holes – the darn thing would never start. Robbie had a tem-
> per and he'd grab a hammer from the side of the boat, bang that engine with the
> hammer, then throw it as far as he could. Sometimes it would bounce around then
> land in the drink. The next day he'd go and buy another hammer. There must have
> been forty hammers lying around somewhere. He was a character – there was nobody
> like Robbie.[4]

Elaine and Gretna worked with Robbie in the summer months. During the winter for a few years they went to St. Petersburg, Florida, and worked at Leland Thorp's hotel. Leland was a Fish Creek native. In May they would return to Sister Bay and again help Robbie in his fish business. The three of them became good friends and were almost inseparable. After some time working for Robbie, Elaine and Gretna thought they might try fishing on their own. Elaine explained:

> **W**e finally got into our own – or thought we could – while we were still working with Robbie. We were using Robbie's steel skiff on the lake side out of Sand Bay. We were setting some perch nets, and I thought there must be some way to fillet these things. I had a chub knife, so I put the perch on a stone and sat there with seven perch and decided I was going to learn how to fillet them. We decided to try a few more (practice makes perfect), so we began filleting our own perch, and we actually started going from door to door peddling our perch fillets. By 1953 we used a 17-foot skiff from Melvin Knudsen, who fished pound nets from Sister Bay, and our Uncle Rueben Bergwin's 5-horse outboard motor and began fishing for perch. We bought some cotton nets from a Washington Island fisherman. I paid him for the nets one day, and he died the next. We took those nets and cut them in half and made shorter nets. I built a bunch of small boxes to hold our nets and soon we began fishing on our own out by the Sister Islands.[5]

The two women would go out in the skiff early in the morning with their modified gill nets. Once they got out near the Sister Islands approximately a mile off the village of Sister Bay, they would remove the outboard motor, and one would row while the other set the nets. Then they would switch jobs. It was the same procedure lifting the nets, which they did entirely by hand. Usually, they would get in by mid morning and fillet their fish before helping Robbie the rest of the day. Elaine recalled:

> **W**e'd fish early in the morning then come in and would have to go wake Robbie up – he tended to be a late riser. Robbie was the darndest guy – we could never seem to get him out of bed. We'd go over to his place, drag him out of bed, and then go get breakfast to get him going.[6]

Elaine and Gretna sold their perch door to door. They were out fishing in their skiff every chance they got and have fond memories of being out in the bay during the summer and early fall months. They always had good rapport with other fishermen in the area. Elaine recalled times they'd run into Howard and Emery Weborg out in the bay:

> **G**retna and I would be out near the Sister Islands. We would bring a couple of boxes of small mesh gill nets, which were enough for us to handle, and we'd set them around the islands. Sometimes I'd row and Gretna set or she'd row and I would set. We would see Howard and Emery coming in with the *Skipper*. We could hear that old Kahlenberg chugging with its distinctive sound, and they'd see us out there in just our underwear, you know. All of a sudden that gol darn stack would be blowing black smoke as they put the boat on her full gait. They'd come in there as close as they could and the hatch door would fly up. Emery would stick his head out the port hole and sometimes we, being smartalecks, would both turn around and give them a

surprise. So when they'd see us out there they made it a point to come in close by us.[7]

Elaine and Gretna always caught enough perch to provide for their customers, and in the late 1950s they began selling perch to restaurants. As restaurants began to place large orders, they bought fish from other fishermen. They bought perch from Stuart Woerfel, Frank Teskie, Sr., Cliff Wenniger, and Homer Albertson (who fished from Sand Bay). Homer fished alone in a small skiff. Elaine commented on his incredible physical strength:

> **H**omer had a little skiff he used for catching perch. He would go all over with that little skiff, which wasn't more than 17 feet. I remember one day [we were] coming down to Sand Bay and saw Homer coming in – the water was pretty low. I can still remember him standing in that rocking skiff. I don't know how many boxes of wet nets he had, but he picked up one of those big boxes, and that old boat was rocking and swaying. I don't know exactly how much it weighed, but I suppose it was 240 pounds wet, and he picked that thing up, lifting it up well over shoulder height, and threw it on the dock. I'll never forget the strength that man had.[8]

At that time, perch were going for six cents a pound. Elaine and Gretna gave the fishermen ten cents a pound, and then sold them for fifty cents a pound. Elaine recalled:

> **I**n 1958 we went to the Hillside to see if the new owners Doris ("Duffy") and her husband Ken Paul would like to buy some perch. We offered to sell her 5 pounds of perch for a perch fry and she wasn't sure they would sell, but she bought five pounds from us anyway. We gave her a price of forty-five cents a pound for the perch. It went over really well. She sold a plate of three perch, french fries, coleslaw, rye bread, and a glass of beer for seventy-five cents. The next week she bought 15 pounds of perch, and later on she was buying 70 pounds of perch a week.[9]

"Northern Light Fish Company" became the moniker of their small business, which included their good friend Robbie Kodanko. Elaine told about the night the Northern Light Fish Company came to be:

> **W**e stopped one night for a beer at the Hillside. We decided we were going to fillet a bunch of perch and put an advertisement in the paper and sell them to the local people around here. It was Gretna, Robbie, and I sitting there that night wondering what to call ourselves. Charlie Jonas was in there drinking – he liked his beer and had quite a snoot full. He overheard us and in a slurred voice stammered, "How about the Northern Light Fish Company? Robbie said, "Hey, I kind of like that – that's a good name." He had it lettered on the side of his old truck and after he died, we continue to have that name for our company today.[10]

Robbie Kodanko played a big part not only in Elaine and Gretna's lives but in the community as well. He was a well-known and well-liked person who lived his life as he saw fit. Robbie was a friend to many, and anyone who knew him remembers him for his infectious laugh that could be heard across the bay. He was a fisherman, a bachelor, a man who saw life through youthful eyes. Robbie's life was cut short on January 5, 1963. Robbie, his brother Ed, and Everett Sitte finished setting nets out on the ice and were returning home in Robbie's truck when it broke through the ice. Elaine described that day:

When our dear friend Robbie died that day, it was a big loss for us. Robbie, his brother Ed, and Everett Sitte were out on the ice and were coming back in from setting nets. Eddy was sitting in the back and Everett was in the front with Robbie. They always drove with the one door open. Everett said they stopped for just a little bit and for some reason he just drove onto that black ice – he didn't know why really, but the truck went down. Robbie always wore those buckle overshoes, so when he grabbed a wooden net box, it was upside down and the net had come out of the box, and the webbing had gotten caught in the buckles of his boots and of course that weight was pulling him too. He held on to the bottom of the box as long as he could, then told Everett that he couldn't hang on any longer and let go, slipping under the water as the net pulled him down. A breeze kind of picked up and the monofilament came up to the top of the water. Eddy and Everett were lying on the ice and managed to grab onto the net and began to pull up the net, and there was Robbie in it. They pulled him onto the ice but he was already gone.[11]

The following is an article written by Keta Steebs as a tribute to Robbie and published in the *Door County Advocate*:[12]

Big- Hearted Robbie was Everyone's Friend

The Captain of the *Osprey* is gone. The President of the Northern Lights Fish Company is no more. Our children have lost their Pied Piper. Robbie Kodanko is dead.

He died as he lived, on the bay he loved so well. No disease felled Robbie, no automobile struck him down, and no bullet ended his life. It took a far more formidable foe to vanquish him – a foe he had met and bested on his own terms most of his life. We like to think he would have wanted it that way.

Few 40-year-old bachelors will be missed and mourned the way we will miss Robbie. He had no children of his own, yet he occupied a particular spot in the heart of every child who knew him. He was their Captain Kidd, Robin Hood, and Daniel Boone. He was Robbie the invincible, the courageous, the daring. Little boys were his equals in every sport they shared and he treated them as such. Whether stalking the elusive deer, netting hard-to-get whitefish, or sailing the high seas, Robbie gave no quarter and they asked for none. Once you boarded the *Osprey*, you became a man. Mothers and fathers might treat children as children, but not Robbie. To him, they were his partners, his comrades, his life. Small wonder they idolized him.

Robbie was not a rich man, nor a handsome man, nor a prominent man. Yet many a rich, handsome, prominent man might well have envied Robert Kodanko, for he was a truly happy man. He lived his life as he saw fit. He worked hard at the work he loved best, but only at his convenience. Robbie obeyed no alarm clock, punched no time clock and didn't own a wristwatch. Time was a commodity to use at his own discretion, not to become a slave to it. He was his own man in everything he did and answered only to the dictates of his own conscience. Not too many men living in this day and age can say the same.

Perhaps his casual disregard for schedules dates back to his early youth. Robbie had no easy time of it as a boy. His father died when he was twelve, leaving Robbie (the oldest) to take care of brother Jake, brother Connie and brother Ed (as he always called them). Brother Robbie automatically became head of the household and helped support the family by trapping, woodcutting, farming, etc. Far from resenting such early responsibility, he thrived on it. The more he had to do at home – the more school he missed and the less he saw of school – the better he liked it.

Robbie ignored most official communiqués mailed him, but the one he received in 1943 with "Greetings" as the salutation, he decided to obey. Again, however, only on his own terms. It had snowed and drifted the night before he was due to appear at the Sturgeon Bay induction center, and he had to walk from his farm home into town (a distance of approximately 2 1/2 miles) in drifts up to his knees. "By the Crimeny," he said, "if I get a ride, I'll report for duty. If not, I'm going back to bed." He did get a ride, and he did report for duty and served honorably for two years, but if that car hadn't come along, Robbie would have gone back to bed.

People warmed to Robbie on sight. His famous laugh was known throughout the county. Perfect strangers joined in the general hilarity once they heard it. "Hearty" is the only adjective to describe it, and, after consulting Webster's dictionary, we realize that a perfect description it is - not only of his laugh, but of Robbie himself – "pertaining to the heart, warm cordial, energetic. Exhibiting strength, sound, healthy, nourishing, abundant. Also enjoying abundant food."

Robbie had a heart all right and a big one. He asked nothing of anyone, but gave of himself freely. No favor was ever refused, no request turned down. He was our Santa Claus, our parade float driver, our Christmas tree bearer, our fish boiler, our baby sitter, our venison provider – the list is endless because Robbie was many things to many people.

As a fish boiler, Robbie had no peer. No man had quite the flair for the dramatic when it came to pouring the kerosene on the fire and lighting the heavens with a rosy glow as R. Kodanko. To the uninitiated, a fish boil is simply boiling fish and potatoes in a kettle. But, for friends of Robbie, a boil was "dinner at the Waldorf", the "Mardi Gras" and a Hawaiian luau all rolled into one. He could start fire with green wood, boil ice cold water, and toss in salt with abandon – laughing all the while – and still end up with the most delectable meal mortal man has ever tasted.

Oh, he was a colorful character, that Robbie Kodanko. You couldn't miss seeing him go sailing through town in his little rattletrap truck held together by binder twine and growing deer horns through the roof. (He actually had three trucks, but as they were all alike, and most people thought he only had one.) He dressed the same winter and summer, and putting on an extra red, plaid shirt was the only concession he made to zero weather. For formal occasions he wore a buck skin jacket and knotted tie around his red, plaid shirt. Yet, when he went out – which was often – many a smartly dressed influential man went out of his way to shake Robbie's hand.

Robbie was not a religious man, and he would have been the first to admit it. Yet, he was more religious than even he realized, for he "did unto others" every day of his life. It takes a good man to live by the Golden Rule.

Robbie left a mother, three brothers, five dearly beloved nieces and nephews and a host of friends.

We said goodbye to our fisherman friend today, and it was hard parting. Our only consolation, dear Robbie, is that you are now safe at home with the greatest fisherman of all.

After Robbie died, Elaine and Gretna provided fish for Robbie's customers as well as their own, including his main customers, Al Johnson's Swedish Restaurant and the Hotel Du Nord. They also sold fish to the Cottage and the C & C Club. The perch were beginning to decline by 1965, so they began providing more whitefish than perch. As their customer base grew, so did the demand for fish, prompting them to import Canadian trout which was sold for the local fish boils. They used one of the buildings on their uncle's farm for their processing center, and their Uncle Reuben helped out with the processing. Gretna and Reuben would scale the fish while Elaine did all the filleting. Elaine recalled:

When our fathers died, our uncle Reuben became more of a father figure. He was with us all the time. We fished together, laughed together, and worked together. He was a good friend as well as our uncle. We lost him in 1980 when he died of a heart attack.[13]

Elaine and Gretna bought a general store in Sister Bay in 1964 which they called Beach Road Market. Gretna tended more to working in the store while Elaine kept the Northern Light Fish Company going. "There were many times Gretna threatened my life," said Elaine jokingly – Elaine was adamant about providing fish for her customers, leaving Gretna to run the store, but it all worked out well for both of them. They sold the store in 1974 and continued with the fish processing, selling the perch that were once again beginning to show up in the bay. By this time they had over twenty accounts and were processing 70,000 to 90,000 pounds of perch and whitefish a year.

In 1974 Elaine and Gretna helped form an association of commercial fishermen to voice their grievances about the new regulations and restrictions the DNR was implementing. "In the beginning we had our own little group. We were the whitefish people around here," says Elaine. "To the south, from Algoma down to Racine, they were the chub fishermen, and southern Green Bay was known as the perch fisheries, so we had our own little associations before we unified and went into a state association."[14] Meetings were held in Green Bay, and in 1974 the Northeast Wisconsin Commercial Fisheries Association was formed. Jeff Weborg was elected president and Elaine Johnson was elected secretary. Gretna helped out at the meetings by taking notes. Elaine became an unofficial spokesperson and went to bat for the association. She recalled:

> I love all commercial fishermen and respect them. They are a special group among men. They had to be mechanics, electricians, carpenters, welders, and really had to do many things to keep their fishery going. When all these new regulations came up – a fisherman can withstand fluctuations in the stock, but when you got to fight the DNR and the regulations, besides the fluctuations, it puts a tremendous challenge on a fisherman.[15]

Elaine was involved in writing newsletters, corresponding with the DNR and political heads, and voicing the concerns of the commercial fishermen. When the association started there were around three hundred members, though that number dropped significantly in the next few decades, especially with enactment of Senate Bill 409 and the limited entry program. Some say it was both a blessing and a curse, but Elaine believes that it was more a curse for fishermen. She remarked:

> When Senate Bill 409 was in the early legislative stage, there was a legislative history before the bill that stated there had to be scientific data presented to warrant or adopt a regulation or an administrative code. They really never had that or needed it. We met with Senator Jerry Van Sistine many times at Sturgeon Bay and added our input, and of course, as it always was with legislation, we thought we were writing something to protect the fisheries. But really we were not aware that maybe we were putting a noose around the fishermen's necks to wipe them out. We never realized that they were going to have limited entry.[16]

Elaine remained involved with the association for many years and saw a lot of changes in the fishery, some good and some bad. When limited entry and the quota system came on the scene, there were considerable changes to the commercial fishery and changes among the attitudes of commercial fishermen. She commented:

> Commercial fishermen tend to be very independent and every one of them seems to know more than the next guy. We all have that certain element of greed, being humans, and you know when they came out with limited entry then the fishermen thought one fisherman would get more quota than the other one. They were so busy seeing if they couldn't get somebody out of the fishery so their quota could be big-

ger; that's when I got out of it.[17]

In 1982 the cousins worked out a deal with Jeff Weborg to run their processing business from the Weborg processing shed. Elaine recounted:

We started working with the Weborgs and worked out a deal with Jeff. He said, "Why don't you come down here to our shed and give us a dock price and we'll help you process your fish so you can take on more customers and help us process our fish." Gretna and I talked it over and we agreed. We were with them for eighteen years and sold our business to them in April of 2000. I had a lot of good memories working there, especially of Marvin Weborg. He was a very dear friend of ours. I remember one day the boys lifted and got back early that day. It was one of those very hot summer days – sultry as could be. We were going to take a break for lunch, and you have to know Marvin, temperate as could be. I looked at him and said, "Marvin, could you lend me $5." He said, "Well yeah," and reached into his back pocket, pulled out his billfold and said, "What are you going to do with $5 now?" I said "I'm going to go down to the Hillside and grab a handy pack (meaning a six-pack of beer)." He looked at me for a minute, then slapped his billfold shut, put it back in his pocket and said, "You see that water spigot over there?" I said, "yes sir." He said, "You go over there and get a drink. We call that Gills Rock Light." When he died it was a big loss for us, he was a dear man.[18]

As of 2006, Elaine and Gretna enjoy retirement on the homestead where their family lived for many generations. They are active in the community and are proud of what they accomplished in their lives. "Those were wonderful years," remarked Elaine. "Being part of the fishery was a privilege and a blessing really. We worked hard at it and made many friends. I will say it again – I love all the commercial fishermen and respect each and every one of them. They are a special and unique breed of people."[19]

Fish Creek

Fish Creek, formerly the site of an old Menominee and Ojibwa village called, Ma-go-she-kah-ning meaning trout fishing.[20] Asa Thorp, who is credited with establishing the community, was a cooper by trade. He learned the craft when he was a teenager living in Milwaukee. In 1844, Asa was working with his father as a lock tender on the Erie Canal. One day he climbed on a scow bound for Buffalo, New York. From there, he boarded a lake steamer that was destined for Milwaukee, Wisconsin. During his sojourn in Milwaukee, Asa learned the trade of making tubs, wooden ware and butter firkins. A drifter by nature, Thorp moved to the town of Rubicon in Dodge County, where free land was available for farming and where he met a traveler who told him of a place in northern Lake Michigan around Washington and St Martin islands. The man said to Asa, "You ought to quit that puttering with butter firkins and come with me to Rock Island and make fish barrels." "Rock Island!" said Asa, "What county is that in?" "Dunno," said the stranger, "we aint got no county down there." "What state or territory is it in?" "Dunno that," replied the stranger, "and what's more, don't care. We have no state, county or town organization. We pay no taxes, and have neither lawyers nor preachers. But we have fish, and we have money. It will keep you busy twenty-four hours a day to make fish barrels at your own price. If you want to make money, come with me."[21]

It didn't take long for Asa to pack up a few belongings and begin his journey north. He hitched rides on freight wagons and ox-teams and made it as far north as Fort Howard (now called Green Bay). In the spring of 1845 he boarded one of the "Buffalo boats" that plied the waters of the Great Lakes between Buffalo and Chicago and was dropped off at Rock Island where there was a sizable fishing village. He set up shop and was soon making barrels for fishermen. Coopering was a special skill and coopers were valued craftsmen. Special bolts of wood had to be cut from timber to make barrel staves. White ash was used for the hoops, and they were simmered or steamed in a tank until they were as pliable as rope. Staves were split from white-oak bolts with a small adze (called a froe) and hardened in a fire. A barrel, or "package," was assembled using a jig, with the staves upright inside a starter hoop, and the hoops were driven down snugly around the outside using a wooden mallet and a hardened block. The barrel then was filled with water so that it swelled to form a watertight seal. A barrel had to be tight enough to keep the contents sealed.[22]

When the fishing slowed down in late fall, Asa closed his cooper shop and headed to Fort Howard on one of the boats that picked up fish for the markets. On the way to Fort Howard, as the boat followed the coast of the Door Peninsula, he overheard the captain complain about not having enough refueling stations where he could get wood for the boat's steam engine. He had to find a safe place to moor every few days to replenish their supply of wood for the boilers. Asa remembered seeing a picturesque cove with a small creek and one lone cabin when he was heading to Rock Island, and this gave him the idea of establishing a refueling station and lumber camp or fishing village. As soon as he landed at Green Bay, he headed for the Federal Land Office in Appleton, where he filed an application for all the shore lands around the cove. He called the place Fish Creek.[23]

The winter of 1853, he sold his land in Rubicon, fetched his fiancée from New York, and he and his future wife, along with his brother Jake Thorp, began their new life at Fish Creek. Asa and his brother hired men and began felling trees and constructing a series of log cribs which they sledded out onto the ice, placed in a row, and partially filled with large chunks of limestone. They then chopped through the ice around the cribs, which allowed them to sink to the lake bottom, and finished filling the cribs with limestone blocks. They then built a pier supported by the cribs. They worked on the pier throughout the winter, and when spring thawed the ice on the bay they were ready for business. By summer they had a pier, a warehouse, a sawmill and stacks of pine lumber ready for shipment, and, over the next several years, Fish Creek began to prosper and grow.[24]

By the turn of the twentieth century, fishing was by far the biggest industry in Fish Creek. Herring was the mainstay for most of the early fishermen in Fish Creek, as the market for whitefish in the early 1900s was almost nonexistent, and lake trout typically were only caught through the ice during the winter months. Most of the herring were harvested with pound nets and either shipped fresh in the round or salted and packed in wooden kegs, or packages. These kegs were built locally by local coopers like John Brown and a man by the name of Peter Weborg who had a cooperage at

Weborg's Point. Several hookers of the Hill Company and the Hart Transportation Company picked up herring at the Fish Creek dock and carried them to wholesale markets in either Green Bay or Marinette. The Seidel Fish Company in Marinette was at one time, the biggest buyer of herring.[25] However, during the winter, sleighs drawn by horses carried most of the freight. After freeze-up, there was always a road on the ice over to Marinette marked with evergreen trees cut and placed on the ice to mark the way. Many farmers in the region would travel the eighteen miles to Marinette to haul fish, apples, cheese, and other produce to market and bring freight and personal items back. Some farmers even covered their wagons with tarps and had stoves in them.[26] Years later, with the advent of the automobile, most of the fish were shipped to Green Bay and Chicago markets via the Anderson Transportation Company based in Ellison Bay.

Some of the fishermen in the early years at Fish Creek were Martin Kinsey and his sons Roy and Pat; John Pelletier; Don and Ray Chambers; and Stuart Woerfel, to name only a few of the dozen or so fishermen who had fisheries at Fish Creek over the years. Besides the herring fishery, many fishermen in the late 1920s converted to gill nets and to hook and line rigs for lake trout. By the early 1930s, whitefish were making a healthy return, which prompted many fishermen to use gill nets. By the 1940s, perch were being caught in large numbers, where they once had been considered trash fish. By the mid 1900s, Fish Creek and the other bayside communities had thriving fisheries. In the winter many fishermen set gill nets through the ice, and some set pound nets as well.

Setting a gill net through the ice was easier than setting a pound net. Gill nets were set under the ice near the shore to catch herring that were following the shoreline. First, a hole was cut through the ice large enough to insert a board 16 feet long, 4 inches wide, and an inch thick, and the board was pushed along under the ice. Once the board was fully extended, another hole was cut to retrieve the other end of the board. Then the top maitre was attached to the board and pulled through, and the process continued until the entire length of the net was strung out.[27] Setting pound nets was a more laborious task, since it involved cutting out a large enough area of ice to set the pound net. The pound net was suspended in the water by cutting channels in the ice for the lead and heart, and then a large area was cut out for the pot. To lift the net, any newly formed ice was removed and the pot was lifted.

Fish Creek Fishermen

John Pelletier moved from Little Sturgeon Bay to Fish Creek in the spring of 1930. He followed the trout north, moving his nets as the ice left the bay. He found the waters off Fish Creek teeming with trout, and decided to move his operation there. John had a small pound-net boat, which he used both for gill nets and pound nets. He fished from Fish Creek for many years and was well known in the community.

David Stuart Woerfel, called Stuart, grew up in Fish Creek. Upon completing high school, he began to fish with John Pelletier. He had a long career as a fisherman; both commercially and in the sport fishing arena, where he ran a charter service during the summer months. Stuart fished with John for several years for lake trout, which in the 1930s were abundant in the bay. Stuart remembered harvesting trout in the spring of the year when the water was so cold that fish they pulled from the nets did not need to be iced down to stay fresh.[28]

In time, Stuart bought nets of his own to set along with John's to make a little extra money. Eventually, he saved enough to purchase his own rig and he bought a boat called the *John* from Alfred Anclam, a fisherman from Baileys Harbor. It was a small, 28-foot wooden fish tug with a two-cylinder Straubel engine. Stuart began fishing on his own with his small tug and a few nets for perch and herring. In 1936, Stuart sold the *John* and bought another boat called the *Helen D.* In 1942, he sold the *Helen D* and acquired yet another boat, a 43-foot wooden fish tug, the *Amelia D.* that had been built at Suamico in 1938. She was built of white oak and had an 85-horsepower Buda engine, and Stuart paid $3500. He fished with the *Amelia D.* for almost forty years – in the 1940s and 1950s for perch in southern Green Bay, then for lake trout off Racine until the lake trout disappeared, and also for chubs from Algoma. The *Amelia D.* once sat south of Sister Bay along Highway 42.

Besides fishing gill nets, Stuart bought a steel pound-net boat called the *Sue* from a fisherman in Suamico. After buying pound nets, he began fishing for herring, which were very abundant during the 1950s in the bay. He had several nets set out off Cottage Road. Late one fall. he took his rig up to Washington Island and fished from Jackson Harbor with the Nelsons. Russ and Spencer Nelson told him that they had a large run of herring there, so Stuart brought his pound-net boat, the *Sue* as well as the *Amelia D.* Stuart recalled:

> One time we took in 15,000 pounds in one day! We had the gill net boat, *Amelia D*
> to haul in supplies. We hauled the fish in, weighed them, and threw them in boxes.
> Didn't have to dress them or anything. The Washington Island freighters would take
> them to Green Bay.[29]

For a few years in the 1960s Stuart had a contract for alewives, which were used for dog and cat food. He also fished for smelt near Algoma. During the summer months he rented his pound-net boat, equipped with a house, to sport fishermen. He also rented cottages, which he and his family bought in the early 1960s (Dun Rovin Cottages), through the 1960s and 1970s. He sold the cottages in 1978, and by 1980 he retired from fishing.

Martin Kinsey settled in the Fish Creek area around 1900. He grew up in the Juddville area and learned fishing from his father who was a farmer and a fisherman. Martin began fishing the bay with a sail-powered Mackinaw boat built by Larsen Brothers of Marinette, Wisconsin. Later, when the marine gas engines came on the scene, he converted his Mackinaw to gas power. Martin was a farmer, but fished herring with pound nets off Cottage Road in the spring and the fall of the year. When his sons Roy and Pat were old enough, they accompanied their father out on the lake. Martin continued to fish well into his eighties.[30]

Over the years there were fewer and fewer fishermen as the ecology of the lake began to change. Most of the early fishermen gave up fishing and moved on to other things. Some of the early fishermen who operated from the Fish creek area were the Rockendorf brothers, Carl Olson, John Melvin, Roy Thorp, the Duclons, Don and Ray Chambers, the Hills, the Carlson brothers, and John and Andrew Anderson. One of the last fishermen of the Fish Creek area was Stuart Woerfel.

Time has brought many changes to these quaint bayside communities. Where once commercial fishing, logging, and farming were the main sources of one's livelihood, now restaurants, condominium developments, and gift shops catering to tourists support the regional economy.

Chapter 13 notes

[1] Lauren Mittermann, "Stuart Woerfel: A Fish Creek Fisherman", *Door County Almanac No.3*, (Sister Bay, WI: Dragonsbreath Press, 1986), 83.

[2] This entire section of text comes from several interviews with Elaine Johnson and Gretna Johns: December 16, 2003, January 16, 2003, February 3, 2003, March 3, 2003, February 4, 2004.

[3] Interview with Elaine Johnson and Gretna Johns, January, 16 2003.

[4] Ibid.

[5] Ibid.

[6] Ibid.

[7] Interview with Elaine Johnson, March 3, 2003.

[8] Interview with Elaine Johnson, June, 2003.

[9] Interview with Elaine Johnson and Gretna Johns, January 16, 2003.

[10] Interview with Elaine Johnson, April 4, 2003.

[11] Interview with Elaine Johnson and Gretna Johns, January 16, 2003.

[12] Keta Steebs "Big – Hearted Robbie was Everyone's Friend", *Door County Advocate*, January 1963.

[13] Interview with Elaine Johnson, April 3, 2003.

[14] Interview with Elaine Johnson and Gretna Johns, January 16, 2003.

[15] Ibid.

[16] Ibid.

[17] Ibid.

[18] Interview with Elaine Johnson and Gretna Johns, February 3, 2003.

[19] Ibid.

[20] Robert E. Guard and L.G. Sorden, *The Romance of Wisconsin Place Names* (New York, NY: October House Inc. 1968), 43.

[21] Ibid.

[22] Duncan Thorp, "The Thorp Family" *Fish Creek Voices* (Ellison Bay, WI: WM Caxton Ltd. 1990).

[23] "Fish Creek's Perfect Natural Harbor," Article from the *Green Bay Press Gazette*. Fishing file found in the Laurie Room, Sturgeon Bay Public Library.

[24] Ibid.

[25] Ann Thorp, "Martin Kinsey"; *Fish Creek Voices*; (Ellison Bay, WI: WM Caxton Ltd 1990), 170.

[26] Ibid.

[27] Allen Schreiber, "Fish Creek Memories," *Fish Creek Voices* (Ellison Bay, WI: WM Caxton Ltd 1990), 82.

[28] Lauren Mittermann, *Door County Almanac No. 3*, 85.

[29] Ibid, 84.

[30] Ann Thorp, "Martin Kinsey"; *Door County Almanac No. 3*, 148-149.

Pic. 13.1 The irrepressible Robbie Kodanko in his old fish truck. Circa 1960. (Photo courtesy of Elaine Johnson and Gretna Johns)

Pic. 13.2 The "Fisher Ladies" of Door County. L to R Gretna Johns and Elaine Johnson.

Pic. 13.3 Don Chambers in the background lifting a pound net near frying pan shoal aboard the *Morning Star* September 27 1933. (Photo courtesy of Door County Maritime Museum and Lighthouse Preservation Society)

Pic 13.4 Crew of the *Morning Star* at Fish Creek July 1925. (Photo courtesy of the Door County Maritime Museum and Lighthouse Preservation Society)

Chapter 14

Baileys Harbor Fisheries

Baileys Harbor is located on the eastern shore of the Door County peninsula. During the mid nineteenth century, when schooners and other sailing vessels plied the waters of Lake Michigan, this harbor proved a safe haven during heavy seas and sudden squalls. One such storm forced a schooner skippered by Captain Justice Bailey to seek shelter there in the late summer of 1848. He had delivered a cargo of wheat to Buffalo, New York, and was returning with immigrants bound for Milwaukee. The schooner was owned by Alonson Sweet, a Milwaukee businessman who hauled stone and lumber to Buffalo and to Detroit, Michigan. After passing through the Straits of Mackinac and turning southward, Captain Bailey found himself in a northeasterly gale. By the time he made it to the Door peninsula, the top-heavy schooner had lost most of its canvas and was being inundated by a heavy sea. The passengers were terrified, and Bailey sought the nearest sheltered cove or harbor. He espied the broad opening of what came to be called Baileys Harbor, but he wasn't sure of its depth or whether there were reefs to be avoided, since his charts showed no details regarding it. He took his chances and made it in without incident. The next day, the storm had subsided and he went ashore to take a look around. He found abundant limestone and dense stands of pine, maple, and beach trees which he knew would interest his employer.[1]

The following spring Mr. Sweet sent a crew to build a pier where the Brann pier and store eventually would be located. He also set up a sawmill and also soon had a stone quarry in operation. It wasn't long before several log cabins had been built and a road cut through the forest, west towards the Green Bay shore. That year, Sweet's crews cut and milled 2,500 cords of wood that were shipped to Milwaukee.

In 1851, Sweet persuaded the U.S. government of the need for a lighthouse in the area, and one was built that year on the east side of the harbor. That lighthouse operated until 1868, when the government installed a range light system in the harbor. The original lighthouse was abandoned and years later, was sold to a private owner. It can still be seen today with its unusual "birdcage" top projecting over the tops of trees on the east side of the harbor. It is one of only three lighthouses in the United States that were built with a dome, or "birdcage" style top.

In 1851, Alonson Sweet sought county status for this region from the Wisconsin legislature. He made his settlement the first county seat and named it Gibraltar, after the great rock at the western entrance to the Mediterranean, because of the limestone bluffs behind the shoreline. However, that name was not popular with local residents, and the settlement continued to be known unofficially as Baileys Harbor. In 1857, Sturgeon Bay became the county seat, and all of Door County north of Sevastopol was organized as a single town called Gibraltar. Thus, when the area around Sweet's hamlet was organized as a town in its own right, it lost the name Gibraltar and reverted to Baileys Harbor.[2]

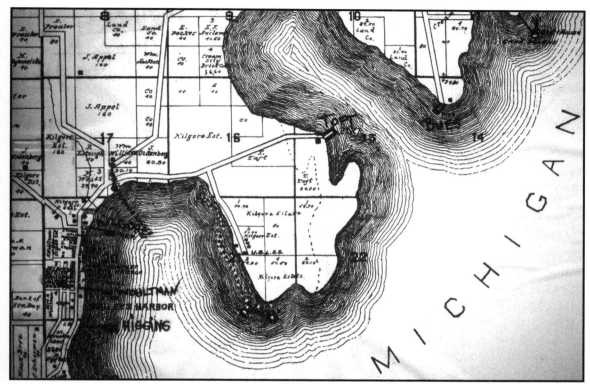

Fig. 14.1 Baileys Harbor circa 1880's showing the docks and piers. (Courtesy of Mary Ann Johnson)

Early Fisheries

After 1857, Baileys Harbor became almost a ghost town. Sweet's mill burned down, the dock fell to ruin, and only the lighthouse kept vigil over the harbor. However, by the early 1860s, more and more settlers from Norway, Sweden, Denmark, Poland, England, Germany, and Ireland were coming to this area. They cleared the land for farming and built cabins. By the late 1860s Baileys Harbor had become a well-populated area. In 1860, Moses Kilgore came to Baileys Harbor, built a pier, and began shipping out timber and cordwood. He was in the timber business until 1870, when his pier collapsed from the weight of 800 cords of green maple that were piled on the dock. He had spent $5,000 the previous year for an extension to his pier. After the ice broke up, the wood was scattered along the Lake Michigan shoreline.[3] After that, Moses pursued other interests away from the timber business. Among other things, he became a prominent local businessman, a stage coach driver, and served as a member of the County Board for many years. Moses was instrumental in procuring funds for public improvements. He promoted the idea of an improved road between Baileys Harbor and Sturgeon Bay, and, after he got himself elected to the state legislature, he got the state to appropriate the funds to build the road, which is now State Highway 57.

By the mid 1870s, Baileys Harbor was bustling with activity. There were three piers where schooners frequently called to load wood and other products. The large steamships plying the Great Lakes between Buffalo and Chicago, known as the "Buffalo boats," also made regular stops. Fredrick Woldtman, a kind-hearted German had a little store and pier, (the future Anclam pier). William Higgins and his son Allen had a pier, sawmill, and hotel, and the community was locally known as "Frogtown."

Early settlers in this part of the peninsula took advantage of the abundance of fish in the waters around Baileys Harbor, and some of the first commercial fisheries operated from Mud Bay, now called Moonlight Bay, around 1854. Some set a few pound nets from their Mackinaw boats and found Mud Bay teeming with whitefish. Early accounts tell of two fishermen, Adam Hendricks and Ernest Bues, who often caught so many fish that they would be nearly waist deep in them standing in their boat. They took their catch to Baileys Harbor where they would be shipped to market on the schooners and steam vessels.[4]

A few miles north of Moonlight Bay lies North Bay, deeply indented into the Peninsula but rather shallow. In the 1920s, a few fishermen operated from near Reibolts Creek in North Bay. Two brothers, Frank and Bill Innas, and their partners Charlie Rohrbuck and Bart Retty had a fishery called North Bay Fish Company. Bart eventually dissolved the partnership and embarked on his own fishing business, which he called the Independent Fish Company. Henry Williams and his son Floyd had a dock just south the North Bay Fish Company and fished with pound nets. However, by the 1930s, most of these fishermen had quit fishing from North Bay.

Prior to 1900, there were only a few fishermen in Baileys Harbor. Most were farmers who set a few pound nets and fished part time. The Paehlers, originally from Cedar River, Michigan, fished out of Baileys Harbor in the early 1850s. They used pound nets with stones and floats as well as seine nets for herring. Godfried Nelson, a farmer who lived just west of town, occasionally fished with a hook and line rig and was quite successful. He was a brother-in-law to Adam Hendricks, who fished out of Mud Bay. Alfred Olander came to Baileys Harbor from Finland in 1878 and fished for many years from his dock and shed on the east side of the harbor. He fished with gill nets in a small wooden boat named after his daughter, Alene. Besides being a successful fisherman, he was active in the town government and served as a town supervisor for several years.[5]

After 1900, Baileys Harbor grew steadily, and the number of fishermen increased as well. For the next seventy years Baileys Harbor boasted many successful commercial fisheries as it was close to one of the best fishing grounds for whitefish in Lake Michigan. Around 1910, two older Danish fishermen, Paetchaw and Fredrickson, fished with hook and line rigs from their boat *Una*. Their fishery was just north of the old Moses Kilgore pier (later the Brann pier) at the north end of town. Alfred Kalmbach, a prominent local fisherman and fish buyer from Sturgeon Bay, had a crew operating out of Baileys Harbor for several years. He hired men from the area to run his boats, which were moored at a dock on the east side of the harbor.

John Anclam, a prominent early citizen of Baileys Harbor, fished many years from his pier in Baileys Harbor. In addition to fishing, John was also a storekeeper, postmaster, and wood supplier. He used a hook and line rig and also had a few seine nets that he set close to shore for Menominees (a small variety of whitefish) and suckers. When the fish schooled near the shore, he and a few other men would encircle them with seine nets, and a shore crew would reel the nets in using large reels. John had five sons, and two of them, George and Lester, helped their father in the fishing business.[6]

Alfred (another son of John's) and George Anclam began fishing on their own in the early 1920s. They had two pound-net boats, *Mike* and *Rosy* from which they set pound nets in the harbor. After a few years, George left Baileys Harbor, leaving Alfred to fish alone. Alfred worked for Bill Andregg for a while before acquiring property on the east side of the harbor where he built a dock and fish sheds. Alfred continued fishing with pound nets, but he also began using gill nets after acquiring a 35-foot wood gill net boat called the *John*. After a few years he sold the *John* to Stuart Woerfel and bought the *Pelican*, a 55-foot gill-net boat built by the Lotti Brothers. Alfred was known to convert automobile engines into marine engines for his boats and then replace them with marine engines when he could afford to buy one. His last boat was the *Pat*, which was only 35 feet long. Over the years, Alfred fished for whitefish, perch, chubs, and lake trout. He fished alone and would employ other men to help out when the fishing was good. Marvin Weborg and his father used Alfred's dock and fished with him for several years in the 1940s. Alfred continued to fish until he was well into his seventies.

Bill Andregg came from Algoma and began fishing from Baileys Harbor in the 1920s. He formed a partnership with another fisherman named Buck Lauscher. They had a wooden gill-net boat called the *Silver Leaf*. Bill later dissolved his partnership with Buck and he and another fisherman from Kewaunee, Wencel Horack, began fishing together. They had Ernest Anclam, John Anclam's brother, build them a boat which they named *America*. Ernest built many fishing boats and rowboats and was known for producing good sea-worthy craft. He always used heavy hardwood for the hull material and built his boats to withstand the Lake Michigan seas. To help preserve the boats, he mixed fish oil in with the paint, which he used to finish them.[7]

Vernon Miller began working at the age of nine after his father passed away. He first worked for Lois Prueter, who ran a shingle and lathing mill in Baileys Harbor, and he began working for Bill Andregg when he was twelve. When Vernon was sixteen years old, he moved to Sturgeon Bay with Bill Andregg, who began fishing from there. Soon after moving to Sturgeon Bay, Vernon formed a partnership with Ole Meunier, and they purchased a wood hull gill net tug called the *Dorothy*. Vernon subsequently married a woman named Gen, and she began helping Vernon in the business after they bought out Ole's share. This was the beginning of a long-term husband and wife team in the fishing business. They sold the *Dorothy* and bought another fish tug called *Maggie*. Finally they had their own boat built for them. Vernon called it the *Gen*, after his wife.[8]

As word spread in the early 1900s of the bounty of fish around Baileys Harbor, Mud Bay, North Bay and Whitefish Bay, many fishermen came to Baileys Harbor from Algoma. Ole Meunier was one of those Algoma fishermen. He and his brother-in-law, Oscar Peterson, fished for several years from Baileys Harbor. Oscar was known for using a wheelbarrow to transport his nets to and from the dock to his home, where he reeled, dried, and mended his nets. In the winter months he rigged skis to his wheelbarrow. Ole Meunier also fished with nets under the ice during the winter months.

Another Algoma fisherman who came to Baileys Harbor was Minor "Dag" Dagneau. He arrived in 1912 and started out fishing with Ole Meunier. In 1919, he formed a partnership with Oscar Peterson and Ole. A short time later he bought Oscar Peterson's and then Ole's share in the partner-

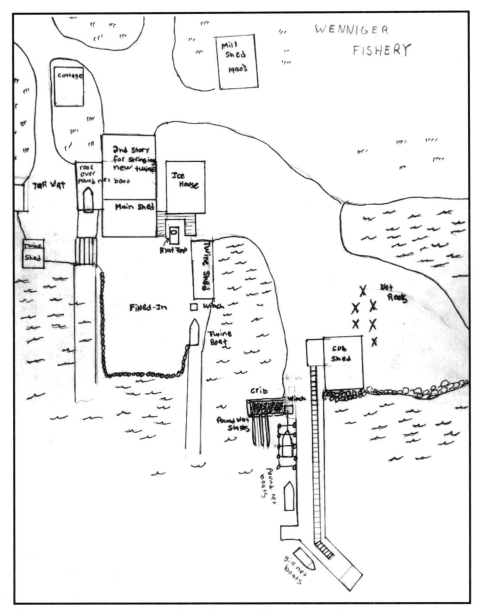

Fig.14.2 Wenniger docks and shed layout. (Courtesey of Pat Orsted)

ship. During the 1920s, Dag began fishing with Charley Heald, who had fished with Bert LeClair out of Jacksonport before moving to Baileys Harbor; they formed a partnership that lasted nearly twelve years. One year, in ten days they came in with 10 tons of whitefish. They hired anyone who was willing and able to work to help dress the fish. There were so many fish that Charley Anderson's truck-ing company couldn't keep up, so they hired Herb Olson to haul the fish to the Chicago markets. Dag retired from fishing in the early 1930s and bought a saloon in Jacksonport.[9]

Charley Heald continued to fish from Baileys Harbor with his son Eugene, who began fishing with his father at the age of seventeen. They used the north leg of the Brann brothers pier located on the west end of the harbor, this was a long pier that ran out diagonally from the shore and then hooked north. Many fishermen used this dock over the years. Later, Charley and Gene moved to the east side of the harbor where they bought property and built a dock and some fish sheds just north of Alfred Anclam's pier and south of Cliff Wenniger's pier. Charley and Gene fished together for many years until Charley suffered a heart attack and died while out fishing one day in 1934. Gene con-tinued to fish for a while, but then sold the rig and began fishing for Cliff Wenniger.

Wenniger Fishery

Cliff Wenniger was born in Algoma, Wisconsin, in 1899 to George and Theresa Weber Wenniger. He began his long and illustrious career as a commercial fisherman at the age of thirteen and had one of the largest fisheries on Lake Michigan. His father George passed away in April 1912 when Cliff was 13 years old and had completed the eighth grade. He had to take over his father's fishery in Algoma to provide for the family. He began fishing with his father's Mackinaw boats *Fae* and *Clifford W*. He later built houses on them and installed gasoline engines for power. In the 1920s, he fished the Whitefish Bay area of northern Door County.

In October 1930, Cliff married Mabel Kuhlhanek, and the next spring decided to move his oper-ations to Bailey's Harbor. He knew this was one of the best whitefish grounds in Lake Michigan. Cliff bought the Jack Stoneman property on Lighthouse Point, on the east side of Baileys Harbor. Some say Cliff actually acquired the property in a card game.[10] Cliff improved the land and dock for his extensive operations. He built nearly all the buildings on and around his dock. The pier ran out 300 feet to the west, then doglegged slightly to the southwest. The main shed, located northeast of the pier, was used for fish processing. In the back, on the main floor, was the cooler room. The main shed had a second story used for stringing new twine for pound nets. On the main floor was a work station with a compressor, workbench and tools. Cliff later installed an ice crusher in the main shed. The icehouse was next to the main shed. If good ice could not be harvested in the harbor, Cliff and his crew got it from nearby Kangaroo Lake.

The harbor side of the main shed was filled in with limestone held in place by cedar cribs. In a small slip between that area and the main dock boats unloaded the fish. That was also where fisher-men washed the pound nets with a hose attached to a high-pressure pump.

A shed on the dock which they called the "cub shed" was used for washing and reeling nets. The reels were stored in front of the shed. Nets were reeled outside in the warmer months and inside if the weather was bad. A wood stove stood at the entrance of the shed under the roof. The shore crew would repair pound nets on the mending lot located north of the main shed. There the pound nets were treated with tar to preserve them and stored in the twine shed near the water. The gill net boats were moored at the end of the dock, while the pound net boats were near shore. Cliff did not want to relocate his family to Baileys Harbor and chose to commute every day from Algoma. His wife Mabel and two daughters, Pat and Liz, came and stayed in Baileys Harbor during the summer months.

Cliff was an innovator. One of the first things he did was to install tracks from the end of the dock to the fish shed. A cart that ran on the tracks was used to haul the boxes of nets, ice, and the catch of the day. Another famous Cliff invention was what the crew called "flat tops." These were stripped down automobiles, late 1920s and 1930s models. On each of them, Cliff built a raised flat-bed built on the chassis running from the front of the vehicle and extending 8 or 10 feet behind the drivers seat and 2 feet out from both sides of the vehicle. They were used for hauling fish boxes and twine. The beds were typically three to four feet from the ground in order to make loading and unloading fairly easier. Cliff typically had four of these built and running at any given time. At first, Cliff bought his fish boxes from Barney Haefert, who operated a sawmill in Baileys Harbor. Later, in the 1940s, Cliff built his own sawmill where a few men made wood fish boxes during slow times or in the off season. There was always a task to be done.

Cliff employed a number of engines for various tasks. One was attached to a winch that was used to pull the pound net boats out of the water at the end of the season. The boats were suspended on timber frames during the winter months. Another engine powered a pump to provide lake water for washing out the boats and net boxes. Cliff's grandson, Greg Orsted, found out the hard way about the power of the water coming from that pump:

> I think I was around sixteen years old, and I worked for my grandfather during the summer months. One day I was with Pete Husby and a few others and we were going to clean one of the nets that were clogged with scum. Grandpa had a 30-horsepower engine hooked up to a pump and a three-inch pipe that ran overhead and down to a fire hose, which was very powerful. Of course, being a dumb sixteen year old [I didn't know] when a practical joke was coming down the road. The guys went and shut down all the bypass valves, so when it came on it flopped me around like a rag doll. I was only about one hundred fifty pounds so you can imagine what it did to me. Then it got stuck underneath my oilers, so I got thoroughly doused, and then it flew out of my hands and flopped around before it broke. Everyone was laughing at me. Grandpa's only comment was, 'Wrecked a perfectly good hose.' That was some ordeal.[11]

Cliff Wenniger had the largest fishery in northern Door County, and he employed more than fifty different men over the years. He had crews operating gill-net boats and crews working pound nets. His daughter Pat Orsted said that she thought her father worked harder in his later years than he did when he was younger. It was somewhat ironic that Cliff couldn't swim a stroke and rarely skippered his boats, preferring to be part of the crew helping out or shouting orders. Phil Albertson, a long-time skipper of one of one gill net crew remembered:

> Cliff had five gill-net boats in operation and would run four pound-net boats at one

time. He was always buying and selling and was always with us on the lake. He would always holler through a bullhorn that he had. He would never steer or run the boat, and if you'd ask him to steer, he'd just walk away.[12]

Elaine Johnson recalled a time she had the pleasure of going along with Cliff one day to retrieve some perch nets on one of his gill-net boats:

I went out with him one day out near Hat Island. He was lying up in Fish Creek with one of his gill-net boats. In those days Gretna and I were buying perch from the fishermen. So I said, "Gee, Cliff, I'll go along with you if you don't mind. I'm not afraid of picking perch." I think we lifted four or five hundred pounds of perch that day. I was going to buy them all from him. Well anyway, we were heading back and coming around by the dock. I kept hollering to him, "Put 'er in reverse Cliff! Put 'er in reverse!" I seen he wasn't going to, so I grabbed onto whatever I could. Then Ker-Blam! We hit the dock hard. I'll never forget that day.[13]

When he began his operation in Baileys Harbor, Cliff had the gill-net boat the *Beaver*, which was built in 1926. Cliff acquired her in 1930, before moving his operation to Baileys Harbor. She was a 40-foot wood hull boat, as were most of his gill-net boats. From his first boat the *Clifford W*, which he proudly nicknamed the "Wooden Shoe", to his last gill net boat, he had a love for wooden boats. Phil Albertson said that Cliff had most of his boats built with wood hulls and then he and his crew would build the houses on them. Cliff had the *Cub* built at Little Suamico, Wisconsin, in 1936. It was a wood hull boat with a length of 34 feet and was different from other fish tugs in that the engine was located in the forward section with the shaft running all the way through the hull to the aft section. *Cub* was a very well-built boat and fared well in big seas. The original engine was a Chrysler Marine engine that lasted only a year before it had to be replaced. This boat was a workhorse for the gill net operation and provided service until 1953 when Cliff sold it to his brother Francis "Toots" Wenniger of Algoma.

Phil Albertson worked for Cliff for nearly thirty-five years. He worked on all of Cliff's boats and for many years skippered the *C.G.* Phil later bought the *C.G.* and operated out of Sheboygan for many years. The first boat he fished from was the *Cub*. During the winter, he fished her out of Racine and Kenosha. Phil recalled:

When I brought the *Cub* up from Kenosha, it took Buster and me three days to get up to Algoma. When we left Kenosha it was 35 degrees below zero. We got into Racine and the only open water was near the shore. We came in the back way and some of the guys there were surprised we made it in at all. We stayed over in Racine until 9:30 the next morning where the temperature was still around 30 degrees below zero when we left the dock. The lake wasn't steaming quite as bad as the day before, although it did take us two days to make it up to Manitowoc, where we had to gas up. We got stuck in the ice trying to get in there and had to shut the engine down. We just sat there. Then there was a car ferry that came out and passed us, and then turned around and came back as another one was coming out and made a circle around us breaking up the ice before towing the other car ferry back in. It must have had trouble getting through the heavy ice. When we finally got into the Manitowoc River it was blowing a gale from the northeast. We ended up staying there two days as it blew hard and dumped three feet of snow, but fortunately for us it broke up all the ice out of the river so we could get out. So we finally made it to Algoma where Cliff had the *C.G* almost ready to take up to Baileys Harbor. It was almost a week before we took off from there.[14]

In 1939, Cliff had another gill net boat, the *Bear*, built at Little Suamico. This boat was a 36-foot wood-hull vessel that replaced the *Beaver* in his gill net fleet. His next boat was the *C.G* built in Green Bay. Cliff had only the hull built and then shipped it up to Baileys Harbor where he and his crew fabricated the house. The *C.G* was 45 feet in length and had an International diesel engine in her. Phil Albertson and then Laurence Daubner skippered the *C.G* for a while in the 1960s. Most of the gill netters were used for harvesting chubs and would sometimes go as far as the Manitou islands. During the winter, the crews would move them south to lower Lake Michigan and fish for chubs. Phil Albertson recalled:

I remember the first time we were sent over to the Manitou Islands, my brother and I, to fish chubs. The Coast Guard plotted me the course, which included the compass heading and time from the range lights here in Baileys Harbor. They figured our time to get over there to South Manitou Island to be three hours and forty-five minutes. Well, that's where we wanted to go. There's a town of Empire on one of the islands. We set ten boxes of nets. We threw the buoy in and it hit bottom right away. It was foggy that day and we weren't too sure where we were, so we set the nets and headed back on that heading the Coast Guard gave us. The next morning we went back out and found our nets and had only a box and a half of chubs from lifting the first half gang of nets. We were also getting some Menominee whitefish. It ended up we were only in six fathoms of water with part of our nets. There was a reef out there on the outside. Our actual time there was only two hours and fifty-five minutes. We went through just a little north and found the rest of the nets in ninety-five fathoms where we were getting the deep water chubs, which have all but disappeared now.[15]

During the winter months Cliff shut his fishing operation down after the last of the pound nets were removed from the water or when the ice set in the harbor. Some of his gill net crews would operate his boats out of Algoma or some of the southern ports on Lake Michigan. Cliff would resume his fishing operations back in Baileys Harbor in April or after ice-out. This was the time when his pound-net crews were busy setting stakes and running twine. He had five pound-net boats with three to four man crews to operate the pound-net fishery. The Northport crew set a half dozen pound nets in and around Death's Door. Those were 70-foot and 90-foot pound nets to accommodate the deep water of the Door, and the crew also had to deal with strong currents while they set the stakes and twine. Orval Orsted remembered:

Yyou had to get there early and get your lift or set up, because sometimes those currents made it a bear to work. If you got there after eight in the morning the twine was almost lying flat from the current. Oscar Knutson knew just how to work the ropes on the "nigger head" [fishermen's term for a winch to pull the ropes on the nets]. He knew enough how to slip the rope so they wouldn't snap.[16]

Cliff's Baileys Harbor crew set pound nets in Moonlight Bay, North Bay, and Whitefish Bay. Cliff also sent a crew out to Minneapolis shoals, but his nets were sabotaged by local fishermen, who cut the twine, rendering the net useless. (This sometimes happened to fishermen who set nets in different areas of the lakes. Local fishermen were often very protective of their fishing grounds, and, if local fishing grounds were invaded by so-called transient fishermen, their nets were often vandalized.) Cliff also had a crew setting nets near the Manitou Islands. Boats were coming and going at a steady rate from the Wenniger dock. During the 1960s, when whitefish were scarce and the herring were gone, Cliff harvested alewives. Even if the fishing was poor or the markets unstable, Cliff always made a go of it.

Pound nets were set in April, taken out in August for maintenance, then reset in mid to late September for the fall run of whitefish coming into the shallow waters of the bays and harbors to spawn. Cliff processed whitefish roe for caviar in his processing shed, and he smoked chubs and trout.

Cliff's crews were all hard-working men and he always treated them well. He once said, "Give a lazy man a job to do, and he'll find an easy way to do it." The boats left the dock promptly at 7:00 a.m. Elaine Johnson told about a time when Eddie LaPlant, who worked for Cliff, was a little late one morning:

Eddie was a great guy and a hard worker but wasn't very bright. One morning he arrived a little late and Cliff was already pulling away from the dock. Cliff saw Eddie running on the dock and hollered, "Get aboard! Get aboard! Eddie stopped when he heard Cliff holler. He turned around, headed back toward the shed and grabbed a one by six board and started back down the dock. Cliff shouted back, "No, you old fool, I mean get on the boat – jump on board.[17]

On Friday afternoons during the warm days of early fall, it wasn't uncommon for Cliff to throw a fish boil for his crews, friends, and the families of the fishermen. He had cold beer and fresh whitefish or trout, to offer them. Pat Orsted, Cliff's daughter, remembered these events fondly. Cliff always made sure his crews were paid weekly, and he liked to pay them in cash. Later on in the fall, he had venison to give to the men.

Some of Cliff's pound-net boats were all-steel boats with unusual names, such as *Spot, Rastus, Can, Liza, Lulu, Tub,* and *Bo.* Some are still in service today and are used by other fishermen in the county. The *Tub* found a new life with Jeff and Mark Weborg as the *Heather* J. The *Rastus* was sold to

Wallace Weborg in Gills Rock and was used for many years for a pound-net operation. Hickey's have a few of the old pound-net boats resting quietly near their sheds, out of service but standing as a reminder of days gone by.

Longtime crew members and friends of Cliff include Oscar Knudson, Eddie LaPlant, Lexie Nelson, Norman Ostreum, Lloyd "Futsy" Ostreum, "Rusty" Meyer, Pete Husby, Bill Apple, Orval Orsted, and Phil Albertson. In 2006, only a few of these men are still alive.

Many fishermen couldn't swim a stroke and never wore a life vest. Moreover, they rarely thought about drowning or falling overboard. Over the forty years the Wenniger fishery existed, there were few mishaps. The only fatal incident involved the loss of two men and occurred within a half-mile of the dock. Laurence Daubner was one of the crew members to escape death that day. He told the story to Leonard Peterson:

> At the time, we were fishing for Cliff Wenniger in Baileys Harbor. We were fishing for those alewives. We had nets over by Cana Island. When we pulled in the nets, a lot of water also came into the boat. There was an automatic self-bailer that removed the water when it became too deep. We were accustomed to loading the boat quite heavy, which was the case that day. On our return trip, Norman Ostreum was steering the boat, and so Glen Sitte and I decided to go into a place under the cabin to eat our lunch. It wasn't long before we saw Willy Carlson out on the deck meddling with the floorboards with a pail in his hand. As soon as we had our lunch, we went out on the deck to see if there was any trouble. When we inquired, he replied that the self-bailer wasn't working and the water hadn't been pumping out. Furthermore, with the wind as it was, a little water kept lapping into the stern of the boat because it was lying so low, and the stern was sinking more and more. I stood on the deck boards to hold them down so the fish wouldn't float out, until I saw it was useless. The motor was up in the front and working well so we felt that all was still right. It wasn't long, however, before the stern of the boat was one-third under water and I was still trying to hold the boards with my weight. When the boat was about one-half under and pitched at about a twenty degree angle, I hollered to Norman that he should head for shore in case there was danger of sinking, and I, too, went up front where it was still dry.
>
> I could see we were in danger and I tried to decide if I should leave my high boots on or take them off. Before I had time to make up my mind, the motor stopped. I told Norman, "Don't check 'er down, 'keep 'er going." He assured me he hadn't cut the motor. (We figured out later that the motor wouldn't draw the gas up at such a steep angle.) She went backwards, down like a bullet, in about twenty feet of water. None of us were "chicken" enough to put on life preservers which were hanging there within reach, but Glen and I just dove in the water and headed for shore, the last few feet being the worst because it was deep inside the reef and there was a terrific undertow. When we got to shore we were exhausted but shouted to some people at a cottage who notified the Wenniger's of our plight.

Looking out at the sinking boat they saw it was still afloat a little at the bow. Willy and Norman were still on it. It was only a few minutes before the bow also went under, leaving the two remaining crewmembers at the mercy of the sea. We knew Willy couldn't swim. All we saw was a few splashes and he disappeared. Norman started to swim and was doing well until he came past the reef when the undertow took him under and he didn't come up. We thought it strange that he never came up, which usually happens, especially if one can't swim. We found out why he didn't.

When the Coast Guard found him, his foot was stuck in a crevice and he was standing upright in the water. That was what held him from coming up.It was a tragic accident. The boat was recovered the next day and it was discovered that the bilge pump had become clogged and was unable to pump the water from the boat.[18]

Orval Orsted told about a time when he and his son Ervin were out on the lake to bring in twine and anchors from a pound net before the onset of winter. Ervin was in the twine net boat *Lulu*, and Orval was in another near Cana Island:

There was one boat that nearly cost me my life towards the end of my career. Cliff had put a reduction gear in one of his pound-net boats – I can't recall which one it was now – and when he put it in, he moved the engine ahead a few feet. It was almost like a snowplow in the water with the engine moved ahead, [because] it made the boat bow-heavy. My son Ervin ("Goober") and I were heading back in from pulling some twine on a pound net. He was ahead of me with the *Lulu* and we started hitting some big rollers, damn near the size of this house, you know. I damn near panicked. The waves were beginning to overcome the boat, then it dawned on me to idle it down. I rode those big rollers real slow like a piece of wood. One of those big combers spun the boat and threw me from the side of the house clear over to the other side of the boat, almost knocking me overboard. You should have seen when we got back in. All the flooring was pushed way up in the bow. As soon as I tied her up I opened her up to get the water out of her. I was shaking so badly, I really didn't think I was going to make it back in – I thought that was it. I still get shivers when I think back on that day. That area out by Cana Island, if there's only a ripple in the water anywhere else, it always seemed to be pounding out there. I sure have a great respect and fear for the lake now, I'll tell you.[19]

During the 1960s, many fishermen in Door County suffered low harvests of whitefish, but that didn't deter Cliff. Being a man who knew how to improvise, he began harvesting alewives. The fish were processed into feed for mink and for dogs and cats. He shipped the alewives to Pensaukee, Wisconsin, on an old dump truck that they nicknamed the "Pensaukee Queen." Pat Orsted told of a time when Jeff Hickey was making a run up to Pensaukee with a load of alewives:

Jeff was on his way up there and had to stop for gas. The truck was fully loaded with fish and you can imagine what it smelled like, especially after the fish were sitting for some time in the heat of the day. Jeff went into pay for the gas and the owner said to Jeff, "I appreciate your business, but the next time you stop for gas I wouldn't mind at all if you'd stop at my competitor's station." It was not so much the smell as it was the slime that was oozing out of the back of the truck and leaving a mess in the lot.[20]

Nearly all of Cliff Wenniger's life was spent on the lake as a commercial fisherman. By the late 1960s and early 1970s, Cliff's grandchildren were working for him and were on their way to learning the craft he loved. Cliff sold his dock property to Bill Wilde, and it later became the Baileys Harbor Yacht Club. He sold it with the stipulation that he could fish from there for five years. Cliff's daughter Pat explained: "My Dad didn't think he was going to live much longer than that so that's why he made a five year deal."[21]

Some of the buildings such as the twine shed and saw mill were moved up to where the Hickey's have their fishery now. The other buildings were removed to make way for the Yacht Club.

Cliff's health began to fail by 1974 and it became harder for him to go out on the lake. Orval remembered how Cliff, in his waning years and declining health, still tried to go out and fish:

> You think you could've kept him on shore? There wasn't really anything that could keep him from going out and fish. He went as far as welding a piece of flat iron on the inside of the ribs of the boat for a platform he could step on to work. But it took one guy to watch over him so he wouldn't fall. He just got to be in the way. So it was hard to see him give up something he loved.[22]

Cliff died in 1975. His pound net gear, gill nets, and pound net boats were purchased by Dennis and Jeff Hickey who had began their fishery some years earlier. They had worked for Cliff for a season and when they were in high school.

Hickey Brothers Fishery

Baileys Harbor has a rich history of logging, farming, and commercial fishing, and the waters nearby have proven to be one of the best whitefish grounds in Lake Michigan. In the past, many fishermen found an ample harvest of whitefish, lake trout, and chubs within fifteen miles of Baileys Harbor, and in 1900 it would not have been uncommon to see a dozen pound-net rigs in the harbor. Now, a century later, pound nets have all but disappeared from the waters of Lake Michigan. Two local commercial fishermen, Dennis and Jeff Hickey, are the last commercial fishery on Lake Michigan to still use (and with great success) a pound-net rig for whitefish. They have been using pound nets since they began fishing on their own in the late 1960s. Dennis Hickey commented:

> [A pound net is] a tremendous piece of gear for fishing. It's our best type of gear for fall fishing. We used to fish pound nets in the spring and summer, but the cormorants got to be such a problem, they literally ruined our spring and summer fish-

ery. In the spring, the cormorants get in the nets and spear all the whitefish, slashing and chasing them. It actually drove the whitefish to deeper water, so we gave up the pound nets until the fall of the year, and we use our trap nets in the spring and summer months.

The pound nets are ideal for us. Some say using pound nets, that's old time stuff. Well the catch per unit effort is five to one over a trap net. It's definitely more of a volume-type fishery and, compared to the trap nets, it's a lot easier to handle the fish, especially when you have to release the salmon and trout. We stay within fifty feet of water with our pound nets. We used to go over that, but we were getting too many trout and couldn't handle all of them. Now that the whitefish stocks go deeper in the summer, the best time to catch whitefish is in the fall of the year when they come into the shallows to spawn. We take 70 percent of our quota in the fall of the year.[23]

The Hickey Brothers' fishery is located on the east side of Baileys Harbor, just south of the Yacht Club & Condominiums. From the Hickey dock flies the American flag along with a Norwegian and a Swedish flag, indicative of their ancestry. Moored to the dock is their well-maintained fleet of boats, consisting of two gill-net boats, the *Southwester*, and *Hickey Brothers*, which is in dry dock but not quite retired yet, and their trap-net and pound-net boats *Norska, Sheepshead*, and *Leif*, which is used as their anchor boat. Both trap-net boats have been rebuilt and modified by Dennis and Jeff to accommodate their needs and to optimize their fishery.

Dennis and Jeff Hickey are third generation fishermen following in the footsteps of their grandfather Martin Hickey. Martin grew up on Rennesøy Island, off the coast from Stavangar, Norway. When he came of age, he began sailing on schooners that hauled mahogany to the Caribbean. After a few years he gave up sailing and headed up the Mississippi River. In the early 1850s, he settled in Baileys Harbor.[24]

Martin lived in a small log cabin for a few years near what is now the Lutheran church, and began fishing small pound nets in the harbor. He had a sail-powered mackinaw boat which he used to set hooks. He used hook and line rigs and pound nets for many years before setting gill nets. He had a small pound-net rig to catch herring, which were used as bait for lake trout that were so abundant in the lake at that time. In the early 1860s, Martin bought the Moses Kilgore house and farm in Baileys Harbor. Moses had built the house two years earlier. It once stood where the town hall is today.[25]

Martin Hickey was industrious. He acquired land from the federal government both around Mud Bay and west of Baileys Harbor, where he began farming as well as running a logging operation. Martin built a dock just north of the Brann pier that ran northeast out into the harbor. He had an icehouse and another shed for packing fish and storing nets. The fish were shipped out in the early days on the hookers that frequented Baileys Harbor and other ports along Door County.

In 1915, Martin Hickey acquired the *Pathfinder* after many years of fishing with a mackinaw boat. The *Pathfinder* was built in1905 by master boat builder H. R. Burger and was originally named the *Minnie R.* In 1914, she collided with the *Pere Marquette 17* near Kewaunee where four people were rescued.[26] It was dropped from the registry then was put back into service after Martin purchased it. The

Pathfinder was a 32-foot wood-hull boat, equipped with a two-cylinder Straubel engine. A few years later he had a Crossley lifter installed on the *Pathfinder* that allowed him to double the number of his gill nets and increase his harvest of fish. Martin fished with the *Pathfinder* until 1929. It was dropped from registry in 1930 after running aground in Baileys Harbor.[27]

Martin Hickey married Lena Schermer, daughter of a German immigrant farmer who had settled west of Baileys Harbor. Martin and Lena had four boys, Martin Jr., Dewey, Lewis, and Bill. The boys helped on the farm and in the fishery. They fished together for five years, until Martin Sr. decided to get into the tavern business and built the Cape Cod Inn. He ran the tavern while his sons ran the fishery. Each eventually went out on his own. Lewis became a life saving officer in the Coast Guard, as did Martin's brother Reinhard Hickey after coming over to America from Norway. Martin persuaded his brother to come to this new land where the fishing was good and land was cheap. Reinhard and Martin fished together for awhile before Reinhard took a job working at the Baileys Harbor Life Saving Station located on the east side of the harbor.

After Lewis quit fishing, Dewey moved to Sturgeon Bay and began fishing with the Allies. Martin Jr. and Bill continued fishing together until 1929 when they had to make a decision. The country was in the midst of the Great Depression, and they were forced to sell some property or the fish rig. They decided to part with the fish rig and they sold the *Pathfinder* and all the gear to a fisherman from Egg Harbor. "They had to make a tough choice," said Dennis Hickey, son of Bill Hickey. "During the depression they had to decide to either keep the fish rig or keep the land. They kept the land and we're damn glad he did." Martin Jr. moved on to Two Rivers and Bill continued farming and fishing with other fisherman. He worked for Cliff Wenniger for a few years then took a job during World War II at the shipyards in Sturgeon Bay, building boats for the war effort.[28]

After the war, Bill worked for the Allies fishery in Sturgeon Bay and then for Roy Nelson from Fayette, Michigan, who fished with pound nets. Later, he fished out of Milwaukee for Kohlbeck fishery. Bill was a hard worker, supporting his wife Ruth and four boys, Dennis, Jeff, John, and Dean. Besides running the farms, Bill continued to fish until 1973, though there was a period of nearly eight years when he didn't fish at all because the fishing was very poor.

After high school, Dennis Hickey spent four years in the U.S. Navy. Jeff, who was a year and a half younger, worked for Public Service after he graduated from high school. After serving in the Navy, Dennis went to the National School of Meat Cutting in Ohio and then headed west to California and joined the Safeway Foods team. Dennis recalled:

It was a great job, I made a good living working in Idaho and California for Safeway Foods. I lived in southern California with my twin brothers, Jeff and John. We had a great time out there. I wasn't married at the time. But Jeff and I [soon] had enough of California, with four lanes of traffic and all the people. We decided to come back home. John stayed out there and still lives out there today.[29]

In the spring of 1965, Dennis and Jeff left the West Coast and came back to Baileys Harbor. Dennis recalled:

After we got back we hadn't thought about fishing. We were just having a good time that summer. Cliff Wenniger spotted us one day and said to us, "Why don't you boys come and help me for the summer." They were fishing for alewives that summer, which were finding a market for fertilizer and animal food. The first week working for him we went and cut some trees for pound net stakes up by his land and brought them over – he was getting ready to set some pound nets for alewives, so we brought them over to his dock. He was gone for most of the day, and when he returned around 4:00 in the afternoon we had that whole pile of pound net stakes stacked and peeled. He drove in the driveway looked down at them, then at us. He got this big smile on his face. I can look back and still remember him saying, 'Oh Boy! Do I have a crew now!'"[30]

Dennis and Jeff worked that summer for Cliff doing various jobs on shore and on the lake. Jeff drove the truck dubbed the "Pensaukee Queen "to haul alewives to a place in Pensaukee where they processed into oil for paint and fish meal used in animal feed. That fall, Dennis and Jeff decided they would strike off on their own and start their own fishery. Dennis Hickey said:

That summer working for Cliff kind of grew on us. We got hooked on it. One thing we noticed that kind of swayed us to get into the business was that while we were catching the alewives in the pound nets we were noticing quite a few 6-inch whitefish, which during the 1960s were pretty scarce. These little whitefish were in with the alewives and our dad said, "You know, those whitefish are going to start coming back in a couple of year's time." I think that same fall or the following spring we bought a gill-net boat and had a couple of lifts of 100 to 200 pounds.[31]

In the fall of 1965, the Hickey Brothers Fishery came to be. Dennis and Jeff began fishing for alewives with pound nets in the harbor. They got a little more than one cent a pound for alewives. Their first gill-net boat was called *Pathfinder*, aptly named after their grandfather's boat and purchased in the spring of 1966. It was a 40-foot wood hull gill-net tug. Dennis recalled:

She was a good boat to start out with, a fairly modern wood boat built in 1955. It had a new Cat diesel engine and a stainless steel bottom and stainless steel shaft. It was a long narrow boat; however it was fairly heavy, with heavy planking. It rode pretty nice for being a narrow boat, of course wooden boats ride nicely any how. Dennis's brother Jeff added:

We had a boat within a year after working for Cliff. It was after I got married and was working for Public Service. Dennis was still fishing, so we decided to look for a boat for ourselves. We looked all around the lake and finally found a boat we could afford. We found it in Marinette but it was originally built in Bessemer, Michigan.

We could have bought the *McDonald Brothers,* but we decided that it was too much money. I'm glad we went the route we did. You can over invest and get caught up in a big overhead, which can drown you if you don't watch out. You have to keep an eye on the return in your investment.[32]

The Hickeys began fishing gill nets with the *Pathfinder.* In 1966, they had some substantial lifts of whitefish after their father, Bill, suggested that they try pound nets. They followed their father's advice and began to set a few pound nets with his help. Success prompted them to buy a few more. Bill was very familiar with pound nets, having fished with them throughout his career as a commercial fisherman.

In 1972, they bought their second gill-net boat, which they named the *Hickey Brothers.* It was a 35-foot boat built by Marinette Marine that they bought in Benton Harbor, Michigan. It originally was called the *James E.* They kept the *Hickey Brothers* tug a long time, though at the end it sat on land behind the dock where it once was moored. Said Dennis:

> There is nothing wrong with her. We used it for setting float nets in the fall. It's excellent for that purpose, but if you have to handle a lot of nets and fish it gets a little cramped in there. She's not a very big boat. For a two-man crew she's real nice. [But] there just isn't enough room for all our equipment.[33]

In 2005, Jay Virlee purchased the boat and renamed it the *Net Worth.*

The year they bought the *Hickey Brothers,* 1972, they also had a pound-net boat built by T.D Vinette Boat Company in Escanaba. Michigan. It was a 35-foot all-steel boat with a Volvo engine that they originally used for gill nets. They named the boat the *Leif* after Jeff Hickey's son. Jeff commented:

> When we bought the *Leif*, it was used for setting gill nets up in Michigan and everyone said, "You can't make a pound-net boat out of a boat that big, and you're putting a diesel engine in besides." Now it's considered small by today's standards.[34]

The *Leif* was used for setting pound nets and is still in service in 2006, although it is used as their anchor boat and for setting the stakes. In the past 6 years the Hickey Brothers Fishery has grown into a substantial fishery. Dennis and Jeff are adept mechanics and are constantly modifying and revamping their fish rigs and apparatus to their own specifications. They began using hydraulics for tasks such as driving pound net stakes. The basic principal was using hydraulic winches and the weight of the boat to drive the pound net stakes into the lake bottom, as opposed to using pile drivers with derricks, as they did in the early 1900s.

In 1974, Cliff Wenniger was in poor health. He still had a sizable fishery with a large number of gill nets, pound nets and a small fleet of boats, along with the land and buildings, but, due to his poor health, the fishery wasn't being utilized as it once had been. Cliff respected and liked Dennis and Jeff Hickey. Cliff was not expected to live much longer, so Cliff's wife Mabel made the Hickeys an offer and they worked out a deal in which the Hickeys purchased some of Cliff's rigs and equipment.

The Hickey's fishery began to grow and they were able to set more pound nets. In 1974, trap nets were legalized, and Dennis and Jeff began setting a few trap nets. Before buying the land where their dock is now, they moored their boats on the west side of the harbor. Their cousin had a dock where the town marina is now. They used the yacht club pier for some time before buying a piece of land south of the yacht club on the east side of the harbor. They had a few more pound-net boats and what was left of the buildings, such as the old sawmill and net shed, which stand across from the Hickey's processing building. Dennis and Jeff modernized most of Cliff's rig or used bits and pieces of it for their own rig, and they acquired Cliff's pound-net boats. Said Jeff:

W e had our pound-net boat the *Leif.* Then we bought Cliff's rig with his boats like

the *Lulu, Can,* and *Bo,* and we had the *Worm* for a while, which we got from the Allies, but it was too small for what we needed it for. The *Lars,* which was another of Cliff's boats, and the *Lulu* [weren't] really big enough for us. We now have two nice pound-net and trap-net boats. Most of what we got from Cliff we changed or modified.[35]

Dennis and Jeff always kept their fishery well maintained and manageable. They did not believe in having a large crew and typically used part-time and weekend help. In the early days, they had a small crew for each gill-net boat. Bob Dewitt and Bill Lindal fished the *Hickey Brothers* tug for them, while Dennis and Jeff fished with the *Pathfinder.* They also had help from Cliff Wenniger's grandsons, Keith and Mark Orsted in the 1980s. Dennis' and Jeff's sons helped out too. In particular, Jeff's son Leif and Dennis' son Lars were always working and learning the craft. Lars and Leif took different paths after high school. Leif went into the Navy and Lars went to college to pursue a business career. But, someday they might be back to carry on the family tradition. Dennis commented, "Lars knows this business like the back of his hand. He and Leif fished with us as they were growing up. I want to see if he can handle it in the city. I hope someday he will want to fish, although he can earn a better living with the career he has chosen."[36]

The Hickeys always had a hard-working crew. In 2006, they have several young guys working with them, though most are weekend or seasonal help. Dennis Hickey's son-in-law, Todd Stuth, worked for them part-time while going to college. He graduated with a degree in international marketing and works for Hickey Brothers full time now. Dennis said he has a good business sense which helps as the fishery heads into the future.

Another enthusiastic and hard-working young man who works with the Hickeys every chance he can get is Jay Virlee. Jay has his commercial fishing license and a small quota and hopes to break into the trade, though he knows the difficulties of the commercial fishing business. Dennis and Jeff are helping Jay out with the use of their boat and dock until Jay can buy his own rig. Dennis commented:

T hese young guys that work for us, like Jay, Steve, and Todd – we have all the equip-

ment here and everything [and] we just let them run some of our stuff – better than making that big investment. Then eventually they can veer off and go on their own. They gain experience at our expense, which we don't mind at all. They are good guys and good workers. We began working for Cliff Wenniger, but not for very long. When we got into the business we mechanized a lot of it ourselves with new equipment, hydraulics, and modifying our gear. We changed all the twine from cotton over to nylon, and now marlex.[37]

In 1981, the Hickeys bought the gill net tug *Amy Jo,* which they renamed the *Southwester.* Asked how they got the name, Dennis responded, "We named her the *Southwester* after a good southwest blow one day. We got enough whitefish in our pound nets to almost pay for the boat." The boat became the pride of their fleet of gill-net tugs, a 50-foot all-steel boat built in 1946 by the Burger Boat Company of Manitowoc, Wisconsin. It was originally built for Paul Jensen who fished out of Muskegon, Michigan, and was called the *Jensen Brothers*. It was sold to Jerome Peterson from Manistique, Michigan, and renamed the *Amy Jo*. Then, a year later, Dennis and Jeff acquired the boat. Its original 75-90 Kahlenberg engine was later replaced with a more modern 343 Caterpillar diesel engine. During the winter months, the ice could be quite heavy in the harbor, which prompted the Hickeys to install a bigger and more powerful engine for winter operations. Dennis said:

> **W**hen you get a prevailing northwest wind coming across that harbor it can make 2 feet of ice overnight. That's why we repowered the boat. We installed a 343 Caterpillar diesel engine with a 4 1/2-inch reduction gear – a big bull gear like a river tug that can give us up to 600 horsepower, which we needed for breaking ice in the harbor – it can be a bear breaking ice in here some days. Some days we are the only ones who can get out, but you don't make any money breaking ice. If we do have to break ice, Jeff will only run it at a third throttle. Some days Jeff will go all the way around an ice flow rather than breaking through it. We still have the original 56-inch Kahlenberg wheel in the boat.[38]

Anyone who has had the pleasure of joining the Hickey's for a day in the *Southwester* had better come equipped with ear protection. An all-steel boat with that big Cat diesel engine purring can get awfully noisy. The *Southwester*, albeit noisy, is a fine all-weather boat used for whitefish and chub fishing with gill nets. A furnace mounted over the engine compartment provides heat during the cold winter months, and heat is supplied to the pilothouse porthole windows to keep them ice free. In the pilothouse are all the modern navigational aids such as a Loran C unit, radar, sonar, radio, and fish finders, and even the old compass, which still sits behind the wheel, is an important piece of equipment.

Located in the forward section of the boat are a mechanical net lifter and sorting table. Here, fish are removed from the gill net when it is brought in by the net lifter. This is also the position from which Jeff Hickey steers and operates the boat. He maneuvers the boat to keep the net directly underneath the lifter, which is a challenge when the seas are building. When the net comes across the drum of the lifter, Dennis and the other crew members pick out the whitefish and chubs and throw any other fish back into the water.

The rear or aft section of the *Southwester* is the location from which the crew sets the nets. Typically, two crew members set nets. The nets are usually set at the normal gait of the boat, which means they are really flying out of the box. Jeff Hickey commented: "You can see why you don't wear loose clothing, rings, wrist watches, or bracelets while setting nets. It can literally carry you overboard if you get caught in the net."[39]

Between 1998 and 2003, the Hickey Brothers added two more boats to their fleet. Both are used for trap nets and pound nets, and both have been lengthened to make them more suitable for this work. The *Norska* originally was a charter boat that they bought in Algoma and then spent two years modifying it to suit their purposes. They removed the original house and stripped the boat down. They first intended it to be used as a twine-net boat, but, as they worked on it, they realized it had potential as a trap-net boat. So they cut off the aft section and lengthened it to 44 feet.

In the year 2000, they acquired a research boat that was put out for bids by the DNR. They put in a bid on the last day of the bidding, and their offer was accepted. The boat was called the *Sheepshead*. It was a fishing boat before the DNR had it, and had been used for trawling sheepshead on Lake Winnebago. The Hickeys didn't have to do much to it. It had an over-hauled 3306 Caterpillar diesel engine for ample power. The only modification they made was installing new hydraulics. Their fleet then consisted of two gill-net boats, one anchor boat, and two trap-net boats. Early in 2003, they began lengthening *Sheepshead*. They added 4 feet to make it a total of 40 feet long.

Dennis and Jeff are proud of the product they market. They take special care to send only the best fish to their markets. They only fish for what they need or what the market demands. Sometimes they set only a third of their trap nets or a limited number of pound nets. There are times they throw many fish back because the market is flooded. Dennis said:

> That's the advantage of live entrapment. You fish for the market. They're better off in the nets than in the coolers getting soft. Some days we don't set as many nets, because we're not sure what the market is going to be. The Indian fishery in Michigan, the way it is, they generally flood the market, so that's what we're competing with. We have a nice trap-net fishery and pound-net fishery, but what's the sense of setting all those [if] you end up flooding the market, and some days the market won't even take them. I'd sooner fish less for more money.
>
> Dave Peterson does our marketing and shipping for us. He's been in the fish business for a long time, and furthermore he's a good businessman and has a great personality. He'll start arranging shipments and tells us how much we need. We talk all day long. That's how we fish – for what we need. It's an entirely different approach than what many people think. They think you just go out there and take all you want. Well you can take all you want, but you have to put it all together as a package and know how to market it. The average person thinks that you try to catch as many fish as you can, but that isn't what it's all about.[40]

The Hickeys once belonged to a Co-op with a few other commercial fishermen but they now do their own marketing. They have a large investment in processing fish – a number of coolers, a smoke house for smoked fish, and a room for processing chub and whitefish roe, which is quite a task in itself. Whitefish and chub roe is sold as caviar in many European countries, but especially in Norway and Sweden. Dennis Hickey said:

> I got to know some people in Sweden real well and we work with their marketing system. That's a different clientele entirely – a different culture. You don't do business like you do American style. When I ship the roe over there, I don't even ask the price. I don't even talk price because they will give us the best price they can. We

know that because we will give them the best product we can. That's our job. It's our job here to make sure it's a good product. When we get all that taken care of, we ship it over there and they'll take care of their end as soon as it's sold.

With the roe, they need this stuff for the holidays. The chub roe, which we produce in December, January, and February, they need for the Christmas holiday the next year – it's always a year late. The whitefish roe is mainly sold to the cruise lines that run between Norway, Sweden, and Denmark. They sell our roe in the summer months to the tourists, so they don't need this roe until the following spring – everything is a year late.[41]

The Hickey Brothers Fishery is going strong and growing. Dennis and Jeff look to the future with optimism and plan to fish as long as possible. With all the challenges that confront fishermen, the Hickeys, like the highly adaptable whitefish, try to find ways to survive and adapt to the changing times and ecology of the lake. In the 1950s, said Dennis Hickey, "They got more money then than we do now. I have some old catch records, all the way back to 1929. In 1929 they were getting $1.00 a pound. That was a great price. We now have to learn to fish smart and keep our overhead down to make any profit."[42]

Ted Eggebraaten

Ted "the Captain" Eggebraaten is one of the youngest of the Door County fishermen. He got into the business in 1999 after buying Jacob Ellefson's rig at Washington Island. The sale included Jake's boat the *Miss Judy*, one hundred boxes of nets, some ice nets, and Jake's quota. Ted said:

I had talked to Jake before he got out of the business, and he said he was probably going to get out and he told Dennis [Hickey] that he had first offer on the rig. Then Dennis told me about it, since I was always looking to get into the business. I bought the boat and the nets. Jake's rig was one of the few rigs that were fairly reasonable and had quota, nets and the whole works.[43]

Ted has a degree in fish biology from the University of Wisconsin at Stevens Point, and he met the Hickey Brothers while he was working on a study of burbot (fresh water codfish, locally known as "lawyers") in Door County. Ted had worked for a fishery in Alaska for more than eight years, but he was tired of fishing there and decided to move back to Wisconsin. That fall and winter he fished for chubs and then worked in Idaho for a time, before returning once again to delve into the commercial fishing business. During the summer of 1999, he was on Washington Island and met with Jake Ellefson. He remembered one of the best lifts Jake got before he sold his rig and retired:

The summer I bought the *Miss Judy* from Jake, I think he said they were getting some pretty small lifts, only about 100 or 200 pounds. I was up there and went out with him one day and we came in with about 1,400 pounds. Jake was about as happy as you could get.[44]

After buying the *Miss Judy*, Ted stripped off the paint and repainted it. He also modified the gear ratio 2 1/2 to 1, which was the limit without changing the wheel. Ted uses the Hickey brothers' dock and does his processing at the Hickey brothers' facility.

A Day In the Life of A Pound-Net Fisherman

The following is an account of a day the author spent in the fall of 2003 working with the Hickey brothers and their crew harvesting whitefish from both a trap net and a pound net. It was written shortly afterward:

It was one of those days in mid October that one cherishes and carries with them through the cold winter months. The early morning air was crisp, the trees were donning their orange and yellow garments of leaves, and a slight wind was blowing out of the south, generating a gentle mist over the harbor. I rolled into the Hickey's dock before sunrise and saw the boats resting peacefully in the placid waters of the slip. The only boat missing from her mooring and presumably out on the lake already was the *Miss Judy* and her newfound skipper, Captain Ted. It was apparent the captain liked to get an early start, or maybe it was the *Miss Judy* that had somehow lured her captain to get an early start, like her previous captain, Jake Ellefson. Jake was an early riser and was known to head out in the predawn hours.

After sunrise, I left the dock and headed down the gravel road and over to the Hickey Brothers processing shed, or Mission Control. Dennis and Jeff were already loading luggers and ice on the back of their truck. They had a crew of two men assembled for the days run, Jay and Jack. When everything was loaded and our oilers had been slipped on over our clothing, we headed back down to the dock, where nearly thirty luggers (2 foot by 3 foot plastic bins for loading whitefish) were loaded on the waiting boats, *Norska* and the venerable old *Leif*. Jeff Hickey fired up *Lief's* Volvo diesel engine and headed out, ahead of Dennis and the crew in the *Norska*.

As soon as we left the slip, Dennis throttled up the big Volvo diesel in the *Norska* and we were on our way. An entourage of a hundred seagulls followed in close pursuit and immediately surrounded us, hoping for a free meal. It was a nice ride out of the harbor. The lake was quiet and the morning sun gave the water a diamond studded glow. Our first stop was a trap net set nearly a mile east of Cana Island. Dennis pointed east and said, "Look, there's the Captain and the *Judy*." We strained to look but couldn't see her. Dennis said, "How could you not see a big boat like the Judy." Then, sure enough, we saw her on the horizon, just under the rising sun, shimmering in the sun glade, a water steed racing through the morning mist. We knew that somewhere in the confines of her hull was her famous Captain Ted reaping a harvest of jumbo whitefish. We all felt at ease knowing the captain was out there. It was going to be a good day.

As we headed out, we passed a myriad of trap nets and floating trap nets that had been set by fishermen from further on up the county. This area is bustling during the whitefish run since it's considered to be one of the best fishing grounds for whitefish when they come into the shallows to spawn. There were other boats on the horizon. Dennis figured one them to be Weborg's. Another was Rick Johnson in his trap-net boat the *Joyce*, and Charlie Henriksen was probably there as well. Like the Hickey Brothers, they were trying to harvest whitefish before the season closed for a month on October 25. There seemed to be nets everywhere, as the bright orange buoy flags dotted the waters like gravestones in a cemetery.

After a twenty-minute ride, Dennis located his trap net and maneuvered the *Norska* in close to the buoy that marked the pot. This particular trap net was a "thirty, which means the pot was 30 feet in depth. The pot is made of a new synthetic material called marlex that is replacing the old nylon twine because it requires less maintenance. The crew pulled the pot up to the boat and opened a hatch, or zipper line, to the pot that allows the fish to be scooped out. Trap net rigs are relatively fast and easy to operate. Once the pot had been pulled up so that the whitefish collected in the bottom, Jay and Jack began scooping out fish with hand nets on a pole. It was a fairly good lift. The fish were loaded into luggers, and the pot was zippered back up and pushed over the side.

As we finished this work, Jeff joined us in the *Leif*, and both boats moved on to a pound net located northeast of Cana Island near North Bay. After a short boat ride, I saw the pound net stakes rising from the water, looking almost like an old shipwreck with the masts poking up out of the water. This particular pound net was a fifty, which means that the depth of the pot was fifty feet and the rig was set in approximately fifty feet of water. The pot was 40 feet square and was suspended on seven sticks (stakes) arranged in a square configuration. Four stakes on one end held the tunnel, and where the heart and lead came into it, they had a frame pole about eight feet above the water. The heart and lead twine ran in to the shore. On top of the stakes, which rose about sixteen feet out of the water, were several cormorants stoically perched and poised for an easy meal of whitefish. Dennis said they had become a serious problem around here, especially to fishermen. They dive down and chase the whitefish around the pot causing them to get entangled in the twine. Many whitefish have severe scarring from the cormorants slashing at them, and many fall prey to the cormorants. As we drew closer, the cormorants flew off.

Dennis tied up the *Norska* to the corner stake, and we all climbed aboard the *Leif*. Once we were aboard, Jeff maneuvered the *Leif* up next to the sticks and killed the engine. Then we unfastened lines from the cable and lowered the net so that the boat could be pulled into the pot area. Once inside, we tied the boat to the stakes on the opposite side, just under the frame pole, and the crew began raising the net to gather the fish in one end of the pot. As the net was lifted, it was secured to the gunwale of the *Leif* with pins. This kept the twine in place while the men worked the fish towards one end of the pot. This operation took about fifteen minutes.

When the fish were gathered in a confined area of the pot, the water seemed to boil with trapped whitefish. Armed with scoop nets, Dennis, Jay, and Jack extracted the lively whitefish. Those over seventeen inches long were loaded into luggers, while undersized whitefish and any species besides whitefish were thrown back into the lake. It was amazing to see nearly three thousand pounds of whitefish harvested in about an hour.

Chapter 14 notes

[1] Hjalmar R. Holand, *History of Door County, Vol. 1* (Chicago, IL: S.J. Clark Publishing Company, 1917) 385-387.

[2]. Ibid.

[3] Holand, "The Oldest village in Door County"; *Old Peninsula Days*; (Twayne Publishers 1959), 70.

[4] Catherine McArdle, "Commercial Fishing in Baileys Harbor, *Door County Almanac, No. 3*, 311.

[5] Catherine McArdle, "Commercial Fishing in Baileys Harbor," *Door County Almanac, No. 3*, 311-312.

[6] Ibid.

[7] Ibid.

[8] Ibid, 315.

[9] Ibid, 136; Catherine McCardle an evening of Story telling "Baileys Harbor Fisheries" hosted by Mary Ann Johnson; videotaped 1997; Courtesy of Pat Orsted.

[10] Interview with Pat and Orval Orsted June 30, 2003. Not a definite fact but that was how some people heard it.

[11]. "Baileys Harbor Fisheries," video cassette narrated by Mary Ann Johnson, 1987.

[12]. Interview with Phil Albertson, March7, 2003.

[13]. Interview with Elaine Johnson, June, 2003.

[14]. Interview with Phil Albertson, March 7, 2003.

[15] Ibid.

[16]. Interview with Pat and Orval Orsted, June 30, 2003.

17. Interview with Elaine Johnson, June 2003.

18. Leonard Peterson, *Rowleys Bay: Reliving the Heritage of Northern Door County*, 1991,

19. Interview with Pat and Orval Orsted, June 30, 2003.

20. Interview with Pat and Orval Orsted, February 27, 2003.

21. Interview with Pat and Orval Orsted, June 30, 2003.

22. Interview with Pat and Orval Orsted, July 10, 2004.

23. Interview with Dennis Hickey, October 12, 2002.

24 Interview with Dennis Hickey, February 24, 2004.

25 Holand, *Old Peninsula Days*; 70

26 Paul J. Creviere, Jr., *Wild Gales and Tattered Sails*, (1997), 128.

27 Ibid.

28. Interview with Dennis Hickey, 10 February 2003.

29. Interview with Dennis Hickey, 14 December 2002.

30. Ibid.

31. Ibid.

32. Interview with Dennis and Jeff Hickey, 18 October 2003.

33. Ibid.

34. Ibid.

35. Ibid.

36. Ibid.

37. Interview with Dennis and Jeff Hickey, 30 January 2003.

38. Interview with Dennis Hickey, 27 September 2002.

39. Interview with Jeff Hickey, 18 October 2003.

40. Interview with Dennis and Jeff Hickey, February 10, 2003 & October 18, 2003.

41. Ibid.

42. Ibid.

43. Interview with Ted Eggebraaten, January 30, 2003.

44. Ibid.

Pic. 14.1 Cliff Wenniger standing at the dock next to his fish tug the *Fay* at Algoma. Next to him are his sister Fay and Cliff's Mother, Theresa. (Photo courtesy of Orval and Pat Orsted)

Pic.14.2 Cliff Wenniger with one of his pound net crew securing a line on a pound net. (Photo courtesy of Orval and Pat Orsted)

Pic. 14.3 Pound net crew taking a lunch break L to R, front left, Norman Ostreum; behind Norman is his brother Lloyd "Futzy Ostreum, laying on the roof is George Lindal, and Rusty Meyer. (Photo courtesy of Orval and Pat Orsted)

Pic. 14.4 Phil Albertson dressing chubs aboard the gill net tug *C. G.* (Photo courtesy of Orval and Pat Orsted)

Pic. 14.5 Cliff Wenniger's crew scooping whitefish from a pound net. Ryne Goetz scooping and Pete Husby standing at right. (Photo courtesy of Orval and Pat Orsted

Pic. 14.6 Wenniger dock looking west. Notice the tracks on the left running along the dock and the cart in the foreground used for hauling net boxes, fish boxes and ice to and from the boats. Pound net boats on the right and the Gill net boats were moored up at the end of the dock. (Photo courtesy of Orval and Pat Orsted)

Pic. 14.7 Cliff Wenniger often threw parties down by the dock The young girl to the right is Cliff's daughter Pat Orsted. At the beer pump are Emil Herbst and Ohm Mueller. To the far right is Alfred Anclam standing alone. To the far left is Gene Heald holding his child, and behind him is Bill Hickey. Ca. 1942. (Photo courtesy of Orval and Pat Orsted)

Pic. 14.8 Drawing close to a pound net that Cliff used extensively. (Photo courtesy of Orval and Pat Orsted

Pic. 14.9 A Wenniger crew busy cleaning fish on a pound net boat. From left to right - standing on the dock, Ryne Goetz; standing in the boat, Pete Husby; cleaning fish, Cliff Wenniger and Orval Orsted. (Photo courtesy of Orval and Pat Orsted)

Pic. 14.10 The *Southwester* coming into Baileys Harbor during an October blow. (Tryrgvie Jensen Photography

Pic. 14.11 Scooping whitefish from a pound net in North Bay. (Trygvie Jensen Photography)

Pic. 14.12 Hickey Brothers and crew working a pound net in North Bay. (Trygvie Jensen Photography)

Pic 14.13 Bringing in the buoy line at the lifter station, inside the gill-net tug, *Southwester*. Jeff Hickey at the forward steering station, while Jay Virlee and Dennis Hickey await the gill net. (Trygvie Jensen Photography)

Pic. 14.14 Hickey Brothers dock in Baileys Harbor. (Trygvie Jensen Photography)

Pic. 14.15 Dennis Hickey standing on the rail of the *Leif* tying off a line on a pound net stake. (Trygvie Jensen Photography)

Pic. 14.16 Jeff Hickey at the forward steering station in the gill-net tug, *Southwester.* (Trygvie Jensen Photography)

Chapter 15

The Jacksonport Fishery

The 1654 Jesuit Chronicles state that fishing was a means of survival for the Potawatomi Indians of the Door Peninsula. They tell of a large Potawatomi village near what is now Jacksonport. Two French fur traders found their way to this area around 1654, and they told the Jesuits that they had their headquarters in a large Potawatomi village in the northern part of Door County that contained some 3,000 indigenous Americans. The village was located at the mouth of Hibbards Creek, north of Jacksonport.[1]

In 1656, the fur traders arrived in Montreal accompanied by a large flotilla of Indian canoes laden with valuable furs. They returned to the Door Peninsula with thirty other Frenchmen, including two priests, Father Gabriel Dreuilettes and Leonard Gareau, who were going to establish their mission of St. Michael among the Potawatomies.[2] Raddison and Grosoillers, who were part of the entourage, spent a winter with the Native Americans and noted that fishing was major means of subsistence for the Potawatomies. They fished from birch-bark canoes using a variety of methods from spearing to hook and line. The Frenchmen also noted that the Potawatomies called the village they stayed in *Mechingan* and called what is now known as Hibbards Creek, *Medemoyaseebe,* meaning "old woman creek."[3]

One of the first European settlers at Jacksonport was a Scotsman by the name of Neil Blair, who settled here in 1850. He became the first commercial fisherman in this small village and fished with pound nets in a Mackinaw boat. Besides fishing, Neil also was farming. Another man, P. M Kirtland, came to the area from Connecticut in 1866 and established himself in the fishing business. He and a partner, Jared Jones, fished together for several years. In 1876, they sent over 600 barrels of whitefish to market.[4] By the 1860s, quite a few people were settling into this quiet lakeshore village. Perry Hibbard moved there from New York in 1858 and settled at the mouth of what is now called Hibbard's Creek, which eventually was named after him. He built a home there along with a barn and a blacksmith shed, and he eventually started several businesses – a general store, a boarding house, and a sawmill. In the beginning he made a living as a fisherman, fishing the bountiful waters off Jacksonport with a Mackinaw boat and a few gill nets.[5]

By 1867, more people were finding the area rich in both fish and timber. Three men from Madison, Wisconsin – Andrew Jackson, Colonel Charles Harris, and John Reynolds – took a special interest to this area. They moved there and formed a land company to harvest timber along the lakeshore. They built a pier and a sawmill and shipped their lumber on schooners that plied the waters of Lake Michigan. They were also instrumental in forming the Town of Jacksonport, which was named after Andrew Jackson because they decided that he was the one who had proposed the plan in the first place. An 1869 article in the *Door County Advocate* documented some of the activity in the small community:

There are two good piers and 80 vessels were loaded there during the season. Many cedar posts, railroad ties, telegraph poles, and many cords of wood were shipped out. In addition one hundred barrels of fish were shipped out of the community that year.[6]

Joseph LaMere arrived in Jacksonport in 1875 at the age of eighteen from Two Rivers, Wisconsin. He became a successful businessman and played a major role in the town's affairs for several decades. When he first came to the community he began fishing, and he continued in the fishing trade until 1885, when he built a store and became a merchant. He marketed trout and whitefish either fresh or salted. By 1880, herring had found markets and were being harvested with pound nets a short distance from the shore. During the 1880s there were some twenty-five pound nets in operation in the Jacksonport region.[7]

LeClair's

In 1853, Victor LeClair moved to Jacksonport from Mishicot, Wisconsin. In 1850 he worked as a logger in Quebec Canada, and had heard that the logging and fishing were good in Wisconsin. His grandson Joe LeClair comments:

My grandfather came from Quebec, Canada and settled in Mishicot. That's where you get all the LeClair's from, Two Rivers. Two of his brothers stayed there, and after two years grandpa came up here. He and his brothers were all woodsmen from Canada and they all came here to work in the woods, as Door County was known at that time for being a large timber producer. After he arrived here, he soon found out the fishing was good and decided he would try fishing. They used seine nets right off the shore in June and July. They would use horses to pull the seine nets back into shore. In those years they would end up with a lot of sturgeon in their nets and at the time there wasn't any market for them so they would dig holes on the beach and bury them. After some time they progressed into pound-net fishing for herring and bought a mackinaw boat, which was popular in Two Rivers.[8]

In the 1870s, Victor LeClair built a good pier for his fishery. The pier ran out some seventy-five yards and was protected by a break wall. The dock was built on the old pilings of Joseph LaMere's dock, a commercial fisherman, who came to Jacksonport in the 1860s. Joseph married Victor LeClair's daughter, Almira. Joseph LeClair recalls:

We had a good dock for many years with net sheds, icehouse, and later, my smoke-house. It was hard to hold a dock in there, especially in the winter time. My dad built the piers out here on the old LaMere dock, which ran out quite a ways where they used to load the schooners. The sticks were all in there yet so my dad removed them and built the breakwater right over the old pilings. That dock remained there for a long time, but they're gone now – that was a hard place to fish out of, but there is good fishing grounds all the way out from here.[9]

Bert LeClair was born in 1882 and fished with his father at a young age. He continued to fish until the age of eighteen, that's when he decided to join the Coast Guard. After a few years of service, he returned to Jacksonport and returned to what he knew best, fishing. He found a partner, a man named Charlie Heald, and they began fishing together. The first boat they bought was named the *Coila,* a 35-foot wooden boat that had a single-horse Straubel engine, which was relatively new at the time. They began fishing with hook-and-line rigs then gill nets. Back then, they didn't have a mechanical net lifter for the gill nets. It was all done my hand. Joe recalled:

Before the lifters came out, we did it by hand. I remember my dad had this big roller they'd throw out over the side of the boat. The rollers were 4 to 5 feet long and 6 inches in diameter and the nets were pulled in over them – boy, that was hard work. My mother made special leather mitts to go over their hands to keep from getting tore up. They could only handle four or five boxes of nets.[10]

Bert and Charlie fished together for several years, and then they decided to move over to Baileys Harbor. Bert began fishing with Richard Strege, and the two formed a partnership together. Joe tells the story of the time Richard nearly lost his life on the *Coila,* "One time my dad's partner Richard Strege fell, or actually slid off while they were setting nets. He just managed to grab the cork line. My dad ran down and shut the engine off, and began pulling the nets back in to the boat. Old Richard hung on for dear life and was pulled back into the boat from the freezing water." A few years later, they lost the *Coila* in a bad storm when it broke from its moorings.

The next boat they bought came from Frankfurt, Michigan called the *R & D*. It had more power with a two-cylinder Straubel engine. The *R&D* was 33 feet long and was equipped with a mechanical lifter, which was becoming a popular piece of equipment. They were very excited about this new apparatus, which doubled the amount of gill nets they could handle, increasing their harvest of whitefish and trout. "We all worked with our father at a very young age," says Joe LeClair. "We were raised around fishing when we were young. We mended nets, reeled nets, scalded nets, and helped out on the boat when we were a little older."

Bert had seven sons, John, Joe, Gilbert, Louis, Richard, Robert, and George. In 1934, Bert bought out Richard Strege's interest. His oldest son John worked with his father, and in 1937, John joined the Coast Guard. After John left, Bert's sons Joe and George helped in the family business. In 1941, Joe was drafted in the Army, and served five years overseas, in World War II. After Joe went into the army, Bert's son Louis replaced him to keep the fishery going. They bought a bigger boat called the *Bub* that was an all-wood constructed vessel, measuring 45 feet long. Joe recalled, "When we bought the *Bub* in 1942, she was open in the back, then we built a stern house on to it. They used to stand out on those decks, exposed to the weather – they even had the lifter out on the deck, before we enclosed it." In 1946, Joe returned back home, and he and his brother Louis took over their father's fishery. For many years their fishery was geared up for harvesting lake trout. By the time Joe had returned from the war, most of the lake trout were decimated by the lamprey. The next few years they were harvesting less trout, eventually they were gone.

They toughed it out for five or six years, and finally Joe realized there just wasn't any point to beat a dead horse. By the 1950s, the lake trout were nearly depleted from Lake Michigan. In 1951, they sold the *Bub* and Joe turned his interest towards the smoke chub business. By this time more fishermen began switching gears and going after chubs. Joe recalled the lean years:

When I quit fishing – I never missed it. I was young when I got into the fishing business and when I got out of the army, I was back into it for five or six years. Fishing wasn't that good anymore; the trout were all gone and that's what my dad was geared up for. I remember my dad telling me they used to make their own nets. My dad used to fish big mesh for trout – he used 5" inch mesh. Trout were always hard on the nets. They'd get their teeth in there and wind them up and tear them all to hell. Anyway, by that time, when there wasn't any trout left, I wasn't going to buy a whole new rig – so I just gave it up, and that's when I went into the smoke fish business.[11]

For twenty-two years it was a good business. We smoked them here in Jacksonport. I had a wholesaler in Appleton, Oshkosh, and Rockford Illinois. I tell you, we turned out some fish. When I got into my smoking business I would sometimes smoke 2,000 pounds of chubs a day for awhile. I had three smoke houses where I could put five hundred pounds in each one, and some days we would go through two batches like that. Fishermen would bring the chubs in dressed, and then I would smoke them and ship them to Rockford once a week. On the way home, I was empty, so I would stop in Racine where they were known to catch a lot of chubs, and I would buy them from the Strege's , Alvin Anderson, and Lorman Greenfeldt.

When you hear about smoked fish, they're not only smoked, they're cooked too, but you get the smoke taste, and if you have good, dry wood, you get the good color. We brought the fish in from the fishermen and soak them in salt brine for seven or eight hours, depending how strong you made the brine. My sons did all this – when I got home from picking up the fish, they had the salt brine all made. We then soaked the chubs overnight and smoked them the next day for three or four hours. We smoked for three days, and then I would go on the road for one day to deliver them to the markets. We used mostly maple for smoking the fish. I would get my wood from a furniture shop at Oshkosh, which was all kiln tried. That's the key to smoking fish – using good dry wood – so you can get the heat.[12]

Joe ran a successful business until 1972, but the DNR put a ban on chub fishing, which in effect ended his twenty-two year smoke fish business. Joe knew what he had to do and once again began fishing. Since the early 1970s, the whitefish were abundant. Joe bought a boat called the *Peter W.*, and went back into the fishing business with his brother George. The *Peter W.* was a wooden hull gill-net boat, which he later sold to a fisherman named Jack Schmiler, at Ellison Bay. In 1974, he and George bought the *De Vet, F, And Sons* fish tug from a fisherman at Fayette, Michigan, which they renamed the *Shelly,* after his daughter. The *Shelly* was a 42-foot all-steel hull vessel, built at Sturgeon Bay

Shipbuilding and Dry Dock Co. in 1937. After Joe bought the boat, he replaced the three-cylinder 75-90 Kahlenberg engine with a bigger engine. Joe recalled:

> When we took that old Kahlenberg out we had to cut a hole in the roof of the house and remove it with a crane. We then installed the *Shelly* with a 400 hp super-charged Volvo engine. That thing really had power – we could now break through a foot of ice with no problem at all. We kept the same Kahlenberg wheel and propeller in her.[13]

Joe continued fishing into the early 1980s and then retired from the business.

Bob and Louis LeClair fished together until 1955. However, after several storms severely damage their dock, they moved their operation to Baileys Harbor. Every day they transported their nets and boxes from Jacksonport to Baileys Harbor, and they began using Alfred Anclam's dock. Bob and Louis fished from that location with their fish tug *Bremen*, which was a wooden hull gill-net tug, equipped with Gray Marine engine. The next boat they bought was named the *Buccaneer*, in which Bob's brother John became a silent partner. The 39-foot wood hull fish tug was built at the Burger Boat Company at Manitowoc, Wisconsin, and was equipped with a Kahlenberg engine. At that time, they had Raymond Strege working with them, and they moved to the Cliff Wenniger dock.

The last boat Bob and John had was a 42-foot steel hull Burger boat named the *Mercury*, equipped with a Kahlenberg engine. After a few years, they replaced the Kahlenberg engine with a Cummins diesel engine. The Cummins gave them more power for breaking ice. Bob became ill for awhile, but in 1966, he was able to fish once again. He and his two sons fished until the early 1980s. After they quit fishing, Bob sold the *Mercury* to a fisherman named Ray Strege, who needed a smaller boat, after selling his boat, the *Bonnie S*. Ray's father had once fished with Bert LeClair. In 1989, Ray sold the *Mercury* to Charlie Henriksen after his health declined.

Grovogel and Sons Fishery

Another fishing family established in Jacksonport was the Conrad Grovogel family. In the mid 1880s, Conrad and his wife, two daughters and three sons, moved to Chambers Island. They lived for several years where Conrad fished the waters of the bay. After a brief stay, Conrad had heard the fishing was good at Jacksonport, and he moved his family there. When his sons came of age, they accompanied their father on the boat and helping out on shore duties. His oldest son John eventually got his own rig and fished on his own before going to work for the Albert Kalmbach fishery at Sturgeon Bay.

In the early years, they fished pound nets for whitefish and herring. They had a dock with a break-wall near St. Michael's church. Years later, they built another dock a quarter of a mile north of their original dock. Most of the fishermen, who fished from that area found it challenging to keep a dock in the shallow water off of Jacksonport. The water is shallow for at least several hundred yards; moreover the bottom is sandy and during some good southerly blows sand bars would form. Winter ice always wreacked havoc with the docks and break walls. However, the break walls did offer some protection, but over the years storms and ice-shoves took its toll on them. By the 1950s, most of the fishermen were gone from Jacksonport, and so were the piers.[14]

Conrad's second oldest son fished with him as a youngster, and he too, eventually went on his own, and bought a fish rig, until he lost his dock and boat in a severe blow. After that in 1906, he joined the Coast Guard and served thirty years at the Baileys Harbor Life Saving Station. Conrad's younger sons, George and Bill fished together with their father for many years. They continued fishing pound nets then fished for whitefish, after they built another dock and sheds. They bought a wooden gill-net boat called the *Julia Coates*. The next gill net boat was called the *Sally Lou*. She was built by master boat builder, Fred Peterson, who was the founder and owner of the Peterson Boat Company at Sturgeon Bay. This was Fred's first large boat that he built. Joe LeClair relates the story of how it came to be:

> The Grovogels had the wood gill-net boat *Sally Lou*. That was the first boat built by Fred Peterson and it was built right here. He had some men travel to southern Wisconsin and cut down some white oak, which they brought back and was sawed into material to build the *Sally Lou*. Fred and his dad used to build skiffs. Fred eventually built bigger boats – and more of them – that's when he formed the company. During World War II the government subsidized them where he built many boats for the war effort and eventually it grew into a substantial company.[14]

After Conrad died, George and Bill continued the Grovogel and Sons fishery for many years. Bill served in World War I, where he was wounded in a battle. After Bill returned home, he could no longer go out on the boats due to his disability, but he helped out on shore duties the best he could. Bill's son Leo took over helping his uncle on the boat, and after George passed away, Leo moved the operation to Racine. The Grovogels fished out of Jacksonport for nearly seventy years. Bill and George continued their father's business and fished together for at least 50 years.

A Few other Jacksonport Fisheries

Charley Olson was a Swedish immigrant who came to Door County in the late 1800s and settled in Sister Bay. He and his brother farmed and fished the waters of Green Bay. Charley and his family moved to Jacksonport and bought a farm, and soon began farming and fishing. The following spring, Charley bought a fishing rig, and he and his sons began fishing from the Grovogel dock. They started out with a hook and line rig and fished for lake trout. They fished lake trout in Lake Michigan as well as the bay, and went as far as whaleback shoals. During the winter months, they fished lake trout through the ice on Green Bay.

Art Weborg and his sons, Orville, Marvin, and Lawrence left Sand Bay and fished in Jacksonport until 1938. They built a shed on the LeClair dock and fished from there with their gill net tug named the *Dierssen*. Joe Cote was another fisherman who fished from Jacksonport for a period of time. He fished with his nephew Leo Grovogel and also fished with his father-in-law, Art Weborg. Ed Kohls did some fishing around the waters off Jacksonport. He mainly fished close to the shore for perch and

Menominee whitefish. Ed also helped in his son-in-law Joe LeClair's smoke fish business for many years. By the late 1950s, the fishing was poor, and most of fishermen retired, got out of the business, or moved elsewhere. The docks were gone, after years of clashing with the storms that eventually took their toll on the break-walls and docks. By the 1960s, commercial fishing was non-existent in Jacksonport.[16]

Chapter 15 notes

[1] HR Holland, "The Marco Polo of the West", Peninsula Historical Review, (Door County Historical Review 1930), 10.

[2] Ibid.

[3] H.R. Holland, "The Marco Polo of the West", Peninsula Historical Review (Door County Historical Society 1930), 10.

[4] Ibid.

[5] Joan LeClair, "Jacksonport Fishing Industry," *Door County Almanac, No. 3*, 165-166.

[6] Door County Advocate, March 1869.

[7] Joan LeClair, "Jacksonport Fishing Industry"; *Door County Almanac*, 165-166.

[8] Interview with Joe LeClair, January, 2002.

[9] Interview with Joe LeClair January, 20, 2003.

[10] Ibid.

[11] Ibid.

12 Ibid.

13 Joan LeClair, "Jacksonport Fishing Industry," *Door County Almanac, No. 3*. (Dragonsbreath Press, 1986), 328

14 Interview with Joe LeClair, January 10, 2003.

15 Joan LeClair, "Jacksonport Fishing Industry," Door County Almanac, No. 3, 329.

16 Ibid.

Appendix A

Jackson Harbor Fisheries

Fishery	Years	Crew	Boats	Years In Service:
McDonalds:	**1904 - 1962**	Jim Boyce	*Fish Hawk*	1890 to1904
Charlie		Jim Cornell	*Stewart Edward*	1903 to 1920
Ray		Hans Hanson	*Maritana*	1924 to 1934
Dennis		Harold Zoelner	*Fred*	1934 to 1935
George		Lester Greenfeldt	*McDonald Brothers*	1945 to 1960
		Alfred Johnson		
Jacob Ellefson & Sons:	**1907 - 1999**			
Everett (Steve)		Maynard Oleson	*Claude S.*	1952 to 1958
Klemmet		Bert Hahnkuper	*K.E.M Jacob*	1929 to 1948
Jacob		Chuck Goodlet	*Esther C.*	1948 to 1965
		Roy Richter	*Miss Judy*	1965 to 1999
		Dale Bjarnarson	*Billy Jean*	1947 to 1991
		Walt Jorgenson		
		Rupert Johnson		
		Fred Bjarnarson		
		Randy Sorenson		
B & H Fishery:	**1934 - 1970**			
Oliver Bjarnarson		Wes Peterson	*Sea Queen*	1935 to 1939
Hannes Hanneson		Dale Bjarnarson	*Clara C.*	1939 to 1953
		Dick Bjarnarson	*Esterlou*	1953 to 1970
		Chuck Goodlet		
		Walt Jorgenson		
		Roy Richter		
		Angus Swenson		

Rasmus Hanson & Sons 1932 - 1947
    Hans Hanson & Art Hanson

Chuck Goodlet	*Welcome*	1928 to 1932
Irv Goodlet	*Gloria*	1932 to 1947
Sam Goodlet		
Ervin Gunnlaugsson		

George Nelson & Sons 1904 - 1989
    Russ Nelson
    Spencer Nelson

Thorwald Johnson	*Rambler*	1926 to 1934
Ervin Gunnlaugsson	*Darlene*	1924 to 1926
Hannes Hanneson	*Sea Queen*	1934 to 1935
Cecil Anderson	*Nelson*	1928 to 1942
Dave Cota	*Jane*	1942 to 1989
Neil Gau		

John Christianson   1902 - 1956
    Curt Johnson

Andrew Nelson	*Pirate I*	1908 to 1921
George Hanson	*Pirate II*	1921 to 1956
Gerald, James & Ned		

Tom Goodman & Sons 1942 - 1965
    Harold Goodman
    Paul Goodman
    Brud (grandson)

Orville Wylie	*Welcome*	1905 to 1911
Tom Johnson	*Big Peder*	1911 to 1926
Rupert Johnson	*Hans*	1926 to 1959
Chuck Goodlet	*Charlene*	1960 to 1970
Ervin Cornell		

Dan Lindal   1930's - 1956
    Steve Ellefson (partners) George Hanson

George Hanson	*Helen C.*	1940 to 1947
Lloyd Orman	*Billy Jean*	1947 to 1956
Tom Johnson	*Jeanette C.*	
James Llewellyn	*R.E. Helen*	1956 to
Vic Goodlet	*Gloria*	

Goodmander & Johnson 1948 - 1964

Albert Goodmander	Hannes Thorainson	*R.E. Helen*	1915 to 1936
Haldon Johnson	Royal Johnson	*Islander*	1936 to 1960
Rupert & Percy (sons)	Ray Hansen		
	Roger Hagen		

Fred & Percy Young   1938 - 1959

	Jack Young	*Sea Queen*	1939 to 1953
	Alvin Cornell	*F.D. Roosevelt*	1953 to 1959
	Vic Goodlet		

Art & Lloyd Young   1938 - 1955

Cliff Young	Stuart Sorenson	*Darlene*	1913 to 1924
	Jack Young	*Rainbow*	1924 to 1953

Greenfeld Fishery   1938 - 1962

Anker (father)	Leland Johnson	*Jane Elizabeth*	1916 to 1941
Harold		*Yankee*	1941 to 1947
Lorman		*Betty*	1945 to 1956
		Falcon	1957 to 1962
		Majestic	1956 to 1957

Greenfeldt & Young   1962 - 1981

Harold Greenfeldt	Jack Young	*Ranger*	1953 to 1972
Clifford Young	Charlie McDonald	*Ranger II*	1972 to 1981
	George McDonald		
	Butch Gordon		

Lorman Greenfeldt

	Betty	1945 to 1956
	Majestic	1956 to 1957
	Kathy	1958 to 1966
	Viking	1954 to 1965
	Faith	1963 to 1964

			Kathy II	1966 to 1974
			Sea Bird	1976 to 1978
			Shrimp	1980s
			Connie J	1979 to 1985
			Energy	
			Ginny (Alex C.)	

Jim Cornell   **1945 - 1972**

Doris Cornell	Royal Johnson	*Don Deloris*	1941 to 1945
	Roy Richter	*J.N Cornell*	1945 to 1950
	Tom Johnson	*Welcome*	1950 to 1972
	Marvin Bjarnarson		
	David Goodmander		
	Alvin Cornell		
	Fred Young		

Bjarnarson & Johnson   **1953 - 1957**

| Fred Bjarnarson | *Sea Queen* | 1953 to 1954 |
| Ben Johnson | *Osprey* | 1954 to 1957 |

Glen & Alvin Sorenson

	Yankee	1947 to 1948
	Falcon	1953 to 1953
	Velox	1952 to 1954
	Sorenson Brothers	1947 to 1953

Zoellner & Ellerbrock   **1948 - 1953**

| Harold Zoellner | *Ranger* | 1948 to 1953 |
| Len Ellerbrock | | |

Lucke & Dulong

David Lucke	*Hagen*	1947 to 1953
Milton Dulong	*Loise* (blew up)	
Carmen Lucke		

Lawrence & Arnold Hahnkuper		*Darlene*	1926
		Claude S	1947
Bert Hahnkuper		*Omar*	
Jack Young			
	Monty Williamson	*Thora Ann*	
	Larry Goodlet	*Connie J*	
	Don Johnson		
Roger Hagen	**1974 - 1992**		
	Marvin Bjarnarson	*Alex C.*	1974 to 1992
	Walt Jorgenson		
	Lon Jorgenson		
Alex Koyen & Sons	**1970 -**	*Welcome*	1972 to 1986
Harvey Koyen		*Sea Diver*	1986 to 2004
Tom Koyen			
Ken Koyen			
Randy Sorenson	**1989 - 1997**		
Rob Carr		Harold Greenfeldt *Jane*	1989 to 1997
Lorman Greenfeldt		Oliver B.	
		Walt Jorgenson	
Jeff McDonald	**1998 - 2004**		
	Jeff Hagen	*Jane*	1999 to 2004
	Jake Ellefson	*C&R*	2003 to

Appendix B:

Washington Harbor Fisheries

Fishery	Boats	Years in Service
Furlong Dock		
J.B Young & Sons	*Darlene*	1913 to 1924
Lloyd & Arthur	*Rainbow*	1924 to 1953
Anker Greenfeldt	*Jane Elizabeth*	1925 to 1941
Harold	*Yankee*	1941 to 1947
Lorman	*Betty*	1945 to 1956
Fred & Percy Young	*Sea Queen*	1939 to 1953
Fred M Hanson	*Celia M.*	
	Rosemary	
Tim & Tom Guinan	*Liberty* (steam tug)	
	Unknown (steam)	
Sievert & Bess Helgeson	*Gertrude*	
Elzie Cornell	*Lady Grace*	
Jim Cornell	*Don Delores*	1940s
Toddy Jensen	*Unice*	1930s
Henry Bilton	*Mabel*	

Gasoline Town (Foss Dock)

Matt Foss	*Laura*	1897 to 1909
	Irma Jeanette	1909 to 1913

Hagen Brothers Fishery	*Darlene (Viking)*	1904 to 1912
Charlie	*Irma Jeanette*	1913 to 1920
Jule	*F. Hunter*	1916 to 1954
Harry		
Harry Hagen	Majestic	1925 to 1956
Swara Hagen	*Mascot*	1915 to 1926
	Hagen	1926 to 1946
Tom Goodman	*Welcome* (steam)	1905 to 1911
	Gertrude	1907 to 1911
	Big Peder	1911 to 1926
	Hans	1926 to 1959
Goodmander & Johnson	*Darlene*	
Albert Goodmander	*R.E. Helen*	1915 to 1936
Haldon Johnson	*Islander*	1936 to 1960
John Ellefson & Sons	*Viking* (Charlie Hagen)	1904 to 1910
Swarra, Julian, & Ernest	Ragna	1910 to 1915
	Mayflower	1915 to 1927
Hannes Johnson & Sons	*Sea Bird*	1912
John (Yonsie) & Hannes Jr.	*Hazel Jeanette*	1910 to 1927
	Service	1925 to 1932

Detroit Harbor Fisheries

Detroit Island:

Fred Richter & Sons	*Pearl*	1906 to 1909
Roy & Earl	*Two Brothers*	1909 to 1927
	Fred	1927 to 1934
	Maritana	1934 to

Charlie Allen & Sons	*Elsa M.* (steam tug)	
Carl & Frank Richter	*Iona Estelle*	1905 to 1917
	Shine On	1930 to 1931
	Welcome	1931 to 1950
Chris & Nels Sorenson	*Crystal*	1910 to 1914
Fred Young & Robert Young	*Messenger* (steam)	1900 to 1906
	Clifford (steam)	1906 to 1914
	Nor	1914 to ?
	Carolyn	
Berend Andersen & son	*Gladys*	
Milton "Cap"	*Liberty*	
	Namycush	

Detroit Harbor & Lobdell's Point

Pat Chambers & Sons	*L.P. Hill*	1890 to 1914
Walter, Cliff, & Lloyd	*Search*	1913 to 1944
	Chambers Brothers	1929 to 1948
J.W Cornell & Sons	*Henry Gust* (steam tug)	1905 to 1918
George	*Clara C.*	1918 to 1939
Claude	*J.W. Cornell*	1920 to 1950
Bub	*Bub*	1922 to 1924
	Sunrise	1925 to 1936
Leon Cornell	*Bub*	1924 to 1940
	Velox	1926 to 1944
Leslie Cornell	*Leila C.* (sunk)	1926 to 1926
	Dawn	1928 to 1966

Henry Einarson	*Petroilia*	
Al & Leon Shellswick	*Shine On*	
George Johnson & Sons	*Energy*	1934 to 1944
George Jr. & Don	*Georon*	

West Harbor & West Side

Torger Engelson and Sons	*Express*	1899 to 1902
	Jessie Jackson	1902 to 1904
Martin	*Tillie E* (steam)	1904 to 1921
Bill	*Buick* (steam)	1921 to 1934
	Dora	?
Hiram Cornell	*Lettie Mae*	
Jake & Lars Bilton	*Lettie Mae*	
	Ethel Mae	
Carl & Walter Jorgenson	*Myrtle*	
	Leo B.	
Dorsey & Vernor Greenfeldt	*Edna*	
	Celia M.	
John Larson & Jacob Young	(Skiff)	
Charlie McDonald	*Fish Hawk*	1890s to 1903

Appendix C

The Men of the Wenniger Fishery

Albertson, Dale
Albertson, Homer
Albertson, Phil
Anclam, Alfred
Anderson, Elmer
Anderson, Emmet
Bohman, "Skipper"
Carlson, Bill
Cory, Mel (Algoma)
Daubner, Lawrence
Daubner, Leo
Daubner, Robert
Dehos, Ed
Dehos, Leland
Erickson, Ed
Evanson, Marvin
Franke, Arnold
Franke, Ralph
Gerckie, Henry
Goetz, Ryne
Grovogel, George Jr.
Grovogel William
Hatrwig, Hohn
Heald, Gene
Herbst, Robert
Hickey, Bill
Hickey, Dennis
Hickey, Jeff
Hugenroth, Clem
Husby, Pete
Issacson, Ed
Issacson, Emil
Johnson, Clayton

Kadonko, Ed
Kadonko, Robbie
Klenke, Kermit
Knudson, Herbert
Knudson, Oscar
Larson, Emery
Larson, Norman
LaPlant, Eddie
Laurent, John B.
LeClair, Lewis
Lindal, George
Madden, Vernon
Mauer, Clarence
Meyer, Herbert
Mueller, Omer
Nelson, Walter
Ohnesorg, Otto
Olson, Delor
Olson, Everet
Orsted, Orval
Orsted, Greg
Orsted Ervin
Ostreum, Lloyd
Ostreum, Norman
Page, George
Pagel, Bill
Peil, Hans
Peterson, Harry
Schmidt, Tom
Schultz, Robert
Strege, Ray
Weborg, Allen
Weborg, Lawrence

Weborg, Orville
Weigand, Warren
Wickman, Wally
Woerfel, David
Zak, Martin
Zastrow, Ed
Zipple, Curtis

Bibliography

<u>Books</u>

Becker, George C. *Fishes of Wisconsin. Madison*, Wisconsin: University of Wisconsin Press, 1983.

Bogue, Margaret Beattie. *Fishing the Great Lakes: An Environmental History 1783-1933.*Madison, Wisconsin: University of Wisconsin Press, 2000.

Chiarappa, Michael J, and Kristin M. Szylvian. *Fish For All: An Oral History of Multiple Claims and Divided Sentiment on Lake Michigan.* East Lansing, Michigan: Michigan State University Press, 2003.

Creviere, Paul J. Jr. *Wild Gales and Tattered Sails.* Paul Creviere, 1997.

Curtis, Kay, prep, *Island Tales an Anthology.* Privately printed, 1948.

Eaton, Conan Bryant. *Washington Island 1836 – 1876.* Washington Island, Wisconsin: Eaton, 1972.

Eaton, Conan Bryant. *Rock Island The Island Series.* rev. add. Washington Island, Wisconsin: Eaton 1979.

Gearhart, Clifford Ross. *Pity the Poor Fish then Men: Fifty Years of Upper Great Lakes History.* Au Train, Michigan: Avery Color Studios Printing, 1987.

Goodlet, Irvin "Gibby". *Kill The Umpire: Memories of Door County Baseball and Life on Washington Island.* Washington Island, Wisconsin: Goodlet family, 2001.

Holand, Hjalmar R. *Old Peninsula Days.* 8th ed. New York: Twayne Publishers, 1959.

Holand, Hjalmar R. *History of Door County. Vol. 1.* Chicago, Illinois: S.J Clark Publishing Company, 1917.

Holmes, Fred L. *Old World Wisconsin: Around Europe in the Badger State.* Madison, Wisconsin: Wisconsin House LTD Publishers.

Karges, Steven. *Keepers of the Lights: Lighthouse Keepers and Their Families Door County, Wisconsin 1837-1939.* Ellison Bay, Wisconsin: WM Caxton Ltd, 2000.

Kuchenberg, Tom. *Reflections In A Tarnished Mirror: The Use and Abuse of the Great Lakes.* Sturgeon Bay,

Wisconsin: Golden Glow Publishing, 1978.

Martin, Charles I. *History of Door County*. Sturgeon Bay, Wisconsin: Sturgeon Bay, 1881.

McDonald, Raymond E. *Four Islands: A History of Detroit, Rock, St Martins, and Washington Islands*. Sturtevant, Wisconsin: Wolfsong Publications, 1984.

Nelson, Sylvia. *Fishermen and Their Boats*. Washington Island, Wisconsin: Jackson Harbor Press, 1999.

Olsenius, Richard. *Distant Shores*. Two Harbors, Minnesota: Bluestem Productions, 1990.

Peterson, Leonard. *Rowleys Bay: Reliving the Heritage of Northern Door County*. Rowleys Bay, Wisconsin: Leonard Peterson, 1991.

Prothero, Frank. *Men 'N' Boats: The Fisheries of the Great Lakes*. Port Stanley, Ontario: Great Lakes Fisherman.

Purinton, Richard. *Over and Back: History of the Washington Island Ferry Line*. De Pere, Wisconsin: Independent Prtinting, 1990.

Schreiber, Edward and Louis. *Fish Creek Voices: An Oral History of a Door County Village*. Ellison Bay, Wisconsin: WM. Caxton Ltd, 1990.

Whitney, *Anne T. Let's Talk About Washington Island 1850 – 1950*. Washington Island, Wisconsin: Town of Washington, 1995.

Wilke, Wendell. The Real Shanty Days. Vol. II. Algoma, Wisconsin: Wendell Wilke.

Articles, Manuscripts and Published Documents

"All Bodies Found By Coast Guard." *Door County Advocate* 1935. DCA; microfilm, Brown County Library.

Anderson, Hannes. Washington Island Through the Years (Ice Harvesting) *Washington Island Observer*. March, 2000. Washington Island Archives.

"Battle Heavy Ice to Save Fish Boat." *Door County Advocate*. 1933. Brown County Library microfilm.

Brown, Edward H. Jr., Ronald W. Rybicki, and Ronald J. Poff. "Population Dynamics and Interagency Management of the Bloater (Coregonis Hoyi) In Lake Michigan 1967 – 1982." *Technical Report No. 44*. Ann Arbor, Michigan: Great Lakes Fishery Commission.

"Charge ad hoc Task Force Report." *Door County Advocate*. Laurie Room. Sturgeon Bay Public Library.

" Charlie McDonald Colorful Personage." *Paul's Netting Gazette*. September 1925.

"Commercial Fishing History of the Fishing Industry in Ellison Bay." *A Century in Gods Country 1866 – 1966*, Centemn's Historical Committee.

Davis, Tom. "To Preserve a Way of Life." *Door County Almanac* No. 3 Sister Bay, Wisconsin: Dragonsbreath Press, 1986. 98-106.

Dayton, Scottie. " Kahlenberg Brothers Built Engines For Some of the Toughest Boats in the World." *New Month Magazine*. March/April/97.

Eaton, Conan Bryant. "Kitty Gaylord." *Door County Almanac* No.1 30-32.

Eaton, Conan Bryant. "Door County Fisheries: The First Fifty Years." *Door County Almanac* No. 3. 1986. 25-33.

Enigl, John. "Fish Box Business Was a Spinoff for Ted Wester." *Door County Almanac* No.3 , 1986. 142-147.

"Fishing Industry at Washington Island." *The Sheboygan Press*. Washington Island Archives.

Gorden, Lorel. Fishing "A Young Family Tradition." *Door County Almanac*. No. 3, Sister Bay, Wisconsin: Dragonsbreath Press, 1986, 65-69.

Hansen, Michael J. and James W. Peck. "Lake Trout in the Great Lakes."

Hirthe, Walter M. and Mary K. "The Conversion from Manpower to Steam Power in the Fishing Industry." *Door County Almanac*. No.3, 1986. 34-37.

Holand. Hjalmar R. "Early Life Among the Indians of the Door County Peninsula." *Peninsula Historical Review*, Publication of the Door County Historical Society for the years 1927, 1928, 1929, &1930.

Holmes, Fred L. Icelandic Fishermen Go Seafaring Washington Island." *Old World Wisconsin*. 217-227.

"Island Had Good Fishing in 1934." *Door County Advocate.* March 1934.

Kopitzke, Lon. "An Interview with Marvin Weborg Along With His Son Mark." *Door County Almanac* No.3 156-158.

Krejcarek, Eugene. "Fishing In Manitowoc County," *Manitowoc County Historical* Society. Occupational Monograph 9 1969 series. Joseph Mann Library, Two Rivers Wisconsin.

Magnusson, Sarah. "Washington Island's Veteran Sailor Has Many Tales To Tell." *Door County Advocate.* Washington Island Archives.

McCardle, Catherine. "Commercial Fishing In Baileys Harbor." *Door County Almanac* No.3 116-117.

Mittermann, Lauren. "Stuart Woerfel: Fish Creek Fisherman." *Door County Almanac* No. 3. 81-86.

Steebs, Keta. "Big Hearted Robbie was everyone's friend." Door County Almanac No.3. from *Door County Advocate.* January 1963.

"The Lake: A Times Special Report". April 20, 1997.

Thorp, Ann. "Martin Kinsey." *Fish Creek Voices: An Oral History of A Door County Village.* 170 – 173.

Toerpe, Gail. "Harvesting Ice for the Icebox." *Washington Island Observer.* May, 2000. Washington Island Archives.

Weimer, Linda. "Pound Nets Impractical Says DNR Fish Manager." *Door County Advocate.* January 22, 1976. Laurie Room. Door County Library, Sturgeon Bay, Wisconsin B-7.

Unpublished Manuscripts and Material

Commercial Fishing Regulations Order No. F – 405 (1939) Washington Island Archives.

Frenzell, Mary Jeanne (McDonald) and Kathleen Rae Bennett, comp, and ed. "From One Island to Another: From Emerald Isle to Washington Island. " *McDonald Family Biographies. 1853-2003.*

Hagen, Percy, comp.& ed. *Hagen/Gudmundsen Story.*

Gagnon, Evan. "When The Mackinaw's Sailed The Upper Lakes." Lester Public Library. Two Rivers, Wisconsin.

Gagnon, Evan. "The Point Beach Fishing Community." Lester Public Library. Two Rivers, Wisconsin.

Meader, Cathy comp & ed. *Hagen Family 1883 – 2005: Hagen Family Biographies and Stories*, 2005.

St. Martins Island Census. 1870. Courtesy of Jim Cornell.

Washington Island Platt Maps, 1850, 1871, 1879, 1899, & 1903. Washington Island Historical Archives.

Wilke, Wendell. *The Real Shanty Days: Algoma, Wisconsin.* Vol.II.

Interviews and Letters

Albertson, Phil. Personal interview. One interview, March 2003; 4 hours.

Anderson, Alvin "Gabby". Phone interviews. Five interviews. Jan 2003- Feb. 2004; total 7 hours.

Bjarnarson, Richard & Marilyn. Personal and phone interview. Two interviews, Dec, 2001, & March, 2002; total 3 hours.

Cornell, James. Phone interview & Personal interview. Two interviews, December 2001, & July 2002; total 3 hours.

Eggebratten, Ted. Personal interview. One interview February 2003; 1 hour.

Ellefson, Jacob. Two letters, personal interviews. Six interviews from Oct 2001 to September 2003; total 12 hours.

Foss, Kirby. Personal interview. One interview; 2 hours.

Foss, Howard. "Recorded by Paula (Hansen) McDonald late 1960's." 2 hours.

Gibson, Mary Ann. Phone interview, February 2004. 0.5 hours.

Goodlet, Irvin "Gibby". Personal interview. One interview, July 2002; 2 hours.

Greenfeldt, Harold. Phone and personal interviews. One phone interview, and five personal interviews. From January 2002 to July 2003; total 4 hours.

Gunnlaugsson, Joy, Letter of stories on Wahington Island among fishermen. Phone interview. February, 2003; 0.5 hours.

Hagen, Bennett, phone interview, one phone interview, January, 2002; 2 hours.

Henriksen, Charlie. Personal interviews and phone interviews. One phone interview, Feb. 2003. Two personal interviews from Dec. 2002 and Dec. 2003; total 3.5 hours.

Hickey, Dennis and Jeff. Personal and phone interviews. Three phone interviews and nine personal interviews. Between September 2002 to February 2004; total 14 hours.

Johnson, Rick. Phone and personal interviews. Two phone interviews, January 2003 and January 2004; personal interview, January 2004; total 2 hours.

Johnson, Elaine and Gretna Johns. Phone and personal interviews. Three phone interviews and four personal interviews from January 2003 to Fubruary 2004; total 9 hours.

Jorgenson, Walter. Personal interview. July 2002. 0.5 hours.

Jornt (Chambers) Carol. Personal interview. July 3 2004. 2 hours

Koyen, Carolyn. Personal interviews. Two personal interviews. May and July 2003; total 4 hours.

Koyen, Ken. Personal interviews. Three personal interviews, May 2002 to July 2003; total 2 hours.

LeClair, Joe. One personal interview, January 2003; 3 hours.

McDonald, Jeff. One personal interview, October 2003; 1 hour.

Moy, Phil. One personal interview, December 2002; 1.5 hours.

Nelson, Sylvia, two personal interviews. October 2001 and July, 2002; total 4 hours.

Orsted, Pat and Orval. Six personal interviews. January 2003 February 2004; total 8 hours.

Richter, Arni J. Personal interview. June 12, 2004. 1 hour

Peterson, Dorothy. Two phone interviews, January 2003 and Febuary 2003; total 1 hour.

Teskie, Neil One personal interview, July 2003; 3 hours.

Voight, Donald. three personal interviews, June 2003, Sept 2004 July 2005; 4 hours.

Voight, Leon and Lyle. One phone interview, March 2003; and one personal interview, December 2002; total 1 hour.

Weborg, Jeff. One phone interview January 2003; and two personal interviews September and December 2002; total 5 hours.

Weborg, Ruby. Two phone interviews, Feb and March 2003 and three personal interviews January 2003 to July 2003; total 5 hours.

Weborg, Tim. One phone interview, March 2003; 3 hour.

Young, Gert. One personal interview May 2002; 2 hour.

Young, Robert. One personal interview, May 2003; 1 hour.

Video:

"Baileys Harbor Fisheries," hosted by Mary Ann Johnson, Videotaped 1997.

Meader, Kathy "Hagen Family Reunion." Video interview with Bennet Hagen talking about the erly gas town fisheries. 1998.

"Fishing the Inland Seas", Manitowoc Maritime Museum.

Miller, Charlie. " An Evening of Story telling" Video at the Wagon Wheel Resort with Jeff Weborg, Laurence Daubner, and Howard Weborg. 1999.

On Line Sources and Websites:

Guinan, John A. and Ralph E. Curtis, "A Century of Conservation." NMFS April 1971. http://www.nefsc.noaa.gov/125th/history/century.html

"Sea Lamprey Control". Great Lakes Fishery Commission. http://glfc.org/lampcon.htm.

"Lake Michigan Facts and Figures." GLIN. Great Lakes Information Network. http://www.great-lakes.net/lakes/ref/michfact.html

"Lake Superior Facts and Figures." GLIN.

"Lake Huron Facts and Figures." GLIN.

"Lake Superior Facts and Figures." GLIN.

"Lake Huron Facts and Figures." GLIN.

INDEX

INDEX

INDEX